D0268316

The Poet's Role

AMSTERDAMER PUBLIKATIONEN ZUR SPRACHE UND LITERATUR

in Verbindung mit

PETER BOERNER, BLOOMINGTON; HUGO DYSERINCK, AACHEN;
FERDINAND VAN INGEN, AMSTERDAM; FRIEDRICH MAURER†,
FREIBURG; OSKAR REICHMANN, HEIDELBERG

herausgegeben von

COLA MINIS†
und
AREND QUAK

147

AMSTERDAM – NEW YORK, NY 2001

The Poet's Role
Lyric Responses to German Unification by Poets from the G.D.R.

Ruth J. Owen

The paper on which this book is printed meets the requirements of "ISO 9706:1994, Information and documentation - Paper for documents - Requirements for permanence".

ISBN: 90-420-1207-2
©Editions Rodopi B.V., Amsterdam – New York, NY 2001
Printed in The Netherlands

To the memory of my grandfather Don Amor

ACKNOWLEDGEMENTS

My first thanks go to Karen Leeder, who has taught me so much about poetry, about better ways of reading and better ways of writing. She has been a brilliant and insightful D.Phil. supervisor. I am also grateful to Katrin Kohl for first encouraging me to do graduate studies and for her unstinting moral support and guidance over many years. To all the librarians at the Taylorian, Oxford, and at the Deutsches Literaturarchiv, Marbach, I owe a debt of gratitude for their assistance, but especially to Jill Hughes and to Jutta Bendt. I thank the poets and academics in Germany who gave their time and comments. For major financial support I thank the British Academy, without which I could not have undertaken this research at all, and also the Heath Harrison fund, which enabled me to spend a year in Germany. The writing of this study was largely undertaken at Oriel College, to which I am grateful for its supportive academic environment and for a scholarship and travel grants.

CONTENTS

Abbreviations...xi

1. Introduction...1

2. The Poet's Role in the GDR 1949-1989...27

3. History and Poetry: 'Wende-Zeitgedichte'...75

4. 'Die Stimmen der Verlierer': Post-Unification Poetry by ex-GDR Poets....135

5. The End of a Role: Volker Braun's Post-'Wende' Poetry....................191

6. The Beginning of a Role: Durs Grünbein's Post-'Wende' Poetry............233

7. Conclusion...273

Bibliography...285

Index of Names...357

Index of Subjects...363

ABBREVIATIONS

FAZ	Frankfurter Allgemeine Zeitung
FR	Frankfurter Rundschau
GLL	German Life and Letters
GM	German Monitor
GR	Germanic Review
ND	Neues Deutschland
ndl	neue deutsche literatur
NR	Neue Rundschau
NZ	Neue Zeit
SDZ	Süddeutsche Zeitung
SGCS	Studies in GDR Culture and Society
SuF	Sinn und Form
SZ	Stuttgarter Zeitung
TuK	Text und Kritik
WB	Weimarer Beiträge
ZfG	Zeitschrift für Germanistik

CHAPTER 1
INTRODUCTION

This study concerns the relationship between a corpus of contemporary poetry and a historic shift in political power. Essentially, it examines the work of poets from the German Democratic Republic (GDR) and their reactions to German unification in 1990. When socialism fell in Eastern Europe in 1988/89, the Soviet Union and its satellites – countries such as Poland, Hungary, Czechoslovakia and the GDR – changed ideologically and economically. Subsequently there were also geographical repercussions: the Soviet Union broke up into its constituent states, Czechoslovakia became two independent nations and the 'Bundesrepublik' embraced the territory of the former GDR. After a month in which the 'Volk' took to the streets of the GDR to campaign for change, the breaching of the Berlin Wall on 9 November 1989 heralded the fall of the 'Sozialistische Einheitspartei Deutschlands' (SED). In German this development was called the 'Wende', a great change or U-turn, which brought both an end to socialist dictatorship and ultimately the GDR's subsequent unification with West Germany. Such events offer gripping material to writers: GDR literature had responded to the civil uprisings of 17 June 1953 and the 1968 Prague Spring, but 1989 brought much larger repercussions.[1] In the words of the GDR poet Bert Papenfuß, 'wenn ein staat ins gras beißt, singen die dichter'.[2] In another line of poetry, the GDR playwright and poet Heiner Müller declared, 'Aufstände und Staatskrisen: guter Stoff'; in 1990 the GDR writer Kerstin Hensel stated in an essay, 'Wir haben allen Grund zum Schreiben'; the GDR writer Kurt Drawert reiterated this too in an interview: 'Und der Untergang eines Weltimperiums, also wenn das kein Stoff sein soll... Was nützt einem ein Talent, wenn man keinen Stoff hat!'.[3] Abundant, vast material also, however, presents a daunting prospect and the question of how precisely one can deal with multi-facetted, proximate events, whose full effects are still unfolding. Nonetheless, the 'Wende' seemed to be a new muse for the writer Wolfgang Hilbig:

---

[1] See, for instance, Heinrich Mohr, 'Der 17. Juni 1953 als Thema der Literatur in der DDR', in *17. Juni 1953: Arbeiteraufstand in der DDR*, ed. by Ilse Spittmann and Karl Wilhelm Fricke (Cologne: Edition Deutschland Archiv, 1982), pp.87-111.

[2] Bert Papenfuß, *mors ex nihilo* (Berlin: Galrev, 1994), unnumbered pages.

[3] Heiner Müller, 'Klage des Geschichtsschreibers', *Die Gedichte, Werke*, i, ed. by Frank Hörnigk (Frankfurt a.M.: Suhrkamp, 1998), p.246. Kerstin Hensel, 'Ohne Angst und an allen Dummköpfen vorbei', *Angestaut: Aus meinem Sudelbuch* (Halle: mdv, 1993), pp.54-61 (p.61). Andreas Herzog, 'Erinnern und erzählen: Gespräch mit Kurt Drawert', *ndl*, 42 (1994), No.4, 63-71 (p.71).

Die 'Wende' muß natürlich schon aus dem Grund Teil meines Schreibprozesses werden, weil ich die Welt seit diesen Ereignissen nicht mehr so sehen kann, wie sie einmal war. Richtig heißen müßte es: Die 'Wende' nimmt an meinem Schreibprozeß teil.[4]

In this view the 'Wende' personified became a new participant in the act of writing. For many poets it meant that they could no longer see the world as it had been and, for a time, the 'Wende' would be at the centre of their poetry.

This study will explore whether a literary turning-point coincided with the political one of 1989/90. The end of the political prescriptions which had conditioned literary production, distribution and reception in the GDR, represents one kind of turning-point. In 1989/90 censorship and the state's monopoly of publishing ended. Before this, although to some extent the SED's model for the writer's place had failed to prevent an increasing diversity of literary enterprises, it still provided the official framework for writers' self-understanding, or a position against which their opposition was defined.[5] In order then to be better understood, poetry since the 'Wende' is set against the background of GDR poetry, in this study. The retrospective Chapter 2 surveys the role which poets had in the GDR. 'GDR poetry' is understood to include not only writers who stayed in the GDR, but those who emigrated, left temporarily, or were forcibly expatriated. Émigré writers' GDR origins and their GDR inheritance often continued to characterize their work.[6] For the purposes of this study however, most attention is given to the poets who remained in the GDR to its end. In looking back, works published within the GDR are distinguished from those which had to be published in West Germany, but both are included here as GDR literature.[7] Within the GDR the 'Dichter im Dienst' on the one hand and the 'Aussteiger' on the other traditionally constituted two poles, between which the majority of works, and those receiving most critical attention, were perceived to form a literature of political dissidence (although in retrospect, perceptions have changed).

---

[4]Wolfgang Hilbig, 'Zeit ohne Wirklichkeit: Ein Gespräch mit Harro Zimmermann', *TuK* (1994), No.123, 11-18 (p.13).
[5]Colin B. Grant sees the diversification of GDR literature as a response to the rigidity of ideological discourse and 'an anticipatory articulation of its collapse' in *Literary Communication from Consensus to Rupture: Practice and Theory in Honecker's GDR* (Amsterdam and Atlanta: Rodopi, 1995), p.154.
[6]Günter Kunert, Wolfgang Hilbig and Uwe Kolbe are important figures of GDR poetry who left the state between 1979 and 1989, and retained a dialogue with the GDR in their work.
[7]This is in line, for instance, with Anneli Hartmann's conclusions in 'Neuere Tendenzen in der DDR-Lyrik', *deutsche studien*, 22 (1984), 5-29, where she talks of a GDR literature constituted by writers living on both sides of the border.

1989/90 brought a period when the future of the official publishing houses and literary institutions was uncertain. Piles of GDR books were thrown out and the mechanisms of official literary production and distribution frozen. Writers' contracts became invalid as institutions closed and privatization and western takeovers began. Wolfgang Emmerich, author of the *Kleine Literaturgeschichte der DDR*, describes the literary scene experiencing 'Zusammenbruch, Kahlschlag und "Abwicklung" funktionierender Einrichtungen'.[8] According to the GDR writer Brigitte Burmeister, the 'Wende' was 'der Wechsel in eine Gesellschaft, in der Vorstellungen wie die vom "schriftstellerischen Auftrag", vom "Bund zwischen Autor und Leser", vom "Leseland" und "Gebrauchtwerden" einigermaßen fremd anmuten'.[9] These ideas about the writer's role, which were crucial throughout the GDR's existence, became redundant in 1989/90. The 'Wende' also meant changes for the publishing scene which had operated outside the state-controlled sphere. Mainstream publishing houses would henceforth apply various aesthetic criteria rather than blanket political ones: an 'alternative' would not be necessary. Birgit Dahlke describes the underground scene experiencing 'Funktionsverlust mit dem Fall der Mauer'.[10] Antonia Grunenberg looks back in 1993 and also sees an endpoint:

> Von 1989/90 an veränderte sich mit den Produktionsbedingungen das Selbstverständnis der Künstler und Künstlerinnen so einschneidend, daß ein Teil der Produktion nicht mehr fortgeführt wurde bzw. werden konnte (so die meisten Zeitschriften, aber auch Mappenproduktionen und Künstlerbücher).[11]

The change in the conditions of literary production thus altered the self-understanding of both official and unofficial GDR writers. Although some expressed a sense that marketability was as insidious a concern in judging literature as socialist loyalty, most ex-GDR poets have been able to publish work since 1990. In addition, much unofficially published material, from the 1970s and 1980s, has been collected, catalogued and republished since

---

[8]Wolfgang Emmerich, *Kleine Literaturgeschichte der DDR*, rev. edn. (Leipzig: Kiepenheuer, 1996), p.436.
[9]Brigitte Burmeister, 'Schriftsteller in gewendeten Verhältnissen', *SuF*, 46 (1994), 646-654 (p.652).
[10]Birgit Dahlke, ' "Die Chancen haben sich verschanzt": Die inoffizielle DDR-Literatur-Szene der DDR', in *Mauer-Show: Das Ende der DDR, die deutsche Einheit und die Medien*, ed. by Rainer Bohn, Knut Hickethier and Eggon Müller (Berlin: Sigma Bohn, 1992), pp.227-242 (p.229).
[11]Antonia Grunenberg, ' "Vogel oder Käfig sein: Zur "zweiten" Kultur und zu den inoffiziellen Zeitschriften der DDR', in *Eigenart und Eigensinn: Alternative Kulturszenen in der DDR (1980-1990)*, ed. by Forschungsstelle Osteuropa (Bremen: Edition Temmen, 1993), pp.75-92 (p.80).

unification.[12] The smaller, newer publishing houses (such as Galrev and Kontext) which grew out of the GDR underground scene, cater for some of the most esoteric new texts. Equally however, the privatized eastern publishers Aufbau and Mitteldeutscher Verlag publish poetry and the prestigious western house Suhrkamp has taken up a remarkable number of young ex-GDR poets. Nevertheless, the GDR had been promoted as a 'Literaturgesellschaft' and 'Leseland', a country of readers for whom literature was important.[13] And there was some truth to the mythical 'culture of reading'. More people read literature in the GDR than in western European countries, even if this was largely as a result of tight controls on public life and restricted possibilities for personal consumption. At unification, GDR writers thus experienced the utter demolition of established notions about literature's importance to society or, in Rolf Sprink's words, 'der doppelte Abschied vom Leseland DDR'.[14]

Besides changes to the publishing industry, the developments of autumn 1989 brought an emancipation of language, which the prominent GDR writer Christa Wolf described in a public speech at the time: 'Jede revolutionäre Bewegung befreit auch die Sprache. Was bisher so schwer auszusprechen war, geht uns auf ein Mal frei über die Lippen'.[15] This statement suggests a linguistic 'Wende'. Eugen Voss described the language of communist rule in Eastern Europe as an 'Un-Sprache'. At the 'Wende' he used the image of a vacuum filling, to express the change to language: 'Kaum war der Druck der Un-Sprache weg, als diese Vertiefungen sich mit dem Inhalt der lebendigen Sprache füllten'.[16] As Voss presented the shift from stagnation to vitality as a shift from non-language to true language, so Wolf personified language leaping free of propaganda and officialdom: 'Ja: Die Sprache springt aus dem Ämter- und Zeitungsdeutsch heraus, in das sie eingewickelt war, und erinnert sich ihrer Gefühlswörter'.[17] This living and

[12]See for instance Klaus Michael and Thomas Wohlfahrt, eds., *Vogel oder Käfig sein: Kunst und Literatur aus unabhängigen Zeitschriften in der DDR 1979-1989* (Berlin: Galrev, 1992); Forschungsstelle Osteuropa, ed., *Eigenart und Eigensinn*.
[13]Johannes R. Becher (1956) and Klaus Höpke (1982) quoted in Ulrich Schmidt, 'Abschied von der "Literaturgesellschaft"? Anmerkungen zu einem Begriff', in *Literatur in der DDR: Rückblicke*, ed. by Heinz Ludwig Arnold (Munich: TuK, 1991), pp.45-52 (p.45 and p.48).
[14]Rolf Sprink, 'Zur Situation der neuen Verlage', *ndl*, 39 (1991), No.8, 188-191(p.190).
[15]Christa Wolf, 'Sprache der Wende: Rede auf dem Alexanderplatz', *Im Dialog: Aktuelle Texte* (Berlin and Weimar: Luchterhand, 1990), pp.119-121 (p.119).
[16]Eugen Voss, quoted in Wolf Oschlies, *Wir sind das Volk: Zur Rolle der Sprache bei den Revolutionen der DDR, Tschechoslowakei, Rumänien und Bulgarien* (Cologne: Böhlau, 1990), p.11.
[17]Wolf, 'Sprache der Wende', p.120.

emotional language is understood as a 'different' language from the everyday, in the same way as is poetic language from political language. Indeed, the GDR critic Peter Geist saw a kind of poetry in the slogans and mottoes of the people's demonstrations: 'Im 89er Herbst war Poesie in Zwischenrufen und auf Tapetenrollen transparent'.[18] Karl Otto Conrady concluded too that poetry was on the streets at the 'Wende': 'Die Lyrik war auf die Straße ausgewandert und dort zuhause, in Losungen und witzig-ironischen oder beißend scharfen Sprüchen auf Plakaten und Transparenten'.[19] He described the effect which this 'poetry of the streets' had on the role of professional poets and writers:

> Als im deutschen Herbst des Jahres 89 die Demonstrationen begannen und sich große Teile des Volks öffentlich in griffigen Parolen artikulierten, war es gewiß keine Zeit für Gedichte nach dem Motto der Mörikeschen Zeile "Was aber schön ist, selig scheint es in ihm selbst." Anderes war an der Zeit: konkret veränderndes Tun, direkt politisches Handeln. (p.175)

This statement suggests that the moment demanded political action, not high-flown sentiments; the active type of poetry would have a function in the moves for change.[20] At the same time, and increasingly in the months that followed, the linguistic 'Wende' made one of the GDR writer's traditional roles defunct: the people could now articulate their ideas directly and no longer needed writers to mediate on their behalf. The emancipation of language thus threw into crisis established notions of the poet's role.

My primary material in this study consists of a body of poetry in collections and anthologies written in 1989-1996 by ex-GDR poets. As well as the collections, I include poetry printed in German newspapers at the time and in the literary journals *neue deutsche literatur*, *Sinn und Form* and *Temperamente*. Out of this broad acquaintance with poetry by ex-GDR poets, some work stood out as the most rewarding on repeated reading. Concentrating on this work, I have sought to illustrate common trends and characteristics. The study aims to strike a balance between an overview of the period and a focus on individual poets who seem particularly interesting: to this end, chapters 3 and 4 are thematic and chapters 5 and 6 focus on single poets. Chapter 3 locates GDR poets on the stage of history as events unfolded in 1989/90 and analyses poems directly reflecting those events. Chapter 4 then

---

[18]Peter Geist, ' "mit würde holzkekse kauen" - neue Lyrik der jüngeren Generation nebst Seiten- und Rückblicken', *ndl*, 41 (1993), No.2, 131-153 (p.136).
[19]Karl Otto Conrady, 'Deutsche Wendezeit', in *Von einem Land und vom andern: Gedichte zur deutschen Wende 1989/1990*, ed. by Karl Otto Conrady (Leipzig: Suhrkamp, 1993), pp.173-248 (p.175).
[20]See *Eine Zukunft ohne Kriege: 13 Plakate für den Frieden* (Berlin, GDR, and Weimar: Aufbau, 1986) for examples of texts by Volker Braun, Heinz Kahlau, Thomas Böhme, and Gisela Kraft as political posters.

identifies subsequent developments in poetry, which point to more distanced, considered reactions to the new German situation. It can be difficult to separate out the themes: a poem about ruins may be also a poem about time and a poem about consumerism, for instance. However, I aim to show examples which isolate the most common trends. Whilst alert to the discontinuities, one must also acknowledge the continuities: with respect to language much is new, but inevitably poets also fall back on familiar techniques. At the same time as poems respond to 1989/90, they may also respond to other events – from a personal divorce, say, to general *fin de siècle* feeling – and each of these may be used to reflect and comment upon the other. Still, there are numerous indications – dates, places, slogans and sights, which link the poems to 1989/90, and I have tried to be guided by these in the main. Some pragmatism is also required when it comes to chronological distinctions within the period: there may be relevant differences between a poem of 1989 and one of 1991 which are set alongside one another for the purposes of a thematic treatment. Broadly, I distinguish between the earlier poetry of events, mainly written in 1989-1991, and the later poetry.

What is striking in the later 'Wende' poetry is the frequency of poetological reflections – an acute concern with the poet's role. Poets have always addressed their own role, of course, but this tendency was given new urgency by the constellation of events in 1989/90. It is particularly interesting that some very different poets have this in common. Against the antinomies of resident/exiled, older/younger and official/unofficial, this treatment shows the work of individual ex-GDR poets to have common characteristics which cross and re-cross the binary oppositions. Another binary category with which this project is not concerned is a male/female contrast. The study concentrates instead on figures who are at the centre of the contemporary German poetry scene. Chapters 5 and 6 address the particular cases of two outstanding poets writing in German, Volker Braun and Durs Grünbein. Braun, the older, longer established, is the 'classic' GDR writer, who published poetry in the GDR from the mid-1960s. He epitomizes the entangled relationship between poetry and GDR politics, and in some respects typifies the sense of loss expressed in poetry after 1989/90. That caesura seems to become the obsessive centre of his writing. Grünbein on the other hand, linked to the alternative publishing scene in Dresden and East Berlin, published his first collection in 1988 in the West. He is identified as a leading poet in Peter Geist's important article, dated November 1992, on new work by young poets.[21] Grünbein's renown is a post-GDR phenomenon, built upon three substantial collections. He articulates something different from other ex-GDR poets after 1989/90: his poetry

---

[21]Geist, ' "mit würde holzkekse kauen", pp.150-153.

reflects not an ending, but a beginning to his role as a poet.

It cannot be assumed that poetry follows responses to the 'Wende' in other genres, be they essays and diaries, or novels, stories and drama (although, of course, some aspects bear comparison). Several books claim to explore post-GDR literature, but in fact overlook poetry. Volker Wehdeking's *Die deutsche Einheit und die Schriftsteller: Literarische Verarbeitung der Wende seit 1989*, for instance, would appear to pertain directly to 'Wende' responses in poetry, but in the entire book 'Wende' poetry is represented only by four poems.[22] A chapter devoted to Wolfgang Hilbig's post-'Wende' work omits his long poem 'prosa meiner heimatstraße'. Furthermore, Wehdeking's model of GDR and post-GDR literature lacks proper contextualization: he describes GDR literature as an encoded literature of dissidence and suggests that an East-West dialogue develops in literature after 1989 which articulates a broad acceptance of unification as a favourable development. In contrast to this, and more in accordance with the direction of my research, are the editorial comments in *Die Zeit danach: Neue deutsche Literatur*.[23] This 1991 book claims to be 'die erste Sammlung von neuen literarischen Texten nach dem Ende der deutschen Teilung' (back cover), although it is almost entirely prose. Interesting nonetheless is the editors' observation of 'neue Konstellationen für das kulturelle Bewußtsein, das Verhältnis von Ästhetik und Politik, für das Selbstverständnis der Literatur' (p.11). Analysing the manuscripts for the collection, the editors perceive 'ein wesentlicher Unterschied in der ästhetischen Grundhaltung von Autoren aus West und Ost' (p.11). Former GDR writers seem 'direkter', writing 'aus einer konflikthaften Situation heraus, mit einem Adressaten vor Augen und in gewisser Weise auch *über* einen konkreten, sie unmittelbar betreffenden Gegenstand' (p.12). My interpretation of the poetry also points to a direct expression of historical rupture in the East, but the sense of conflict (conflict with western materialism and commercialism, for instance) and of a particular addressee (such as the 'Volk') apply to smaller, specific groups of poems within the corpus.

A few articles drew early attention to German 'Wende' poetry: in particular articles by Gerrit-Jan Berendse, Anna Chiarloni, and Christiane Zehl Romero suggested useful starting-points. In all cases, however, the number of poems discussed was a minute proportion of the corpus in question. Berendse's thesis is that after the 'Wende' writers withdrew into a local and intimate discourse in poetry: when the closed borders opened up, writers

---

[22]Volker Wehdeking, *Die deutsche Einheit und die Schriftsteller: Literarische Verarbeitung der Wende seit 1989* (Stuttgart, Berlin and Cologne: Kohlhammer, 1995).
[23]Helga Malchow and Hubert Winkels, eds., *Die Zeit danach: Neue deutsche Literatur* (Cologne: Kiepenheuer & Witsch, 1991).

reacted by drawing back from the 'fraying', contourless world at large.[24] This points to the way in which reactions to the end of the GDR feed into more general reactions to life at the end of the twentieth century and at the end of a millennium. But it also, though less specifically, indicates the kind of withdrawal which I present as a concern with self and with one's own writing (and which, it must be said, was also present before 1989). Berendse looks at disorientation and the search for identity in two post-'Wende' texts: Heiner Müller's 'Selbstkritik' and Volker Braun's 'Das Eigentum', which are rightly identified as two of the most significant 'Wende' texts. He sets these poems against a background of regionalism and of a 'kommunikative Wende' in the earlier 1980s. These poems also demand, it seems to me, to be interpreted with reference to literary communication and the role of the poet throughout the GDR years. They both specifically thematize their writers' earlier work and earlier sense of role. Chiarloni includes the same two poems as Berendse in looking at a range of 'Wende' poems by theme.[25] She picks out three thematic complexes (but again, only in a limited number of texts): firstly, the exodus of summer 1989 (6 poems), secondly, Berlin in November 1989 (3 poems) and thirdly, the dissolution of the GDR and the problems of unification (7 poems). Refuting the media contention of the day that intellectuals were silent at unification, Chiarloni draws an interesting distinction between earlier and later 'Wende' poems: 'Der strahlenden Novemberlandschaft der früheren Texte folgt jetzt ein Szenarium, das durch rote Fahnen, Floskelfetzen und staubige Versatzstücke aus der ehemaligen Republik geprägt ist' (p.97). This suggests that the fallen GDR may return in poetry, a topic I particularly address with respect to the notion of 'Floskelfetzen'. Romero also identifies a writerly concern with the GDR past.[26] She begins by discussing a critical approach to post-GDR literature and claims that literature is 'uniquely qualified to articulate the strangeness, represent the approaches and congruences, and, perhaps most importantly, recall and question the past' (p.142). Nevertheless, the emphasis in this article is on writers' statements and essays rather than literature (Romero refers to only four poems: Gabriele Stötzer's untitled poem from *grenzen los fremd gehen*, Christa Wolf's 'Prinzip Hoffnung', Braun's 'Das Eigentum' (in a throwaway line) and Hans-Eckart Wenzel's 'Unlust und Schwermut') and it deals equally with Austrian, West German and other

---

[24]Gerrit-Jan Berendse, ' "Ändern sich die Umstände, zeigen sich die Konstanten!" Deutsche Lyrik in der "Wende" zum Regionalen', *GR*, 67 (1992), 146-152.
[25]Anna Chiarloni, 'Zwischen gestern und morgen: DDR-Gedichte aus der Zeit des Mauerfalls', *SGCS*, 11/12 (1993), 89-103.
[26]Christiane Zehl Romero, 'No Voices - New Voices? Literature and Literary Climate in the Former GDR since the Wende', *SGCS*, 13 (1994), 139-164.

writers, as well as those from the GDR. Her conclusion, however, seems to concur broadly with my interpretation of the ex-GDR poets: 'While 1989 constitutes an important turning point and subject, it neither ends older trends nor begins a new literature' (p.164). One point I seek to demonstrate through close readings of post-GDR poems is that 1989/90 is this 'important turning point and subject' for poetry. I am also concerned, however, to look beyond the first wave of 'Wende' poems to developments after 1991.

Contemporary literature will never be accompanied by a vast corpus of research and criticism: most of the secondary material directly related to my study consists of reviews of single post-'Wende' collections. There are, however, works relevant to this project in other ways, which pertain to poetry in the historical process and to poetological reflections in poetry. In so far as it identifies the poet's self-understanding as a central lyric theme, my project might, for instance, be seen as a postscript to Walter Hinck's survey *Magie und Tagtraum: Das Selbstbild des Dichters in der deutschen Lyrik*.[27] In thirty chronological chapters, Hinck examines reflections on the production and on the reception of poetry, from the entire canon of German poetry. As Hinck states, poetological poems are always primarily lyric and linguistic works of art: the moment of reflection on the poet's role is dependent on the poem (and collection) which contains it. Furthermore, and this I think is important, Hinck picks out the moment of poetological reflection as an exemplar of poetry's particular distinction from prose:

> Indem das poetologische Gedicht auch im Nachdenken über das Poetische noch Poesie bleibt, macht es zugleich auf exemplarische Weise deutlich, daß sich der Ausdrucksgehalt von Dichtung nie ganz in die Interpretation auflösen oder in ihr einfangen läßt. (p.11)

A poem makes a statement in a way that cannot be entirely measured out in analysis. Not only the poetological poem, but also the historical poem particularly foregrounds the generic implications of writing poetry as against prose. Hinck makes this point in the essay 'Das lyrische Subjekt im geschichtlichen Prozeß oder Der umgewendete Hegel: Zu einer historischen Poetik der Lyrik', in which he discusses how the topic and intention of a poem can be determined by historical reality.[28] While it is important to explore the timelessness of the post-'Wende' poems and their connections with literary tradition, the poems also demand to be considered in their specific historical context, taking full account of the events to which they explicitly refer. The interpretation of a poem as a poetological or a historical utterance becomes

---

[27]Walter Hinck, *Magie und Tagtraum: Das Selbstbild des Dichters in der deutschen Lyrik* (Frankfurt a.M. and Leipzig: Insel, 1994).
[28]Walter Hinck, *Von Heine zu Brecht: Lyrik im geschichtlichen Prozeß* (Frankfurt a.M.: Suhrkamp, 1978), pp.125-137.

This suggests that poetry's intimacy makes it the genre in which to address post-unification shame and one's own part in history. In addition, Müller's lyric identification at this time with various 'Geschichtsschreiber' raises the question of genre. Müller, although a literary writer of contemporary history, finds an affinity with ancient historians, from Tacitus to Mommsen.

Despite the continuities in poetry, many doubts have been expressed in the 1990s about its continued existence after the paradigm shift from modernism to postmodernism. Considerations about the place of poetry in contemporary Germany have included both defences and condemnations of contemporary work. Some critics voice prescriptive concern about readability and current tendencies to ignore some poetic traditions. Even a critic such as Erk Grimm, who makes a positive response to recent poetry, commences his piece on its readability by asking, 'Ist "das Gedicht" in unserem Informationszeitalter überhaupt noch haltbar?' and later states, 'Das Gedicht in der Ära unserer anhebenden *Cyberculture* spricht kühl zu uns, es spricht von den allgegenwärtigen Telegeräten und den Körper-Phantomen, beispielsweise von der Television'.[43] For Grimm, this interest in the media, as a subject and as a provider of forms which are imported into the poem, signals the end of poeticizing: 'Das neueste Gedicht ist eigentlich und wesentlich kein Gedicht mehr, das heißt, es arbeitet drängend gegen die Poetizität des Poetischen' (p.293). In fact, the poem has long ceased to adhere to a 'poeticizing' language: in the 1970s, for instance, Nicolas Born and Jürgen Theobaldy (representing the movement of 'Neue Subjektivität') rejected the 'scented words' which poeticized life. Grimm also, however, describes a departure from the great lyric topoi of nature, love and the human soul. These subjects are still well-represented in German poetry, nonetheless, including in the work of Durs Grünbein which Grimm holds up only as an example of the 'new' obsession with the virtual. He is not alone, however, in perceiving a coldness in contemporary poetry. Hans-Jürgen Heise has lamented a tendency towards unmoving, academic poetry and emotional escapism.[44] Poetry has, he suggests, become the intellectual sport of 'der geklonte Poet' (p.195). He uses an image of the genre drifting further and further away from human life: 'Die lyrische Gattung ist ins Abseits gedriftet, weil sie aufgehört hat, ein Arsenal menschlicher Erfahrungen zu sein' (p.193). Peter Maiwald decries a loss of verse form: 'Das Handwerk der Verskunst ist derart in den Verruf gekommen,

---

[43]Erk Grimm, 'Das Gedicht nach dem Gedicht: Über die Lesbarkeit der jüngsten Lyrik', in *Deutschsprachige Gegenwartsliteratur: Wider ihre Verächter*, ed. by Christian Döring (Frankfurt a.M.: Suhrkamp, 1995), pp.287-304 (p.287 and p.288).
[44]Hans-Jürgen Heise, 'Die verdrängten Inhalte: Zur Lyrik unserer Zeit', *die horen*, 40 (1995), 193-196.

daß unter den jüngeren Dichtern immer weniger zu wissen scheinen, daß ein Gedicht nicht aus Worten, sondern aus Versen besteht'.[45] Contemporary poetry is associated, by critics like Grimm, Heise and Maiwald, with a decay of poetic language. They seem to regret a diversifying of poetic language to include many different styles and registers. In some ways this diversifying is due to an intermingling of genres, and of high culture with popular culture, but literature and its genres have always been fairly conceptually unstable. What is known as postmodernism now signals radical indeterminacy and the self-conscious, parodic articulation of scepticism towards the old certainties in intellectual and political life. In 1991, Hanns-Josef Ortheil perceives in the latest poetry 'nichts als ein hilfloses Fließen von Wahrnehmungspartikeln, die längst nicht mehr zu großen Symbolen verdichtet werden'.[46] At the root of much of the criticism of contemporary poetry is a dislike of this mode of the moment. Nevertheless, where poetry is a montage of particles, it can be an extreme resistance to the regimented and ordered symbols of an external reality. Its rejection of the symbolic and metaphorical is a type of witness. Czeslaw Milosz has particularly conceived of poetry bearing witness to individual lives and societies.[47] He describes poetry participating in social discourse:

> Poetry is an art of rhythm but is not primarily an affective means of communication like music. Its language enables it to participate in and to dominate "the incessant transformations of religious, political and social thought". (p.25)

Milosz attributes a type of dialogism to poetry here, which is perhaps most manifest in closed and regimented societies. Although poetry may not primarily be an affective means of communication, it is closer to music than the novel or drama, in its use of the rhythm and sounds of language to move people, separately from any moving representation which may be the subject of the text. Poetry, particularly that in traditional verse-forms, has a musical quality and in the modern era, when these are not taken for granted, metre and rhyme are particularly a way of foregrounding the choice of an affective genre. The patterns of impulse and ebb create a rhythm and an audible structure, so that the poem is not some 'hilfloses Fließen'.

As well as considering poetry as a genre of writing, one can also consider its place as a national institution. At unification, GDR writers

[45]Peter Maiwald, *Wortkino: Notizen zur Poesie* (Frankfurt a.M.: Fischer, 1993), p.108.
[46]Hanns-Josef Ortheil, 'Zum Profil der neuen und jüngsten deutschen Literatur', in *Spätmoderne und Postmoderne: Beiträge zur deutschsprachigen Gegenwartsliteratur*, ed. by Paul Michael Lützeler (Frankfurt a.M.: Fischer, 1991), p.36.
[47]Czeslaw Milosz, *The Witness Of Poetry* (Cambridge, Massachusetts and London, England: Harvard University Press, 1983).

experienced an acute confrontation with the intrinsic conflict between literature and society. In capitalist, technology-ridden Europe, poetry is at odds with the main aspirations of society. When the socialist bloc was first established, however, the situation there appeared to be potentially different. Rather than being obviously at odds, poetry here apparently embodied the same 'alternative' espoused by the mainstream. Under socialism 'otherness' was to be the project of a whole society and poetry taken up into a project much larger than itself. Because of the legacy of Nazism and the antithetical division of Germany, GDR intellectuals cherished this idea longer than intellectuals in the rest of the socialist bloc. I shall briefly outline some points of comparison between the case of the GDR and that of Czechoslovakia and Poland, as described by Ludvik Kundera and Leszak Szaruga, in order to indicate that although the GDR was part of a larger collapse across the former Warsaw Pact countries, the literary reaction to the end of the GDR showed something peculiarly German.

For Czech literature, 1989 brought 'Chaos' according to the Czech writer Ludvik Kundera and a dearth of poetry: 'Die neue dichterische Produktion, welche unmittelbar auf die Revolution des Jahres 1989 reagiert, ist aber wirklich arm, sehr arm'.[48] He attributes this paltriness to poets' involvement at civic meetings in November and December 1989. Kundera points out that Czech writers began expressing themselves in newspapers, radio and television rather than literary genres. To some extent this applies too to a GDR poet such as Lutz Rathenow who was also a dissident political campaigner. Emmerich suggests furthermore that in 1989/90 there was generally 'keine Zeit für Lyrik' in the GDR.[49] My chapter on the 'Wende-Zeitgedichte' challenges this point however. Rather, the 'Wende' seems to have inspired and become a subject of German poetry. Kundera's analysis does highlight other problems, however, which GDR poetry articulates too, such as a sense of the professional writer's words being supplanted by the slogans and mottoes of revolution. Generally however, the politics of culture in the GDR were more ambiguous than in the rest of the socialist bloc. The dominant model in Poland was that of a 'Kampfkultur', according to Leszak Szaruga.[50] In the 1980s, Polish poets were active in the public and underground 'Solidarnosc' movement: 'Das Pathos des Handelns reimte sich

---

[48]Ludvik Kundera, 'Die lyrische Reaktion auf die stillen Revolutionen von 1989/90 in Ost- und Südosteuropa', in *Lyriker Treffen Münster 1987-1989-1991*, ed. by Lothar Jordan and Winfried Woesler (Bielefeld: Aisthesis, 1993), pp.515-542 (p.539).
[49]Emmerich, *Kleine Literaturgeschichte der DDR*, p.510.
[50]Leszek Szaruga, 'Danach (Alles Vorbei). Die polnische Lyrik um die Wende', in *Lyriker Treffen Münster*, ed. by Jordan, pp.543-548 (p.547).

in den achtziger Jahren mit dem Pathos der damals entstehenden Lyrik' (p.546). Writers' political dissidence led to a moral paradox Szaruga suggests: their silence seemed to be the most complete renunciation of the state's programme. In 1989 in Poland there was therefore an explosion of 'saying' and a spirit of freedom in poetry. Both the vacuum in Czech literature and the newfound freedom in Polish literature after 1989 reflect the impact of dissident politics in literature in these countries. GDR literature had been characterized as a dissident political literature too, but retrospectively this was rejected, in 1996 for instance by Ernst Hannemann:

> Die DDR-Literatur war jedoch zum größten Teil keine Dissidentenliteratur, obwohl sie von der westdeutschen Kritik gemeinhin so interpretiert wurde. Denken und Handeln der Intellektuellen der DDR beruhte häufig auf utopischen statt auf jenen pragmatischen Prämissen, wie sie sich in die westliche Mentalität eingeschliffen hatten.[51]

Much GDR literature rested on utopian premises, which distanced it from the type of literature of political opposition which predominated in Czechoslovakia and Poland. Emmerich and Probst's collection of essays on the status of intellectuals and writers from the GDR places contemporary writers against a background of utopianism in the GDR and in eighteenth-century Germany.[52] Emmerich also sets 'die abstrakte Konservierung der Utopie' alongside misplaced political enthusiasms (for the Third Reich, Stalin or the First World War) harboured by certain German writers of other eras. He describes the 'Wende' of 1989 as 'der Höhepunkt ihrer [GDR writers'] Illusionen' (p.7) and suggests that writers suffered a 'nachfolgender Rollenverlust' (p.7). No evidence from literature itself is adduced to support this: rather, Emmerich and Probst seek to describe a social history and characterize the GDR writers psychologically. Invoking Freud, Emmerich links a writerly tendency to utopian aspiration with melancholy: loss of utopian ideals results, in Freud's words, in an 'außerordentliche Herabsetzung des Ichgefühls'.[53] I shall argue that this relationship between a loss of utopia and a loss of self becomes tangible in poetry. This was not only a disillusionment going on in writers' heads however: in a reassessment, published in 1995, the Germanist Edwin Kratschmer, for instance,

---

[51]Ernst Hannemann, 'Geschichtsschreibung nach Aktenlage? Bemerkungen anläßlich der Debatte um die Stasikontakte von Christa Wolf und Heiner Müller', *GM*, 38 (1996), 19-34 (p.20).
[52]Wolfgang Emmerich and Lothar Probst, *Intellektuellen-Status und intellektuelle Kontroversen im Kontext der Wiedervereinigung* (Bremen: Universität, 1993).
[53]Sigmund Freud, 'Trauer und Melancholie', *Studienausgabe*, x (Frankfurt a.M.: Fischer, 1969), p.430

characterizes the whole of GDR poetry in terms of a 'Sündenfall', a fall from grace, or an original sin.[54]

After unification, two linked debates about such 'sins' of GDR literature began, which have been subsumed under the term 'der Literaturstreit' and which are of importance for understanding the way GDR poetry has been read since 1989.[55] The first ignited at the publication of Christa Wolf's story *Was bleibt* in June 1990, and the second at Wolf Biermann's revelation in October 1991 that the Prenzlauer Berg poet Sascha Anderson had been an unofficial agent for the 'Staatssicherheit' (Stasi).[56] Arguments took place in newspapers, literary journals and on television about the role of ex-GDR writers like Wolf and Anderson in the bipolar ideological system. In the discussions, writers were still judged by their positions with respect to political power: in Stephen Brockmann's words, they were seen as 'representatives of institutional systems, rather than as creators of texts'.[57] The reception of Wolf's *Was bleibt*, a book particularly attacked by the West German critic Frank Schirrmacher in the *FAZ*, reflects this point.[58] Wolf was accused of opportunism for publishing a piece of 'Schubladenliteratur' only when it was advantageous to do so, a decade after it was written. Reading *Was bleibt* as an autobiographical account of a period when Wolf was under surveillance by the Stasi, Schirrmacher furthermore criticized Wolf for casting herself as a victim of the state regime, when she now looked more like a privileged luminary. Schirrmacher's position was received sympathetically by other western commentators such as Ulrich Greiner, writing in *Die Zeit*, and Karl Heinz Bohrer, writing in the journal *Merkur*. However, Wolf and her allies felt that her literary work had been unfairly attacked. The West German critic Uwe Wittstock argued for a judgement on aesthetic grounds which would be untroubled by any 'morality of publication': 'Welche moralischen oder ideologischen Sünden ein Schriftsteller auch auf sich geladen hat, das

---

[54]Edwin Kratschmer, *Dichter Diener Dissidenten: Sündenfall der DDR-Lyrik* (Jena: Universitätsverlag, 1995).
[55]For a detailed description see Bernd Wittek, *Der Literaturstreit im sich vereinigenden Deustchland: Eine Analyse des Streits um Christa Wolf und die deutsch-deutsche Literaturstreit in Zeitungen und Zeitschriften* (Marburg: Tectum, 1997).
[56]Christa Wolf, *Was bleibt: Erzählung* (Frankfurt a.M.: Luchterhand, 1990). Wolf Biermann, 'Der gräßliche Fatalismus der Geschichte', in *Büchner-Preis-Reden 1984-1994*, ed. by Deutsche Akademie für Sprache und Dichtung (Stuttgart: Reclam, 1994), pp.176-189 (p.184).
[57]Stephen Brockmann, 'German Literary Debates after the Collapse', *GLL*, 47 (1994), No.2, 201-210 (p.201).
[58]Frank Schirrmacher, 'Abschied von der Literatur der Bundesrepublik', *FAZ*, 2 October 1990, Buchmesse Beilage, p.1.

Urteil über seine künstlerischen Qualitäten bleibt davon unberührt'.[59] The colloquium 'Kulturnation Deutschland', held in Potsdam in June 1990, articulated a defence of GDR literature, represented by Wolf, Stefan Heym, Walter Jens and Günter de Bruyn. As Ulrich Greiner was eager to point out, this 'old guard' had enjoyed 'ein massenhafter, seit Jahrzehnten nahezu einhellig jubelnder Opernchor abgrundtiefer Zustimmung' in the West.[60] He argued that GDR authors had no reason to bemoan their lot, given the significance of criteria such as courage which, Greiner supposed, had inflated regard for their texts. He was particularly riled by Wolf's apparent criticism of western editors for subjecting scripts to 'censorship'. Greiner now believed that émigrés such as Biermann and Kunert deserved attention: he no longer saw Wolf as a freelance writer at all but as part of the oppressive regime. Greiner closed his article by dismissing writers like Wolf: 'Die toten Seelen des Realsozialismus sollen bleiben, wo der Pfeffer wächst'. Although he is not named in Greiner's article, Volker Braun quotes this line in his post-'Wende' poem 'Das Eigentum': 'Und ich kann *bleiben wo der Pfeffer wächst*'.[61] He clearly associates himself with Wolf as the target of western commentators. In some ways, it seemed that the poets who had remained in the GDR, and most were socialists if anything, were suddenly to be cast out with the Party apparatchiks, as though the two groups were indistinguishable. The revelation that poets such as Heiner Müller and Heinz Kahlau had once passed information to the Stasi seemed to further amalgamate socialist intellectuals with state-dictacted socialism. In fact, the critic Karl Deiritz interprets the 'Literaturstreit' as a general, undifferentiating attack on socialism per se: 'Die sogenannte Literatur-Debatte ist eine Anti-Sozialismus-Debatte. Es geht um das Bekenntnis zum Westen'.[62] In a sense then, the 'Literaturstreit' was a rejection of GDR intellectuals' socialism and their anti-western sentiments.

This first debate, which Frauke Meyer-Gosau has called 'der westdeutsche Literaturstreit', concerned the older living writers, such as Wolf

---

[59]Uwe Wittstock, 'Die Dichter und ihre Richter. Literaturstreit im Namen der Moral: Warum Schriftsteller aus der DDR als Sündenböcke herhalten müssen', *SDZ*, 13/14 October 1990 and reprinted in *"Es geht nicht um Christa Wolf": Der Literaturstreit im vereinten Deutschland*, ed. by Thomas Anz (Munich: Spangenberg, 1991), pp.198-207 (p.205).
[60]Ulrich Greiner, 'Der Potsdamer Abgrund: Anmerkungen zu einem öffentlichen Streit über die Kulturnation Deutschland', *Die Zeit*, 22 June 1990, p.59.
[61]Volker Braun, 'Das Eigentum', *Die Zickzackbrücke: Ein Abrißkalender* (Halle: mdv, 1992), p.84.
[62]Karl Deiritz, 'Zur Klärung eines Sachverhalts', in *Verrat an der Kunst? Rückblicke auf die DDR-Literatur*, ed. by Karl Deiritz and Hannes Krauss (Berlin: Aufbau, 1993), pp.11-17 (p.15).

and Braun.[63] Schirrmacher was by date of birth a member of the younger generation, which was characteristically sceptical of political engagement, with respect both to GDR literature and also to the dominant post-war trend in West Germany. This idea of the 'Literaturstreit' as a generation conflict, rather than an attack by western critics on GDR writers, is outlined in Brockmann's article 'A Literary Civil War':

> Frank Schirrmacher's criticism of Christa Wolf was, in fact, criticism of an entire post-war German literary generation that had, as he saw it, staked its literary career on coming-to-terms with a specifically German Nazi past.[64]

In this view, literature's articulation of left-wing politics was no longer a legitimate development after the Second World War, but a tainting or polluting of German literature. As J.H. Reid has argued, there is a contradiction between the two aspects of the 'Literaturstreit' outlined so far: on the one hand Wolf and others were attacked for not criticizing the GDR regime sufficiently. (Had *Was bleibt* been published in 1979, it would have been bold political criticism.) At the same time, their political literature was deemed not to be proper literature at all.[65] Schirrmacher, Greiner and in particular Bohrer, were suggesting that unification would 'normalize' German literature, making it 'aesthetic' as opposed to 'political'. Subsequently Germanists criticized this polarity: T.J. Reed, for instance, rejects the notion of 'außerliterarische Themen' and describes the polarity as 'the most impermissible disconnection'.[66] In Germany, however, this idea of an exclusive opposition between aesthetics and politics still had currency in the early 1990s. It seemed to be a continuation of the stance adopted by those younger GDR writers, who typically sought autonomy and freedom from having to confront political issues. After the discrediting of the apparently co-opted authors of Wolf and Braun's generation, the unofficially published literature of the alternative scene looked set to emerge as the 'true' GDR literature.

---

[63]Frauke Meyer-Gosau, '"Linksherum nach Indien!" Zu einigen Hinterlassenschaften der DDR-Literatur und den jüngsten Verteilungskämpfen der Intelligenz', in *Literatur in der DDR*, ed. by Arnold, pp.267-279 (p.276).

[64]Stephen Brockmann, 'A Literary Civil War', *GR*, 68 (1993), 69-78 (p.73).

[65]J.H. Reid, 'Right hand, left hand - both hands together: German writers and the challenges of unification', in *The New Germany: Divided or United by a Common European Culture?* ed. by B. Ashbrook and P. P. Hasler (Glasgow: Goethe Institut, 1992), pp.1-24.

[66]T.J. Reed, 'Disconnections in the 1990 "Literaturstreit": "Keine akademische Frage"?', in *Connections: Essays in Honour of Eda Sagarra*, ed. by Peter Skrine, Rosemary E. Wallbank-Turner and Jonathan West. (Stuttgart: Heinz, 1993), pp.211-217 (p.215).

The Prenzlauer Berg literary phenomenon, orchestrated by Sascha Anderson and Rainer Schedlinski, was re-assessed in a new light, however, in the second stage of the 'Literaturstreit'. Biermann's shocking revelation that Anderson was an 'Informeller Mitarbeiter' (IM) discredited the idea that the underground scene had preserved artistic autonomy. Anderson and Schedlinski were not widely suspected until the Stasi files were opened. After this however, some critics found references in Anderson's texts to his activity as an IM. The title poem of his first collection 'jeder satellit hat einen killersatelliten' was for instance re-interpreted: Brockmann designates Anderson the killer satellite of oppositional culture.[67] It began to look as though the entire alternative scene had been underpinned by the Stasi itself, perhaps in order to release pressure in society and to demonstrate that the GDR could foster art of all kinds. Any evasion of a political imperative in literature now seemed to have been an illusion. In this, as in the earlier debate, critics equated 'Geist' with 'Macht', in this case 'Geist' of the younger generation. The two stages of the 'Literaturstreit' seemed to condemn both generations of living GDR writers for colluding with political power. The extrapolation from individuals to literary generations applied in these debates was, however, a broad generalization. As Uwe Kolbe's book *Die Situation* suggests, Anderson cannot simply be equated with Prenzlauer Berg.[68] There were other young Berlin writers who are not implicated and others still who were not connected with the Berlin scene in the first place, but were involved in alternative scenes in Leipzig, Dresden, Halle and Karl-Marx-Stadt. Why then was there such hostility to GDR writers in general in the early 1990s? Robert von Hallberg suggests that the 'Literaturstreit' reflects a closing down of any scepticism about unification:

> Now to learn that a new nation cannot be founded, even a highly advanced democratic country, without reducing the dissent of writers – this is a big surprise.[69]

Such reducing of writers' non-conformity would seem to be a reaction to their social importance in 1945-1990: there was a sense that, in Bohrer's words, 'Eine aufgeklärte Gesellschaft kennt keine Priester-Schriftsteller'.[70] Ian Wallace's idea of the 'Literaturstreit' demonstrating how unification meant a

---

[67]Brockmann, 'German Literary Debates', p.203. Sascha Anderson, 'jeder satellit hat einen killersatelliten', *Jeder Satellit hat einen Killersatelliten* (Berlin, FRG: Rotbuch, 1982), p.50.

[68]Uwe Kolbe, *Die Situation* (Göttingen: Wallstein, 1994).

[69]Robert von Hallberg, 'Introduction', in *Literary Intellectuals*, ed. by Hallberg, p.36.

[70]Karl Heinz Bohrer, 'Kulturschutzgebiet DDR?', *Merkur*, 10/11 (1990), 1015-1018 (p.1017).

kind of Judgement Day for writers echoes Thomas Schmid's perception of it as the twilight of false idols.[71]

Inasmuch as the 'Literaturstreit' illustrated the isolation of writers within society, it paralleled that crisis of literary self-understanding, which unfolds in poetry after unification. The sense in which it was a reduction of writers' status and a twilight of their important political role seems especially apposite in the light of poetic themes which point to the poet's identity disconnecting from the fate of the nation and poetry becoming 'Voices from No-Man's Land'.[72] In contrast to the 'Literaturstreit', however, and seeking to negotiate the extra-literary suspicions that dogged German reception of work by GDR writers, this study emphasizes the poem as a poem and examines its particular linguistic effects. The view writers take of writing is brought out, rather than the perspective of critics and the general population (which propelled the 'Literaturstreit'). The poetry seems to point to an acute sense of being an ex-GDR poet and to an identity thrown into question by unification. In an important article, Ian Hilton, for instance, writes about a reflection of 'verfehlte Identität' in poetry of the early 1990s.[73] German literature in 1989/90 is addressed by Arthur Williams et al. under the rubric *German Identity in Literary Perspective*, and identity is one of the watchwords for their volume *The Individual, Identity and Innovation*.[74] In this title, identity is symbolically located between the individual and innovation. In the GDR, poetic identity had been officially tied up with the nation rather than the individual and more with tradition than innovation, as is suggested by the title

---

[71]Ian Wallace, 'Deutscher Literaturstreit aus britischer Sicht', *ndl*, 39 (1991), No.3, 150-155 (p.151). Thomas Schmid, 'Pinscherseligkeit', *Die Zeit*, 10 April 1992, pp.13-14.

[72]Peter Geist, 'Voices from No Man's Land: Recent German Poetry', trans. by Friederike Eigler, in *Cultural Transformations in the New Germany: American and German Perspectives*, ed. by Friederike Eigler and Peter C. Pfeiffer (Columbia, South Carolina: Camden House, 1993), pp.132-153.

[73]Ian Hilton, ' "Erlangte Einheit, verfehlte Identität": Reflections on lyric poetry of the 1990s', in *The New Germany: Literature and Society after Unification*, ed. by Osman Durrani, Colin Good and Kevin Hilliard (Sheffield: Sheffield Academic Press, 1995), pp.252-273.

[74]Arthur Williams, Stuart Parkes and Roland Smith, eds., *German Literature at a Time of Change 1989-1990: German Unity and German Identity in Literary Perspective* (Bern, Berlin, Frankfurt a.M., New York, Paris and Vienna: Lang, 1991). Arthur Williams and Stuart Parkes, eds., *The Individual, Identity and Innovation: Signals from Contemporary Literature and the New Germany* (Bern, Berlin, Frankfurt a.M., New York, Paris and Vienna: Lang, 1994).

of a book on the GDR novel, *Identity, Community, Continuity*.[75] The shifting of identity after 1989/90 must be set against concepts and realities of the poet's role in the GDR, and these are examined in the following chapter.

---

[75]Dennis Tate, *The East German Novel: Identity, Community, Continuity* (Bath: Bath University Press, 1984).

CHAPTER 2
THE POET'S ROLE IN THE GDR 1949-1989

> Die Autoren waren halbe Helden, zwischen
> Hoffen und Bangen, zwischen Zweifel und
> Zynismus, halbiert vom Kalten Krieg, von
> Westveröffentlichung und Ost-Utopie.[1]

This chapter will trace the roots of poets from the GDR, in order to provide the background to their writing after 1989. The oldest poets writing in the post-'Wende' period were published in the GDR from the late 1950s, but even the youngest came to some recognition in the course of the 1980s and had confronted the peculiar situation for writers in the GDR. Though differentiated, the poets' understanding of literature falls into patterns, which all seem to bear on the existence of the socialist state. An investigation of the historical relations between these poets and political power accounts for how the fall of the GDR disrupted their writing practices. The first part of this chapter shows three stages of development in the place of poets and poetry in the GDR over its forty-year history.[2] At each stage, poetry provided an innovative impulse. It also continually ignited debates in the GDR about the relationship between art and politics. Initially, this relationship was largely in accordance with official policy: the poet's role was to be a public educator and in this there was apparent congruence between poets and policy-makers. From the mid-1960s, however, poetry voiced a more overt challenge to cultural policy and seemed to serve as a counter-discourse. By the 1980s, this in turn reached declarations of total autonomy and a rejection of all political discourse, in the poetry of the 'outsiders'. GDR poets fell roughly into three generations which have been characterized according to these three relationships to the state. The situation was, however, rather more complicated than this model suggests. Whilst setting up common denominators, it will also be necessary to acknowledge both that the chronological categories have blurred edges and that the practice of individual poets often suggests a fluid sense of their role. Towards the end of the chapter I therefore look broadly at the issue of poetry and power in the GDR, putting aside the model of three

---

[1]Karl Deiritz and Hannes Krauss, 'Ein deutsches Familiendrama', in *Der deutsch-deutsche Literaturstreit oder "Freunde, es spricht sich schlecht mit gebundener Zunge": Analyse und Materialien*, ed. by Karl Deiritz and Hannes Krauss (Hamburg and Zurich: Luchterhand, 1991), pp.7-12 (p.8).

[2]A wide ranging discussion of the place of poetry throughout the GDR years is provided in Kratschmer, *Dichter Diener Dissidenten*.

generations. To begin, however, the poet's role unfolds as a series of chronological ideas.

In the wartime words of the then exiled poet Bertolt Brecht, the Nazi years constituted a 'Schlechte Zeit für Lyrik'.[3] They were also years which would have great influence over future cultural policy in the GDR. At the end of the war, exiled writers returned to Germany eager to find consensus with political authority and to help in establishing a better German state. They sought to be 'Volkserzieher und Wegweiser in einer sozialistischen Welt' (Kratschmer, p.136). Whereas in exile, socialist literature had only needed to provide ideals and a vision of opposition, it was now to be engaged in building up a real state. The metaphor of 'Aufbau' became a common expression for the enterprise undertaken by state and literature:

> Die Werke der Wissenschaftler, Schriftsteller und Künstler müssen die gesellschaftliche Realität widerspiegeln, sie müssen dem Volke verständlich sein und eine friedliche Aufbaumoral festigen.[4]

The criteria for a state-approved work of literature were based on the model of Soviet socialist realism, which had been pursued in the Soviet Union since 1934. Under these criteria works had to show 'Parteilichkeit und Volksverbundenheit':[5] literature was to be accessible to the average literate citizen and portray the socialist success story. Thus Brecht's defiant 'Aufbaulied' of 1948 includes the rousing lines 'Weg der alte, her der neue Staat. / Fort mit den Trümmern / Und was Neues hingebaut!' (36-38).[6] This poem, set by Paul Dessau, became a well-known song of the Freie Deutsche Jugend (FDJ), the socialist youth organisation.[7] The 1949 poem 'Sagen wird man über unsre Tage' by Kurt Barthel is a typical expression of hope in 'der Anbeginn' (26).[8] The following extract from this poem exemplifies the state's projected success represented as a building project:

> Und man wird die junge Stadt zu Füßen liegen sehn
> und wird sagen:

---

[3]Bertolt Brecht, 'Schlechte Zeit für Lyrik', *Gesammelte Werke*, ix (Frankfurt a.M.: Suhrkamp, 1967), pp.743-744.
[4]'Dokument 30' (1950), in *Dokumente zur Kunst-, Literatur und Kulturpolitik*, ed. by Elimar Schubbe (Stuttgart: Seewald, [1972]), p.133.
[5]Hans Koch, ed., *Zur Theorie des sozialistischen Realismus* (Berlin, GDR: Dietz, 1974), p.566.
[6]Bertolt Brecht, 'Aufbaulied', *Gesammelte Werke*, x, pp.955-956.
[7]'Aufbaulied', *Lieder der FDJ*, ed. by Zentralrat der FDJ (Berlin, GDR: Lied der Zeit, 1979), pp.34-35.
[8]Kuba (Kurt Barthel), 'Sagen wird man über unsre Tage', in *Die eigene Stimme; Lyrik der DDR*, ed. by Ursula Heukenkamp, Heinz Kahlau and Wulf Kirsten (Berlin, GDR, and Weimar: Aufbau, 1988), pp.76-77.

Die den Grundstein dazu legten,
wurden ausgelacht und hungerten,
und doch
planten sie und bauten und bewegten
Trümmersteine.   (lines 11-17)

A representative commentator from the new city of the future is imagined for rhetorical effect. His words ennoble the present, especially vis-à-vis western mockery (14), and make moving 'Trümmersteine' a metaphor for achievement. The building project which was literally undertaken in many spheres of society was also a literary enterprise. The name of the Aufbau publishing house reflected its ideological motivation: literature was to further the successful founding of a socialist Germany.

The first way in which GDR literature, and indeed the new GDR state, defined itself was as the antithesis of fascism. In 'Fünf Schwierigkeiten beim Schreiben der Wahrheit' of 1935, Brecht had emphasized the writer's responsibility to declare the anti-fascist truth.[9] This imperative was not so keenly felt in other socialist countries and to a large extent accounts for the differences between the relationship of literature to power in the GDR and that in those other countries. The cultural policy-makers of the GDR applied this criterion retrospectively, by claiming for the new state a 'Kulturerbe' (curiously a mirror image of the Nazis' appropriation of literature). They thus combined an emphasis on literary continuity (unlike the West German 'Stunde Null' or 'Kahlschlag'), with the key concept of 'Umerziehung'. German art and literature was to be used for anti-fascist re-education. The 'Zentralkomitee' (ZK) of the SED declared specific years to be commemorative for Goethe (1949), Bach (1950), Beethoven (1952) and Schiller (1955). A natural path, it was claimed, linked Goethean ideals to the establishment of the socialist state. This was formulated in the SED manifesto for the 'Goethe-Jahr':

Die großen Ideale, die Goethe in seinem Werk und seinem Leben verkündete, werden durch die sozialistische Arbeiterbewegung in die Tat umgesetzt werden.[10]

From the beginning, GDR literature therefore saw itself as the legitimate heir to the humanist tradition in German literature. Within this evolutionary concept, fascism was seen as an anachronistic deviation. In constructing an 'Ahnenreihe' from Goethe, including Büchner, Feuerbach, Fontane and Heine

---

[9]Bertolt Brecht, 'Fünf Schwierigkeiten beim Schreiben der Wahrheit', *Gesammelte Werke*, xviii, pp.222-239.
[10]'Manifest', quoted in Wolfram Schlenker, *Das Kulturelle Erbe in der DDR: Gesellschaftliche Entwicklung und Kulturpolitik 1945-1965* (Stuttgart: Metzler, 1977), p.71.

to proletarian-revolutionary writers of the twentieth century, the GDR also laid claim to German literary history in a way that reduced West German literature to an inheritor of the 'deviant' trend. GDR literature thus defined itself against West German literature, which it saw as the voice of a retrograde, futureless social order. Socialist national literature was a stand against West Germany. It was important for national identity, at once embedded in a rich tradition, yet simultaneously marking the inception of something new.

The special relationship between literature and politics in the dictatorship stemmed from a theoretical alliance between 'Geist' and 'Macht', between intellectual and political power. In a speech of 1951 entitled 'Die Kunst im Kampf für Deutschlands Zukunft', the Prime Minister Otto Grotewohl stated, 'Die Kunst hat eine wichtige führende Rolle im gesellschaftlichen Leben zu spielen. [...] Die Kunst *erzieht* die Menschen, indem sie in bestimmte Ideen des Lebens einführt, indem sie sich auf eine bestimmte Seite stellt'.[11] In poetry, Mayakovsky's Russian poems of revolution were translated and promoted. Contemporary poets too were to have 'eine anfeuernde Funktion' (Kratschmer, p.147) and continue to show the way. On the one hand, literature was ascribed great power as a formative influence on people's minds: the author was once more an authority. Literature was the subject of rousing speeches by the powerful; it was discussed and directed at government meetings and on committees, just as were production plans for the chemical industry or agriculture. At the same time, however, literature was reduced to a tool of government. Grotewohl explicitly stated that political criteria were to outweigh artistic criteria in the judging of artwork (Grotewohl, p.208). In practice 'Geist' was subjugated by 'Macht'. Thus whilst the GDR was the antithesis of Hitler's Third Reich in that it actively opposed everything fascist, common to both eras was the totalitarian party dictatorship, which made claims to eternity and persecuted non-conformists. Both systems monopolized the life of their citizens and demanded from literature not only submission but reverence. At the time, however, the majority of writers did not perceive parallels between the new GDR and the old Nazi Germany. Antifascism as a state order, including the utopian potential of a unity between 'Geist' and 'Macht', and practical support for the arts, attracted writers to move to the GDR. Amongst others such writers included the young poets Wolf Biermann in 1953 and Adolf Endler in 1955, who within the next ten years became increasingly vehement critics of the system (as it became more illiberal), but initially believed wholly in its enterprise.

---

[11]'Dokument 54', in *Dokumente*, ed. by Schubbe, pp.205-209 (p.207).

Alongside Brecht, Johannes R. Becher was the major GDR poet of the early years, publishing five collections of poems in the first decade of the GDR. The former Expressionist poet became a key figure in post-war GDR poetry in his position as Minister of Culture. In the 1950s he was one of many poets who, amongst other types of poetry, wrote panegyric poetry to socialism. This included eulogies to Stalin and to the GDR leader, Walter Ulbricht. The sonnet 'Der Staat' is typical of Becher's exaltation of the GDR; its closing lines demonstrate the ideal unity of poet and people:[12]

> Ein Staat, der so geliebt ist und geehrt,
> Ist unser Staat, und dieser Staat sind Wir:
> Ein Reich des Menschen und ein Menschen-Staat. (lines 12-14)

Repetition in these lines creates a pseudo-logic which equates state, people and humane behaviour. Equally effusive praise is bestowed upon the party with religious terms. The poem 'Partei, du bist Friede auf Erden!' (*Gedichte 1949-1958*, pp.462-464) uses the patriotic motifs of dream, peace, flag and triumph, culminating with the line 'Dir alle Macht, der Sieg ist dein, Partei!'. Becher's published work from this period, like his exile poetry, evokes dream-like memories of a pre-Nazi Germany and culture, with topoi such as the 'Volk', liberation and 'Heimat' being presented against pseudo-religious motifs of salvation, sanctity and eternity. Glorious battle unto victory is a recurrent theme, which is addressed through exclamations such as 'O Fahne rot im Blauen!' and 'Der Sieg des Sozialismus!' ('Lied vom Bau des Sozialismus', *Gedichte 1949-1958*, p.307). Becher's poem 'Auferstanden aus Ruinen' (*Gedichte 1949-1958*, p.61), which became the GDR national anthem, uses the motif of a better Germany rising from the rubble of the Second World War:

> Auferstanden aus Ruinen
> Und der Zukunft zugewandt,
> Laß uns Dir zum Guten dienen,
> Deutschland, einig Vaterland. (lines 1-4)

The call to serve and the address to 'du' make these lines a prayer to the fatherland, in the style of a prayer to God the Father. The exuberant tone is typical of Becher's public poetry of the time. The unity of purpose between poet and nation reflects the *zeitgeist* of the GDR in the 1950s. Many people felt that to support the state was to support 'Aufbau' instead of destruction, peace instead of war. Poets were writing 'im Bann einer großen Aufgabe'.[13]

---

[12]Johannes R. Becher, 'Der Staat', *Gedichte 1949-1958, Gesammelte Werke*, vi (Berlin, GDR: Aufbau, 1973), p.89.

[13]Rüdiger Thomas, 'Selbstbehauptung', in *Jenseits der Staatskultur: Traditionen autonomer Kunst in der DDR*, ed. by Gabriele Muschter and Rüdiger Thomas (Munich: Hanser, 1992), pp.11-42 (p.14).

The legacy of fascism was a binary kind of thinking which would continue to make the role of the GDR intellectual unique within the socialist bloc. In the 1950s the ideas of the unorthodox Marxist Ernst Bloch were appealing in this context and began to gain common currency: as a professor of philosophy at Leipzig from 1949, he propounded, and in 1954 first published *Das Prinzip Hoffnung*.[14] A principle of hope meant that belief in the future was stronger than doubts about the present. Hope and optimism seemed valid after the throwing off of the Nazi past. Hanns Cibulka's 1959 poem 'Zwei Silben' is an expression of such patriotic idealism and hope.[15] Its final stanza particularly captures the sense of being at a crucial point in history:

> Ein kleines Stück
> der neuen, großen Welt,
> voll von dem, was verging
> und was noch kommen wird,
> eine Landschaft
> voll Arbeit und Frieden,
> und zwei Silben Sehnsucht –
> Deutschland   (lines 23-30)

The recurrence of 'voll', at the beginning of lines 26 and 29, emphasizes a sense of abundance. The new world is clearly that of socialism, but the two syllables and the build-up to 'Deutschland', thematize German division too, as does Becher's anthem quoted above.

A contrast to Becher's published eulogies is provided by his own unpublished poetry from the same period, such as the poem 'Der Turm von Babel'.[16] Here the tower's fall is foreseen, unlike in the Bible, and the murderer Cain is not cursed, but celebrated as godly. Becher seems to have felt that doubts about the socialist building project, such as those which he articulates in this poem, were untimely and he therefore withheld this poem from publication. Brecht's last poetry reveals that he was not an unambiguous supporter of the GDR state either. Most of the *Buckower Elegien* are terse and without any features of conventional form.[17] Many are allegories, perhaps written as subjects for meditation. These are poems written in and for the GDR, but they are different from Brecht's exile poetry in that they find no

---

[14]Ernst Bloch, *Das Prinzip Hoffnung* (Frankfurt a.M.: Suhrkamp, 1959). Written 1938-47.

[15]Hanns Cibulka, 'Zwei Silben', in *Wir, unsere Zeit: Gedichte aus zehn Jahren*, ed. by Christa and Gerhard Wolf (Berlin, GDR: Aufbau, 1959), pp.189-190.

[16]This critical Becher poem is highlighted and well interpreted in Hans Mayer, *Der Turm von Babel: Erinnerung an eine Deutsche Demokratische Republik* (Frankfurt a.M.: Suhrkamp, 1991).

[17]Bertolt Brecht, *Buckower Elegien, Gesammelte Werke*, x, pp.1009-1016.

panacea in the founding of a socialist Germany – instead he doubts the new institutions. The poem 'Die Lösung' (pp.1009-1010), for instance, responds to the historical worker's uprising in East Berlin on 17 June 1953: it treats with irony the 'Schriftstellerverband', whose secretary in the poem embodies the distance between the writers and the people. Brecht did not release this poem for publication during his lifetime. 'Die Wahrheit einigt' (pp.1011-1012) from the same collection, however, was a poem sent by Brecht to Paul Wandel, the Minister for Education. This poem is in one way an appeal to good socialists for 'ein kräftiges Eingeständnis'. Yet the appeal contains implicit criticism in the use of the subjunctive: 'Freunde, ich wünschte, ihr wüßtet die Wahrheit und sagtet sie!'. The poet seems to be warning his readers, perhaps his fellow writers and politicians; he has no confidence that they can speak the truth. Brecht wrote the poem to be used by the government and it reflects his commitment to the social usefulness of poetry.

Some other poets became relatively marginalized in the GDR's first decade because their work was felt to be socially unhelpful. Erich Arendt, for example, expressed humanist convictions in his work without promoting the GDR and its cult figures. His poetry, which had been first published in the Expressionist magazine *Sturm*, distils a bitter sadness at the destructiveness of mankind and seems hermetic in its reduction of language to short, single words and isolated metaphors. Arendt influenced many subsequent GDR poets, including the Prenzlauer Berg scene, from where Endler quotes a 'Punk-Poet' exclaiming, 'Ein ganzer Opium-Laden, dieser Arendt!'.[18] Arendt's work was not favoured in the GDR of the 1950s however, where he was accused of 'mystifizierende Ideologie' and 'außerrationale Sprache'.[19] Such rejection of the twentieth-century Avant-garde and its experimental spirit was a significant element in the early debates about art and politics, and was justified by the importance of 'Verständlichkeit': literature had to be accessible for the 'Volk'.

The first Bitterfeld Conference in 1959 promoted the integration of writers into the industrial world and encouraged writers' circles amongst factory workers. The two maxims of the conference summarize this unifying of arts and 'Volk': 'Schriftsteller an die Basis!' and 'Greif zur Feder, Kumpel!' (quoted in Kratschmer, p.154). The Avant-garde motto of 1919 'Kunst und Volk müssen eine Einheit bilden' would appear to be echoed by the SED line of 1969: 'Die Kluft zwischen Kunst und Leben, zwischen Künstler und Volk – von Kapitalismus und Imperialismus bewußt vertieft –

---

[18] Adolf Endler, *Tarzan am Prenzlauer Berg* (Leipzig: Reclam, 1994), p.54.
[19] Quoted in Emmerich, *Kleine Literaturgeschichte der DDR*, p.167.

wird geschlossen'.[20] The difference between this programme and that of the Avant-garde lies in the propagandistic use of the term 'Volk' in the GDR: 'Volk' was equated not only with the working class but by extension with the party, and thus with the SED leadership. The state remained very much an authority or father-figure: the relationship between the party and the people was thus an unequal alliance in which the state was 'vormündlich'. The tenets of the Bitterfeld Conference mark the restrictive policy which culminated in the building of the Wall two years later. By the middle of the 1960s however, writers were in practice articulating a reaction against the closed state as sole representative and sole voice in the GDR. The young Günter Kunert for instance, whose first collection, descriptively entitled *Wegschilder und Mauerinschriften*, had been enthusiastically received by Brecht and Becher, dropped the positive didacticism from his poetry: it instead became characterized by a growing scepticism and pessimism.[21]

Commentators identified the mid-1960s with a 'Lyrikwelle' in the GDR: seventy poetry collections were published in the GDR by GDR poets between 1961 and 1968. The American academic John Flores perceived a 'new specifically East German poetry' in the 1960s.[22] The poet Sarah Kirsch referred to the 'Teamwork-Attitüde' of the young poets, who formed 'unsere Truppe', a natural grouping, not one imposed from above.[23] This 'different' collective, retrospectively dubbed the 'sächsische Dichterschule', was centred on Leipzig, Saxony, and a student group around Georg Maurer.[24] The group, which included Wolf Biermann, Volker Braun, Heinz Czechowski, Adolf Endler, Elke Erb, Rainer Kirsch, Sarah Kirsch, Reiner Kunze and Karl Mickel, to a great extent defined the emergent image of GDR poetry. These poets began to question, in their work, the state's political and literary programme, heralding literature as counter-discourse. They expressed a concept of poetry overcoming 'Unmündigkeit'. The 1965 collection *Provokation für mich,* by Volker Braun, exemplifies the shift towards constructive challenge to

---

[20]'Dokument 384', in *Dokumente*, ed. by Schubbe, pp.1420-1421 (p.1421).
[21]Günter Kunert, *Wegschilder und Mauerinschriften: Gedichte* (Berlin, GDR: Aufbau, 1950).
[22]John Flores, *Poetry in East Germany: Adjustments, Visions and Provocations 1945-1970* (New Haven and London: Yale University Press, 1971), p.23.
[23]Sarah Kirsch, quoted in Emmerich, *Kleine Literaturgeschichte der DDR*, p.225.
[24]There is good analysis of the work of this group of poets in Gerrit-Jan Berendse, *Die "Sächsische Dichterschule": Lyrik in der DDR in den sechziger und siebziger Jahre* (Frankfurt a.M.: Lang, 1990). For a discussion with more emphasis on the theoretical debates surrounding poetry at this time, see Karl Heinz Wüst, *Sklavensprache: Subversive Schreibweisen in der Lyrik der DDR 1961-1976* (Frankfurt a.M., Bern, New York, Paris: Lang, 1989).

orthodoxy.[25] In one poem from that collection, 'Anspruch' (pp.51-52), the 'hier' is that of the new generation of young writers: 'Hier herrscht das Experiment und keine steife Routine'. Poets were no longer prepared to submissively accept prescriptions passed down from above. In his prose notes, Braun took up Brecht's statement 'Es genügt nicht die einfache Wahrheit' (*Texte*, i, pp.236-238). Poetry too would not simply echo the ideologue, but rather presented a poet who was located at a remove from society's official representatives. Braun was typical of young poets who were idealistic 'angry young men' in this period. Some poets broke with the state's truth to a greater degree. In 1969/70 writing was conceived of by Uwe Grüning, for instance, as an unguided wandering:[26]

> Unsere Irrfahrt gilt einer
> nicht von den Dingen bezwungenen Sprache. (lines 4-5)

Literature was declared, in the words of Cibulka's 1973 title, 'losgesprochen', freed from the contract with the state.[27] Poems by the younger poet Siegmar Faust show an overt defiance vis-à-vis cultural policy and again a rejection of the discourse imposed from above:[28]

> mit welchem recht zwingt ihr mir eure sprache auf?
> was gehen mich eure maßeinheiten und strafgesetze an?
> was soll ich mit euren plänen normen und medikamenten?
> ich verweigere jede unterschrift jede zusage jede beteiligung
> wenn ich etwas zu sagen hätte: ich hätte nichts zu sagen. (lines 23-27)

The omission of commas in these interrogative lines serves to further emphasize the question marks. The questions articulate the dilemma that saying nothing was the ultimate rejection of the political burden placed on writers by the state regime. This was a marked departure from the role of the first GDR writers, and this period established a new model of GDR literature, namely that of literary generations.

The generation of the 'sächsische Dichterschule' came to prominence through an increasing number of poetry readings and anthologies. Stephan Hermlin first introduced their work at a controversial reading in the

---

[25]Volker Braun, *Provokation für mich, Texte in zeitlicher Folge*, i (Halle and Leipzig: mdv, 1989-93), pp.49-101.

[26]Uwe Grüning, 'In unserer Sprache', *Spiegelungen* (Berlin, GDR: Union, 1981), and reprinted in *Ein Molotow-Cocktail auf fremder Bettkante: Lyrik der siebziger/achtziger Jahre von Dichtern aus der DDR: Ein Lesebuch*, ed. by Peter Geist (Leipzig: Reclam, 1991), pp.336-337.

[27]Hanns Cibulka, *Losgesprochen: Gedichte aus drei Jahrzehnten* (Leipzig: Reclam, 1986).

[28]Siegmar Faust, 'Ich bin kein Tier kein Gott und kein Genosse', in *Ein Molotow-Cocktail*, ed. by Geist, pp.180-181.

'Akademie der Künste', Berlin, on 11 December 1962. They were introduced in print with the anthology *Sonnenpferde und Astronauten* edited by Gerhard Wolf in 1964, and Endler and Mickel's anthology *In diesem besseren Land* in 1966.[29] In the summer of 1966, *In diesem besseren Land* ignited a 'Lyrikdiskussion': a notorious debate developed in the official FDJ magazine, *Forum*, about the new generation's poetry and its contribution to socialist progress.[30] Although some hardliners were dismissive, the period brought new outlets for poetry. The *Auswahl* series of anthologies, produced from 1964 (until 1988), sought expressly to bring new poets to the public's attention.[31] In the words of the academic Anthonya Visser, poetic innovation brought 'Blumen ins Eis': the anthologies reflected both the freezing and the thaws of the GDR literary climate.[32] Braun's poem 'Jazz' (*Texte*, i, p.60) can be seen as an expression of the young poets' challenge to the rigidity of cultural prescriptions. Their reaction is conveyed in verbs of destructiveness: 'ausbrechen', 'zertrommeln', 'sezieren', 'zersprengen'. The jazz band, provocative in its embodiment of western decadence, serves as a metaphor for the relationship between the individual and the collective: 'Du hast das Recht, du zu sein, und ich bin ich'; here the individual's free creativity is part of the harmony of the whole. The younger generation believed in the value of such constructive challenge, but was still fundamentally socialist. They had been youngsters in the Third Reich, naive or unwitting participants in Nazism, and so as adults in the newly-formed GDR, these writers felt a loyalty to the anti-fascist Germany. This loyalty informed their self-understanding as artists. In his 1992 autobiography, Heiner Müller states in reference to his attitude in 1961, 'Ich konnte mir eine Existenz als Autor nur in diesem Land vorstellen, nicht in Westdeutschland'. He explains this attitude by calling the totalitarian dictatorship of the SED 'eine Diktatur gegen die Leute, die meine Kindheit beschädigt hatten'.[33] Heinz Czechowski's expression 'in diesem besseren Land' was a motto for those who shared this sentiment in the 1960s and 1970s, and in a poem of 1995 his childhood experience of Nazism still leaves 'diese Bitterkeit auf der Zunge'.[34]

[29]Gerhard Wolf, ed., *Sonnenpferde und Astronauten: Gedichte junger Menschen* (Halle: mdv, 1964). Adolf Endler and Karl Mickel, eds., *In diesem besseren Land: Gedichte der DDR seit 1945* (Halle: mdv, 1966).
[30]For details of the positions taken in this debate see Visser, *"Blumen ins Eis"*, pp.37-63.
[31]*Auswahl 64: Neue Lyrik - Neue Namen* (Berlin, GDR: Neues Leben, 1964).
[32]Visser, *"Blumen ins Eis"*.
[33]Heiner Müller, *Krieg ohne Schlacht: Leben in zwei Diktaturen* (Cologne: Kiepenheuer & Witsch, 1992), p.181.
[34]Heinz Czechowski, 'Brief', *Wasserfahrt: Gedichte* (Halle: mdv, 1967), pp.97-101

Certain metaphors and images betray poets' mixed loyalties to the GDR, however. The journey, originally an image appropriated by GDR state propaganda to describe progress, became a solitary wandering and even a process of dying, in literature critical of GDR power. Yet the retention of the journey reflects too the retention of socialist idealism; the new generation of poets expressed belief in the goal of socialism, although that goal lay far from the contemporary reality. The journey is a metaphor particularly linked to the idea of social and technological progress towards utopia. A section of the anthology *In diesem besseren Land* entitled 'Reisen' provides examples, such as Franz Fühmann's poem 'Der Seefahrer' (pp.74-76):

nun dies: In den Raum zu reißen
die Zeit, die einst sein wird,
die Mannschaft zum Ziel zu weisen:
sie haben sich doch nicht verirrt. (lines 69-72)

Simple, familiar rhythm and rhyme, with the internal alliteration and assonance, reiterate the sense of an uncomplicated course. Here the poet affirms the projected future and seeks to guide society to its goals. Czechowski's 'Ode auf eine Motorradfahrt' (pp.84-86), first published in 1962, illustrates utopian hope meeting technologies of travel:

Denn klein sind auch heut noch die Freuden der Menschen,
Die sie sich stiften, aufbauend so
Aus Kleinem die Größe der Welt, in die hinausführen werden:
Straßen. Oder darüber
Das dröhnende Werk eines Rotors: denn
Uns erwartet der Flug.   (lines 58-63)

Here, projections of a better future are offered as compensation for a present life which seems too confined. Streets to the wide world and flight seem ironic metaphors for the GDR enterprise, given the closure of the border to the West in 1961 and the lack of freedom to travel. However, flight in particular, and its association with Soviet space missions, remained a popular image for socialist success.

Writers and politicians shared a common ideological end, but they had different ideas about how it would be achieved and how literature could be useful. Antagonism developed between writers on the one hand and the official guardians of culture and policy on the other. Despite the fact that freedom of expression was enshrined in the constitution, literature was in practice

---

(p.101), and 'Die Bitterkeit auf meiner Zunge', *ndl*, 43 (1995), No.2, 38.

rigorously censored.[35] The 1960 parable-poem 'Das Ende der Kunst' by Reiner
Kunze examines the senseless lack of artistic freedom:[36]

> Das Ende der Kunst
> Du darfst nicht, sagte die eule zum auerhahn,
> du darfst nicht die sonne besingen
> Die sonne ist nicht wichtig
>
> Der auerhahn nahm
> 5   die sonne aus seinem gedicht
> Du bist ein künstler,
> sagte die eule zum auerhahn
>
> Und es war schön finster

Prohibition stands alone at the beginning of this poem, in its first three words.
The dramatic title suggests what is implied but left unsaid in the laconic fable
that follows. This poem reflects the importance for GDR writing of artistic
activity as a theme in itself. Kunze's volume *Sensible Wege*, which could only
be published in the West, harbours a bitter tone that displays a loss of faith in
the state and a new awareness of loneliness, scepticism and despair. The young
poets were repeatedly criticized in the press for the bleakness and scepticism
expressed in their work. The hardline GDR critic Hans Koch, for instance,
condemned Kunze, Mickel, Braun, Kunert, Kirsch and Jentzsch, using
categories such as illness, decadence and ugliness. He reproached them for
cultivating angst and for a lyric 'ich' asserting itself in opposition to society.[37]
An example of the state's judgement of the new poetry is provided by Sarah
Kirsch's poem 'Schwarze Bohnen' (1968), which was criticized for not being
optimistic and positive about the socialist enterprise. Despite such criticism,
the same poem was, four years later, honoured as a component of
Zaubersprüche, which in 1973 won Kirsch the prestigious Heinrich Heine
prize in the GDR.[38] This is an indication of how the bounds of acceptability in

---

[35]See Ernest Wichner and Herbert Wiesner, eds., *Zensur in der DDR: Geschichte,
Praxis und "Ästhetik" der Behinderung von Literatur. Ausstellungsbuch* (Berlin:
Literaturhaus, 1991) and same eds., *"Literaturentwicklungsprozesse": Die Zensur der
Literatur in der DDR* (Frankfurt a.M.: Suhrkamp, 1993).
[36]Reiner Kunze, 'Das Ende der Kunst', *Sensible Wege: Achtundvierzig Gedichte und
ein Zyklus* (Reinbek bei Hamburg: Rowohlt, 1969), p.14.
[37]Manfred Jäger, *Kultur und Politik in der DDR 1945-1990* (Cologne: Edition
Deutschland Archiv, 1995), p.133 and p.203.
[38]Sarah Kirsch, *Zaubersprüche* (Ebenhausen Isartal: Langewiesche-Brandt, 1974).

GDR literary culture loosened in the early 1970s. A relaxation of the strictures was famously expressed by the leader Erich Honecker in his 'keine Tabus' speech of 1971.[39] In practice there were still many taboos nonetheless.[40] The period of thaw was shortlived, but there was a growing acknowledgement that poetry would no longer offer only concrete 'Wegschilder', but also 'Zaubersprüche'.

In the late 1960s and early 1970s there was much discussion in the GDR literary journals *neue deutsche literatur*, *Sinn und Form* and *Weimarer Beiträge* about the role of the 'klassisches Erbe'. Braun complained in 1968 of 'Die Goethepächter': 'Sie haben seine Schwellen gebohnert – aber wagen sich nicht mehr darüber' (*Texte*, ii, p.248). The classical heritage extolled by the state authorities in name only was also a source which poets drew from in their work. One distinctive feature of GDR literature is the prevalent treatment of this heritage. Portrait poems of writers from the past became increasingly popular from the 1970s onwards. The past was brought into relation with the present, portraits of eighteenth-century writers simultaneously being self-portraits. Braun's poems using quotations from Hölderlin, Kunert's poems to 'Bruder Kleist' and to Heine, and Czechowski's poems about Kleist, Novalis, Mörike and Hölderlin exemplify the genre.[41] They imply an affinity and sense of solidarity between the GDR poet and literary predecessors from the Romantic era. The selection of subjects for portrait poems reflects a concern with the question of literature's place in society and the role of the poet. The portrait poem 'Klopstock in Langensalza' by Annerose Kirchner presents, for instance, a poet opposed by the restrictive and philistine society of 1748.[42] It is a place where the poet cannot breathe easily, where all value is measured in terms of money. Typical is the representation of tension between the ideal and reality. The GDR critic Achim Trebeß interpreted this poem as a poem about the past, in which the present recedes and the writer's social interest is never

---

[39]Erich Honecker, 'Hauptaufgabe umfaßt auch weitere Erhöhung des kulturellen Niveaus', in *Dokumente zur Kunst-, Literatur und Kulturpolitik 1971-1974*, ed. by Gisela Ruß (Stuttgart: Seewald, 1976), pp.287-288.

[40]For discussions of how restrictions remained in place, despite Honecker's speech to the contrary, see Ian Wallace, ed., *The Writer and Society in the GDR* (Tayport: Hutton, 1984), and Alexander Stephan, 'Cultural Politics in the GDR under Erich Honecker', in *The GDR under Erich Honecker 1971-1981*, ed. by Ian Wallace (Dundee: GDR Monitor, 1981), pp.31-42.

[41]Günter Kunert, *Ein anderer K.: Hörspiel* (Stuttgart: Reclam, 1977) and 'Bruder Kleist', *Stilleben: Gedichte* (Munich and Vienna: Hanser, 1983), p.64.

[42]Annerose Kirchner, 'Klopstock in Langensalza', in *Ästhetik heute*, ed. by Edwin Pracht (Berlin, GDR: Dietz, 1978), p.90.

made clear.[43] The stifled poet would, accordingly, represent the antithesis of the present. Yet it seems beyond doubt that the portrait expresses solidarity with Klopstock, a poet who struggled to assert artistic ideals in the face of a 'difficult' publishing situation. Like Klopstock, the treatment of Hölderlin as a figure in literature is typical of the GDR's reception of German Romanticism. Hölderlin's life and works were officially taken into the canon in the 1970s and interpreted as a legitimation of the GDR state. The words of ideologue and cultural policy-maker Alexander Abusch exemplify the way in which Hölderlin was hailed as an eighteenth-century revolutionary whose visions were being made manifest by a socialist Germany:

> In unserer Deutschen Demokratischen Republik wird der visionäre Traum des jakobinischen Dichters durch die wissenschaftlich begründete, revolutionäre Tat vollzogen: die Einheit von Friedrich Hölderlin und Karl Marx als Produkt der Dialektik der Geschichte.[44]

Where the official discourse took up the visionary dream, poets drew on the fact that Hölderlin spent the last forty years of his life in a tower in Tübingen, isolated and apparently insane. In poetry, Hölderlin thus became a symbol of existential alienation. It is in this way that Biermann, whose work was banned in the GDR from 1965, identifies with Hölderlin in 'Das Hölderlin-Lied' of 1972:[45]

> In diesem Land leben wir
> wie Fremdlinge im eigenen Haus   (lines 1-2)

The text is both Hyperion's interior monologue and the GDR poet's commentary. As in many portrait poems, interest focuses on the biography of an ostracized individual: there seems to be a preference in portrait poems for poets who suffered and died young. (Kleist committed suicide; Heine suffered exile and many years of paralysing illness.) Perhaps the selection of subject reflects the fact that many GDR writers were increasingly unable to identify with the social process, especially in the light of the crushing of the Prague Spring in Czechoslovakia in 1968.

---

[43]Achim Trebeß, ' "wir würschten" in den Kämpfen unserer Zeit: Porträtgedichte junger Autoren', in Lyriker im Zwiegespräch: Traditionsbeziehungen im Gedicht, ed. by Ingrid Hähnel (Berlin, GDR, and Weimar: Aufbau, 1981), pp.312-344 (p.321).
[44]Alexander Abusch, 'Hölderlins poetischer Traum einer neuen Menschengemeinschft', WB, 16 (1970), No.7, 10-26 (p.26).
[45]Wolf Biermann, Alle Lieder (Cologne: Kiepenheuer & Witsch, 1991), pp.198-199. On Hölderlin reception, see Karen Leeder, 'Towards a Profane Hölderlin: Representations and Revisions of Hölderlin in some GDR Poetry', in Neue Ansichten: The Reception of Romanticism in the Literature of the GDR, ed. by Howard Gaskill, Karin McPherson and Andrew Barker (Amsterdam: Rodopi, 1990), pp.212-231.

Biermann himself became the epitome of the marginalized, alienated writer after his enforced expatriation of 1976.[46] This landmark judgement laid bare a harsh cultural policy which criminalized many writers, and in the wake of the outcry from fellow writers, others were forced to leave the GDR, such as Siegmar Faust in 1976, Reiner Kunze and Sarah Kirsch in 1977 and Günter Kunert in 1979. The first five years of Honecker's leadership, which had brought a relaxation of censorship, were followed by a policy stricter even than during the worst years under Ulbricht. Censorship was rigorous and many writers could only publish in the West. Nonetheless, poets did not seek to be 'Menschen ohne Zugehörigkeit'.[47] They still saw the poet's role in terms of a social usefulness and, in their own way, attempted to further the 'building' of socialism. Rather than allowing the ideology to dictate to literature, ideology was lent justification in literature. In many ways poetry became the preserver of the socialist dream that the GDR was failing to make real. Whilst subversive of 'real existierender Sozialismus', poets also saw the socialist experiment as incomplete, an 'Unvollendete Geschichte' or 'Unvollendeter Tag'.[48] They articulated their criticism of reality against a projection of the completed triumph of the socialist dream.

The preservation of this dream in poetry can be seen in the theme of nature. The motif of a natural landscape is well represented in work by the middle generation of poets, as well as some of the earliest poets such as Johannes Bobrowski.[49] The nature metaphor had also been important in the influential philosophical works of Bloch and Adorno.[50] As Marianne Schwarz-Scherer has pointed out, Becher's poem 'Vollmond' is typical of the embracing harmony in nature portrayed by poetry of the 1950s.[51] The utopian-

---

[46]See Bernd Wagner on the 'Biermann-Ausbürgerung' as a major turning-point for GDR literature, in Bernd Wagner, *Der Griff ins Leere: Elf Versuche* (Berlin, FRG: Transit, 1988), pp.109-111.

[47]Volker Braun, 'Der Mensch ohne Zugehörigkeit', *Das Argument* (1986), No.57, 327-329.

[48]Volker Braun, *Unvollendete Geschichte* (Frankfurt a.M.: Suhrkamp, 1977). Steffen Mensching, 'Unvollendeter Tag', *ndl*, 38 (1990), No.3, 50-56.

[49]The preoccupation with nature is reflected in the titles of the following collections: Günter Kunert, *Unschuld der Natur* (1966); Uwe Greßmann, *Der Vogel Frühling* (1967); Kito Lorenc, *Struga, Bilder einer Landschaft* (1967); Heinz Czechowski, *Wasserfahrt* (1968).

[50]See the discussion of the nature metaphor in Marx, Bloch, Adorno and Marcuse in Silvia Volckmann, *Zeit der Kirschen? Das Naturbild in der deutschen Gegenwartslyrik: Jürgen Becker, Sarah Kirsch, Wolf Biermann, Hans Magnus Enzensberger* (Königstein/Ts: Forum Academicum, 1982), pp.24-33.

[51]Marianne Schwarz-Scherer, *Subjektivität in der Naturlyrik der DDR (1950-1970)*

anticipatory nuances of this type of poetry correspond to a sense of the GDR offering hope of true 'Heimat'. From the following decade, nature was often portrayed   as   mechanized   and   instrumentalized,   as   in   Braun's 'Durchgearbeitete Landschaft' (*Texte*, iv, pp.88-89):

> Hier sind wir durchgegangen
> Mit unseren Werkzeugen   (lines 1-2)

The landscape is marked by the progress of the socialist collective, 'wir', a band of tool-bearing workers. In the 1970s, Uwe Kolbe's 'Hineingeboren' describes in a nature poem a different GDR.[52] This landmark poem sets a harmony between landscape and 'ich' in the first stanza against its abrupt reversal in the second:

> Kleines grünes Land enges,
> Stacheldrahtlandschaft.
> Schwarzer
> Baum neben mir.
> Harter Wind.
> Fremde Vögel.   (lines 7-11)

The adjectives 'schwarz', 'hart' and 'fremd' constitute an indictment of the poet's home country. Exposure in a landscape either post-apocalyptic or just vast and inhuman is part of a general sense of retreat from 'Aufbau' and other engagement in society. The title of the collection *Abschweifungen über Bäume* by Kristian Pech uses an allusion to Brecht's poem 'An die Nachgeborenen' to make the landscape metaphor political.[53] In the 1970s and 1980s, ecological concerns focused literary interest in polluted landscapes; the natural world became a site of threat in GDR poetry, as it did in West German poetry. In 1982, Silvia Volckmann stated in connection with this point, 'Wer heute von Natur spricht, äußert sich politisch aus'.[54] This had always been true in the GDR. Biermann's melancholy poem 'Der Herbst hat seinen Herbst' reveals this in its antithetical conclusion, in the turning to the social 'wir':[55]

> Der Herbst hat seinen Herbst
> Bald
> blüht schon der Winter
> Eins nach dem andern

(Frankfurt a.M.: Lang, 1992). Johannes R. Becher, 'Vollmond', *Glück der Ferne leuchtend nah* (Berlin, GDR: Aufbau, 1955), p.180.
[52]Uwe Kolbe, 'Hineingeboren', *Hineingeboren: Gedichte 1975-1979* (Berlin, GDR, and Weimar: Aufbau, 1980), p.46.
[53]Kristian Pech, *Abschweifungen über Bäume* (Rostock: Hinstorff, 1976). Bertolt Brecht, 'An die Nachgeborenen', *Gesammelte Werke*, ix, pp.722-725.
[54]Volckmann, *Zeit der Kirschen*, p.17.
[55]Wolf Biermann, 'Der Herbst hat seinen Herbst', *Mit Marx- und Engelszungen: Gedichte Balladen Lieder* (Berlin, FRG: Wagenbach, 1968), p.20.

Es betet ihren Rosenkranz
und gelassen die Natur

Wir aber
Ja, aber wir   (lines 8-15)

The seasons move on like the beads of a rosary, but this is the antithesis of the human collective's progress. Neither the natural order and peacefulness of nature, nor religious prayer, are mirrored in human society. Generally at this period, the poetic subject who is increasingly thrust out into a natural environment for solace, also expresses the poet's sense of displacement from the political centre.

The 1980s saw, in the work of poets born in the GDR, a resistance to the enterprise of the 'sächsische Dichterschule'. 'Eingreifen', optimism and hope in change were superseded in the new poetry by disillusionment and a playfully irreverent approach to GDR literary norms.[56] The official view, as articulated by Honecker at the tenth 'Parteitag der SED', still idealized the relationship between writers and the SED: 'Im Gegensatz zur bürgerlichen Gesellschaft vereinen sich Geist und Macht'.[57] Rather than feeling themselves bound to the socialist state, however, the latest generation seemed to have no allegiance. The esoteric discourse and relatively difficult poetic language of the young poets of the 1980s were regarded as escapism by some older poets: perhaps to opt out of overtly critical discourse was a 'safer' option than direct confrontation with the mechanisms of the state. Braun disliked the 'Neutöner' for their purported disinterest in social responsibility and their refusal to participate in a battle over the breadth of literary realism:

> Unsere jungen Dichter, Kinder der administrativen Beamten, suchen auch das Loch in der Mauer. Sie verbrauchen ihre Fantasie an Tunnels und Fesselballons, ihre "monologe gehen fremd". Fluchten wieder, aber auf Hasenpfoten.[58]

Braun interprets the poetry as newfangled rather than innovative. The young poet Jan Faktor takes a contrastingly positive view in 1988 of the new generation's poetry: 'Es gibt Zeitabschnitte in einem Leben usw., in denen man das Gefühl hat, daß die Dichtung eine Zukunft hat'.[59] For Faktor, Berlin

---

[56]For discussion of the new poetry of the 1980s as the work of a new young generation, see Karen Leeder, *Breaking Boundaries: A New Generation of Poets in the GDR* (Oxford: Clarendon, 1996); Ekkehard Mann, *Untergrund, autonome Literatur und das Ende der DDR* (Frankfurt a.M., Berlin, Bern, New York, Paris and Vienna: Lang, 1996).
[57]Erich Honecker quoted in *ND*, 12 April 1981.
[58]Volker Braun, 'Rimbaud. Ein Psalm der Aktualität', *SuF*, 37 (1985), 978-998 (p.983).
[59]Jan Faktor, 'Was ist neu an der jungen Literatur der 80er Jahre?', in *Vogel oder Käfig*

in the early 1980s was just such a time, when the writer's sense of social resonance, of the personally healing process of writing and of not being alone, coincided to give poetry a new impetus. Rather than the loss of aura which Peter Bürger associates with the Avant-garde, Faktor would here seem to be highlighting a resurrection of literary aura.[60] The new poets showed a concern with global issues of the human condition, rather than a special sense of being a GDR writer. These younger writers often had roots in the rock and punk music scenes, in theatre and performance art, or worked in collaboration with graphic artists and painters. The GDR academics Gabriele Muschter and Rüdiger Thomas describe them as 'resistent gegen ideologische Verheißungen, skeptisch gegen gesellschaftliche Utopien, widerspenstig gegen eine antimodernistische, volkstümelnde Ästhetik, fasziniert vom Anspruch der internationalen Avantgarde'.[61] Young GDR poets no longer identified with Romanticism, as the previous generation had done, but with twentieth-century Modernism and the Avant-garde. And rather than describing in portrait poems the forefathers to whom they looked, the young poets sought to participate directly in the modernist tradition. Where Endler and Mickel, editors of *In diesem besseren Land*, had preferred expressions of pathos in hymns, elegies and odes, the new poetry displayed a decay of traditional structure. Language itself became of overriding interest to poets such as Bert Papenfuß-Gorek, Jan Faktor and Sascha Anderson. Wittstock summarizes the generation change as 'Nach den Weltveränderern kamen die Sprachveränderer'.[62] Many poems of the 'sächsische Dichterschule' were concerned with changing the world; much of the younger poets' work was concerned with changing language. The form and language of this new work was often deliberately irritating. The new consensus about the origin and function of poetic language corresponded to the following description in a 1987 issue of the unofficial magazine *schaden*: 'die bearbeitung des vorgefundenen, des trivialen, des mißachteten, verachteten, geringgeschätzten rückt in den mittelpunkt der betrachtung'.[63] Was this then the end of the state as a point of orientation for poets?

The notion of political orientation was anathema to those poets of the 1980s who were labelled the 'Prenzlauer Berg Szene'. In the derelict districts

---

sein, ed. by Michael, p.367.
[60]Peter Bürger, *Theorie der Avantgarde* (Frankfurt a.M.: Suhrkamp, 1974).
[61]Gabriele Muschter and Rüdiger Thomas, 'Vorwort', in *Jenseits der Staatskultur*, ed. by Muschter, pp.7-10 (pp.8-9).
[62]Uwe Wittstock, *Von der Stalinallee zum Prenzlauer Berg: Wege der DDR-Literatur 1949-1989* (Munich: Piper, 1989), p.227.
[63]'Editorial Materialschaden', in *Vogel oder Käfig sein*, ed. by Michael, pp.351-352 (p.352).

of the major cities and most famously in Prenzlauer Berg, East Berlin, poets declared their art to be apolitical, neither affirmation of, nor opposition to, the state. Alexander von Bormann has described the resulting situation as 'eine Gegen-Kultur, die von keinem "Gegen" mehr wissen wollte, sondern nur von Selbst-Bestimmtheit'.[64] Although from the perspective of the 1990s, the allegiances of the 'Szene' poets look more ambiguous, Bormann represents the insiders' view and the view which predominated in the 1980s. As far as the younger generation of poets was concerned, the older GDR poets writing in the 1960s had been engaged in a dialogue with power which only compromised their art. Now writing was no longer to be undertaken against the dominant discourse, but in closed circles of like-minded artists. This late GDR phenomenon sought to supersede the culture of dialogue, with a refusal to negotiate with cultural policy. Stefan Döring's poem 'willelei' reflects this new enclave mentality:[65]

> ich habe euch nichts zu sagen
> ihr habt mir nichts zu sagen
> ihr macht was ihr wollt
> ich mache was ich will   (lines 1-4)

This poem is reminiscent of an exercise in a language learner's text book (as are some poems by Jan Faktor, such as 'wie praktisch ist unsere haut' of 1982).[66] Paradoxically, literary communication is established in order to reject communication. In this, the poem cannot be apolitical: rather, it suggests what James Mellis calls these poets' 'awareness of themselves as dissident intellectuals'.[67] Thomas Böhme's anti-authoritarian 'Elegie' of 1984 evokes the lifestyle of youth and uses humour to subvert the expectations of an elegy:[68]

> Narkotisiert unter lindenschatten
>   laufen wir durch vernieselten sommer
> So mekkafern, strafzettel an die regenmäntel
>   geheftet für wiederholtes radfahren

[64]Alexander von Bormann, 'Wege aus der Ordnung' in *Jenseits der Staatskultur*, ed. by Muschter, pp.83-107 (p.83).
[65]Stefan Döring, 'willelei', in *Sprache und Antwort: Stimmen und Texte einer anderen Literatur aus der DDR*, ed. by Egmont Hesse (Frankfurt a.M.: Fischer, 1988), p.91.
[66]Jan Faktor, 'wie praktisch ist unsere haut', *Georgs Versuche an einem Gedicht und andere positive Texte aus dem Dichtergraben des Grauens* (Berlin, GDR, and Weimar: Aufbau, 1989), pp.28-33.
[67]James Mellis, 'Writers in Transition: The End of East German Literature?', in *The New Germany: Social, Political and Cultural Challenges of Unification*, ed. by Derek Lewis and John R. P. McKenzie (Exeter: University of Exeter Press: 1995), pp.220-242.
[68]Thomas Böhme, 'Elegie', in *Vogel oder Käfig sein*, ed. by Michael, p.31.

> Im park, denn wir hatten geglaubt
> an die narrenfreiheit der radfahrer   (lines 1-6)

These humorous lines suggest an alternative 'wir', one that takes drugs because there is no other escape from ridiculous restrictions. 'Unter lindenschatten' evokes the park, but also the main avenue in East Berlin, Unter den Linden. The word 'mekkafern' is both an ironic comment on the weather, and also points to being far from the destination of a pilgrimage or a centre of faith: Mecca here is another way of referring to utopia. Papenfuß-Gorek's poem 'dem einkaufen & eingehen dieser tage' also makes a moral point:[69]

> es soll kein wert
> mehr mehrwert sein
> denn wert ist mir
> was du mir weh & ach
> & ueberhaupt antust
> wert ist was ich dir
> an tu tu an tu an
> was gilt ist nich geld   (lines 12-19)

This poem is about value and worth, playing on the aural connection between 'Geld' and 'gelten'. The lines are driven by sound and a rocking repetition, which makes the text sound like a litany. Where this poem uses no punctuation, Matthias BAADER Holst's 1985 poem 'mondvögel-stumpfsinnig' overuses full-stops; both techniques create barriers to a first reading:[70]

> du wirst nicht verlassen. man hält den löffel. an die schläfe.
> um das umrühren einer tasse. kaffee. aufgeben zu können.
> man sitzt im trockenen. eines nie erreichten. vormittags. jemand liest
> aus verlorenheit. eigne sätze. betrachtet den schutt. einer
> frau. keines eingezeichneten landes.   (lines 13-17)

Despite the assertion in the first line quoted here, there is a predominant atmosphere of desolation. The gesture with the spoon is both an allusion to compulsive behaviour and 'aufgeben' in a wider sense. A morning that never comes and the rubble of lives and buildings constitute an indictment of the GDR, as does the savouring of 'eigne sätze', a phrase emphasized by the use of full-stops. The old, pre-1945 Germany not drawn on any map becomes a symbol of being lost. Clearly these lines evoke a certain social milieu, even a literary milieu (in lines 15-16), which in itself is a political reflection on the GDR. The critic Birgit Dahlke has pointed to a dissident political discourse in

---

[69]Bert Papenfuß-Gorek, 'dem einkaufen & eingehen dieser tage', *dreizehntanz: Gedichte* (Berlin, GDR, and Weimar: Aufbau, 1989), p.118
[70]Matthias BAADER Holst, 'mondvögel-stumpfsinnig', in *Vogel oder Käfig sein*, ed. by Michael, p.134.

the Prenzlauer Berg scene: 'tabuisierte Themen wie Staat, Partei, Macht, Presse, Rituale oder Ausgrenzungspraktiken wurden hier zum Gegenstand von Kunst und Literatur'.[71] This statement refutes the poets' own claims that their literature was not a political discourse. However, Dahlke's listed themes were also in fact represented in officially published literature, by writers like Braun. The taboos which the new poetry broke were not primarily thematic, but rather publishing taboos and language taboos.

The new writing broke publishing taboos by existing in a niche outside state jurisdiction in the small print-runs of magazines which the artists published themselves. Adolf Endler has called these magazines 'Heftpublikationen' over which the poets exclaimed, 'Klein, aber mein!'.[72] The first of the 'samizdat' magazines, issued in 1981, was *Der Kaiser ist nackt*, edited by the young poet Uwe Kolbe. The title recalls the fairytale in which a boy alone dares to speak the obvious truth and mock the king. In the foreword to the anthology of magazine issues which were put together for West German readers, Kolbe wrote 'wir wollten einfach eine andere Öffentlichkeit'.[73] This new kind of publication was very limited, but it was the only alternative publication within the GDR. Typically, the unofficial magazine *Entwerter-Oder* was first produced in only four copies of fifteen sides each, in Berlin in February 1982. In retrospect, its editor stated, 'Am Beginn dieser originalgrafischen Zeitschrift "Entwerter-Oder" stand der Versuch, dem "Für-den-Schreibtisch-Schreiben" ein Ende zu setzen'.[74] Previously, writers who were rejected by the state could produce only exile literature from abroad, or remain in the GDR and consign their work to a desk drawer. Although circulation was small, the underground publications provided a new possibility of reaching a GDR readership. In 1979 almost all important new GDR books had been published in West Germany alone. Writers were in the East: their texts were with an unknown public in the West. Wolfgang Hilbig's collection *abwesenheit* (published in the West) thematizes his own absence from the GDR and the absence of the collection.[75] Kolbe has interpreted the underground literary scene of the 1980s as a reaction against the 'abwesenheit' of GDR literature:

---

[71]Dahlke, ' "Die Chancen haben sich verschanzt" ', p.229.

[72]Endler, *Tarzan am Prenzlauer Berg*, p.262.

[73]Uwe Kolbe, Lothar Trolle and Bernd Wagner, eds., *Mikado oder Der Kaiser ist nackt: Selbstverlegte Literatur in der DDR* (Darmstadt: Luchterhand, 1988), p.106.

[74]Uwe Warnke, 'Entwerter-Oder: Statement des Herausgebers', in *Vogel oder Käfig sein*, ed. by Michael, p.339.

[75]Wolfgang Hilbig, *abwesenheit* (Frankfurt a.M.: Fischer, 1979).

Großgeschrieben wurde, daß es darum ginge, etwas HIER zu "machen", HIER aufzubauen, zu unternehmen. HIER, in der allemal schäbigen DDR, sollte produziert und anwesend, das längst Vorhandene sichtbar gemacht werden.[76] This comment suggests that the Prenzlauer Berg poets who rejected a dialogue with official policy nonetheless had a GDR identity and wanted to write as GDR poets, albeit not in the state-sanctioned mode. Some GDR commentators close to the unofficial scene have described it as the extension and completion of GDR culture. Christoph Tannert thus described the unofficial magazines as 'initiativen einer ergänzungskultur' and Peter Böthig refers to their function as 'eine notwendige Ergänzungskultur'.[77]

The badge of this culture was the linguistic mutation typical of the underground poets, an extreme rejection of the need to be 'volksverständlich'. Papenfuß-Gorek, Döring and Faktor are described by Endler as 'die "Jandlianer" der DDR', that is a group of poets whose language can resemble that of the Austrian concrete poet Ernst Jandl.[78] Strategies employed by Döring, Papenfuß-Gorek, Sascha Anderson, and Rainer Schedlinski include montage, the distortion of traditional metaphors, strings of metonyms, consistent capitalization or consistent 'Kleinschreibung', the favouring of 'f' instead of 'v', the elimination of umlauts, and the replacing of 'und' with the emptier '&'. These devices became the hallmarks of the underground. Whilst the new poetry involved the kind of linguistic play with words that the title of Döring's collection *Heutmorgestern* demonstrates, the avant-garde forms do not obscure all communication.[79] Exchanging of the letters 'f' and 'w' in Döring's poem 'wortfege' (p.103), for example, means another text co-exists beneath the surface one, but the key to the code is not difficult. This poem is about 'fortwege', about staying or leaving the GDR. The effect of the playful manipulation of words is to lend buoyancy to Döring's serious and often bold statements. The experimental, often hermetic poetic forms coming out of GDR cities in the 1980s correspond to Viktor Shklovsky's definition of art as

---

[76]Kolbe, *Die Situation*, p.18.

[77]Christoph Tannert, 'Frischwärts' (1986) and Peter Böthig, 'Aufbrüche in Vielfalt' (1988), in *Zellinnendruck*, ed. by Egmont Hesse and Christoph Tannert (Leipzig: Eigen+Art, 1990), pp.6-7 (p.6), and pp.9-10 (p.10).

[78]Endler, *Tarzan am Prenzlauer Berg*, p.68. See the concrete poems by Papenfuß-Gorek, Michael Wüstefeld, Elke Erb and Johannes Jansen in *wortBILD: Visuelle Poesie in der DDR*, ed. by Guillermo Deisler and Jörg Kowalski (Halle-Leipzig: mdv, 1990).

[79]Stefan Döring, *Heutmorgestern* (Berlin, GDR, and Weimar: Aufbau, 1989).

'ostranenie', a making strange, a renewal of perception.[80] All art might seem to involve a renewal of perception, a negation of existing habits, but not all art draws such attention to its devices as does avant-garde art.

Innovations in poetry of the 1980s correspond to the general notion of literature's function as a breaking of boundaries. Ludwig Wittgenstein had understood language as a boundary marker: 'Die Grenzen meiner Sprache bedeuten die Grenzen meiner Welt'.[81] This is echoed in Anderson's poem entitled 'lettern schwarz auf weissem grund', which closes with the lines 'ich habe ausser meiner sprache keine / mittel meine sprache zu verlassen'.[82] Papenfuß-Gorek's experimentation with words made them lose established meaning in this way and gave them a fresh conceptual context; his writing shows a mistrust of everything handed down by the GDR, and seems aimed at provoking conservative sensibilities about what a poem should be. For such poets, the poetic text does not mean an ideal distance from language, nor an aesthetically closed product, but rather working in, and with, words: Papenfuß-Gorek has described language as a 'kampf-tanz' between the senses and the cultural rules. He gave the language he reclaimed for himself its own name, 'arkdichtung'. This assertion of a personal language contradicted the socialist primacy of the collective. Geist has summed up the creative language which emerged in the cities of the GDR at this time as writing which 'favoured the process of writing over the finished product and promoted the blasphemous, scurrilous and humorous deconstruction of fixed meanings'.[83] To give more importance to the performance of writing than to the finished text evades fixed meaning. The young poets' dissection and defamiliarization of language exposed what was hidden or suppressed, undermining the apparent authenticity of grammatical language. This correlates with Mikhail Bakhtin's general notion of language as a site of struggle for individuals trying to wrest words away from the dominant authority and out of previous contexts. Verbal expression is a struggle to be able to use words for one's own purposes without their being tainted with the 'taste' of the party.[84] Böthig describes the wild,

---

[80]See Frederic Jameson, *The Prison-House of Language: A Critical Account of Structuralism and Russian Formalism* (Princeton: Princeton University, 1972), pp.50-51.
[81]Ludwig Wittgenstein, *Tractatus logico-philosophicus: Tagebücher 1914-1916. Philosophische Untersuchungen* (Frankfurt a.M.: Suhrkamp, [1969]), p.140.
[82]Sascha Anderson, 'lettern schwarz auf weissem grund', in *Ein Molotow-Cocktail*, ed. by Geist, p.243.
[83]Geist, 'Voices from No Man's Land', p.136.
[84]Mikhail Bakhtin, *The Dialogic Imagination*, trans. by Caryl Emerson and Michael Holquist (Austin: University of Texas, 1981), p.293: 'All words have the "taste" of a profession, a genre, a tendency, a party, a particular work, a particular person, a

agrammatical language as 'ein kollektiver prozeß des mündigwerdens'.[85] Again then, GDR literature seemed to be about 'speaking out' and rejecting infantilization by the SED.

The GDR 'Szene' poetry of the 1980s is regarded as neo-avant-garde, following on and reworking the principles of early twentieth-century Avant-garde poetry in several respects. Prenzlauer Berg was perhaps comparable to the Lower East Side, New York, as a place which became renowned as a centre of bohemian culture and avant-garde language. In the 1980s Jack Kerouac, Alan Ginsberg and other American 'beat' poets were popular amongst 'Szene' poets of the GDR. The 'Manifeste der Trivialpoesie', drawn up by Faktor in 1982 and 1983, also resemble Dadaist manifestos.[86] The GDR manifestos were persiflage of cultural prescriptions and of the idea that the avant-garde was trivial. They also point to the heritage with which the new poets identified, namely Expressionism, Cubism, Surrealism and Dada (poets like Kurt Schwitters for instance). Kolbe has also expressed a debt to the Expressionist anthology *Menschheitsdämmerung* as the source of his poetic language: 'Da kommt meine Sprache her, die hat keinen anderen literarischen Ursprung'. Frank-Wolf Matthies sees the influence of Surrealism and Dada on his work as a natural consequence of the peculiar situation created by the state's machinations in the GDR: 'Hineingeboren in eine surrealistische Umwelt werden wir fast schon zwangsläufig Surrealisten'.[87] In Matthies's view then, experience of life in the GDR involved the collision of incompatible realities, the breaks in context and in logical sequence, that constitute surrealism. In 1962 Hans Magnus Enzensberger suggested that a neo-avant-garde writer could be accused of banal mimicry.[88] Rather than merely a belated catching-up, the GDR avant-garde used in a new context the central ideas of an avant-garde as a militant break with established norms, as an attack on the institution of art and as a 'true' lifting of distinction between art and life. For the GDR in the 1980s this was in opposition to the official understanding of literature's place, but also a playing with the absurd as a response to an absurd social reality. In September 1989, Durs Grünbein

---

generation, an age-group, the day and the hour. Each word tastes of the context and contexts in which it has lived its socially charged life'.

[85]Peter Böthig, 'die verlassene sprache', in *Die andere Sprache: Neue DDR-Literatur der 80er Jahre*, ed. by Heinz Ludwig Arnold (Munich: TuK, 1990), pp.38-48 (p.40).
[86]Faktor, *Georgs Versuche an einem Gedicht*, pp.87-102.
[87]Kolbe and Matthies quoted in Anneli Hartmann, 'Der Generationswechsel - ein ästhetischer Wechsel? Schreibweisen und Traditionsbezüge in der jungsten DDR-Lyrik, *Jahrbuch zur Literatur in der DDR*, 4 (1985), 109-134 (p.128 and p.129).
[88]Hans-Magnus Enzensberger, 'Die Aporien der Avantgarde', *Einzelheiten* (Frankfurt a.M.: Suhrkamp, 1962), pp.290-315.

aspired to poetry which would be 'absolut ätzend und unzitierbar'.[89] Such an aspiration offers an interpretative starting-point for some of the more experimental and disjointed poetry. It also accommodates a type of ambivalence and obscure symbolism as counter-response to the appropriation of literature by German politics. The 'Kultivierung des Fehlers' sabotaged the rules of the language and of 'der vormundschaftliche Staat'.[90] This is at the root of David Bathrick's conclusion that even this generation of GDR poets was in dialogue with state power:

> Even at the level of poetic utterance, the Prenzlauer Berg poets were in dialogue, regardless of their disavowal of any participatory role within what they disparagingly called a *Gesprächskultur*.[91]

If the experimentation was a response to, and a rejection of state power, it would seem to define itself against the discourse which necessitated it.

As far as Faktor is concerned, even in the 1980s poets did not achieve some kind of niche between and beyond the political system: 'Die Tragödie der DDR-Literatur ist ihr von vornherein verlorener Kampf um Autonomie'.[92] Experimental poetic language was still a 'Sklavensprache'.[93] In his texts Papenfuß-Gorek can seem to write from 'eine freche Sklavenposition' (Kratschmer, p.300). The unresolvable duality referred to in Papenfuß-Gorek's 1985 poem 'man kann nie wissen' can be read as his own statement of an ambiguous struggle for autonomy:[94]

ich steck mit beiden beinen
im dualismus & krieg's im kopp
nicht zusammen, meine haut zu retten
[...]
ich bin mir nicht staats sicher
aber yck byn eher so'n bardo-typ (lines 4-6 and 13-14)

The poet is 'nicht staats sicher' in the sense that he is not safe from the state and in the sense that he is unsure about its aims; the state cannot rely upon him (including as a co-opted member of its security service), but equally he is still

---

[89]Durs Grünbein, 'Ameisenhafte Größe', *Die andere Sprache*, ed. by Arnold, pp.110-113 (p.113).
[90]Gerrit-Jan Berendse, 'Outcast in Berlin: Opposition durch Entziehung bei der jungeren Generation', *ZfG*, N.F.1 (1991), 21-27 (p.24). Rolf Henrich, *Der vormundschaftliche Staat: Vom Versagen des real existierenden Sozialismus* (Reinbek bei Hamburg: Rowohlt, 1989).
[91]David Bathrick, *The Powers of Speech: The Politics of Culture in the GDR* (Lincoln, USA: University of Nebraska Press, 1995), p.240.
[92]Faktor, 'Was ist neu an der jungen Literatur der 80er Jahre?'.
[93]'Sklavensprache' is a term widely used (e.g. by Mayer and by Wüst) to refer to literary language in the GDR.
[94]Bert Papenfuß-Gorek, 'man kann nie wissen', *dreizehntanz*, pp.154-155.

caught up in the duality. 'Bardo' is a term from the Tibetan Book of the Dead which refers to the intermediate spiritual state of death, in which the soul chooses between a bright light (nirvana) or lesser, coloured lights which lead the soul back to rebirth in the relative world of samsara. The lyric 'ich' is thus between two states of being. The young poet Steffen Mensching also thematizes duality and contradictions in his poem 'Aus Gesichtern älterer Freunde':[95]

> Ja sagen
> Die Worte, Nein die Gesichter.
> Falten der Schrecken, Falten
> Des Glücks. Zwischen
> Auftrag und Selbstaufgabe
> Vergleich und Verrat
> Leben wir und beobachten wir uns und unsere
> Bitterkeiten. Aus denen
> Der älteren Freunde
> Lese ich, mein Scheitern
> Ist hier noch nicht gründlich genug.   (lines 28-38)

These lines suggest self-analysis: references to 'Worte', 'Auftrag' and 'lesen' indicate that this lyric subject is a writer, who is located 'zwischen', between the poles. The 'yes' of the words and the 'no' of the faces represent the contradiction between literary ideals and experienced realities. At the close of this poem the lyric voice anticipates only a growing sense of failure and resignation as he gets older. The inclusion of the word 'hier', in the last line quoted, seems deliberately to point to Germany's division too.

The youngest generation was in some ways practising the same 'Balance-Akte zwischen dem Bedürfnis nach Autonomie gegenüber dem Staat (der Gesellschaft) und dem Wunsch nach Zugehörigkeit zu ihm (zu ihr)' (Faktor, p.367), just as previous generations of GDR writers had. Indeed, the so-called 'outsiders' were not completely invisible inside the official literary scene. Döring is represented, for instance, in several anthologies of the mid-1980s, including *Vogelbühne* (published in the GDR) and *Berührung ist nur eine Randerscheinung* (prepared in the GDR, but finally published in the West). His poems of 1979-1988 are collected in *Heutmorgestern*, which was published in the GDR in pre-'Wende' 1989 in the 'Außer der Reihe' series. That series, which began to appear at the end of 1988 from the Aufbau Verlag, is an indication of the relaxation of official restrictions. The Prenzlauer Berg poets Papenfuß-Gorek, Faktor, Schedlinski and Gabriele Kachold were each

---

[95]Steffen Mensching, 'Aus Gesichtern älterer Freunde', in *Ausdrückliche Klage aus der inneren Immigration: Texte und Grafiken aus der DDR*, ed. by Asteris Kutulas and Udo Tietz (Luxemburg: Edition Phi, 1992), unnumbered pages.

published in this series too and thereby brought both to the attention of a wider audience and under the umbrella of institutionalized culture. From 1988, the Aufbau Verlag also published work by writers who had left the GDR and gone to West Germany.[96] Despite, or perhaps because of, official liberalization and diversification, there remained a strong political element to literature's place in society. Generally, authors' readings still provided somewhere for those who identified with the authors' political views to meet and discuss matters in a way that was otherwise possible only under the aegis of the Church. Thus Silvia Volckmann describes all poetry in the GDR as a taking up of position with respect to political power: 'Im Unterschied zu dem westdeutschen hat der ostdeutsche Lyriker einen klaren Bezugspunkt: In wie unterschiedliche Weise auch immer, jedes in der DDR entstandene Gedicht bezieht – direkt oder indirekt – Stellung zu dem Staat DDR, zu den (kultur-) politischen Postulaten und Direktiven der SED, zu den Problemen des sozialistischen Aufbaus'.[97]

The role of the writer in the GDR was always caught up with the possibilities of autonomy on the one hand and social resonance on the other. These possibilities have provided one way of discussing GDR literary history. One can see that each generation consciously distanced itself further from cultural policy than the last and rejected the artistic undertakings of its predecessor generation. Hermann Korte's description of 'volle historische Unordnung' seems to me to overstate the case.[98] Rather, a gradual emancipating of GDR literature occurred. The history of the writer's self-understanding in the GDR can be seen as the history of his or her attempt to take the essence of literature further from state politics. In the light of the three stages of innovation identified with the development of GDR poetry, a general principle emerges: poetry, as a basic exploratory activity, means making an effort to say what cannot be said in the language except metaphorically. When acceptance catches up with it finally, then poetry takes a new 'deviant' path. By the 1980s therefore, GDR literature was diverse. Within this diverse literature, the concept of the poet's role had shifted and proliferated. By this decade, poetry had come far from the explicit 'Parteilichkeit und Volksverbundenheit', far from the didactic purpose and social dialogue, of the 'original' GDR text. In Braun's image of 1985, recent GDR poetry offered a multi-layered and uncharted path:

---

[96]See Carsten Wurm, *Jeden Tag ein Buch: 50 Jahre Aufbau-Verlag 1945-1995* (Berlin: Aufbau, 1995), pp.84-85.
[97]Volckmann, *Zeit der Kirschen*, p.237.
[98]Hermann Korte, 'Vorwort', *Geschichte der deutschen Lyrik seit 1945* (Stuttgart: Metzler, 1989), p.x.

Ästhetische Wanderkarten helfen nicht weiter, wir müssen einen unbekannten
Pfad finden durch die Bedeutungsschichten. ('Rimbaud', p.997)
The only exception to this was the poetry which still followed the SED's well-
charted path, and was represented by a few anthologies of workers' poems,
FDJ poetry and by a small number of remaining 'Dichter im Dienst'. Antonia
Grunenberg also characterizes 1980s literature in the GDR by its multiplicity:
'Ein einheitliches, gar representatives Bild von der Literatur der DDR in den
achtziger Jahren läßt sich nicht gewinnen. Prägend ist der Eindruck, daß es
viele Literaturen und nicht eine Literatur in der DDR gibt'.[99] The GDR
publishers on the one hand and the alternative publishing scene on the other
brought together poets who had contrasting ideas about poetry: their common
acceptability or unacceptability should not, in the long run, conceal their
individual poetics. With this widening of the GDR poet's place came
increasingly diverse ideas about poetic language. Although the image of the
alternative scene was largely coloured by Papenfuß-Gorek's type of radical
language experimentation, there was actually great diversity within the young
generation: poets such as Grünbein, Mensching and Drawert were using quite
different poetic languages, and some young women poets were doing
something different again.[100] Between the various strands of GDR poetry then
there were numerous poetic voices. Formal diversity can also be seen in the
many traditional forms, alongside the avant-garde forms for which GDR
poetry of the 1980s was renowned.

   Despite great diversification, it was only with the end of the socialist
regime that GDR writing was beyond the jurisdiction of political power. The
three chronological stages of new developments can each be characterized by
a certain conception of the relationship between 'Geist' and 'Macht'. In the
cases of individual poets these three strands tend not to be clearly delineated
however. State culture and non-state culture are more analytical tools
describing fields of activity than two distinct realms. In 1972, Werner
Brettschneider located GDR literature 'zwischen Autonomie und
Staatsdienst':[101] it is also true to say that for individual poets, their work
shifted between the same two poles. With different texts and different

---

[99]Antonia Grunenberg, 'Entgrenzung und Selbstbeschränkung: Zur Literatur der DDR
in den achtziger Jahren', in *Liebes- und andere Erklärungen: Texte von und über DDR-
Autorinnen*, ed. by Christel Hildebrandt (Bonn: Kleine Schritte, 1988), pp.137-156
(p.155).
[100]On female poets in the alternative GDR publishing scene see Birgit Dahlke,
Papierboot: Autorinnen aus der DDR - inoffiziell publiziert (Würzberg: Konigshausen
und Neumann, 1997).
[101]Werner Brettschneider, *Zwischen Autonomie und Staatsdienst: Die Literatur in der
DDR* ([Berlin]: Schmidt, [1972]).

collections a poet would move about within the spectrum, for instance writing satirical, combative verse and then something more visionary and existential, which had no engagement with political reality. Dieter Schlenstedt describes this shifting within the spectrum as a game:

> Die Autoren hatten einen bestimmten Bezugspunkt, ob sie den nun wollten oder nicht; und was sie sagten, welche Bilder sie zeigten, war zu bewerten am Maß des Aufgehens in oder der Distanz zu diesem offiziellen ideologischen Raum. Ein Spiel von Nähe und Ferne zu dem, was offiziell galt, wurde gespielt, von Lesern und Autoren, auch wenn über die Regeln dieses Spiels nicht gesprochen wurde.[102]

Alongside the gestures of literary autonomy which became acute by the mid-1980s, state policy remained a visible presence. The 'Vorstandsmitglieder' at the tenth congress of the writers' union in November 1987, for example, included the poets Czechowski, Mensching, Heinz Kahlau, Rainer Kirsch and Richard Pietraß. Sitting on the platform, writers alternated with Politburo members, whilst the President Hermann Kant opined, 'Wir haben einen Auftrag'.[103] Antonia Grunenberg identifies a dependence on the state's position, amongst all GDR writers. Even at this late stage she discerns 'das Phänomen einer auch psychischen Abhängigkeit des einzelnen von dem Machtgestus des Staates und der SED'.[104] Paradoxically then, the state was still some kind of orientation point for GDR writing, amidst its great diversity.

Since the fall of the socialist regime in 1989, revelations and reassessments concerning the role of the poet in the GDR have centred on new equations of 'Geist' and 'Macht'. Writers have been implicated in power, as informers and as instruments of state rule through their work. In the early 1990s, it emerged that writers such as Kant, Anderson, Schedlinski, Kahlau, Wolf, and Müller passed information to the Stasi. When Anderson and Schedlinski's involvement with the Stasi came to light, critics rejected the underground publications' assertions of artistic autonomy. What had been taken as an apolitical avant-garde movement became suspicious. It seemed that in fact there had been no 'alternative' nor an authentic underground, and this impression damaged perceptions of GDR literature. But can literature in fact be guilty of collusion or falsification? Responses to this question depend largely on how congruent poet and poem are perceived to be. The lyric persona in modern theory tends to be a shifting concept that is repeatedly

---

[102]Dieter Schlenstedt, 'Integration-Loyalität-Anpassung: Über die Schwierigkeit bei der Aufkündigung eines komplizierten Verhältnisses', in *Literatur der DDR*, ed. by Arnold, pp.172-189 (p.176).
[103]Details from Burmeister, 'Schriftsteller in gewendeten Verhältnissen'.
[104]Antonia Grunenberg, *Aufbruch der inneren Mauer: Politik und Kultur in der DDR 1971-1990* (Bremen: Edition Temmen, 1990), p.236.

reconstructed, depending on whether the poem is read by one reader or another or, for instance, whether it is presented at a public reading by the poet. Nonetheless, judgements of literature from the GDR have tended to be author-based. This applied to the reception of GDR writing both in the West, where writers' dissenting political attitudes were crucial for popular acclaim, and in the East, where for many years the right to publish entailed having conformist political attitudes. Although initially there were clear guidelines as to what could and could not be published in the GDR, censorship and permission to publish became increasingly arbitrary, based less on the text in question and rather on the reputation and political allegiances of the writer. Subsequently, in the 'Literaturstreit' outlined in my introduction, textual criticism continued to be overshadowed by the political activities of writers.

Creative achievements become problematic under an oppressive regime, where literature is constantly confronted with a choice between affirming or opposing the state. Although literature may be a space outside this political duality, many GDR writers seemed to be forced back to choose between complicity and dissent. Writers such as Braun and Müller had always drawn on a discourse which was not that of the regime, but was close to it, a discourse of alternative Marxism provided by Marx himself and other political philosophers such as Walter Benjamin and Ernst Bloch. The writers sought thus to be accepted by the regime, despite undermining its monoculture. David Bathrick describes this kind of accommodation as creating a 'heretical discourse' which, intended as an impulse for reformation and revision, functioned as a forerunner to the 'Wende' democracy movement:

> Simply to dismiss the East German literary opposition on the basis of their philosophical roots within a political culture of Marxism or their efforts to work from within is to ignore their *function* within the evolution of a much broader, democratizing process.[105]

This suggests that the way to be an oppositional, alternative voice, to survive without being crushed by the Stasi, was to 'work from within'. Thus Bathrick sees GDR literature as an instance of 'rewriting some master code from within the code itself' (p.19). Others have seen the poetry from outside the code as a forerunner of the 'Wende': in discussing Papenfuß-Gorek's linguistic 'revolution', Achim Trebeß states, 'Die Spracheuphorie und -phantasie der Demos im Oktober und November 1989 scheint mir auch ein wenig geprägt durch die Vorarbeit dieser Lyrik'.[106] The connection made by Bathrick and Trebeß between two kinds of GDR poetry and the emergence of alternative

---

[105]Bathrick, *The Powers of Speech*, p.229.
[106]Achim Trebeß, ' "im rechten augenblikk das linke tun": Spracherneuerung in Texten von Bert Papenfuß-Gorek', *WB*, 36 (1990), 617-636 (p.625).

politics points to the 'alternative' implicit in all poetry as a genre. Thus the distinction between being inside and being outside was effectively a consequence of pervasive censorship: until the late 1980s, poets had to work within the code otherwise they could not work officially in the GDR at all.

In order to reach a GDR readership some kind of compromise with power was unavoidable, it seemed. Questions of compromise usually came up first in negotiation with a publishing house: even the most dissident GDR writers nearly always tried in the first instance to have their work accepted for publication in the GDR. This negotiation often resulted in substantial reworkings of the author's original material for the sake of political correctness. It also inevitably precipitated a type of self-censorship, at an earlier stage: writers who endeavoured to write within the guidelines had effectively internalized the state. Wolf saw such censorship as a practice which precluded self-understanding. The GDR censor deleted the following lines from Wolf's 'Vier Vorlesungen' of 1983, which deal precisely with the impact of censorship:

> Wie verhängnisvoll erweisen sich jetzt jene Lücken in unserem Denken und Fühlen, wie verhängnisvoll alles, was uns zu sehen, hören, riechen, schmecken, empfinden und zu sagen nicht erlaubt wurde und wird.[107]

At root Wolf expresses a belief that what compromise will not allow one to articulate, one cannot fully conceive. Heiner Müller, speaking about the integrity of the writer in a dictatorship, casts compromise in another light:

> Es gibt einfach Prioritäten. Ich bin Schriftsteller zu allererst. Das Wesentliche ist, die Möglichkeit zu finden, das zu schreiben, was ich schreiben will und was nur ich schreiben kann. Das ist die erste Moral. Danach kommt alles andere.[108]

A different morality can seem to apply to the writer. Müller made this statement in the context of talking about prizes and money which he received from the SED. It suggests that to remain in the GDR showed a greater allegiance to one's art and one's readership than leaving. It may also suggest that artists have different commitments. GDR writer Horst Drescher also places commitment to writing above all else and sums up the problems in an exclamation:

> Ein Künstler, wenn er diesen Namen verdient, nimmt jede, aber auch jede Demütigung hin, um sein Werk schaffen zu können. – Aber dann![109]

Certainly, some writers endured humiliation during the GDR years in connection with their writing, but others were also humiliated in the aftermath

---

[107]Quoted in Wichner, ed., *Zensur in der DDR*, pp.109-110.
[108]Heiner Müller, ' "Ich bin kein Held, das ist nicht mein Job" ', *SDZ*, 14/15 September 1991, p.15.
[109]Horst Drescher, *Aus dem Zirkus Leben: Notizen 1969-1990* (Berlin and Weimar: Aufbau, 1990), p.6.

when the Stasi revelations brought condemnation. Drescher's exclamation 'Aber dann!' alludes to the problems for self-understanding and for the finished product, if an artist's loyalty to his art is above integrity. State control over writers not only manifested itself through censorship and the politics of discourse, however. Every book published in the GDR required a license: the manuscript had to be approved by 'die Hauptverwaltung Verlage und Buchhandel', directed from 1973 by Klaus Höpcke, which also oversaw the distribution of books and the distribution of materials and equipment for their production. Even to publish abroad, writers were under a legal obligation to offer their manuscript first to a GDR publishing house and, if it was rejected, to proceed via the 'Büro für Urheberrechte'. Fines and imprisonment were meted out to authors who contravened the publishing procedures or produced texts which could be construed as 'staatsfeindlich'. The Stasi particularly monitored artists and writers:

> Das MfS hatte dafür zu sorgen, daß die Bezirksliteraturzentren und deren Beiräte personell "richtig" besetzt wurden. Ferner waren durch den "Einsatz von geeigneten Inoffiziellen Mitarbeitern in Schlüsselpositionen in den Bezirksliteraturzentren" systematisch die "loyalen" Autoren zu fördern, während bei nicht förderungswürdigen Personen Verträge mit Verlagen, Redaktionen, Massenmedien sowie die Aufnahme als Kandidat im Schriftstellerverband verhindert werden sollten.[110]

Part of the defined task of the Stasi was then to penetrate cultural life. Evidence of this is provided by the numerous writers who were closely watched and the numbers who, like Kunze and Kunert, were hounded out of the country. The effect of spying was to thwart some artistic activity within the GDR. The Stasi was also a strange judge of literature, spies in effect producing reviews which judged 'bad' writing as that which could be construed as 'konterrevolutionär'.

The problems of censorship only became public in the GDR in 1987 when they were raised at the tenth 'Schriftstellerkongreß'. On this occasion, Christoph Hein openly described censorship as 'überlebt, nutzlos, paradox, menschenfeindlich, volksfeindlich, ungesetzlich und strafbar'.[111] For Kunert, the state's control over literature eventually made writing impossible:

> Die Folgen einer restriktiven Kulturpolitik in der DDR haben dazu geführt, daß über Jahrzehnte hinweg Schriftsteller den Ort der geistigen Mumifizierung

---

[110]David Gill and Ulrich Schröter, *Das Ministerium für Staatssicherheit: Anatomie des Mielke-Imperiums* (Berlin: Rowohlt, 1991), pp.162-163.
[111]See Carsten Gansel, *Das Parlament des Geistes: Literatur zwischen Hoffnung und Repression 1945-1961* (Berlin: BasisDruck, 1996), p.36.

flohen, um nicht die Zahl der abgestorbenen Talente zu vergrößern.[112] He describes the prospect of remaining in the GDR as a slow death for a writer. In the 1987 collection *Berlin beizeiten* he returns in poetry to the city which he had been forced to leave in 1979.[113] It is a place marked by 'Reglosigkeit' (p.34), 'teuer erworbene Katatonie' (p.32) and 'lustlose Menschen' (p.34). Kunert seems fascinated by images of humanity petrified: he uses the legends of Golem, Medusa and Pygmalion; poems focus on Sodom's column of salt, on fossils, and on the stone figures of Bomarzo. In 1986 Bernhard Greiner identified a general 'Motiv der Metamorphose' in Kunert's work.[114] In *Berlin beizeiten* it is a negative metamorphosis that curtails movement and saps life. Kunert himself, in his essay 'Schreiben in einem Deutschland', rejects anecdotes about writers outwitting the censors, because such tales imply that writers could live under censorship and remain unscathed.[115] Elsewhere Kunert uses evolution as a metaphor for the effect of writing under censorship. This follows on from the political interpretation of Kunert's earlier poem 'Wie ich ein Fisch wurde'.[116] Kunert believes that the author exposed to censorship is forced into compromises which change him irrevocably into a different creature. Self-censorship becomes, Kunert claims, the defining attribute of the writer in a dictatorship: 'In der Rolle des Zensors schlüpfend, beurteilte er seine Arbeit' ('Schreiben in einem Deutschland', p.41). For Kunert the poet in the GDR took the role of a censor: to survive he had to adapt to what would be accepted and think one step ahead of the external censor.

Many writers, like Kunert, were forced to leave the GDR because writing became impossible for them. Many other writers and poets persevered, however, and were able to continue to write under the perculiar conditions imposed by the GDR regime. Are we to conclude that the political and ideological pressure could also foster creativity? GDR poet and poetry editor Richard Pietraß likened GDR censorship to roulette, a game of chance, reflecting the gamble of submitting one's work and waiting to see if it was accepted. Often poets might submit a few highly provocative texts in a

---

[112]Günter Kunert, 'Deutsch-deutsches Exil. Nachwort', in *Aus fremder Heimat: Zur Exilsituation heutiger Literatur*, ed. by Günter Kunert (Munich: Hanser, 1988), p.105.

[113]Günter Kunert, *Berlin beizeiten: Gedichte* (Munich: Hanser, 1987).

[114]Bernhard Greiner, *Literatur der DDR in neuer Sicht: Studien und Interpretationen* (Frankfurt a.M.: Lang, 1986), p.224.

[115]Günter Kunert, 'Schreiben in einem Deutschland' (1991), *Der Sturz vom Sockel: Feststellungen und Widersprüche* (Munich: Hanser, 1992), pp.39-52.

[116]Kunert, 'Vorwort', *Der Sturz vom Sockel*, pp.7-9 (p.7). Günter Kunert, 'Wie ich ein Fisch wurde', in *Kunert lesen*, ed. by Michael Krüger (Munich and Vienna: Hanser, 1979), pp.63-64.

collection which they hoped would absorb the censor's interest and allow the rest to pass without changes. The arduous processes of censorship in a dictatorship might also however promote certain favourable qualities in censored literature, Pietraß suggests. The 'gamble' could bring a gain, the honing of literary skill, as well as the more obvious losses:

> Das Versteckspiel mit der Zensur und der Macht weckte und verfeinerte sprachliche Kräfte, domestizierte und deformierte aber zugleich, so daß wir das Ende der DDR als dreiste Krüppel erlebten. In der unlösbaren Verquickung von Skandal und Ruhm waren wir Opfer der Zensur und ihre stillen Nutznießer.[117]

GDR writers were able to assume their readership would pick up reworkings of slogans, parodies of official tone and motifs from the works of the officially-sanctioned canon. The population had knowledge of the censorship 'game' and expected to find in literature an engagement with politics, which writers used. Perhaps in the development of satire, irony, certain metaphors and images, one can see the censor as a spur to creative writing. Ultimately, however, Pietraß acknowledges that censorship was also a crippling force which tamed and disfigured literature. The domesticating of literature, which he alludes to, points to it becoming parochial and unable to press back against reality. Even when a work was published, its reception could be tightly controlled, as Mensching indicated in an interview:

> Bestimmte Dinge wurden zugelassen und bestimmte Bücher wurden gedruckt, aber sie wurden nicht besprochen oder in geringen Auflagen verteilt und dergleichen – abgewürgt wurde sozusagen hintenrum.[118]

Lutz Rathenow was one of the most political and most oppositional GDR writers, who despite the sanctions against him, did not leave the GDR. According to his own statements he found the battle with the state was productive for his work. This contradicts Kunert's experience of perpetual opposition as a petrification of literature. A number of Rathenow's poems relate directly to his experience of being held in a prison cell. In the 1981 poem 'Der Rest des Lebens' for instance, imprisonment and freedom apply to his arrest.[119] The theme also addresses being in the GDR or outside it: the italicized words '*Drinnen*' (8) and '*Draußen*' (1,4,9) draw attention to this representation of the GDR itself as a prison. Freedom is also the theme of Rathenow's poem 'Erbe des Ikarus' (p.63) where Icarus embodies the futile hope for metamorphosis and flight:

---

[117]Richard Pietraß, 'Lyrisch Roulette: Zensur als Erfahrung', in *"Literaturentwicklungsprozesse"*, ed. by Wichner, pp.178-198 (p.198).

[118]Steffen Mensching and Hans-Eckardt Wenzel, 'Entwürfe einer anderen Welt: Ein Gespräch mit Frauke Meyer-Gosau', *TuK* (1990), No.108, 86-94 (p.87).

[119]Lutz Rathenow, 'Der Rest des Lebens', *Verirrte Sterne oder Wenn alles wieder ganz anders kommt: Gedichte* (Gifkendorf: Merlin, 1994), p.86.

So steht er da und hofft,
daß sein Arm ein Flügel werde.   (lines 1-2)
The freedom to fly represents both literary freedom and freedom to travel: the
state rejected Rathenow's numerous visa applications; he was expelled from
the University of Jena in 1978 because of his subversive writing, and when his
work was published in the West from 1980, he was convicted in the GDR for
publishing illegally. Having contributed to a 'Friedensanthologie', he was
amongst about one hundred members of GDR peace groups who were arrested
on 4 November 1983. Rathenow's poetry was thus part of a political stance
and allied to his opposition to the oppressive regime, as is made clear in a
programmatic poem after the Russian poet David Samoilov:[120]

> Nach David Samoilow
> Das Gedicht: Bescheiden
> als obs ein knorriger Ast wär
> Auf dem Weg, den ich geh
> dients mir als Stütze
> 5   Und zum Erschrecken der Hunde
> zum Taktschlag beim Laufen
> Kahl ists, ohne Verzierung
> schmucklos (wen störts)
> Es dient mir als Stütze
> 10   und zum Schlag ist es gut

This 1979 poem pinpoints Rathenow's aesthetic. His poems of the 1980s are
indeed bald, often unlyrical pieces which tend to relate explicitly to 'der Weg,
den ich geh' (3). They serve as a support to him (line 4 above), as personal
'Lebenshilfe'. Equally, the poem is for beating (10), violently attacking the
circumstances of life in the GDR and perhaps defending oneself from the
blows meted out to the writer by the authorities. The reality of the state in
which Rathenow lived determined the object and intention of the poem. It was,
as he saw it, a historical situation which offered only very limited scope for
lyric subjectivity. Rathenow, like Brecht before him in the 1930s, saw
historical reality determining the possibilities of poetry.
    Like Rathenow, Kolbe was a young poet resisting the state's
interference in poetry and struggling to get his work heard in public. For

---

[120]Lutz Rathenow, 'Nach David Samoilow', in *Vogelbühne: Gedichte im Dialog*, ed. by
Dorothea von Törne (Berlin, GDR: Verlag der Nation, 1984), p.41. In the same year as
this poem by Rathenow, the Russian poet's work appeared in the GDR's
"Poesiealbum" series. See David Samoilow, *Poesiealbum 145* (Berlin, GDR: Neues
Leben, 1984).

Wittstock, writing in 1989, these two poets are representative of 'die zornigen Jungen'.[121] Some of Kolbe's poems of 1975-1979 were collected in the 1980 volume *Hineingeboren*, a title which gave a label to his generation. Kolbe has expressed a strong sense that the experiences of his generation alienated the young citizens from the state's projected image of itself. In an interview of 1989 for instance he declared, 'Für uns ist dieses "bessere Deutschland" einfach eine sehr mickrige Variante des Daseins, die wir mehr oder weniger ignoriert haben'.[122] In 1981 Kolbe submitted the text 'Kern meines Romans' for an anthology.[123] No censor nor lector initially recognized the irreverent acrostic within it. This political gesture involved the appropriation of the poem to carry a subversive message, in a way that departed from the programme of *Hineingeboren*: 'Protest ist keines meiner Worte' (p.34). It seems that the poet who had no wish to be involved in politics eventually found protest unavoidable. Kolbe had taken a year's course at the 'Literaturinstitut', but found difficulties getting his work accepted by the state-sanctioned publishing houses. 'Kern meines Romans' perhaps reflects the frustration of this situation. He both became a founding figure of the underground publishing scene in 1980s Berlin, and was also allowed to publish two further collections in the GDR officially, in 1983 and 1986 respectively, before he moved to West Germany in 1987 on a temporary visa.[124] This blurring of the boundaries in Kolbe's case, between the state-published writer, the unofficial writer and the dissident émigré is a typical consequence of GDR censorship. Some poems in *Bornholm II*, such as 'Was in einem Tag zu denken ist' (pp.79-80) indicate Kolbe's growing protest against his restrictive state:

zu viele Besucher schneiden in dieses dünne Brot des Gesprächs,
hungern so wölfisch
in diesem Kleeland und Zaunland, Kuhland und Huhnland,
inmitten der ganzen Geschmacklosigkeit:
viel zu wenig fliegende Fische.   (p.80)

The list of compounds with '-land' emphasizes the absence of the name 'Deutschland'. Here the poet decries the GDR for being narrow and philistine:

---

[121]Wittstock, *Von der Stalinallee*, p.225.

[122]Uwe Kolbe, interview with Konrad Franke, quoted in *"Es geht nicht um Christa Wolf"*, ed. by Anz, p.14.

[123]Wichner, ed., *Zensur in der DDR*, p.185.

[124]Ironically, these collections were published by the 'Aufbau Verlag'. Uwe Kolbe, *Abschiede und andere Liebesgedichte* (Berlin, GDR, and Weimar: Aufbau, 1983), and *Bornholm II: Gedichte* (Berlin, GDR, and Weimar: Aufbau, 1986). Kolbe marked the censorship process on the title of the latter collection: *Bornholm II* is the cut version and the censored 'Bornholm' poems are published later in *Vaterlandkanal: Ein Fahrtenbuch* (Frankfurt a.M.: Suhrkamp, 1990).

the lack of choice food is linked to, and exceeded by, the lack of cultural 'tastes' and diversity. Christine Cosentino interprets Kolbe's poems as an expression of his role as a poet: 'Der Dichter sieht seine Aufgabe darin, der erstarrten "Fertigkeit" der DDR-Gesellschaft an die Wurzel zu gehen und das "Unfertige" zu schreien'.[125] In Kolbe's poem 'Renaissance, im Gegenteil' (pp.15-16), the socialist ideal is a 'fremde Verheißung' that has cooled and now lies 'im Grundeis'. Instead there are the nightmarish elements 'das grinsende Lügen' and 'das monotone Klopfen grundloser Hoffnung'. Kolbe plays off the old socialist promises against a reality of stupidity and dilapidation 'im erstmals geeigneten Staat eines deutschen Glücks'. In this context poetry, however, can become a salvation:

> [ich] suche mein Heil in Gedichten,
> [...] deute ohne Wahl zu weit,
> zu eng – bei Ansicht der Instrumente. (p.16)

These lines exemplify the condensation and quite complicated nature of some of these poems. Texts point 'zu weit' where they are written and read in a politicized context: the last line of the quotation is reminiscent of Brecht's Galilei, who recants at the sight of the instruments of torture and does not speak the truth. This goes to the heart of writing in a dictatorship. The poem can scarcely avoid being Rathenow's stick, or a kind of salvation for its author. In Kolbe's 'Ein Gedicht, worum es mir geht' (pp.7-8) the poem is the antithesis not only of the GDR state discourse, but of both German discourses:

> So winzig beginnt das Gedicht, emfatisch
> erstickt es, erklärt nichts außer sich selbst,
> verweist, wie stets, auf seinen Widerstand
> den beiden deutschen Übersprachen   (p.8)

Here the poet aspires to writing poems which explain nothing beyond themselves. Wittstock has particularly noticed Kolbe's 'Assoziationskraft' in this collection.[126] Wittstock also however strings together phrases from different poems to illustrate what he argues to be Kolbe's aggressive attack on socialism. In their true situation in the poems these phrases do not seem to me to be always so unambiguous. A subjective mood and a subjective sense of metaphor characterize many poems in the volume. In the words of the poem 'Aus Rundungen des Kopfes' (p.97), 'Hermetische Gedichte wachsen an berliner Bäumen'. Kolbe seems to be conjuring up an alternative realm, more imaginary, more lively. Although he might not, to judge from the lines quoted above, wish for it, this too can of course be seen as a political gesture. As Wittstock concludes:

---

[125]Christine Cosetino, 'Gedanken zur jüngsten DDR-Lyrik: Uwe Kolbe, Sascha Anderson and Lutz Rathenow', *GR*, 60 (1985), 82-90 (p.85).
[126]Wittstock, *Von der Stalinallee*, p.281.

Die von Alltagsschlacken gereinigte, durchgeformte Sprache wird für ihn zu einem berauschenden Gegenentwurf, der ihm Zuflucht gewährt. (*Von der Stalinallee*, p.281)

The idea of poetic language as 'Zuflucht' points to a drawing back into introversion, a fleeing from the outside world into a withdrawal inwards.

A remarkable number of poems written in the 1980s in the GDR thematize an opposition between being outside and being inside. Papenfuß-Gorek's poem entitled 'Ausdrückliche Klage aus der inneren Immigration' locates the poet in inner withdrawal.[127] From here, he announces his anger and calls for justice: the poem opens, 'aus sieche, schimpf & scham erhebe ich meine klage'. Motifs of grief, the beloved and God, alongside the gesture of legal complaint, echo the late medieval text *Der Ackermann aus Böhmen.*[128] In effect, Papenfuß-Gorek's poem, a lament for truth and knowledge, is a monologue addressed to the closed state. The 'inner immigration' of the title seems to provide a space from which to articulate accusations against the power whose authority he rejects, but it is not an escape from under the aegis of that power. In a discussion of the magazines unofficially produced in the GDR, Brian Keith-Smith has referred to 'inner emigration': ' "Small is beautiful" had become a key to forms of inner emigration and restrained protest before the *Wende*'.[129] It was only after the fall of the GDR that critics began to refer to some GDR poetry as having undergone an inner emigration, or exile within the GDR, as Keith-Smith does here.[130] It is a problematic term, primarily used of German writers in the Nazi period. The concept does, however, seem to be implicit in the GDR poetic discourse of borders and

---

[127]Bert Papenfuß-Gorek, 'Ausdrückliche Klage aus der inneren Immigration', in *Ein Molotow-Cocktail,* ed. by Geist, pp.221-222.

[128]Johannes von Tepl, *Der Ackermann aus Böhmen* (Oxford: Blackwells, 1950).

[129]Brian Keith-Smith, 'Little Magazines from the former German Democratic Republic: A Survey', *GM*, 26 (1992), 65-93 (p.65).

[130]See for instance Jürgen Senke, *Zu Hause in Exil: Dichter, die eigenmächtig blieben in der DDR* (Munich and Zurich: Piper, 1998), which counts amongst those 'in exile at home' Richard Leising, Heinz Czechowski, Harald Gerlach, Thomas Rosenlöcher, Kurt Drawert and Horst Drescher. Arrigo Subiotto, in an aside, refers to Volker Braun being 'in this inner "exile" '. See Arrigo Subiotto, 'Volker Braun: Literary Metaphors and the Travails of Socialism', in *Socialism and the Literary Imagination: Essays on East German Writers*, ed. by Martin Kane (New York and Oxford: Berg, 1991), pp.195-212 (p.197).

boundaries.[131] Within that discourse, withdrawal inwards is an alternative to enforced expatriation, because the 'border area' has been made uninhabitable. Keith-Smith sees poet Sascha Anderson pointing to inner emigration in the following lines from the poem 'Elegie':[132]

ich habe alle fenster geschlossen
denn ich habe angst
vorm verschwinden der enden
einfacher sätze in niegedachten
labyrinthen.   (lines 4-8)

Closing the window is here a gesture of withdrawal inwards. The lyric subject's fear of being swallowed up into labyrinths is a postmodern anxiety about language. A rare full-stop after 'labyrinthen' corresponds to the closing of the windows. The enclosed room can be interpreted psychologically and as a reflection of the social situation, especially for the writer. Such ambiguity about being inside or outside can be traced with respect to a number of poetic motifs in poetry written in the 1980s, but I would like to illustrate it with respect to the window. Earlier instances of the window as a crucial poetic motif seem to occur predominantly in the work of poets who were to leave the GDR in the 1970s, such as Reiner Kunze and Sarah Kirsch. In the late 1960s the window motif was suggestive in Kunze's collection *Sensible Wege* (p.39, p.73, p.87). In contrast to Anderson's closed window, an escape through the window is the subject in Sarah Kirsch's 1979 poem 'Trennung' (*Ein Molotow-Cocktail*, p.26):

Trennung
Wenn ich in einem Haus bin, das keine Tür hat
Geh ich aus dem Fenster.
Mauern, Mauern und nichts als Gardinen
Wo bin ich denn, daß

---

[131]For 'Grenzen' as the motto of the 1980s, see Wolfgang Rath, 'Entgrenzung ins Intersubjektive: Zu den literarischen achtziger Jahren', in *Tendenz Freisprache: Texte zu einer Poetik der 80er Jahre*, ed. by Ulrich Janetzki and Wolfgang Rath (Frankfurt a.M.: Suhrkamp, 1992), pp.258-276 (p.268), and Karen Leeder, ' "ich fühle mich in grenzen wohl": The Metaphors of Boundary and the Boundaries of Metaphor in Prenzlauer Berg', *GM*, 35 (1995), 19-44

[132]Sascha Anderson, 'Elegie', *u.s.w.* (1984), No.3, and quoted in Keith-Smith, 'Little Magazines', p.70.

This window is an alternative way out. Cosentino has interpreted this poem's image as that of a house with no door to shut, so that it is open to attack.[133] A door is also a way out, however. Kirsch's title points to the separation between inside and outside, and to German-German division which is also thematized in the repetition of 'Mauern' (3). 'Gardinen' (3) suggest the net curtains of the impersonal city, but also the 'schwedische Gardinen' of a prison. The last line, in italics, seems to be a despairing statement of social criticism: the 'ich' becomes speechless in mid-sentence. Whereas the opposition between inside and outside brought a gesture of introversion in Anderson's poem above, Kirsch's poem suggests a gesture of transgression.

The title of the important anthology *Ein Molotow-Cocktail auf fremder Bettkante* comes from Harald Gerlach's poem 'Interieur, anarchisch' *(Ein Molotow-Cocktail*, p.285). Here inner immigration is a withdrawal into the anarchy inside one's own, alternative space. The paradoxical juxtaposition of violence (the Molotov cocktail) with domesticity thematizes inner immigration as a rebellion. This connects with suggestions that literature was part of the preparation for the 'Wende' itself:

> Der bis 1989 unvorstellbare Akt der friedlichen Selbstbefreiung von einer Diktatur hatte sicher viele Wegbereiter. Zu ihnen zählen auch die Autoren, die nicht selten unter physischer und psychischer Belastung der Sprache einen individuellen Freiraum erhalten haben.[134]

But in Gerlach's poem the 'Freiraum' is not for revolution, but a space in which to consider utter resignation:

> Vorm Fenster die
> verschlissenen Inhalte, übermüdet, zählen die Tage
> bis zur Veteranenrente.   (lines 16-18)

The mood created by dusk, 'gardegrau' (1), 'vertrocknet' (10), 'tot' (10), 'verlassen' (11), 'leer' (12) and 'trostlos' (15) is one of passive despondency. This corresponds to what is viewed from the window: the title of the poem suggests that something else, altogether less passive and acquiescing exists within. Looking out of the window from an enclosed room to the world outside can perhaps be interpreted as a gesture of alienation.[135] Looking through a window is an urban phenomenon, contrasting isolation (inside) and

---

[133]Christine Cosentino, *"Ein Spiegel mit mir darin": Sarah Kirschs Lyrik* (Tübingen: Francke, 1990), p.101.

[134]Groth, *Materialien zu Literatur im Widerspruch*, p.47.

[135]Concerning the window motif in general see Gotthardt Frühsorge, 'Fenster: Augenblicke der Aufklärung über Leben und Arbeit: Zur Funktionsgeschichte eines literarischen Motivs', *Euphorion*, 77 (1983), 346-358, and Heinz Brüggemann, *Das andere Fenster: Einblicke in Häuser und Menschen: Zur Literaturgeschichte einer urbanen Wahrnehmungsform* (Frankfurt a.M.: Fischer, 1989).

participation (outside). It can be the attitude of a contemplative observer, introverted and melancholy. This contemplative, inactive poet in the city is perceptible behind Schedlinski's untitled poem (*Ein Molotow-Cocktail*, p.197) which begins as follows:

> das fenster ist geöffnet
> der hund bellt nicht
> das wetter ist ernst
> alle menschen sind sterblich   (lines 1-4)

This inventory reflects a depressed mood and recalls Jakob van Hoddis's Expressionist poem 'Weltende'.[136] The window is open but there is no breeze, nothing at all comes in. Grünbein's 1980s poem 'Etwas das zählt' illustrates the presentation of another isolated person at the window.[137] Here the negative mood is set by the dusk, autumn and rain:

> Du
> im Museumszwielicht am Fenster kaust
> Kaugummi, weil es die beste
> Arznei ist gegen
> Barockphobie. Punktlich wird Herbst,
> kommen die Depressionen
> von Stuhlreihen vor einer
> leeren Freilichtbühne seit Regen-
>
> gedenken nicht mehr bespielt.   (lines 7-14)

Where one seems to stand in a museum or before an empty stage, existence is slow and lifeless. This poem exemplifies boredom and depression, which are a central motif of Grünbein's whole collection *Grauzone morgens*.[138] The human figure at the window seems to symbolize the need to look outside, beyond the narrow confines of the GDR. Drawert's poem 'Augenblick am Fenster' also conveys time slowed.[139] Lines drip like the dripping washing described.

> Augenblick am Fenster
> mit schwarzen Rahmen,
>
> in dem eine Frau steht

---

[136]Jakob van Hoddis, 'Weltende', *Menschheitsdämmerung: Ein Dokument des Expressionismus*, ed. by Kurt Pinthus (Berlin: Rowohlt, 1993), p.39.
[137]Durs Grünbein, 'Etwas das zählt', *Grauzone morgens: Gedichte* (Frankfurt a.M.: Suhrkamp, 1988), p.11
[138]Durs Grünbein, *Grauzone morgens: Gedichte* (Frankfurt a.M.: Suhrkamp, 1988).
[139]Kurt Drawert, 'Augenblick am Fenster', *Zweite Inventur: Gedichte* (Berlin, GDR: Aufbau, 1987), p.52.

und alt wird. Und der Tag

ist die Sehnsucht
nach vergangenen Tagen,

5   die als Wäsche
auf dem Hof hängt

und erbarmungslos
austropft.

Ageing takes place at this window and that location is again associated with
wistfulness here. The window is a border between past and future time.
Mensching addresses the theme of being trapped versus free, in the poem 'Wir
standen am Fenster' (*Tuchfühlung*, p.75), dedicated to the revolutionary Ernst
Toller, who wrote *Das Schwalbenbuch* whilst in prison in the Weimar
Republic in 1922. Here however, the GDR experience which is reflected on at
the window is one of freedom. Mensching addresses to the captive Toller a
description of idyllic love. The lyric 'ich' and a girl are happy, free and secure
in the GDR:

Wir standen am Fenster, Toller, das
Mädchen und ich
und sahen die Schwalben
ihr Nest bauen, wir erwachten des Morgens vom Geschrei
5   der hungrigen Jungen,
freuten uns auf die Welt, tranken eiskalte Milch.
Die größte Schwalbe nannte ich Ernst, aber Toller
sagte, im Ernst,
das ist das Weibchen, das Mädchen sagte, ihr habt beide
10   einen Vogel,
wir lachten, gingen hinaus, wußten noch nicht wohin.

Here, looking from the window is part of a present mood of freedom. The
nesting and freely flying swallows are symbols of a human idyll, and the
freedom to depart is unusual in GDR poetry of the 1980s. The break of the
fourth line above however, so that 'Geschrei' falls in a position of emphasis at
the end of the line, renders the hungry young an uncomfortable element in the
image of an idyll. In contrast, Kerstin Hensel writes an overtly discomforting
window-love-poem. A connection is established between 'Verbot' and
'Fenster' in Hensel's Romeo and Juliet poem 'Das Verbot' (*Ein Molotow-
Cocktail*, p.47):

Das Verbot
Und als ich noch mal wiederkam,
ihm zu begegnen, seinem Verbot
uns zu sehen, es war der Tod
für mich um ihn und ich hörte
5   mich rufen
(Der Abend war wie lila Milch)
Und wirklich im Fenster,
hinter dem er wohnte oder
sich vergrub, schien das Licht,
10   und er öffnete und
sah mich und da
brach
schon die Nacht.
Daß ich meine Arme nicht
15   aufhielt, wie sonst, wenn er kam,
wußte ich
jetzt erst, reglos wie er.

The window in the context of this love poem is a dividing line between lovers. The Romeo and Juliet scenario is inverted in two ways: the female is outside and the male waiting inside, and the 'Verbot' is not external, but is a command from the beloved himself. This man hides himself away and is characterized as 'reglos'. The 'Verbot' is associated here with unreality, which is conveyed in the lines 'und ich hörte / mich rufen' (4-5), whereas the window is where things are 'wirklich' (7). The window is a point of realization where symbolic light and darkness are manifest. The portrayal of individual isolation and the resignation at the poem's close are typical of the mood in other window-poems discussed here. The window is a cross-over between the inner and the outer, but also a source of natural light by which to 'see'.

In Gabriele Kachold's untitled 'Großstadtgedicht' which begins 'diese stadt ist eine insel voller ungeheuer' (*Ein Molotow-Cocktail*, p.67), the window is again a place of intuitive realization:

es ist nicht das faßbare an dem ich dich fühlen kann
es ist das was du dir selber verschweigst
und das ich manchmal ahne wenn ich eine minute still
aus dem fenster sehe   (lines 12-15)

This poem is addressed to a disloyal partner, 'du'. The first part of the poem describes city houses where one is 'verfängt und bleibt und dorrt und skelett wird' (5). The lyric voice describes being trapped and dying in an urban house. A window is also linked to the wasted and arid in Wolfgang Hilbig's poem 'verwüstet'.[140] Far from being a socialist utopia, the notion of dream is an imaginative transgression in this 1986 poem:

> verwüstet vertrocknet
> am fenster in der drift meines zimmers
> begann ich plötzlich einen dammbruch zu träumen (lines 1-3)

This is a dream of breaking out, a desire to see a watery torrent destroying a desert, perhaps a cultural desert. It is inspired by the sense of encroaching doom: 'vor mir der tod' (7) alludes to the room as the place where the lyric subjest will experience nothing but death. Again then, the window motif in 1980s poetry is a specific expression of being trapped at a boundary, which the lyric subject longs to traverse, indeed which he is inspired to imagine traversing. The lyric subject behind the window dreams of a natural disaster, a dam breaking, a flood engulfing the present and changing it utterly. In part at least, this is an expression of literary and poetic possiblities.[141]

In Barbara Köhler's prose poem written in 1983-1989 and entitled 'Kurzer Brief über die Abwesenheit', the walls of a room are huge windows in effect, made of glass:

> angst ist das baumaterial der wände ein nebeltrübes glas das die bewegungen draußen zu schattenspielen geraten läßt. silhouetten entfernen und nähern sich werden bedrohlich groß oder verschwimmen ganz und gar. der eindruck gegenwart entsteht aus angenommenen reaktionen: nachbildungen zu vor-bildern. die dornröschen sitzen schlaflos im traum ihrer erlösung harrend (die ihnen zusteht wie sie wohl wissen).[142]

These window-walls are explicitly metaphorical in that they are made of fear, a connection perhaps implicit in other instances of the window motif discussed above. The distorting, mediating impact of the glass on one's vision is likewise spelt out in this text, whereas elsewhere it is perhaps implied in the use of the window image in conjunction with a sense of profound unease. The figures inside are here Sleeping Beauties dreaming of their escape: this corresponds to the passivity of other lyric subjects at the windows of their rooms, not acting in the present but rather resigned to imaginary break-outs and dreams of release.

The window, as a metaphor in poetry, locates the individual trapped at the borderline, at once forced to recede inwards, yet also seeking to escape

---

[140]Wolfgang Hilbig, 'verwüstet', *zwischen den paradiesen: Prosa. Lyrik*, ed. by Thorsten Ahrend (Leipzig: Reclam, 1992), p.304

[141]*Offene Fenster* was also the title of an anthology series of poems and graphics by young people in the GDR, which was edited by Margret and Edwin Kratschmer and Hannes Würtz. Mensching, Pietraß and Hensel published there. Eight issues came out, the last in 1984.

[142]Barbara Köhler, 'Kurzer Brief über die Abwesenheit', *Deutsches Roulette: Gedichte 1984-1989* (Frankfurt a.M.: Suhrkamp, 1991), pp.35-37 (p.35).

outwards beyond the immediate world. It becomes a prevalent metaphor in poetry by different generations of writers in the 1980s and can perhaps be regarded as emblematic for poets in the GDR in the years immediately prior to the 'Wende'. It might indeed encapsulate a sense of the poet's position in the GDR at that time, reflecting how the censor-poet, who internalized the state's restrictiveness, was trapped. Power was articulated and contested in the GDR through language: GDR writers could scarcely write a line without being representative and speaking for the state or for the 'Volk' or for dissidents. They could not move without being located in a political landscape. As a poetic motif, the window relates to the images of building a new house from the rubble, images which were prevalent in the early GDR years and remained significant as part of the GDR's foundation narrative. The lyric subjects at the windows in the 1980s are implicitly inhabiting the building whose construction poets had eagerly portrayed in the 1950s. In the later decade, however, there is negligible sense of a home or a community (Mensching is an exception in portraying such positive resonances in the poem quoted above); rather, the building is predominantly a confining space, limiting the individual and inspiring new dreams of escape, where earlier the dreams had been of finding a secure home. The window motif is thus in part a development of, and a response to, the GDR's cherished foundation myth. Even in the 1980s then, there is compelling evidence of how official disocurse continued to be a crucial touchstone for a wide variety of literary writers in the GDR. Although from the early years when poets were happy to see themselves as 'Dichter im Dienst' to a time when they felt themselves to be 'Aussteiger', poets distanced themselves from the political centre, still the presence of state policy shaped almost all literary reception. Strict control of the production and availabilty of literature made the state an unavoidable force. Those who wished to publish in the GDR had to accept the state censor; those who sought to bypass the state (by publishing in the West or underground) were still defined by this stance. Thus there was a sense that however literature might provide a window to another world, the writer remained fundamentally confined, a melancholy observer, looking beyond yet unable to cross so many of the SED state's boundaries. Cosentino's conclusion with regards to Kolbe, Anderson and Rathenow in 1985, rings true for other poets at this time:

> Sie alle haben sich ideologisch abgenabelt; sie alle aber sind in irgendeiner Form gesellschaftlich orientiert, sei es auch aus der Ambivalenz oder aus dem Negativum her.[143]

Using the past participle 'abgenabelt' points to an image of the writer as a child born with an umbilical connection to the parent-GDR. The paradox of

---

[143]Cosentino, 'Gedanken zur jüngsten DDR-Lyrik', p.89.

disconnecting from the state yet being finally unable to extricate oneself might typify the position of GDR writers in the last decade of the state's existence. By the 1980s writers were increasingly aware of being trapped both literally and figuratively: literally by the impenetrable border and figuratively by the existence of political prescriptions for literature. This has been seen as a defining theme of the decade:

> In der Lyrik und Theorie der Achtziger geht es um die Innen-Außen-Problematik eines Textes. Darüber hinaus ist dies eine Problematik der Grenzen.[144]

Many poems of the 1980s indeed discuss being inside or being outside and this theme reflects an interest in addressing in poetry the poet's awkward place with respect to society. The window motif, for instance, is an indication of the fact that, in life and in their work, poets were émigrés who left the state behind, whilst at the same time they also remained perpetual negotiators of its boundaries. Barbara Köhler's line of verse 'Ich harre aus im Land und geh, ihm fremd' encapsulates the paradox of remaining in the GDR yet simultaneously, through writing, leaving it and cheating on the marriage to the state.[145]

In order to assess the impact of the 'Wende' on poetry, it is necessary to have a sense of what came before, particularly in terms of the earlier work of specific poets writing after 1989 and in terms of broad trends which characterize poetry in the mid- to late-1980s. Two features – an inescapable relationship to the state and a wide range of poetic 'paths' – stand out in the poetry written in the years leading up to 1989. They provide a way of understanding why the 'Wende' was not only a series of historical events, but also a turning-point for poetry. The poet's role had been an unavoidably political question throughout the history of the GDR; the loss of the state would turn upside down many poets' understanding of their enterprise and inevitably alter conditions of literary production in various respects. It would also undermine the established reception of GDR literature and call into question its historiography. At the same time, the diverse strands of GDR poetry would be drawn together, for a time, by shared concerns about the sudden, political upheaval and about the re-assessments and new perspectives on writers' past role and their past writing. In the 1980s, the lyric identification with standing at windows might be interpreted as waiting to cross a transparent boundary; it was a wait which would end dramatically in autumn 1989, casting

---

[144]Patricia Anne Simpson, 'Entropie, Ästhetik und Ethik im Prenzlauer Berg', in *MachtSpiele: Literatur und Staatssicherheit im Fokus Prenzlauer Berg*, ed. by Peter Böthig and Klaus Michael (Leipzig: Reclam, 1993), pp.50-59 (p.56).
[145]Barbara Köhler, 'Rondeau Allemagne', *Deutsches Roulette*, p.63.

writers out into a freedom they had long sought, but also, more ambiguously, removing them from the secure, familiar house (of the GDR), from whose windows they had been looking out.

CHAPTER 3
HISTORY AND POETRY: 'WENDE-ZEITGEDICHTE'

> Denn Verse sind nicht, wie die Leute meinen,
> Gefühle (die hat man früh genug), – es sind
> Erfahrungen.[1]

This chapter concerns the poems which first, and most directly, represented the events of the 'Wende' and German unification. The upheavals of 1989/90, epitomized by the fall of the Berlin Wall, constituted a historic shift which numerous poets put at the centre of their work at that time. The first manifestations of the 'Wende' in the GDR consisted of exodus and protest on a larger scale than ever before. Hungary began dismantling the Iron Curtain in May 1989 by removing the barbed-wire along its border with Austria. Thousands of GDR citizens fled over this 'grüne Grenze' and, when the armed border patrols stopped on 11 September, twenty-five thousand GDR citizens left in the few days before the GDR government banned travel to Hungary. Meanwhile, there was another exodus via West German embassies in Bucharest, Prague and Warsaw. Hundreds of GDR refugees occupied the diplomatic missions until they had to be closed, and then people climbed over perimeter fences. Eventually, they were taken through the GDR to Bavaria in sealed trains. In September and October 1989 large numbers of other GDR citizens began to demonstrate their demands for greater freedom by marching through the streets and gathering at rallies. On 7 September, for instance, eighty people were arrested at Alexanderplatz, East Berlin, as they protested against fixed elections. Increasingly large demonstrations took place in all the major cities, particularly calling for freedom of speech and freedom to travel: demonstrators carried placards and banners, containing new slogans which were characterized by humorous rhyme, 'Volkswitze' and parodies of SED gesturing. Their mottoes included 'Wir sind das Volk!', 'Keine Gewalt' and 'Freiheit, Gleichheit und Ehrlichkeit'.[2] In the retrospective words of Uwe Kolbe, 'Die Mehrheit war tatsächlich Opposition geworden'.[3]

Many writers and intellectuals were amongst that majority as the protests got underway. In Berlin, Volker Braun took part in demonstrations

---

[1]Rainer Maria Rilke, *Die Aufzeichnungen des Malte Laurids Brigge* (Wiesbaden: Insel, 1952), p.25.
[2]Six hundred 'Wende' slogans are contained in Ewald Lang, ed., *Wendehals und Stasi-Laus: Demo-Sprüche aus der DDR* (Munich: Heyne, 1990). These examples, p.5, p.31 and p.20.
[3]Uwe Kolbe, 'Die Heimat der Dissidenten: Nachbemerkungen zum Phantom der DDR-Opposition', in *Der deutsch-deutsche Literaturstreit*, ed. by Deiritz, pp.33-39 (p.39).

and signed appeals, Heiner Müller spoke on public platforms for reform, and Durs Grünbein was arrested at a street demonstration on 9 October 1989. In other GDR cities the poets were also caught up in historic events: in Leipzig, Kurt Drawert and Heinz Czechowski joined the 'Montagsdemonstrationen' and Johannes Jansen issued the appeal 'bleibt auf der straße'.[4] In autumn 1989 Steffen Mensching and Hans-Eckardt Wenzel were touring the GDR with their 'clown cabaret': 'Diese Auftritte, vor vollen Häusern, in angespannter Atmosphäre, immer unter Druck des Verbots, hatten durchaus demonstrativen Charakter, aber eben nicht nur'.[5] Barbara Köhler took part in the Round Table Talks in Karl-Marx-Stadt. In Dresden, Czechowski and Thomas Rosenlöcher heard the West German chancellor Helmut Kohl addressing the crowds in December 1989. The location of GDR poets at the 'Wende' reflects their role as witnesses of change, as participants in it and even as exiles: Uwe Kolbe, for example, watched the Wall come down on television in Texas. In October 1989 the poets who had stayed in the GDR, however, seemed to represent the principle of 'Einmischung', an involvement in public life.[6]

The 'Wende' poems are the most immediate literary responses to 1989/90. Many capture an apparently spontaneous reaction, which conveys a fresh hopefulness and an emotional truth which is not expressed in the later poems, written in the aftermath, rather than amidst the events. 'Wende' poems are 'Gelegenheitsgedichte' in the sense that many are written in response to a certain occasion; some are even written to be read as part of the occasion. *Occasio* as a muse, the poet's inspiration and ultimately as the focus of the poem, has a long poetic tradition.[7] In classical literature the *occasio* was usually a significant birth, marriage or death: the 'Wende' could be said to be all three. The 'Wendegedichte' correspond to two ideas in the modern tradition of the 'Gelegenheitsgedicht': firstly, the poem inspired by a historical experience, a public 'Gelegenheit', as opposed to the poem which has a private trigger; and secondly, the idea of the unassuming poetry of the everyday, or what Wulf Segebrecht terms the 'Casualgedicht'.[8] Here the event or occasion is sufficient for the poem; it does not aspire to be timeless and

---

[4]Johannes Jansen, 'bleibt auf der straße', *Temperamente*, (1990), No.1, 130.
[5]Letter to me from Steffen Mensching, 9 December 1998.
[6]Compare the title of Stefan Heym's collection of 'Wende' speeches and essays, *Einmischung: Gespräche, Reden, Essays* ([Munich]: Bertelsmann, 1990).
[7]See Wulf Segebrecht, *Das Gelegenheitsgedicht: Ein Beitrag zur Geschichte und Poetik der deutschen Lyrik* (Stuttgart: Metzler, 1977) and Helmut Heissenbüttel, 'Zum Gelegenheitsgedicht', in *Lyrik-Katalog Bundesrepublik: Gedichte, Biographien, Statements*, ed. by Jan Hans, Uwe Herms and Ralf Thenior (Munich: Goldmann, 1978), pp.440-443.
[8]Segebrecht, *Das Gelegenheitsgedicht*, p.20.

eternal. The term 'documentary poem' is perhaps also useful for some 'Wende' poems, in that they represent the poet as a reporter of history and as a citer of historical utterances. A better term, however, is perhaps 'Zeitgedichte', poems inspired by and written for a particular time, analogous with titles such as Kurt Drawert's 'Zeitmitschriften' or Christa Wolf's 'Schreiben im Zeitbezug'.[9]

Poems whose theme is a political event, such as the 'Wende', can seem to become quickly dated and less interesting. They may be dismissed as having value only as historical documents, rather than as enduring literature, but even where a poem is written for the moment, it can both be a monument to that moment and also be read as an expression of more general, existential issues. I intend to demonstrate how selected poems cast history in a new light: they offer a viewpoint that is unfamiliar, and may be very private. They can reveal how the poet conceives his or her role, and make the reader address history afresh. History books tend to see the 'Wende' as a process, a broadly linear development out of the people's demonstrations and Soviet-led change throughout Eastern Europe. This development included monetary union and culminated in the political union of the two Germanies on 3 October 1990. In a short form like poetry we will see not this linear development, but rather the flashpoints – scenes which have struck the imagination – and summary images which capture a feeling about the whole process. There are other differences between history's record of events and poetry's record: the Dutch critic Gerd Labroisse emphasizes poetry's personal voice as against the collective, objective voice of historical report:

> Lyric poetry, as the most personal and subjective of literary genres, offers another possibility of reacting directly to events. Astonishingly, there are only a few poems in which the "time of change" (or Wende-Zeit) is obviously articulated.[10]

Some 'Wende' poetry does indeed illustrate the possibilities of poetry to be very private in its handling of public themes, or to be an expression of subjective experience. GDR tradition, however, preferred the poem as a statement on behalf of society and this is equally represented after 1989. Labroisse's contention that there are but few poems about the 'Wende' stems from the fact that, at the time he made this comment in 1990, many had not been published and the most important anthology of 'Wende' poetry was still three years away. The 'Wende' has given rise to countless poems, some of

[9]Kurt Drawert, *Haus ohne Menschen: Zeitmitschriften* (Leipzig: Suhrkamp, 1993). Christa Wolf, 'Schreiben im Zeitbezug: Gespräch mit Aafke Steenhuis', *Im Dialog*, pp.131-157.
[10]Gerd Labroisse, 'The Literature of the GDR and the Revolution of 1989/90', trans. by Ian Wallace, *GM*, 26 (1992), 37-49 (p.39).

them merely well meant, but others genuinely moving, precise in their description of the situation, and aesthetically satisfying. This chapter identifies focal points in the representation of 1989/90 in poetry. What I am concerned to establish is how the 'Wende' and unification are represented in poetry in German. Naturally this subject is of greater concern to poets from the GDR than from elsewhere, and they have in fact written the majority of 'Wende' poems. My project focuses on poets from the former GDR, but in this chapter some poems by poets from West Germany are referred to in footnotes by way of comparison.

The first critical presentation of 'Wende' poetry was published in the *GDR Monitor* by Anna Chiarloni under the title 'Die Dichter und die Wende'.[11] These texts, collected in July 1990, form what she terms 'eine Art lyrisches Tagebuch' (p.1). The following GDR poets are represented in the fifteen poems: Volker Braun, Holger Teschke, Gisela Kraft, Harald Gerlach, Kurt Drawert, Heinz Czechowski, Thomas Böhme and Hinnerk Einhorn. Two important, larger sources are the 'Wende' anthologies *Von einem Land und vom anderen: Gedichte zur deutschen Wende 1989/1990* and *Grenzfallgedichte: Eine deutsche Anthologie*.[12] Both anthologies juxtapose poems by writers from different generations and different ideological viewpoints. They contain both diary-like and report-like poems, as well as more indirect reflections of recent history. The hundred or so poems in *Grenzfallgedichte* pertain mainly to the period from autumn 1989 until autumn 1990, but about a quarter of the poems originate before the period with which I am concerned. The *Von einem Land* anthology contains around 130 poems, of which all but four were written between October 1989 and 1993. Many of these poems first appeared in German newspapers shortly after they were written and chart poets' impressions of the historic events they witnessed. In December 1989 Christa Wolf wrote, 'Wir befinden uns wirklich in einem Ausnahmezustand: alle unsere Gedanken und Gefühle werden völlig durch die gesellschaftlichen Prozesse vereinnahmt'.[13] The sense of an exceptional social change, which is completely preoccupying, is reflected too in the poetry. Lyric expression does not simply echo journalistic expression, however. As Wolfgang Ertl states in his review of *Grenzfallgedichte*, 'Einige der Gedichte schürfen auf knappem Raum tiefer als die so aufregenden Berichte in der Presse und die notgedrungen langatmigeren Prosastücke, die inzwischen zum

---

[11]Anna Chiarloni, 'Die Dichter und die Wende', *GDR Monitor*, 23 (1990), 1-12.
[12]Karl Otto Conrady, ed., *Von einem Land und vom anderen: Gedichte zur deutschen Wende 1989/1990* (Leipzig: Reclam, 1993). Anna Chiarloni and Helga Pankoke, eds., *Grenzfallgedichte: Eine deutsche Anthologie* (Berlin and Weimar: Aufbau, 1991).
[13]Wolf, 'Schreiben im Zeitbezug', p.139.

Thema erschienen sind'.[14] It is however as literary works, rather than as press reports, that I am interested in these texts. The poet's language is both familiar and strange: we are culturally disposed to know that a poem is to be read 'against the grain of the manifest and, because of that requirement, *good* poems about historical crises speak a different language from historical record and historical myth'.[15] Part of my literary analysis involves describing that 'different language'. Conrady too refers in the essay 'Deutsche Wendezeit', which he appends to his *Von einem Land* anthology, to 'die besondere Sprache des Gedichts'.[16] Unlike everyday speech or descriptive prose, this language counters the manifest, rather than clarifying it. It is language with more than one dimension. Close textual analysis will be my means of exploring this and, through that language, the poet's role.

From the time of the earliest demonstrations poets responded to the new social climate, in their writing. I shall start by looking at some early poems of ending, or so-called 'WEnde' poems, by four very different poets: one of the newest (Oliver Tietze) and one of the oldest (Hanns Cibulka), a poet associated with the 'sächsische Dichterschule' (Uwe Grüning), and one associated with Prenzlauer Berg (Matthias Holst). Oliver Tietze's poem 'Berlin – 5. Oktober 1989' is a report of one day, as its title suggests.[17] This is a typical 'Wende-Zeitgedicht' recording the occasion because, as the poem itself explains, national television is not broadcasting the events. The poem makes transparent its function as a substitute for free journalism. The poet behind the text presents himself as a passive recorder, who seeks to report on the situation in his own country, whilst the state reporters ironically report from abroad. The Gethsemane church in East Berlin, the candles, western television cameras and the 'Volkspolizei' are typical sights at the demonstrations and the poem evokes these in an apparently naturalistic manner.

Berlin – 5. Oktober 1989
Immer mehr Leute gehen
bei Rot über die Straße.

---

[14]Wolfgang Ertl, 'Grenzfallgedichte', *GR*, 67 (1992), 183.
[15]Frank Kermode, *Poetry, Narrative, History* (Oxford: Blackwell, 1990), p.67.
[16]Conrady, 'Deutsche Wendezeit', p.175.
[17]Oliver Tietze, 'Berlin - 5. Oktober 1989', *Temperamente*, (1990), No.1, 46. In Berlin on the same date the reformist statement 'Wir müssen unsere Angelegenheiten selbst in die Hand nehmen! Aufruf der "Initiative für eine vereinigte Linke" an alle Werktätigen der DDR' included the declaration 'Wir hören jetzt häufig, die "Wende" sei da, und manchmal schon sei unumkehrbar'. The inverted commas around 'Wende' point to this usage still being new.

Im Abendlicht
vor der Gethsemanekirche
5   flackert, brennt
ein Meer aus Kerzen.

Vor Westkameras
frieren
Volkspolizisten.

10   Die Sender des Landes
berichten
aus Rom.

The opening description of disregard for traffic lights constitutes an image of wider transgression, of breaking the normal rules. There are other layers of meaning to the description however. For instance, the first line on its own refers to the exodus of GDR citizens to the West. 'Rot' (2) is the traffic light but also the communist 'reds', and the red sunset of the 'Abendlicht' (3). This warm light and the candles contrast with the frozen policemen. Burning candles became a potent symbol of peaceful protest, as candlelit vigils were being held for political prisoners, and in 1990 Jörg Swoboda called the 'Wende' period 'die Revolution der Kerzen'.[18] In line 5 of Tietze's poem, the heightening from 'flackert' to 'brennt' suggests that the candles represent flickering hope growing stronger. Only a few days later however, on 9 October, the Gethsemane church issued a statement criticizing police violence and the imprisonment of protesters there the preceding day.[19]

Early awareness of historic change is reflected too in Uwe Grüning's poem 'Heimfahrt von Prag', also written in October 1989.[20] The poem is sensitive to an imminent caesura: Grüning uses the image of Czechoslovakia sinking beneath the sea and on fire. Czechoslovakia had been one of the most

---

[18]Jörg Swoboda, *Die Revolution der Kerzen* (Wuppertal and Kassel: Oncken, 1990). The candle is also a motif in the following 'Wende' poems: Hans-Christian Braun, 'zusehen', in *Grenzfallgedichte*, p.102, and Reiner Kunze, 'Demonstranten', *ein tag auf dieser erde: gedichte* (Frankfurt a.M.: Fischer, 1998), p.59. See also Kathrin Schmidt's retrospective 'Wende' poem 'vierzigster und einundvierzigster oktober', *Flußbild mit Engel: Gedichte* (Frankfurt a.M.: Suhrkamp, 1995), p.17, in which the candle is a lone light of hope inside her head: 'ich hatte eine kerze in meine stirn gestellt es tropfte / ein wenig wachs ins angsthaben'.
[19]See *Temperamente*, (1990), No.1, 70. In *Stern*, 22 March 1990, p.44, the Gethsemane church was referred to as 'eine der Wiegen der Revolution in der DDR'.
[20]Uwe Grüning, 'Heimfahrt von Prag', *Von einem Land*, pp.8-9.

repressive communist regimes yet, unlike the GDR, it had a relatively powerful opposition movement, organized by groups such as Charter 77. Many demonstrations took place in 1988 and 1989, especially in Wenceslas Square, Prague, where on 15 January 1989, five thousand citizens gathered to remember the self-immolation of Jan Palach twenty years before. Most of these demonstrations were broken up by police violence. Unlike the historical record, this poem focuses not on the police and protesters' actions, but on what is left, broken and smashed, afterwards. The synonymous adjectives in lines 12-14 are symbolic of monolithic power being shattered:

Heimfahrt von Prag
Es dämmert.
Libussas
versinkendes Königreich
blinkt auf den Wellen.

5   Eine Epoche,
       die alle Schätze zu haben versprach,
       schleicht sich als Bettler fort wie der Abend.
       Wir fanden
       Papier und Lebensmüll
10   vor dem Palais;
       Limousinen
       mit zerschlagenen Scheiben,
       aufgebrochenen Türen,
       zersplitterten Leuchten,
15   standen,
       ein trostloser Treck,
       auf dem schmalen Asphaltweg,
       der hinauf in die Gärten führt,
       und Obstbäume
20   neigten die herbstlichen Zweige
       über die Dinge, welche die Erde
       zu keinem neuen Leben erweckt.

       Und ein Gefühl von Fremdheit und Angst
       fiel mich an
25   mit dem Schwermutsglanz des Oktobers,
       als ich heimfuhr,
       im Rücken
       Libussas flammendes Königreich
       und vor mir
30   den Eisenhimmel des Ostens.

(Anmerkung: Vom 3.-6. Oktober 1989, als der zweite Flüchtlingsstrom das Palais Lobkovic überflutete, waren wir in Prag und konnten das Ende der Ära Honecker sehen.)

The poem opens in the present tense, then becomes retrospective from line 8 to the end. The retrospective is interrupted however by present tense verbs in lines 18 and 22, which make 'der schmale Asphaltweg' something timeless and the non-awakening a general principle of death. The present vision of descent beneath the waves seems to contrast with the memory of a path ascending to gardens and fruit trees. In religious imagery the moral path is the narrow path, and gardens and fruit trees are associated with Eden paradise. In Grüning's poem, however, there is now no solace and no 'neues Leben'. The aborted socialist journey leaves only 'ein trostloser Treck'; the Czechoslovakia personified by Princess Libuse and promising treasures, is now personified by a departing beggar. Even at the beginning of October 1989, Grüning expresses the fear and loss which are more prevalent in poetry after unification. This is especially so from line 23, where the poem becomes more personal. The 'Wende' October (25) invites an implicit comparison with 'Der Große Oktober' (Brecht) of the Russian Revolution.[21] Grüning draws on evening and autumn to illustrate the sense of an ending, even whilst the GDR is not yet itself a burning kingdom. References to 'Königreich', 'Limousinen' and 'Palais' suggest a class revolution, however, rather than the end of socialism. The title also describes an ironic reversal of direction from that in the headlines at this time: GDR refugees were fleeing to West Germany via Czechoslovakia, as the poet's 'Anmerkung' indicates, but the lyric 'ich' goes home.[22] Later 'Wende' poems would describe the break-up of the 'Eisenhimmel des Ostens' which is still intact here over the GDR.

In contrast to both the previous poems, "matthias" BAADER holst (this is how his name is printed with this poem), again in October 1989, composes a satirical 'Wende'-Loreley poem, a different type of poetic response to the same historical period:[23]

ich weiss nicht was soll es bedeuten das ich so
glasnost bin ich küsse auf der strasse schon jedes

---

[21]Bertolt Brecht, 'Der Große Oktober', *Gesammelte Werke*, ix, pp.675-677.

[22]Compare a typical reference to 'die Ausreise ehemaliger DDR-Bürger aus Prag über das Territorium der DDR in die BRD' in *Junge Welt*, 9 October 1989, p.15. See also Michael Andrew Kukral, *Prague 1989: Theater of Revolution* (New York: Columbia University Press, 1997).

[23]"matthias" BAADER holst, 'ich weiss nicht was soll es bedeuten', *Temperamente*, (1990), No.1, 33.

doppelkinn
ich höre auf zu schreiben denn fühl mich viel zu frei
5   was gestern deutlich unrecht schluck heut wie süßen brei
und all die toten tanzen wer toter noch
der träumt die knuten bluten frohsinn
bei uns wird aufgeräumt
pardon wird nicht gegeben
10   gib pfötchen dissident!
vergessen all die jahre
ins offne messer rennt
ein jeder frisch beseelt

Holst replaces the word 'traurig' in Heine's 'Lorelei' line with 'glasnost' (1), Mikhail Gorbachev's reformist principle of openness and transparency.[24] Holst uses the skipping rhythm of Heine's famous Rhine poem, and also works against it by using contrary line breaks. Rhyme is part of the mocking tone, for instance where Heine follows 'bin' with 'Sinn', Holst has the one-word line 'doppelkinn', and 'brei' follows 'frei'. The abandonment of rhyme at the poem's close pulls the reader up short and leaves the satirical phrase 'frisch beseelt' hanging in the air. Positive feelings of freedom, reconciliation and hopefulness are undermined in this poem: the poet declares himself now too free to write and too gullible (5). The continuation of Heine's lines seems to be implicit in Holst's poem, namely 'Ein Märchen aus alten Zeiten / Das kommt mir nicht aus dem Sinn'; he still refers to the GDR role of the writer as a dissident who identifies injustice. Holst represents the people's euphoria as a resurrection in this poem: the dead can dance. But such resurrection is ironized by the subsequent comparative: 'wer toter noch / der träumt' (6-7). Paradoxically, the happy are lashed and bleeding (7), and with renewed hope (for a better life under capitalism) rush into a suicide bid (12).[25] Enjambement and a lurching between satirical rhymes mirror this idea of a crazy lurching towards fatal political changes.

The three early 'Wende' poems discussed here are 'Zeitgedichte' which reflect the arrival of social change. They also, however, reflect the GDR 'Zeit', with motifs that would disappear in later 'Wende' poetry: literature as a substitute for GDR journalism (Tietze), the sky as an 'Eisenhimmel' over the

---

[24]Heinrich Heine, 'Die Lorelei', *Penguin Book of German Verse*, ed. by Leonard Forster (London: Penguin, 1959), pp.328-329. Mikhail Gorbachev articulated his principle of glasnost in *Perestroika: New Thinking for Our Country and the World* (London: Collins, 1987), especially pp.75-80.
[25]Suicide is a motif in a number of 'Wende' poems, but Matthias Holst also in fact apparently committed suicide on 1 July 1990.

East (Grüning) and, however ironically, poets as political dissidents (Holst). In
Hanns Cibulka's 'Wende' poem 'Ohne Titel' the GDR past seems to be
represented by China, where heavenly peace is the name of a square, not a
reality of communist rule, and where the ancient emperors lived apart in the
Forbidden City.[26] Cibulka's lyric subject evokes Tienanmen Square, Beijing,
where in June 1989 the Chinese army crushed a peaceful protest by students,
brutally killing many. A reporter-'ich' then describes what he sees in the GDR.
All this lyric subject can do is observe: in the second section, the echo 'sehe
ich'/ 'ich sehe' links the two strophes and the two scenes.

Ohne Titel
I
Auf dem Platz des Himmlischen Friedens
Genickschüsse.

Barmherziger als der Mensch
sind die Bäume,
5   die geben uns Schatten.
II
Wie die Fürsten haben sie gelebt,
die Hüter der Arbeiterklasse,
voller Zorn sehe ich ihre Weinkeller,
die mit Edelholz getäfelten Zimmer,
10   die Fußbodenheizung
in der Jagdhütte.

Ich sehe wie die Menschen
von einem Land ins andere gehen,
die Luft ist kalt geworden,
15   die Krähen kehren heim in Scharen,
wo ist der Ort
um niederzuschreiben was wahr ist?

The first section is Brechtian in its brevity and its stark contrasting of heavenly
peace with violence, mercy with brutality, trees with humans. This aphorism
on China is superseded by anger and bad omens (cold, crows) when the 'ich'
turns to his own country. Despite the apparent distance between the GDR and
China, in early October 1989 a parallel was rightly feared: a ministerial
circular to East Berlin students hinted that Tienanmen-like repression could be

---

[26]Hanns Cibulka, 'Ohne Titel', in *Die sanfte Revolution: Prosa, Lyrik, Protokolle,
Erlebnisberichte, Reden*, ed. by Stefan Heym and Werner Heiduczek (Leipzig and
Weimar: Kiepenheuer, 1990), p.296.

expected in the GDR too. In the run-up to Gorbachev's visit to East Berlin for the GDR's fortieth anniversary celebrations, Soviet tanks were indeed stationed around the 'Volkskammer'. The GDR leaders enjoyed a life of secret luxury in enclaves such as the Wandlitz 'Waldsiedlung', near East Berlin.[27] Cibulka's poem focuses on an image of them as timeless aristocrats, their wine-cellars and wood-panelled hunting lodge, an ironic antithesis of socialist architecture. By calling the poem 'Ohne Titel' Cibulka gives the impression that a full understanding or overview is not yet possible. One can however observe: the crows go homewards whereas the people are leaving their homes. The issue, as in Grüning's poem above, is the perpetuation of upper class privilege, but also here a matter of revelation. The open ending of this poem, however, reflects uncertainty on the lyric subject's part: he does not know where to write down the truth.

In October 1989 more established poets than Tietze or Holst were writing 'Zeitgedichte' of a different kind. Rather than seeking to report on the exodus and civic unrest, these texts were written as demonstrations themselves. These poets were not anxious like Grüning, nor were they Cibulka's powerless observer; rather they still showed belief in poetry's social usefulness. They knew places in which to publish their 'truth'. Two poems by prominent GDR writers were read out in public by their authors and participated directly in the changes: Heiner Müller's 'Fernsehen' and Volker Braun's 'Prolog zur Eröffnung der 40. Spielzeit des Berliner Ensembles am 11. Oktober 1989'. These are poems which were part of the 'Wende' events themselves.

Braun's 'Prolog' is a four-part poetic text from the time of the exodus of many GDR citizens via Hungary to the West and the time of the first mass demonstrations in the GDR.[28] Braun refers to these developments as 'die Beben der Völker' (p.37) and uses other images of natural turmoil such as storm, flood and landslide. A prose section of his poem describes the GDR citizens panicking in a struggle against the elements: 'Sie sehn sich auf eine Insel versetzt umspült von einer reißenden Strömung, oder ist es das Hochwasser eines heftigen Frühlings, und die rammen Wellenbrecher in die Wiesen oder nehmen blindlings Platz im letzten Ikarus' (p.38). Flood and earthquake in Braun's poem also relate to a resumption of temporal movement after standstill:

[27]See Peter Kirschey, *Wandlitz/Waldsiedlung – die geschlossene Gesellschaft: Versuch einer Reportage, Gespräche, Dokumente* (Berlin: Dietz, 1990).
[28]Volker Braun, 'Prolog zur Eröffnung der 40. Spielzeit des Berliner Ensembles am 11. Oktober 1989', *Die Zickzackbrücke*, pp.37-39. Also published as 'Zur Wiedereröffnung des Berliner Ensembles am 11.Oktober 1989', in 'Die Dichter und die Wende', pp.2-3.

Lange schien es, als stünden die Zeiten
Still. In den Uhren
Der Sand, das Blut, der abgestandene
Tag. Jetzt bricht er an
Der jüngste wieder und unerwartet.

Wo geht es lang oder, bescheidner gefragt
Weiß wer was vorn und hinten ist?
Die Strategien verschimmeln
Wie naß abgebrochne Zelte
Hinter den Flüchtlingen.   (p.37)

Tension is conveyed by the juxtaposition of 'wieder' and 'unerwartet' at end
of the first stanza and by breaking the phrase 'der Jüngste Tag' across two
sentences and two lines. An end to stagnation, the movement of time and of
refugees bring new uncertainties. In the past, the GDR had believed it knew
what lay ahead, namely the socialist utopia (which was commonly represented
as a house or other concrete building). Now on Judgement Day its strategies
are represented by Braun as mouldering, damp tents, something temporary and
inadequate, which the people have fled. Another image which Braun uses in
this poetic text is that of trucks on fixed tracks colliding into one another:

Der Planwagen der Händlerin
Und der Eisenwagen der Genossen
Stoßen aufeinander. Was für alte
Fahrzeuge, die nicht wenden können! (p.39)

This is a reference to the intractable opposition between capitalism and
communist socialism, which Braun seems to mock in this image, implying that
some third, more flexible system could now exist. 'Der Planwagen' is an
allusion to Brecht's *Mutter Courage und ihre Kinder* where the imperative to
make money is the driving force of life.[29] 'Der Eisenwagen' refers to Braun's
own parable about the vehicle of socialism.[30] The play on 'Wende'/'wenden'
is a bitter joke at the inability of both these vehicles to adapt in the changing
political climate of the late 1980s. At the close of this poem, read for the re-
opening of Brecht's theatre, Braun hopes for civic debate:

Eröffnen wir
Auch das Gespräch
Über die Wende im Land. (p.39)

The poem functions as a public statement here, calling for political dialogue.
At this stage many writers and intellectuals participated in the new climate of
openness and celebrated change. They were often involved in direct, political

---

[29]Bertolt Brecht, 'Mutter Courage und ihre Kinder', *Gesammelte Werke*, iv, pp.1347-
1443.
[30]Volker Braun, 'Der Eisenwagen', *Monatshefte*, 78 (1986), 7-10.

dialogue between the people and the authorities. Christa Wolf, for instance, sat on a commission investigating the police's violent treatment of demonstrators on 7 and 8 October 1989.[31] Commenting on the following months in the interview of 11 December 1989 entitled 'Schreiben im Zeitbezug', she referred to how busy she was with such activities, which related to the new developments underway in GDR society.[32] Wolf Biermann, as another example, demonstrated just how much an exiled GDR poet remained part of the GDR with his poem 'Mein Bauch ist leer', written on hunger strike with the citizens occupying the archive of the East Berlin Stasi building in September 1990.[33]

Heiner Müller's tripartite poem 'Fernsehen' was first read in public in early October 1989 at the 'Theater im Palast der Republik', East Berlin.[34] Müller's play *Quartett* was due to open there, but an actor and the producer had fled to the West. In a gesture of solidarity with those who remained in the GDR, 60-year-old Müller read the play to the audience himself. He interrupted a monologue by Valmont to read 'Fernsehen', in which the lyric voice is another reporter. The first section of the poem draws a 'Panzerspur' (4) again linking the streets of the GDR to Tienanmen Square. The second section of Müller's poem evokes Budapest in 1956, another civil uprising against communism. The Hungarian politician Kadar, who died in 1989, had been tortured by the Nazis, and in 1956 betrayed his fellow socialist Nagy. After a show trial, Nagy had died in 1956, and was exhumed in 1989 for a state funeral. Müller evokes this history in 1989 as another illustration of the brutality and betrayal which has accompanied socialism:

1 GEOGRAFIE
Gegenüber der HALLE DES VOLKES
Das Denkmal der toten Indianer
Auf dem PLATZ DES HIMMLISCHEN FRIEDENS
Die Panzerspur

2 DAILY NEWS NACH BRECHT 1989
Die ausgerissenen Fingernägel des Janos Kadar
Der die Panzer gegen sein Volk rief als es anfing
Seine Genossen Folterer an den Füßen aufzuhängen
Sein Sterben als der verratene Imre Nagy
Ausgegraben wurde oder der Rest von ihm
BONES AND SHOES das Fernsehn war dabei

---

[31]See also Christa Wolf, 'Brief an den Generalstaatsanwalt', *Im Dialog*, p.92.
[32]Wolf, 'Schreiben im Zeitbezug', p.139.
[33]Wolf Biermann, 'Mein Bauch ist leer', *Alle Lieder*, pp.429-430.
[34]Heiner Müller, 'Fernsehen', *Temperamente*, (1990), No.1, 31, and reprinted in *Grenzfallgedichte*, p.55.

Verscharrt mit dem Gesicht zur Erde 1956
WIR DIE DEN BODEN BEREITEN WOLLTEN
FÜR FREUNDLICHKEIT
Wieviel Erde werden wir fressen müssen
Mit dem Blutgeschmack unserer Opfer
Auf dem Weg in die bessere Zukunft
Oder in keine wenn wir sie ausspein   (lines 1-19)

Both elements in the title of the second section are characteristic for the many 'Wende' poems which trace 'daily news' and are Brechtian in form. Brecht's 1938 poem 'An die Nachgeborenen' is cited by Müller in lines 14-15.[35] Many GDR poems took up this particular Brecht poem and identified themselves with Brecht's addressees.[36] The 'wir' in Müller's poem, however, are less the generation which followed Brecht and more witnesses of the same 'dark' years with 'keine bessere Zukunft'. References to torn-out fingernails (7), being strung up by the feet (9) and the corpse which is now 'BONES AND SHOES' (12), attest to the brutalized human body. In November 1990 Müller commented in an interview, 'im Namen von Utopien wurden die schlimmsten Terrorstrukturen errichtet'.[37] The violent images of such terror in his 1989 poem are linked to the title 'Fernsehen' in the sense of 'looking far' over time. After the global links of the first section, and the human bodies of the second, the poet then turns to himself as an individual, in the third section of the poem, 'SELBSTKRITIK':

Meine Herausgeber wühlen in alten Texten
Manchmal wenn ich sie lese überläuft es mich kalt Das
Habe ich geschrieben IM BESITZ DER WAHRHEIT (lines 21-23)

There is a great sense of personal failure here (a theme which I explore in depth in the next chapter). The title 'SELBSTKRITIK' indicates self-criticism but also, more specifically, the poet as a critic of his own texts. Television has become the medium of truth, which corrects that offered by writers and intellectuals. This is reinforced by the use of quotations, and especially by the recourse to English words in lines 6 and 12. Youth saw the founding of the poet's identity and the founding of the GDR: the perspective of 1989 however brings torment and disorientation, in respect of both personal and national identity. The contrast between then and now is drawn with respect to the truth about socialism.

Several poems associate November 1989 with revelation and a new understanding of the truth. In Kathrin Schmidt's 'novemberalmanach' the

---

[35]Brecht, 'An die Nachgeborenen', *Gesammelte Werke*, ix, pp.722-725.
[36]See Silvia Schlenstedt, 'Fragen der Nachgeborenen', *SGCS*, 9 (1989), 85-99.
[37]René Ammann, 'Eine Tragödie der Dummheit', *Freitag*, 16 November 1990, p.3.

'Wende' is a 'kehren', a turning of language; an old statement is broken into pieces, which show up its falsity:[38]

    der satz zerbrach
    wenn du ihn kehrtest
    in gelebte stücke und stimmte nicht (lines 23-25)

The 'gelebte stücke' are fragments of past life, but also perhaps plays or performances, something acted, not real. Günter Kunert's poem 'November' associates November 1989 with truth as opposed to the empty promises of the past:[39]

    Alles Versprochene zeugt
    alsobald Ekel wie Worte
    glitschig vom Sabber
    endlosen Gebrauchs: Prothesen
    aus Allerweltsmündern.
    Jetzt im November stattdessen
    das pathetische Rauschen
    so kalt und so schneidend
    wie Wahrheit   (lines 5-13)

Kunert describes a new language which is not slippery or prosthetic, but like truth. 'Rauschen' is a natural sound, of a river, perhaps here the sound of change sweeping in, although it is also unclear – not the distinct articulation of words. Oddly, this indistinct, truthful language seems knife-like where it is described as cold and cutting, a language that can do violence, like Armin Richter's 'Sprache aus Steinwürfen'.[40] Annerose Kirchner's poem 'Zwischen den Ufern' suggests the new language was simpler and undeceiving, the language of conscience:

    Dein Gewissen, mündig gesprochen,
    schwört auf einfache Worte,
    und die oftmals betrogene Zunge
    probiert den Hymnus verlorner Freiheit (lines 5-8)

The anthem mentioned here was perhaps Beethoven's setting of Schiller's 'An die Freude', which was reworded as 'An die Freiheit', an ode to freedom, and

---

[38]Kathrin Schmidt, 'novemberalmanach', *Flußbild mit Engel*, pp.18-19.

[39]Günter Kunert, 'November', in *Fremd daheim* (Munich: Hanser, 1990), p.28. Later the poem was read differently, as satire. A slightly altered version of it appears as 'Ja zum November', in *Nie wieder Ismus! Neue deutsche Satire*, ed. by Christine and Manfred Wolter (Berlin: Eulenspiegel, 1992), p.58. The 'alles Versprochene' later seemed to refer to 'Wende' promises too. The simile 'wie Wahrheit' also suggested that the new language only resembled truth, but was not actually truthful.

[40]Armin Richter, 'Herbstsonate 89', *Die kleinen mecklenburgischen Meere: Gedichte 1988 bis 1990* (Frankfurt a.M.: Fischer, 1991), p.47, and reprinted in *Von einem Land*, p.10.

conducted by Leonard Bernstein at the Deutsche Staatsoper on 27 December 1989. Although Kirchner's lines point primarily to past deception and freedom lost in the past, they are actually more ambivalent: 'verlorne Freiheit' could refer to freedom now lost, and the implication of 'oftmals' is perhaps scepticism about the present.

It is clear in these poems that from the first, poets were concerned about truth. On 28 October 1989, some seventy writers, artists and intellectuals gathered at Berlin's 'Erlöserkirche' under the motto 'Wider den Schlaf der Vernunft' (after Francisco Goya's etching of the sleeping writer, 'El sueño de la razon produce monstruos'). Simultaneously, at the 'Deutsches Theater' the actor Ulrich Mühe read from Walter Janka's Schwierigkeiten mit der Wahrheit, a book eagerly read and passed from hand to hand in autumn 1989.[41] These gatherings included Müller, Wolf and the novelists and playwrights Christoph Hein, Stefan Heym, Stephan Hermlin, Günter de Bruyn and Helga Königsdorf. Janka, one-time head of the Aufbau Verlag, was imprisoned in 1956 under false accusations that he had conspired to oust the Ulbricht government. The 1989 event represented the rehabilitation of those, like Janka, who had been victims of the state's Stalinist paranoia and oppression. Wolf held up Janka's book as an aid to rectifying what she saw as the moral crisis of GDR society: 'Wir müssen unsere eigenen "Schwierigkeiten mit der Wahrheit" untersuchen'.[42] In 1978, Václav Havel described the power of revelation or truth-telling against apparently solid totalitarian power:

> The crust presented by the life of lies is made of strange stuff. As long as it seals off hermetically the entire society, it appears to be made of stone. But the moment someone breaks through in one place, when one person cries out 'The emperor is naked!' [...], the whole crust seems then to be made of a tissue on the point of tearing and disintegrating uncontrollably.[43]

'Der Kaiser ist nackt', the phrase Havel refers to here, was taken as a title by one of the underground magazines produced in the GDR. However, not only the unofficial GDR writers, but officially recognised writers, like Braun and Müller, were also part of this truth-telling. At the congress of the GDR writers' union held in November 1987, the last before unification, speakers had voiced

[41]Walter Janka, Schwierigkeiten mit der Wahrheit (Berlin and Weimar: Aufbau, 1990).
[42]Christa Wolf, 'Wider den Schlaf der Vernunft: Rede in der Erlöserkirche', Im Dialog, pp.98-100, p.100.
[43]Václav Havel, 'The Power of the Powerless', trans. by P. Wilson, in Václav Havel or Living in Truth, ed. by Jan Vladislav (London: Faber and Faber, 1987), pp.36-122 (p.59).

unheard-of opposition to censorship.[44] Hein declared, 'Die beste Propaganda ist die Wahrheit'. This ambivalent declaration encapsulates both a radical accusation of false propaganda, and also indicates the idealized view of socialism which Hein and other writers harboured. A scandal ensued as writers called for a debate about glasnost and environmental concerns. Braun spoke against 'gewohnte Enge' and eagerly looked forward to the beginnings of change: 'Jetzt spüren wir aber die Bewegung, das heißt, etwas kommt in Fluß: und das Fragen beginnt'.[45] In 1987 this was a premature anticipation of the 'Wende' and a relatively isolated incident.

By November 1989, however, a mass movement was taking place on a daily basis across the whole country. The huge East Berlin rally on 4 November at Alexanderplatz, a demonstration for freedom of speech and the press, involved a million citizens. Writers and intellectuals took the platform; indeed, Wolf saw it as the climactic culmination of years of interplay between critical literature and civic action: she called this demonstration 'der Punkt der größtmöglichen Annährung zwischen Künstlern, Intellektuellen und den anderen Volksschichten'.[46] Those who addressed the assembled crowd included Wolf and Heym. Müller read out a flyer demanding independent trade unions. Hein declared that Leipzig, where the 'Montagsdemonstrationen' had been an inspiring force for change, was a city of heroes, a 'Heldenstadt'. Heym spoke for, as well as to, the people: 'Freunde, Mitbürger! Es ist, als habe einer die Fenster aufgestoßen, nach all den Jahren der Stagnation, der geistigen, wirtschaftlichen, politischen'.[47] This metaphor of the 'Wende' as a breath of fresh air after years of stagnation became a commonplace. In 1988 Czechowski had already echoed Gorbachev, the leader of change, in lines from a long poem, which use fresh air as a simile:[48]

Wir brauchen die Demokratie
Wie die Luft zum Atmen. (Gorbatschow)

Und die Luft zum Atmen
Wie die Demokratie.   (Czechowski)   (p.73)

[44]Details of this congress are given in Dieter Schlenstedt, 'Der aus dem Ruder laufende Schriftstellerkongreß von 1987', *GM*, 40 (1997), 16-31.
[45]Volker Braun, in *X. Schriftstellerkongreß der Deutschen Demokratischen Republik, Berlin 24.-26- November 1987*, ndl, 36 (1988), No.3, 44-47 (p.46).
[46]Christa Wolf, 'Zwischenrede', *Im Dialog*, pp.158-162 (pp.158-159).
[47]Stefan Heym, 'Rede auf der Demonstration am 4. November', *Einmischung*, pp.257-258 (p.257).
[48]Heinz Czechowski, 'Tag um Februar', *Mein Venedig: Gedichte und andere Prosa* (Berlin, FRG: Wagenbach, 1989), pp.69-74.

Here the poem resembles a slogan on a placard, in its concision, use of inversion and invocation of Gorbachevian reform. Czechowski's reversal also makes an environmental point, in tune with the emerging 'alternative' politics of the time. At this stage in 1988, the poet articulated demands for reform as if speaking for the people.

Kolbe described the demonstrations of autumn 1989 as 'ein Akt der Mündigkeit', the people speaking for themselves.[49] One manifestation of this maturity lay in the public use of satirical slogans such as 'Ruinen schaffen ohne Waffen – 40 Jahre DDR' and the adulteration of socialist clichés: 'Je stärker der SED, um so sicherer die Massenflucht' modelled on 'Je stärker der DDR, um so sicherer der Friede'; 'So wie wir heute demonstrieren, werden wir morgen leben' modelled on 'So wie wir heute arbeiten, werden wir morgen leben'; and 'ZK = Zirkus Krenz' instead of 'Zentralkomitee'.[50] The numerous slogans on banners at the Alexanderplatz rally, which famously included 'Wir sind das Volk', suggested the clarity of the people's will for change.[51] Some expressed general revolutionary sentiments such as 'Skepsis bleibt die erste Bürgerpflicht' or 'Privilegien für alle' (p.76); many were anti-SED slogans: 'SED allein – das darf nicht sein', 'Pässe für alle – der SED den Laufpaß' (p.78). The people demanded dialogue – 'Krenz zu Tisch' – and action – 'Wir wollen endlich Taten sehen, sonst sagen wir Auf Wiedersehen' (p.78). Use of rhyme, humour and word-play was evident, as the following banners, combining 'Wende'-demands with the language of environmental campaigning, illustrate: 'Öko-Daten ohne Filter', 'Kein Artenschutz für Wendehälse' and 'Sägt die Bonzen ab – nicht die Bäume' (p.78). The apparent vocality which the population had suddenly found would become crucial to writers' later reactions to the 'Wende'. The author Fritz Rudolf Fries stated in 1990 that at the 'Wende' writers could only follow after the masses: 'Die Autoren konnten ihnen die Parolen nur nachsprechen'.[52] In the words of François Bondy, 'Da die Schriftsteller nicht mehr in und zwischen den Zeilen

---

[49]Uwe Kolbe, 'Gebundene Zungen. Ein offener Brief', in *Die Geschichte ist offen: DDR 1990: Hoffnung auf eine neue Republik: Schriftsteller aus der DDR über die Zukunftschancen ihres Landes*, ed. by Michael Naumann (Hamburg: Rowohlt, 1990), pp.85-90 (p.86).
[50]Wolfgang Thierse, *Mit eigener Stimme sprechen* (Munich and Zurich: Piper, 1992), pp.305-306.
[51]Hannes Bahrmann and Christoph Links, eds., *Wir sind das Volk: Die DDR im Aufbruch - Eine Chronik* (Berlin and Weimar: Aufbau, 1990 and Wuppertal: Hammer, 1990), p.78. Further page references follow in the text.
[52]Fritz Rudolf Fries, 'Braucht die neue Republik neue Autoren?', in *Die Geschichte ist offen*, ed. by Naumann, pp.53-57 (p.55).

die "Stimmen der Stummen" waren, ging ihr Wort im Stimmengewirr unter'.[53] Rather than a sense of GDR literature paving the way for the demonstrations, some poems suggest that slogans paved the way for literature. B.K. Tragelehn's poem 'Die Losungen des Jahres' for example quotes demonstrators' slogans:[54]

> Die Losungen des Jahres
> Eben hat er noch um sich geschlagen der Staat
> Obwohl versprochen war und er immer gewußt hat
> Er soll verschwinden, wuchert und wuchert er bis
> WIR SIND DAS VOLK
> 5   Er beim Wort genommen und endlich enteignet gleich
> WIR SIND EIN VOLK
> Über die eigene Grenze springt. Und wie bereits
> Stalin gesagt hat: Die Honecker kommen und gehen
> Denn alles hat ein Ende nur die Wurst hat zwei
> 10 Und ICH BIN VOLKER
>   1989

The GDR's closed border, a literal restriction on travel and a symbol of the other boundaries on freedom, became the focus of the people's protest. In this poem, the state is personified as a figure finally leaping over its own border (7), essentially Honecker himself (8). The Stalin quotation was originally displayed in 1945 in the Soviet occupied zone and actually ran, 'Die Hitler kommen und gehen, das deutsche Volk, der deutsche Staat bleibt'. Tragelehn's poem thus links 1989 to 1945 and Honecker to Hitler. It works with an opposition, rather than an identity, between 'Staat' and 'Volk'. The first two quotations in capitals were commonplace cries at different stages of the demonstrations, but all three capitalized mottoes form a witticism which also came from the demonstrations. Within the text, the lyric voice is interrupted by the voice of the people on the streets. But the poem also preserves their mottoes after the placards have gone: the title points to fashion, as though by the following year the sentiments would be invalid (as in fact they were).[55]

Holger Teschke's 'Berliner November' also exemplifies the importation of street slogans into the poem. In the opening lines the poet

---

[53]François Bondy, 'Nach dem Zusammenbruch der DDR - deutscher Intellektuellenstreit', *Schweizer Monatshefte*, 70 (1990), 710-715 (p.710).
[54]B.K. Tragelehn, 'Die Losungen des Jahres', *ndl*, 43 (1995), No.5, 5.
[55]'Viel zu schnell verschwanden die originellen Losungen, die wunderbaren Demo-Bilder', *Leipziger Andere Zeitung*, 1 March 1990, p.1.

speaks with 'we' the people: line 3 quotes two slogans of the demonstrations.[56] 'We' and 'our', long keywords of the SED's rhetoric, now exclude the ruling regime. Historic change in this poem is conveyed breathlessly: here the suddenness and energy of the 'Wende' are articulated in the runover lines and lack of punctuation.

Berliner November
Alles auf einmal brüllten wir heraus
Auf unsern Straßen Unter diesem Himmel
Sägt Bonzen ab statt Bäume Stasi raus
Aufriß der Himmel wie in alten Filmen
5   Im ungarischen Herbst Im Prager Frühling
Und keine Panzer kamen von Karlshorst
Aber als sich einer auf die Barrikade ging
Das Holzgerüst am Alexanderplatz
Auslachte unsern Kindertraum Tapetentanz
10   Anstatt den Hunderttausenden zum Maul zu reden
Aussprach was Herren aller Länder fürchten Streik
Da gellten Pfiffe War der Spaß zu Ende

The 'Wende' in the GDR is compared to the Hungarian Uprising of 1956 and the Prague Spring of 1968 and is, as in Müller's 'Fernsehen', the heir to those demands for reform. Whereas these earlier civil revolts were suppressed, the tanks of the Red Army do not descend on East Berlin. The 'Tapetentanz' was a response to Neues Forum's appeal 'Schreibt Eure Forderungen auf Tapetenrollen und bringt sie zur Demo mit'.[57] The sky is torn open (4): this is at once an expression of liberation and the break up of the 'Eisenhimmel' (Grüning). In the second half of Teschke's poem the positive assertions of the first are countered by an 'Aber'. Manning the barricades (an image from the French Revolution of 1789) is inspired by a childhood dream which soon pales: the verbs 'auslachen' and 'aussprechen', pushed to the beginning of lines and with their separable prefixes unseparated, pre-empt the demonstrations becoming exhausted, 'aus'. The last line deflates the drama, paralleling the end of the 'Tapetentanz' (9), as the demonstrations threaten to be superseded by strikes. On 1 December 1989, for instance, Neues Forum called for a general strike.

---

[56]Holger Teschke, 'Berliner November', in 'Die Dichter und die Wende', p.4 and in *Von einem Land*, p.13. See the list of slogans in Bahrmann, ed., *Wir sind das Volk*, p.78.
[57]Julia Michelis, ed., *Die ersten Texte des Neuen Forum* (Berlin: Neues Forum, 1990), p.13. On 10 September 1989 'Neues Forum' was formed as an umbrella organization for GDR opposition groups.

As in Teschke's opening lines 'Alles auf einmal brüllten wir heraus / Auf unsern Straßen', many poems evoke the city streets as a metonym for popular protest:

The streets became a veritable laboratory for the reconstruction of democratic forms as the previously "passive objects" aspired to shape the structures in which they lived.[58]

The streets suggest a place outside the buildings and corridors of established power. They constitute an image which, as Anna Chiarloni states, is linked to a more general sense of moving forward: 'Das dynamische Fortschreiten der Deutschen in der Geschichte bringt oft das Bild der Straße in den Vordergrund'.[59] In November 1989 they are the starting point for Harald Gerlach's 'Aufbrüche, deutsch' or 'November'.[60] This poem again invokes the famous slogan 'Wir sind das Volk' and the candle-lit marches. The first strophe provides an image of history coming down from grand plans to the realistic level of pot-holed streets:

Der Ort, an dem Geschichte
sich einholt zwischen Schlaglöchern:
die Straße.

Ich bin, du bist, wir sind.
Das Volk, meine Herrn.

Gesichter mit dem Abglanz
der Romantik. Kerzen schmelzen
das Schwert zur Pflugschar   (lines 1-8)

The glowing faces reflect peaceful demonstrations but perhaps point to a naivety on the part of those who envisaged a wondrously better life for themselves in the future. In the 1980s a peace movement developed under the church's auspices, with the biblical motto 'Schwerter zu Pflugscharen'. Stephan Hermlin and Volker Braun praised the movement, which was also increasingly supported by the young. Using the motto in the poem suggests how it seemed that people's ideals would now be realized. For Gerlach, autumn 1989 was a time for imagination: 'Im warmen Herbst blüht Phantasie' (12). Mostly, the poem celebrates the renewal of hope and imagination, although on repeated reading there seems to be ambiguity about how realistic this hope might be.

---

[58]Mike Dennis, 'Civil Society, Opposition and the End of the GDR', *SGCS*, 11/12 (1993), 1-18 (p.10).
[59]Chiarloni, 'Zwischen gestern und morgen', p.95.
[60]Harald Gerlach, 'Aufbrüche, deutsch', in *Von einem Land*, p.11, or 'November', in *Grenzfallgedichte*, p.67.

The streets were an important image of the remarkable protests, but also of the border opening. On 9 November 1989 ZK spokesman Günter Schabowski was answering journalists' questions at a press conference when he stated that, 'Privatreisen nach dem Ausland können ohne Vorliegen von Voraussetzungen (Reiseanlässe und Verwandschaftsverhältnisse) beantragt werden'.[61] As people heard this statement on the television news, they set out to see for themselves; border guards in Berlin, at first unsure what to do, eventually had to give way to the gathering throng. Armin Richter's poem 'Rotes Kirschlaub' begins with a transformation of the streets: [62]

> Plötzlich sind Straßen wieder
> Wie fließende Gewässer
> Münden in alle Orte der Welt
> Und in die Straßen
> Wo noch das mächtige hilflose Volk steht
>
> Feuersignale der Hoffnung (lines 1-6)

The co-existence of fire and water points to elemental change and corresponds to the oxymoronic description of the 'Volk'. The concrete streets became fluid.

Alongside the streets, some 'Wende' poems also take up organic images from nature, implying hope and new growth. In Richter's poem 'Rotes Kirschlaub', 'Hoffnung', a word concomitant with a certain strand of Marxist philosophy, is apparently to be realized now in 1989:

> Feuersignale der Hoffnung
> Flammen von den Ahornen
> Der nahen Chaussee herüber
> Das Kirschlaub im Garten
> Errötet davon   (lines 6-10)

These lines seem less persuasive than others, due to their echoes of unreflecting political panegyric. The title 'Rotes Kirschlaub', referring to the autumnal maple trees, connects with the fire image, red being the colour of anger and revolt, but also in 'erröten' (10) the colour of blushing faces. Autumn 1989 was a season of new hope, as the altered word-order of line 17 allows the alliteration of 'Herbst' and 'Hoffnung' to accentuate:

> Noch ist Herbst
> Der Hoffnung Früchte
> Wer wird sie ernten(lines 16-18)

These lines follow Brecht's lines 'Noch die Ernte / Ging in die Scheuern der Herren' in the poem 'Der Große Oktober', which plays on the spring and

---

[61]Text reprinted in Bahrmann, ed., *Wir sind das Volk*, p.91.
[62]Armin Richter, 'Rotes Kirschlaub', *Die kleinen mecklenburgischen Meere*, p.48, and reprinted in *Von einem Land*, p.12.

summer as metaphors for socialism's preparation period and equates October with 'Hoffnung'. In Richter's poem, 'Noch' seems to imply a renewal of the October Revolution which established communist Russia. As the last line of the poem, the unmarked question indicates an unknown future. Yet harvesting the fruits of hope is a strong, positive image of a natural process. In 'Herbstsonate 89', Richter again draws on nature images, linking 'Herbst' and 'Hoffnung':

> Wie gelassen wie unbeschadet
> Der Herbst die Baüme färbt
> Und sich schließlich im Nebel verleugnet
>
> Gleichzeitig fallen Herzblätter
> Von ihren Stammbäumen
> Vergeßne und wiederentdeckte Gefühle
> Arten aus in nie gekannte Leidenschaften
>
> Volksfeststimmungen
> Wermuträusche
> Absingen des Prinzips Hoffnung (lines 1-10)

The seasons change naturally, without damage to the cycle of life, here suggesting political change as equally natural. Trees, fruits and mists, like 'fließende Gewässer', are images of nature which are relocated in the city. Leaves falling are likened to emotions expressed as Germans from East and West cried and celebrated on the streets of Berlin.[63] The trees become family trees, symbolic of a sense of kinship.

In Michael Wüstefeld's unsettling 1990 poem 'Gegenwärtige Vergangenheit', nature is part of the Dresden setting of the poem, in the Elbe valley, but also urban protest and exodus respectively in the first two stanzas.[64] The people are 'das KrähenVolk', wild birds which had been caged:

> Gegenwärtige Vergangenheit
> 1)
> Am Elbhang die Lichter
> vergrößern den Käfig der Nacht
> in der Stadt und den AbSteigen
> Im Dürrholz der Bäume
> 5   das KrähenVolk wacht

---

[63]Compare Richter's 'Volksfeststimmungen / Wermutsräusche' to West German poet Hans Magnus Enzenberger's poem 'Aufbruchstimmung', in *Von einem Land*, p.31, which refers to champagne, vermouth and valium on the streets.
[64]Michael Wüstefeld, 'Gegenwärtige Vergangenheit', *Deutsche Anatomie: Gedichte* (Schöppingen: tende, 1996), p.59.

ein schwarzer Flügelreigen

Das ElbTal voll Ahnung
zu viele haben weggewollt
aus der Stadt unter dem Schweigen
10   Der Tag fragt: Sind wir schon
ein Raum ohne Volk
wollen die Krähen noch bleiben

2)
Auf allen Bäumen kahlen Landes
blühen die Krähen

15   Mit schwarzen Mänteln hängen sie
im Wind und rufen
Wir sind das Volk
Wir sind ein Volk

The most famous slogans of the 'Wende' and unification respectively are located in nature here, as though they were natural cries, the voice of Nature itself. The traditionally ominous crows seem to be an ambiguous metaphor in conjunction with the positive image of blossoming in a barren landscape. Likewise, the darkness of night, black wings and black coats is ambiguous: symbolic darkness is tempered by the fact that the demonstrations took place after dark, during the winter months when days were short. 'Raum ohne Volk' is not only a reflection of exodus however, but a reversal of and reference to 'Blut und Boden' ideology.[65]

In Kirchner's poem 'Wolfsspur' the lyric 'ich' follows the traces of wolves in a natural wasteland.[66] The phrase 'der aufrechte Gang' (16) was used in public discourse at the 'Wende' to refer to the GDR people's new self-respect.[67] (The discussion of Volker Braun's poetry in Chapter 5 will develop this point.) Ceasing to walk upright in the last stanza of Kirchner's poem suggests a going back to nature, to the wild. The wolves have fled, as has the border, and the traces left behind are the dust and dry grass of the wolves' lair.

---

[65]Hans Grimm, *Volk ohne Raum* (Munich: Langen, 1928).
[66]Annerose Kirchner, 'Wolfsspur', *Literatur Bote*, 5 (1990), No.20, 27.
[67]See Dieter Herberg, Doris Steffens and Elke Tellenbach, *Schlüsselwörterbuch der Wendezeit: Wörter-Buch zum öffentlichen Sprachgebrauch 1989/90* (Berlin and New York: de Gruyter, 1997), p.214: 'Das Lexem *aufrechter Gang* mit seiner verbalen Entsprechung *aufrecht gehen* stellt [...] insofern eine Besonderheit dar, als es in übertragener Bedeutung in der Vor-Wendezeit nur ganz vereinzelt gebraucht wurde und erst in der Wendezeit usuell wird'.

As these wolves are the GDR 'Genossen', so snapped telegraph poles speak of the 'Wende' storm.

Wolfsspur
Im schütteren Zwielicht
Staub auf vertrockneten Grasbüscheln –
die fliehende Grenze
von zitternden Fingern
5   in die Luft gezeichnet.

Wer alte Schlupfwinkel
noch beim Namen nennt,
spricht über vergeßne Topographie:
Die Wölfe zogen nach Norden
10   und ließen ihre Legende zurück.

Querfeldein entdeck ich
Schutthalden und Schneegitter.
Geknickte Telegraphenmaste
summen Nachrichten aus dem Jenseits.

15   Am stinkenden Wasserloch
verlier ich den aufrechten Gang,
und mein Atem wittert
die verspätete Nacht.

1989/1990

This poem does not quite come into focus. References to twilight, the border and 'das Jenseits' however suggest images which correspond to the transgressive dating '1989/1990', and the change from one condition to its opposite. Postponed nightfall is an ambiguous image: the 'Wende' means the resumption of normal quotidian exchange after the relentless day, dawn and light of socialism, but also the beginning of night and darkness.

Nature provides not only the positive metaphors of trees and harvest, or ambiguous images of crows and night, but also metaphors of devastation. Apocalyptic landscapes in Kurt Drawert's 'Tauben in ortloser Landschaft' represent the dying GDR: 'mein kleines, aufgeschlitztes Land' (1) 'modert, // und verendet nicht' (4-5). The 'ortloser Landschaft' suggests a metaphorical endpoint, a nowhere. Drawert's first line in an article of 1995 also echoed these sentiments: 'Wir sind am Ziel: nichts mehr findet statt'.[68] His jaundiced,

[68]Kurt Drawert, 'Osten, Westen, Finale', SuF, 47 (1995), 499-504 (p.499).

poisonous 'Tauben', once the birds of mythical hope, associated with the biblical flood, are now just the urban birds. The wasted landscape echoes ecological poetry, its decay symptomatic of the modern condition. In the 1990s, harmony and latent potential in nature have been replaced long ago by utter loss and hopelessness. In Kirchner's poem 'Legende', the GDR environment will not sustain human life at all: the lyric subject is overwhelmed by crumbling clay, dust and cinders.[69] A post-apocalyptic vision here symbolizes extinction. The ruptured ozone layer and destroyed environment are accompanied by the breaking of an hour-glass which symbolizes another rupture. The human is adrift between dream and reality: 'Zwischen Bettpfosten und Tür / beginnt die Wüste zu wandern' (4-5). Here the perspective suggests someone lying in bed, perhaps feverish, and dreaming this vision of apocalypse.

Amongst the 'Wende' poems which use nature imagery, many focus on water images – rivers, seas and floods. In the poem 'Zwischen den Ufern' by Kirchner, the river rushing between two banks is an image of the force of historical change in which the human subject is swept up: 'Zwischen den Ufern verliert sich / der eigene Lebenslauf'.[70] This flowing river recalls the 'reißende Strömung' in Braun's 'Prolog'. The flux and movement of the larger process overwhelms the individual's course. Two banks represent a duality echoing Germany's division, but are also places of solidity which the subject leaves, so that by the penultimate line the imperative is to swim: 'Schwimm gegen die steigende Flut' (13). This rising water is reminiscent of the biblical flood, which totally destroyed the old order, so that the late stab at defiance in this line is likely a futile gesture.[71] Flood is also of course a Brechtian motif familiar from poems such as 'Das Schiff', 'An die Nachgeborenen' and 'Lied vom Glück'.[72] In December 1989, Czechowski's lyric subject hears a coming flood in the demonstrators' cries:[73]

Wenn ich die Augen schließe,

---

[69]Annerose Kirchner, 'Legende', *Literatur Bote,* 5 (1990), No.19, 29, and reprinted in *Grenzfallgedichte*, p.27.

[70]Annerose Kirchner, 'Zwischen den Ufern', *Literatur Bote*, 5 (1990), No.19, 30, and reprinted in *Grenzfallgedichte*, p.97.

[71]Rising water is also an image of impending threat in the quite different context of Hanns Cibulka, 'Jahrgang 20', in *Die sanfte Revolution*, ed. by Heym, p.297. The 'wir' is here that of a particular German generation which suffered various torments: the rising water in the present day is the culmination of these.

[72]Bertolt Brecht, 'Das Schiff' and 'Lied vom Glück', *Gesammelte Werke*, viii, pp.179-181, and x, pp.997-998.

[73]Heinz Czechowski, 'Historische Reminiszenz', in 'Die Dichter und die Wende', pp.7-8, and reprinted in *Grenzfallgedichte*, pp.74-75.

Hör ich die Rufe der Masse
Wie Brandung.   (lines 10-12)

The sound is only a memory now, however. The sea coming to inland Europe is a metaphorical tradition in poetry: in 1977 Hilbig for instance had concluded a poem with the following vision: [74]

ich weiß das meer kommt wieder nach sachsen
es verschlingt die arche
stürzt den ararat.   (p.283)

In his poem 'april ohne datum' of 1989 it is already raining: 'regen' and 'regnen' appear five times in this 14-line poem.[75] Barbara Köhler's 'Meer in Sicht', dated 2.1.90, looks to the sea bringing seafood and sailing boats to Bohemia.[76] Here the water represents a positive change; it is a vital element that will quench a desert. In Drawert's poem 'In dieser Lage' however, the historical upheaval is likened to a shipwreck.[77] The GDR had long used the ship as a metaphor for its quest: as late as 21 September 1989, the SED organ *Neues Deutschland* was echoing Karl Liebknecht's statement, 'Unser Schiff zieht seinen Kurs fest und stolz dahin – bis zum Sieg'.[78] In Drawert's poem this ship sinks without trace. A 'wir' has been saved, but somehow left stranded and bereft. A paradoxical sense of loss is suggested by the repetition of 'kein':

Keine störenden Zeichen
drangen nach oben und bewegten
das friedliche Wasser. Keine Reste
von Luft und von Gasen. Kein letzter Befehl,
der uns drohend als hilfloses Blubbern erreichte.   (lines 6-10)

The loss of 'Zeichen' may be especially resonant for a writer. Primarily however, these lines provide an image of the GDR leaders' demise and the alliteration equating 'Befehl' and 'Blubbern' mocks their commands. The tense change to the present in the last two lines of this poem suggests that a remnant of the original ship survives:

Wir sprechen uns Mut zu und peilen
Den Mond an. Unter uns ein letztes Stück Holz. (lines 19-20)

---

[74]Wolfgang Hilbig, 'das meer in sachsen', *zwischen den paradiesen*, pp.280-283.
[75]Wolfgang Hilbig, 'april ohne datum', *zwischen den paradiesen*, p.311.
[76]Barbara Köhler, 'Meer in Sicht', *Deutsches Roulette*, p.83.
[77]Kurt Drawert, 'In dieser Lage', *Wo es war: Gedichte* (Frankfurt a.M.: Suhrkamp, 1996), p.12.
[78]Dieter Brückner and Heiner Schulz, 'Unser Schiff zieht seinen Kurs fest und stolz dahin – bis zum Sieg', *ND*, 21 September 1989, p.3. Erica Fischer and Petra Lux, *Ohne uns ist kein Staat zu machen: DDR-Frauen nach der Wende* (Cologne: Kiepenheuer & Witsch, 1990), p.128, reports a woman's statement, 'Ich habe das Gefühl, mitten in einem riesigen Ozean auf einem kleinen Schiff zu sein'.

Ironically, given the journey to utopia as a GDR metaphor, this post-GDR 'wir' steer towards the moon, as though still trying to escape and navigate towards utopia. The shipwreck is clearly an image of the demise of the GDR which recalls Brecht's 'Ballade auf vielen Schiffen' and also recalls Grüning's image, cited above, of Czechoslovakia sinking beneath the waves.[79] Kunert's 1990 poem 'Atlantis' draws on the same image of a city sinking beneath the sea, a means of ironically universalizing the 'Wende'.[80] Plato described Atlantis as a utopia, a mythical Lost City of riches and marvels, which Francis Bacon invoked anew in *The New Atlantis* of 1626. Because it was lost, Atlantis becomes a 'Gelegenheit' for poetry.

> Und einige die Gelegenheit ergriffen
> zu einem Gedicht: Spätfolge
> von Untergängen die allein durch Ortsnamen
> der Unterscheidung sich fügen.   (lines 21-24)

These lines by Kunert turn on its head the idea of an astonishing, unique collapse. They also ironize the rush to write poems, of which there are many which use particular 'Ortsnamen'.

In the preceding discussion of nature imagery, it becomes clear that what makes these 'Wende' poems and not just nature poems is the use of slogans, the dating and the development of commonplace metaphors for socialism, in order to anchor mythical poetic elements in the concrete experience of 1989/90. Certain places have emblematic value in the discourse of 1989/90 and poets use their names to mark stages of the 'Wende'. This is illustrated in poems above by Tietze's 'Berlin' and 'Gethsemanekirche', Cibulka and Müller's references to Tienanmen Square and Teschke's 'Karlshorst' and 'Alexanderplatz'. Tragelehn's poem 'Plan von Berlin', written in 1990, uses place names in the second stanza to evoke key events of the 'Wende':[81] Lichtenberg, the district of the Stasi headquarters, Werderscher Markt where the ZK building was located, 'Alex' or Alexanderplatz where the largest demonstration took place on 4 November, and Bornholmer Brücke where the border first opened between East and West Berlin on the night of 9-10 November 1989.

> In Lichtenberg die Liebe der Spinne für alle
> Am Werderschen Markt das geschmeichelte Lächeln
> Des Idioten gewählt von Idioten
> Die andere Seite die andere
> Auf dem Alex die Leute

---

[79]Bertolt Brecht, 'Ballade von vielen Schiffen', *Gesammelte Werke*, viii, pp.219-222.
[80]Günter Kunert, 'Atlantis', *Fremd daheim*, p.117.
[81]B.K. Tragelehn, 'Plan von Berlin', *NÖSPL: Gedichte 1956-1991* (Basel and Frankfurt a.M.: Stroemfeld, 1996), p.142.

Das Phantom der Freiheit
Über die Bornholmer Brücke entschwindend
1989   (lines 9-16)

These lines take up various elements of 'Wende' discourse. On 13 November 1989 in his last public appearance as a minister, an apparently confounded Erich Mielke, the departing head of the Stasi, declared to the 'Volkskammer', 'Ich liebe doch alle'.[82] Line 9 compares with Friedrich Schorlemmer's designation of the Stasi casting 'ein Spinnennetz' over the GDR.[83] The idiot is Krenz who was elected leader by the ZK on 18 October. Lines 11-13 perhaps echo Brecht's poem after the 17 June 1953 uprising, which closes 'Wäre es da / Nicht doch einfacher, die Regierung / Löste das Volk auf und / Wählte ein anderes?'.[84] Tragelehn refers not to the 'Volk' of SED government propaganda, but to 'Leute'. The phantom disappearing is that of the united GDR citizenry: between 9 November and 2 December 1989, over 10 million GDR citizens visited West Germany.[85]

Outside poetry, the Brandenburger Tor, at the end of East Berlin's main avenue, Unter den Linden, was *the* symbolic location of the 'Wende'. GDR émigré Ulrich Schacht's poem 'Das Brandenburger Tor' seems to romanticize a period of experience as historic, but the date at the end of the poem, 28.2.90, shows that this lyric subject is not crossing the border at the historic moment, on 9/10 November 1989 at all.[86]

Das Brandenburger Tor hab
ich nun auch durchschritten und
dachte dabei so sind sie die
historischen Stunden: Nicht
immer geht alles im Gleichschritt (lines 1-5)

The word 'revolution' has from the first been used to describe the changes of 1989/90 in historical accounts.[87] In poetry, however, the sense of a historic movement can also be ironized. In the subsequent years Schacht's statement here, about everything not coming at the same time, became increasingly apposite, as the GDR seemed to lag behind the West for so long. Nonetheless, passing through the border is passing into another era: the lyric subject's

---

[82]Jochen von Lang, *Erich Mielke: eine deutsche Karriere* (Berlin: Rowohlt, 1991), p.188.
[83]*Berliner Zeitung*, 5 September 1990, p.1.
[84]Bertolt Brecht, 'Die Lösung', *Gesammelte Werke*, x, pp.1009-1010.
[85]Figure in *Der Tagesspiegel*, 3 December 1989, p.1.
[86]Ulrich Schacht, 'Das Brandenburger Tor', in *Von einem Land*, p.40.
[87]For example Anne McElvoy, *The Saddled Cow: East Germany's Life and Legacy* (London: Faber and Faber, 1992), p.192; Karl-Dieter Opp and Peter Voß, *Die volkseigene Revolution* (Stuttgart: Klett-Cotta, 1993), p.56.

footsteps are the metaphorical steps of history, which defamiliarize even the recent past.

> Hier gings mal nicht
> durch. Sagen Passanten in jener
> Zukunft, zwölf Monate könnte die
> nah sein, und wundern sich über
> sagenhafte Ideen von einst: Stadt
> Mauern hießen die, und ab und zu fiel
> einer von den Zinnen. In Chroniken
> müßte das stehn. Von damals   (lines 9-16)

Allusions to the legendary, to battlements and to chronicles suggest medieval history, alongside the recent GDR past. Lines 15-16 make a programmatic statement about the importance of oral history, and spoken language is imported into the poem, in the constructions with 'hab' (1), 'sie' (3) and 'gings mal' (9). The last lines seem to imply that recent history could soon be erased and forgotten if it is not chronicled.

In 1989 the 'Nikolaikirche' in Leipzig became an important centre of demands for change and a symbol of resistance. Its weekly 'Friedensgebet' was politicized and became the starting point for regular street demonstrations. Priests and churches were repeatedly connected in such ways with the moves to reform. Gerlach alludes to all this with his title 'Nikolaikirchhof'.[88] He has written a whole collection of 'Wende-Zeitgedichte' which alternate with a literary diary in prose, dated from October 1989 to March 1990. The poems too form a kind of diary, in the present tense and precisely located in Leipzig.

> Nikolaikirchhof
> Blechern, eine unübersetzbare Sprache,
> pressen Lautsprecher das Friedens-
> bitten zwischen die gedrängten Landeskinder.
>
> Wie kostbar es sein kann, Menschen
> 5   zu berühren mit Blicken.
>
> Im Schweigen der Lichter liegt
> Einverständnis. Bestehen meint:
> vor sich selbst.
>
> Selten genug im langen Wechsel
> 10   von Zeitläuften erhebt sich die Reinheit,
> zeigt lächelnd ihr offnes Gesicht,

---

[88]Harald Gerlach, 'Nikolaikirchhof', *Einschlüsse. Aufbrüche: Blätter zu sechs Monaten deutscher Geschichte* (Rudolstadt: burgart, 1991), unnumbered pages.

unangefochten vom Kamerasurren.

Nichts in der Welt war mir näher
als jene kleine Hand, die
15   flüchtig mich streift, verkrustet
vom abtropfenden Wachs.

Poetry can make sense of change in a way which does not involve economic factors or statistics, but rather moral values. This poem evokes a new language, new communion and new purity. Although it is poem is about humanity, direct reference to people is withheld until the end of the third line. This is part of the mystical abstraction of the human, which is shown by strange juxtapositions – language and 'blechern', lights and silence; there is a face, but it is the face of personified purity. The 'Landeskinder' (3) and the child's hand compound the impression of purity and innocence. In another poem Gerlach goes further in this direction, evoking not only the pure child, but an angel. His 'Angelus Novus', with quite different characteristics to Paul Klee's or Walter Benjamin's, is an angel of history in Leipzig:[89]

Angelus Novus
Der Engel der Geschichte
montags auf dem Opernplatz
spricht sächsisch. Die geschleifte
Unikirche läutet ihre
5   eingeschmolznen Glocken.

Mit solchen Stimmen melden
die Trümmer sich zu Wort,
wenn Barbarei zerfällt.

Fingerdick am Hals des Engels
10   die Ader zeigt die Mühe, alte
Entzweiung laut zu übertönen.
Was geschieht, wo der Schrei verklungen
und das Schweigen noch nicht
eingekehrt ist?

This angel appears on Mondays, a reference to the 'Montags-demonstrationen'. Ruins are alluded to, which may be remnants of the Second

---

[89]Harald Gerlach, 'Angelus Novus', *Einschlüsse. Aufbrüche*. See Klee's 'Angelus Novus' picture and Benjamin's description of this 'Engel der Geschichte' being blown by history, in Walter Benjamin, *Gesammelte Schriften*, ed. by Rolf Tiedemann and Hermann Schweppenhäuser, i/2 (Frankfurt a.M.: Suhrkamp, 1974), p.697.

World War, but also as though the Cold War were a literal war. Here what was razed, melted and ruined comes back to life. The image of the angel straining to cry out is a metaphor for the people's struggle to voice their wishes. Religious imagery of angels and new life conveys wonder and hope at the 'Wende', but again a question at the poem's close points to the unknown outcome.[90] Müller's terse poem 'Glückloser Engel 2' is an altogether different type of 'Wende' angel:[91]

> Glückloser Engel 2
> Zwischen Stadt und Stadt
> Nach der Mauer der Abgrund
> Wind an den Schultern die fremde
> Hand am einsamen Fleisch
> 5   Den Engel ich höre ihn noch
> Aber er hat kein Gesicht mehr als
> Deines das ich nicht kenne

This poem follows on from Müller's 1958 prose poem 'Der glückloser Engel', in which the angel beats his wings in vain, 'wartend auf Geschichte', and his 1979 text 'Ich bin der Engel der Verzweiflung' where the motif of the abyss occurs: 'Mein Flug ist der Aufstand, mein Himmel der Abgrund von morgen'.[92] In the 1991 poem 'Geschichte' and 'Aufstand' have come and gone. The sound of the angel now seems to be just an echo; there is nothing more to await. Loneliness in the crowds is evoked by Müller, not unity. The same motifs of the wind, the stranger's hand and the angel occur as in Gerlach's poems above, but take on an ominous aspect here beside 'fremd', 'einsam' and the unknown 'du'.

Many poems dealing with the mass protests and ideas of unity paradoxically focus on the loner in the crowd: Richter's poem 'Herbstsonate 89' closes on this kind of ambiguous note:

> Unter tausenden Gesichtern
> Such ich eins das mich ansieht
> Vergebens   (lines 20-22)

Impersonality is the negative side to the noisy, intoxicating unity of the demonstrations. Gerlach's poem 'Exodus' also foregrounds the lone individual

---

[90]Compare the angel motif in Schmidt, 'Flußbild mit Engel', in *Grenzfallgedichte*, p.83 and Drawert, 'Engel', *FAZ*, 10 February 1997, p.29. See also West German poet Jürgen Theobaldy's 'In der hellsten Nacht', in *Von einem Land*, p.14.
[91]Heiner Müller, 'Glückloser Engel 2', in *Von einem Land*, p.77.
[92]Heiner Müller, 'Der glückloser Engel' and 'Ich bin der Engel der Verzweiflung', *Die Gedichte*, p.53 and p.212.

not joining in. Here the departure of many GDR citizens in 1989 is implicitly likened to the biblical exodus and Honecker is a King Lear figure who stumbles through a void.[93] Freedom has brought a vacuum into which a westerly wind rushes:[94]

> Ein Westwind trägt
> Gesangfetzen herüber: Frei-
> heidiheidoheida!

>   Fassungslos irrt
> der König durch die Leere. Und du,
> fragt er einen Mann, der
> seinen Rosenstock häufelt gegen
> den Winter, gehst du nicht auch?

> Mein Leben, sagt der Mann, hat
> der König zerstört. Unwiederbringlich.
> Nun will ich bleiben, mit ihm
> meine Bitternis teilen.   (lines 7-18)

Symbolically, the word 'Freiheit' (from the national anthem of the 'Bundesrepublik' or from the 'Wende' anthem, 'An die Freiheit') does not quite carry and gets lost on the breeze (8-9). In this poem there is no mood of euphoria, but rather emptiness and bitterness. There is a sense of freedom coming too late for an older citizen. A connection between the lone individual and a problematic freedom is drawn in other poems too. A similar sense of not having been brought up to live in the new circumstances precipitates doubts in Johannes Jansen's untitled poem dated 'nov.89':[95]

> hätte ich einfalt gelernt vor der freiheit
> wär mir die freiheit frei
> das letzte wort im gelächter
> aber unwissend bin ich (lines 5-8)

Line 6 here implies that the so-called free world has not brought freedom. Furthermore, the lyric subject feels that he carries with him 'ein kleines ende'(4); celebration of unity seems 'fragwürdig' (12) and yet to question it 'unwürdig' (14). The poet is sceptical but prefers to see this as a fault in himself and, on the contrary, hopes he will be proved wrong. As King

---

[93]Harald Gerlach, 'Exodus', in 'Die Dichter und die Wende', p.11 and in *Grenzfallgedichte*, p.58. Compare Honecker as Lear in Volker Braun's 1990 prose piece 'Lear oder Der Tod der Hundeführer', *Texte*, x, pp.28-29.
[94]Compare the wind motif in Barbara Köhler's 'Endstelle', *Deutsches Roulette*, p.39, where 'IM WINDE KLIRREN Wörter, Hoffnungsfetzen'. And in Ulrich Schacht's 'Das Brandenburger Tor'.
[95]Johannes Jansen, 'zusammen gekommen', in *Grenzfallgedichte*, p.72.

Honecker above is 'fassunglos', so this lyric 'ich' describes himself as
'unwissend'.

Many poems in fact articulate a sense of great uncertainty. In Armin
Richter's 'Jahrzehntewechsel', the New Year 1989/90 is emblematic of the
entire 'Wende'.[96] Blackness and grey fog indicate the inability to see ahead.
An allusion to confetti suggests the wedding of East and West:

> Jahrzehntewechsel
> Das Feuerwerk leuchtet die Nacht nicht
> Den Himmel nicht aus
> Vom Jubel verweht treibt Konfetti
> In die verblendete Schwärze
>
> 5   Der erste Tag im neuen Jahrzehnt
> Zieht sich in sich selber zurück
> Unter bleiernes Nebelgefieder
>
> Die Hügel harren jeder Regung enteignet
> Im unausgenüchterten Grau
> 10 Selten platzt eine verspätete Rakete
>
> Nur im Hirn wetterleuchtet es noch
> Und im Ohr klingt das leise Brandungsgeräusch
> Mit den Gezeiten des Herzschlags
>
> Überall Undeutlichkeiten
> 15 Die zu Prognosen verleiten
> Spieler machen erste Einsätze
>
> Was anderes sollte man jetzt auch tun

Lines 11-13 allude to storm, seas and seasons as in the nature poems discussed
above, but now these are only a memory, inside the body. There is no full
illumination; all remains unclear, like the outcome of a bet, and the
unanswered question raised at the end expresses resignation. The sense of
waiting is projected onto the hills in line 8 and here there is already the
keyword 'enteignen', to dispossess, a word which is increasingly common in
poetry of the years after unification. Unification is a gamble here which may
or may not pay off.

The sense of not knowing, of being unsure about the apparent
liberation, is the theme of Czechowski's poem 'Die überstandene Wende',

---

[96]Armin Richter, 'Jahrzehntewechsel', *Die kleinen mecklenburgischen Meere*, p.49.

which is the motto poem for Conrady's anthology.[97] In this Brechtian-style poem, the 'Wende' is a moment of revelation to be suffered. This is a reserved reaction, revealing implicit doubt about Germany's imminent future:

Die überstandene Wende
Was hinter uns liegt,
Wissen wir.
Was vor uns liegt,
Wird uns unbekannt bleiben,
5 Bis wir es
Hinter uns haben.
(November 1989)

This is a typical representation of a turning-point in time and in experience. A wishful distance from events is reflected in the cold rationality, in the balance of 'vor' and 'hinter', 'wissen' and 'unbekannt'. The notion of a cusp or fulcrum is illustrated in a number of other 'Wende' poems such as Braun's 'Der Reißwolf' where a shredder, eating up 'mein friedliches Leben' (7), stands at the same focal point between past and future:[98]

Die vergangenen ruhigen Tage beginnen zu rennen
In einen Abgrund. Auch die Zukunft
Reißen sie mit hinein.   (lines 1-3)

The GDR past and the socialist future that had been expected are effectively eaten up, and the present brings a gap, another 'Abgrund' (2), like Müller's. The end of the quiet days and the start of the rat-race represent a frightening loss of control.

Liberation is represented as a release which precipitates an uncontrolled freefall in a number of poems. Czechowski's 1990 prose poem 'Der stürzende Ikarus' uses a summary image of the fall of the GDR, which makes explicit the extraordinariness of this experience.[99] Icarus, who fell from the sky as he flew too near the sun, becomes an image of the GDR. His fall is

dieser Sturz, der alles vorwegnahm, was uns noch bevorsteht. Wir aber, / selbst schon gestürzt, / wundern uns nicht: / der Flug, der zum Fluch wurde, / ist uns vertraut. Jetzt beschweren wir uns mit dem Blei, / das uns zur Verfügung gestellt ist, und / diesen Misthaufen, in den Ikarus stürzt, / nennen wir einfach Geschichte.

Flight was an established metaphor for the GDR future. There is a sense here that high-flown ideas of a collective 'wir' are no longer possible. The

[97]Heinz Czechowski, 'Die überstandene Wende', in *Die sanfte Revolution*, ed. by Heym, p.420, and reprinted without the second line-break in *Von einem Land*, p.7.
[98]Volker Braun, 'Der Reißwolf', *Die Zickzackbrücke*, p.90.
[99]Heinz Czechowski, 'Der stürzende Ikarus', *ndl*, 43 (1995), No.2, 32.

opposite, namely the realities of history, are represented by a leaden burden. This seems to convey some implicit regret. Furthermore, history is ingloriously reduced to a 'Misthaufen', in which the GDR-Icarus lands. Czechowski is drawing on the established Icarus motif, which Karen Leeder describes as used in different ways by two different generations of GDR poets:

> If in the early poetry of the GDR he was taken to represent the utopian aspiration of flight (Arendt) or the victorious ascent of *Aufbau* (Becher), the poetry of the younger generation demonstrates a marked shift in emphasis. [...] In general, one can say that it is either the attempt of Icarus to escape the tyranny of slavery and the labyrinth, which is emphasized in much of the young writers' work, or his inheritance: age, disillusionment and impotence, which mean that he will never fly.[100]

At the 'Wende' it is not these things which are emphasized, but Icarus's fall from the sky. The link between Icarus and Hölderlin in Czechowski's poem particularly recalls Biermann's Icarus motif in 'Hölderlin im Turm'.[101] Biermann's earlier 'Ballade vom preußischen Ikarus' (1976) is also an interesting point of comparison with Czechowski's Icarus poem, in that it explicitly links Icarus's fall to the experience of being forced out of the GDR.[102] In the first two verses of Biermann's ballad, the Prussian Icarus does not fly away or fall, but in the final verse and chorus this changes and the third-person Icarus becomes an 'ich'-Icarus. Czechowski's 'Wende' poem follows the Icarus poetry of the GDR and in particular Biermann's Icarus poetry of expatriation.

Images of the lyric subject falling are frequent in 'Wende' poetry and often, as in Czechowski's prose poem here, presuppose past ascent. In Walter Werner's poem 'An einem siebten Oktobertag' it is the demonstrations which precipitate fall – here, a fall from the escalator of time:[103]

> Von der Rolltreppe
> der Jahre gefallen, haben wir
> im Sturz den roten Tagstern
> mitgenommen, die Fahnen losgelassen. (lines 9-12)

This fall is ambiguous, a release, but also a descent after the ascent of progress. A falling 'wir' take socialism, symbolized by the red star, down with them, rather than vice versa. The star falling from the firmament is a bad

---

[100]Leeder, *Breaking Boundaries*, pp.60-61. On Icarus in GDR poetry, see also Theo Mechtenburg, 'Von Odysseus bis Sisyphos: Zur Rezeption und Brechung mythischer Gestalten in der DDR-Lyrik', *Deutschland Archiv*, 18 (1985), 497-506 (pp.503-504).
[101]Wolf Biermann, 'Hölderlin im Turm', *Affenfels und Barrikade: Gedichte/Lieder/Balladen* (Cologne: Kiepenheuer & Witsch, 1986), pp.107-108.
[102]Wolf Biermann, 'Ballade vom preußischen Ikarus', *Preußischer Ikarus: Lieder/Balladen/Gedichte/Prosa* (Cologne: Kiepenheuer & Witsch, 1978), pp.103-104.
[103]Walter Werner, 'An einem siebten Oktobertag', in *Grenzfallgedichte*, p.56.

omen, but the other symbol of socialism – the flags, which are released – point to concomitant liberty. Compare Grünbein's 'ich fiel' in 'Vorm Fernseher die Toten':[104]

Dann halfen mir Hände, zogen mich langsam herauf
Ins Blitzlichtgewitter wo ich nackt stand, ich fiel
Rückwärts in Zeitlupe herab. (lines 39-41)

The dream sequence of being raised up by others and then falling backwards, naked and alone, becomes a metaphor for the GDR experience as a whole. The words 'ich fiel' are made prominent by their separation at the end of the line. Slow motion is part of the experience of falling and also indicates a trauma.

Images of the lyric subject falling are part of a more general concern with fantastical and dream images in 'Wende' poetry. The fantastic corresponds to the sense of surprise and unreality associated with the 'Wende'. Deadpan presentation of the bizarre is exemplified in Annerose Kirchner's poem 'Sonntag', which was written in the summer of 1990:[105]

> Sonntag
> Fliegende Teppichhändler tauschen
> eins zu eins
> Hanswürste gegen Zinnsoldaten.
>
> Mein Verstand denkt deutsch
> 5 und probiert Maulkörbe, die es gratis gibt,
> 13 gehn auf ein Dutzend.
>
> Morgen, flüstert mir
> eine besoffne Stimme ins Ohr,
> wandern wir aus.
>
> 1990

Economic and monetary union of the two Germanies came into effect on 1 July 1990. The Deutschmark became the unit of currency in the GDR and Ostmarks were exchanged at a ratio of 1:1.[106] This is transformed into a fantastical setting in Kirchner's poem. Allusion to fairytale and toys creates the impression of a childlike perspective. There is a sense of a lyric 'ich' bowled over by the free gifts, but the drunken voice is ambiguous. It refers to

[104]Durs Grünbein, 'Vorm Fernseher die Toten', *Schädelbasislektion*, pp.36-37.
[105]Annerose Kirchner,'Sonntag', *Literatur Bote*, 5 (1990), No.19, 28, and reprinted in *Grenzfallgedichte*, p.76.
[106]The ratio of 1:1 applied to savings of up to 2,000 Marks and to salaries. Otherwise the ratio was two Ostmarks to one Deutschmark.

the new freedom to leave, but one suspects that 'morgen' might also bring disillusionment, such is the wonder, the 'Sunday feeling'. In a Grünbein poem, the 'Wende' is the product of a magic trick, a magician's spell: [107]

> Was für ein Trick: Eins zwei drei...n,
> Schon war das Kollektiv verschwunden.
> Eben noch Schweigemasse, schwerer Schlaf,
> Appell ans Nichts in Reißbrettstädten,
> 5   Fata Morgana im Beton... genügt
> *Ein* falscher Ton es zu zerstreuen.
> Das Karussell von Putsch und Polka
> Dreht sich im Leeren weiter, sonntagsruhig.

Here history is a careering merry-go-round, which spins on quietly after the 'Wende'. This is another surreal, dream image, as if on waking from the deep sleep of line 3. The GDR is a mixture of opposites, weightiness ('Masse', 'schwer', 'Beton') and mirage ('Nichts', 'Reißbrett', fata morgana). The collective destroyed by a single 'wrong note' is a strange representation of the street demonstrations. Grünbein's image implies dissolution achieved with blithe simplicity. There is a levity of tone, emphasizing 'genügt' (as a present tense after past, as a verb ahead of its nominative subject) and '*Ein*' (which is both italicized and begins the line). That '*Ein* falscher Ton' might be said to be the cry 'Wir sind ein Volk', which contradicted the false assertion that people believed in a separate, socialist GDR. References to a trick, putsch and the void convey a sense of instability. Besides the equation of putsch and polka, the tension between the image of continuity and 'verschwunden' and 'zerstreuen' above, also compounds this. As the drunken voice in Kirchner's 'Sonntag' undermines its own projection of tomorrow, so one feels that 'sonntagsruhig' at the end of this poem is only a temporary peacefulness.

Dream images recur in many 'Wende' poems with a sense both of the miraculous and of the nightmarish. An expression of hope and resolution is the climax of Richter's early demo-poem 'Rotes Kirschlaub':

> Ich habe das Gefühl
> Als träume die Wirklichkeit
> Gegen alle Zweifel an (lines 13-15)

Reality is personified as a dreamer: after the GDR years of discrepancy between dream and reality, the 'Wende' is here a reconciling of the two. But the 'ich' expresses this not as a certainty, but as his own subjective feeling, in

---

[107]Durs Grünbein, 'Die leeren Zeichen, 6', *Schädelbasislektion*, p.74. Compare the allusion to 'Hokuspokus ohne Hexerei' in Lutz Rathenow's poem 'Dezember 89', in *Von einem Land*, p.29.

the subjunctive. Dream and reality, especially in terms of the 'Volk' for whom the regime supposedly spoke, were commonplace measures of the GDR. They are also Richter's measures of the 'Wende'. A more sinister presentation of dream is exemplified by Braun in 'Der 9. November'.[108] In this poem, the historic moment was not one of involved celebration but of the bizarre.

Der 9. November

Das Brackwasser stachellippig, aufgeschnittene Drähte
Lautlos, wie im Traum, driften die Tellerminen
Zurück in den Geschirrschrank. Ein surrealer Moment:
Mit spitzem Fuß auf dem Weltriß, und kein Schuß fällt.
5   Die gehetzte Vernunft, unendlich müde, greift
Nach dem erstbesten Irrtum... der Dreckverband platzt.
Leuchtschriften wandern okkupantenhaft bis Mitte. BERLIN
NUN FREUE DICH, zu früh. Wehe, harter Nordost.

The explicit references to dream (2) and to a surreal instant (3) are backed by strange juxtapositions: water is 'stachellippig' (1), mines become kitchen plates and neon signs walk. Lines 1-4 describe the barbed-wire cut down, the mines cleared and the end of shooting at the border, yet the neon signs seem to be a new army of occupation. Braun uses the historical utterance 'BERLIN / NUN FREUE DICH' (7-8) ironically. This quotation from the Mayor of West Berlin, Walter Momper, on 10 November 1989, is rendered hollow by the closing lament, 'Wehe, harter Nordost'. This is a reference to the GDR territory in north-eastern Germany, but also echoes the first two lines of Friedrich Hölderlin's famous 'Andenken', 'Der Nordost wehet, / Der liebste unter den Winden'.[109] 'Wehe' is thus not only a woeful interjection, but also an imperative calling for a wind to blow from the East, to counter that from the West. The dream-poem amalgamates Hölderlin's words with the figure of reason (5), which is personified as a hounded, desperate person, held together by a dirty bandage, which splits.[110]

Dream-like experience is also addressed through film metaphors, which reflect the sense of unreality and the importance of visual imagery in many 'Wende' poems. The television screen is a motif which Müller evoked in the poem 'Fernsehen' and Teschke's poem 'Berliner November' uses the simile 'wie in alten Filmen'. Foreign television was a source of truth about what was

---

[108]Volker Braun, 'Der 9. November', in *Von einem Land*, p.21.
[109]Friedrich Hölderlin, 'Andenken', *Poesiealbum 17* (Berlin, GDR: Neues Leben, 1969), pp.27-29.
[110]Weary personified 'Vernunft' recalls the title of the writers' gathering on 28 October 1989 'Wider den Schlaf der Vernunft' after the picture by Goya.

really happening in a country where national sources could not be trusted. Paradoxically, it embodied both this type of reality and the surrealism of mediated experience and a mediated identity.[111] In Grünbein's poem 'Vorm Fernseher die Toten' the lyric 'ich' is writing at night, falling asleep in front of the television and hears the cries 'Wir wollen raus' before the border opened:[112]

> Es war wie ein Film
>
> Der *Das Ende des Wartens* hieß. Amigo, erleichtert
> Sah ich, es war vorbei, die Geduld verbraucht.
> "Wir wollen raus hier, hört ihr. Wir wollen raus."   (lines 42-45)

The dead of the title may be figuratively lifeless, stagnating in the GDR. The demonstrators' demands for freedom signal the end of patiently waiting for change and the 'ich' is relieved. This poem reflects Jens Reich's idea that 'Milliarden erleben Geschichte als Videoclip'.[113] The demonstrations are another film, but a silent one, in Grünbein's second poem in the cycle 'Die leeren Zeichen':[114]

> Schwachsinn, zu fragen wie es dazu kam
> Es war der falsche Ort, die falsche Zeit
> Für einen Stummfilm mit dem Titel *Volk*.
> Die Luft war günstig für Vergeblichkeit,
> 5   Das Land weit übers Datum des Verfalls.
> "Alles was schiefgehn kann, wird schiefgehn"
> War noch der kleinste Nenner wie zum Trost
> Das Echo, anonym "Ich war dabei…"

After all the negative words – 'Schwachsinn', 'falsch', 'stumm', 'Vergeblichkeit' and 'schiefgehn' – only the presence of the lyric 'ich' at the historical turning-point remains. Grünbein mocks the idea of the people's voice emerging at the 'Wende'. The grumble of line 5 and the anonymous echo of a witness are all that is left of the demonstrators' hope. There is a

---

[111]The mediated, second-hand nature of experience is also conveyed in West German poet Thomas Kielinger's 'Eingeschaltet', in *Von einem Land*, p.97.
[112]Compare Herbert Wagner, 'Die Novemberrevolution 1989 in Dresden: Ein Erlebnisbericht', in *Ursachen und Verlauf der Deutschen Revolution 1989*, ed. by Konrad Löw (Berlin: Duncker & Humblot, 1991), pp.9-15 (p.11): 'Am 5. November 1989 versammelten sich erneut Ausreisewillige und skandierten "Wir wollen raus!" '.
[113]Jens Reich quoted in Klaus Hartung, *Neunzehnhundertneunundachtzig: Ortsbesichtigungen nach einer Epochenwende* (Frankfurt a.M.: Luchterhand, 1990), p.22.
[114]Durs Grunbein, 'Die leeren Zeichen, 2', *Schädelbasislektion*, p.70.

sense that everything went wrong – the GDR in 1989/90 was the 'wrong' place and the 'wrong' time (2), but a better reading of line 2 perhaps points to a false place and a false sense of time. In later poetry, film images also describe life in the new Germany. In Drawert's poem 'Man kann nichts machen dagegen', individual impotence is expressed in an image of the self swept up into a film: [115]

Auch ich bin nur Gast
eines laufenden Films
und ausgesetzt worden
ohne Bestimmung.   (lines 25-28)

Alienation is articulated as a sense of being a guest in one's own life here, abandoned and without purpose.

The prime televisual image of the 'Wende' was the breaking up of the Berlin Wall, either by citizens chipping at it or by bulldozers removing concrete slabs. Walls are an old motif in poetry, but they obviously had special resonances in the GDR: the Berlin Wall was suited as a poetic motif which addressed the theme of German division and GDR identity.[116] As the Wall became an increasingly taboo subject in the GDR, many poets exploited the implications of merely alluding to it. In 1989/90 Gerlach writes of the fallen Wall not as a concrete barrier, but as a wall of fear:

Gefallen ist die Mauer
aus Furcht, die das brüchige Reich
zusammenhielt.   ('Exodus', lines 5-7)

The Berlin Wall stands for the entire communist border to the West here. It extends to an architechtonic representation of the Soviet empire, which the dividing wall was, paradoxically, holding together. Furthermore, Gerlach inverts the idea of monolithic socialism and instead suggests that the Soviet bloc was always fragile. Kunert's poem 'Jericho, kürzlich', later called 'Jericho 1989', parallels the fall of the Berlin Wall with the biblical fall of the walls of Jericho.[117] This poem refers to the dawning of a new day:

Jericho, kürzlich
Anschwellender Ton
aus Mündern gleichgestimmter
Schall

[115]Kurt Drawert, 'Man kann nichts dagegen machen', *Wo es war*, pp.15-16.
[116]Wulf Segebrecht, 'Gedichte über die Mauer. Wie Lyriker aus der DDR die Mauer berührten und von ihr berührt wurden oder: Zur Geschichte eines Syndroms', in *Lyriker Treffen Münster*, ed by Jordan, pp.285-305.
[117]Günter Kunert, 'Jericho, kürzlich', *Akzente*, 41 (1994), 106. Here the Jericho poem is one of five Berlin poems by Kunert dated from 1949 to 1993. 'Jericho 1989', *Mein Golem: Gedichte* (Munich and Vienna: Hanser, 1996), p.56.

```
        Stachel Lebenssucht
5       Glücklicher Wahn
        Menschen verkörpern eine Menge
        Massenhaftes Geschiebe
        Leibliche Lava sprengt
        alle Regeln alle Bande
10      Gitter wie Mauerwerk
        Und erst zum Morgendämmer hin
        im Schleppschritt der Geschichte
        kehrt zage
        ein Befremden heim.
                                        19.11.90
```

Barbed-wire replaced by a barb of 'Lebenssucht' expresses the 'Wende' here. History personified comes 'im Schleppschritt', as though history is the 'leibliche Lava' above. However, mass unity is 'Wahn', a delusion or illusion. The 'Wende' is an eruption of sound and joyful madness: the demonstrators as a lava flow recall the imagery in Braun's 'Prolog'. Biblical reference to Jericho's walls felled by trumpeting and marching is matched in the rest of the poem by the metaphor of breaking free from bonds. Swelling sound, expelled debris and lava as liquid rock contrast with the monoliths in Kunert's earlier works, for instance 'das Gestein deiner Tage', 'dieses Bauwerk', 'Pyramide', and 'Monument' in the poem 'Bauwerk'.[118] 'Jericho, kürzlich' also explicitly follows on from the imperative in Kunert's earlier poem 'Schofar':[119]

        Wenn der Atem wegbleiben will
        oder die Hoffnung:
        Gedenke Jerichos.   (lines 6-8)

In 1989 this stoicism seemed vindicated. The 'gleichgestimmte / Schall' (2-3) is reflected in the alliteration, such as in lines 6-7 and in line 8. In contrast to the mass marching, the close of Kunert's poem, however, introduces a lone personified displeasure – akin to the loner identified above at the end of Richter's 'Herbstsonate 89'.

        In the year after the Wall fell, ambivalent feelings about unification were reflected in the idea of other, invisible walls remaining. The wall internalized appears for example in Reiner Kunze's poem 'die mauer: zum 3. oktober 1990':[120]

---

[118]Günter Kunert, 'Bauwerk', *Unterwegs nach Utopia* (Munich and Vienna: Hanser, 1977), p.9.
[119]Günter Kunert, 'Schofar', *Unterwegs nach Utopia*, p.47.
[120]Reiner Kunze, 'die mauer: zum 3. oktober 1990', in *Von einem Land*, p.86. See also West German poet Adelheid Johanna Hess's 'Verfehlt', in *Von einem Land*, p.89, which illustrates again the motif of invisible barriers remaining.

Als wir sie schleiften, ahnten wir nicht,
wie hoch sie ist
in uns (lines 1-3)

At the close of this unification-day poem the Wall reflects continued division and personal guilt; it had become a limited horizon beyond which one did not have to think, or a barrier one hid behind:[121]

Nun stehen wir entblößt
jeder entschuldigung (lines 9-10)

Unification day sends the poet back to the Wall. Kunze's poem reflects on how attitudes to its fall shifted between November 1989 and October 1990.

In some poems ruins represent the experience of history in 1989/90, although of course there was no 'Trümmerlandschaft' as after 1945. This image relates instead to 'Aufbau' as the economic, political and cultural development of the socialist state. Drawert's post-'Wende' poem 'Tauben in ortloser Landschaft' is set 'in den Ruinen der Republik'.[122] A human 'wir' are 'verschüttet in den Trümmern / der Bau-auf-Konstrukteure' (p.8). A second post-war landscape is attributed to the 'Bau-auf-Konstrukteure' here, the ideologues of socialism. In the following lines from Czechowski the lyric 'du' was a builder himself:[123]

das Haus,
An dem du gebaut hast,

Zerfällt. (lines 7-9)

History is presented as processes of construction and destruction. Derelict or empty buildings represent the failure of the GDR and epitomize what Müller has termed 'die Frustration im Schrott der Utopien'.[124] The ruins are not the starting-point for hope that they had been after fascism, but embody only failed hope. In some ways this is a re-play of disillusionment in the GDR. For example, in the pre-'Wende' poem whose first line is 'aufgestanden und

---

[121]See also West German poets: Frank Hodjak, 'die wende des winds', in *Von einem Land*, p.88, a poem in which the Wall is also an excuse, 'das alibi'. And Matthias Buth, 'Berlin 91' in *Von einem Land*, p.107, where the Wall, personified as a female 'Geiselnehmerin' and 'Mutter Tod', is killed. As in some of the poems above, the Wall has an internal manifestation, here 'Narben unter der Haut'. The personification is taken up again in the representation of 'die warme / Umarmung von Beton und Trauer'.

[122]Kurt Drawert, 'Tauben in ortloser Landschaft', *ndl*, 43 (1995), No.6, 5-11 (p.5).

[123]Heinz Czechowski, 'Nahe und fern', *Nachtspur: Ein Lesebuch aus der deutschen Gegenwart: Gedichte und Prosa 1987-1992* (Zurich: Ammann, 1993), p.185. Compare the same image in Ralph Grüneberger, 'Der Verfall meines Hauses' and 'Es war Sonntag', *ndl*, 40 (1992), No.11, 81 and 82.

[124]Heiner Müller, 'Bautzen und Babylon', *SuF*, 43 (1991), 664-665.

ruiniert', it is already time to play a *danse macabre*.[125] Here Stefan Döring
plays on lines from the GDR national anthem composed by the 'original' GDR
poet Johannes R. Becher. The poet, 'meister im flötenspiel', is a Berlin
Orpheus crossing into the land of the dead. Döring's 1985 poem contrasts with
the words of reformist pastor Friedrich Schorlemmer at the 'Wende' rally of 4
November, which echoed rather than inverted Becher's sentiments: 'Im Herbst
1989 sind wir auferstanden aus Ruinen und der Zukunft neu zugewandt'.[126]

Ancient ruins inspire Teschke's 'Elegie nach Virgil', a title invoking
the classical lament.[127] Teschke evokes Roman ruins in a context which
compares the fall of Rome and the fall of the GDR: like the Romans, many
GDR citizens thought their state would last forever. The opening scene in
Teschke's poem is one of collapsing pillars and smoke, a demolition of
edifices. The close of the poem offers an image of suicide, a recurrent theme in
'Wende' poetry, which occurs here as suicide by sword:

> Elegie nach Virgil
> Kaum stürzten die Säulen Kaum hat der Rauch sich verzogen
> Da ziehn übers Forum salbadernd die neuen Augurn
> Sehn dem Adlerflug nach überm Fluß Stochern in Därmen
> Aufsteht aus seinen Trümmern der alte Senat
> 5   Der Wolf bleibt Bote im Tempel der Juno Moneta
> Bald fallen die Römer still in ihr herbstliches Schwert

Like Kunert's 'Jericho' above, this poem uses an exemplum or model to show
that the 'Wende' has parallels in history. Augurs poke the entrails to predict
the future, an ancient, superstitious rite that ironizes the commentators on
Germany's political future. Reference to Juno Moneta points to materialism.
Her lupine messenger and the eagle, which is traditionally associated with war
gods and is a German imperial emblem, represent predatory western and
nationalistic values. Ancient Rome in this poem is a fallen empire, a place of
ruins, ancient superstition, emerging commercialism and imminent suicide. By
conjuring up ancient civilization and implicitly drawing parallels with the most

---

[125]Stefan Döring, 'neue zehnzeiler und ein romantisches gedicht', in *Vogel oder Käfig sein*, ed. by Michael, p.112, and reprinted as 'auferstanden und ruiniert', *Zehn* (Berlin: Galrev, 1990), unnumbered pages.
[126]Friedrich Schorlemmer, in *"Wir sind das Volk!" Flugschriften, Aufrufe und Texte einer deutschen Revolution*, ed. by Charles Schüddekopf (Reinbek bei Hamburg: Rowohlt, 1990), pp.211-213 (p.211).
[127]Holger Teschke, 'Elegie nach Virgil', in *Von einem Land*, p.64. In West German poet Hans-Jürgen Heise's 'Schwer rumpelt die Erdkugel', in *Von einem Land*, pp.44-45, the Pink Floyd concert at the Wall in summer 1989 is likened to the Great Fire of Rome, marking the end of an era.

recent history of the GDR, the contemporary poet points to an underlying pattern of ruin in history.

Teschke's collapsing pillars resemble Kunert's 'leere Häuser' and Drawert's 'Haus ohne Menschen' as architectural images of the fall of the GDR.[128] Both these are images of the 'Wende' as the emptying of a house that is left behind, whilst the inhabitants perhaps move to a new one. They focus on the negative aspect of destruction. Walter Werner's empty towers in 'Die verlassenen Türme' are, in contrast, overtly positive. Here the turning-point of the 'Wende' ends militarism and, in particular, a heavily guarded border: [129]

> Jetzt kann jeder in die Kanzel steigen,
> aus seinem Blick das Schußfeld streichen,
> die Soldatenstiefel von der Brüstung werfen,
> die Wächter in die Schranken weisen. (lines 12-15)

The 'Wende' brings an end to the 'Feindbild-Dasein' (17) embodied by the guard towers along the border. Energetic, alliterating verbs in this poem and its democratic 'jeder kann' convey an easy dispensation with the past. More ominous is the past with which Schacht's 'Rosenhagen am Meer' begins:[130]

> Die Türme sind
> leer entschärft der
> Zaun getrocknet das
> Blut: Wir gehen
> durch die
>
> November
> Schneise ins
> Dorf das schweigt (lines 1-8)

This poem functions as an action against the prevalent sense of forgetting which it describes. The word order, which makes the reader fall heavily onto 'leer', 'Zaun' and 'Blut', makes the past reality of the guarded border shocking again. November is associated with 'Schneise' (6), dividing lines, which cut off the past when the towers were occupied and the fence barbed and electrified.

The appropriateness of the ruin motif seems to have drawn Grünbein to the famous Shelley poem 'Ozymandias'.[131] The ex-GDR poet includes in *Schädelbasislektion* the original and his translation of Shelley's poem of 1817: a colossal, crumbling statue, toppled from its pedestal, on which the

---

[128]Drawert, *Haus ohne Menschen*. Günter Kunert, 'Durch die leeren Häuser: Vier neue Gedichte', *NR*, 104 (1993), 147-150.

[129]Walter Werner, 'Die verlassenen Türme', in *Grenzfallgedichte*, p.68.

[130]Ulrich Schacht, 'Rosenhagen am Meer', in *Von einem Land*, p.142.

[131]Percy Bysshe Shelley, 'Ozymandias', and Durs Grünbein, 'Transsibirischer Ozymandias', both in *Schädelbasislektion*, p.58.

inscription declared greatness, is revived as an ironic image which marks the end of communism in Eastern Europe.[132] The encroaching desert and the traveller in this poem are motifs in later 'Wende' poetry too. A sense of time bringing a new imperative to bear on the extant poem is reflected by a number of other texts, including Müller's poem dedicated to Erich Honecker.[133] Müller's text is a translation of a poem by the American Ezra Pound, which was itself a translation from the Chinese.[134] The poem is read in a new way because of its dedication, but at the same time, the appropriating poet draws attention to the timelessness of its central motif. This poem also illustrates the choice of the quiet and contemplative, rather than hope and euphoria:

>   Leichter Regen auf leichtem Staub
>   Die Weiden im Gasthof
>   Werden grün werden und grün
>   Aber du Herr solltest Wein trinken vor deinem Abschied
> 5   Denn du wirst keine Freunde haben
>   Wenn du kommst an die Tore von Go
>
>   (für Erich Honecker nach Ezra Pound und Rihaku)

The 'Herr' becomes Honecker himself in Müller's poem, his 'Abschied' an allusion to Honecker's flight to Moscow in 1990.[135] The poem is spoken as the 'Herr' is about to pass through a point of no return. Rain falling on arid land also indicates the point of transition for the country he leaves behind. Line 3, not the simplest translation of Pound's line (which would be 'werden immer grüner werden'), carries a resonance from Brecht's lines 'O Lust des Beginnens! O früher Morgen / Erstes Gras, wenn vergessen scheint / Was grün ist!'.[136] The green thus indicates a fresh start for the country left behind. History lends Pound's poem a new function in the context of Germany. For the same reason, Tragelehn takes up another nineteenth-century poem in

---

[132]The fallen statue motif also occurs in Gisela Kraft's poem 'Bitte des Karlmarxkopfes an das rotliegende Chemnitz', in 'Die Dichter und die Wende', p.5, and in Armin Richter's poem 'Ein Monument', *Die kleinen mecklenburgischen Meere*, p.86.
[133]Heiner Müller, *Gedichte* (Berlin: Alexander, 1992), p.93.
[134]Pound's translation is a motto to 'Four Poems of Departure' amongst his *Cathay* translations from Rihaku. See Ezra Pound, *Collected Shorter Poems* (London and Boston: Faber and Faber, 1984), p.137.
[135]Honecker was brought back to Germany in 1992 to stand trial for shootings along the GDR border and in 1993, released from prison due to illness, he went to Chile. He died in May 1994.
[136]Bertolt Brecht, 'O Lust des Beginnens', *Gesammelte Werke*, ix, p.771.

English, namely Christina Rossetti's 'Song' of 1848.[137] In the German version, the death of the individual takes on resonances of the demise of the GDR:

Wenn ich tot bin, seid so gut
Singt mir nicht Lieder nach (lines 1-2)

These lines reject obituary-poetry for socialism though this poem is, of course, precisely that. And the address to a general 'ihr' becomes an address to the GDR people, perhaps from the poet himself who feels forgotten:

Und wenn ihr wollt, dann denkt an mich
Und wenn ihr nicht wollt, vergeßt (lines 7-8)

These translated versions by Grünbein, Müller and Tragelehn foreground history's effect on a text, its ability to create a new poem.

At the 'Wende' writers also became aware of how the changing conditions of life create a change in the way their own poems are read: a number of pre-'Wende' or early 'Wende' texts have been published anew because they can be re-read as more contemporary poems. As Chiarloni has pointed out, a second, 1990 version of 'Fernsehen' appears in Müller's collection of poems published in 1992.[138] This redefines the original text by supplying a prologue in American English and an epilogue in prose. An undefined female figure, 'Margarita', now introduces the piece by making the American millionaire Howard Hughes into an emblem of the TV nation. The text now denounces western civilization, where television mediates experience. The new final part to the text brings in the figure of Honecker as powerful head of state, as a prisoner in a Nazi prison, and as a broken, elderly man who is being turned into a scapegoat. This part of Müller's poem is also based on the opening lines of his 1977 play *Hamletmaschine* (a literal 'wühlen in alten Texten'):[139]

HAMLETMASCHINE: der Hamletdarsteller ohne Gesicht, im Rücken eine Mauer, sein Gesicht eine Gefängniswand. Bilder, die keine Aufführung einholen konnte. Wegmarken durch den Sumpf, der sich schon damals zu schließen begann über dem vorläufigen Grab der Utopie, die vielleicht wieder aufscheinen wird, wenn das Phantom der Marktwirtschaft, die das Gespenst des

[137]B.K. Tragelehn, 'Beim Abschied zu singen, nach C.G. Rosetti [sic]', *ndl*, 43 (1995), No.5, 6.
[138]Anna Chiarloni, 'From the Ramparts of History: Two Versions of a Poetic Text by Heiner Müller', in *Heiner Müller: ConTEXTS and HISTORY: A Collection of Essays from the Sydney German Studies Symposium 1994*, ed. by Gerhard Fischer (Tübingen: Stauffenburg, 1995), pp.243-248. Heiner Müller, 'Fernsehen', *Gedichte*, p.94-96.
[139]At the 'Wende' Müller stated, '*Hamlet* ist im Moment das aktuellste Stück der DDR [...]. Es beschreibt den Abgrund hinter jeder Politik'. See Heiner Müller, ' "Nicht Einheit, sondern Differenz": Gespräch zur Revolution in der DDR', *Deutsche Volkszeitung / die tat*, 24 November 1989, pp.13-14 (p.14).

Kommunismus ablöst, den neuen Kunden seine kalte Schulter zeigt, den
Befreiten das eiserne Gesicht seiner Freiheit. (pp.95-96)

Social utopia, the market economy, and communism, are each personified as
immortal spirits, which appear and disappear throughout history: Müller
suggests that the idea of utopian society is not dead, but will return, despite the
end of the GDR. Contradictions thus frame the poem and suggest an enduring
awareness of the dialectic of history. This redefinition of the original poem
indicates a desire on the poet's part to write a poem for the moment.

Conversely, the poem can re-cast historical statements of a certain
moment. As Braun's poem ironizes Momper's comment 'Berlin, nun freue
dich', casting it in a different light from that in which it was uttered, so
Drawert's 'Politisches Gedicht, Januar 1990' re-casts the words of another
prominent 'Wende' figure, Egon Krenz:[140]

> Politisches Gedicht, Januar 1990
> "Krenz erklärte abschließend,
> er habe 'wieder von unten
> in der Partei anfangen' wollen.
>
> 'Das geht jetzt auch nicht
> 5   mehr. Andere Arbeit zu finden,
> ist sehr schwierig. Ich werde
>
> wohl Schriftsteller.' "

When in October 1989 he replaced Honecker, Krenz tried to imply that moves
for change were a joint venture between the SED leaders and the 'Volk'. On
December 6 however, he also resigned his position as head of state and was
replaced by Manfred Gerlach, the chairman of one of the minority parties in
the 'Volkskammer'. The poetic form of Drawert's poem not only preserves
Krenz's comments, but exposes their full irony. They refer tangentially to the
dissolution of the SED, to unemployment in the 'neue Länder' and to the role
of the writer, which has now become the last resort of failed politicians.[141] The
entire poem, however, is contained within speech marks, suggesting it is a

---

[140]Kurt Drawert, 'Politisches Gedicht, Januar 1990', in 'Die Dichter und die Wende',
p.6 and in *Die sanfte Revolution*, ed. by Heym, p.172.
[141]Honecker in fact published poems (which are of negligible literary interest) in *Tiefe
Eindrücke und andere Gedichte von Erich Honecker*, ed. by Hans Wald (Siegen:
Universität, 1993) and Krenz a book of memoirs, *Wenn Mauern fallen: Die friedliche
Revolution: Vorgeschichte – Ablauf – Wirkungen* (Vienna: Neff, 1990).

found, or overhead, text.[142] This seems to point to the poet as a documentor, not of the obviously historic comments (say, the opening of the border or the resignation of Honecker) but of the telling, throwaway lines, such as those in this poem.

Some 'Wende' poems particularly undermine the historic by avoiding key dates and events in the period and instead focus on 'the inbetween'. Often there is a sense that the old has fallen, but the new has not yet established itself. Czechowski's poem 'Historische Reminiszenz' articulates a sense of negative continuity between past and present. This poem marks the occasion of a Christmas 1989 speech made by Helmut Kohl before a crowd of Dresden citizens:

> Heute, so scheint es,
> Ist wieder ein Tag,
> Wo man uns einreden will: Nun
> Wird alles gut! (lines 6-9)

Czechowski compares the false promises of the socialist government with those promises being made about unification by Kohl, another Iron Chancellor, following Bismarck who brought about the 1871 unification of Germany. The historic moment proclaimed by Kohl becomes a point in limbo, at the end of the poem:

> Die Dresdner Bank,
> Dank sei dem Eisernen Kanzler! –
> Zieht jetzt Bilanz in der dreimal
> Zerstörten Stadt an der Elbe, während das Volk
> Sich zu streiten beginnt, um sein Anteil
> An einer Ordnung, von der niemand weiß,
> Wer *nun* den Kopf hinhalten wird
> Für die Vergangenheit des immerwährenden
> Historischen Augenblicks: demokratischer Aufbruch
> Ins Niemandsland
> Zwischen gestern
> Und morgen. (lines 30-41)

In 1990 Dresden, destroyed by fire in 1685, by the Seven Years' War in 1760 and by the Second World War in 1945, becomes synonymous with its bank. In these lines, Czechowski emphasizes ironic continuities and sets against them the name of the new opposition organization 'Demokratischer Aufbruch', which was founded on 12 September 1989. 'Niemandsland', a commonplace of GDR literature, here takes on a positive connotation, a space unclaimed by

---

[142]Compare Rolf Dieter Brinkmann's similarly titled poem 'Politisches Gedicht 13. Nov. 74', *Westwärts 1&2: Gedichte* (Reinbek bei Hamburg: Rowohlt, 1975), pp.160-167, which uses many fragments of quotation.

anyone.[143] In Hilbig's 'prosa meiner heimatstraße' the phrases 'in den zwischenzeiten' and 'in der zwischenzeit' allude to the interregnum period between the old GDR years and the new Germany. This time in limbo began 'in der leere der november', when the SED regime fell and there were the first inklings of an emergent reality amidst the unreality:[144]

> es fehlte mir etwas: realität knirschte
> mit dem sand der sätze
>   doch tauchte nicht auf   (p.92)

Language as grains of sand recalls the idiomatic phrase 'Sand im Getriebe', something that disrupts the planned course.[145] Here reality is audible, but it has not yet fully appeared. The lyric subject is left dissatisfied, lacking 'ein einziger wirklichkeitsbeweis im wahnhaften sein'. Replacing the expected throwaway phrase 'im wahrhaften Sinn' with 'im wahnhaften Sein' emphasizes the predominant sense of a mad, surreal experience.

Thomas Böhme's 1990 poem 'die kuckucks verschweigen den mai' alludes to silence, sleep and vacation also to suggest a waiting period between two worlds.[146] This poem is about what comes after revolution and the opening of the border, namely stillness and langour:

> die kuckucks verschweigen den mai
> die tafel runde ist schlafen gegangen
> als gäbe es nichts mehr zu retten
> in den städten. die jakobinerclubs haben frei.
>
> 5   über dem land wogt die china hitze
> um mauergeripe summt weiß der monsun
> manchmal stürzt eine türken taube
> über die grüne grenze nach hüben. '
>
>   kinder drücken die zuckerlippen
> 10   in den bördelrand ihrer coca büchsen
> manchmal stürzen sich altgediente
> fluchtpioniere von den häuserklippen.
>
>   (mai 1990)

---

[143]By contrast, in Richter's poem 'Zwischenräume', *Die kleinen mecklenburgischen Meere*, p.53, the places inbetween represent an inability to find 'Heimat'.
[144]Wolfgang Hilbig, 'prosa meiner heimatstraße', *NR*, 101 (1990), 81-99.
[145]Duden, xi (1992), p.605.
[146]Thomas Böhme, 'die kuckucks verschweigen den mai', in 'Die Dichter und die Wende', pp.10-11, and reprinted in Thomas Böhme, *ich trinke dein. plasma november: 2 dreizehnzeilige und 100 zwölfzeilige gedichte (1987-1990)* (Berlin and Weimar: Aufbau, 1991), p.61.

The Round Table talks of 1989/90 become a sleeping Arthurian Round Table and the revolutionaries (the Jacobins) take a holiday. Repetition of 'manchmal' and 'stürzen' contrast the dove's benign border-crossing with the old guard's suicide. The young pioneers become 'altgediente Fluchtpioniere'; ironically the old guard who had prevented citizens from fleeing now flee life themselves. The edge with which the children are concerned – not a political 'rand', not 'grenze' – is that of the Coca Cola can, the symbol of America.

Despite the predominant sense of an interregnum period, a number of dates stand out as key points of change. On 18 March 1990 free elections took place in the GDR for the first time in its forty-year history. They meant the formation of a new 'Volkskammer', the implementation of a truly multi-party system, and the separation of legislature from judiciary. Victory belonged to the CDU, which dominated the conservative 'Allianz für Deutschland' of CDU, DSU and 'Demokratischer Aufbruch' that won 47.7% of the vote. This was effectively the mandate for unification. The SPD took 21.8% and the SED-PDS 16.3%. 'Bündnis 90', the party formed out of the opposition movement of autumn 1989, won only a negligible 2.9% of the vote. Steffen Mensching's first epigram of 'Berliner Elegien 2' pertains to this election.[147]

       Ich hatte die Wahl
       Gab meine Stimme
       Ab in die Urne Trat
       Stumm auf
5   Die Straße zurück

Line breaks emphasize the double meanings in this text. 'Die Wahl' is both the election and a choice, 'Stimme' vote and voice, 'Urne' ballot box and funeral urn. The prominence given to 'stumm' (4) brings out the contrast in meaning with the words with which it alliterates, 'Stimme' and 'Straße'. The departure of the lyric subject co-exists with the image of the election as a step backwards: the lyric subject returns to the streets, the symbolic site of protest. In Kirchner's poem 'Halbzeit' the term 'die Urnen' again links funeral rites to voting for unification. This poem concludes with physical death: 'Mein Körper stirbt / bedeckt von Sand der Urnen.' (11-12).[148] Journeys in Kirchner's 'Halbzeit' are 'Passagen en gros ins gelobte Land' (4). The commercial phrase 'en gros' points forward to the payment of 'Schweigegeld' and provides an uncomfortable contrast to the biblical metaphor of a promised

---

[147]Steffen Mensching, 'Ich hatte die Wahl', *Berliner Elegien* (Leipzig: Faber & Faber, 1995), p.21.
[148]Annerose Kirchner, 'Halbzeit', in *Von einem Land*, p.151.

land. Unification meant adopting consumerism and commercialism. Heinz
Kahlau captures this in 'Tag der Einheit' in the image of advertisements and
payment demands:[149]

> Ich war ummüllt von Werbung und von Briefen,
> die Geld von mir verlangten   (lines 3-4)

By analogy with 'umhüllen', Kahlau creates the verb 'ummüllen' to express
the paper and packaging, tokens of buying and selling, engulfing the
individual. Rather than any description of the unification ceremony, this poem
responds to the modest reminiscences of an ordinary individual. It is not
concerned with the political stage, but with the domestic sphere. The dating of
Czechowski's 'Brief nach L.' reveals that this is in fact a unification-day poem
and the married couple thus represent the two Germanies:[150]

> Mir jedenfalls
> Ist, als wäre heut Weihnachten,
> Dieses verlogene Fest,
> Wo sich die Ehepaare
> Versöhnen, um sich zu streiten und
> Sich wieder zu versöhnen. Die Wahrheit
> Ist janusköpfig, wie je.   (p.160)

Mixed feelings are clearly conveyed here: references to Christmas, Janus and
'das kommende Jahr' (p.161) point to a new year beginning on 3 October
1990 (Kirchner's poem 'Zwischen den Ufern' is also concerned with a
'Jahreswechsel' (4)), but this is set against the laconic expression 'wie je'.
Like some of the earliest 'Wende' poems, this text articulates a concern about
truth. Here it is personified as double-faced, like the two faces of Germany,
East and West.

Amongst the poems written by ex-GDR poets about 1989/90 there are
actually remarkably few which represent unification itself. Rather, there is
emphasis on the 'Wende' demonstrations and the collapse of the GDR.
Similarly, although Czechowski uses the word 'Umsturz', this is a rare
instance: the titles of poems often invoke November, but hardly ever refer to
revolution as such. These things reflect the fact that poetry better approaches
history obliquely and unconventionally; it finds history in fragments rather
than in treaties and coherent movements. Only the GDR-émigré poet-singer
Wolf Biermann and the minor GDR poets Jürgen Rennert and Friedrich
Dieckmann have written poems directly representing German unification as
two entities growing together. Biermann's 'Dideldumm' categorically declares
the paradox of united Germany's duality:[151]

---

[149]Heinz Kahlau, 'Tag der Einheit', in *Von einem Land*, p.95.
[150]Heinz Czechowski, 'Brief nach L.', *Nachtspur*, pp.159-161.
[151]Wolf Biermann, 'Dideldumm', in *Von einem Land*, pp.82-85.

Nun endlich ist mein Land wieder eins
Und blieb doch elend zerrissen
Aus Geiz und Neid. (lines 1-3)
The reason for divison is no longer imposed from without but is a meanness
within people. In the 'dideldumm dumm dum' refrain of this song-poem
Biermann suggests German stupidity. Social division, which constitutes 'ein'
Riss' (13), has replaced the concrete barrier:
Darin ist schon mancher ersoffen
Er fiel in die Brühe aus Resignation und
In Jauche aus falschem Hoffen (lines 16-18)
The horror with which the poet views the disunity of united Germany is
captured in this striking image of a Germany 'zerrissen' (2) and 'zerschnitten'
(12) with a cesspit in the middle in which people are drowned: 'die
Menschheit geht ganz zugrunde'. Rennert's representation of the two
Germanies as siblings makes their unification incestuous.[152] Here the GDR
sister is stripped and submits to her stronger brothers, an act of union which
suggests barbaric immorality.

In Friedrich Dieckmann's poem, unification is an operation to separate
Siamese twins.[153] Here the historical developments are not likened to nature
taking its course, but rather to a human intervention:

<pre>
     Deutsche Einheit
     Die Operation ist geglückt die lebens-
     gefährliche lebens-
     notwendige Verbände decken
     Die Wunde die beiden
5   Abgewandt miteinander
     Verwachsnen nach zwei
     Seiten sich Streckenden
     Strampelnden in unauflöslicher
     Verbundenheit sie sind
10   Endlich getrennt mühsam mit
     Langgezogenen Schnitten. Sich wendend beide sehn sie
     Einander zum ersten Mal und tief
     Befremdet: einer dem andern
     Wie aus dem Gesicht geschnitten dem nie
15   Erblickten. Sie sehen
     Sich im Spiegel sie
</pre>

[152]Jürgen Rennert, 'Lied vom fröhlichen Inzest', in *Von einem Land*, p.55. This poem's
imagery echoes that in some contemporary cartoons. See Susan S. Morrison, 'The
Feminization of the German Democratic Republic in Political Cartoons 1989-1990',
Journal of Popular Culture, 25 (1992), No.4, 35-51.
[153]Friedrich Dieckmann, 'Deutsche Einheit', *ndl*, 43 (1995), No.2, 72.

Reiben sich den Rücken es
Juckt –

Unification is paradoxically here a separation: the two Germanies are likened
to twins joined along their backs so that they could not see one another, nor
their similarity. The closing image of the two looking into a mirror indicates
questions about identity, and the wound and itching seem to symbolize an
uneasy East-West relationship.

The poets' predominant concern with 1989/90 as the end of the GDR,
rather than as the beginning of a new Germany, is reflected in the importance
of the Stasi files as a lyric theme. Although in name replaced by the 'Amt für
Nationale Sicherheit' (AfNS) in November 1989, many Stasi structures
remained in place into 1990. Citizens' strikes and demonstrations in January
and February 1990 created an atmosphere of pressure and fear amongst ex-
Stasi operatives who had been taken into the new services. Files continued to
be destroyed periodically.[154] Christiane Grosz's compelling poem 'die blonde
frau auf der behörde' encapsulates the ordinary citizen's fearful confrontation
with the files' version of the past:[155]

> die blonde frau auf der behörde
> hat eigentlich schon mittagspause
> geht kommt gleich wieder
> muß erstmal ans telefon
> sucht in der akte
> 5   tut was in ihren kräften steht
> weiß auch nicht was werden wird
> muß sich täglich was anhörn
> hat hautausschlag zwischen den fingern
> macht nächste woche eine woche urlaub
> 10   bleibt aber zu hause
> sagt es aber keinem
>
> (26.2.90)

The dating at the end and the line 'sucht in der akte' (4) signal the 'special'
context that is underplayed by the poem's seemingly innocuous subject. The
technique of beginning each line with a verb creates the impression of a simple
narrative; it also focuses attention on the character of the title, 'die blonde
frau'. Her sole distinguishing feature literally marks her skin: a rash on her
hands (8). Prominent verbs suggest her mental anxiety which, with the secrecy

---

[154]For a full account, see Michael Richter, *Die Staatssicherheit im letzten Jahr der DDR*
(Weimar, Cologne and Vienna: Böhlau, 1996).
[155]Christiane Grosz, 'die blonde frau auf der behörde', in *Von einem Land*, p.39.

alluded to at the end (11), diagnose the broken skin as stress-related. 'Big' topics of 'Verrat', revelation and revision are here subsumed under the little narrative of a humble, human figure, another individual alone. In the ninth of Grünbein's poems in the cycle 'Die leeren Zeichen', going to read one's files is a remnant of GDR experience; it brings back memories of encounters with GDR authority:[156]

> Ein schattenloser Raum, ein Akten-Trakt
> In dem das typisch Surreal-Banale,
> Beamte, Schreibmaschinen, Brillen, Tische,
> Die kichernden Klischees der Macht
> 5   Im Schluckauf hoch und runter fuhren
> Wie mit dem Fahrstuhl, *Paternoster*
> Kopfunter murmelnd, steif in Uniform,
> Stichelnde Bilder aus der Stummfilmzeit.

A lack of shadows, a faintly religious atmosphere, the 'kichern' (4) and 'murmeln' (7) echo Kafkaesque representations of faceless power. The oxymoron 'surreal-banal' conveys the strangeness of the experience, yet there are echoes of the poet's own realm in 'Schreibmaschinen, Brillen, Tische' (3): 'Die Macht' (4) was also engaged in writing.[157] The Latin *'Paternoster'* and the 'Stummfilmzeit' are references to the GDR's paternalism, its 'religion' of Marxism and its desire to speak for its citizens, thus keeping them 'stumm'. The 'Stummfilmzeit' is also a black-and-white past, a different kind of time.

An irreversible division between past and present, a caesura in time, was a crucial theme in 1989/90. The commentator Klaus Hartung termed the 'Wende' a return from the future, implying that utopian dreams in the GDR were symptomatic of an unnatural deviation from the present.[158] Realities in the GDR became obscured by a focus on a relentlessly projected future. Reversing the cultural historians' representation of progress in the GDR, stagnation became an established metaphor for life: the GDR was 'ein großer Wartesaal', 'auf dem Abstellgleis der Zeit'.[159] Leeder describes the 1980s as 'a kind of historical parenthesis'.[160] In Drawert's 'Tauben in ortloser Landschaft', the GDR is identified with a realm outside normal time, 'wo die Geschichte /

---

[156]Durs Grünbein, 'Die leeren Zeichen, 9', *Schädelbasislektion*, p.77.
[157]Compare this theme in Lutz Rathenow, 'Was für kein Gedicht', *Verirrte Sterne*, p.11.
[158]Hartung, *Neunzehnhundertneunundachtzig*, pp.16-17 states 'Eine Hälfte Europas kehrt aus der Zukunft zurück'.
[159]Heiner Müller, *Rotwelsch* (Berlin, FRG: Merve, 1982), p.51. Steffen Mensching, *Erinnerung an eine Milchglasscheibe* (Halle-Leipzig: mdv, 1984), p.17.
[160]Leeder, *Breaking Boundaries*, p.53.

anders zurückläuft' (p.7), 'jenseits der Zeit' (p.8). Its people are now lemurs, ghosts or spirits of the dead members of the household, who according to Roman religion, come back to haunt the house. In Hilbig's 'prosa meiner heimatstraße', GDR petrification extends to the 'ich': he is a mummified shadow, repeatedly 'erstarrt in erwartung'.[161] Here, Hilbig has taken the classical idea of shadows waiting in the ground, for the flesh, the life, to return:

> wie fleisch
>   wie königsfleisch
> das in den grund zurück will wo ihm seine schatten harren (p.82)

The 'Wende' marked the end of such waiting. Poetry traces this shift from stagnation to a surreal speeding of time. In Mensching's poem 'La vie ou la vite' the tramp dancing is an image of the era in which experience is mediated through the screen.[162] The French title here allows a witty equivalence of 'life' and 'speed' which is represented in a montage:

> Epochenschrott säumt die *Allee*
> *Der Kosmonauten. Welcome*
>
> *To the machines* im Radio. Schnellste Gegenwart
> Der Weltgeschichte. Ein *Pin-up-girl*
>
> Mit ausrasierten Achselhöhlen, blond
> Und geschmacksneutral wie ein Drei-Minuten-Menü
>
> Aus der Mikrowelle. Sternschnuppen
> Über dem *Nürnberger Todesdreieck.*
>
> Zerbeulte Leitplanken. Tempo 130. Richtung
> Atlantik. In die Radarfalle.
>
> Im Zyklotron. Im Schnellkochtopf,
> *Time is money*, honey, totsein können wir
>
> Noch lange genug. Pappeln im Gegenlicht,
> *Fastfood*, Zivilisationskritik mit Senf.　　　(lines 3-16)

The principle adopted is now a foreign, American one (14). Interpolated references to convenience food in lines 8, 13 and 16 illustrate the minimization of natural human requirements, like sustenance, because of the quickening of time. Past time has left only 'Epochenschrott'; present time seems surreally

---

[161]Hilbig, 'prosa meiner heimatstraße', p.82.
[162]Steffen Mensching, 'La vie ou la vite', 'Simulis simulis', *ndl*, 40 (1992), No.4, 35-36.

fast. Both descriptions suggest human bewilderment and dismay. Peter Geist has accorded these themes a special place in poetry by ex-GDR writers:

> It is due to the specific type of socialization in the GDR that the creeping dismay about the currently (i.e., after unification) accelerating expropriation of biographies, of time-spaces [...] and of authentic experiences, has become part of the more recent poems.[163]

Although the subject is the commonplace western world, the acute sense of speed and acceleration in poem by poets from the GDR, and the portrayal of simulacra, articulate a GDR perspective.

Events moved with what was generally perceived to be bewildering rapidity.[164] Less than a year separated the abortive attempt of the GDR to celebrate its fortieth anniversary from full political integration with the 'Bundesrepublik'. Whilst people in the East lived in the same flat, had the same pot-holed roads and heated their flats using the same briquettes of brown coal, suddenly the media, the products available and the education system became western. Gone were the Lenins and the socialist proverbs; in came new cars, advertisements and banks. Drawert has expressed this experience as a revelation of historical instability:

> Gerade die letzten Jahre haben der Welt gezeigt, was bereits überwunden zu sein schien: daß die unterschiedlichsten Systeme in Beschleunigungen geraten können, deren Folgen nicht mehr absehbar sind und alle Prognosen verlassen.[165]

This seems to coincide with the catastrophe theory to which Jens Reich refers: the GDR 'was more ideologically conformist, looked more stable, less surmountable, much more rigid than any other of the European communist regimes'.[166] It is difficult to move out of the stable condition, but once an avalanche is released, everything cascades rapidly into another stable condition. In the case of eastern Germany, the new stability was realized through unification.

Titles of some post-1989 poetry point to the disruption of history at the 'Wende'. Rathenow's title *Verirrte Sterne* exemplifies cosmic irregularity and Braun's *Die Zickzackbrücke* points to the unforeseen twists and turns of

---

[163]Geist, 'Voices from No Man's Land', p.144.
[164]For instance see Lothar Baier, *Volk ohne Zeit: Essays über das eilige Vaterland* (Berlin: Wagenbach, 1990).
[165]Drawert, *Haus ohne Menschen*, p.112.
[166]Jens Reich, 'Reflections on becoming an East German dissident, on losing the Wall and a country', in *Spring in Winter: The 1989 Revolutions*, ed. by Gwyneth Prins (Manchester and New York: MUP, 1990), pp.65-97 (p.82).

history. Mensching's third epigram of 'Berliner Elegien, 3' offers a related image of history's new disorder:[167]

> Der eiserne
> Vorhang gefallen. Das Labyrinth
> Wieder offen   (lines 2-4)

This experience of history as non-linear and labyrinthine has an effect on the function of poetry: there is a need to capture an impression of the moment. The title of a poem by Drawert, 'Zustandsbeschreibung. Zwischenbericht', epitomizes this sense of the poem fixing a point in time. This also applies to Czechowski's direct reflection of contemporary events in the poem 'Historische Reminiszenz', which is precisely placed in 'Dresden, 19.12.1989'. As Ian Hilton has highlighted, there is a 'preoccupation with time': the poet attempts 'to make his verses into marker-buoys in the fast-flowing tide of life in post-'Wende' Germany. To this end, many poems are given a specific date – not merely a year, but often a month and day'.[168] Grünbein's telegram poems particularly exemplify this by their titles.[169] Other examples include 'Herbstsonate 89' (Richter), 'novemberalmanach' (Schmidt), 'Berliner November' (Teschke), 'Der 9. November' (Braun), 'Dezember 89' (Rathenow) and 'die mauer: zum 3. oktober 1990' (Kunze). The lyric subject is a 'Zeitzeuge' both in the sense of a witness of his or her historical times and in the sense of a witness of time. Drawert comments on the importance of date for his poem 'Andere Arbeiter, ein anderer Herbst' as a result of the 'Wende':

> Allein das Entstehungsdatum entscheidet nunmehr das Schicksal des Gedichtes, es ist quasi der 19. und entscheidende Vers.[170]

This statement applies to other poems of this period, where the dating appended to the text conditions how it is read. Many 'Wende' poems have a year appended (of those mentioned above: Kirchner's 'Zwischen den Ufern' and 'Halbzeit', Kahlau's 'Tag der Einheit', Czechowski's 'Nach dem Umsturz', Drawert's 'Ortswechsel'). Others have a month and year (Czechowski's 'Die überstandene Wende', Grüning's 'Fahrt zum Palast der Republik'), but some have a precise date (Grüning's 'Heimfahrt von Prag', Grosz's 'die blonde frau', Schacht's 'Das Brandenburger Tor', Rennert's 'Lied vom fröhlichen Inzest' and 'Mein Land ist mir zerfallen'). Such dating points to the function of the poem as a diary-like record of a particular day. Czechowski has generally tended to conceive his recent poems to be

---

[167]Steffen Mensching, 'Berliner Elegien, 3', *Berliner Elegien*, pp.43-46.
[168]Hilton, ' "Erlangte Einheit, verfehlte Identität" ', p.266.
[169]Durs Grünbein, 'Sieben Telegramme', *Schädelbasislektion*, pp.59-65.
[170]Drawert, 'Veränderung des Hintergrundes', p.53.

'Gelegenheitsgedichte': in his 1989 poem 'Nimms, wie es kommt, nimm es leicht', he explicitly links the poem to a day-by-day diary:[171]

das Gedicht
Ersetzt mir das Tagebuch, Stenogramme
Des täglichen Lebens   (lines 4-6)

These lines distil the sense that the situation was changing on a daily basis, that the pressure of extraordinary change rendered poetic language a kind of shorthand and the poem an aide-mémoire. Many of the poems discussed here in fact foreground place and time, fixing the poem with respect to daily life and simultaneously fixing that daily life as a series of poems. Czechowski's lines here point to GDR literature's function as a substitute for a free press being superseded by a more modest substitute function: thus the diary also embodies the shift from public writing to private writing. Real scenes such as the 'Nikolaikirche', the Wall and candle-lit marches are evoked in 'Wende' poetry, but also images of nature, miracles and angels. And unlike a diary account, the 'Wende' in poetry is a moment, not a process. It utilizes many symbols of movement, flux and shifting, but is aware above all of the shifting of words and statements, the shifting of poetry itself. Functional ambiguity is important in poetry's account of history, both for undermining pathos and romanticizing, but also questioning the satirical and cynical perspective. What do these poems then say about the role taken by GDR poets at the 'Wende'? Poems come obliquely at history, not straight on, so they can approach history from close to it. They can be a way of making sense of events, especially by linking the present to the past, and can sometimes act on events and opinions. These two possibilites do not dominate this poetry, however. Rather, there is a desire to record, especially those things not otherwise recorded, and to bear witness, including to the ravages of time on truth. Poems dated for the 'Wende' and unification are also of course about life changes more generally; any reader can identify with the broadest experience which the GDR poets distil, of the old falling away and something new coming in its place. Metaphors of movement, such as exodus, walking through the border, the seasons, water-flow and speed, relate after all to time-flow. These poems demonstrate how the 'Wendegedichte' are often 'Zeitgedichte' both in the sense that they thematize the historical events at a particular time, but also in the sense that they represent time itself.

---

[171]Heinz Czechowski, 'Nimms, wie es kommt, nimm es leicht', *Nachtspur*, p.145.

CHAPTER 4
'DIE STIMMEN DER VERLIERER':
POST-UNIFICATION POETRY BY EX-GDR POETS

> In the political jargon of the day 'intellectual' was an
> expletive. It designated a person who failed to understand
> life and was cut off from the people.[1]

This chapter examines the poetry which came after the 'Wende-
Zeitgedichte' of 1989-1991, mostly in the period 1991-1996. Whilst no hard and
fast deadline exists, from about 1991 there is a natural development in the way
poets respond to the historic changes: the poetry of events tails off. The caesura
of 1989/90 continues nonetheless to be the prevailing reference point dividing
'then' from 'now'. My examination of what is thus the later 'Wende' poetry
focuses on how this caesura threatens the poet's writing and identity. I intend to
examine lyric responses to the new Germany and through this, the role of the
poet. For a brief period between the onset of the 'Wende' and the final
resolution brought by the unification treaty, a special situation existed for
GDR writers and intellectuals. During the period in limbo, many poets
believed that the failings of the regime, which 'critical' literature had exposed
over many years, were about to be redressed. They looked to the realization of
a 'better' socialist GDR, because they believed that a Third Way might still
exist. A middle road between the socialism of their experience and the
grasping capitalism of the West would, they thought, combine the best features
of both systems. As suggested in Chapter 3, the most prominent GDR writers at
the 'Wende' took to political platforms. In a speech of April 1990, the former
GDR academic Hans Mayer recalled the resurrection of cultural idealism at
this time:

> Einen kurzen, unvergessenen Augenblick lang durften wir alle hoffen, daß der
> tiefe Wunsch aller großen Deutschen, das Ernstnehmen deutscher Denker und
> Dichter, des Geistes, [...] nicht nur von der jeweiligen Macht anerkannt werden
> würde, sondern daß der Geist selbst zur Macht werden konnte.[2]

Rather than an end to claims of an alliance between 'Geist' and 'Macht', some
writers and intellectuals hoped to extend their role in society and politics. The
'wir alle' in Mayer's statement was deceptive however; it applied only to the
writers and intellectuals, and not, as had so long been presumed, to the general
populace. In a piece published in January 1990, in a volume which was

---

[1]Milan Kundera, *The Book of Laughter and Forgetting*, trans. by Michael Henry Heim
(London: Faber, 1982), p.5
[2]Hans Mayer, quoted in Deiritz, 'Zur Klärung eines Sachverhalts', p.17.

subtitled *DDR 1990: Hoffnung auf eine neue Republik*, the poet Heinz
Czechowski also articulated the enduring idea of a utopian unity between
intellectual and political power:

> Das entwertete Wort von der Einheit von Geist und Macht könnte als
> neugeprägte Münze wieder in Umlauf gesetzt werden. Nämlich dann, wenn
> eine neue, frei gewählte Regierung der DDR damit begänne, die besten Köpfe
> der Intelligenz zu ihren Beratern zu machen, sie zu Botschaftern und
> Kulturattachés zu ernennen.[3]

In January 1990 this socialist principle seemed as attractive as it had been at
the beginning of the GDR. Czechowski states his resurrected belief in the
importance of intellectuals and artists for political life. Subsequently however,
in reality, writers and intellectuals became redundant as political figures. In an
article of 1993, Czechowski hints at a concomitant 'Krise des Schreibens'.[4] Is
there a general tendency to express in poetry an anxiety about writing practices
and about the future role of the poet? The GDR writer Werner Heiduczek has
stated, 'Es gibt Leute, die gehören immer zu den Siegern der Geschichte.
Schriftsteller aber gehören auf Dauer immer an die Seite der Verlierer'.[5] This
seems to have been particularly felt by GDR poets after unification. Many lost a
utopian vision, economic security and social status: the familiar literary
institutions ceased to exist.[6] Angela Krauß's definition of literature is
interesting in connection with this experience of loss: 'Literatur – ob man sie
nun schreibt oder liest – hat damit zu tun, daß einem etwas fehlt. Die zur
Verfügung stehende Wirklichkeit reicht nicht'.[7] Certain things were missing in
the GDR, particularly a free press and freedom of expression. The things lost
to the new Germany are of a different order, so Krauß's statement suggests
that this difference will have consequences for poets' writing practices. In
1991 the poet Kerstin Hensel includes in her programmatic poem 'Poetik' the
same relationship between loss and literature:[8]

---

[3]Heinz Czechowski, 'Euphorie und Katzenjammer', in *Die Geschichte ist offen*, ed. by
Naumann, pp.31-43, p.39.
[4]Heinz Czechowski, 'Abgebrochene Biographien, vergessene Orte', *ndl*, 41 (1993),
No.10, 27-34 (p.28).
[5]Werner Heiduczek, quoted in Deiritz, 'Zur Klärung eines Sachverhalts', p.17.
[6]For details of the fate of GDR literary institutions from 1989 onwards, see Emmerich,
Kleine Literaturgeschichte der DDR , pp.435-456, and Volker Lilienthal, 'Links liegen
gelassen: Die Buchverlage der ehemaligen DDR', in *Mauer-Show*, ed. by Bohn,
pp.243-256.
[7]Angela Krauß, 'Das Poetische am Politischen', *Monatshefte*, 82 (1990), 403-407
(p.405).
[8]Kerstin Hensel, 'Poetik', *ND*, 20/21 April 1991, p.14 and reprinted in *Gewitterfront:
Lyrik* (Halle: mdv, 1991), p.88.

Was wir erleben ist Licht
Was wir schreiben Verlust. (lines 13-14)

Literature, for these writers, is not about the light but the darkness, not about what can be experienced in reality, but what is lost and missing from that experience. This general paradigm took on an acute historical reality in 1989/90. I shall investigate how poets write the losses of 1989/90 and, through this, examine poets' self-understanding. In Heinrich Mohr's words, poetry by reform-socialists is composed of 'die Stimmen der Verlierer'.[9] This chapter will examine whether the voices in the poems by ex-GDR poets show this particular kind of self-presentation.

The position of the reform-socialist intellectuals was reflected in their public appeal on 26 November 1989 entitled 'Für unser Land'.[10] This document presented a choice between realizing a dream and selling out: the signatories urged the GDR not to relinquish the dream in the face of an encroaching western reality.

> Noch haben wir die Chance, in gleichberechtigter Nachbarschaft zu allen
> Staaten Europas eine sozialistische Alternative zur Bundesrepublik zu
> entwickeln. (p.240)

This appeal was made even as the exodus of citizens to the West continued and those still on the streets were beginning to call for unity with the West. It was signed by the writers Braun and Wolf, and also, in a cynical move to reclaim power, by Politburo members Krenz and Modrow. In a letter to the Rowohlt publishing house on 20 November 1989, another signatory, Christoph Hein, wrote 'Es gibt eine Chance für unsere Hoffnung, allerdings ist es die erste und gleichzeitig die letzte. Wenn wir scheitern, frißt uns McDonald'.[11] Writers like Hein were arguing against western life under capitalism. For such writers, unification meant their hope had no chance of realization. The critic Harold James describes this literary generation as the losing group at German unification: 'The losers in 1989-90 were the semi-oppositional, semi-official intellectual elite of the old GDR, the Christa Wolfs and Stefan Heyms who wanted a reformed socialism'.[12] For the German critics Karl Deiritz and Hannes Krauss, the reform-socialists are characterized by the failure of their ideals: they

---

[9]Heinrich Mohr, in *Von Abraham bis Zwerenz: eine Anthologie*, ed. by Bundesministerium für Bildung, Wissenschaft, Forschung und Technologie, i ([Berlin]: Cornelsen, 1995), pp.12-17 (p.15).

[10]'Aufruf für eine eigenständige DDR vom 26. November 1989', in *"Wir sind das Volk!"*, ed. by Schüddekopf, pp.240-241.

[11]Christoph Hein, 'Brief an den Rowohlt Verlag', *Die fünfte Grundrechenart: Aufsätze und Reden 1987-1990* (Frankfurt a.M.: Luchterhand, 1990), p.210.

[12]Harold James, 'The landscape that didn't bloom', *Times Literary Supplement*, 13 June 1997, 5-6 (p.5).

138   Lyric Responses to German Unification

are 'die Gescheiterten: Volker Braun, Christoph Hein, Heiner Müller, Christa Wolf. Noch viele mehr'.[13] Similarly, Andreas Huyssen writes of the 'failure' of German intellectuals at the 'Wende', with respect to their misunderstanding of the popular mood.[14] History proved the socialist intellectuals wrong; it contradicted their Third Way. The unification treaty made a mockery of their utopian visions. In this sense they became losers, that is, in the contest between ideologies they were seen to be on the 'wrong' side.

The failure of the socialist dream of a better world is the subject of Hein's post-'Wende' story 'Kein Seeweg nach Indien'.[15] Hein uses Columbus's sea-journey as an allegory and parallels the 'Schiffsvolk' with the citizens of the GDR. The emphasis is on their failure to find India, but with a crucial qualification:

> Einige der Schreiber sagten nun, nur der Kurs der Schiffe sei falsch gewesen und hinter dem Ozean warte noch immer ein reiches Land auf seine Entdeckung. Und sie nannten es weiterhin Indien oder Amerika oder auch Utopia. (p.18)

India represents the socialist utopia which was never found in the GDR. A longing to believe that a utopia is nonetheless possible was typical of reform-socialist writers at the 'Wende'. At the end of Hein's voyage, there is a sense of relief: 'Und die Schreiber konnten endlich zu ihren Schreibpulten zurückkehren und wieder ungestört ihre Arbeit verrichten' (p.18). In reality, it was not the case, however, that GDR writers simply returned to their writing, undisturbed by the failure of the GDR and the loss of the utopian project. A cartoon in the *Deutsches Allgemeines Sonntagsblatt* of 9 March 1990 entitled 'Aufbruch ins Ungewisse' showed another sea-bound vessel: worried faces on a little boat represent the GDR 'Schriftstellerverband', which is floating out to sea, its 'SED' moorings severed.[16] This illustration captures the uncertainty and sense of being cut adrift, which came with the end of GDR institutions and the end of any aspiration to unify intellectual and political power. Harald Gerlach's 'Wende' poem, 'Utopia' reflects on this aspiration.[17] The poem contrasts a dream of a 'Republik der Gelehrten' where the poet is a high priest, with the commercial

---

[13]Karl Deiritz and Hannes Krauss, 'Ein deutsches Familiendrama', in *Der deutsch-deutsche Literaturstreit*, ed. by Deiritz, pp.7-12 (p.8).
[14]Andreas Huyssen, 'After the Wall: The Failure of German Intellectuals', *New German Critique*, 52 (1991), 109-143. This article is a useful summary of the position of writers and intellectuals in 1989/90, and the rift between writers and the people.
[15]Christoph Hein, 'Kein Seeweg nach Indien', in *Christoph Hein. Texte, Daten, Bilder*, ed. by Lothar Baier (Frankfurt a.M.: Luchterhand, 1990), p.13-19.
[16]The cartoon is reproduced in Ludwig Fischer, 'Zwischen Aufbruch und Zukunftsangst: Beobachtungen und Dokumente zur Situation der Künstler in der Noch-DDR', *deutsche studien*, 28 (1990), 122-142 (p.137).
[17]Harald Gerlach, 'Utopia', in *Von einem Land*, p.73.

reality of the new Germany. Dream and reality inform and criticize one another:

Utopia

Um die Gipfel kreisen
die Adler. Und mein Traum wies
im Lande ein Feld: Republik
der Gelehrten. Dort, Diotima,
5   laß uns sein. Sinclair, mein
Präsident! Gehüllt in den Mantel
der Poesie schreitet
dein Hohepriester. Auf eilig
verhökertem Boden. Vorbei. Vorüber.

10   Nebel. Das Reich der Gedanken
bleibt landlos.

DRINK

COCA COLA LIGHT! So kam ich
unter die Deutschen. Handwerker
15   fand ich ... Allianzversichert.
Shake hands, Scardanelli.

The ideal of an intellectuals' republic, akin to the 'Gelehrtenrepublik' envisioned by Klopstock and Hölderlin in the eighteenth century, is now hopelessly untimely: it represents a failing on the part of intellectuals, as well as a failing of the materialistic world. The intellectuals' utopia is 'landlos'. This corresponds to the disillusionment, and sense of homelessness, amongst reform-socialist writers after unification. The most striking strategy in this poem is the use of quotations, especially from Hölderlin, a GDR poets' poet, whose intellectual ideals and disappointments are so often evoked in GDR poems.[18] Gerlach draws on Hyperion's lines 'So kam ich unter die Deutschen [...] Handwerker siehst du, aber keine Menschen' as a parallel for contemporary disillusionment with human aspirations.[19] Unification prompts a confrontation with the final, undeniable loss of a long-awaited utopia.

In the six short lines of Christa Wolf's poem 'Prinzip Hoffnung' utopian hope is irretrievably nailed to the past.[20] The title of this poem quotes Bloch's title, a cipher for the position of many intellectuals throughout the GDR years.

---

[18]Many are collected in the anthology Hiltrud Gnüg, ed., *An Hölderlin: Zeitgenössische Gedichte* (Stuttgart: Reclam, 1993).
[19]Friedrich Hölderlin, *Hyperion oder der Eremit in Griechenland* (Stuttgart: Reclam, 1980), p.171.
[20]Christa Wolf, 'Prinzip Hoffnung', in *Von einem Land*, p.134

Wolf's poem offers a single image of excruciating pain. It deals with the physical agony of crucifixion, rather than with the salvation which the cross primarily represents in Christianity:

> Prinzip Hoffnung
> Genagelt
> ans Kreuz Vergangenheit.
>
> Jede Bewegung
> treibt
> 5   die Nägel
> ins Fleisch.
>
> (Dezember 1991)

Horst Domdey reads in this poem Wolf's self-aggrandizement: she presents her lyric subject as the ultimate martyr, a crucified Christ. Claire Baldwin emphasizes, on the other hand, the expression of vulnerability.[21] Both interpretations reflect the position of established GDR writers like Wolf. In the prose piece 'Nagelprobe', this poem is reprinted in the context of an 'ich's vision of walls of nails closing in on her.[22] The 'Nagelprobe' is also associated with 'die Frau, die nun endlich bereit war, einzugestehen, daß sie als Hexe mit dem Bösen getrieben hatte' (p.34), that is, with a fairytale transference of Wolf's role in the 'Literaturstreit'. Heinz Kahlau's poem 'Folter' of 1989 is remarkably similar in theme and form to Wolf's.[23] Where Wolf redefines hope as torture, Kahlau redefines torture as the pain inflicted by hopes.

> Folter
> Wenn dir
> bei schöner Abendröte
> die Splitter
> deiner Hoffnungen
> 5   unter die abgebissenen
> Nägel getrieben werden.

As in Wolf's poem, pain is located in the hands – perhaps a reflection of the writing hands of the poet. These poems describe an existential crisis, which can

---

[21]Horst Domdey, 'Feindbild BRD', *Kursbuch*, 109 (1992), 63-79. Claire Baldwin, ' "Nagelprobe": On German Trials', *Colloquia Germanica*, 27 (1994), 1-11.
[22]Christa Wolf, 'Nagelprobe', *ndl*, 40 (1992), No.5, 34-44 (p.44).
[23]Heinz Kahlau, 'Folter', *Kaspers Waage: Gedichte* (Berlin and Weimar: Aufbau, 1992), p.27.

be accounted for in terms of what the commentator Joachim Fest calls socialism's 'pseudo-religion': 'Zur großen Verführungsmacht des Sozialismus gehörte zeit seines Bestehens, daß er ein pseudoreligiöses Welterklärungssystem bot, eine große Verheißung mit der Hoffnung auf Gerechtigkeit, Frieden, Glück'.[24] Fest argues that the end of Nazism in 1945 and socialism in 1989 were failed utopias which heralded 'eine schwierige Freiheit', because of the indifference of liberal capitalism to the meaning of modern life: 'Und wie 1945 die Parteigänger der einen, so hatten 1989 die Anhänger der anderen Seite den Zusammenbruch ihrer Hoffnungen als eine Art metaphysischen Verlust erlebt' (p.415). In the Wolf poem especially, the metaphysical is indeed absent; the end of hope is inscribed on the body as physical torture which has no higher meaning.

A mournful, sometimes wounded tone in post-'Wende' poetry in part explains the negative reactions of some readers. In early 1990, the critic Ludwig Fischer wrote an article about the situation of GDR intellectuals after the collapse of socialism, in which he identified 'eine bisher so nicht gekannte kunstfeindliche Stimmung'.[25] Fischer emphasized the climate of self-pity and fearfulness about the future amongst writers in the GDR. Even the exiled poet and singer Wolf Biermann was unsympathetic to these writers, declaring 'Es stinkt im Osten nach Selbstmitleid'.[26] The academic Ernst Hannemann describes the 'Wende' heralding 'eine Periode der Larmoyanz'.[27] Czechowski's 1992 poem 'Trägheit des Herzens. Stimmungsverlust.' illustrates such a lachrymose mood.[28] After a catastrophe, a woeful, confessional voice articulates the sense of vacuum:

Trägheit des Herzens. Stimmungsverlust.
Das Lied
Will nicht mehr ins Ohr.
Was ich
Zu schreiben hatte,
5   Hab ich geschrieben. Jetzt
Zerspiele ich
Die Begriffe. Brot-
Arbeiten.

---

[24]Joachim Fest, 'Nach dem Scheitern der Utopien: Probleme der offenen Gesellschaft', *SuF*, 49 (1997), 410-421 (p.410).
[25]Fischer, 'Zwischen Aufbruch und Zukunftsangst'.
[26]Wolf Biermann,'Nur wer sich ändert, bleibt sich treu', in *"Es geht nicht um Christa Wolf"*, ed. by Anz, pp.139-156 (p.141).
[27]Hannemann, 'Geschichtsschreibung nach Aktenlage?', p.26.
[28]Heinz Czechowski, 'Trägheit des Herzens. Stimmungsverlust.', in *Nachtspur*, p.208.

        Kahlschlag in Dresden, Kahlschlag
10   In Leipzig. Amokläufe
        Gegen die Leere, Spazier-
        Gänge durch
        Kleingartenanlagen:
        Vielleicht
15   Hilft dir der
        Angekündigte Regen...

        (1992)

This poem characterizes the caesura of 1989/90 as 'Kahlschlag' (9), a term
which echoes the clearing of ideological attachments in 1945.[29] Juxtaposition of
nouns in lines 7-13 without connecting verbs reiterates the directionlessness of
the 'ich'. It is also a strategy for creating ironic discrepancy: the banality of
strolling through allotments hardly equates with 'Amokläufe'. The confiding,
slow-moving voice tends to focus attention on inherent verbal ambiguity as it
lingers over every word: 'Was ich / Zu schreiben hatte, / Hab ich geschrieben'
(3-5) can be a statement of conformity or of exhaustion. Rain, coming to cleanse
and refresh, is apparently a hopeful flourish at the poem's close, yet 'vielleicht'
is in a position of prominence, occupying a whole line, and 'angekündigt' has
more significance than the noun it describes. The effect is one of sarcasm which
mocks the self's inability to cope with unannounced change. Gerd Labroisse
describes Czechowski's poetry from the 1990s as characterized by 'eher eine
sarkastische als eine elegische Note'.[30] This poem exemplifies both sarcastic and
elegiac tones. It may suggest that writing poetry has become 'Brot- / Arbeiten'
(7-8), as though that is all writing can be in the western world.[31]
        Gerlach, Wolf, Kahlau and Czechowski belong to the same generation. It
was not only these older writers, born before 1945, that lost a utopian vision
however. For a brief period at the onset of the 'Wende', many younger writers
believed that the failings of the SED regime could now be redressed. Joseph
Pischel attributed this belief to the majority of authors who remained in the GDR

---

[29]See Czechowski's earlier poems about bombed Dresden in *Auf eine im Feuer
versunkene Stadt* (Halle-Leipzig: mdv, 1990), which thematize a return to a childhood
place, but also a return to the post-war milieu.
[30]Gerd Labroisse, 'Verwortete Zeit-Verflechtungen: Zu Heinz Czechowskis neuen
Texten', *GM*, 32 (1994), 29-85 (p.83).
[31]See also the more positive equation of words with 'bread' and with the 'bread of life'
in Czechowski's earlier poem 'Brotarbeiten', in *Scharfe und Sterne: Gedichte* (Halle:
mdv, 1974), p.93.

in 1989:

> Die Mehrheit derer, die in der DDR geblieben sind (ja selbst viele von denen, die
> ausgereist waren oder ausgegrenzt wurden), haben bis zuletzt und trotz aller Ent-
> Täuschungen an der Hoffnung festgehalten, die zentralischpolitbürokratischen
> Herrschaftsstrukturen könnten durch innere Wandlungen aufgebrochen oder
> durch Gewalt von unten zerschlagen werden, und es könnten so noch Potenzen
> des Sozialismus freigelegt werden, die mit ihren Entwürfen von menschlicher
> Emanzipation und Mündigkeit in Übereinstimmung zu bringen wären.[32]

Younger intellectuals, who never claimed identification with the GDR state, did
not support unification with the 'Bundesrepublik' either. Kerstin Hensel, for
instance, hoped for socialism: in an interview of November 1989 she said,
'Meine Hoffnung ist, daß ein konstruktiver Kern sich formiert, der wirklich den
Sozialismus will'.[33] Kurt Drawert also hoped for the third alternative in 1989,
stating in an interview of 1994, 'Ich hatte schon auf einen dritten Weg gehofft.
[...] Ich habe gedacht, daß die in der DDR gewachsene Widersstandskultur etwas
hervorbringt, das nicht die DDR und auch nicht die Bundesrepublik sein wird'.[34]
The Germanist Peter Geist used the biblical metaphor of a splinter in the eye in
attributing such hope to a deep-seated attraction to utopia.[35] He suggested, in
1992, that young writers picked this up as an integral part of a GDR upbringing:

> Viele der heute Dreißig- bis Vierzigjährigen haben, das ist in Gedichten von
> Barbara Köhler, Uwe Kolbe, Kerstin Hensel, Steffen Mensching oder Hans
> Brinkmann nachzulesen, in den fortschrittseuphorischen Jahren ihrer Kindheit
> noch genügend Utopiesplitter ins innere Augen eingepflanzt bekommen.

The 'Utopiesplitter', Geist claimed, affected the vision of even the youngest
GDR poets. Jan Faktor has also described hope prevailing in unofficial literary
circles. In 1993 he compared the illusions of young, alternative writers in East
Berlin with the Czech intellectuals who had given up all socialist faith after
1968: 'Meine Ostberliner Freunde hatten eine Gläubigkeit unverwechselbarer
Prägung'.[36] Faktor attributed this retained hope to the influence of West German
intellectuals. He suggested that the unofficial GDR literati imported western
literary theories and, along with them, left-wing western attitudes about
socialism. Clearly then, there are indications that GDR utopianism was not

---

[32] Joseph Pischel, 'Das Ende der Utopie? Zur aktuellen Diskussion um die DDR-Literatur
und zum Streit um Christa Wolf', *ndl*, 38 (1990), No.9, 138-147 (p.139).
[33] Kerstin Hensel, 'Ich teste meine Grenzen aus', *Deutsche Volkszeitung / die tat*, 3
November 1989, p.9.
[34] Herzog, 'Erzählen und erinnern', p.65.
[35] Geist, ' "mit würde holzkekse kauen", p.148.
[36] Jan Faktor, 'Realität von nebenan: Der besondere Stand der jungen, linken DDR-
Intellektuellen im ehemaligen Ostblock', in *Über Deutschland: Schriftsteller geben
Auskunft*, ed. by Thomas Rietzschel (Leipzig: Reclam, 1993), pp.73-81 (p.77).

confined to Wolf's and Braun's generation.[37] Rather, younger poets, and those who largely denied political allegiances, also hoped that the 'Wende' would reform socialism.

In poetry, the two young poets Kerstin Hensel and Steffen Mensching, for example, have set themselves in sympathy with older poets from the GDR. This strategy has implications for the poet's role as it is represented by the poetry. It is particularly interesting against the generally accepted model of a young literary generation in the GDR rejecting the premises on which the older generation wrote. Hensel has for instance stated, 'Mich hat kein Staatssystem geprägt'.[38] She has argued that the change of political system has not been important for her, because her interest in general human questions remains unaltered. She emphasizes continuity: 'Schreiben war für mich ein Abenteuer. Das ist es heute noch' (p.20). At the same time, she also regrets that the desire to make the world a better place has become a cliché, and in poetry, she identifies with Braun. Her poem 'Im Stau' expresses a solidarity with the older poet's bitterness and disappointment: [39]

> Im Stau   (für V. Braun)
> Noch rot hinter den Ohrn und aufgesessen!
> Die Kluft im Nischel: Freisein oder Fressen.
> Es rollt sich aus in was
> Wir nimmer wollten.
> 5   Die Räder stehn. Es strampeln die Revolten.
> *Denn hier ist keine Heimat - Jeder treibt*
> Und festgeflochten in das Lenkrad Zeit
> Dem Ziele zu, das sich verrammelt, so
> Kriecht unser Troß dem Nichtigen entgegen:
> 10   Der süßesten Verzweiflung saurer Regen.
> Jetzt stehn wir, Volker, gut am Pißwald, was?
> Über den Rand, den wir nicht halten, wächst das Schneidegras
> Und fröhlich hupt der Chor der Ungetrübten.
> Wie hieß das, was die Köpfe einstens übten?
>
> 15   Komm, laufen wir, als ob uns nichts mehr hält.
> *Denn jede Straße führt ans End der Welt.*

---

[37]Even in 1993, the young poet Steffen Mensching declared in an interview, 'Von der Alternative Sozialismus als einer humaneren, zivilisierteren, ausbeutungsfreieren Welt verabschiede ich mich nicht'. See Günter Görtz, 'Die Maske paßt', *ND*, 30 April 1993, p.17.

[38]Kerstin Hensel, 'Das Eine und nicht das Andere. Zum Thema: Schreiben in der DDR', *ndl*, 43 (1995), No.4, 19-23 (p.19).

[39]Kerstin Hensel, 'Im Stau', *Angestaut*, p.64.

The street, the site of protest in 1989, has led to the end of the world – an ambiguous description of the end of socialism as an arrival in paradise on the one hand but, on the other, a terrible destruction. The 'wir' of this poem is that of the self and Braun, united against 'der Chor der Ungetrübten' (13). Hensel develops a jaunty tone by using colloquial phrases (as if writing to overcome the sense of being 'getrübt'). 'Noch rot hinter den Ohrn', for instance, plays ironically with a suggestion that socialism is something one grows out of. The term 'Nischel' recalls Günter Gaus's well-known designation of the GDR as a 'Nischengesellschaft'. Whereas Gaus's interpretation was positive, Hensel's 'Nischel' is now rent and *'hier ist keine Heimat'*. Line 5 ironically echoes Georg Herwegh's 'Bundeslied für den Allgemeinen deutschen Arbeiterverein' of 1863, an SED song which calls upon the 'Mann der Arbeit' to recognize his own power: 'Alle Räder stehen still, / Wenn dein starker Arm es will'.[40] The GDR past alluded to in line 14 is contrasted with the image of the poets on a wagon creeping slowly towards the trivial. Whilst Hensel identifies with Braun's regret (3-4), her lyric subject is also irreverent. Line 11 illustrates this. Hensel's traffic jam is in part a rebuttal of ideas of progress, but it also contrasts standstill in the new Germany with a metaphor of progress under socialism. Against this, 'Im Stau' ends with an evocation of abandon and the imperative to run freely. This may be a simulated freedom however ('als ob uns nicht mehr hält'). Hensel expresses loss here but not despair, perturbation but also the will to move on. This ambivalence recurs in her poem 'Der neue Ton':[41]

> Die Aufklärer abgeklärt, die dunnemals wilden
> Gelage, was traute ich denen und trauer
> Denen nicht nach.   (lines 14-16)

Here Hensel plays on the aural affinity between 'trauen' and 'trauern'. The word 'nachtrauern' suggests following 'die Aufklärer' and mourning, despite the fact that this poet was sceptical about their enterprise.[42] Such following is explicit in the poem 'Reiseleiter' (*Freistoß*, p.39). Hensel refers to Braun's post-'Wende' poem 'Das Theater der Toten' (*Die Zickzackbrücke*, p.91): she takes up the concluding lines 'Im übrigen bin ich der Meinung / Daß der Sozialismus zerstört werden muß und / Mir gefällt die Sache der Besiegten' and amends the statement of resignation to one of attack:

---

[40]Georg Herwegh, 'Bundeslied für den Allgemeinen deutschen Arbeiterverein', *Werke in einem Band*, Ausgewählt und eingeleitet von Hans-Georg Werner (Berlin, GDR: Aufbau, 1967), pp.232-233 (p.233).
[41]Kerstin Hensel, 'Der neue Ton', *Freistoß: Gedichte* (Leipzig: Connewitzer Verlagsbuchhandlung, 1995), pp.60-61.
[42]Hensel's poem 'Trauer Arbeit' (*Freistoß*, p.11) portrays grieving as scrubbing out the stalls of slaughtered cows. The work is unnecessary and unrewarded, but it is a way for the lyric 'ich' to forget 'die Not'.

Im übrigen bin ich der Meinung daß Karthago
Zerstört werden muß. (lines 18-19)
This culmination of Hensel's poem is a rejection of the West, using the name of
Carthage which Braun had juxtaposed with New York in his poem. These lines
are also the closing words of the Roman statesman and writer Cato the Elder in a
speech to the Roman Senate, in which he argued that Carthage represented a
dangerous trading rival to Rome.[43] Historically, Carthage was indeed, of course,
later destroyed.

Mensching's poetic response to Czechowski shows similar identification
with the poet of an older GDR generation.[44] Like Hensel, Mensching also uses
literary allusions (to Klopstock, Auden, Yeats, Freud, Kleist, Poe, as well as
Czechowski), whilst developing a familiar, witty tone. 'Öde an einen
klemmenden Buchstaben und Heinz C.' plays on the typewriter having a faulty
key, so that the letter 'o' must be replaced by other vowels. 'O' is of course for
'Ost', so 'Ich wohne im Osten' has become 'Ich wahne im Esten!' (13).
'Genossen' has become 'Genussen' (13), a transformation which goes beyond
humorous distortion. The broken key suggests an injury to the poet's vocabulary,
but he can make a virtue out of necessity: 'Schließlich geht es auch ahne' (23) –
without the GDR too, that is. In this text, the young poet compares himself to his
despairing friend 'Chechöwski' (19) who writes odes. Mensching's lyric 'ich'
would follow the tradition of which Czechowski is a contemporary exponent, but
he falls into a more distanced perspective: the younger poet cannot write an ode
exactly, but an 'Öde'. The frivolous wit plays against the reasons for a GDR poet
to despair:[45]

wenn ich
Anstatt des wunderbar uffenen Lauts
Lauter Nullen einsetze, fällt das hier
Siewiesau
Keinem mehr auf. (lines 25-29)
Even in an apparently light-hearted text like this, there is a note of anguish at the
end, in the recognition that the poet will no longer have the social resonance
which he previously secured in the GDR. Mensching identifies with the
despairing Czechowski, and uses humour to confront the idea that no-one takes
notice of poetry any longer. This new lack of resonance is an important motif in
the later 'Wende' poetry.

For writers who had remained in the GDR, unification brought a

---

[43]Duden, xii (1993), p.82.
[44]Steffen Mensching, 'Öde an einen klemmenden Buchstaben und Heinz C.', *Berliner
Elegien*, p.11.
[45]Mensching's designation (in a letter to me of 9 December 1998) of himself as 'nicht
der ernsthafteste Dichter' seems pertinent here.

sudden confrontation with a commercial, media-rich society. In the book *Die deutsche Einheit und die Schriftsteller*, Volker Wehdeking asserts that amongst writers from East and West there is broad acceptance of unification as a favourable development.[46] Poetry by ex-GDR writers gives a demonstrably contrary impression however. Referring to GDR poets in the immediate aftermath of unification, the Germanist Christiane Zehl Romero states, 'All have to confront a very different Western way of life and are at varying stages of an uneasy adaptation'.[47] Some poems thematize a profound crisis amongst poets, however, not just an uneasy adaptation to western life. In the collection *Berliner Elegien* by Steffen Mensching, and in Heiner Müller's posthumously published poetry, there is in fact a striking rejection of capitalism. These poets have tended to interpret unification in terms of conquest and exploitation by the West.[48]

Müller's 'Mommsens Block' can be read as an expression of resentment at the western takeover.[49] The lyric subject expresses 'Ekel am Hier und Heute' (p.262). In a good restaurant he overhears businessmen, whom he ironically calls 'Helden der Neuzeit' (p.262), talk about buying off an employee. He voices his disgust to Mommsen: 'Tierlaute Wer wollte das aufschreiben' (p.263). Nonetheless, such antipathy has been overcome – the poem quotes extensively the 'Tierlaute' of the capitalist city. The compulsions of commerce are emphasized in the repetitions of 'müssen' in the businessmen's dialogue:

Diese vier Millionen / Müssen sofort zu uns // Aber das geht nicht // Aber das fällt gar nicht auf // Wenn Du diese Klaviatur nicht beherrschst / Bist Du verloren Das hast Du an X gesehn / Er hat sie nicht beherrscht // Die mußt Du ihm / Einhämmern [...] Aber wenns an die Knochenarbeit geht ... // Dann muß ers in andre Hände geben // Aber dann ist die Frage Sind unsre Hände so gut / Daß sie den Spieß umdrehn können // Man muß ihn auf Vordermann bringen // Wir müssen ihn kaufen für die Deutsche Bank (pp.262-263)

Subsequent description is equally cynical: sirens mark where the poor beat up the poorest, while the gentlemen have cigars and cognac. The strong invective allows only this clichéd view of western society. Müller's poem 'Herz der Finsternis nach Joseph Conrad' (*Die Gedichte*, p.234), like 'Mommsens Block', uses a named addressee, in this case Gregor Gysi, a member of the commission which temporarily succeeded Krenz in the run-up to unification. Müller takes as

---

[46]Wehdeking, *Die deutsche Einheit und die Schriftsteller*, pp.38-39.
[47]Romero, 'No Voices - New Voices?', p.144.
[48]Braun's poem 'Der 9. November', in *Von einem Land*, p.21, already described neon signs appearing 'okkupantenhaft' in Berlin-Mitte.
[49]Heiner Müller, 'Mommsens Block', *SuF*, 45 (1993), 206-211 and reprinted in *Die Gedichte*, ed. by Hörnigk, pp.257-263. Page references in the text refer to the latter edition.

a motto Gottfried Benn's phrase 'Schaurige Welt, kapitalistische Welt'. The title borrowed from Conrad's story clearly equates capitalism with colonial exploitation.[50] In the story, Kurtz's last words before he dies are 'The horror! The horror!', from which Müller derives the last line of his poem: 'THE HORROR THE HORROR THE HORROR' (25). The arrival of capitalism in the GDR is presented through certain human figures – again, colonizing businessmen, but also the 'Hure Gastarbeiterin' (3) and infants festooned with signboards, advertising the fact that they were in the West on 9 November 1989. The poet's own horror is clear in the crass characterization: capitalist woman is an exploited whore and capitalist man a brash City-type, carving up Asia. As this poem presents an invented quotation from the businessmen's dialogue, so an untitled poem of 1993 (*Die Gedichte*, p.273) presents the voice of a New York taxi driver:

Ein Taxifahrer in New York ein Rumäne
Sagte zu mir YOU GERMAN GERMANY GOOD
DO YOU KNOW THAT HITLER WAS CRAZY YES
Sagte ich BUT DO YOU KNOW WHY
Sagte er BECAUSE HE DIDNT KILL ALL JEWS   (lines 12-16)

The poet echoes the words he purports to have heard and can only conclude with irony, 'So wird die Welt verständlich das Leben / Leicht' (24-25). The shocking, warped rantings of this immigrant American reflect the warped world, as Müller perceives it; a far cry from Marx, with whose name the poem began. The brutality, which is quoted without commentary, is elsewhere conveyed in laconic descriptions of death, such as the poem 'Stadtverkehr' (*Die Gedichte*, p.265).

Stadtverkehr
Eine Frau beim Warten auf Grün an der Kreuzung
Prüft ihre Fingernägel Ein Bild aus der Werbung
Zehn Minuten später wird sie tot sein Und steht
Morgen in der Zeitung zum erstenundletztenmal
20.1.1993

Death as casual and meaningless is part of the indictment of a world of speed and images. Life is an advertising image and death mediated by the newspaper. The proximity of death ironizes the woman's vanity and moment of fame.

Mensching's collection *Berliner Elegien* portrays the West within the same parameters as Müller's poetry: it is invariably represented as exclusively urban, rushed and overly full (with glittering advertisements and virtual

---

[50]Joseph Conrad, *Heart of Darkness, Three Short Novels* (New York: Bantam, 1960), pp.1-94.

images). In the poem 'Gefühlsstau A9' (*Berliner Elegien*, p.36) driving in traffic is a metaphor for western life (as it is in Hensel's poem 'Im Stau' discussed above). Assonance and a tripping rhythm push one's reading onwards: the imperative to get on ('das Rennen') is embodied in the poem's form.

<u>Gefühlsstau A9</u>

Bei Dessau, im Stau, schöne Fata Morgana, dein Name,
JA-NA, dein Bild, im Qualm, auf dem Nummerschild
Eines LKW, mitten im Pulk. Ein Wink, ein Zeichen
Der Götter, ein Ulk? Blasse Mauritius, seltenstes Stück
5   Der Erfahrung, zu dir, zum Glück, zur Natur, muß ich nur,
Raus aus dem Rennen, zum Ursprung zurück. Nomen
Est omen. Singende Gnomen, ins Strauchwerk gedrückt,
An den Straßenrändern: *Du mußt, du mußt dein Leben
Ändern.* Hört sie denn keiner? Zehntausend Rainer,
10   Marias und Rilkes rufen hupend die Polizei, zur Hölle
Mit euch! Kupplung und Gas und vorbei und vorbei.

The poem expresses bitterness and anger at the spiritual poverty of modern life: in the fumes of a traffic jam the lyric subject sees a lorry's number plate as an omen. Rilke's prescription (8-9) from the first poem of *Der Neuen Gedichte anderer Teil* is drowned in car horns, unheard by all except the lyric subject.[51] By another metaphorical motorway where everyone else is rushing on their way, a man who feels redundant commits suicide, in Mensching's poem 'Der Frührentner' (*Berliner Elegien*, p.43). Lack of a suicide note and the apparent oblivion of the wife illustrate his utter isolation. The death notice by an omniscient poet is reminiscent of Müller's 'Stadtverkehr':

Der Frührentner, der über das Leergut gebeugt,
Die Tabletten einsteckt, die Frau küßt, sagt, warte
Nicht mit dem Mittag und, Wochen später,
Entdeckt wird, in einer Schonung, nah der Autobahn,
5   Ohne Abschiedsbrief, neben einem Nylonbeutel
Mit leeren Flaschen und Reiseprospekten

The grammatical construction of the poem, as a series of relative clauses describing the subject, sets up expectation of a main verb which never appears. This effect, and the many commas breaking up lines, create unease. The objects of the final line have symbolic value: they recall the utopian

---

[51]Rainer Maria Rilke, 'Archäischer Torso Apollos', *Der Neuen Gedichte anderer Teil* (Leipzig: Insel, 1923), p.1.

implications of 'Flaschenpost' in GDR discourse and a population 'Unterwegs nach Utopia'.[52] This piece and 'Stadtverkehr' are laconic glimpses of everyday deaths. Circumstances are described without comment, reflecting the pitiless world.

Mensching includes eleven portrait poems of artists in *Berliner Elegien*, many of which reflect capitalist, materialistic society of the present day. The portrait poem 'Rimbaud 1' (*Berliner Elegien*, p.48) pertains to a poet's place in this world.[53] Mensching's portrayal of Rimbaud on a television talkshow recalls Franz Kafka's humanized monkey in 'Ein Bericht für eine Akademie' rather than Braun's invocations of him as a literary forefather.[54] The poet, 'Wunderkind von Charleville' (2), who had passionately denounced materialistic existence, abandoned literature at the age of twenty, travelled to Africa and concerned himself with becoming rich. Addicted to drugs, ego and money, vomiting blood in this poem, Rimbaud declares himself 'Ein Beispiel für Alles / Und Nichts' (12-13). These lines ironically recall Rimbaud as the great, inspiring poet ('Ein Beispiel für Alles'). Mensching renders Rimbaud an ultimately meritless example and typical: he sold out, as the GDR did, and embraced colonial exploitation. In C.A. Hackett's words, Rimbaud 'lived out the values of a materialistic age to their absurd and terrible conclusion' as a trader in coffee, skins and ivory (akin to the trader of Conrad's *Heart of Darkness*, whom Müller invokes above).[55] In the second Rimbaud poem, 'Rimbaud 2' (*Berliner Elegien*, p.49), he is part of the post-unification opposition between losers and victors: the opening phrase in effect describes the poem as 'der Spleen der Verlierer' (1), whereas at the end, Rimbaud is 'ein verlorner Mann / Der in der Haut des Siegers tanzen kann' (15-16). In both Rimbaud portrait poems, Mensching uses the figure of Rimbaud to address conversion to materialism, and the barbaric quality of western civilization.

Mensching's post-GDR poems show a fascination with the crass face of capitalism, similar to that in Müller's. The poem which begins 'Rot hat verloren' (*Berliner Elegien*, p.43) invites the equation of red and communism; it suggests life is literally a gambling table where the bank clears up:

[52]For example, Harald Gerlach, 'Flaschenpost', in *Ein Molotow-Cocktail*, ed. by Geist, p.284; Günter Kunert, *Unterwegs nach Utopia*.
[53]For the prevalence and implications of portrait poems in the 1980s, see Wolfgang Braune-Steininger, 'Das Fremde im Eigenen: Zur lyrischen Biographie der achtziger Jahre', in *Lyriker Treffen Münster*, ed. by Jordan, pp.250-271.
[54]Franz Kafka, *Sämtliche Erzählungen*, ed. by Paul Raabe (Frankfurt a.M. and Hamburg: Fischer, 1970), pp.147-155. Braun, 'Rimbaud: Ein Psalm der Aktualität'.
[55]C.A. Hackett, *Rimbaud* (London: Bowes and Bowes, 1957), p.91.

Rot hat verloren. Die Bank
Räumt ab. Jetzt setzt man
Auf Schwarz. *Fait votre jeux.*
Die Kugel rollt weiter.
5   Nichts gilt mehr, Genossen, adieu.

Tragically, all is chance, the roulette ball rolls again and the old is no longer valid.[56] Like the traffic, an unnoticed suicide and colonialism in the three poems above, gambling is a caricature of western life. Such caricatures express the poet's alienation. In 'Während der Regen' (*Berliner Elegien*, pp.38-39) Mensching uses the image of being trapped by a new wall: 'eine neue Mauer [...] / Die ich nicht mehr begreife / Die mich schmerzt und festhält / In dieser anderen Welt' (33-36) reiterates the experience of 'Fremdheit', as in Müller's poem 'Schwarzfilm' (*Die Gedichte*, p.275) where 'Alles Menschliche / Wird fremd' (12-13).[57] Life is virtual in Mensching's 'Simulis simulis' (*Berliner Elegien*, p.15).[58] This title evokes simulation and imitation; the poem goes on to describe life as the 'unerschöpflicher Fundus / der Automatenhersteller' (1-2). Computer jargon implies a pervasive virtual reality: everything, including labyrinths and 'Himmel' (5), is reduced to the span of the screen. Quotations from Hamlet and from Marx allude to literature and ideology, whilst exemplifying how meagre and reductive this appropriation is: '*Online* sein oder nicht sein, / *Basic* und Überbau' (6-7). When however, 'der Fehler' (10), the system error, occurs, all action is in vain, the human 'du' is a mere passenger who can do nothing. Impending doom is also announed by the title 'Liquidation totale'.[59] Here Mensching evokes with sarcasm the sordid, hedonistic side of western commercialism, putting Hegel on television as he did Rimbaud above.

Liquidation totale
Euphorie , Katzenjammer. Freundliche Marktlage
Für einfache Kausalketten.

---

[56]Roulette is also a metaphor for German history in the title of Barbara Köhler's 1991 collection *Deutsches Roulette* and Gabriele Stötzer's collection *Erfurter Roulette* (Munich: Kirchheim, 1995).
[57]Compare the awful ambiguity expressed in Mensching's earlier poem in *Tuchfühlung: Gedichte* (Halle-Leipzig: mdv, 1986), p.24 in the lines 'mehr als ich wünsche, weggehen zu können / möchte ich hier bleiben müssen'.
[58]'Simulis simulis' is also the title of a set of poems from the collection which were published earlier in *ndl*, 40 (1992), No.4, 31-36.
[59]Steffen Mensching, 'Liquidation totale', in *Von einem Land*, pp.112-113, and reprinted in *Berliner Elegien*, pp.70-71.

Herr Hegel, Philosophieprofessor, Berlin, gewinnt
Alle Ratespiele im Frühstücksfernsehn.

5   Davon ab. Etwas Bescheidenheit
Steht dir ganz gut zu Gesicht, insofern

Das Schlachtfeld mit Augen
So genannt werden kann.

Oversized, oversized. Modische Kapriolen,
10 Overalls, Schultern wie *Superman.*

Ansonsten alles eine Nummer kleiner, geschrumpft
Auf menschliches Maß. Ego ist in.

Morus-Campanella-Sonnenstaat AG, klimatisiert
Und vorgebräunt zu den globalen Wühltischen.

15 Davon ab. *Was Sie wirklich suchen,*
Finden Sie hier. Headline

Im Schaufenster, Sexshop Bahnhof Zoo.
Leicht gesagt. Schwer

Von der Hand zu weisen. Ach, führe uns
20 Nicht in Versuchung. Apropos,

Der Spielautomat, Pizzeria Winsstraße
Heißt *Utopia.* Weiblicher Schlitz

Für harte männliche Münzen.
Faß das nicht an, das

25   Wirst du nicht los. O Gott
O Schrott

Nimm deinen weißen Arsch
Und tanz die Tarantella.

The selection of words and impressions conveys a rejection of capitalism as cheap and immoral. The phrase 'Davon ab', interpolated twice, intimates the habit of switching between television channels. The name of the limited company in line 13 alludes to two visions of the impossible, ideal state, namely Thomas More's *Utopia* of 1516 and Thomas Campanella's *Civitas*

Solis of 1623. A marketing motto, '*Was Sie wirklich suchen / Finden sie hier*', points to the bankruptcy of values. A line from the Lord's Prayer (19-20) is ironically interpolated amongst the temptations to gamble and spend, and God is just an exclamation which rhymes (25). Accumulated tokens of modern living recreate a contemporary world, that has reached an apotheosis of superficiality and indifference. The poem 'In der Peep-Show' (*Berliner Elegien*, p.44) also renders voyeuristic, mediated eroticism a representative aspect of this world. Women, sex, even shame, have become commodities to be purchased. The location 'Rosa-Luxemburg-Straße' (1), a street in Berlin-Mitte, ironically evokes the young communist martyr, a heroine of socialism. She is implicitly compared to the strippers, 'arbeitslose Kommunistinnen' (2).[60] A mocking voice addressing 'meine Herren' (3) is the counterpart to that seedy, cynical voice in 'Liquidation totale' which declared 'Nimm deinen weißen Arsch / Und tanz die Tarantella'. The tesserae of these poems together portray a place characterized by Emile Durkheim's 'anomie'.[61] A cascade of impressions shows what shocks the poet from the GDR. His poems reflect back the external world. Comparing his recent with his earlier poems, Mensching has posited, 'Möglicherweise sind die jüngeren Texte einsamer, ihre Wut abgeklärter, ihr Schmerz kälter'.[62] The poems discussed here exemplify these characteristics. The human self has become merely an implied 'surface' on which gathers a welter of projected images and borrowed words. This lyric voice is like the 'ich' in Kristian Pech's poem, 'Fotos', 'Ich der voyeur der sammler der nostalgiker / [...] Ich der fotoästhet ich der fernsehzuschauer'.[63]

Bert Papenfuß's long poem *mors ex nihilo* parallels Mensching's 'simulis'-poetry in criticizing the modern world through the evocation of a cheapened existence dominated by commerce.[64] The clarity of this theme and the poem's language represent a marked departure from Papenfuß's earlier work, as though the urgency of the theme precludes the most indulgent

---

[60]Compare Mensching's earlier love poem to Rosa Luxemburg entitled 'Traumhafter Ausflug mit Rosa L.', in which she is 'meine Freundin'. See *Poetenseminare 1970-1984*, Poesiealbum Sonderheft (Berlin, GDR: Neues Leben, 1985), pp.49-50
[61]See *Readings from Emile Durkheim*, ed. by Kenneth Thompson (England: Ellis Horwood, 1985), p.108-112. In discussing suicide, Durkheim concludes that when society is disturbed, either by a painful crisis or by favourable but abrupt changes (and the 'Wende' has been interpreted as both of these), then it temporarily ceases to be a regulating authority over people's actions. Anomie is a state of deregulation, a lack of human law and moral discipline.
[62]Letter to me, 9 December 1998.
[63]Kristian Pech, 'Fotos' in *Ein Molotow-Cocktail*, ed. by Geist, p.89.
[64]Papenfuß, *mors ex nihilo* (Berlin: Galrev, 1994).

phoneme-games. *Mors ex nihilo* is addressed to 'genossen', 'kamaraden' and 'kollegen' (4-5):

> genossen, unterdruß im unterschlupf,
> kameraden, verrat ist unaufhaltbar; kollegen,
> lassen wir uns nicht lumpen: alles wird teurer,
> wir aber, im einklang mit unserer zielgruppe,
> senken unsere preise: das kapital ist machbar,
> herr nachbar, "big bank take little bank":
> bekannt durch fresse, buschfunk, rundflunk &
> teleflax: sarg-discount christburger bietet an:
> selbstbestattungen aller arten, erledigung
> aller formalitäten, sämtliche pietätsartikel,
> drucksachen, blumendekoration, heraldische
> elemente, überurnen, memoiren, literarischer
> nachlaß, copyright-probleme, auf wunsch
> hausbesuche   (lines 4-17)

Papenfuß parodies commercial offers, in the role of a cabarettist. Death, literal and metaphorical, is the main theme, here the commercialization of death for instance, and at the end of the passage above, the commercialization of literature (with echoes of the role of the Stasi and the censor in the GDR). Death characterizes the quotations in English in the poem: they are the words of a murderer and of men about to be executed: 'I thought it would be a good thing for this / country to kill the president, I done my duty' (197-198), 'this is about as good a day as any to die' (289), and 'I came here to die not make a speech' (306). The poem closes with 'dulce et decorum' (484), already taken up as the 'old Lie' in Wilfred Owen's First World War poem on death.[65] Again, the death of the GDR is thematized as murder and suicide in the new state, in stupid scenarios which mock clichéd obituaries:

> 7.12.92: tod des gauleiters von balkenbiege-
> klingespring durch totlieben unter vielen
> schwerthieben; in allen ehren
> 9.12.92: tod des betagten buletten-orjes
> vom alexanderplatz durch propangasbrand
> von proletenhand; gott zum gruße [...]
> 13.12: tod des präfekten & heerführers von
> ausbau-west durch gift, dolch, aufschwung ost
> & auftakt-nord; in liebe und dankbarkeit (lines 227-232, 239-241)

The notion of poetry which sets out to be offensive and tasteless is familiar from Papenfuß's earlier work, but this is a more sophisticated poem which departs from earlier play with phonemes. It is published alone, with no page

---

[65]Wilfred Owen, 'Dulce Et Decorum Est', *The Collected Poems* (London: Chatto & Windus, 1968), p.55.

numbers, but line numbers, and consists of three parts: 'prolog auf dem schirm' (1) (rather than a Goethean prologue in heaven), 'der eigentliche mors' (54) and 'nachspiel im stall' (436). The text is not continuous, but broken by epigrams and sayings which can stand alone in the middle of a page, such as the following:

> *ein blick auf den zins, gesell*
> *blick sie auf den DAX, mademoiselle*
> *der rentenmarkt tendiert ohr über's fell* (lines 87-89)

Papenfuß uses a montage of language, typically parodying the language of financial markets and of popular idioms, and mocking middle-class values. Some of the language becomes abstruse and inaccessible, but even this fits the theme of a society which has lost touch with art and has reduced language. Numbers (for dates and for prices) and abbreviations (DAX, dm, ggf., MEGA, u.a.w.g., m.b.h., TWAR) clatter through the poem as ciphers of this reduction. Snapshots of news items, such as the homeless man who broke into the queen's apartment at Buckingham Palace or the Lillehammer winter games, break into the text, but it is mostly located in areas of East Berlin, whose street names and districts are scattered as adjectives. Papenfuß rescues many GDR words in this piece and uses language which generally withdraws from immediate comprehension, as if setting up poetic language in resistence to the new society. The reviewer Jürgen Engler describes the poem as an anarchic death-dance: 'Das Poem ist eine Art anarchischer Totentanz, ein Tanz der Worte, Wahrnehmungen, Assoziationen, wie sie einem durch den Kopf schießen'.[66] A cascade of attacks on different aspects of society conveys the anarchic anger of 'der bandit' (307).

Alison Lewis attributes attacks on the immorality of capitalism to an experience of the GDR regime: 'A tendency towards moralistic asceticism is also very much a legacy of SED socialism'.[67] Anti-capitalist gestures in poetry by Müller, Mensching and Papenfuß, however, can hardly be attributed to the SED: on the contrary, it is the legacy of GDR utopianism, not the real, existing SED regime, which influenced these writers, different as they are. Müller, Mensching and Papenfuß express horror at the wantonness of western society. They also echo the denigration of consumerism and commerce, which has been articulated by some western intellectuals.[68] In the surge of romantic, anti-

---

[66]Jürgen Engler, 'Vom Herzversagen der Poesie', *ndl*, 43 (1995), No.5, 152-155 (p.154).
[67]Alison Lewis, 'Unity begins together: Analyzing the Traumas of German Unification', *New German Critique*, 64 (1995), 135-159 (p.151).
[68]See for instance poetry by Günter Grass, Bruno Hillebrand, Yaak Karsunke and Thomas Kielinger.

capitalist feeling there is perhaps solidarity, or what Lewis terms 'an imagined sense of identity that is anti-Germanic, antimodernist and antimaterialist' (p.159). This is an interesting idea in relation to the identity of GDR intellectuals and writers after unification. The role of the poet seems to be inextricable from the culture versus civilization conflict, which was articulated intermittently throughout the GDR years. In the 1990s the poet takes the role of cabarettist, attacking society's crass materialism.

A number of poems of the period parallel the poet and the beggar in united Germany, expressing solidarity with a victim of capitalism, as in Hensel's beggar poem 'Auskunft gewünscht' (*Freistoß*, p.8). Here the beggar's voice breaks in in italics, '*HassemaneMark?*' (3) and '*HassemaKleingeld?*' (8). The poem makes an ironic play on the name 'Gesundbrunnen' (a place where beggars congregate in Berlin) in order to forefront the plight of the underclass. In Michael Wüstefeld's 1992 poem 'Wie ich aus Amsterdam nach Dresden zurückgeholt wurde', the lyric subject is taken for a beggar by tourists: [69]

> Sie verstehen die Sprache meiner Frage nicht
> Und legen mir einen Gulden in die sprachlos offene Hand (p.43)

A different kind of identification with figures from the underclass is implied in Mensching's poem 'Panem et circenses' (*Berliner Elegien*, p.26). These 'Trickkünstler' (7) become metaphors for the writer-artist. The Latin title is a line from one of Juvenal's *Satires* in which he mocks the people for their new obsession with bread and circuses.[70] Juvenal's renowned *saeva indignatio* is not unrelated to Mensching's satire on the greed and wantonness of the new Germany. Mensching's poem focuses on the immigrants who take bets on matchbox tricks (they can be seen at Alexanderplatz, Berlin). Three aspects are picked out in the poem: deception, the nomadic life, and gambling and losing. The tricksters are 'Psychologen / Des Alltags' (3-4), 'Verlierer' (6) and 'Nomaden mit zweifelhaften Papieren' (7). Their art is the dance of matchboxes and sleight-of-hand, for the sake of deceiving:

> alle Köpfe hier
> Wissen um den Betrug. So ist das Leben. Den Betrüger betrügen. (lines 10-11)

Their 'art' of deception is an indictment of the new society but also of art itself, which is somehow dodgy or not entirely honest.[71] Kurt Drawert's poem 'In

---

[69]Michael Wüstefeld, 'Wie ich aus Amsterdam nach Dresden zurückgeholt wurde', *Deutsche Anatomie*, pp.42-43.
[70]'The people that once bestowed commands, consulships, legions and all else, now meddles no more and longs eagerly for just two things - bread and games!' Juvenal, *Satires*, x, 'The Vanity of Human Wishes', line 81, in *Juvenal and Persius*, trans. by G. G. Ramsey (London: Heinemann, 1918), p.99.
[71]In *Berliner Elegien* Mensching's lyric 'ich' articulates personal shame, whereas various anti-bourgeois artist figures (Beckmann, Courbet, Klee) earn his respect.

Wien' draws together 'Penner' and poetological statement in a more personal way:[72]

Dichtung,
sagen freundlich die einen

zu den falschen inneren Bildern,
die man, mit gebrochener Stimme,
verkaufte. Dichtung, sagt man freundlich
sich selbst und schaut
auf beschriebene Seiten.   (lines 4-10)

These lines imply an unspoken shame – the lyric subject understands himself as a poet who sells false images which are indulged with the title 'Dichtung'. Drawert's usage implicitly plays on the opposition between 'Dichtung' and 'Wahrheit'. The word 'verkaufte', delayed by the insertion of a prepositional phrase, falls in a position of emphasis at the beginning of line 8. Across the sentence break it forms 'verkaufte Dichtung'. This lyric subject's social solidarity is expressed as a memory:

Ich hatte den Penner
vor Augen, vor einem Schuhgeschäft
auf der Habsburgergasse, im Schneidersitz
hockte er friedlich am Boden,
versöhnt mit der Kälte des Tages,
versöhnt mit allem, was keinen Sinn gibt (lines 22-27)

The hopeless tramp reflects the 'Wende' revolution:

Es war ein Blick wie von Hunden,
die keine Zukunft mehr haben,
so wie man ihn oft auch nach Revolutionen
zu sehen bekommt.   (lines 37-40)

Müller also expresses unhappiness at social inequalities around him and draws attention to this in poetry, for instance in 'Müller im hessischen Hof' (*Die Gedichte*, pp.253-254):

Der schlafende Penner vor ESSO SNACK&SHOP
Widerlegt die Lyrik der Revolution
Ich fahre im Taxi vorbei (p.253)

This poem, dated 'Frankfurt, 3.10.1992', sets the figure of a tramp against the material well-being that the revolution was to achieve. It articulates personal shame, and a sense that the 'poetry of revolution' failed. The title invites an equation of lyric 'ich' and poet, which heightens the seriousness of this expression of shame. And this has implications for the role of poetry:

MÜLLER SIE SIND KEIN POETISCHER GEGENSTAND
SCHREIBEN SIE PROSA Meine Scham braucht mein Gedicht (p.254)

---

[72]Kurt Drawert, 'In Wien', *Wo es war*, pp.61-62

This shame is not about the past (as in Braun's 'ich schäme mich, mit Schweinen gekämpft zu haben' or Müller's own 'welches Grab schützt mich vor meiner Jugend')[73], but about a present in which the poet drives by in a taxi, like a passer-by in the story of the Good Samaritan. Indeed he calls himself a 'Lehrstück', an illustration of what is wrong with the world. The poem serves as a means to still the conscience, a new type of 'useful' poetry.[74] 'Lernprozess' (Die Gedichte, p.269) juxtaposes Lenin with a self who is learning not to notice beggars and the plight of the homeless. This poem too is hijacked by personal guilt. Vilified along with the discredited ideology in 1989/90, intellectuals have had to come to terms with a new identity. One element of that identity is being the defeated. But the personal sense of shame in the poetry has its origin less in relation to writing under the old GDR regime and more in relation to being a published writer in the new Germany.

In Mensching's Berliner Elegien and Müller's late poetry there is remarkable use of quotations. These particularly come from advertisements and from foreign languages, usually English. In either case, the use of such quotations introduces strange, 'other' languages to the poem.[75] I have already alluded to Müller's quotations from Conrad's English narrator and from a taxi driver in America. Even where he purports to quote German-speaking businessmen in 'Mommsens Block' and in 'Herz der Finsternis nach Joseph Conrad', he effectively quotes a 'foreign' language, the dispassionate language of business. In Mensching there is recycling of television blurb: the warning which accompanies television adverts for pharmaceuticals, 'Über Risiken und Nebenwirkungen, lesen Sie die Packungsbeilage oder fragen Sie Ihren Arzt oder Apotheker', is taken up in the poem 'Äh' (Berliner Elegien, p.27), and television news items feature in 'Drei Grauwale' (Berliner Elegien, p.37). Mensching's

---

[73]Volker Braun, 'Schreiben im Schredder', ndl, 43 (1995), No.4, 5-7. Müller, 'Fernsehen', Die Gedichte, p.233.

[74]Compare Heinz Czechowski's description of the conscience heard above all the news and information, in his poem 'Gestörte Verhältnisse' (Nachtspur, pp.177-179):

> Mein schlechtes Gewissen
> Richtet sich auf. Im Überfluß
> Aller Nachrichten hör ich auf meine innere Stimme. Dies,
> Wie fast alles, hat keine
> Allgemeine Bedeutung. (p.179)

[75]For theoretical discussions of quotation see Peter Horst Neumann, 'Das Eigene und das Fremde: Über die Wünschbarkeit einer Theorie des Zitierens', Akzente 27 (1980), 292-305; Volker Klotz, 'Zitat und Montage in neuer Literatur und Kunst', Sprache im technischen Zeitalter (1976), No.57, 259-277; Klaus Laermann, 'Vom Sinn des Zitierens', Merkur 38 (1984), 672-681; Steven Taubeneck, 'Zitat als Realität, Realität als Zitat', Arcadia, 19 (1984), 269-277.

poem 'Tabula rasa' (*Berliner Elegien*, pp.5-6) takes up ciphers from contemporary life: the brand names 'Doktor Oetker' and 'Beate Uhse', 'Alzheimer' a cipher for memory-loss, 'Sean Connery als Thomas von Aquino' a cipher for the glib gloss of Hollywood. In addition, the poem 'Nix Kühnheit nix' (*Berliner Elegien*, p.25) is a montage of different languages, including German, English, French, Spanish and Latin. In 'Liquidation totale', English 'Fremdwörter' ('oversized', 'Superman', 'Sexshop', 'Headline', 'in') suggest modish American imports. The use of quotation in these instances dominates whole poems and thematizes a distinction between what is owned and what is alien. The German poet is using language newly imported into the culture of eastern Germany, language which seems strange in a poem and which thus points to an alien colonizing of the East. Imported expressions also call into question the poem itself which is overrun and colonized.

Other poets beside Müller and Mensching use quotation, for instance Gerlach in 'Utopia' where the words 'Shake hands' and 'Coca Cola' signal the American-influenced western world. Quoting here involves breaking off a fragment which can stand for a whole. In the same way, Drawert quotes Ludwig Uhland's line 'Nun muß sich alles, alles wenden' from 'Frühlingsglaube' to embody the sense of hope and purpose alive in the Enlightenment.[76] (Not only is the 1812 poem 'Frühlingsglaube' about imperative change, but Uhland himself was a politically active poet, social reformer and spokesman for German unification.) Other signals of this Enlightenment world are 'Sinclair' and 'Diotima' in Gerlach's 'Utopia'. As 'Wir sind das Volk' signals the 'Wende' demonstrations or an extract from the GDR national anthem 'Auferstanden aus Ruinen' signals socialist aspirations, quotations can flag particular points in history, or call up particular historical moods. At the same time, reproducing an extant phrase interrupts the poem, drawing attention to its construction and the poet's labour in writing it. Prevalent quotation thus reflects writing itself as a theme of the post-unification period.

Writing is a crucial theme in Müller's 'Mommsens Block', which uses quotation on a large scale. Horst Domdey has stated, 'The emphasis in *Mommsens Block* is less on coming to terms with the failure of socialism (apparently the 'product of a false reading') than on the rejection of the West'.[77] Whilst rejection of the West is emphasized in the final quarter of the text, I

---

[76]Drawert, 'Das bleibt nun so', *Wo es war*, p.75. Ludwig Uhland, 'Frühlingsglaube', in *Das Oxforder Buch der deutschen Dichtung vom 12ten bis zum 20sten Jahrhundert*, ed. by H.G. Fiedler (Oxford: OUP, 1930), p.247.

[77]Horst Domdey, 'Writer's Block, or 'John on Patmos in the Haze of a Drug High': Heiner Müller's Lyrical Text Mommsens Block', trans. by Colin Hall, in *Heiner Müller: ConTEXTS and HISTORY*, ed. by Fischer, pp.233-241 (p.239).

would argue that more dominant in the poem as a whole is the theme of writing itself. Socialism is indeed attributed to wrongly reading Marx and capitalism in the new Germany is said to follow another textbook. The poem begins with Mommsen's unwritten book and ends in his library. The whole is a protracted identification with the 'Geschichtsschreiber', Theodor Mommsen, who won the Nobel Prize for Literature in 1902 for his *History of Rome* (published in three volumes, 1854-1856), which was incomplete. 'Mommsens Block' is a mental block which stops Mommsen writing the missing fourth volume. It is also the plinth on which Mommsen's statue stood, epitomizing petrification.[78] The 'ich' in the new Germany experiences history as a petrifying 'Schreibhemmung' (p.263). This inability to write is inscribed on the writer's body as a wound, from which blood, the very symbol of life, pours: 'der ungeschriebne Text ist eine Wunde' (p.263). In a sense this bleeding is the opposite of petrification: paradoxically, Mommsen's unwritten volume of his *History* inspired Müller to write his poem. As Gerd Labroisse indicates, Müller was also inspired by the book constructing Mommsen's unwritten volume from students' notes made at Mommsen's lectures on the Roman imperial period.[79] Frequent use of quotation from this volume supports a characterization of Müller's poem as concerned with writing and text. Thematization of 'Schreibhemmung' however prompts Labroisse to conclude, 'Hier entlarvt nicht bildkräftige Literatur die laufende Wirklichkeit, vielmehr entlarvt diese Heiner Müller in seinem Nicht-weiter-Kommen' (p.247). It seems to me that Müller does 'go further', particularly in exploring the relationship between writing and history. At the beginning of his poem, he sets the heaviness of history and politics against the weightlessness of literature. Later, Mommsen's library goes up in smoke, like the Alexandrian libraries destroyed by Christians thousands of years ago. The link emphasizes the fragility of literature. A rumour that Mommsen had written a manuscript is taken up by Nietzsche. The fire reported by newspapers and the story, told in Nietzsche's letter, becomes 'Ein Dokument' (p.260). Müller plays here with concepts of literature as epistle, reportage, document, myth, rumour and history. Intellectuals' responsibility is articulated in reference to texts which have been scanned by soldiers' boots. War and dictatorship are 'Produkt / Einer falschen Lektüre' – this is the danger of text – 'und fälschlich genannt / Sozialismus nach

---

[78]Compare Günter Kunert's discussion of 'der Sturz des Schriftstellers in Ost wie in West von seinem ihm bisher unbestrittenen Sockel', in Kunert, *Der Sturz vom Sockel*, p.68.
[79]Gerd Labroisse, 'Heiner Müllers "Endzeit" oder Wie die Wirklichkeit den Schriftsteller verrät', *GM*, 32 (1994), 229-247. Barbara and Alexander Demandt, eds., *Römische Kaisergeschichte. Nach Vorlesungs-Mitschriften von Sebastien und Paul Hensel 1882/86* (Munich: Beck, 1992).

dem großen Historiker / Des Kapitals' (p.261). The discrepancy between Marxism and its manifestation as the GDR is alluded to here, whilst Marx is implicitly compared to Mommsen by the epithet 'der große Historiker'. Three strands of history inform one another in 'Mommsens Block': Müller's own time in the new Germany, Mommsen's place in Bismarck's Germany, and ancient imperial Rome. These strands are linked by texts – an unwritten book, the constructed text in its place, and the poem of 1992 quoting the constructed text. It is the theme of text which thus inspires and structures the poem.

Müller's poetry is concerned with other historians, such as the writers of ancient history in the poems 'Rechtfindung' and 'Feldherrngefühle' (*Die Gedichte*, p.274 and p.289). In 'Klage des Geschichtschreibers' (*Die Gedichte*, p.246), the 'ich' identifies with Tacitus.

> Klage des Geschichtsschreibers
> Im vierten Band der ANNALEN beklagt sich Tacitus
> Über die Dauer der Friedenszeit, kaum unterbrochen
> Von läppischen Grenzkriegen, mit deren Beschreibung er
> Auskommen muß, voll Neid
> 5   Auf die Geschichtsschreiber vor ihm
> Denen Mammutkriege zur Verfügung standen
> Geführt von Kaisern, denen Rom nicht groß genug war
> Unterworfene Völker, gefangene Könige
> Aufstände und Staatskrisen: guter Stoff.
> 10   Und Tacitus entschuldigt sich bei seinen Lesern.
> Ich meinerseits, zweitausend Jahre nach ihm
> Brauche mich nicht zu entschuldigen und kann mich
> Nicht beklagen über Mangel an gutem Stoff.
>
> 16.8.1992

The ostensible point is ironic, for the topic of this poem is not in fact 'Aufstände und Staatskrisen', but the poetological matter of having a topic for writing. Müller is concerned with his role as a writer of history. He takes up a pose in this poem, saying he cannot complain about his material, but implying thereby that he has other complaints about 1989/90, or that good material can make it difficult to write too.

Confrontation with the new Germany seems to throw into question writing practices generally. Writing, it is stated in 'Mommsens Block', is undertaken 'ins Leere' and 'für die Toten' (p.260). Müller even self-consciously inserts the remark, 'Wer ins Leere schreibt braucht keine Interpunktion / Gestatten Sie daß ich von mir rede' (p.260). In Drawert's poem 'Geständnis', the poet 'ich' feels that he too is engaged in an 'Umgang / mit Toten' (*Wo es war*, p.42) and the lyric subject in Czechowski's 'Gestörte Verhältnisse' (*Nachtspur*, pp.177-179) declares 'hier teile ich meine Erinnerungen mit den Toten' (p.179). Such morbid reflections about the purpose of writing are typical of poetry by ex-GDR poets in the early 1990s. In Czechowski's poetry, which includes many poetological reflections in this period, there is also a 1992 poem ('Schreibtage', *Nachtspur*, pp.186-187) whose subject is poems about poems:

> Gedichte über Gedichte: so
> Verhurt man die besten Stunden des Tages.   (lines 6-7)
> [...]
> Was also sollen
> Die Tage, am Schreibtisch verbracht,
> Um Gedichte zu schreiben,
> Die nichts beweisen?   (lines 39-42)
> [...]
> Ich habe Mühe,
> Nicht zu sagen: So
> Ist das Leben. Doch was hat das Leben
> Mit meinen Gedichten zu tun?   (lines 49-52)

Poems where the lyric subject is a poet, clearly invite parallels betweeen the text-'ich' and the poet-'ich'. This kind of recuperation of the poet's presence could express a desire for stable categories in a profoundly destabilized historical context. In the vacuum, the poet feels he has no addressees and nothing to 'prove', writing has no bearing on life and becomes meaningless self-gratification (see the first two lines quoted above). Drawert's poem 'Ein goldener Herbst. Erfolgreiche Zeiten' (*Wo es war*, pp.18-19) addresses the writer's role, against a general sense of break-up:

> die Ideen des Jahrhunderts
> demontierten sich eben,
> wie Laubfall so etwa   (lines 5-7)

The end of ideology is here a demolition which is inextricable from contemporary problems of writing: the only writers now are 'echt coole Typen' (36) with whom the lyric subject does not identify himself. They were birds singing on the political telegraph wires, he claims bitterly, who now fly away to 'bessere Welten' (42).

> während du mit deinem versauten
> Verhältnis zur Wahrheit
> prompt in die Leerzeilen stolperst (lines 43-45)

A pre-'Wende' poem by Drawert asserted the concept of a shifting truth: 'Was Wahrheit ist, / ändert sich stündlich'.[80] The self in the poem of the 1990s cannot, it is implied, accept this and without the old relationship to truth he only produces 'Leerzeilen'. Müller in 'Besuch beim älteren Staatsmann' (*Die*

---

[80]Kurt Drawert, 'Vom Gehen und vom Zurückbleiben', *Privateigentum: Gedichte* (Frankfurt a.M.: Suhrkamp, 1989), pp.73-74.

Gedichte, pp.255-256) concludes that if truth is not the subject of literature then there is nothing:

Nichts fühlte ich nichts nichts nichts nur die bittere Leere
Beim Zuhören hinter Gerüchten Mythen Legenden
Tauchen die Nachrichten auf wird mein Blick
Auf seine Hände zum Spiegelblick [...]
Was geht mich die Welt an Ich
Esse ihre Bilder Die Wahrheit WAHRHEIT
Ist kein Gegenstand   (p.256)

Müller, like Drawert, expresses a sense of vacuum after the disillusionment with truth as a stable category. The look reflected back, the 'Spiegelblick', indicates a sense of nothing outside; one is only turned back to oneself. In Müller's 1995 poem 'Vampir' (*Die Gedichte*, p.317) mirrors have replaced walls:

Statt Mauern stehen Spiegel um mich her
Mein Blick sucht mein Gesicht Das Glas bleibt leer (lines 8-9)

A vampire is an image of a dark, blood-sucking 'ich'. The image of the hall of empty mirrors, part of the vampire myth, also expresses a loss of self here. This lyric subject is trapped by myriad reflections of his own emptiness, which is attributed to the break-up of political power:

Zerstoben ist die Macht an der mein Vers
Sich brach wie Brandung regenbogenfarb (lines 4-5)

Now, it is implied, there is no solid object to write against, but a vacuum. After unification there is no need for writers to assume political responsibility and no need for contraband. Colin B. Grant states that the collapse of the system in 1989/90 'deprived some writers of the polar (attracting) opposite of their writing and jeopardized the dynamic of their writing practices'.[81] Müller's image reflects this point.

The sense of losing a purposeful topic is conveyed in several other poems. Drawert entitles a poem 'Nichts' (p.66) and the word recurs in both the first two lines. After the loss of truth and utopia, the poem itself becomes a directionless wandering:

Auf nichts ein Gedicht,
schön wie nichts tun,
vielleicht noch ein langsames,
zielloses Gehen,

eine kurze Empfindung,
die man für sich selber
benötigt oder der Liebe
an einem Nachmittag schenkt (lines 1-8)

Poetry has humble aspirations here: it is written for almost no-one, just the poet

---

[81]Grant, *Literary Communication*, p.156.

himself or perhaps for his beloved. As one long sentence of six stanzas, flowing across line- and stanza-breaks, this poem exemplifies the 'zielloses Gehen' (4), which might be of value in itself. In Hensel's poem 'Der neue Ton' (*Freistoß*, pp.60-61) gestures of inactivity include writing about nothing:

Und nun – groß durchatmen
Im abgefuckten Jahrhundert, die Hände
Tief in den Hosentaschen, vom Nichts
Dichten   (lines 1-4)

The deep breath of the opening blew away hope, even though hope was a big sign in capital letters 'das Stoppschild / HOFFNUNG' (22-23). This playful image conveys the idea that the hope, which gave writing direction, is gone. Günter Kunert's post-'Wende' poem 'Bekennerbrief' focuses on an ex-GDR poet's disorientation.[82] The poet is 'leer' (1) and 'erblindet' (2). Alienation from human society is a theme that can be traced through the words 'verlassen' (3), 'Einsamkeit' (9) and 'unbeachtet' (12). An image of empty houses particularly draws on the complex of images of structure and edifice in Kunert's earlier work, and again reflects the loss of the GDR project.[83] Lines 6 and 7 show the ambiguity of the poet's new freedom: 'Kein Wort lohnt mehr / Die Bewachung'. Once, every word a poet wrote was carefully scrutinized. Now a lack of any solid, certain entity to say 'ich' or 'du' or 'wir' suggests a lack of self. The lyric 'ich' of Kunert's 'Biographie' finds he is 'selber entronnen'.[84] It is as if the writer's whole identity lay in the struggle against the censor and against the Stasi.

In 1992 Jan Faktor declares, in a long poem, 'wir brauchen eine neue lyrik', implying that the old poetry is now invalid.[85] Characteristically for Faktor, this text is structured by repetition, here the repetition of 'lyrik die' at the opening of lines. The poem describes the new poetry which he seeks. Personification points to poetry itself needing to become a solid figure:

wir brauchen eine neue lyrik [...]
lyrik die mit würde holzkekse kauen kann [...]
lyrik die logarithmische kurven mit fußnoten verunstaltet [...]
lyrik die bei bedarf tief in die eigenen kniekehlen schaut [...]
lyrik die vormittags beim kohleschleppen hormonell-hysterisch wird [...]
lyrik die sich auf unzulässiger art und weise sich bückt   (pp.4-8)

---

[82]Günter Kunert, 'Bekennerbrief', 'Durch die leeren Häuser der Dichter: Vier neue Gedichte', *NR*, 104 (1993), 147-150, p.149, and reprinted in *Mein Golem*, p.19.
[83]The empty houses of 'Bekennerbrief' are empty cattle sheds in Hensel's 'Trauer Arbeit' and empty rooms in Hilbig's 'prosa meiner heimatstraße'.
[84]Günter Kunert, 'Biographie', in *Grenzfallgedichte*, p.98.
[85]Jan Faktor, 'wir brauchen eine neue lyrik', *Litfass* 16 (1992), No.54, 4-9. Despite the demand for a new poetry, this text bears a striking resemblance to Faktor's earlier manifestos. See for instance 'Manifeste der Trivialpoesie', in *Georgs Versuche an einem Gedicht*, pp.87-102.

This sample of lines from the poem conveys the personification of poetry as a fallible human: what begins as a manifesto, pointing to bold, provoking poetry, becomes a sarcastic rendition of human failings. As the inventory goes on, it becomes a mockery of a poetry that would suit the new Germany. In many poems then, the purposefulness of writing is called into question. Poets bitterly suggest that their subject is Nothing and their addressees are dead; their writing is no longer truth set against others' lies, but an undirected and thus directionless activity, which is ultimately hopeless.

This shift in the status of writing is illustrated by the development after 1989/90 of one motif which was associated with the poet's role in the GDR. Sisyphus, for whom the gods devised a famous punishment, was a figure recurrently appropriated by GDR poets from the mid-1970s onwards.[86] His task, of rolling up a hill a stone which always rolls down just before the summit, provides an image of endless labour. This was employed as a metaphor for the GDR poet's enterprise. Uwe Kolbe spoke out in the 1980s as a member of the young literary generation casting the older generation's political engagement as 'Sisyphosarbeit'.[87] Kolbe's poem 'Sisyphos' from his 1980 collection also exemplifies the association between Sisyphus and the archetypal writer.[88] The lyric 'ich' in this poem is a writer who identifies his writing with Sisyphus's stone: it always ends up back at the beginning. Günter Kunert's 1977 poem 'Aufgabe' plays with an equation of 'Hoffnung' and 'jener Marmorblock, / der mir immer aufs neue entglitt'.[89] In Hans Brinkmann's poem 'Sisyphos' from his *Poesiealbum* collection of 1981, Sisyphus's stone also embodies hope: '[er] sieht die Hoffnung zu Tal fahrn'.[90] In the GDR (though rarely elsewhere), Sisyphus's labour encapsulates perseverance: hope should keep being raised anew by the socialist writer. Sisyphus is then a figure explicitly related to the GDR writer and the 'Prinzip Hoffnung'. This association is maintained in some post-'Wende' poems and provides a way of discussing the changes made to the poet's role. In Drawert's contemplative poem 'Sisyphos' (*Wo es war*, p.10), Sisyphus's labour is over.[91] The stone associated with the GDR writer's enterprise has gone:

Das waren noch Zeiten,

---

[86]See also the discussion of the Sisyphus theme in Leeder, *Breaking Boundaries*, pp.110-112 and Mechtenburg, 'Von Odysseus bis Sisyphos', pp.504-506.
[87]Quoted in Berendse, 'Outcast in Berlin', p.21.
[88]Uwe Kolbe, 'Sisyphos', *Hineingeboren*, pp.48-49.
[89]Günter Kunert, 'Aufgabe', *Unterwegs nach Utopia*, p.88.
[90]Hans Brinkmann, 'Sisyphos', *Poesiealbum 170* (Berlin, GDR: Neues Leben, 1981), p.8.
[91]In the article 'Mein arbeitsloser Sisyphos', *Freitag*, 17 January 1997, p.2, Drawert offers an interpretation of his own poem. He chooses to emphasize an association with social unemployment in the 'neue Bundesländer'.

als es einen Gegenstand gab,
den es zu bewegen galt.   (lines 1-3)

Here, identification of Sisyphus's stone with writing in the GDR encapsulates both the notion of bearing a burden and of having a sense of purpose. The object to be moved might also be the entrenched state bureaucracy. Lines 8-9 refer to the status of Sisyphus's labour as a punishment executed in the Underworld. It was 'ein Flop' (4): the jarring modern 'Fremdwort' dismisses high-flown notions of 'der Auftrag' (4). It also points forward to the reductive suggestion of the GDR as 'eine Unterwelt' (9) 'in der Dilettanten am Werk sind' (10). The status of the past 'Auftrag' shifts in the course of the poem. A sentimental tone in the first half is created by the first line and by the mocking familiarity that reduces 'der Auftrag' to 'ein Flop'. From line 11 the tone becomes bitter. Praising 'die Lust / auf Wiederholung' (11-12) and 'keine Gerichtsbarkeit, // die er ernst nehmen mußte' (15-16) may be a show of irony, but the closing gesture – that of Sisyphus staring into his empty hands – is quite serious: the visual image captures the bewilderment of loss. The last line, 'Wieder und wieder', ironically indicates a new type of repetition, one following no longer from activity now but rather from inactivity.

Lutz Rathenow's two Sisyphus poems from *Verirrte Sterne* also associate Sisyphus with the writer, and the end of the GDR with the removal of Sisyphus's stone.[92] Both the poems, 'Sisyphos bleibt zurück' and 'Sisyphos. Wechselnde Einstellungen', come from the second section of the collection, which is made up of poems from the time of the 'Wende'. In the first, the Sisyphus-poet is left behind, ailing:

          Sisyphos bleibt zurück
          Krank von der Sucht, Bilder zu finden.
          Der Stein der Weisen gesprengt,
          tausend Kieselsteine –
          knirschen dem einen die Ohren voll,
5   tausende abertausende Kiesel
          schnippen die Kinder ins Meer

This is a poetological crisis, more than the loss of a state-imposed 'Auftrag'. Sisyphus's stone is here the Philosopher's Stone, which is shattered into thousands of pebbles. The fragmentation is part of a general sense of break-up and instability, of an irrevocable loss of authority: the children's innocent game disperses the fragments forever. This type of connection between the fall of the GDR and a more general loss of certainties and stable categories at the end of the

---

[92]Lutz Rathenow, 'Sisyphos bleibt zurück' and 'Sisyphos. Wechselnde Einstellungen', *Verirrte Sterne*, p.50 and pp.52-54.

millennium is made in other poems of this period. Rathenow's numbered strophes entitled 'Sisyphos'. Wechselnde Einstellungen' incorporate resonances of a poetological crisis whose emblem is the end of Sisyphus's labour. This Sisyphus is also identified with the writer who has a given 'Aufgabe' (p.53) and is 'zum Ruhm verpflichtet' (p.54). As a symbol of purpose, the stone not only refers to the GDR writer's ordained task, but to writing as a source of meaning for one's existence:

Wieviel Seiten Papier braucht es, daß sie
zusammengepreßt den Stein fürs Leben ergeben? (p.54)

Behind this question is the sense of literature providing the 'Stein fürs Leben', replacing the ideology and the 'Hoffnung' (to make Kunert and Brinkmann's connection) which is now gone. The second strophe casts Sisyphus with his head in his hands and in the tenth strophe the writer adopts the same posture:

Den Kopf zwischen den Händen. Seine Finger-
spitzen an den Schläfen. (p.54)

This posture issues from the loss of the stone at the end of the labour; it is also a typical posture of despair. The correlation set up in the poem between Sisyphus's stone, the writer's texts and his head plays off the old burden against the new:

Sisyphos, von einer Zelle träumend.
Schön klein soll sie sein. Hineinsperren soll man ihn.
Da paßt der Stein nicht mit rein. (p.52 and p.54)

This motto from Rathenow's earlier collection *Boden 411* opens and closes the post-'Wende' text: the writer has escaped the stone, but his space is reduced to that of the cell.[93] The Sisyphus-poet no longer contends with a repetitive and futile labour nor with an ordained task that is literally a burden to move. Now he is not moving at all, but rather sits either staring into his empty hands or with his head in his hands. This is the classical attitude of the melancholic, as in Albrecht Dürer's engraving *Melencholia I* which Emmerich uses to illustrate what he perceives as the 'status melancholicus' of modern writers and intellectuals and especially the experience of those from the GDR.[94] The Sisyphus-poetry above is typical of lamenting 'Verlierer' voices for whom the end of the GDR brings a loss of purpose: a historical shift forces poets from their familiar task and makes them address their own role anew. In the 1970s Kunert had used another classical hero, Atlas, as an image of the poet who is relieved of his 'Auftrag'.[95]

---

[93]Lutz Rathenow, *Boden 411: Stücke zum Lesen und Texte zum Spielen* (Munich: Piper, 1984). The cell is a characteristic feature of Rathenow's writing.
[94]Wolfgang Emmerich, 'Status melancholicus', *Die andere deutsche Literatur*, pp.175-189, p.175.
[95]Günter Kunert, 'Atlas', *Unterwegs nach Utopia*, p.77. This poem exemplifies how a GDR poet forced to the West (Kunert left in 1977) can be seen as a forerunner of those GDR poets who found themselves lost as a result of unification with the West in 1990.

Having carried the burden of social responsibility, he is still 'gebeugt', itself an attitude of servitude. He is shocked by 'der Verlust der Last', the loss of the political burden. Kunert's lines 'Plötzlich überflüssig / ein nackter Überlebender seiner Aufgabe' describe precisely the position of the GDR poet after 1990, as it does of the writer who left the GDR and emigrated to the West in the 1970s.

Poems of self-address particularly show the reduced significance suffered by the post-GDR poet. The commentator Martin Meyer observes a general concern amongst contemporary intellectuals with their own position in the world: 'Zu beobachten ist die Lage, daß sich die Intellektuellen häufiger als nötig mit sich selbst beschäftigen. Die Reizbarkeit wendet sich nach innen'.[96] Emmerich states of the GDR author after the 'Wende', 'Ohne Fesseln war er nun, aber auch ohne Bindung, ohne Auftrag. Das ist, so merkten viele DDR-Autoren, schwer zu ertragen – eine nicht geringe narzißtische Kränkung'.[97] Injured narcissism is articulated in poems addressing the self. Poems of address to the self particularly thematize the way to survive after the loss of role. Mensching's 'Doppelsonett in den Spiegel gesprochen' (*Berliner Elegien*, p.19) is such a dialogue with the self, in which the mirror pinpoints the narcissistic nature of the poem. We overhear the poet persuading himself to come to terms with the new era. This is a 'du' characterized by 'Verzweiflung, stumpfer Haß' (1), by 'dein Kummerblick, die Leidensmiene' (7). The new age brings an unwelcome 'holy trinity' of ailments – 'Fettleber, / Weltschmerz, Herzinfarkt', but the lyric subject tells himself to be content: unification is 'dein Sprung, die weiche Landung' (2). He acknowledges that he has food and money and should try to forget great visions:

Schweig still, halt's Maul, mein Freund, vergiß es,
Wie du es immer drehst und wendest, du verwendest,
Am Tag der Pleite, als Verlierer auf der Siegerseite   (lines 12-14)

The paradox of being a loser on the winning side points up the contrast between the theme of defeat after unification and the socialist victory-poetry of the 1950s. Characterization of the self as a loser, who would be wise to keep quiet, implies censure from outside. Self-address conveys the same advice in Kahlau's poem 'An den Rasen' (*Kaspers Waage*, p.7), which was written in 1991.

Sei still, mein Freund,
laß alle Hoffnung fahren.

---

[96]Martin Meyer, 'Intellektuellendämmerung?', in *Intellektuellendämmerung? Beiträge zur neuesten Zeit des Geistes*, ed. by Martin Meyer (Munich and Vienna: Hanser, 1992), pp.7-12 (p.9).
[97]Emmerich, *Kleine Literaturgeschichte der DDR*, p.16. Alison Lewis recognizes too in the loss of ideals amongst ex-GDR Germans the same type of 'narzißtische Kränkung' which the Mitscherlichs perceived amongst Germans after the end of the Second World War. See Lewis, 'Unity begins together'.

Besinne dich
auf deine Fähigkeit,
die Ruhe und
den Anstand zu bewahren
und halte dich
heraus aus Zank und Streit. (lines 1-8)

In this poem the lyric voice advises the relinquishing of hope, for the sake of survival. Again it is not a rousing programme, rather the self should keep quiet and shrink into obscurity: 'Du überstehst nur / in der kleinsten Größe' (9-10).[98] The close of the third and final stanza however is hopeful (making clear that 'Hoffnung' in the first stanza was not a general hopefulness but specifically hope for a better world):

Wir sind das Gras,
das unterm Schnee noch treibt.
Die Wiese hat
die Zeit auf ihrer Seite.
Das Harte bricht,
das Zarte lebt und bleibt. (lines 17-22)

Beneath the frozen surface lies new growth. The switch to the collective subject 'wir' and echoes of Brecht's grass metaphor for hope indicate that the self in question has a socialist identity.[99]

Poets' socialist allegiance is at odds with the aspirations of the majority of people in the new Germany. The 'Wende' exposed a latent estrangement between writers and the general populace. As Antonia Grunenberg has argued, many GDR writers had remained 'Vermittler', however critical they were of the regime, and had difficulty relinquishing this function in 1989.[100] The GDR had essentially seen itself at one with the people, and embued its writers with this sense of social representativeness too. Crucially, this understanding of their role was retained by writers even when they criticized 'der real existierende Sozialismus': in taking a position constructively critical of the state, they understood themselves to be aligned with ordinary people and the tribulations of their everyday lives. Although the unofficial publishing scenes in the 1980s formed more inward-looking literary circles, some of these young poets too aspired to 'enlightening' people through their art. Hensel, part of both the official

[98]Compare also Kahlau's 1990 poem 'Zeitbegriffe' (*Kaspers Waage*, p.46) in which 'die Genossen' climb into a deep freezer, in order to wait out the current era. This quirky, playful poem thematizes the long-term survival of socialism by means of cryonics.
[99]Brecht, 'O Lust des Beginnens', *Gesammelte Werke*, ix, p.771.
[100]Antonia Grunenberg, ' "Ich finde mich überhaupt nicht mehr zurecht...": Thesen zur Krise in der DDR-Gesellschaft', in *DDR: Ein Staat vergeht*, ed. by Thomas Blanke and Rainer Kirsch (Frankfurt a.M.: Fischer, 1990), pp.171-182 (p.181).

and the unofficial publishing scenes in Leipzig and East Berlin, stated in an interview of summer 1988, 'Ich glaube, letztlich will ich, wie viele mehr, nichts als Aufklärer sein'.[101] Such 'Aufklärer'-aspirations seemed dashed at unification, in that the GDR people chose material well-being above intellectual ideals.[102] A number of poets express in poetry 'der Verlust ihrer aufklärerischen Rolle'.[103] Some poems trace the poet's loss to the people's demonstrations: there is a sense of the writer being superseded by the 'Volk' in Hilbig's 'prosa meiner heimatstraße', for instance:[104]

> mit einem mal haben chöre von stotternden die plätze erobert-
> o zeilen: die abgebrochnen stimmen stehlen sich den abend
> schön ist ein volk in waffenlosem aufruhr (p.96)

'Chöre' at once indicates a musical harmony, but the 'stotternde' are the inarticulate, those whose use of language is not their profession. These choirs are also represented as a wave which swamps the individual: 'jetzt gleicht er einem schwimmenden schrei / unbeachtet in der dunklen massenwoge' (p.96). Peter M. Stephan also sees the erstwhile relation between writer and 'Volk' thrown into disarray by the 'Volk' seizing the linguistic and political initiative at the 'Wende':[105]

> Wir lebten wie Lenz so dahin bis alles in einem Ruf auf der
>   Straße explodierte und unsere leibeigenen Trümmer
> uns ins Gesicht flogen ins neue Jahrzehnt Jahrhundert
> Wir sind das Volk
> Wir sind das Volk nie   (lines 23-27)

In this poem, Stephan draws a comparison between GDR writers and the archetypal 'lost' writer, J.M.R. Lenz, who (as Georg Büchner portrays him)[106] was cut off from society and tortured by the projections of his own mind. In Stephan's poem the 'Wende' cry 'Wir sind das Volk' is an explosion that blows up the unity of poet and people. The 'wir' of the 'Volk' becomes a different 'wir' from that of the writers. Distance from the people is implied by the

---

[101]Karin Néy, ' "Letztlich will ich nichts, als Aufklärer sein..." Ein Gespräch mit Kerstin Hensel', *Temperamente* (1989), No.3, 3-7 (p.4).

[102]See Uwe Wittstock, 'Ab in die Nische? Über die neueste deutsche Literatur und was sie vom Publikum trennt', *NR*, 104 (1993), No.3, 45-53. Wittstock compares the relation between poet and society to that between an old married couple: one talks on but the other simply does not listen anymore. He also highlights broken communication in asking the question, 'Natürlich darf sich ein Autor in der Rolle eines Rufers in der Wüste gefallen — aber kann sich das eine ganze Autorengeneration leisten?' (p.46).

[103]Grunenberg, ' "Ich finde mich überhaupt nicht mehr zurecht" ', p.182.

[104]Hilbig, 'prosa meiner heimatstraße', *NR*, 101 (1990), 81-99.

[105]Peter M. Stephan, 'In den achtziger Jahren', in *Von einem Land*, pp.145-146.

[106]Georg Büchner, *Lenz, Sämtliche Werke*, i (Frankfurt a.M.: Deutsche Klassiker, 1992), pp.223-250, of which the last sentence is 'So lebte er hin' (p.250).

mediation of the television screen in Müller's poem 'Fernsehen' (*Die Gedichte*, pp.232-233):

Auf dem Bildschirm sehe ich meine Landsleute
Mit Händen und Füßen abstimmen gegen die Wahrheit
Die vor vierzig Jahren mein Besitz war   (p.233)

The writer is an onlooker, who does not participate with his compatriots in voting for unification. With such distance from society comes dispossession. Socialist belief was Müller's possession, 'mein Besitz', when the GDR was first established: the writer-intellectual could be an oracle then. In a poem of 1994 Müller writes of now having no audience for his drama ('Fremder Blick: Abschied von Berlin', *Die Gedichte*, p.287): the victors, that is the West and the people who voted for unification, are deaf to the writer:

Aus meiner Zelle vor dem leeren Blatt
Im Kopf ein Drama für kein Publikum
Taub sind die Sieger die Besiegten stumm (lines 1-3)

Clearly the lyric subject counts himself amongst the defeated who cannot speak nor write. In this poem, and others after unification, the text as a 'Gespräch ohne Ende', between reader and writer, seems to be in doubt.[107]

Michael Wüstefeld's prescriptive poem 'Leihweise Manifestation' of 1987/88 was a pre-'Wende' call for the people's voice to be made manifest.[108] Here the writers could not be the sole providers of 'ways out':

Nicht Dichter nur alle
            Alle
öffnet Fenster öffnet Türen
äfft die Affen nicht länger nach
Die Väter sind tot   (p.71)

This call was answered in effect by the 'Wende' initiatives. In Wüstefeld's post-'Wende' poem 'Will ich noch reden mit euch' the poet addresses the 'ihr' of the 'Volk' in order to voice his doubts about the future relation between the two parties.[109] There is a latent sentimental longing for the old relationship:

Will ich noch reden mit euch
von den alten Geistern verlassen
von den nächsten bedrängt
Kann ich reden mit euch
in unserer heimlichen Sprache

---

[107]Uwe Kolbe, 'Gespräch ohne Ende' (September 1979), in *Berührung ist nur eine Randerscheinung: Neue Literatur aus der DDR*, ed by Sascha Anderson and Elke Erb (Cologne: Kiepenheuer & Witsch, 1985), p.39.
[108]Michael Wüstefeld, 'Leihweise Manifestation', *Stadtplan: Gedichte* (Berlin and Weimar: mdv, 1990), p.70-73.
[109]Michael Wüstefeld, 'Will ich noch reden mit euch', *SuF*, 44 (1992), 835-836, and reprinted in *Von einem Land*, pp.58-59.

    die einmal jeder verstand

        Soll ich heulen mit euch
        Wenn das Kalb den Goldzahn fletscht
        die Kursbücher den Konkurs bestimmen
        und der pornographische Hund sich in den eigenen Schwanz
        beißt

    Soll ich noch reden mit euch
    die ihr zu schweigen gelernt habt
    Keiner vergoldet das Silber der Wörter
    Keiner beweist des Schweigens Gold (lines 17-30)

Marginalized in capitalist society, with the covert language inspired by censorship now defunct, the 'ich' of the writer is wracked by self-doubt. He perceives the new society's materialism and immorality as a threat to the currency of words. Repetition of construction, variations with 'will ich' replaced by 'soll ich' and 'kann ich', trace the writer's search for a meaningful position with respect to the 'Volk'. Any question mark is withheld until the last line, making the whole poem one long question about whether there will be dialogue between the writer and the 'Volk'. The poem closes with an allusion to how democracy and technology have altered the role of literary communication:

    Kann ich noch reden mit euch
    wenn die Stuben längst von Vertretern besetzt sind
    Anrufungen automatisch beantwortet werden
    Kann ich so noch reden mit euch?   (lines 42-44)

This poem follows on from Wüstefeld's poem 'Ihr könnt mit mir reden' which was published in 1987.[110] The title statement is repeated throughout the 1987 poem as a type of refrain. This earlier poem sets up an ideal of spontaneous dialogue between the lyric 'ich' and the 'ihr', a dialogue which is possible anywhere and at any time. It closes, however, with a suggestion that the writer's ideal may not be shared by his addressees:

    Immer könnt ihr mit mir reden
    Jedenfalls spreche ich so zu euch. (lines 15-16)

A tentative retraction of the ideal in these last lines of the 1987 poem becomes overwhelming doubt about the possibility of dialogue in the post-'Wende' text. Wüstefeld's poem 'Absage' of 1991/1993 allows the reader to overhear one side of another dialogue between 'ich' and 'ihr'.[111] It seems to be an unspoken reply, constructed as a weaker party imagines arguing with a stronger party, but never actually speaks. The lyric 'ich' opens defensively and aggressively:

---

[110]Michael Wüstefeld, 'Ihr könnt mit mir reden', *Heimsuchung* (Berlin, GDR: Aufbau, 1987), on book cover only.
[111]Michael Wüstefeld, 'Absage', *SuF*, 46 (1994), 108-111.

Was fragt ihr ob ich gelebt habe
Wo glaubt ihr daß ich gelebt habe
Woher wollt ihr wissen wie mein Leben war   (lines 1-3)

The poem is a rejection of the perspective of an undefined you-plural. The 'ich' refuses to discard his past life. Rather, he delivers a sarcastic 'Geständnis': 'Jetzt gebe ich meinen Decknamen preis // Ich gebe zu ich bin Ingenieur geworden' (16-17). The 'Deckname' implies activity as a Stasi IM, but the following line is no sincere admission, but sarcasm. Yet it also recalls Stalin's designation of the socialist writer as an engineer of the soul. Perhaps it is also as a writer then, caught up in the machinations of the state, that the 'ich' has been judged. He responds with indignation:

Wer hat das Recht zu urteilen
zu verurteilen den Stil meines Gehens   (lines 27-28)

The 'ihr' is identified by the introduction of 'wir': the 'ihr', persecutors and inquisitors, are the West. The lyric 'ich' begins to speak on behalf of the East with sarcastic repetition of 'ihr steht uns bei':

Die ihr uns beisteht
uns den Brüdern und Schwestern
habt euch das eure Väter gelehrt
Evaluieren Abwickeln Liquidieren
Ihr steht uns bei
bis es uns aus den Schuhen tropft   (lines 37-42)

In the earlier poem 'Leihweise Manifestation', Wüstefeld declared the fathers to be dead. Here, their teaching (40) seems to live on. The poem becomes an aggressive retort to the West. Verbs of business takeovers are actions applied to people directly and thus convey torture which is overseen by the West. Repetitions of the imperative 'Sagt nicht' reveal the West's half of the dialogue, in particular a demand to desist from poetry and to forget: 'Sagt nicht ich sollte die Verse vergessen' (72), 'Sagt nicht ich sollte das Erinnern abwerfen' (104). The last line of the whole emphasizes the rejection: 'Sagt so etwas nicht' (114). This poem harbours no naivety or nostalgia for the old dialogue, but creates a new, angry dialogue with the West.

In Drawert's poem 'Geständnis' (*Wo es war*, pp.35-42), the dialogue enacted between the writer 'ich' and a you-plural is more formal:

Ich lehne Ihre Probleme ab.
Ich habe Ihnen nichts, was ein Trost wär, zu sagen. (p.38)

The 'ich' addresses 'Sie', the people of united Germany, rejecting any engagement with their problems as a new society. Instead, the 'ich' sends them away to disappear 'in Ihre Geheimzahl', 'in Ihre Software' (p.38), 'in Ihre Brieftasche, / in Ihren Diätplan, in Ihren Volkshochschullehrgang' (p.39). The lyric voice takes a satirical tone, repeating four times on one page (p.41) that the country is 'einfach herrlich'. He enjoys the 'Land der Verwöhnten' (p.35) and the 'Wirtschaftswunder' (the word occurs nine times in the poem). The openings 'Ich gestehe' and 'Ich sage', which are repeated throughout, emphasize the individual's perspective, but there is also contemplation of ideas of 'Zeugenschaft' and 'Zuständigkeit' with respect to the 'Sie'. These considerations reflect on the old relationship between poet and 'Volk' in the GDR. The poet now asserts 'Ich bin kein Botenjunge' (p.41). This is a translation of the poem's motto, taken from W.B. Yeats (p.35). The poet will not be the messenger-boy of a new society. Indeed he asserts the enduring value of his literary endeavours: 'Mein Denken hat keinen Schaden genommen, // meine Sätze haben keinen Schaden genommen' (p.37). In Drawert's poem, 'Ortswechsel' (*Wo es war*, p.83), there seems to be no possibility of being a messenger: communication is broken. The isolation of the lyric 'ich' is established at the outset:

Meine Freunde im Osten
verstehe ich
nicht mehr, im Landstrich
zwischen Hamme und Weser

kenne ich keinen.
Gelegentlich grüßt mich
der taubstumme Bauer   (lines 1-7)

The poet's sole human contact is with a farmer who is deaf and dumb, clearly another outsider who epitomizes blocked communication and isolation. The poet feels that he was and is nowhere: 'Nirgendwo bin ich angekommen. / Nirgendwo war ich zuhaus.' (13-14). Memories of smell and past conversations are unbearably insubstantial, 'wertlos', 'in alle Winde / verkauft' (27-29). 'Verkauft' again has resonances of the 'Wende' as a sell-out. The 'ich' in Drawert's poem was one of the 'Voyeure / des besseren Wissens' (29-30). As a voyeur, he was a passive onlooker, faintly immoral, 'mit schönen Sätzen' (34) that hint at falsity or lies. Now the poet addresses 'Ihr', a new you-plural, just as the 'ich' is also changed:

Jetzt also spreche ich Klartext:
Ihr habt mich getäuscht. Ich
bin ein anderer gewesen

im Zentrum der beschädigten Jahre.
Doch wenn ich, für die Sekunde,
meinen Namen vergesse,
dann verstehe ich wohl

diesen Grabgang
der Sprache und möchte bedauern   (lines 47-55)

Rimbaud's positive Modernist statement 'Je est un autre' is taken up as a negative statement.[112] The caesura is a moment of realization when the lyric subject sees that he experienced a loss of self in the GDR years. Being nowhere is now mirrored by the loss of language (54-55). Yet there is a tension between the non-location of the 'ich' and the assertion, 'Das stelle ich fest' (16-17), a tension which indicates that the writing of the poem is a way of recapturing some substantiality. A stark contrast between past and present is highlighted in the line, 'Jetzt also spreche ich Klartext' (47).[113] This indicates a new way of speaking, but also (in line 48) the poet's damaged relationship to the people. At the poem's close the death of language is accompanied by images of ending and obscuring: 'Verwesung', 'Herbst', 'Abend' and 'Nebel' are, however, romantic images too. On the one hand, the end of the poem indicates a respite from fraught anxiety about past and present: 'mein Körper / ist ruhig geworden' (66-67). On the other, it heralds the death of the poetic self.[114]

The loss of relationship which prompts the search for dialogue in the poetry above is an unassailable silence in Wüstefeld's 1993 poem 'Warten'.[115] Here the lyric subject waits in silence, with a blank page, in anticipation of a communication from outside:

Ein Ruf müßte kommen jetzt durch den Draht
der sich verbündet mit meinem Schweigen
der ein Widerwort wäre dem stummen Papier
der mich verbindet   entbindet dem Hoffen (lines 1-4)

In waiting he anticipates various sounds: a knock at the door, scratching fingers and toes, a pebble against the window. Increasingly his anticipations become metaphorical (singing birds in the postman's pocket) or fanciful (the cry of a whale or a fly). Any cry would be 'eine Antwort' (12), a response to fill the void. Memory becomes crucial: Wüstefeld's lyric 'ich' desperately awaits 'ein Staubkorn gegen die Vergeßlichkeit' (24) and 'der Geruch des Erinnerns' (16). The lyric subject also seeks to be taken somewhere outside himself, by '[ein Ruf] der mich einnimmt   mitnimmt irgendwohin' (21). The poem is structured as a series of possibilities, each introduced by 'oder': the last possibility is that the lyric 'ich' goes deaf, blind and dumb. Even then he

---

[112]Arthur Rimbaud, 'Lettre à Paul Demeny', *Oeuvres* (Paris: Classiques Garnier, 1991), pp.346-352 (p.347).

[113]Compare also *Fraktur*, the title of Drawert's collection of pre- and post-'Wende' writing: the word embodies the sense of history, language and identity fracturing, but also the sense of 'Fraktur reden', which means the same as 'Klartext sprechen'. The term 'Klartext' also has particular 'Wende' resonances, perhaps because it was the title of a magazine programme which began on GDR television in November 1989.

[114]In reviewing Czechowski's *Nachtspur*, Drawert comments on the opposition between literary language and 'Klartext'. See Drawert, *Haus ohne Menschen*, p.81.

[115]Michael Wüstefeld, 'Warten', *SuF*, 46 (1994), 107-108.

anticipates 'der Ruf' and at the end we find that this has all been a search for identity:

    dann
    müßte der Ruf kommen aus blindem Schmerz
                        aus taubem Gestein
                        aus stummem Lied
    erst dann könnte ich sehen
                        hören
                        sagen
    wer ich wirklich bin   (lines 51-58)

The silent song, or unspoken poem, is equated with blind pain and deaf stone. Wüstefeld has inverted the familiar metaphors of blinding pain and of stone deafness. The silence and the empty page are, in a fairly commonplace irony, overcome in the act of lamenting these. Identity is to be found in writing, but writing first needs some stimulus from outside. This is not necessarily a successful wait: identity is still only a prospect at the end.

In Czechowski's 1991 poem 'Nach dem Umsturz' the poet's location is unchanged by 1989/90 and his identity unusually intact:[116]

    Meine Freunde
    Gingen über
    Die Grenze. Ich

    Bin geblieben. Hier,
    Wo ich bin,
    Wird keine Revolution
    Mein Leben verändern.

    Man lebt nicht
    Unter dem Schirm
    Irgendeiner Regierung.   (lines 26-35)

He refers to the broken community of writers after the expulsions and emigrations of the 1970s and 1980s, and also perhaps to ex-GDR writers who moved to western Germany after unification (such as Drawert). But this lyric subject locates himself outside the political realm, in a space apparently untouched by change. Nonetheless, in the closing stanza, the 'ich' laments his blank page, without accounting for this inability to write anything down. In Czechowski's poem 'Nachtrag' of 1994 however, the poet-'ich' has crossed into a void.[117] Here he finds no answer (3), no progress (9) and no echo (18). The first line of the poem pinpoints this relationship between the writer and the lost GDR: 'Ich bin aus dem Kontext genommen.' The GDR provided the context in which

---

[116]Heinz Czechowski, 'Nach dem Umsturz', in *Von einem Land*, pp.132-133.
[117]Heinz Czechowski, 'Nachtrag', in *Fragebogen Zensur*, ed. by Zipser, pp.82-83.

the writer's identity and his writing made sense. Both past and future now fall away: the future is 'immer fragwürdiger' (27) and the past 'brachgelegt' (35). Correspondingly, there is no language for the past (35-36) nor the future (26-28). The process of censorship is one focus of this poem. It created a politically charged context in which 'Keine Antwort ist auch eine Antwort' (14). Another paradox replaces this paradox when the politically charged context is gone:

Wer alles sagen kann,
Sagt überhaupt nichts.   (lines 15-16)

Total freedom of expression is experienced as a vacuum: it is at once a dreamt-of freedom, yet also the white wall (17), the blank sheet of paper.

Ein echoloses
Schriftstellerleben, wer
Erträumte es nicht? Jeden Morgen

Stehe ich auf, um das weiße Papier zu beschreiben. Doch wer
Kauft mir ab, was ich schreibe? So
Verzweifle ich letzten Endes doch
An meiner Fähigkeit, die Natur

Zu begradigen, und
Zensiere immer noch mich.   (lines 18-26)

The writer-'ich' despairs about who will buy his writing but also who will believe him ('abkaufen' implies both of these). As Robert von Hallberg has written, 'the greatest privilege enjoyed by writers and scholars in East Germany was altogether immaterial: they felt a sense of consequence'.[118] The writer's subsequent crisis of confidence after the loss of this double-edged privilege is understood in Czechowski's poem as a type of self-censorship. The closing lines encapsulate the sense of a trade-off:

Geblieben ist aber
Immer noch diese vergebliche Suche
Nach einer Stimme, die sagt, was sie meint,
Und die dennoch gehört wird...   (lines 41-44)

The writer is concerned with being heard: his own writing seems to depend on being in dialogue. (The noun 'Antwort' occurs seven times in this poem of forty-four lines.) Czechowski's evocation of a literary scene where dialogue and 'Freunde' are important recalls the closeness of the 'sächsische Dichterschule' of the 1960s and 1970s, of which he was a part. Now the poet experiences a conflict between poetry and communication.

Unification threw into crisis not only literary communication, but also the matter of where writers were going from here. It prompted a review of the

---

[118]Hallberg, *Literary Intellectuals*, p.8.

writer's location – where had writers located themselves within the GDR and where, if anywhere, was their place now that the GDR was gone? Czechowski's space beyond political frontiers is an exception. The subject of his poem 'Nahe und fern' (*Nachtspur*, p.185) is a 'Wanderer' figure, going into exile:

Nahe und fern: Syrakus
Gibt es nur in den Büchern, jetzt
Nimm deinen Stab, der dich
An den Rand der Grube gebracht hat, erwandre

Dir deinen Tod oder
Dein neues Leben: Kontoauszüge
Begleiten dich ins Exil   (lines 1-7)

The word 'Kontoauszüge' indicates the particular context of this exile. The old, non-existent destination, and an equation of the new life with death, are common motifs in poetry of the 1990s.[119] Now the lyric subject is an exile in the domain of banks and bank accounts. The 'ich' in Drawert's poem 'Geständnis' (*Wo es war*, pp.35-42) finds himself in a new location by chance:

Ich bin herübergefallen
wie eine Frucht vom anderen Grundstück.

Ich komme her von dem Land der gesplitterten Baüme,
der verdorrten, der gebrochenen Baüme.
Ich komme nirgendwo her.   (p.36)

Here the GDR is a land of splintered trees, suggesting a barren wasteland. Now the grieving 'ich' comes from nowhere. Dislocation is asserted too in Drawert's poem 'Tauben in ortloser Landschaft' (*Wo es war*, pp.103-110) where the 'ich' occupies 'diese namenlos weite, / ortlose Landschaft'. The area of the former GDR becomes a nameless no-place where '[wir] können gut ohne Hoffnungen bleiben' (p.110). This landscape suggests 'Kahlschlag', as after 1945.[120] In the poem, 'Träume' are inextricable from what is now 'morsch', 'abgestellt' and 'tot' (p.106), and the GDR people with whom the lyric subject identifies are orphaned:

und [wir] gehen abverlangt krumm
mit unseren Akten im Arm

---

[119]Clearly the exilic experiences of writers during the GDR years of Germany's division were reflected in poetry at that time. See the theme of exile in poetry by Günter Kunert, Wolf Biermann and Reiner Kunze, for instance.

[120]This landscape also echoes the image of memory in *Haus ohne Menschen*, p.16 as 'eine öde, eingeäscherte und begriffslose Landschaft' (p.16). Compare too earlier use of a landscape metaphor to refer to feelings, in Drawert's poem 'Mannequin', *Zweite Inventur*, pp.40-41, where he refers to 'die Zerstörung der inneren Landschaft' (p.40).

durch die vereinten Betriebe
wie flache, schwarze Figuren
im Schattenspiel eines Illusionisten.
Was müßte gesagt sein

an dieser Stelle, daß wir am Wegrand
der Geschichte ausgesetzt wurden
und Findelkinder sind, Bastarde,
Waisen bei befleckter Empfängnis

und bei keinem Namen zu nennen,
eine Kasper-Hauser-Legion   (pp.106-107)

The set of associations expresses homelessness and stigma. The GDR people are offspring without origin, from 'nirgendwo', 'Nachgeburt kalter Kriege', 'hingefickt lieblos' (p.107). Concerns for a place of origin are part of the sense of being exiled and unhoused: these are recurrent themes in post-unification poetry in connection with questions of identity. Like the abandoned orphans left on the mountains, the 'wir' are in exile too in an untitled poem (*Wo es war*, p.45):

...*vielleicht sind wir alle*
verlorene Exilanten
eines Gefühls   (lines 1-3)

This exile concurs with the dispossession and emptiness expressed in other poems by ex-GDR poets. [121] Empty spaces are a recurrent motif in Drawert's collection *Wo es war*: the title itself suggests this. For instance, the poem 'Leer und sehr blau' (*Wo es war*, pp.67-68) describes a lyric 'ich' in domestic emptiness, surrounded by 'Stille' (2) and 'nichts' (6), 'und selbst der Gedanke / an eine Bewegung // verlor sich' (14-16). The line 'leer und sehr blau' describes both a lover's eyes and the 'Himmel'. There is no human spirit to touch nor a divine spirit here. Such disconnectedness in the present accompanies disconnections from the human subject's own past. Gaps in biography are alluded to in the poem 'Vom Endprodukt her' (*Wo es war*, pp.20-21):

Tauschen wir,
wennschon die Tage
im Videotext enden,
Ereignisrelikte, Erfahrungen aus
im Umgang mit leeren Stellen. (p.20)

---

[121]Furthermore, Kunert responded to the above quotation with the remark, 'Zumindest sind wir, und das verbindet mich graduell mit Kurt Drawert, "Umsiedler" besonderer Art, Weltenwechsler, Platztauscher'. See 'Zu Kurt Drawert', *Akzente*, 41 (1995), 107-108 (p.107).

In an article, Czechowski connects the caesura of 1989/90 with 'ein Riß [...]
durch meine Biographie'.[122] In the lines quoted above such a rent biography is
represented as gaps and as the virtual ('Videotext') replacing the real text of life.
Drawert's title 'Wo es war' quotes Sigmund Freud's statement 'Wo Es
war, soll Ich werden'.[123] The founding of an 'Ich', an identity which counters the
emptiness, is central to many poems. In Wüstefeld's 1995 poem 'Mein
Inventar' the inventory in question is 'das Ich-Inventar', which recalls both
Günter Eich's post-war stocktaking and the loss of 'ich'-identity typically
expressed after 1989/90.[124] Drawert's poem '...doch' (*Wo es war*, p.101)
challenges the pervasive sense of loss, albeit with increasing desperation:

> ...doch
> es muß auch eine Hinterlassenschaft geben,
> die die Geschichte des Körpers,
> auf die ich selbst einmal, denn das Vergessen
> wird über die Erinnerung herrschen,
> 5   zurückgreifen kann wie auf eine Sammlung
> fotografierten Empfindens, und die die Geschichte,
> denn das innere Land
> wird eine verfallene Burg sein
> und keinen Namen mehr haben und betreten sein
> 10   von dir als einem Fremden
> mit anderer Sprache, erklärt.

The self is now a stranger, using another language. This poem is about the
dilemma of losing part of one's origins: a breathless voice insists that there
must be a legacy which offers explanation. The verbs 'zurückgreifen kann' (5)
and 'erklärt' (11) are long withheld, a strategy which has the effect of
qualifying and relativizing the possibilities of reaching back. Alienation from
the past is compounded by 'Vergessen' (3). In Barbara Köhler's 'Hotel Vörös
Csillag', the poem also appeals for remembering after 'das ende': 'vergiß dich
nicht / zu erinnern'.[125] The line break sets off the little irony of remembering to
remember: the play on the name of the flower becomes a command to

---

[122]Heinz Czechowski, 'Das Vergängliche überlisten? Ein lyrisches Ich am Ende des
zweiten Jahrtausends', in *Das Vergängliche überlisten: Selbstbefragungen deutscher
Autoren*, ed. by Ingrid Czechowski (Leipzig: Reclam, 1996), pp.60-75 (p.68).
[123]Sigmund Freud, 'Neue Folge der Vorlesungen zur Einführung in die Psychoanalyse',
Studienausgabe, i, p.516.
[124]Michael Wüstefeld, 'Mein Inventar', *Deutsche Anatomie*, pp.17-20 (p.20). Günter
Eich, 'Inventur', in *Seventeen Modern German Poets*, ed. by Siegbert Prawer (Oxford:
OUP, 1971), p.82.
[125]Barbara Köhler, 'Hotel Vörös Csillag', *Deutsches Roulette*, p.82.

remember who one is. Drawert's lyric subject seeks 'fotographiertes Empfinden' (6), an impossible visual record, to escape the sense of vacuum. He hopes to overcome alienation from feeling and emotion by a search for 'die Geschichte des Körpers' (2). In the poem 'Mit Heine' (*Wo es war*, p.87) his country's name is burnt onto the body of the lyric subject forever. This branding is an image of the GDR's importance for identity. In a number of poems the lyric subject returns to childhood places in order to remember who he is. In Czechowski's poem 'Abgebrochene Biographien' (*Nachtspur*, pp.297-298) the 'ich' goes back to the place of his schooldays, comparing the time of the GDR's founding with the present.[126] At the poem's close, the friendly atmosphere of a bar reminds him nostalgically of the past:

> das stille
> Einverständnis der hinterbliebenen Trinker
> Gedenkt jener Zeit,
> Als wir noch unter uns waren. (p.298)

In the title poem of Drawert's collection (*Wo es war*, p.80), the returning lyric 'ich' resembles a post-war 'Heimkehrer' figure.

> Wo es war
> Ich wußte nicht mehr, wie wir uns trafen,
> damals, in den Städten, in denen heute
> die Hymnen verwaist
>
> ihr Vaterland suchen. In den Ruinen
> 5   des letzten Krieges war eine friedliche,
> vaterlose Stille zu finden.
>
> Hier kam ich als Kind her, verstört,
> hier ging es uns gut, hier war die Sprache
> außerhalb des Körpers geblieben.
>
> 10   Später, an einer empfindlichen Stelle
> der Biographie, brach, wie dem einen
> die Stimme, dem andern
>
> das Rückgrat, erinnere dich,
> mir war das Glück des Verstummens
> 15   gegeben, wo es war.

---

[126]See also Czechowski's poem 'Bauernsterben' (*Nachtspur*, pp.255-256) which thematizes a return to a childhood place which is now deserted and desolate. In this poem there is clearly no reconciliation with the past and the lyric 'ich' leaves again, 'ungetröstet' (p.256).

Wo es war, hat das Gras schon zu wuchern
begonnen. Die kleine Senke im Boden,
in der ich von Liebe geträumt haben muß,
ist mit Schotter gefüllt, Lachen von Flußtang
20   und Öl, zerdrückte Aluminiumdosen,

ein Brandfleck. Auch diese Erde
hat ihre Geschichte verleugnet. Schon lange
war es dunkel geworden, als ich noch immer
bewegungslos dastand. Was ich hörte,
25   war fremd. Was ich dachte. Und es war Tag.

The GDR childhood of the lyric subject is now alien to him. Adjectives such as 'verwaist' (3) and 'vaterlos' (6), applied to abstract things, reflect the orphaned self.[127] His voice breaking was not a coming of age, but literally broken speech, a means of survival, 'das Glück des Verstummens'. Writing as remembering corresponds to Drawert's statement 'Wir müssen alles erst einmal sprechen, um es dann zu verlassen'.[128] Emergence from darkness into light at the poem's close suggests that the lyric subject has now been able to do this and take leave of the past.

Hilbig's 'prosa meiner heimatstraße' describes another journey back: 'der rückweg' follows the lyric 'ich's 'heimatstraße' to his home and origins.[129] This five-part poem traces the journey to find identity, culminating in the final part entitled 'ankunft': simultaneously the process of writing is that journey.[130] The poem begins in a wasteland of the present:

asche. schattenwelt der asche...
flachland der asche... seit jahren vertagt
der rückweg bis auf diesen grund: schwierige wörter
haben mich gehindert (p.81)

---

[127]See the GDR as 'Vaterland' and the past represented by a father-figure in Kurt Drawert, *Spiegelland. Ein deutscher Monolog* (Frankfurt a.M.: Suhrkamp, 1992).
[128]Drawert, *Spiegelland*, p.11.
[129]Wolfgang Hilbig, 'prosa meiner heimatstraße' ['die einleitung' and parts 1-3], *NR*, 101 (1990), 81-99 and completed [part 4, 'ankunft'], *Sprache im technischen Zeitalter* (1991), No.119, 99-102.
[130]Compare Thomas Rosenlöcher, *Die Wiederentdeckung des Wanderns beim Gehen: Harzreise* (Frankfurt a.M.: Suhrkamp, 1991) and Wolfgang Hilbig, 'Grünes grünes Grab', *Grünes grünes Grab: Erzählungen* (Frankfurt a.M.: Fischer, 1993), pp.99-122. Rosenlöcher's narrator in this story is 'ein Fremder im eigenen Land' (p.10) who relates his journey into the mountains in search of identity. Hilbig's narrator is a poet who undertakes a journey to his childhood home at the time of the 'Wende'.

In part 1, there is silence: 'kein echo', 'kein zähneknirschen', 'kein schuß', 'kein rauschen' (p.84). The enumeration of the lack of audible traces corresponds to a text which is washed-out 'und die lettern schweigen – versiebt, verschlungen, vergraben' (p.84). The poet's writing and his self-understanding are submerged in ash, and his language 'verrottet' and 'verworfen vom tod' (p.85). The lyric subject has lost even 'die mickrige silbung meines namens'.[131] This symbolic loss of identity suggests the insubstantial self; in part 2 the 'ich' is a void, an empty space:

> in der leere
>
> selbst schatten nichts als leere nichts
> als leergefärbte schatten hinter scherbenjalousien
> licht- und schattenstaffeln eines ausgeräumten zimmers (p.89)

Repetitions of 'leere' and 'schatten' (in addition to echoes of both in the word 'scherben') recreate an echoing emptiness. The journey back to substantiality is specifically linked to the act of writing after the loss of one's own story, one's own text: the first obstacles to return were 'schwierige worte' in an environment of 'tonnen zermürbter papiere' and 'waben und adern der schrift' (p.81). The return of the lyric subject to his past facilitates the return of the 'ich' through writing:

> in prosa kehre ich wieder
> in wiederholungen zuletzt
> in bildern manchmal unsichtbar (p.91)

The poet must pick up 'die fäden des vergessens', 'die speichelfäden' (p.87), which like Ariadne's threads, give the route back. These 'fäden' are superseded by 'garne' (p.88), to which he compares 'der stoff von poesien'. Travelling, with the emphasis lent by the rhyme of 'kreisend' and 'reisend', becomes a nomadic search for words:

> kreisend
> reden wir langsam reisend
> kreuzend durch die trübe schwindsucht der ebene
> quer zu den sätzen worte suchend (p.90)

The image recalls Drawert's poem as a 'langsames, zielloses Gehen'. In Hilbig's poem, this process of writing is also 'den leichnam [...] befruchten', 'aus der schmiede zerbrechen', bringing life to the dead, breaking up that which has been forged. The journey began with a leap into the abyss: at the

---

[131]Namelessness, an ultimate dispossession, comes up again and again in Drawert's *Wo es war*. The anonymous lover's ('Nichts', p.66 and 'Leer und sehr blau', pp.67-68) is one of many missing names in the collection: names are lost from gravestones in 'So gehen die Unsterblichkeiten' (pp.26-27), a name is lost by data bank technology in 'Bleib sitzen' (p.28), nameless orphans feature in 'Tauben in ortloser Landschaft' (pp.103-110), and a nameless inner self in '...doch' (p.101).

end of the introduction the lyric 'ich' is Shakespeare's Lear, the blind and insane king, who comes to tragic realization of his own misjudgement and misguided loyalties:

> am ende am abgrund ließ ich mich fallen
> ein lear in lumpen am fuß einer klippe von mist. (p.82)

The lyric subject goes back to his childhood (part 1), and writes it in the third person. The journey is described as 'splitternde stiegen nach oben in der nacht in der unzeit' (p.83). Allusions to great fires, 'brände', 'fallböen blutiger feuer' suggest a vista with biblical resonances of the fiery lake and Judgement Day, or Dante's road through the circles of Hell beneath the surface of the earth. Various mining terms are woven into the text: 'flözen des asche', 'sinter des nichts', 'kohlehalden' suggest location in the earth's core (pp.84-85). Omens of death, 'schlingen', 'salamander' and 'raben' (p.85), indicate Hades, but these depths also facilitate renewal through memory:

> ah! und es steigen endlich
> gefieder von erinnerungen aus der toten luft
> die das land vermummte.   (p.85)

Hilbig draws on the Platonic cycle of *corruptio* and *generatio*. Continuance of the cycle is 'seit jahren vertagt', but now his return to the earth is also a restoration of the cycle. The process of return is one of remembering, 'nachdenken' (p.84): memories bring grass sprouting in the fields of ash, the first signs of regrowth. Part 3 of the poem corresponds to the last years of the GDR. 'Wir' here are GDR writers as domestic servants and sirens:

> und wir schrieben unsere verse mit bohnerwachs
> wir fielen nicht auf am fuß der treppenhäuser: einmal
> pro jahr atmeten wir wie kompressoren auf der schwelle
> zwischen den doppeltüren von geist und macht –
> nacht für nacht heulten wir: sirenen in seenot
> und gedachten unsrer in giftschränken faulenden fehlgeburten (p.95)

This image of writers polishing the floors in the corridors of power captures the exclusion of many writers from what was proclaimed to be a symbiotic relationship between 'Geist' and 'Macht'. It also suggests that writers effectively 'polished' the image of the state regime. Their creative writings were not births but miscarriages. Towards the close of part 3, the poet heralds his addressees as the 'Wende' demonstrators:

> und ich rufe euch an: schön seid ihr endlich in der revolte
> die ihr nicht vergessen werdet denn ihr seid gepriesen
> waffenlos gewaltlos rückhaltlos und gepriesen
> die ihr die straße mit euren lange verschütteten worten
> gefüllt (p.98)

The re-emergence of language at the 'Wende' is celebrated as a bacchanal: 'schön ist das bacchanal der toten worte' (p.98). The location of the street, which has run through this text, issues into the 'Wende' image of the street as the site of change: 'mit einem mal haben die wörter die straße betreten' (p.95). Awakening from hibernation, stressed by repetition of 'erwacht'/'erwachte' (p.95) in consecutive lines, is also an awakening of words, whose life is conveyed by personification. Words, which are 'endlich geformt zu zeilen', are implicitly likened to a liberating army, 'schulter an schulter' (p.95). This is where the poet founds his word, like a building amidst 'abschutt' (p.94).

Part 4, published separately, is the 'ankunft', arrival back at the present: 'ah! über küsten und lande kam ich ...' ('ankunft', p.99), 'hier bin ich endlich wieder: hierher blicke ich zurück' (p.101). This is not the end of travel however:

hier laßt mich fahren mehr denn je
                              im gras
        erinnerung wie eine leere landschaft im gepäck:
hier scheiterte der einbaum meiner metaphysischen epoche   (p.99)

With this point in time the lyric subject associates 'das wort meiner hoffnung' (p.100), although it brings exile for him, because he is a poet:

und es war das wort von einer wohnung für alle
und für mich wars ein wort des exils.

denn das vaterland des dichters ist das exil.   (p.100)

The poet is always in exile here; he has no fatherland; he is 'verwaist' and 'unverwandt inmitten der systeme' (p.100). The theme of writing and the poet's location has run through the whole poem, but at the close, the topic is the writing of this poem:

ich widerstand der lockung nicht wie orpheus der nicht widerstand
und sah zurück: ich warf zurück den basiliskenblick
ich schulterte die schuld und schritt verdrehten halses weiter
und ließ das leben hinter mir [...]
(im rückschaun erst verwirklicht sich der tod –   (p.102)

The ex-GDR poet identifies with the singer-poet Orpheus who to rescue Eurydice went down to the Underworld too. The 'basiliskenblick' refers to this story where to look back is to be frozen as a solid pillar. The punctuation of the last line above, the final line of the poem, indicates the unending process of looking back. Yet in another sense this is an ending, for going back has made the death real and facilitated a leave-taking from the GDR years.

Two 'Neue Gedichte' of 1991 use similar imagery to 'prosa meiner heimatstraße'.[132] In Hilbig's poem 'jugend' (pp.5-7) we find the same image of spirits awakening from the dead as words reawaken:

wie schläfer plötzlich

---

[132]Wolfgang Hilbig, 'Neue Gedichte', *ndl*, 39 (1991), No.9, 5-8.

> die ihre schatten neben sich erwachen sehn
> sahn wir: aus äußersten vergangenheiten
> erhoben sich die worte die uns dachten (p.5)

This 'wir' is defined by words from a past, which was a period of hibernation. In the poem 'die aufklärung' (p.8) Hilbig raises the unmarked question 'zu welchem ende sind wir nun erwacht' (23). The awakenings central to 'prosa meiner heimatstraße' are called into question and the poet evokes the timeless motif of a journey to the end of the world, which reveals no utopia:

> morgen brach nicht an
> nachtfarben wie der stoff der segel selbst
> stieß heulender wind uns ins dunkel und
> wir erreichten der welten rand ...
>
>   dort
> war zeit nicht des vergangnen zu gedenken: schrecklich
> schrien kopflose helden nach blut
>   und gellend
> verklagten uns die wüsten sieger aus dem lärm der see
> der sie schwerer schlug als schwerter... (lines 8-17)

This journey of 'die aufklärung' finds only defeat at the hands of 'die wüsten sieger'. It recalls the charge into the void in Wilhelm Bartsch's poem 'Gen Ginnungagap'.[133] Here Bartsch presents barbarians travelling into a bottomless ravine as an image for our times. This title poem of Bartsch's 1994 collection *Gen Ginnungagap* draws on the apocalyptic verses of the Edda to name the void or magic gorge.[134] The journey superseding this charge into the void is the personal one of 'prosa meiner heimatstraße': that poem expresses the end of the Enlightenment journey as an empty wasteland which sends the individual back to find how he got there, and thus who he is. Similarly, the earth rent and the search for home are motifs in Armin Richter's 'Zwischenräume' and the underground biography recurs in Thomas Rosenlöcher's 'Erdsirenen'.[135]

    The journey in search of identity, a crucial motif in post-unification

---

[133]Wilhelm Bartsch, 'Gen Ginnungagap', *Gen Ginnungagap: Gedichte* (Halle: mdv, 1994), p.6.

[134]See *The New Encyclopaedia Britannica: Micropaedia*, iv (Chicago, London, Toronto, Geneva, Tokyo, Manila, Seoul, Johannesburg: Encyclopaedia Britannica, 1974), p.548: 'Ginnungagap (Magic Void) in Norse mythology, is the void that existed between Niflheim, a region of frost and mist, and Muspelheim, a light, hot place, before the earth was formed at the beginning of time. According to the most rational account, three gods, Odin and his brothers, raised up the earth, perhaps from the sea, and placed it in the Ginnungagap, where it was soon covered with green herbage and, later, populated'.

[135]Armin Richter, 'Zwischenräume', *Die kleinen mecklenburgischen Meere*, p.53; Thomas Rosenlöcher, 'Erdsirenen', *ndl*, 43 (1995), No.2, 124-125.

poetry, embraces the opposition between 'eigen' and 'fremd': writing becomes a refounding of identity in the face of all-consuming 'Fremdheit', a means of finding memories and history to make one's own text. 'Eigentum', in the sense of values, an identity and a place of one's own, is central to the poetry of the period. In the poem 'Badlands: Eine Rhapsodie nach dem 1. Korintherbrief, 13' (*Gen Ginnungagap*, pp.67-69) Bartsch's lyric subject finds one type of 'Eigentum' in America:

> Bis zu den Badlands erfuhr ich nichts
> von meinem planetarischen Eigentum.
> Erst das Schlamm-Meer des Missouri erstickte
> meine alten feudalen Grenzen um Herz und Hof.
> Doch dann, wo Grasprärien wie Brotberge aufbrachen
> und vertrocknen, hatte ich es   (lines 1-6)

Not a journey into one's past, like Czechowski, Drawert and Hilbig have portrayed, but rather a journey to a foreign country, brings awareness of this 'Eigentum'. It is planetary 'Eigentum', opening the self to the infinite landscapes of the earth. Seneca, in Müller's words, claims a quite different 'Eigentum', one which closes in on the self. In 'Senecas Tod' (*Die Gedichte*, pp.250-251) the most resonant line is the conjectured thought, 'MEINE SCHMERZEN SIND MEIN EIGENTUM' (p.250). This statement reflects the pained self which recurs generally in poetry by diverse poets from the former GDR. The poem is one of many death poems in Müller's collection: he was dying himself, but in this poem the death theme also represents the end of the teacher's role. Both Seneca as Nero's tutor and the GDR writer are 'Lehrer'. Müller's lyric subject identifies with Seneca as he commits a tortuous suicide, hacking at his various veins. In the 1990s, writing is part of the great search for 'Eigentum', for what one still has, as against what is lost, and for a text of one's own, as against what is 'fremd'.

On the one hand the crisis which these poets articulate is part of a general sense of break-up at the end of the millennium. Czechowski's poem 'Gestörte Verhaltnisse' (*Nachtspur*, pp.177-179), for instance, overtly describes the situation in Germany after the 'Wende', but then opens out this context in the following lines:

> Das plattgewalzte Jahrhundert
> Braucht keine Propheten, quer
> Liegt es unter den Füßen, planetarische Manifeste
> Wird es nicht mehr geben. (p.179)

The articulation of crisis can also, however, be rendered very particular to German poets from the GDR. One aspect of this particularity is the contact between 1989/90 and 1945. The fall of the GDR is represented in ways that echo the end of the Second World War and the fall of the Third Reich. References to 'Kahlschlag', representations of devastation, and 'Heimkehrer' figures in post-unification poetry recall these motifs in post-war literature. Discourse involving father-figures suggests a repositioning with respect to history and authority, which relates the self to the actions of the previous generation.[136] In the poem 'Man kann nichts dagegen machen' (Wo es war, pp.15-16) Drawert rejects Theodor Adorno's famous post-war dictum 'Nach Auschwitz ein Gedicht zu schreiben, ist barbarisch', instead echoing Franz Fühmann's designation of poetry as 'das Andere zu Auschwitz':[137]

> Und so stimmt es: nach Auschwitz
> haben die Deutschen
> nur noch ein Recht
> auf Gedichte   (lines 33-36)

In turning round Adorno's statement, Drawert creates a *bon mot* which makes a point about genre, suggesting poetry cannot be misappropriated. All that is left is poetry, he seems to declare. Two terms established for talking about the post-war period were 'Trauerarbeit' and 'narzissistische Kränkung'.[138] In poems after 1989/90 these terms might be used too to characterize literary responses to the 'Wende' and German unification. There is a sense in which the caesura in 1989/90 sends the poets back to the caesura of 1945, as if that turning-point could only now be fully resolved and confronted.

Finally, I return to the basic idea of poets as 'Verlierer', with which this chapter began. Many writers present themselves in poetry not so much as the losing side in the battle between ideologies, but rather as losers in that they experienced the 'Wende' and unification as a loss – of utopia, of a dialogue, of identity. Poetry becomes concerned with grieving for these losses, and naming what is 'eigen' and what is 'fremd' after the turning-point of 1989/90. In the foreword to his collection of writers' pronouncements on the 'Wende', Michael Naumann stated, '22 Autoren – das sind im Frühjahr 1990 mindestens zehn rückwärtsgewandte Utopisten'.[139] This idea of writers as utopians, encapsulates both their pursuit of utopia and the fact that they ended up literally with 'no place'. Metaphors of homelessness, emptiness and anonymity recur in the poetry, but against these things writing itself is a search to recoup loss: Hilbig's

---

[136]On the subject of the fathers theme in Drawert's prose monologue *Spiegelland*, see Joachim Garbe, 'Hanns-Josef Ortheil und Kurt Drawert: Abschied von den Vätern', in *Deutschsprachige Gegenwartsliteratur*, ed. by Hans-Jörg Knobloch and Helmut Koopmann (Tübingen: Stauffenburg, 1997), pp.167-180.

[137]Theodor W. Adorno, 'Kulturkritik und Gesellschaft' (1949), in *Lyrik nach Auschwitz? Adorno und die Dichter*, ed. by Petra Kiedaisch (Stuttgart: Reclam, 1995), pp.27-49 (p.49). Franz Fühmann, *Der Sturz des Engels: Erfahrungen mit Dichtung* (Hamburg: Hoffmann und Campe, 1982), p.236.

[138]See, for instance, Alexander and Margarete Mitscherlich, *Die Unfähigkeit zu trauern: Grundlagen kollektiven Verhaltens* (Munich: Piper, 1977).

[139]Naumann, ed., *Die Geschichte ist offen*, p.11.

lyric subject in 'prosa meiner heimatstraße' states, 'aus verlornem zieh ich der zeilen gewinn' ('ankunft', p.95); Papenfuß in an interview in 1993 declared, 'Verlust ist eine Herausforderung'.[140] Loss and its challenge to writing is self-consciously thematized by many, different poets. The loner figure identified in connection with the 'Wende-Zeitgedichte' continues to be important, but it shifts as a motif: the loner tends specifically to be a poet who is searching for words and for identity after 1989/90. The psychologist Hans-Joachim Maaz identifies unification with a general sense of loss: 'Werteverfall, Orientierungsverlust und Identitätsbrüchen'.[141] Poetry is concerned with these three themes, but particularly with respect to the poet's own position. Czechowski's reflection on the time after 1989/90 seems typical:

> Ich suchte keine 'neue' Rolle, würde jedoch immer mehr in meinem Selbstverständnis auf mich selbst verwiesen. [...] Ich sehe mich mehr und mehr mit meinen Problemen befaßt, wobei ich, von mir aus gesehen, es nicht aufgehört habe, mich als *zoon politikon* zu begreifen. Deshalb ist die Sprache meiner Gedichte nach wie vor auf die Öffentlichkeit gerichtet, auch wenn mich diese weniger hört.[142]

The collections demonstrate a remarkable prevalence of poetological reflection and self-reflection as reactions to the end of the GDR and the arrival of the new Germany. Ex-GDR poets write as post-war Germans, as new members of capitalist society, as outsiders, but also and above all else as poets, with an overt consciousness of poetic identity and articulating the need to refound that identity after 1989/90.

---

[140]Jörg Magenau and Stefan Reinecke, 'Verlust ist eine Herausforderung: Gespräch mit Bert Papenfuß', *Freitag*, 24 December 1993, p.21.
[141]Hans-Joachim Maaz, 'Die sozialpsychologischen Schwierigkeiten der deutschen Vereinigung', in *Probleme des Zusammenwachsens im wiedervereinigten Deutschland*, ed. by Alexander Fischer and Manfred Wilke (Berlin: Duncker & Humblot, 1994), pp.9-12 (p.11).
[142]Letter to me, November 1998.

CHAPTER 5
THE END OF A ROLE:
VOLKER BRAUN'S POST-'WENDE' POETRY

Having characterized 'Wende' poetry and post-unification poetry generally, I now turn in the next two chapters to look at two poets in greater depth. This chapter examines a 'classic' GDR poet, Volker Braun, so as to identify the impact of the 'Wende' and unification on the particular role he conceives for himself and his writing. I have chosen Braun because he is in many ways more typical of the development of poetry after 1989/90 than others, and because he illustrates its strengths and weaknesses rather more markedly than they do. He also lends himself to special study because few writers of the time produced anything as compelling as the 'Wende' poem 'Das Eigentum', which I discuss in detail below. Braun's position in 1989/90 is set against what came before, for the first months of change seemed to bring the apotheosis of his past role as a poet and the culmination of his writing project to date. In November 1989 a Budapest journalist suggested that Braun had essentially been promoting glasnost and perestroika long before these words were on everyone's lips.[1] The relentless sociological concerns in his poetry can be seen to foreshadow the GDR civil rights discourse of 1988/89. Indeed Braun's title *Training des aufrechten Gangs* became a commonplace metaphor in announcements and headlines at that time.[2] Examining the use of this metaphor at the 'Wende', Bernd Jürgen Warneken traces it to images in Kant's *Was ist Aufklärung?*, but the phrase itself comes from Bloch in the 1960s and Braun's title of 1979.[3] In Bloch and Braun it refers to a training in 'true' socialism: 'ein neues, härteres Training des schmerzhaften und wunderbaren aufrechten Gangs'.[4] The same metaphor occurs in the opening lines of Brecht's poem 'Der Große Oktober':

---

[1]'Darum sieht diese neue Welt so alt aus', *Budapester Rundschau*, 20 November 1989, p.9.
[2]Volker Braun, *Training des aufrechten Gangs* (Halle: mdv, 1979) and in *Texte*, v , pp.57-112. In 1989 the phrase was also the motto for a literary competition in *Temperamente* to mark the fortieth anniversary of the GDR.
[3]Bernd Jürgen Warneken, ' "Aufrechter Gang": Metamorphosen einer Parole des DDR-Umbruchs', in *Mauer-Show*, ed. by Bohn, pp.17-30. Immanuel Kant, 'Beantwortung der Frage: Was ist Aufklärung?' (1784), *Werke*, xi (Frankfurt a.M.: Insel, 1964), pp.53-61. Bloch, *Das Prinzip Hoffnung*.
[4]Braun, 'Höhlengleichnis', *Texte*, v, p.102.

O großer Oktober der Arbeiterklasse!
Endliches Sichaufrichten der so lange
Niedergebeugten   (lines 1-3)

As a motto in 1989, 'aufrechter Gang' was used by the writer Stefan Heym
speaking at the Alexanderplatz rally on 4 November. It was a metaphor for the
resurrected sense of self-respect which people demonstrated in taking to the
streets. Later it also became a metaphor for GDR pride, against crawling to the
West, and a metaphor for GDR guiltlessness as opposed to hanging ones head
in shame. In effect, it thus represented the apparent antithesis of the post-
unification 'Verlierer'. In a newspaper article published on 11/12 November
1989 Braun reprinted part of an earlier poem, which takes up this metaphorical
rising of the crushed:[5]

Frühjahre der Völker. Seltenzeit
Wenn sie ausgehn, aus ihrem Schlummer
Ins Freie. Das Eis
Der Strukturen bricht, und es hebt den Nacken neugierig
Der Unterdrückte.

Braun followed this self-quotation with the statement 'Wir machen die
Erfahrung der Freiheit' (p.163). He interpreted the incipient 'Wende' as a
realization of the awakening described in his 1986 poem 'Der Eisenwagen'.[6]
As the 'Wende' unfolded, Braun eagerly greeted the prospect of social change
as a shift towards the ideals articulated in his work. In Leipzig on 8 November
1989 he gave a reading of texts he had written over the last five to ten years,
under the title 'Texte zur Wende'. The 1971 poem 'Die Morgendämmerung',
interpolated into Braun's 'Leipziger Vorlesung', represents another example
of the 'Wende' as the culmination of Braun's reformist project: the title refers
to the dawn which Braun's writing had long been anticipating.[7] Hope which
had begun to degenerate in the earlier 1980s was renewed. As the
demonstrations grew, Braun identified with the demands being voiced and
sought to encourage those who took to the streets. He interpreted the
beginnings of change in the GDR as a positive conflict which would
reinvigorate socialism.[8] This Marxist idea of fruitful conflict was typical of the
stance Braun had taken throughout the GDR years. Indeed, looking back in
March 1990 to the Alexanderplatz rally, Braun stated, 'Die Zeit war da, auf

---

[5]Volker Braun, 'Die Erfahrung der Freiheit', *ND*, 11/12 November 1989, p.13, and
reprinted in *Texte*, x, pp.163-167 (p.163).
[6]Braun, 'Der Eisenwagen', *Monatshefte*, 78 (1986), 7.
[7]Braun, 'Leipziger Vorlesung', *Wir befinden uns soweit wohl. Wir sind erst einmal am
Ende. Äußerungen* (Frankfurt a.M.: Suhrkamp, 1998), p.29.
[8]This is clear from the interview by Karoly Vörös, 'Lösungen für alle', *Der Morgen*,
28/29 October 1989, and reprinted in *Wir befinden uns soweit wohl*, pp.14-17 (p.16).

die viele von uns, Lebende und Tote, hingearbeitet haben. Das Horizontbewußtsein der Literatur war kein bewußtloses Träumen gewesen'.[9] These words come from the speech Braun made to his fellow writers at the special 'Schriftstellerkongreß' of March 1990. They express a sense of the 'Wende' as a product of literature's utopian vision. Braun felt that GDR writers had led the way to this point and that their dreams would now be vindicated.

Examining Braun's poetry of the 1960s and 1970s, the academic Gerrit-Jan Berendse wrote, 'Braun oder das lyrische Ich Brauns stellt sich selbst als "Brigadier" der "Dichterbrigade" an die Spitze der Erneuerungen'.[10] Perhaps Braun was seeking to do the same thing in autumn 1989. Not only did he use his public profile as a writer to support the demonstrators' demands, he also gave his first unofficially-published poems to the 'alternative' magazine *Bizarre Städte*.[11] Asked about his role in November 1989, Braun responded: 'Ich finde, man muß – zB durch ein bewußtes Auftreten in allen möglichen Foren – all diese Leute ermutigen, die auf die Straße gehen oder ihre eigenen Gruppen bilden. Das ist doch eine aktive Teilnahme, die es lange nicht gab'.[12] Braun's sense of the writer's role as an educator and leader is perceptible in these comments. He was resentful of those who left the country to find what, in his view, was a personal solution, rather than working for 'Lösungen für alle'.[13] On 8 November Christa Wolf read a statement on GDR television which had been signed by Braun, Heym, Hein, and Ulrich Plenzdorf, the theatre director Ruth Berghaus, the conductor Kurt Masur, and various leaders of opposition groups. It was an appeal to citizens who were considering emigrating:

> Wir bitten Sie, bleiben Sie doch in Ihrer Heimat, bleiben Sie bei uns! Was können wir Ihnen versprechen? Kein leichtes, aber ein nützliches und interessantes Leben. Keinen schnellen Wohlstand, aber Mitwirkung an großen Veränderungen.[14]

The artists and intellectuals called for citizens to work with them to effect change in the name of democratic socialism. They spoke as though they were the voice of the nation itself. At that time Braun did not realize that the actual solution chosen would be capitalism. He spoke not in favour of multi-party democracy, but specifically for a more democratic socialism. As the early

[9]Braun, 'Das Unersetzliche wird unser Thema bleiben', *ndl*, 38 (1990), 6-9 (p.6).
[10]Berendse, *Die "Sächsische Dichterschule"*, p.222.
[11]Volker Braun, [7 poems], *Bizarre Städte*, Sonderheft, October 1989.
[12]See interview 'Halbheiten kommen teuer zu stehen', *Unsere Zeit*, 7 November 1989, p.7.
[13]Vörös, 'Lösungen für alle', p.17.
[14]'Dokumente', in Wolf, *Im Dialog*, pp.169-170 (p.169).

weeks went by he still sought a new form of socialism, regardless of the historical reality:[15]

Meint ihr, weil die traditionelle Form des Sozialismus den Bach hinunter floß, und weil sie sich als untauglich erwies, daß das Bedürfnis nach Gerechtigkeit erloschen ist? [...] Meint ihr nicht, daß die alte Sehnsucht nach einer solidarischen und verhältnismäßigen Chancengleichheit wieder aufflammt?

This image of the old yearning for a better world flaring up at the 'Wende' corresponds to Braun's republication of old, visionary poetry at this time. In December 1989 Braun reproduced his 1977 poem 'Vom Besteigen hoher Berge (nach Lenin)' in a journalistic article.[16]

Jetzt geht es nicht mehr vorwärts in dem ewigen Schnee
Formulare / Kies / Versprechungen / kalter Kaffee.
Jetzt hat uns die Höhenkrankheit befallen
[...]
Wo wollen wir eigentlich hin.
Ist das überhaupt der Berg, den wir beehren
Oder eine ägyptische Pyramide.
Warum sind wir so müde.
Müssen wir nicht längst umkehren
Und von unsern Posten herabfahren. (lines 1-3 and 9-14)

Again, he seeks to make poetry 'useful' to the unfolding historical process. Republishing this poem in a newspaper article reflects his sense of the poet's role as a mouthpiece for the people who demonstrated on the streets. Braun adds to his poem in the prose which follows it, interpreting a quite ambivalent text in a markedly positive sense: 'Jetzt sind wir im Tal, mit unsern Rucksäcken, Seilen und Eispickeln' (p.23). After growing disillusionment in the earlier 1980s, Braun finds a new hopefulness in 1989. The insistent repetition of 'jetzt' throughout this poem emphasizes a new potential in the present. In the 'Wende' demonstrations Braun perceives a resurrected 'wir': according to his article, the role of the poet is to be a climber alongside the population. The motif of the bowed head being raised recurs here as looking up to symbolic heights: 'Jetzt im Tal, beschleunigt Hoffnung die Schritte. Das Volk hebt *demonstrierend* den Blick: wohin hinauf?' (p.25). 'Hoffnung', which had been crucial to the intellectuals' stance throughout the GDR years, is felt to be an active force at the 'Wende'. There is a renewed sense of purpose: 'Es ist ein seltener geschichtlicher Augenblick, in dem wir die Macht in Händen haben, die Zukunft zu korrigieren' (p.27). These statements

---

[15]'Halbheiten kommen teuer zu stehen'.
[16]Volker Braun, 'Notizen eines Publizisten: Vom Besteigen hoher Berge oder: Kommt Zeit, kommt Räte', *ND*, 8 December 1989, p.4, and reprinted in *Wir befinden uns soweit wohl*, pp.23-28.

demonstrate astonishing self-belief. Subsequently, great disillusionment would set in. But in late 1989 the republishing of older texts from some twelve years previously, with their metaphors of the crushed arising, of justice flaming up, and of mountaineers setting out to conquer a peak, indicate that Braun was retaining old parameters and re-employing the old language.[17] Events seemed to be vindicating his poetic visions.

Braun was the most prominent reform-socialist poet from the GDR. Overall his poetry largely held to ideal socialism, to the 'Volk' and to a collective 'wir'. Critics have identified Braun as a writer who took 'DDR-Befindlichkeiten' as a starting point for his literary work.[18] He was interested in the GDR as poetic material because he regarded it as a great experiment in modern civilization, according to Walfried Hartinger. Klaus Schuhmann describes the poet Braun as a 'Landgänger und Chronist'.[19] Despite quotations from philosopical, historical and literary works which are timeless and international, the reader is always brought back to the poet's concern with his own country. Even in December 1989 Braun was living out the idea of co-operation between 'Geist' and 'Macht' in the GDR, by publishing a text specifically in order to influence the SED.[20] Another poem 'Tapetenwechsel', which he read out at the writers' gathering 'Wider den Schlaf der Vernunft' at the end of 1989, refers to Kurt Hager's rhetorical question of 1987 vis-à-vis perestroika in the Soviet Union: 'Würden Sie, wenn Ihr Nachbar seine Wohnung neu tapeziert, sich verpflichtet fühlen, Ihre Wohnung ebenfalls neu zu tapezieren?'.[21] In this instance, the poem gestures towards a dialogue with the Politburo and the ZK, of which Hager was a member.

> Tapetenwechsel
> Die Verwaltung erklärt mir
> Sie habe den Umbau längst in aller Stille vollzogen.
> Aber das Haus ist nicht geräumiger
> Die Treppe unbequem

---

[17]Further examples of symbolic mountain heights occur in the pre-'Wende' poems 'Machu Picchú' and 'Benjamin in den Pyrenäen', *Lustgarten Preußen: Ausgewählte Gedichte* (Frankfurt a.M.: Suhrkamp, 1996), pp.56-58 and pp.113-114.

[18]See especially, Walfried Hartinger, 'Gesellschaftsentwurf und ästhetische Innovation - Zu einigen Aspekten im Werk Volker Brauns', in *Volker Braun*, ed. by Rolf Jucker (Cardiff: University of Wales Press, 1995), pp.30-54.

[19]Klaus Schuhmann, 'Landeskunde im Gedicht: Zeitwandel und Zeitwende in der Lyrik Volker Brauns', *ZfG*, N.F. 3 (1993), No.1, 134-145 (p.136).

[20]Braun, *Wir befinden uns soweit wohl*, p.50.

[21]Volker Braun, 'Tapetenwechsel', *Die Zickzackbrücke*, p.15. Kurt Hager, in *Stern*, 9 April 1987, p.140.

5   Und sind die Zimmerchen heller?
      Und warum ziehen die Leute aus und nicht ein?

Braun's epigrammatic poem uses the image of a house in need of renovation, thereby referring to an officially-propounded image of 'Aufbau', in order to counter the claims of the administration. Unanswered questions in lines 5 and 6 represent a political provocation, especially where the last line draws attention to the exodus of GDR citizens.

Clearly, Braun was never a 'Dichter im Dienst', following the SED's every criterion for literature, and yet he did believe in the underlying GDR principle of the writer's socialist responsibility. Having been a defining figure of the 'Lyrikwelle' of the 1960s, Braun had arguably become part of the GDR Establishment by the 1980s. He was a member of the select 'Präsidium' of the GDR writers' union under Hermann Kant's presidency and made a speech in that capacity at the tenth 'Schriftstellerkongreß' in November 1987.[22] To some younger poets in the GDR Braun no longer epitomized daringly critical writing as he had done in the 1960s and 1970s: on the contrary, his membership of the 'Schriftstellerverband' and numerous publications within the GDR implied to some minds an artistic compromise with political power.[23] Braun's case can be seen as representative of the problematic linking of politics and poetry under socialist dictatorship. The ex-GDR writer Brigitte Burmeister termed the relationship between suppression and creativity in the GDR 'eine befremdliche Koexistenz'.[24] As a poet, novelist and playwright, Braun was the typical GDR artist caught up in this uneasy co-existence. Braun himself described the dilemma in *Verheerende Folgen mangelnden Anscheins innerbetrieblicher Demokratie* as an unbearable contradiction: 'Es ist unerträglich, diesen Widerspruch zu leben: eine bedeutende Kulturpolitik mitzutragen und ihr ein Ärgernis zu sein'.[25] Braun was a long-standing member of the union whose statutes stated that its members were 'Schriftsteller der DDR, die in ihrer schöpferischen Arbeit aktive Mitgestalter der entwickelten sozialistischen Gesellschaft sind'.[26] This was the significant

---

[22]Braun's speech is reproduced in *ndl*, 36 (1988), No.3, 44-47.
[23]See for instance Ingrid Pergande, ' "Volker Braun? Da kann ich nur sagen, der Junge quält sich..." New Voices in the GDR lyric of the 1980s', in *Socialism and the Literary Imagination*, ed. by Kane, pp.229-246 and Ursula Heukenkamp, 'Ohne den Leser geht es nicht: Gespräch mit Gerd Adloff, Gabriele Eckart, Uwe Kolbe, Bernd Wagner', *WB*, 25 (1979), No.7, 46.
[24]Burmeister, 'Schriftsteller in gewendeten Verhältnissen', p.652.
[25]Volker Braun, *Verheerende Folgen mangelnden Anscheins innerbetrieblicher Demokratie: Schriften* (Frankfurt a.M.: Suhrkamp, 1988), p.118.
[26]Quoted in Joachim Walter, ed., *Protokoll eines Tribunals: Die Ausschlüsse aus dem*

cultural policy in which Braun believed. Nevertheless, his work was an irritation to the censoring authorities. His major collection of the 1980s, *Langsamer knirschender Morgen* contained his most 'critical' work, especially in the section 'Satiren und Lektionen'.[27] It took years of negotiations with censors before the pruned and tamed collection could be published in 1987.[28] This indicates both that Braun was writing discomforting poetry, and that he was ultimately, if reluctantly, willing to forgo exclusive control over his writing. Furthermore, his perseverance in such a regulated environment showed perhaps greater belief in his art and allegiance to a wide readership, than a withdrawal from GDR literary life. In his 1985 essay on the contemporary innovations in GDR literature, Braun used the image of the state as an overprotective parent in order to criticize cultural prescriptiveness: 'Sie hat uns wie Kinder gehalten, als wir längst Männer werden wollten'.[29] Yet he did not want to escape the state, but rather to engage more effectively in its original enterprise and as a 'Provokateur' stir others, through his writing, to do likewise. His own texts sought to contribute to an incipient 'tomorrow', creating the 'knirschen' of the *Langsamer knirschender Morgen*.

Braun was not only the classic GDR poet by virtue of his established career and of his public statements and republications at the 'Wende'. His new poetry also articulates a response to the 'Wende' that reflects his sense of having a role in the development of the society in which he was living. Braun's 'Wende' collection is entitled *Die Zickzackbrücke: Ein Abrißkalender*. In May 1988 Braun had visited Shanghai and seen its bridge with nine zigzags, which becomes a metaphor for the twists and turns of history in the title of his collection. The zigzag reflects the surprises during the course of 1988-1991, the period of Braun's 'Kalender'. It also reflects Bloch's view that progress through history is not a curve, but 'ein Zickzack, in dem [...] nur die Figur des Chaos ist'.[30] The collection furthermore claims to be an aesthetic zigzag; it includes poems and prose, and documentary material such as interviews, as well as literary texts. But a single aesthetic can also perhaps be seen to unite the material, namely the text as an address to society and a sociological comment. A direct line is drawn between text and society at the outset: in the 1987 poem 'Aus dem dogmatischen Schlummer geweckt'

DDR-Schriftstellerverband 1979 (Reinbek bei Hamburg: Rowohlt, 1991), p.34.
[27]Volker Braun, *Langsamer knirschender Morgen* (Halle: mdv, 1987) and *Texte*, viii, pp.43-122.
[28]See Wichner, ed., *Zensur in der DDR*, pp.161-165.
[29]Braun, 'Rimbaud. Ein Psalm der Aktualität', p.979.
[30]Bloch, *Das Prinzip Hoffnung*, p.231.

(*Zickzackbrücke*, p.9) the dreams of the lyric subject have consequences in reality:

> Du träumst, nicht wahr, du träumst mit Konsequenz. –
> Und auf den Straßen weht die Transparenz.   (lines 7-8)

The lyric subject describes his own visions manifesting themselves as street demonstrations. In May 1988, the poem 'Die Wende' (*Zickzackbrücke*, p.13) looks ahead to a historical turning-point:

> Auf den Hacken
> Dreht sich die Geschichte um;
> Für einen Moment
> Entschlossen.   (lines 5-8)

History itself is personified here as the active subject. Braun declared that this early 'Literatur der Wende' was 'als Herausforderung gemeint'.[31] The calendar of texts goes on to describe a course from such hopes in 1988 and 1989 to disillusionment a year later. The later poem 'Der Reißwolf' (*Zickzackbrücke*, p.90) is typical in its expression of hopelessness:

> Mein altes Schweigen wird zum Gebrüll
> Nicht mehr verständlich. Was bezweckte ich?   (lines 4-5)

The dreams which had seemed to inspire people in the lines quoted above, are incomprehensible now. This incomprehensibility heralds a crisis of purpose for the lyric subject, whom one cannot but identify with the reform-socialist GDR writer. His 'old' silence, a reference to the writer's compromises perhaps, was meaningful in the politically charged context of the GDR.[32] Now that silence sets the writer apart from the people's 'roar' at the 'Wende'. The collection documents such displacement, in effect tracing the 'Abriß' of Braun's role as a socialist poet, rather than the demolition of the GDR.

Both the demolition of the GDR and of the self is conveyed in Braun's 1995 poem 'Der Weststrand' (*Lustgarten Preußen*, pp.150-159). In the following extract from this poem, images of vertical descent and falling into oblivion reverse the earlier mountain metaphors of ascent:

> Ausschreitend auf dieser abschüssigen Bahn Progrès
> War kein Halten mehr
> Ein Riß
> In der Existenz (...) Das Minenfeld
> Deiner Kompromisse
> Geht langsam hoch. Passé
> Politisches Tier
> Vergiß die Witterung des Ziels.
> Abgewickelt

[31]Braun, *Wir befinden uns soweit wohl*, p.42.
[32]See also the motif of the silent writer in the 1975 poem 'Der schweigende Dichter', *Texte*, vi, pp.66-70.

                        ausgeschieden
                                    verrutscht
Ohne Zentralperspective
Fällt dein leichter Leib durch den Rost;
PARTEI UND STAAT, der Kurze Abgang
Der Seilschaft
            Von der Eifer-Nordwand
            Ins Nichts –   (II, p.151)
The layout of this poem mirrors the theme of instability and an uncontrolled
fall. Such woe represents a radical departure for Braun: 'Ein Riß / In der
Existenz' ushers into his poetry a fallen, insubstantial self. This is one of
several post-1989 poems by Braun which articulate the struggle against a loss
of identity.[33] The imagery of the last four lines quoted above is a continuation
of the mountaineering metaphors in earlier poems, such as 'Vom Besteigen
hoher Berge': the north face of the Eiger provides an image of escalating
socialist zeal.[34] A self that had climbed 'die Eifer-Nordwand' of the SED, now
reassesses his position:[35] he has lost all belief in progress towards a utopian
peak.
        In several poems Braun represents the 'Wende' as seismic activity. In
his 'Prolog zur Eröffnung der 40. Spielzeit des Berliner Ensembles am 11.
Oktober 1989' (*Zickzackbrücke*, pp.37-39) Braun referred to earthquakes and
'die Beben der Völker', and in the poem 'O Chicago! O Widerspruch!'
(*Zickzackbrücke*, p.81) the 'Wende' consists of 'die Erdbeben, die wir
hervorriefen'.[36] In an interview, the replacement of socialism by capitalism is
likened to lava flow: 'die eine Struktur schiebt sich über die andere wie
Lava'.[37] To some extent Braun's metaphorical seismic activity is a
continuation of the natural metaphors identified in a range of poetry in Chapter
3. The volcano is, however, a larger natural phenomenon and one which
especially suggests the smallness and powerlessness of the human being.
Braun's 'Plinius grüßt Tacitus (Für Heiner Müller)' (*Lustgarten Preußen*,

---

[33]See also the concept of literature as 'Arbeit gegen Identitätsverlust' in Hannemann,
'Geschichtsschreibung nach Aktenlage?', p.28.
[34]In addition, the word 'Seilschaft' was also a keyword of public discourse at the
'Wende'. See Herberg, *Schlüsselwörter der Wendezeit*, pp.340-341.
[35]Braun had access to the political heights: he was an 'SED-Genosse', a personal friend
of Klaus Höpcke, the high-ranking censor, and in regular contact with Kurt Hager, the
chief Politburo ideologue.
[36]Compare the opening of Jens Reich's *Abschied von den Lebenslügen: Die Intelligenz
und die Macht* (Berlin: Rowohlt, 1992), which uses an image of eastern Europe as a
landscape after a volcanic eruption.
[37]Braun, 'Jetzt wird das Schwächere geplatzt', *Wir befinden uns soweit wohl*, pp.59-63
(p.61).

pp.160-162) locates the lyric subject amid another volcanic eruption. Braun uses the letters of Pliny the Younger who witnessed the eruption of Vesuvius in AD 79 and whose letters are the primary source for the life and death of Pliny the Elder.[38] As Heiner Müller draws on reports of Mommsen's Roman history lectures in his post-'Wende' poem 'Mommsens Block', so Braun draws on the observations in Pliny's letter 6.16: the parallel with Müller is suggested by Braun's dedication. Like Müller, Braun thematizes the writing of history and evokes the ancient Roman world. (Perhaps it is relevant that this was a world of imperial patrons, where literary life was bound up with social, judicial, military and political life, and a writer like Pliny held military command.) The ancient natural disaster is paralleled in Braun's poem with the *'verratene Revolution'* (p.161) in the GDR. The contemporary German poet compares himself to Pliny the Elder remaining in an area of catastrophe. Descriptions from Pliny the Younger about his uncle weathering the volcanic eruption with a pillow tied to his head, taking sips of cold water and shaking off the ash, are taken into Braun's confession as an interior monologue:

> Ich habe den Untergang (bändeweise) beschrieben
> *Nur hin und wieder ein Schluck kalten Wassers*
> Und es wird nur mein eigenes Ende sein
> Während dessen ich bade und speise
> Von der Schlacke einer anderen Katastrophe
> *The Triumph of the West*, written by J.M. Roberts
> Aus der Nähe betrachtet ein Naturereignis
> Bis der Abraum vor der Türe liegt knüppeldick
> Warum verharre ich nicht
> In meiner sicheren Hoffnung an meinem Schreibtisch
> *Man müßte nur ab und zu die Asche*
> *Abschütteln, um nicht begraben zu werden*   (p.161)

The first line here refers both to Pliny the Elder's encyclopaedia *Naturalis Historica* and to Braun's poetry and plays which address the GDR 'Untergang'. A gulp of refreshing water becomes a metaphor for writing. The 'Untergang' of the state is also tied to the writer's own end. Unification is paralleled with a great shifting in the very earth, which the mining terms 'Schlacke' and 'Abraum' make vivid. The fate of Pliny the Elder, who died in the volcanic fumes, becomes a metaphor for the fate of the GDR poet-'ich' in the new Germany. The 'Wende' as a 'Naturereignis' denies human action if anything, reversing the 'Durchgearbeitete Landschaft' of Braun's earlier poem (*Texte*, iv, pp.88-89). The volcano also follows the earlier mountaineering

---

[38]See M. C. Howatson, ed., *The Oxford Companion to Classical Literature*, 2nd ed. (Oxford and New York: OUP, 1989), pp.445-447; Plinius der Jüngere, *Briefe in einem Band*, trans. by Werner Krenkel (Berlin, GDR: Aufbau, 1984), pp.171-174.

images, suggesting that the solid mountain of socialism suddenly explodes, crushing the would-be climbers.

A great shift is also the subject in Braun's poem 'Das Eigentum', which is the classic German poem of the 'Wende'.[39] Here the shift is not a natural disaster, but rather one for which blame can be attributed. This 1990 poem expresses a similar loss of literary communication and loss of purpose to that articulated in 'Der Reißwolf'. As Dieter Schlenstedt indicates, 'Das Eigentum' was the 'Wende' poem par excellence, published in *Neues Deutschland* (twice), *Die Zeit*, read by Braun at readings and on the radio, taken up in numerous anthologies, including *Von einem Land*, *Grenzfallgedichte*, *DEUTSCH in einem anderen LAND*, *Luftfracht* and *Das große deutsche Gedichtbuch*.[40]

> Das Eigentum
> Da bin ich noch: mein Land geht in den Westen.
> KRIEG DEN HÜTTEN FRIEDE DEN PALÄSTEN.
> Ich selber habe ihm den Tritt versetzt.
> Es wirft sich weg und seine magre Zierde.
> 5   Dem Winter folgt der Sommer der Begierde.
> Und ich kann *bleiben wo der Pfeffer wächst.*
> Und unverständlich wird mein ganzer Text.
> Was ich niemals besaß, wird mir entrissen.
> Was ich nicht lebte, werd ich ewig missen.
> 10   Die Hoffnung lag im Weg wie eine Falle.
> Mein Eigentum, jetzt habt ihrs auf der Kralle.
> Wann sag ich wieder *mein* und meine alle.

Despair is articulated as the paradox of losing something one never had, in line 8. The lyric 'ich' has lost the utopian vision, which will now remain unknown and unnamed ('Was'). This understanding of 'Eigentum' echoes that in Hölderlin's 1799 poem 'Mein Eigentum', where it is a longed-for place, 'der Traum', that is never achieved.[41] It also echoes Hugo von Hofmannstal's

---

[39]Braun, 'Das Eigentum', *ND*, 4-5 August 1990, p.1, and reprinted in *Zickzackbrücke*, p.84. The poem has also been reprinted under the title 'Nachruf', in *Grenzfallgedichte*, p.109.
[40]Dieter Schlenstedt, 'Ein Gedicht als Provokation', *ndl*, 40 (1992), No.12, 124-132. The poem has also had resonance within German poetry. It is taken up by the West German poet Dirk von Petersdorff in an untitled poem in *Wie es weitergeht: Gedichte* (Frankfurt a.M.: Fischer, 1992), p.33.
[41]In Hölderlin's poem, though, the homeless soul seeks rootedness in poetry: 'Sei du, Gesang, mein freundlich Asyl!'. See Friedrich Hölderlin, 'Mein Eigentum', *Sämtliche*

'Chandos-Brief', in which already-written texts are 'mein Eigentum'.[42] The
fiefdom of Braun's 1980 poem 'Das Lehen' (*Texte*, viii, pp.75-76) is replaced
by ownership in 'Das Eigentum', reflecting the 1989/90 shift in the poet's
role. The 'Eigentum' in Braun's poem also has resonances of
'Volkseigentum'. In an article Braun wrote two days after the fall of the Wall,
he enthused about the possibility of 'VOLKSEIGENTUM PLUS
DEMOKRATIE'.[43] He put democracy second here, but in the event,
democracy ensured the removal of 'Volkseigentum', for ultimately the citizens
voted for private ownership rather than state ownership. In Braun's poem, it is
also the 'Volk', 'ihr', who have effected the poet's dispossession: 'Mein
Eigentum, jetzt habt ihrs auf der Kralle' (11). The lyric subject is abandoned
by his country (line 1) which is intent, so he claims, on turning back the social
progress brought by the French Revolution. As Schlenstedt points out, line 2
reverses the cry of the French Revolution, a cry taken up in Büchner's 'Der
Hessische Landbote'.[44] Importantly, the GDR is 'mein Land' (1): despite his
criticism of its realities, the GDR was the country to which the poet bound his
identity. Horst Domdey sees in lines 4-5 the writer as a spurned lover, who
decries his GDR-bride for throwing herself away to lust.[45] Typical of reform-
socialists is the perception that the GDR population became gripped by
consumerism and materialistic greed. In this poem the GDR people are
represented as a wanton woman. Frauke Meyer-Gosau interprets the poet-'ich'
in 'Das Eigentum' as a teacher whose class have turned their backs on his
teaching at the first opportunity and given themselves to wantonness. The
poet-schoolmaster 'beklagt als ein Verlassener den Verlust dessen, was nun
sich als ein Phantasma enthüllt: die Gewohnheit, in seinem "Ich" ein "Wir",
im "Mein" ein "Unser" selbstverständlich aufgehen zu sehen'.[46] Braun's poem
closes with a yearning to recapture the sense of a community which embraces
poet and population: 'Wann sag ich wieder *mein* und meine alle' (12). In *The
Grapes of Wrath*, John Steinbeck articulates the same sense that ownership

Gedichte: Studienausgabe in zwei Bänden, ed. by Detlev Lüders (Bad Homburg:
Athenäum, 1970), pp.214-216.
[42]Hugo von Hofmannstal, 'Ein Brief' (1902), *Gesammelte Werke*, vii (Frankfurt a.M.:
Fischer, 1986), pp.461-472 (p.462).
[43]Braun, 'Die Erfahrung von Freiheit'.
[44]Georg Büchner, 'Der Hessische Landbote', *Sämtliche Werke*, ii, pp.53-66. Braun
sought to edit, and provide a commentary on, Büchner's letters in the late 1970s, but
was rejected by the authorities. His commentary appears in *Texte*, v, pp.293-310.
[45]Horst Domdey, 'Volker Braun und die Sehnsucht nach der Großen Kommunion: Zum
Demokratiekonzept der Reformsozialisten', *Deutschland Archiv*, 23 (1990), 1771-
1774.
[46]Meyer-Gosau, ' "Linksherum, nach Indien!".

works against community: 'the quality of owning freezes you ever into "I", and cuts you off for ever from the "we" '.[47] After the 'Wende', Braun's poetry repeatedly defines a loss of utopian possibilities. Here, the final unmarked question captures this in the repetition '*mein*' / 'meine'. Nonetheless the rigid form and the fact that each line of this poem is one complete sentence give the poem a controlled tone, which perhaps indicates the writer maintaining dignity in the face of loss. Could this poem then be read as characteristic of the 'Provokateur'? The allusion to wantonness and the accusation of the penultimate line may be construed as a provocation to those citizens eager for unification. Where Emmerich perceives a certain defiance in this poem, Domdey's analysis suggests the utter misguidedness of the reformer.[48] Braun is presenting a paradigm of the intellectual situation for ex-GDR writers like himself.[49] He aligns himself with Christa Wolf whom the journalist Ulrich Greiner attacked as one of 'die toten Seelen des Sozialismus' in June 1990.[50] Braun conveys their re-appraisal of hope as a treacherous virtue, which caught and trapped socialist intellectuals: 'Die Hoffnung lag im Weg wie eine Falle' (10). The failure to realize socialist ideals had been bearable because of hope that a better society would eventually be achieved by following the current course. Furthermore, 'Hoffnung' had been a word particularly associated by Braun with the early demonstrations in the GDR. The outcome of the 'Wende', literally a U-turn towards unification with the West, invalidated utopianism: hence Braun concludes, 'Und unverständlich wird mein ganzer Text' (7). This is what the shredder in the poem 'Der Reißwolf' (and later in 'Schreiben im Schredder') represents. Meaninglessness affects both the poet's writing and the text of his life, because of the loss of the context in which they both made sense. Comprehensibility has been important to Braun from the beginning; now his claims for socialism become acutely incomprehensible in the light of the historical reality.

Doubt in the continued validity of his writing is a recurrent theme in Braun's post-1989 poetry. Besides the short poems of *Die Zickzackbrücke*, this

[47]John Steinbeck, *The Grapes of Wrath* (London: Arrow, 1998), p.175. First published 1939.
[48]Wolfgang Emmerich, 'solidare - solitaire. Volker Braun: Drei Gedichte', in *Verrat an der Kunst?*, ed. by Deiritz, pp.195-205. This analysis compares 'Das Eigentum' with two earlier Braun poems which also thematize the opposition between solitariness and solidarity. Domdey, 'Volker Braun'.
[49]In Domdey's words, this poem is 'ein Dokument der Bewußtseinslage von Intellektuellen in der DDR', in 'Volker Braun', p.1771. Leeder sees in it 'the fundamental paradigm of the 1990s', in *Breaking Boundaries*, p.1.
[50]Greiner's article 'Der Potsdamer Abgrund' concludes with the sentence 'Die toten Seelen des Sozialismus sollen bleiben, wo der Pfeffer wächst'.

work includes a number of longer, free-verse pieces which appeared primarily in journals. These sprawling forms are dense poems of outpouring, with lines running on and on down the pages. Three of these, and many of the *Zickzackbrücke* poems, were taken into Braun's *Ausgewählte Gedichte* published in 1996 under the title *Lustgarten Preußen*. This old title (taken from an epigram in *Training des aufrechten Gangs*) is an ironically sentimental designation for the GDR, which also echoes the utopian implications of the original garden paradise, Eden.[51] The Lustgarten in East Berlin was also a site of 'Wende' demonstrations by students, such as that on 17 November 1989. Braun's collection, embracing a life's work in poetry from 1959 to 1995, concludes with texts which reject the collection's own validity: on the contrary, they suggest a sense that earlier work is incomprehensible in the new climate. The penultimate poem is 'Schreiben im Schredder' of 1995, a poem of eighty lines whose title indicates the sense that the old writing is now invalid.[52] Here the poem of outpouring reflects the action of the shredder. 'Der Schredder', a symbolic import from English, embodies for Braun the reception of GDR writing in the new, America-influenced Germany. A note in the back of *Lustgarten Preußen* indicates that 'Schreiben im Schredder' draws on a historical incident when hundreds of thousands of books were threatened after the 'Wende'. A priest, Pastor Martin Weskott, sought to save them by removing the books from the Leipzig 'Kommanditgesellschaft' depot and storing them in stables in Katlenburg.[53] This provides Braun with a metaphorical location for GDR literature in the new Germany – amongst the straw and filth of a farm.

> In einem Stall von 100m Länge
> Liegt der Mist bis an die Decke
> MÜLLER MATERIAL MICKEL MAKULATUR
> Eingeschweißt auf Paletten
> Pfarrer Weskotts Aufgesammelte Werke   (lines 1-5)

In line 3 the surnames of two fellow GDR poets represent GDR literature, which is now relegated to the status of its raw materials, no longer a source of social guidance but merely wastepaper. Clearly Braun is also utilizing commonplace expressions of disgust in his montage: there are relentless references to the stink, to history as 'Scheiße' and power as 'Mist'. Literature seems tainted, along with the discarded GDR:

---

[51]Braun, 'Lustgarten Preußen', *Texte*, v, p.69.
[52]Braun, 'Schreiben im Schredder', *ndl*, 43 (1995), No. 4, 5-7, and reprinted in *Lustgarten Preußen*, pp.164-166.
[53]Books stockpiled under the GDR's central planning were sold off by Weskott to aid the charity 'Brot für die Welt'. Braun was one of the 'Müll-Literaten' who gave readings in Katlenburg. See Emmerich, *Kleine Literaturgeschichte der DDR*, p.439.

WARUM SCHWEIGEN DIE DICHTER schämen sie sich
Ihrer Handschrift mit dem Stallgeruch
Des Staats, der in den Schredder kommt
ERRUNGENSCHAFTEN zum Schleuderpreis
Eine DEFA-Vision GESCHLOSSENE GESELLSCHAFT
Was für ein Umweg der Geschichte   (lines 16-21)

The feuilleton headline in capitals 'WARUM SCHWEIGEN DIE DICHTER'
is an accusation which was made at the 'Wende' against writers: the poem also
includes an accusation against readers choosing to read the Stasi files now,
rather than literary works. Books are 'Verfault im Massengrab der Literatur /
Wenn der Sohn keine Oden liest sondern Akten / Die Lektüretips aus der
Gauck-Behörde' (p.166). The father-son opposition thematizes generational
differences, a theme to which German literature returns again and again in the
post-war period. In these lines Braun is particularly quoting Hans Magnus
Enzensberger's poem 'ins lesebuch für die oberstufe' which opens with the
sarcastic imperative, 'lies keine oden mein sohn, lies die fahrpläne'.[54] What
was a sarcastic dismissal of literature in the late 1950s has become a
despairing confrontation with an actual dismissal in the 1990s. Braun's poem
signals the topicality of the 'Gauck-Behörde', which oversaw access to the
Stasi files and was on everyone's lips in the early 1990s. Despite the Stasi
legacy, three repetitious exclamations in the poem nonetheless suggest that
unification is a deviation from progress: the phrases 'Was für ein Umweg des
Geistes' (9), 'Was für ein Umweg der Geschichte' (21) and 'Was für ein
Umweg des Witzes' (78) recall the image of 'die Zickzackbrücke'. Progress
apparently comes not as a straight line, but by a circuitous route or a zigzag.
Braun's 'Umwege' here also recall Bloch's designation of the human as 'das
Umwege machende Tier'.[55] The early 'Wende' sense of standing immediately
below the mountain peak to be conquered is thus superseded by a sense of
deviation and diversion.

Braun's poetry sets society's deviations and digressions against the
lyric subject's own sense of already seeing the goal ahead and the process by
which to achieve it. Archilochus's statement about the fox and the hedgehog
has long been interpreted as a model for two types of thinker: the fox has
many ideas, but the hedgehog has one big idea. If one applies this model to the
role of the poet, Braun is a hedgehog type (whereas Grünbein, the subject of
the next chapter, is a fox type). His 'one big idea' is that of the socially
responsible and enlightening writer who promotes a Blochian 'Prinzip

---

[54]Hans Magnus Enzensberger, 'ins lesebuch für die oberstufe', *verteidigung der wölfe:
Gedichte* (Frankfurt a.M.: Suhrkamp, 1957), p.85.
[55]Bloch, *Das Prinzip Hoffnung*, p.54.

Hoffnung'. This describes Braun's lyric self-understanding before 1989/90 and is the concept he holds to at the 'Wende'. In 1989, in the words of Braun's 'Das Eigentum' poem, he has not moved: 'Da bin ich noch'. Schlenstedt's term for what I have called the 'one big idea' behind Braun's poetry is 'innerer Auftrag'.[56] Schlenstedt indicates that Braun's 'Prinzip Hoffnung' is not imposed from without by the political authorities but is a self-imposed task, a task tied to the poet's inner identity. The 'innerer Auftrag' is perhaps personified in Braun's poem 'Larvenzustand' (*Texte*, v, pp.102-105) from the collection *Training des aufrechten Gangs*. This poem can seem to make a poetological statement:

> Notfalls reiße ich es
> Aus ihren Gurgeln, den notorischen
> Labyrinthen der Brust (und er griff in meine
> Und zerrte mich halb hervor:)   (p.103)

Like Heine's lictor taking blood from the poet's heart in *Deutschland. Ein Wintermärchen*, Braun's lyric 'Doppelgänger' wrenches out his innards.[57] This image suggests the importance of identity to the poet's task: the self is violently plundered for the sake of a larger purpose. The 'innerer Auftrag' can be seen in the grotesque digging around in the skull, jaw and eye sockets, which is described further on in this poem. Here the poetological 'Auftrag' seems to be a task carried out within the body, a violent search for human potential. The poem gives us the poet's battle-cry as dramatic dialogue: 'Du, Larve, schrie er, in deinem Larvenstaat' (p.104). The 'Doppelgänger' identifies the undeveloped individual with the undeveloped socialist state. The 'Larve' image suggests both a frustrating lack of full development, but also a mask which conceals the underlying, true nature. Thus the 'innerer Auftrag' is also perhaps a natural law, by which the larva-individual or larva-state should develop to maturity and become fully itself. Another poem from *Training des aufrechten Gangs* closes with a biblical image of this maturity as a light to lighten the darkness:[58]

> Geh jetzt ins Dunkle: werde selbst das Licht.
> Du mußt das tun, was keiner kann. Entzweie
> Dich von dem toten Leben. Sorge dich nicht.
> Wenn du fällst, wachsen die Schreie.   (p.60)

---

[56]Dieter Schlenstedt, 'Vorwort', in *Im Querschnitt: Volker Braun: Gedichte, Prosa, Stücke, Aufsätze*, ed. by Holger J. Schubert (Halle-Leipzig: mdv, 1978), pp.8-20: 'Man spürt in jedem Werk Volker Brauns den inneren Auftrag' (p.10).

[57]See Caput VII in Heinrich Heine, 'Deutschland, ein Wintermärchen', *Sämtliche Werke*, i (Munich: Winckler, 1969), pp.411-478 (pp.431-434).

[58]Braun, 'Du bist verloren: nun geniess den Hohn', reprinted in *Lustgarten Preußen*, pp.59-60.

This is the language of Bloch's *Prinzip Hoffnung*, especially in the opposition between utopia and death, as well as being the language of religious discourse. The 'du'-poet is a Saviour-figure here, going through metamorphosis and heralding a new life. The final line reveals the 'du's special status which allows him to do this, namely his prominence. This line intimates towards a political strategy: the threat to the missionary 'du' is outweighed by the public outcry which would ensue if he were harmed.

Elsewhere imposition from outside is examined more closely with respect to the 'innerer Auftrag'. In 'Gedankenkinder-Mord' for instance, Braun's topic is his own response to the 'Byzantian aesthetic' of the GDR cultural gurus:[59]

> Meine schamhaften Freunde
> Die das öffentliche Gerede scheuen
> Und vor *Schande* warnen und *Beschmutzung unseres Namens*
> Haben mich angestiftet
> Zum Mord
> An manchem jungen Gedanken
> Eh er geboren war.
> Ich habe Zukunft, die sich meldete
> Nicht zur Welt gebracht.   (lines 1-9)

The personification of thoughts and of the future make their destruction more powerful in this poem. We have a sense of the poet's task in the last lines here as being to give birth to the future, not abort it for the sake of social expedience. In 1970 Braun made this same responsibility for the future explicit in the text 'Wie Poesie':

> Die Poesie, die teilhat an der Emanzipation aller menschlichen Sinne und Eigenschaften, die *wie nichts andres* den Reichtum der gesellschaftlichen Beziehungen bewußt macht, schreibt sich also nicht aus Vergangnem her sondern aus dem Zukünftigen, das in den wirklichen Beziehungen schon enthalten ist.[60]

The future which is incipient in the present recalls the larva image. This linking of poetry and the future particularly contrasts with the predominant concern with the past in post-unification poetry. For Braun, it also led to an interpretation of the early 'Wende' movement as a realization of the alternative articulated by his poetry:

---

[59]Braun, 'Gedankenkinder-Mord', amongst 'Verstreute Gedichte 1959-1968', *Texte*, iii, p.107. Unpublished at the time of writing. Reference to a Byzantine aesthetic implies that anything other than out-and-out praise of socialism is considered treacherous. This is Braun's own term for the censorship of his *Hinze-Kunze-Roman* and *Langsamer knirschender Morgen*. See *Verheerende Folgen*, p.146.

[60]Volker Braun, 'Wie Poesie', *Es genügt nicht die einfache Wahrheit: Notate* (Leipzig: Reclam, 1975), pp.78-83 (p.82).

Nun müssen wir Poesie nicht aus der Zukunft reißen. Wir erleben, wie sie in unserem Augenblick geboren wird, nicht nur als scharfer Text der Tafeln und Transparente, mehr noch im Grundgefühl des Anspruchs auf Austrag der Widersprüche, auf das Ende der Schrecken im Vorschein der Schönheit, den unsere Demonstrationen machen.[61]

Poetry is a model for reality here, specifically a model for the 'Wende' movement, as it was perceived at the time by Braun, as a reform-socialist poet. Braun's one big idea and his missionary poetry were, however, rendered untimely by unification. Indeed, the illusion that these express only 'old', 'GDR' values has led to them being regarded with suspicion. In Braun's long 1995 poem 'Der Weststrand' (*Lustgarten Preußen*, pp.150-159) this reception is suggested by the image of light that is wasted: 'Das Licht verschwenderisch, niederströmend' (p.150). As Berendse points out, Braun's socially-committed poetry has become historically understood after 1989/90.[62] Any confrontation and provocation it once contained now leech away: the light (or enlightenment) is wasted in the 1990s because such social challenges are no longer read as challenges to the present but as the product of certain historical conditions which have ceased to exist. The end of the GDR has brought a change in the reception of socially-interested poetry: how then has poetry itself reacted to this new state of affairs? In Braun's case there is some indication of defiance, but there is also a gnawing despair that poetry cannot have a sociological effect and that a better world cannot be created.

Certain recurrent motifs in the poetry – particularly famine and deserts – betray Braun's rigid rejection of capitalism. In his 'Prolog' (*Zickzackbrücke*, pp.37-39) Braun warns that people will hunger for justice. The vocabulary of mandates, masses and justice points to sociological discourse:

Aber bedenkt
Daß da auch Hunger herrscht
Mit dem Mandat der Massen, Hunger
Nach Gerechtigkeit. (p.38)

Hunger is an important motif which recurs elsewhere in Braun's poetry after 1989. Here it is a hunger mandated by the people. The poem 'Ende Oktober im August' (*Zickzackbrücke*, p.94) opens with the most evocative image of the fall of communism: 'Die Denkmäler Stricke am Hals'. The October of the title is both the Russian Revolution and the 'Wende' of 1989, whilst August is most feasibly August 1991 when there was a putsch in the Soviet Union to oust Gorbachev. Rather than being hanged however, the ultimate communist

---

[61]Braun, *Wir befinden uns soweit wohl*, p.29.
[62]Gerrit-Jan Berendse, 'Fünfundzwanzig Jahre politischer Poesie von Volker Braun: Von einem heftigen Experimentator, der immer neue Wege sucht', *Wirkendes Wort*, 41 (1991), 425-435.

icon survives in a 'Nachwelt': Stalin's corpse dines with the contemporary leaders Gorbachev and Yeltsin. Braun's hunger motif occurs here in references to the 'Magen des Volkes' and 'DIE MAHLZEIT [...] DER FREIHEIT'. It is the statesmen, living and dead, who dine in freedom. In poetry, the old guard lives on 'beyond', dining whilst the ordinary citizens struggle to feed themselves. In 'Tiananmen' (*Texte*, ix, pp.87-89) of August 1989, there is an equation of hunger and hope:

in der Weltmitte
Sitze ich in der wartenden Menge
Und buchstabiere meinen Hunger
Mein Hunger meine Hoffnung (lines 4-7)

The writing lyric subject also suggests an equation of hunger and the literary project. Literature is described as food in the poem 'Schreiben im Schredder' (*Lustgarten Preußen*, pp.164-166) where it would be 'BROT FÜR DIE WELT' (7), providing 'Mahlzeit' (12) and 'Nährwert' (14). The name of the charity 'BROT FÜR DIE WELT' connects metaphorical starving to Third World famine. Braun's motif of 'der Hunger der Welt' embraces practical humanitarian concerns and the role of literature which, as he sees it, was a humanitarian mission now discarded. The phrase becomes something of a motto for Braun after unification, referring to both material and spiritual hunger. The 'Hunger der Welt' motif recurs in 'Die Verstellung' as famine and as hunger for a better future.[63] Braun explicitly links this hunger to a special sense of communism which the ex-GDR traveller carries with him as luggage: 'Sein Kommunismus ist jenseits aller Politik und Ideologie, es ist der Hunger der Welt, den er mitschleppt, der ihm folgt in den Waggon'.[64] In the 1980 poem 'Das Lehen' (*Texte*, viii, pp.75-76) Braun utilizes idiomatic sayings, including the biblical proverb 'Bleibe im Lande und nähre dich redlich':[65]

Ich bleib im Lande und nähre mich im Osten.
Mit meinen Sprüchen, die mich den Kragen kosten
In anderer Zeit: noch bin ich auf dem Posten.

---

[63]Volker Braun's 'Die Verstellung' was first published, with the dedication 'Für Christa Wolf, 18.3.94', in *Ein Text für C.W.* (Berlin: Janus, 1994), pp.18-22. And subsequently in *Theater der Zeit*, 49 (1994), No.3, 2-4, as 'ein Einakter' commissioned by the Staatstheater Braunschweig, to follow performances of Lessing's play *Die Juden*. The text is formally akin to poems such as 'Schreiben im Schredder' and 'Das Verschwinden des Volkseigentums' and I therefore treat it as a poem in this study. Further references are to the *Theater der Zeit* edition.
[64]Rolf Jucker, ' "Wir befinden uns soweit wohl. Wir sind erst einmal am Ende": Volker Braun im Gespräch', in *Volker Braun*, ed. by Jucker, pp.21-29 (p.25).
[65]Psalm 37.3 or see Duden, xi (1992), p.430.

In Wohnungen, geliehn vom Magistrat
Und eß mich satt, wie ihr, an der Silage. (lines 1-5)
This is another, earlier instance of eating as a metaphor for writing. Eating one's fill, albeit of the unappetizing silage, becomes hunger and famine in the post-'Wende' poem. Braun turns around the apparent plenitude of western life and suggests that in a sense people are going hungry:

Was für ein Umweg des Geistes
In die leeren Mägen, Wellfleisch aus Wellpappe
Wieviele Bände der GELEHRTENREPUBLIK
Reclam Leipzig, sind eine Mahlzeit
Man kann die Bücher auch anbrennen
Aber das hat keinen Nährwert   (lines 9-14)

Karl Mickel's title *Gelehrtenrepublik* here evokes the ideal unity of 'Geist' and 'Macht' which has receded from the realms of possibility.[66] Nutrition and sustenance provided by books recalls Braun's recurrent designation of poetry as 'der Stoff zum Leben', the stuff which keeps one alive.[67] This label 'Stoff zum Leben' suggests intellectual 'food', not western materialism, to be what makes life better.

Having looked at the famine motif in Braun's poetry, I turn now to the related motif of the desert, which is equally far removed from the obvious reality of the western world. In 'Die Verstellung' the Gulf War, 'im Wüstensand', provides Braun with the desert metaphor that is developed in other poems at this period. The short poem 'Wüstensturm' (*Zickzackbrücke*, p.86) takes up the name of the American campaign in the Gulf War, but it is also linked to the 'Wüste' of 'Wohlstand' in Braun's poem 'Marlboro is red' (*Zickzackbrücke*, p.93) and the 'Wüste des Widerstands' in 'Ende Oktober im August' (*Zickzackbrücke*, p.94). The desert is a motif which complements the hunger motif as a Braunian metaphor for capitalism. The empty area represented by the desert is described in Braun's long 1991 poem 'Das Verschwinden des Volkseigentums':[68]

Die festen Gebäude zuerst, dann die leeren Flächen
Schließlich die Ackerkrume bis hinab
In die undeutlichen Bodenschätze. Eine Hand
Heißt es, reißt das an sich und läßt nichts zurück
Das zu verwerten wäre, das Grund-
Und das Regenwasser, buchstäblich nichts

---

[66]Karl Mickel, *Gelehrtenrepublik: Aufsätze und Studien, Essay* (Halle: mdv, 1976) and (Leipzig: Reclam, 1990).
[67]Braun, 'Der Stoff zum Leben 1', *Texte*, v, pp.85-105, 'Der Stoff zum Leben 2', *Texte*, viii, pp.63-90, 'Der Stoff zum Leben 3', *Texte*, ix, pp.65-92.
[68]Volker Braun, 'Das Verschwinden des Volkseigentums' (dated 31.12.91), *Freibeuter*, 59 (1994), 125-127. (dated 31.12.91)

Bleibt uns von unserem Eigentum.   (p.125)

The poet takes up the voice of the aggrieved collective 'wir'. There are several layers of allusion at work, some more GDR-specific (the hand of the 'Treuhand' organisation) and others more general human issues (such as the exploitation of natural resources, or human mortality). The possessive is repeatedly brought to the fore, such as in the question, 'Wer gibt uns Nachricht / Von dem Unseren?' (p.126). This is perhaps reminiscent of Braun's earlier motto and title *Wir und nicht sie*. And the possessive is also brought out in hand metaphors and in the inventory-style piling up of nouns. The 'wir' is characterized with the negative terms 'achtlos' and 'ahnungslos' placed prominently at the beginning of line 1 and as a single-word line respectively: 'Achtlos saßen wir darauf' (first line in each of the first three strophes) and 'Ahnungslos / Hielten wir es in den Händen' (10-11). Furthermore, the predominance of passive constructions ('vernichtet werden', 'aussortiert und bearbeitet werden', 'eingeschwärzt werden') and the repetitions of 'müssen' imply collective helplessness and compulsion. Repeated use of 'müssen' also, however, seems to question whether in fact things had to be so. And at the poem's close a 'but' is set against all the compulsion:

> Aber an der leeren Stelle
> Dort wo nichts bleibt
> Nagt eine Ahnung, die nur blaß zu nennen ist
> Von etwas Einfachem, Zugänglichem
> Nur nicht Begangenem
> Das man nicht achtete, das man nicht nutzte
> Und wegwarf wie eine abgetragene Hoffnung
> Etwas Unwiederbringlichem und darum Unvergeßlichem
> Dem unauffälligen
> Eigentum des Volkes.   (p.127)

The image of the desert which occurs in other of Braun's poems, and images of gaps and vacuums in post-GDR poetry more generally, correspond to 'die leere Stelle' in the first line here. In this poem Braun laments the loss of an enterprise for the collective good: socialism had been 'das Einfache / Das schwer zu machen ist'.[69] This 'Eigentum', referring both to abstract ideals and to concrete property we may assume, constitutes the culmination of the lists of adjectival nouns.[70] These nouns, qualifying and describing, talk around the

---

[69]The quotation is from Bertolt Brecht's 'Lob des Kommunismus', *Gesammelte Werke*, ix, p.463. Compare also Braun's prose title *Das Nichtgelebte: Eine Erzählung* (Leipzig: Faber & Faber, 1995).

[70]Compare also the use of 'Eigentum' in Braun's post-'Wende' drama *Iphigenie in Freiheit* (Frankfurt a.M.: Suhrkamp, 1992) where Goethe's symbol of goodness has

subject without naming it, in a manner recalling religious circumspection. Again then, the problem of naming is a motif: 'eine Ahnung, die nur blaß zu nennen ist' echoes 'eine alte gemeinsame Sache, die keinen Namen mehr hat' ('3. Oktober 1990') and the use of 'Was' in 'Das Eigentum' (lines 8 and 9). This unnameable thing is the hope or the utopian future, which is utterly discredited in the new Germany, no longer a peak to ascend, but an empty desert.

Having traced certain continuities in Braun's conception of his moralizing role, I now turn to a different perspective on his self-understanding. The high seriousness of the 'innerer Auftrag', the Saviour-poet heralding the light of an enlightened future, contrasts with another aspect of the poet's role as it is represented in Braun's poetry. That aspect is the role of the fool, a figure with a long literary tradition, who entertains and jests, but also embodies untimely wisdom which allows him to satirize his patrons and mock the society around him. Historically, a fool was part of the feudal structure, dependent economically on those in power. This is directly reflected in Braun's title 'Das Lehen' (*Texte*, viii, pp.75-76). In 1980 Braun is the poet soldiering on at his outpost, still not winning the fief that he seeks from his feudal lord, the SED.[71] This fief seems to represent trust and freedom. Of course irony is evident in the poet making the party into the lord of the manor, part of a social structure which it claimed to supersede. In an article of 1977, Manfred Jäger comes close to identifying Braun with the clever fool where he demonstrates Braun's use of irony and links him to Heine and to Brecht.[72] The role of the fool, it seems to me, goes to the heart of the opposition between the controlling authorities and the poet's 'innerer Auftrag'. Braun was in many ways the servant at court, close to power, but also in a position to play with his patrons' rules and mock the status quo. His use of sayings are, furthermore, typical of a fool, where he modifies commonplace sayings or creates a 'new proverb'. For instance, Braun parodies state propaganda and the voice of the

---

become a wanton GDR-Iphigenie:
        Nimm es dir, Pylades
        Mein Eigentum. Entwaffnet von der Werbung
        Geht Iphigenie handeln mit der Lust
        Und mit der Liebe.   (p.20)
[71]Compare the feudal relationship implied by an analogy between GDR writers and medieval clerics in Jens Reich, *Abschied von den Lebenslügen*, p.25.
[72]Manfred Jäger, 'Das Handeln als Basis und Ziel dichterischer Praxis: Zu Volker Brauns Reflexionen über Poesie und Politik', *TuK*, (1977), No.55, 12-21.

collective in the poem 'Gemischter Chor' (*Lustgarten Preußen*, p.101), with a rhyming litany which also plays on the end of Goethe's *Faust*:[73]

> Gemischter Chor
> Das Unverfängliche
> Gibt uns kein Gleichnis;
> Das Unzulängliche
> Hier wirds *Erreichnis*.
> 5   Das fein Geplante
> Ist doch zum Schrein.
> Das Ungeahnte
> Tritt eisern ein.

Braun's sarcasm is clearly directed outwards to the society around him here. In the poem 'Die Treulose' (*Texte*, viii, pp.45-46), which is a dialogue with Catullus, Braun refers to 'Nachdichtung / Aus einer schlechten Gesellschaft in die andre' (5-6). The GDR writer is advised to give up:

> Laß die laufen
> Nach ihrem Planziel, Volker, jetzt heißts hart bleiben.
> Und was du schon verloren siehst, das gib ganz auf. (lines 9-11)

As utopia recedes, surrender seems imminent, but this too is a challenge. Braun's lyric voice addresses him by name; he is to be 'hart', rigid, and to cut his losses by giving up on the bureaucrats. There is no abject despair in this poetry, still the old energy is conveyed, though there is greater restless dissatisfaction. More generally, Braun mocks the failings of reality against a utopian vision which is never entirely beyond realization. Such ambivalence is captured in the line 'Hoffnunglos die Lage ist nicht ernst' from the poem 'Die Wellen' (*Texte*, viii, p.46). Here the lyric voice states 'Wir ändern die Welt nicht', but then goes on to ask, 'Du weißt es?' This question indicates a slippery hopefulness, but a hope which has not been utterly ousted by cynicism. It is in effect a provocation, but more than that, it is the fool's rueful mockery which tips between seriousness and playfulness. The fool mocks human nature but also his own court. Braun's distance from some of the SED's cultural endeavours is expressed for example in the satirical text 'Verbandszeug' (*Texte*, viii, pp.46-47), where the writers' union is discussing reality – 'Das fehlte uns noch' – and the lyric subject decides to go for a sauna instead of taking part in the meeting. Such texts in *Langsamer knirschender Morgen* reflect the role of the poet as a fool figure, mocking the social authorities.

---

[73]See Johann Wolfgang von Goethe, 'Faust', *Werke*, ii, (Munich: Artemis & Winckler, 1992), pp.7-354 (p.354).

A comparison of one poem from the 1960s with one from the 1990s
illustrates a shift in Braun's sense of his role as a poet. The programmatic
poem 'Meine Damen und Herrn' (*Texte*, 1, pp.72-73) presents a fool-like
figure, who addresses the public directly, in the manner of an entertainer. This
dialogic poem, written in 1964 when Braun was 25 years old, epitomizes the
socially-active poet and an optimistic attitude towards his 'Engagement'.

<u>Meine Damen und Herrn</u>
Noch kann ich zurück
Aus meinen Vorsätzen
Noch spiele ich meine Rolle
Kühl, mit großem Abstand
5   Noch stehe ich über dem Text
Noch ist die Maske nicht ins Fleisch gewachsen
Ich kann nicht mehr abtreten, aber ich hab viele Schlüsse
Meine Damen und Herren
Es ist vieles möglich
10   Ich kann mich verhüllen oder entblößen, wie Sie wollen
Ich kann auf den Haaren laufen oder noch besser
Auf zwei Beinen wie ein Clown
Entscheiden Sie sich
Noch kann ich meine Worte wenden
15   Noch kann ich meinen Mund umstülpen zur Trompete
Und Sie in meinem Blick halten wie in einem Strudel
Noch kann ich aus meiner Haut
Aber entscheiden Sie sich
Noch kann ich Ihnen dienen
20   Also äußern Sie Ihre intimen Wünsche
Sonst müßte ich Ihnen etwas vormachen

Sonst müßt ich mich festlegen auf mich
Sonst müßt ich auf meiner Stelle treten
Und mich einrollen
25   In meiner letzten Rolle.

The mask referred to in line 6 seems to be the party's sense of the writer's
role, which has not yet become synonymous with the lyric subject's own role:
'Noch stehe ich über dem Text' (5). The idiom 'nicht aus seiner Haut können'
is inverted in line 17 as 'Noch kann ich aus meiner Haut', an expression of the
poet's flexibility and freedom. Here, as throughout the poem, the prominent
repetitions of 'noch' suggest both that the poet's relationship to his readers is
intact, and also that it is under pressure: the mask threatens to fix his face to
one expression. The poet-'ich' appeals to his readers to give him a role to play
for them, as a clown or as a trumpeter perhaps. In many ways the GDR poet

continued until 1989/90 to be offered a role from outside. An alternative to the poet's service is playfully suggested in this early poem, in the lines which begin 'Sonst müßte ich'. They point to the alternative being an introversion, a turning back to the 'ich' of self. In a sense the 'letzte Rolle' referred to in the last line here is the role Braun's lyric subject must fall back on after unification. In the 1990 piece 'Verbannt nach Atlantis' (*Zickzackbrücke*, pp.57-60) the 'ich' has changed role completely: instead of being the entertainer, the lyric subject is now a spectator.

> Ich bin Zuschauer. Das ist die Rolle, die ich mir erkämpft habe. Indem der Kampf verloren ist. Ich weigere mich aufzutreten. Das ist nicht mein Stück.
> (p.57)

The theatre metaphor suggests the dramatic nature of events at the 'Wende'. The lyric subject, who feels himself to be on a losing side, has lost his role as active participant and must now passively look on. Nonetheless, he identifies his own words being used by the actors: 'die Bühnengestalten sogenannte Darsteller benutzen meine Worte' (p.57). One might wish to interpret this as a reflection of Braun's social criticisms during the GDR years foreshadowing the people's demonstrations for change. By winter 1990 however the popular movement had, under its own momentum, ignored the course proposed by Braun and instead sought German unification. Thus Braun now refers with irony to the role he had fought to achieve: he had fought for the influence of 'Geist', for the writer as an important voice in society, as a guide, a check on power, as a moral voice. Now he finds that he has no role to play on the stage of history.[74]

By the time unification came, the apparent unity of purpose, which saw the intellectuals making rousing speeches to assembled crowds of demonstrators, was no more. Braun satirized those who fled the GDR by likening them to lemmings.[75] The writer Stefan Heym exclaimed over 'eine Horde von Wütigen, die, Rücken an Bauch gedrängt, Hertie und Bilka zustrebten [...] Welche Gesichter, da sie, mit kannibalischer Lust, in den Grabbeltischen [...] wühlten'.[76] The poet Frank-Wolf Matthies also saw the dash to the cheap supermarkets as a symbol. He describes 'Wiedervereinigung im Aldi-Rausch' and compares GDR citizens to an Old Testament plague of

---

[74]In Braun's *Der Wendehals: Eine Unterhaltung* (Frankfurt a.M.: Suhrkamp, 1995) the 'ICH' is an out-of-work writer. Dialogue between 'ICH' and 'ER', as they walk through the western milieu of Berlin, also thematizes the reduced role of the ex-GDR writer in materialistic society.
[75]Braun, 'Die Lemminge', *Die Zickzackbrücke*, p.33.
[76]Stefan Heym, 'Aschermittwoch in der DDR', in *Die Geschichte ist offen*, ed. by Naumann, pp.71-78 (pp.71-72).

locusts descending on western shopping centres.[77] In this way, intellectuals scorned the people, invoking images of cannibalism and intoxication, and raised a cry of moral outrage. Even in his observations as a 'spectator', Braun's lyric subject raises this cry too and measures the new reality against socialist ideals. The twelve short poems in the seventh section of *Die Zickzackbrücke* indicate the retention of the socialist discourse in their vocabulary: 'Sozialismus' appears in three, 'Hoffnung' in two. Other nouns reflect the Enlightenment tradition and the loss of more general absolutes: 'Gott', 'Vernunft', 'Glaube', 'Zukunft', 'Wahrheit'. Braun's 1990 poem 'O Chicago! O Widerspruch!' (*Zickzackbrücke,* p.81) pinpoints the supersession of these big words by 'das nicht Nennenswerte', something unmentionable and unworthy of a name. Such ironic circumspection with respect to capitalism inverts the religious circumspection found elsewhere with respect to socialism:

> O Chicago! O Widerspruch!
> Brecht, ist Ihnen die Zigarre ausgegangen?
> Bei den Erdbeben, die wir hervorriefen
> In den auf Sand gebauten Staaten.
> Der Sozialismus geht, und Johnny Walker kommt.
> 5   Ich kann ihn nicht an den Gedanken festhalten
> Die ohnehin ausfallen. Die warmen Straßen
> Des Oktober sind die kalten Wege
> Der Wirtschaft, Horatio. Ich schiebe den Gum in die Backe
> Es ist gekommen, das nicht Nennenswerte.

The title is Brechtian, analogous to opening lines such as 'O edle Zeit, o menschliches Gebaren!' or 'O Lust des Beginnens! O früher Morgen!', as well as reminiscent of Brecht's anti-capitalist play set in Chicago, *Die heilige Johanna der Schlachthöfe.*[78] The opening apostrophe to Brecht, long Braun's literary forefather, articulates Braun's own shock. More specifically, Braun's poem is a response to Brecht's poem 'Vom armen B.B.', from which he had

---

[77]Frank-Wolf Matthies, 'Wiedervereinigung im Aldi-Rausch', in *Die Geschichte ist offen,* ed. by Naumann, pp.137-141.
[78]Bertolt Brecht, 'Über Schillers Gedicht "Die Burgschaft" ' and 'O Lust des Beginnens', *Gesammelte Werke,* ix, p.611 and p.771; *Die heilige Johanna der Schlachthöfe, Gesammelte Werke,* ii, pp.665-786. For a discussion of Braun taking up in his poetry the work of Brecht, see Jos Jacquemoth, *Politik und Poesie: Untersuchungen zur Lyrik Volker Brauns* (Berlin: Schmengler, 1990), pp.129-140.

taken up the idea of 'Vorläufiges' in his 1966 collection of that title and from which lines 1, 2 and 9 in the 1990 poem are drawn:[79]

Wir wissen, daß wir Vorläufige sind
Und nach uns wird kommen: nichts Nennenswertes.

Bei den Erdbeben, die kommen werden, werde ich hoffentlich
Meine Virginia nicht ausgehen lassen durch Bitterkeit   (lines 34-37)

In the 1990 poem Braun takes up the allusion to earthquakes and to the poet's cigar going out in bitterness. His lyric subject combines the gesture of a teenage rebel with Hamlet's stoic confrontation with dashed hopes (8). Braun's fourth line echoes the West German television advertising slogan 'Der Tag geht, Johnny Walker kommt', thus implicitly equating socialism with the day and daylight. References to Chicago, chewing-gum and Johnny Walker in this poem coincide with further American borrowings in 'Philemon and Baucis', the next poem in the collection (*Zickzackbrücke*, p.82) – 'streetpeople', 'East 42nd Street Midtown Manhattan', 'Drink'. They are part of the sense of an invasive new world, which the poet finds morally destitute and, especially where they are combined with biblical metaphors, they complement the poet's moralizing tone. The eastern bloc apparently consists of 'die auf Sand gebauten Staaten', akin to the Foolish Man's building in Matthew 7.26. 'Es ist gekommen, das nicht Nennenswerte' closes the poem 'O Chicago! O Widerspruch!' on a note of sad resignation: the future Brecht and Braun dreaded has arrived, despite their efforts.[80] Instead there is a sense of meaninglessness and the end of history. A number of other poems from this time have melancholic final lines; for example the image of death in 'Dann liegen sie nebeneinander in der frischen Grube', or the Hölderlinian apostrophe 'Wehe harter Nordost' (*Zickzackbrücke*, p.82 and p.83). Like the proverbial closing line of 'Das Eigentum', 'Wann sag ich wieder *mein* und meine alle', Braun's last line is frequently highlighted rhetorically and laments loss, especially the loss of socialism.

In effect, B.K. Tragelehn's poem 'Der Rest 2' is addressed to the poet of 'O Chicago! O Widerspruch!'.[81] In the 'Anmerkungen' at the back of the

---

[79]Bertolt Brecht, 'Vom armen B.B.', *Gesammelte Werke*, viii, pp.261-263.
[80]In an interview with Karoly Vörös on 18 October 1989 ('Lösungen für alle', *Wir befinden uns soweit wohl*, pp.14-17), Braun already raised Brecht's line in connection with the outcome of the 'Wende': Soll sich der Osten vom Westen kolonisieren lassen? Noch ist ja nichts bewiesen. Wo leben wir denn - und "wird nach uns kommen nichts Nennenswertes" ?' (p.17). The question is answered in the affirmative in the poem cited.
[81]B.K. Tragelehn, 'Der Rest 2', *NÖSPL*, p.152.

collection *NÖSPL*, Tragelehn's poem is related to Brecht's 'Von armen B.B.',
but much more than that, it seems to be a response to Braun's 'Wende' poem:

> Der Rest 2
> Staaten auf Sand gebaut, also wozu
> Erdbeben. Und die Zigarre, blicket hinan
> Raucht. Wenn der Tag geht, achte darauf
> Daß nicht Johnny Walker kommt, sondern
> 5   Malt. Irgendwann schläfst du ein.

> 1991

Tragelehn rejects Braun's metaphorical earthquakes, and points up an
inconsistency between the states being doomed to fall because of weak
foundations, and their fall requiring earthquakes called forth by a Promethean
'wir'. He mocks Braun's tone further, by equating both Brecht's cigar and the
branded whisky with western provision of every luxury. His poem suggests
that Braun should have a malt whisky and sleep soundly, a suggestion which
rejects identification with Braun's lamenting and his moral outrage, but also
sits uneasily with the tone of reassurance: perhaps one sleeps through the night
in order to escape its darkness.

Relearning socialism is ostensibly the theme of Braun's poem 'Es kann
wieder gelernt werden' (*Zickzackbrücke*, p.87). Here, however, the notion of
history as a learning process is utterly ironized. References to learning, reading
and uniform are taken from the schoolroom into a political frame of reference.
The poet seems to look down as a moral authority on the people, who are no
longer addressed as the 'Volk', but rather as the rabble:

> Es kann wieder gelernt werden
> Der Häftling Honecker DIE MAUER STEHT HUNDERT JAHRE
> Reist aus ins Land, von dem er verlieren lernte
> Perestroika... espero estoica, sagt Castro
> Abwarten... Der Krieg der Lautsprecher
> 5   Verebbt über dem Chinesischen Meer
> Was wollt ihr denn, ihr Pöbel? Kohl in Halle
> Endlich wieder goldene Wasserhähne in Kuweit
> Die armen RUSSEN RAUS
> Lesen aus den deutschen Äckern
> 10   In der Uniform der Roten Armee
> Die steinige Zukunft.

Braun's rabble (6) is effectively the global population: he hops between
references to political upheaval in Germany, China, and the Gulf, as a series of

equally misguided political developments. Socialist solidarity, symbolically invoked not in German but in a foreign language now, comes from Fidel Castro's communist Cuba, which contrasts with the oil-kingdom of Kuwait on the opposite side of the world, the invasion of which triggered the Gulf War. The capitalized cry of line 8, analogous to the archetypal xenophobic cry 'Ausländer raus', suggests that the Soviet army's withdrawal from eastern Europe is as repugnant as racism. Braun turns round the GDR slogan 'Von der Sowjetunion lernen, heißt siegen lernen' in lines 1-2, so that victory turns to both defeat and loss. In January 1989 even Honecker used the term 'die Mauer', which earlier had been taboo in public discourse: 'Die Mauer wird in 50 und auch in 100 Jahren noch bestehen bleiben'.[82] The historic statement became a commonplace irony, the ultimate false prophecy, and as such is invoked in Braun's poem. Here it is part of a succession of things which are simply wrong. In lines 9-11 the fields and stony ground recall the parable of the sower, some of whose seed represented words which fell on barren hearts and minds, in Matthew 13.1-9. The challenge to the poet's own time is summed up in the image of 'die steinige Zukunft', prospective time as a barren land. Here the old idea of the poet's role being concerned with the nature of the future recurs, except that utopia has been replaced by dystopia.

The loss of utopia brings the encroachment of death in Braun's poem 'Das Theater der Toten' (*Zickzackbrücke*, p.91): this is a world of ruins and falsity, peopled by the living dead. The god Jupiter as a broken statue in a museum embodies the 'Götterdämmerung'. Braun's old hope for the living turns to resignation in a single line, with a very human exclamation:

Aber die Lebenden einmal könnten ... ach was
PRIVATPÖBEL. WENN MAN IHNEN NUR ANGENEHM DAS MAUL
                                                                                            STOPFT
Und das Spiel ist gelaufen. Im übrigen bin ich der Meinung
Daß der Sozialismus zerstört werden muß, und
Mir gefällt die Sache der Besiegten.   (lines 8-12)

The cynical view of human nature is capitalized (9), as a quotation from the priest and founding member of Neues Forum, Friedrich Schorlemmer, which dismisses earlier idealizations of the 'Volk'. Previously Braun had typically held up 'die Weisheit / Des Volkes' in the poem 'Lustgarten Preußen' (*Lustgarten Preußen*, p.67). In the poetry of the 1990s the masses are now a 'PRIVATPÖBEL'. The last three lines quoted seem to be an expression of utter resignation. It is difficult to know how to take the assertion that socialism must be destroyed, so completely does it contradict Braun's statements elsewhere. However, the identification with the defeated recalls Brecht's line

---

[82]Reported for example in *Bild*, 10 November 1989, p.3.

from 'Lob der Dialektik', 'Denn die Besiegten von heute sind die Sieger von morgen'.[83] The end of the play in Braun's poem is also the end of the GDR. It seems to bring a symbolic shift from the living to the dead who have defeated them. Unification is associated with the same kind of transfer from life to death in 'Verbannt nach Atlantis' (*Zickzackbrücke*, pp.57-60). Here, the lyric subject has been banished after the revolution:

Verbannt nach Atlantis
Unter Touristen
Die Lava der Revolution
Kalt an den Sohlen
Eine brutale Bühnenanweisung
STASI-LICHT HARTE WÄHRUNG EUROPACK
Der weit hinausverlegte Todesstreifen
Betoniert von muslimischen Leiharbeitern
REIN INS VERGNÜGEN AUSLÄNDER RAUS
Das Paradies der Billigprogramme
Ich stehe rechts in der Gasse Rauch
Steigt aus den Deponien Ein Lebens-
Zeichen
        DU BIST HIER ENGAGIERT DIE ROLLTREPPE
HINAB IN DEN HADES Plastikfraß Edelmüll
Im Kühlschrank die toten Ideen
Lustlos inhaliert Das Lippenrot der Zukunft
Verbrannte Hoffnung der November Laub
Die Demonstrationen Hinweggeweht
DAS HABT IHR GEWÄHLT   (p.57)

The GDR revolution is again a volcanic eruption here, one which sank utopia to the bottom of the sea. The lyric 'du' is given a stage direction, finds himself not among real citizens but tourists, and surrounded by programmes, not real life. These things suggest unreality and pretence. This place is also a deathly, dystopian Atlantis of 'tote Ideen' and with a buried 'Todesstreifen', but it has not been forced upon the addressees; it is what they have elected. The last line quoted reads as an accusation to the GDR citizens who voted for unification. A different Atlantis, one pre-submersion, is also recalled, at greater length, as a metaphor for the GDR in Braun's prose piece 'Atlantis' (*Texte*, x, pp.202-203):

Die Insel war zu meiner Zeit noch bewohnt. Ich selber habe mich darauf aufgehalten, ehe sie versank [...] Man muß sich erinnern, daß Atlantis eine *glückliche Insel* sei, mit weißen flimmernden Stränden und grünen Städten, Gemeinbesitz, und das Volk regiert, und die Natur bestimmt. – Zuletzt aber ein

[83]Brecht, 'Lob der Dialektik', *Gesammelte Werke*, ix, pp.467-468.

gewöhnlicher verkommener Hafen, der wegen schlechter Geschäfte, unerträglicher Bürokratie und der rohen Abwanderung der Schauerleute aufgegeben wurde. (pp.202-203)

From the happy island, to the dissolute port, to a deathly Hades, Braun's Atlantis represents the potential GDR idyll, the bleak GDR reality and the end of the GDR, respectively. In the poem the present is characterized by the adjectives 'kalt', 'brutal' and 'HART' in the first six lines above. Paradise and a sign of life are referred to ironically: instead the lyric subject is working on an escalator descending to Hades. The West is just 'Billigprogramme' and 'Edelmüll'.

The West and its freedom are morally suspect in Braun's post-unification poetry. Montage in 'Wüstensturm' (*Zickzackbrücke*, p.86) makes Saddam Hussein the product of western imperialism and a throwback to Old Testament kingship. Montage also links the Gulf War, the bombing of Dresden in 1945 and the fall of socialism. The poetic technique thus defies historical logic:

Und Bagdad mein Dresden verlischt
OHNE GEWALT der Hoffnungsschrott des Herbstes (lines 9-10)

The 'Wende' motto in capitals, like the reference to religious mores, is ironic. The same kind of historical confluence is illustrated by the poem 'Die Verstellung', where freedom brings 'das Begrüßungsgeld' (p.2) and 'der Begrüßungskrieg' (p.4), the Gulf War. The traveller's 'Selbstbefreiung' is courtesy of the banks; he is released from prison into 'die Freiheit die die Fremde ist / In der ihn keiner kennt und er sich selbst nicht' (p.2). For Braun this is not only a loss of identity because things seem foreign, but the loss of a specific identity, one which represented fairness, goodness and humanitarian compassion. Braun's moral condemnation of the new identity is enounced as a Kafkaesque metamorphosis from human to beetle:

Jetzt liegt er in dem reservierten Sitz
Gelehrig wie ein Käfer auf dem Rücken
Als nützlicher Idiot im zweiten Beruf
Weil er den ersten los ist, den er verschwiegen hat
DAS IST DER ERSTE BERUF EIN MENSCH SEIN
Es war ein schöner Traum der ausgeträumt ist (p.3)

Braun's enduring preoccupation with the dream of ideal socialism is explicit here. Neo-fascism in the incident on the train and the slogan 'ASYLANTEN RAUS' is part of capitalism, according to its presentation in this text; the phrase 'die Glatzen der Treuhand' for instance conflates privatization and fascism, and the businessman's beer can is made to evoke the cans of gas used by the Nazis to kill Jews at Auschwitz. Communists are a persecuted minority like blacks and Jews in the cynical world of this poem, and capitalism is robbery. This is a blatantly old-Marxist view. Braun's argument refines itself, however, in the idea that the traveller is living 'unter seinem Wissen': his knowledge of a better world is 'sein armes Wissen, das er nicht gebraucht hat' (p.3). In an interview Braun stressed this interpretation of his text:

> Der Reisende, der freiwillig Zugestiegne im Reichsbahngebiet, muß sich fragen lassen, wer er ist. Das übersteht er. Er gibt die Frage zurück. Erst wenn der Chef ihn umarmt, "in einem namenlosen Paternoster", weiß er seine Schuld. – Es ist die Komödie der Menschheit, unter ihrem Wissen zu leben.[84]

The poem itself refers to 'die Komödie / Der Menschheit lebend unter ihrem Wissen'.[85] Pervading this text is the sense that the poet, on the other hand, writes at the full level of this social knowledge, from where he looks down with despair on the behaviour of his peers. He is already 'jenseits', that is, beyond the world and apart from it. The lyric subject who is so profoundly troubled by the condition of society does not square with the portrayal of the 'jenseits' poet here. Rather, the apartness occurs in the particular framework of political polarization, which dislocates the lyric subject from society at large. In his poetry, Braun repeatedly characterizes contemporary society as neo-fascist. The title 'Mein Terrortorium' (*Zickzackbrücke*, p.92), to a poem of 1991, amalgamates the Latin 'terra' and 'Terror'. Here the one-time poet-teacher is aghast at skinheads' racism in Hoyerswerda, where the miners of the 'Schwarze Pumpe' live (with whom Braun worked as a young man and whom he immortalized in *Die Kipper*)[86] and which was the setting of Brigitte Reimann's novel *Ankunft im Alltag*, one of the foundational narratives of the GDR canon:

> Heute gehört uns Deutschland nicht mehr / Morgen
> Kurzarbeit Null in Pumpe, Lauchhammer plattgemacht
> Skinheads DIE STIMMUNG HAT VOLKSFESTCHARAKTER:
> Niggerschweine
> Hoyerswerda, wo liegt das? Finsterste Welt
> Lessing im Gulli mit eingetretener Stirne
> Der Lehrer auf dem Marktplatz im reißenden Rudel der Schüler
> ICH HABE IN VIERZIG JAHREN NICHTS GELEHRT   (lines 1-7)

The poet is self-critical here, but does not suggest that his teaching was wrong, only that he failed to instil it in his pupil-readers. Rather, the socialist writer was following the moral didacticism of Lessing and Brecht. 'Finsterste Welt' recalls Brecht's dark world which he hoped would be overcome in the next

---

[84]Jucker, ' "Wir befinden uns soweit wohl" ', p.25.

[85]Braun also articulated this idea in his speech at the X. Schriftstellerkongreß: 'Das Problem der Kunst enthält das Problem unserer Gesellschaft unter ihrem Bewußtsein zu bleiben, unter ihren Möglichkeiten zu leben'.

[86]Volker Braun, *Die Kipper: Schauspiel* (Berlin, GDR, and Weimar: Aufbau, 1972).

generation.[87] Lessing is present in post-GDR Germany in this poem, as a victim of violence. The eighteenth-century anti-racism of his play *Nathan der Weise* is part of the heritage to which the ex-GDR writer lays claim here.[88] Darkness and violence are evoked as if they were new phenomena in the East, attributes of the capitalist 'Marktplatz' alone.[89]

Other of Braun's post-'Wende' poems show the poet's role measured in terms of teaching which failed. In 'Schuldspruch' (*Zickzackbrücke*, p.85) the lyric subject is explicitly a condemned teacher, against whom the Transylvanian writer Richard Wagner raises a capitalized accusation:

> Schuldspruch
> Der siebenbürgische Dichter DU HAST MICH VERFÜHRT
> Mit meinen ersten Versen, den Sozialismus zu glauben.
> Hätte er weitergelesen... Kann ich dafür
> Daß er sitzenbleibt in meiner Schule.
> 5   Ich habe genug zu tun mit meiner eigenen Dummheit
> Und kauen wir nicht den gleichen rohen entsetzlichen Stoff.

The poet is cast as a deceiver for encouraging belief in socialism through his writing (2). From line 3 to the end of the poem, the 'ich' is the poet-accused and 'er' his reader. In the first two lines, however, the referents are unstable: the shifts from 'he the poet' to 'you the poet' to 'I the poet' show that there is not a sharp distinction between deceiver and deceived. This is also the point made in the last line of the poem (6). The poet is not a seer, but in the same position as his erstwhile pupil who stayed down a class. The past role of the writer, drawn on here as a point of comparison with the present, seems to be that of the early GDR years. This role as educator has been described by Ian Wallace as 'a socialist Higgins faced with a nation of Elizas'.[90] Now however, the poet declares his own stupidity (5) and argues that, even as a teacher, he was no more able to digest the 'Stoff' of ideology than those he was to instruct. The pupil's verdict of guilt is thus one that the poet confronts with

---

[87]See the line 'Wirklich lebe ich in finsteren Zeiten!' in Brecht, 'An die Nachgeborenen'.

[88]Gotthold Ephraim Lessing, *Nathan der Weise: Ein dramatisches Gedicht* (Munich: Goldmann, 1979).

[89]In the prose piece 'Die Leute von Hoywoy (2)' (*Wir befinden uns soweit wohl*, pp.65-66) property seems to be the root of neo-fascist vice. Braun begins accounting for the emergence of racist thugs by stating, 'Sie hatten sich eingerichtet in ihrem billigen *Eigentum*' (p.65).

[90]Ian Wallace, 'Teacher or Partner? The Role of the Writer in the GDR' in *The Writer and Society in the GDR*, ed. by Wallace, pp.9-20.

some despair, for although not the deceiving propagandist, he was unfit to be a teacher and guide.

The unfinished sentence from the last poem, 'Hätte er weitergelesen...', points to the poet developing in later years a critical approach to his early poetry. In 1986 Braun spent three months in Hamburg following Lessing and Klopstock, Enlightenment writers with whose sense of role he had long identified. During this time, in an interview with Peter Schütt, he already expressed disillusionment with the ideals he had pursued:

> Ich sehe heute mit großer Distanz auf meine frühen Texte. Damals hab' ich die Heimat der Zukunft gesucht, aber das ließ sich nicht ein Leben lang durchhalten. Irgendwann mußte ich auf dem Boden der Tatsachen landen. [...] Ich bin dageblieben, wo ich gebraucht werde, aber ich bin naturlich in all den Jahren nicht stehengeblieben.[91]

Noticeable here is the importance of purpose and of being situated where he is needed. 'Die Heimat der Zukunft' refers to Bloch's principle of hope, which Braun suggests he has already relinquished at this point. The metaphors of place are interesting in this quotation: the home in the future, the ground of facts and the paradox of staying put yet moving on. They correspond to metaphorical locations in Braun's post-1989 poetry, which takes up displacement as a core theme. Braun's post-'Wende' poem 'Mein Bruder' (Zickzackbrücke, p.89) focuses on parallels between the poet-'ich' and a beggar, as in other poets' beggar poems identified in Chapter 4. This is a displacement to the underclass. The destitute poet laments, 'Nichts als mein Vers ernährt mich und bringt mich ins Bett' (4). Poetry is personified as the last parent figure, who alone provides spiritual nourishment and must also provide for basic material wants. However, the poetry is 'mein Satz, der Aussatz', a disfiguring disease, and 'dreckig und unverhüllt' (5-6). The bohemian poet or tramp-poet is of course a commonplace in poetry. Thus whilst he laments, the ex-GDR poet also links himself to a strong poetic tradition. Braun's comparison between poet and beggar shifts to a personification of 'Worte' as beggars living on the street (6-7) begging for pity. This is an image of poetry itself being unhoused and 'schamlos' (6) in the commercialized world, even perhaps morally destitute. Reducing the poet's role to that of a homeless beggar contrasts sharply with the positive leadership and confident defiance of the earlier Braun. By contrast, in 1990 the poet addresses a gypsy boy begging in the car fumes, saying, 'Nicht einmal eine Hoffnung habe ich dir voraus' (11). 'Hoffnung' again encapsulates the element of idealism which was long retained by writers like Braun. The lack

---

[91]Peter Schütt, 'Trost bei der Nüchternheit der Aufklärer', Deutsche Volkszeitung/die tat, 4 July 1986, p.11.

of hope is a disturbing note to end on and illustrates the loss felt by an ex-
GDR writer who suffers the transition to the West.

In his Rimbaud essay of 1985 Braun already saw the artist as someone
who is part of social discourse and yet forced to the outskirts, like a vagrant:
'Wir müssen, gräßliche Vernunft, Provokateure bleiben. Ich gehöre diesem
Volk an, und bin doch ein Landstreicher: unbediensteter Autor' (p.996). The
role of the writer as both 'Provokateur' and vagrant was Braun's enduring
dilemma in the GDR. This goes to the heart of his hopeful reaction to the
'Wende' and his perception of it as an opportunity for the writer to come in
from the edges to the centre of society. At unification however, he must revert
to his role as a poet-'Landstreicher', according to his statement entitled '3.
Oktober 1990' (*Zickzackbrücke,* pp.48-49):

> Wir werden arbeiten wie die Türken, aber unsere arbeitslosen Seelen werden
> sich der Zukunft erinnern, einer alten gemeinsamen Sache, die keinen Namen
> mehr hat. Mein Luftkoffer, mein politisches Gepäck enthält Erinnerungen und
> Erwartungen, unkontrolliert und subversiv, schwer zu tragen, aber die Schritte
> treibend. (p.49)

Braun swears to commit the vision of a socially just future to memory; it will
be packed up as luggage. He evokes a poet-traveller reminiscent of Heine's in
Deutschland. Ein Wintermärchen who carries his contraband in his head.[92]
Remarkably, Braun suggests that he is even now, after censorship, concerned
with smuggling subversive material. In the 1993 essay '... solang Gedächtnis
haust / in this distracted globe' (*Wir befinden uns soweit wohl,* pp.89-96),
Braun restates the endurance of memory: 'Noch wohnt Gedächtnis in unserem
Trümmerhaupt, kämpfende Erinnerungen an Überlebtes und Erträumtes,
Nichtgelebtes' (p.95). There is a strange paradox in this memory being not of
the past but of 'Nichtgelebtes'. It is also a collective memory, as the plural
possessive 'unser' implies. 'Die Erinnerung' also represents 'ein Boden, ein
Erbe, ein Besitz' (p.93). Memory of the socialist dream is thus solid ground,
against the predominant sense of falling, and a possession for the
dispossessed.

Another post-GDR traveller is the subject of Braun's 1994 poem 'Die
Verstellung'. The contraband of Braun's unification-day statement, those
'Erinnerungen und Erwartungen', re-emerge in the interior monologue of this
traveller. The representative figure travelling 'Aus seinem BESSEREN LAND
in das beste' (p.2) is the GDR and, in the echo of the GDR anthology *In
diesem besseren Land,* GDR literature too.[93] The poem's title suggests the
question of identity at the outset. 'Verstellung' applies to the businessman who

---

[92]Heine, Caput II, *Deutschland,* p.420.
[93]Endler, ed., *In diesem besseren Land.*

is secretly an alcoholic, but also to the minor figures of the poem, the fascist train-guard and the made-up daughter. 'Verstellung' also applies to the '16 Millionen in der guten Stube' and Leipzig as the 'HELDENSTADT' (a 'Wende' designation). Repetitions of 'Wer ist er. Kennt ihn wer' (p.2 and p.4) punctuate the man's search for identity. He finds he is Kafka's *Der Bau, Der Hungerkünstler* and *Die Verwandlung* protagonists rolled into one.

> Jetzt sag ich dir wer er ist:
> Ein Opfer ist er, nämlich Staatsgefangner
> Das edelste Geblüt von Bautzen Waldheim
> Und so weiter, auf der Brust die Orden
> Narben sind es, jetzt hat er es schriftlich
> Vierzig Jahre Bau, es steht bei Kafka
> Der Hungerkünstler nach seiner Verwandlung
> Das Ungeziefer vor dem Widerstand
> Ein Opfer ist er und erfährt es jetzt erst   (p.2)

The subject finds identity as a victim of the GDR. He is also, however, one of the 'Täter': 'aus dem Opfer sich der Täter rekelt' (p.2). This paralleling of 'Opfer' and 'Täter' corresponds to a new ambiguity about Braun's own truth and about his one big idea.[94] In an aside in her 1997 book on Braun's drama, the American Germanist Carol Anne Costabile-Heming identifies a concern with the victim-perpetrator dichotomy in *Die Zickzackbrücke*:

> Volker Braun himself is often at the center of the stage in this poetry. In examining his role as social critic, he brings the *Täter/Opfer* dilemma to the forefront, and acknowledges that he himself played a large part in both the construction and deconstruction of his socialist society.[95]

I would argue that it is not primarily with any sense of having 'a large part' or important role, however, that Braun takes centre stage in this poetry. Rather it is as a confessional voice, re-assessing his self-understanding and finding it was based on illusions. In 'Verbannt nach Atlantis' (*Zickzackbrücke*, pp.57-60) of winter 1990, Braun's lyric alter ego cries 'GIB MIR MEINE ILLUSIONEN WIEDER' (p.48). This is a yearning for regression: the political changes have prompted unwanted self-discoveries and, at the close of the text, the tone is one of resignation: 'Vergiß das Bild einer anderen Welt'.

---

[94]Compare Jacquemoth's characterization of Braun, as reflected in his poetry until *Langsamer knischender Morgen*, as 'ein Wahrheitsfanatiker', in *Poesie und Politik*, p.197.
[95]Carol Anne Costabile-Heming, *Intertextual Exile: Volker Braun's Dramatic Re-Vision of GDR Society* (Hildesheim, Zurich and New York, Olms, 1997), p.206. See also Barbara Miller's discussion of the general re-assessing of identity according to the 'Opfer/Täter' dichotomy, after reading the Stasi files, ' "Wiederaneignung der eigenen Biographie": The Significance of the Opening of the 'Stasi' files', *GLL*, 50 (1997), 369-377.

However the capitalized cry is also self-ironic, for illusions are of course no use, only genuine belief. The command to give up the utopian ideal is reformulated and also answered in the poem 'Marlboro is red. Red is Marlboro' (*Zickzackbrücke*, p.93): here the 'du' of the old, banished self is set against the 'ich' of the new, seeing self. In Theodore Fiedler's words, the poet is 'at odds with himself' in this poem.[96] Relinquishing the dream or the 'Bild einer anderen Welt' is on the one hand imperative, yet also felt to entail the loss of all spirit.

> Marlboro is red. Red is Marlboro
> Nun schlafen, ruhen... Und liegst lächelnd wach.
> Das ist mein Leib nur, der noch unterwegs ist
> Auf irgendwelchen Straßen, ah wohin.
> Das Unbekannte wolltest du umfangen.
> 5   Jetzt kenn ich alles das. Es ist die Wüste.
> Die Wüste, sagst du. Oder sag ich Wohlstand.
> Genieße, atme, iß. Öffne die Hände.
> Nie wieder leb ich zu auf eine Wende.

In 1990 red billboard posters of the Marlboro cowboy in front of a desert superseded the red of socialism. Again Braun presents the image of the traveller, this time ironized as a soulless, empty shell of self, perhaps another façade or 'Verstellung'. He has no destination: this recalls the line 'ICH WEISS KEINEN WEG, ABER ICH GEHE IHN' which refers to futile travelling in a scene originally conceived for Braun's 1992 play *Böhmen am Meer*.[97] The 'du' in the poem is told to be satisfied with the simple, physical elements of life (7). To the old self, such materialism is a spiritual wasteland. The final line of the poem, with its ironic 'nie wieder' taken from socialist discourse, offers no defiance: the gesture of opening one's hands likewise implies shrugging in resignation. Helmut Böttiger suggests that Braun tries to continue with dialectical writing after the GDR.[98] This poem seems to exemplify this in the opposition between two aspects of the self: 'ich' and 'du'. There is also a re-writing of the travel motif: the journey has become a sham.

According to Klaus Schuhmann, the caesura of 1989 is perceptible in Braun's new themes but there is no change to his self-understanding as a

---

[96]Theodore Fiedler, 'Trauma, Mourning, Laughter: Volker Braun's Response to the "Wende" ', *Colloquia Germanica*, 30 (1997), 335-347 (p.336).
[97]Braun, *Böhmen am Meer*, *Texte*, x, pp.61-111 (p.109).
[98]Helmut Böttiger, 'Gebrochen, zerstückelt, versandt', *FR*, 8 August 1992, p.ZB4.

poet.[99] This is an interesting question. Certainly, Braun is still concerned in
poetry with critically measuring his society against socialist ideals. I have cited
a number of poems in which post-GDR society and socialist ideals are central.
Conscious kinship with Brecht and Heine further reflects the humanist,
socialist heritage. A moralizing tone, mocking human nature and use of the
proverbial continue to be characteristic across the caesura. In these instances,
Braun seems to retain his established self-understanding. However, the fool's
authoritarian 'court' has gone. His irony and sarcasm are no longer directed
solely outwards, but increasingly directed inwards, to the self. This is
illustrated by the shift from actor to spectator, represented above in the poems
'Meine Damen und Herrn' and 'Verbannt nach Atlantis' respectively. If one
looks at the poems of self-irony from Braun's post-1989 oeuvre, one reaches a
quite different conclusion from Schuhmann. Braun's poems of the 1990s
reflect a new concern with self.[100] Alongside the poet's loftier, moral role to
which Braun harks back in the earliest post-1989 poems, it looks like a
subsequent crisis of poetic identity. Braun's own sociological visions are
parodied in the following passage from 'Der Weststrand' (*Lustgarten
Preußen*, pp.150-159), which begins by echoing Faust's declaration to
Mephistopheles that 'Das Drüben kann mich wenig kümmern':[101]

> Wir
> Das Drüben konnte uns wenig kümmern
> Dasselbe (bestenfalls) in Grün
>
> Von unserer Insel Utopia
>   (Gemeinbesitz!
> Geld: spielt keine Rolle, Arbeit für alle)
> Vertrieben, aus Mangel an Fantasie,
>   genußunfähig
> Gescheiterte
>   Reale Existenzen, *total mobil*
>   Im prétexte der Simulation. Wir   (IV, p.153-154)

Braun's alterations to Goethe's line replace the present tense with the past and
a first-person-singular speaker with a plural one, thereby emphasizing a
backward-looking, communal perspective. Furthermore, this passage is
stretched between two floating and ironically prominent 'wir's. The

---

[99]Schuhmann, 'Landeskunde im Gedicht'.
[100]Compare Jacquemoth's discussion of Braun's self-understanding in poetry to 1988 in
Poesie und Politik, p.196: 'Er thematisiert relativ selten seine eigene Person, weil er
nicht sich, sondern das Ganze der Gesellschaft, als deren Mitglied er spricht, in den
Mittelpunkt stellt'.
[101]Goethe, 'Faust', p.57.

juxtaposition 'Simulation. Wir' particularly suggests an illusory sense of community. The general opposition in this passage between the real and the imaginary is a parody of Braun's own old perceptions. In many ways it is a parody of his 'wir' voice from the time of the 'Wende'. The island utopia referred to here recalls Braun taking up Rimbaud's utopian metaphor of deepest Africa in his *Langsamer knirschender Morgen* poem 'Das innerste Afrika' (*Texte*, viii, pp.87-90). In that poem, the recession of utopia to a faraway continent symbolized withdrawal inwards from the unpleasant realities at hand. In the 1990/91 poem 'Ambra' (*Zickzackbrücke*, p.88) the subject has heeded the earlier imperative 'Dahin! Dahin'. This almost voyeuristic poem evokes the primitive life he finds. The first half of the text describes what he sees – the 'Herr' with his 'Dattellippen' – and the second half what he speculates:

Wahrscheinlich hat er drei Frauen nachts im Lager
Und sie schonen ihn wie etwas Kostbares
Duftendes, das durch die Finger gleitet
Einen Glauben, der sich im Nachsinnen verflüchtigt.
Aber er nimmt sie achtlos wie abgeriebene
Kaktusfeigen. (lines 8-13)

A lyric voice jealously construes a life alien to him and in particular the retention of patriarchy. Inasmuch as this poem evokes the world of Goethe's *West-östlicher Divan*, it may be an oblique reference to that title.[102] On one level the poem ironizes the idealization of a strange, undeveloped land. It also exposes the observer's warped imagination.[103] Irony becomes a sort of confession woven into the representation: it basically has a corrective function. The poem 'Ende Oktober im August' corrects the lyric subject's relationship to truth. It closes *Die Zickzackbrücke* (p.94) in 'wir' mode, with an apparent declaration of stubborn resistance to capitalism:

DIE EISERNE RATION DES BEWUSSTSEINS, AUFGEFRESSEN
DAS IST DIE MAHLZEIT, GENOSSEN, DER FREIHEIT
Vor der Blendwand aus Weißblechdosen;
So gewiß wie die Kamele in die Sonne
Werden wir in die Wahrheit blicken oder das Ende
Wissen in der Wüste des Widerstands.   (lines 7-12)

Alliteration and word-ordering thrust forward the future tense 'werden' and the verb 'wissen' in order to set doubt against knowing and certainty, and to suggest that one can no longer know what will happen. This poem ironizes

---

[102]Johann Wolfgang von Goethe, 'West-östlicher Divan', *Werke*, i, 323-447.
[103]For a different conclusion concerning the Third World as a motif in Braun's work see the article on his drama of the 1960s and 1970s, Herbert Arnold, 'The Third World in the Work of Volker Braun and Heiner Müller', *Seminar*, 28 (1992), No.2, 148-158.

earlier claims to truth by drawing the comparison with camels. Looking into the sun also blinds a person. The sun of truth is further ironized by the juxtaposition of reference to a wall of blindingly shiny cans, which might be mistaken for the sun. In this allusion and the lines in capitals Braun quotes his 1988 poem 'Strömfeld' (*Zickzackbrücke*, p.19), where the shiny cans are already associated with 'der Hunger nach Wahrheit'. In 'Strömfeld' the lyric subject was not implicated in being blinded and unaware, whereas in the 'wir' of 'Ende Oktober im August' he is. The quotation from the earlier poem is now interpolated ironically.

Braun's shift in self-understanding is made explicit through irony in a number of other poems, such as the personal accusation in 'Schreiben im Schredder' (*Lustgarten Preußen*, pp.164-166):

ich schäme mich
Mit Schweinen gekämpft zu haben
Die ich für meine Gegner hielt, meine Genossen
Gegen die ich antrat ein treuer Verräter
In der schimmernden Rüstung der Worte (lines 28-32)

Braun casts himself with irony as a poet-knight in shining armour. The splendid fighter is 'ein treuer Verräter'. (This oxymoron recalls Jürgen Kuczynski's title to his memoir of life as a GDR writer, *Ein linientreuer Dissident*.[104]) Those SED functionaries against whom Braun once debated, become in retrospect unworthy swine, yet these were also the poet's own comrades. As he here parodies his own earlier ideals of being a saviour, so the close of the poem 'Mein Terrortorium' (*Zickzackbrücke*, p.92) parodies the poet-teacher: 'Ich vor meinen Lesern Helm im Gesicht / Den Plexiglasschild in Händen Tränengas'. The teacher has given up argument and teaching, and resorts to being a riot policeman in order to create peace. The 'Plexiglasschild' is a barrier separating and protecting the poet from the people. This image seems to be self-ironic, propelling the poet onto the side of authoritarian control. Furthermore, his proud designation 'mein Land' has become 'mein Terrortorium': the retention of the possessive gestures towards self-irony. Irony as rhetorical re-enforcement of social criticism is distinct from self-disparaging irony. In such passages as those cited here, Braun re-assesses his earlier hopes and visions, but more than that, he re-assesses his previous writing, its metaphors and imperatives. Now he holds these up to the sarcasm which had formerly been directed towards society.

Braun's new self-irony reflects the destruction of his role as a poet after the end of socialism. Because of the way in which his conception of that role

---

[104]Jürgen Kuczynski, *Ein linientreuer Dissident: Memoiren 1945-1989* (Berlin and Weimar: Aufbau, 1992).

was inextricable from a relationship to the 'Volk' and from a projected ideal of human society, the early months of the 'Wende' resurrected old conceptions of the poet as a public educator and guide. In the course of the 'Wende' and unification period, Braun effectively retraces in poetry what was a gradual decline in faith from the mid-1960s to the mid-1980s as a sudden and more extreme descent. A great sense of his role in October 1989 turned to a defiant, stoical battling in the subsequent months, and then finally to an utter loss of purpose from the early 1990s onwards. After this point, Braun's poetry becomes caught up in recrimination and in the loss of socialism. Thus in retrospect the 'Wende' represented an endpoint for Braun's role as he had defined it. Whilst he continued to write prolifically, he articulated a sense of losing his chosen role as a socialist poet. Through the course of the 'Wende' and unification period, Braun's poetry shifts in its predominant concern, from hope to hopelessness to regarding both these concerns with self-critical distance. In November 1989, Braun exclaimed 'Das Eis / Der Strukturen bricht', but images of solidity return in subsequent poems. Ice is superseded by iron ('Ende Oktober im August'), armour ('Schreiben im Schredder') and acrylic glass ('Mein Terrortorium') in Braun's later, self-ironic poetry. Society's ice cracked, but the poet-'ich' apparently became encased by his own inflexibility and intellectual rigidity (though his self-criticism itself indicates flexibility). Such self-criticism is typical of other poets discussed in Chapter 4, such as Müller and Czechowski, and is linked to the end of a relationship between the poet and the people. After unification, public attention turned away from the old literary Establishment – another endpoint for Braun – and instead towards new poets for the new Germany.

CHAPTER 6
THE BEGINNING OF A ROLE:
DURS GRÜNBEIN'S POST-'WENDE' POETRY

As Braun was received in the mid-1960s as a talented, young GDR poet and the central figure of his literary generation, so Durs Grünbein emerged as the most exciting young German poet in the early 1990s. In 1993 the Germanist Gerhard Wolf described Grünbein as 'der Volker Braun der nächsten Generation'.[1] Both Braun and Grünbein were born in Dresden, and subsequently lived as writers in East Berlin. In 1996 their common birthplace brought their work together in an anthology of Saxon poets.[2] It is the quality of their writing which prompted Wolf's comparison however: Braun and Grünbein share an ability to craft, out of the discourses available to all, an artistic language of maximal density and referentiality, a language of great 'otherness'. In their perceptions of the GDR, the generation gap is telling however. Grünbein's generation only ever knew the GDR with a sealed border, Dresden in a 'Tal der Ahnungslosen', beyond the reaches of western broadcasting, and Berlin divided by the Wall. As a writer, Grünbein only experienced the post-Biermann era of overt conflict between politics and culture. Thus in an unofficially published article of 5 September 1989, Grünbein delighted in the prospect of poetry personified as 'ein übler kleiner Wechselbalg aus Defätismus, frecher Einsicht, Aphasie und Ketzerei':

> Dann erst wäre sie wieder eines der weniger gemütlichen Produkte ihrer Zeit, absolut ätzend und unzitierbar für die Kulturhüter und Rhetorikzwerge an allen Auf- und Abbaufronten.[3]

The desire to be unquotable seems to be a reaction against the appropriation of literature for political agendas. It is a rejection of any co-operation between 'Geist' and 'Macht'. Defeatist and blasphemous writing particularly contrasts as an aspiration with Braun's adherence to hope and to Marxist doctrine. Writing poetry that would be read as literature alone, however, still remained in September 1989 a wish rather than a reality. After he moved to East Berlin in 1986, Grünbein wrote for unofficial, 'underground' magazines such as *ariadnefabrik* and his poetry was circulated in a 'Künstlerbuch' of graphics by Via Lewandowsky.[4] This biographical detail places him in a scene typical for

---

[1]Karl Deiritz, 'Ich halt's halt mit der Kunst: Ein Gespräch mit Gerhard Wolf', in *Verrat an der Kunst?* ed. by Deiritz, p.270.
[2]See Helgard Rost and Thorsten Ahrend, eds., *Der heimliche Grund: 69 Stimmen aus Sachsen* (Leipzig: Kiepenheuer, 1996).
[3]Grünbein, 'Ameisenhafte Größe', p.113.
[4]Durs Grünbein (Texte) and Via Lewandowsky (Grafik), *Ghettohochzeit* (Berlin:

many young poets in the 1980s. As he himself has stated, he could not be a
'GDR poet' in the sense that Braun was:

> Ich habe damals keine Rolle spielen können, weil es mich offiziell gar nicht
> gab. Meine erste Veröffentlichung war 1988 – im Westen. Bis dahin war ich
> ein reines Untergrundphänomen.[5]

Yet Grünbein's poetry has often, and with good reason, been promoted
without reference to the Prenzlauer Berg underground. Whereas the young
Braun was central to the 'sächsische Dichterschule', Grünbein was not a
defining figure of the group which dominated his literary generation in the
GDR. In Emmerich's words, he was 'der Außenseiter unter Außenseitern'.[6]
This gap between Grünbein and Stasi-implicated Prenzlauer Berg has also had
repercussions in the new Germany: whereas writers like Anderson and
Schedlinski, or like Wolf and Braun, became suspect during the
'Literaturstreit' debates, Grünbein was fêted by the literary critics of the
feuilletons and regarded as a leading poet of the new Germany. His poetry has
been grouped with international 'post-poetry', and with that of contemporary
poets Thomas Kling, Lavinia Greenlaw or John Ashbery.[7]

   Through this tendency amongst critics to read Grünbein without
reference to other ex-GDR poets, some worthwhile points of comparison with
Braun have been overlooked. Grünbein's prose piece 'Aus einem alten
Fahrtenbuch' serves as an introduction to ideas which are central in his
poetry.[8] It also relates him to Braun, in that this monologue of an individual in
a tank might be a response to Braun's 'Der Eisenwagen' of 1986.[9] In Braun's
parable the subjects find themselves 'in diesen dröhnenden Panzer verpackt,
den wir uns nicht ausgesucht hatten' (p.8). This 'Eisenwagen', under attack
from without, is GDR socialism:

Ursus, 1988).
[5]Letter to me, 30 November 1998. Grünbein's only official publication in the GDR
consisted of six poems in *SuF*, 40 (1988), 818-824.
[6]Emmerich, *Kleine Literaturgeschichte der DDR*, p.516.
[7]Erk Grimm, 'Das Gedicht nach dem Gedicht: Über die Lesbarkeit der jüngsten Lyrik',
in *Deutschsprachige Gegenwartsliteratur*, ed. by Döring, pp.287-304. Harald Hartung,
'Placebos, Kwehrdeutsch, Vaterlandskanal: Anmerkungen zur jungen Lyrik', *Merkur*,
45 (1991), 1145-1152 (p.1150). Joachim Sartorius, ed., 'Vorwort', *Atlas der modernen
Poesie* (Reinbek bei Hamburg: Rowohlt, 1995), pp.7-16 (p.13).
[8]Durs Grünbein,'Aus einem alten Fahrtenbuch', *Falten und Fallen: Gedichte*
(Frankfurt a.M.: Suhrkamp, 1994), pp.81-91. Jürgen Engler calls it a 'langes
Prosagedicht' in his article 'Nicht heimisch', *ndl*, 42 (1994), No.4, 139-145 (p.142).
[9]Braun, 'Der Eisenwagen', *Monatshefte*, 78 (1986), 7-10.

Die Lokomotive der Geschichte, meine Herren Arbeiter und Bauern. Aber sie war ein Panzerzug. Ihre Waffe der Schrecken. Wir darin: gefangen, verborgen, abgeschirmt. (p.8)

Whereas Braun's subject is amongst comrades, speaking almost exclusively of 'wir', Grünbein's subject is alone. His 'ich' also, however, experiences the tank as not only confining but also protecting: 'hier bin ich geschützt, einzigartig bewehrt' (p.83). Where Grünbein's tank is a 'verrostete Illusion' (p.85) it too seems to be the vehicle of socialism. Grünbein develops the metaphor in a different way however. His tank is a 'Panzer der Sprache', whose steel sides are a 'stabile Grammatik' (p.83). Braun's 'Eisenwagen' is a crucial forerunner nonetheless, which clatters in the background throughout Grünbein's text, perhaps one of the other tanks which the narrator hears outside. Braun's tank of socialism is a technological apparatus: 'Ein sagenhaftes ominöses Gefährt. Eine Apparatur, die alle Funktionen aller Geräte in sich vereinigte und knirschend krachend rasselnd öl- und kottriefend vom Zentrum bis an die ferne reine Küste ratterte' (p.9). This ominous machine finally invades the human body so that Braun's subject, now individual, finds that his skin is the wall of the vehicle: 'In diesem Augenblick empfand ich es als gerecht, daß die Zeit, in der ich es begriff, die Zeit meines Todes war. Der Wagen würde mein Mausoleum sein, mein Grab' (p.10). Comprehension comes at the moment of death: Braun's 1986 tank of socialism is a death chamber which consumes the individual. Grünbein's metaphor of 'gebunkertes Denken' (p.84) suggests his tank is in fact a bunker in which to escape socialism's repression. Here too though the individual 'ich' is lost: 'Spreche ich ernst, ist es vorbei, unaufhaltsam verschwinde ich. Niemand achtet darauf, man verfolgt nur den Panzer' (p.85). Language as the hard shell of a moving machine, autonomous of its poet-driver, is an unexpected image. In discussing his language alongside that of other poets in Prenzlauer Berg, Grünbein said, 'Meine Sprache verstand sich nicht missionarisch, sie war eher ein Schutz nach draußen, eine zweite Haut'.[10] This protective skin is intimated by the image of the tank. Such an image does not set language and culture against science and technology, but sees them as part of the same process of civilization. Grünbein breaks into the sarcastic, sagacious tone and form of 'du'-self-address that is typical of many of his poems:

Und wo ist er geblieben, dein tierhafter Charme. Alle verlernt und vergessen, die lieben Reflexe, Babinsky, Saccadi ... (p.86)

---

[10]Thomas Naumann, 'Poetry from the bad side', *Sprache im technischen Zeitalter* (1992), No.124, 442-449 (p.447).

'Tierhafter Charme' and natural reflexes (here, for instance, the Babinsky reflex of the big toe) are key to Grünbein's poetry of zoology and biology. Suffice it to note at this point that they are set against conditioned love, conditioned anger and conditioned fear. The 'Panzer der Sprache' suggests the ambivalent idea of language as conditioning and training, as that rigid metal shell of the tank, which determines the 'ich's view of his surroundings. The 'ich' sees 'ausschnittweise', 'durch ein Zielfernrohr oder durch schmale Schlitze' (p.86). Sight is conditioned by the direction and speed of the language-vehicle. But this restriction is necessary in order to take in anything at all: 'nur in ihm, meinem Panzer, bahne ich mir einen Weg durch das unermeßliche Sichtfeld' (p.87). 'Der Blick' is, I shall argue, a key concept in Grünbein's poetry.

> Unter den Brauenbögen scheint nur mein Blick das Ziel. Im weiten Umkreis sucht er das Diorama nach festen Körpern ab, ein Bumerang, der zurückschnellt vom Horizont und leicht ins Auge geht.   (pp.86-87)

Here 'das Ziel' is no socialist utopia achieved through popular enlightenment, but rather the individual's ability to see and survey the frozen scene for solid objects. Further on in the piece, the purpose of the language-tank is re-interpreted as 'das Erkennen' (p.91), a word which recurs throughout Grünbein's writing: it will be important to explore what it means in various poems. Here in the prose allegory, it is a discovery of the landscape, whose function as a metaphor for human understanding is indicated in the last line: 'Nicht mehr lange, heißt es, und diese fürchterlich zerebrale Landschaft zerreißt' (p.91). This break-up of the cerebral landscape points to the fragmentation of human ideas in postmodernism. Braun's and Grünbein's tanks allegorize their self-understanding as intellectuals. Furthermore, Grünbein's cycle 'Point of no return', written for Heiner Müller, presents an 'Autopoet', a term which suggests both autonomy and another vehicle, akin to the 'Panzer der Sprache'.[11]

In 1990 Karl Krieg reviewed Grünbein as a poet born into the GDR and concluded, 'ob er sich herausdichten wird, weiß heute noch kein Mensch'.[12] At that time only Grünbein's first collection of poems from 1985-1988, *Grauzone morgens*, had appeared, published in the West in 1988. The 'Grauzone' is recognizably the 'Ostzone', the cities of Dresden and East Berlin. It is also that zone of grey light between night and morning, a

---

[11]Durs Grünbein, 'Point of no return: Für Heiner Müller', *Jahrbuch zur Literatur in der DDR*, 7 (1990), 47-50. The first two parts, with alterations, appear under the title 'Buna 1-2', in *Schädelbasislektion*, pp.144-145.
[12]Karl Krieg, 'Durs Grünbein: Grauzone morgens', *Passauer Pegasus*, 8 (1990), No.15, 137-138 (p.138).

metaphor of resignation: the bright morn that would symbolize hope has not arrived. Grünbein himself has also indicated that he conceives of a grey zone between poetry and prose: 'Grauzone, das war auch der Landstrich in dem Lyrik und Prosa ununterschiedbar verschmolzen im Schweben einer balancierenden Sprechstimme'.[13] The 'Großstadtgedichte' of *Grauzone morgens* describe urban life which is characterized by tiredness, heaviness and slow-motion. A lyric 'ich' observes grim-faced workers (p.10) and a city which, like an old film, is 'ein / Wirbel grauer Pigmente' (p.16). Grey is a symbolic backdrop to a life without anticipation of anything better. Typically for the 1980s, a number of poems focus on environmental destruction where they describe rubbish bins, the polluted Elbe, or a rubbish-filled brook. There is also a recurrent sense of stillness: 'Soviele Tage in denen nichts sich / ereignete' (p.48). Motifs of greyness and mistiness are accompanied by images of being frozen: people have 'total // eingefrorene Gesten' (p.16) for instance. The lyric subject is an urban sleepwalker, 'wie benebelt im Ätherrausch' (p.19). One poem demands, 'Schiefer Nomad, wach endlich auf!' (p.26). Human figures are invariably lone, isolated figures like the single man of 'Mundtot frühmorgens' (p.12), 'Eine hagere Frau' (p.13) found dead, 'Eine von diesen Harpyien (pp.73-74) or the lone Spanish woman of 'Olé' (pp.76-77). Similarly, the self is 'Du, allein mit der Geschichte im / Rücken' (p.53). As a single human figure can provide the focus of the poem, so single objects are prominent in the collection. One poem describes a draught ('Eine Regung', p.54), another a vodka bottle frozen into a pond ('Anderswo', p.55). Like the poem about bath-tubs (p.50), this type of subject points to the depressed mind. It is the antithesis of vision and expansive hope. It also offers a new perspective on disregarded objects. The poem 'Ohne Titel' (pp.61-62) offers an alienating perspective on marriage by situating it on a 'Nebelmorgen' and 'Ermordungstag'. Even in the context of a wedding, the rubbish-heap motif occurs, and again rain, 'Nieselregen'. Amidst such a bleak view of one's surroundings, the following lines seem provocative:

Westwärts zog ein Paar
    kleiner Wolken   (lines 23-24)

They hint at the married couple contemplating a move to the West, as Grünbein did in 1987/88 when he submitted an exit visa application. The poetry in *Grauzone morgens* thus seems to reflect quite clearly the GDR situation Grünbein experienced in the 1980s. He himself has referred to these pre-'Wende' poems as documents of that time: 'Alles vor 1989 Geschriebene

---

[13]Naumann, 'Poetry from the bad side', p.445.

erscheint mir selbst heute als historisches Dokument'.[14] The collection can seem to be confined by the time and place it was written.

With the collection *Schädelbasislektion* Grünbein, to echo Krieg's term, 'writes himself out' of the GDR. His own 'Panzer der Sprache' symbolizes a defiance vis-à-vis the 'Panzers vor dem Bahnhof' which were in evidence in October 1989.[15] It also symbolizes this 'writing a way out'. *Schädelbasislektion* has been recognized as 'eines der bedeutendsten literarischen Werke zum Thema Wende und Wiedervereinigung'.[16] In the cycle 'Die leeren Zeichen' Grünbein find terms for, and thus seems to come to terms with, the GDR experience. Poems 8 and 11-15 particularly draw on Grünbein's 'Wende' imprisonment as a metaphor for the whole of life in the GDR. References to being forced to stand and not being allowed to go to a toilet reflect his experience of custody after he was arrested at a street demonstration on 9 October 1989.[17] The narrowness of the cell is clearly symbolic in a wider sense:

> Ein enger Gang, verbrauchte Luft, das Licht
> So grell daß es die Ohren abstehn ließ.
> Die Adern an der Hand des Nebenmanns
> Traten wie Würmer violett hervor.
> 5   Man war verdammt zum Aufrechtstehn,
> Kein Kniefall half. Das Glück der Schwäche
> Zu überwinden war man streng bewacht.
> Die Szenerie vertraut... ein Polizeirevier.   (No.8, p.76)

> Ein Tote-Fakten-Raum, ein gelbes Loch,
> Die Wände wie mit Gänsehaut bespannt,
> Wo alle Farben per Dekret entfärbt
> Unter dem Anstrich mundtot schwelten.
> 5   Den Ton gab dieses Gelb an,
>   gelber Hohn
> Der sich durch jede Zelle fraß, Urin-
> Delirien die das Denken lähmten...

---

[14]Letter to me, 30 November 1998.

[15]The reference to 'Panzers vor dem Bahnhof' occurs in the tenth 'Die leeren Zeichen' poem, *Schädelbasislektion*, p.78.

[16]Klaus Bednarz, 'Durs Grünbein: Den teuren Toten', in Klaus Bednarz and Gisela Marx, *Von Autoren und Büchern: Gespräche mit Schriftstellern* (Hamburg: Hoffmann und Campe, 1997), pp.204-210 (p.204).

[17]As a point of comparison, see the eye-witness account of another citizen detained in Dresden on the night of 8-9 October 1989, in Bahrmann, ed., *Wir sind das Volk*, pp.12-14.

"Wozu aufs Klo gehn? Pißt euch ein!"   (No.12, p.80)

Horror is made vivid in the yellows and violets and the 'grelles Licht'. Absence of an 'ich' and the laconic description emphasize the sense of oppression. Furthermore, in No.12 the 'Anstrich' image recalls Brecht's designation for Hitler, 'der Anstreicher'.[18] In another poem in this group, the 'ich' lists the names he is given by the state: 'In schneller Folge war ich Demonstrant, / Dann Wirrkopf, Rowdy, Element / Und also Unperson, mit einem Wort / Ein Unding oder schlicht, ein Nichts' (p.83). The self was practically eradicated. These poignant poems recite a terrible experience of repression and brutality using cool, fairly distanced description.

In contrast to other poets who labour over the GDR and its fall, Grünbein quickly seems to free himself from this past. This is indicated in representations of the 'Wende' as an 'Augenblick' in the poems of the cycle 'Die leeren Zeichen' (*Schädelbasislektion*, pp.67-87): the shift is condensed into twenty four hours (p.71), one night (p.72), a lesion (p.72), or an instantaneous disappearance by magic (p.74). In the telegram poems (*Schädelbasislektion*, pp.59-65), the past is 'vorbei wie das stählerne Schweigen' (p.61), 'geplatzt wie der Kürbis' (p.62), or simply 'gesprengt' (p.65). The period of transition becomes a borderline, instantly traversed:

> Seit damals ist ein Wort ein Wort,
> Sonst nichts. Seit diesem einen Tag
> Und dieser Nacht, die am Gehirn fraß.
> Etwas brach ab und etwas neues
> 5   Kann nicht beginnen seither, Ebbe.
> In den verödeten Kanälen treibt
> Nur die Erinnerung an Schlimmeres.
> Gerinnsel, Chlor, ein kortikaler Fleck.   (No.3, p.71)

The first line distils the end of literature's political function as a simple resumption of normality. This straightforward statement contrasts with the painstaking analyses by other ex-GDR poets, such as Heinz Czechowski's 'Nachtrag' discussed in Chapter 4. In Grünbein's poem, juxtaposed repetitions of 'seit', 'Wort' and 'etwas' emphasize the theme of duality, of before versus after. 'Etwas' (4) is deliberately vague (as is 'dazu' in the opening line of the preceding poem: 'Schwachsinn, zu fragen wie es dazu kam' (p.70)). The 'Wende' is measured by fracture and flow, in a cerebral rather than an urban landscape. There is no human subject in this poem, rather the brain is a

---

[18]Brecht uses this term in a number of poems, of which the earliest is 'Das Lied vom Anstreicher Hitler', *Gesammelte Werke*, ix, pp.441-442.

discrete object, like a barometer whose fluid responds to the surrounding atmospheric changes. Memory of the GDR is a physical reaction in the human brain (3 and 8): 'die verödeten Kanäle' (6) suggest city streets or underground tunnels, but primarily here the channels of the mind. In the following poem (p.72), the fourth in 'Die leeren Zeichen', the brain also provides a simile: the night of the 'Wende' separates the past from the present as the two hemispheres of the brain are distinct and different. The poem 'Die meisten hier' (*Grauzone morgens*, p.15, and as 'Zerebralis', *Schädelbasislektion*, p.134) refers to the brain as a resonating chamber which responds to the terror of city life:

> Gehirn
> bloßgelegt
> (Dieses Grau!) und dazwischen
> nichts mehr was eine Resonanz auf den
> Terror ringsum
> dämpfen könnte.   (lines 13-18)

The 'Wende' is represented by Grünbein as this type of resonance in the exposed brain.[19] He seems to be responding as much to an international scientific revolution – namely the developments of cognitive science in the last decade – as to the political revolution of 1989. The nineteenth poem in 'Die leeren Zeichen' (*Schädelbasislektion*, p.87) exemplifies the brain as another cityscape where history plays itself out:

> Nach soviel Aufruhr *up and down* die Nacht,
> Schiffsschaukeln in den Grachten des Gehirns,
> Soviel gestauter Gegenwart, Ideenflucht, Entzug
> Kam früh, wie immer früh, die *Wende*.
> 5   Die Wände hochgekrochen kam und blieb
> Die eigne Frage in Gestalt des Feindes –
> Daß niemand es gewesen sein wird, hieß
> "Das Ganze war ein Zwischenfall, mehr nicht."

Physical states and processes hold this poem together: vertical movement in '*up and down*' (1) and 'schaukeln' (2), and damming up in 'gestauter Gegenwart' (3) represent a lack of horizontal progress. Vertical movement develops into a surmounting of the obstacle in the phrase 'die Wände hochgekrochen' (5), which includes a literal climbing of the Berlin Wall. Several threads of imagery intertwine here: one links the cerebral

---

[19]Compare other contemporary notions of the brain as a millennial symbol in Edward Bullmore, 'The Millennium Brain', *The Independent on Sunday*, 17 January 1999, pp.14-16.

claustrophobia, see-sawing in the brain, 'Ideenflucht' (3), and the figurative sense of 'climbing the walls' as 'going mad'; another points to the image of ships on canals and going through a lock. As in other Grünbein poems, the 'Wende' takes place at night and 'früh, wie immer früh' (4) whilst it is still dark. This recurrence of 'früh' creates a tension because of the clichés of the 'Wende' as a long overdue catching-up, and 'wie immer' indicates a typical occurrence, rather than ascribing uniqueness to 1989. The term 'die *Wende*' (4) actually occurs in this poem, which is unusual for Grünbein. He tends to avoid any designation like 'DDR' or 'Berlin' which would limit the frame of reference. Even here, '*Wende*', italicized as a quotation, immediately becomes its acoustic twin, 'Wände' (5). In the second half of the poem, collapse is not presented as the physical collapse of walls: in line 6, 'Feind' collapses as a concept, for the enemy is revealed to be a projection of the self. The drawn-out future perfect (7) articulates a process of reassessment which reveals 'niemand'. In the final line of the poem the GDR is just 'das Ganze' (8), a characteristically dismissive and unspecific term. The ultimate collapse is the dissolution of a state, a system, a utopia, but all of these become only 'ein Zwischenfall, mehr nicht' (8).

Grünbein's understatement contrasts with Braun's dramatic natural metaphors of earthquakes and volcanic eruption. He does not portray the human subject at the mercy of changes much larger than himself: if anything, the human mind internalizes the shift where the mind becomes a biological barometer. Grünbein's chosen motto to his collected essays of 1989-1995, however, indicates that the GDR experience, at least for a short while, will produce a distinctive sensibility, a 'kurze Wachzeit', in those who are living in the West for the first time: [20]

> Die ihr so weit gekommen seid nach Westen
> Durch tausende Gefahren, Brüder, lohnt
> Die kurze Wachzeit, die den Sinnen bleibt als Rest
> Mit der Erfahrung einer Welt, die unbewohnt
> Hinter der Sonne liegt. (lines 1-5)

These lines from Dante's *Inferno* read, when appropriated by Grünbein, like an address to his ex-GDR compatriots who have experienced the transitions of German unification. 'Eine Welt, die unbewohnt / Hinter der Sonne liegt' becomes the socialist utopia. This 'new' reading signals the timelessness of Dante's lines and thus places the GDR experience in the context of larger patterns which characterize human history. This is typical of the deliberate timelessness of Grünbein's poetry after the fall of the GDR. It is telling that

---

[20]Durs Grünbein, *Galilei vermißt Dantes Hölle und bleibt an den Maßen hängen: Aufsätze 1989-1995* (Frankfurt a.M.: Suhrkamp, 1996), p.7.

lines from Dante constitute Grünbein's only apparent address to the GDR people. The lyric subject is unconfined by the GDR experience in the later collections: as if responding to the cry 'wach endlich auf!' in *Grauzone morgens*, there seems to be an awakening to a diversity of ideas, traditions and languages.

The morning of Grünbein's post-'Wende' dawn-song, 'Alba' (*Falten*, p.95), contrasts with the grey dawns in *Grauzone morgens*. Instead, the night has brought 'das Neue' (13). Against the perpetuated wanderings in the poetry discussed in Chapter 4, Grünbein opens here with the end of the wanderers. These wanderers, firstly mortals, are subsequently revealed to be also poets writing 'Lieder':

> Alba
> Endlich sind all die Wanderer tot
> Und zur Ruhe gekommen die Lieder
> Der Verstörten, der Landschaftskranken
> In ihren langen Schatten, am Horizont.
>
> 5   Kleine Koseworte und Grausamkeiten
> Treiben gelöst in der Luft. Wie immer
> Sind die Sonnenbänke besetzt, lächeln
> Kinder und Alte aneinander vorbei.
>
> In den Zweigen hängen Erinnerungen,
> 10 Genaue Szenen aus einem künftigen Tag.
> Überall Atem und Sprünge rückwärts
> Durchs Dunkel von Urne zu Uterus.
> Und das Neue, gefährlich und über Nacht
> Ist es Welt geworden. So komm heraus
> 15 Aus zerwühlten Laken, sieh sie dir an,
> Himmel, noch unbehelligt, und unten
>
> Aus dem Hinterhalt aufgebrochen,
> Giftige Gräser und Elstern im Staub,
> Mit bösem Flügelschlag, Diebe
> 20 In der Mitte des Lebensweges wie du.

On the one hand the imagery here suggests a park where the lyric subject sees shadows, the horizon, benches, children and old people, branches, sky, grass and magpies. Perhaps the theme of death points rather to a graveyard walk: reference to 'Ruhe' (2) and 'Urne' (12) evokes the graves; the grass and dust

(18) recall biblical descriptions of mortality.[21] The human subject 'du' is scarcely here at all, appearing as a simile in the final line where magpies are 'Diebe [...] wie du' (19-20). He is stealing time, as it were, en route to death. Furthermore, memories (9) and 'kleine Koseworte und Grausamkeiten' (5) may evoke the experience of bereavement. The medieval alba was a type of 'Minnesang', in which morning means lovers must part. Grünbein's 'Alba' suggests a parting brought by death. This is not a gloomy treatment of death, however. The dawning of a new day (fleetingly recalling the 'Wende' perhaps) reveals a new world: the 'du' is called to get up and look at the 'Himmel' (13-16). As the path through the park is also a 'Lebensweg' (20), so this 'Himmel' and 'künftiger Tag' also represent heaven at its end. In the midst of life, the subject finds 'Überall Atem und Sprünge rückwärts / Durchs Dunkel von Urne zu Uterus' (11-12). Children and old people in the previous stanza represent the points of life closest to the two vessels, the grave urn and the uterus. The words 'gelöst' (6) and 'vorbei/lächeln' (7-8) anticipate the sense of a benign process, which is not completely irreversible. The processional preposition 'durchs' stands out in its alliteration with 'Dunkel' and assonance with 'Urne' (12). This is the middle of the poem too. Furthermore, when the poem was published in *Manuskripte*, the stanzas were arranged diagonally descending across the page, giving another impression of the passage through time as a path.[22]

Forward-looking images of awakening and walking on are set beside a backward trajectory (from funeral urne to uterus) in 'Alba'. For one thing this disrupts the socialist teleological paradigm. Braun's 'Der Eisenwagen' does not consist solely of the parable discussed above, but includes a poem (p.7) which is particularly interesting in relation to Grünbein's treatment of the human course. It describes a moment of awakening to 'das Neue' (13) and rising out of oppression:

Frühjahre der Völker, Seltenzeit
Wenn sie ausgehn, aus ihrem Schlummer
Ins Freie. Das Eis
Der Strukturen bricht, und es hebt den Nacken neugierig
5   Der Unterdrückte.

Ist das Bedürfnis groß
Davon die Zeitungen schweigen, tritt es furchtlos hervor
Aus den inwendigen Menschen. Freudig

---

[21]'Denn der Staub muß wieder zur Erde kommen, wie er gewesen ist, und der Geist wieder zu Gott' (Prediger 12.7). 'Denn alles Fleisch ist wie Gras' (I Petrus 2.24).
[22]Durs Grünbein, 'Alba', *Manuskripte*, 33 (1993), No.122, 30.

Gewahren sie es auf der Straße. Sie gewahren es
10   In ihrer Freude.

Durchsichtig die Geschichte
In der sie sich sehen
Läßt sich ein auf das Neue.
Sie kommen aus ihrer Haut.

15   Wie die Liebenden, die sich zu erkennen geben
Alle Scheu fällt von ihnen, amtliches Kleid.
Ihre Lust teilt sich mit, Natur und Maschinen.
Alles versteht sich von selbst.

The break-up of frozen structures (3-4) is accompanied by the removal of all
boundaries: need coming out from within (6-8) is portrayed in these terms
('hervor/treten aus'), as is history becoming transparent ('durch/sichtig'). The
awakening in 'Der Eisenwagen' is a dream of reformed socialism, which was
given new impetus in autumn 1989. The last line of Braun's poem particularly
articulates the idea of a natural human utopia. 'Die Liebenden' without shame
are prelapsarian Adam and Eve figures. Set against this poem, Grünbein's
poem for Elias Canetti (*Galilei*, p.196), in which the human is an 'Untier',
gives a contrastingly cynical view of human civilization.[23]

Sieh dieses Untier auf zwei Beinen, wie es geht
Und hält sich aufrecht, bahnt sich seinen Weg
Auch über Leichen, die sein Blick besiegt
Im Weitergehn. Was liegt, das liegt.

5   Sieh, wie es seinesgleichen froh beiseite legt -
Das schon gefallen ist, und sich noch regt
Am Unfallort. Der schönste Augenblick
Ist der des Überlebens. Was ist Glück?

This poem reproduces the rhythm of walking: Grünbein uses enjambement
and the placing of commas to recreate the striding out and the following-on of
two legs. The walking here is different to that in Braun's poem – Braun
describes stepping into Arcadian human goodness, whereas Grünbein sees a
bestial trampling to survive. The contrast is brought out further in Braun's

---

[23]In the essay with which this poem is published in *Galilei* ('Wir Buschmänner: Eine
Erinnerung an Elias Canettis Masse und Macht', *Galilei*, pp.197-209), Grünbein
indicates the influence of reading Canetti's *Masse und Macht* in the GDR, a book
which analyses the human as a social animal.

'Wende' commentary on his poem, in which he looks to a new, more civilized type of behaviour, again represented by a way of walking: 'Laßt uns eine andere Gangart wählen als die der Räuber, die wir waren. Eine Gangart, mit der wir zu anderen Zielen kommen, zu sanfteren Technologien'.[24] Grünbein rejects this utopian sociological view and instead interprets human beings as 'die Räuber, die wir waren'. 'Über Leichen gehen' is present in Grünbein's poem as a commonplace metaphor, but also as a physical movement, in the relative clause that follows (3-4) and the second stanza. 'Aufrecht' (2) is the posture that physically distinguishes human from animal and not a moral superiority here, for 'Weitergehn' (4) is itself an amoral unconcern for fellow humans, particularly for the fallen and the dead. The question at the end of the poem suggests that happiness and unhappiness are deliberately suspended in viewing the human as an animal: he pursues only his own survival. Therein lies the horror of Grünbein's unanswered question 'Was ist Glück?', which so contrasts with Braun's 'Alles versteht sich von selbst'.

Diverse roaming becomes an important metaphor for writing or thinking in Grünbein's later poetry. It reworks the amoral path, the 'sich seinen Weg bahnen' of the human 'Untier' and the path of Grünbein's language tank. Finding one's own course is a pursuit of curiosity in new, unrelated directions in the eighth poem of the 'Grenzhund' cycle (*Schädelbasislektion*, p.102):

Verstand, wie *Joe* sagt, die Dreigroschen-Hölle
Ist dieser Ort, wo sich das Ich eins pfeift;
Wo sich auf Abstand halten Angst und Neugier.
Die Angst: es könnte bald an seinem Rand
Spurlos verschwinden auf dem Weg der Neugier.
Der Neugier: wie sich's lebt, befreit von Angst.
Daraus ergibt sich leicht ein kleines Drama
Entlang der Grenzen, vom Verstand markiert
Durch immer neues unverwandtes Streunen.   (lines 1-9)

'Die Neugier', teutonically stronger than 'curiosity', means a deep longing for knowledge, literally for new things. Here it is opposite to the fundamental experience of the human in urban chaos, a fear of disappearing.[25] Lines 4-6 create a formal counterpoint – 'Angst', 'Neugier', 'Neugier', 'Angst'. This thematizes a borderline which literature (one sense of 'Drama' above) occupies between knowledge and urban chaos. There is a strong sense of boundaries here, but not political ones. Rather these are one's own boundaries: the words 'Rand' and 'Grenzen', in contrast to Braun's use of them with respect to society, refer here to the extent of the self. 'Unverwandtes Streunen'

---

[24]Braun, *Wir befinden uns soweit wohl*, p.25.
[25]See for instance the cycle 'Niemands Land Stimmen', *Schädelbasislektion*, pp.21-51.

recurs in the poem 'Inframince' (*Schädelbasislektion*, p.16) along the border
between 'Ich' and 'Dinge':
Unverwandt streunend, der Traum eine Lichtung im Ich
Nimmst du die Sprache der Dinge mit unter die Haut.
Jeder in seiner Welt (lines 1-3)
Assimilation of language into the body is a typical idea in Grünbein: language
comes from outside, from the 'Dinge', and traverses the skin-boundary which
divides a person's own private world from the outside world. In the third
poem of the cycle 'Schädelbasislektion' (*Schädelbasislektion*, p.13), the verb
'Streunen' is in a prominent position and its subject, the animal, delayed:
Zwischen Sprache und mir
Streunt, Alarm in den Blicken,
Ein geschlechtskrankes Tier.
Nichts wird ganz unterdrücken
Was mein Tier-Ich fixiert   (lines 1-5)
Here the articulate human is caught between an animal-self and language, in
an uneasy relationship to both, it seems. In the three extracts above, 'Streunen'
is linked to curiosity, language acquisition and to the 'Tier-Ich'. As a
metaphor for the poet's self-understanding, it is a straying from one's training,
a straying beyond the GDR, a mental roaming through the ideas of different
eras and academic fields.

The human as animal is a central theme in Grünbein's poetry: the
human is 'ein Tier, das den aufrechten Gang übt, / Den Gebrauch von
Werkzeug' (*Falten*, p.22). More specifically, the GDR system sought to train
people in socialism and technology. The echo of Bloch's and Braun's
metaphor for socialist decency is typical of Grünbein's re-appropriation of
moral and political metaphors (exemplified above in the cases of 'Wände' and
'Grenzen'). Grünbein's 'Grenzhund' cycle in *Schädelbasislektion* ('Porträt des
Künstlers als junger Grenzhund', pp.93-107) explores questions of human
instinct versus social conditioning. It draws on the behaviourist views of the
Russian physiologist Pavlov, who removed dogs' organs and nerves in pursuit
of the 'unbedingter Reflex' and sought to instil in the animals other reflexes
through training.[26] In the seventh poem of the cycle (p.101), the lyric-'ich'
becomes an absurd and allegorical border-guard dog:[27]

---

[26]Compare too Volker Braun, 'Monströse Banalität', *Die Zeit*, 22 November 1991,
p.63, in which Braun seems to see his own instincts and reflexes as a writer bound by
state power: 'Auch die Macht herausfordern bedeutet, sich mit ihr einzulassen: man
konnte die Mechanismen kennen, und doch hat das herrschende Bewußtsein die
Reflexe gebunden'.
[27]This seems to invert the biographical point of correspondence: whilst doing
compulsory military service, Grünbein refused to undertake border patrol (and for this

Glücklich in einem Niemandsland aus Sand
War ich ein Hund, in Grenzen wunschlos, stumm.
Von oben kam, was ich zum Glauben brauchte.
Gott war ein Flugzeug, wolkenweiß getarnt
5   Vom Feind, mich einzuschläfern, ferngesteuert.
Doch blieb ich stoisch, mein Revier im Blick.
Wenn ich auf allen Vieren Haltung annahm,
Zündstoff mein Fell, lud mich der Boden auf.
Im Westen, heißt es, geht der Hund dem Herrn
10   Voraus.
          Im Osten folgt er ihm – mit Abstand.
Was mich betrifft, ich war mein eigner Hund,
Gleich fern von Ost und West, im Todesstreifen.
Nur hier gelang mir manchmal dieser Sprung
15   Tief aus dem Zwielicht zwischen Hund und Wolf.

By giving a poetic voice to a dog, Grünbein articulates an apparently light-hearted response to the GDR past. This is particulary clear in contrast to Czechowski's lines 'Was mich betrifft / So bin ich ich' which epitomize sincere self-assertion and are echoed by Grünbein in line 12 above.[28] The ironic pride in his 'Revier' and in being 'mein eigner Hund' adds to the humour. At the same time, Grünbein is drawing on the dog as a common metaphor for human degradation (2). The 'Grenzen' are not explicitly German borders between East and West, but rather confines on expression ('stumm', line 2) and on understanding (3-4). This combination of the anthropological-philosophical and the faintly absurd seems to be a strategy typical of Grünbein. In the eleventh 'Grenzhund' poem (p.105) the dog asks, 'Was heißt schon Leben? Für alles gibt's Ersatz / Wo nur Hypnose herrscht und "Dienst ist Dienst" ' (lines 13-14). The 'big' statement of cynicism (13) is run on into the commonplace maxim 'Dienst ist Dienst und Schnaps ist Schnaps' – 'Schnaps' is heard as an echo in 'Ersatz' and 'Hypnose'. Self-contradiction and a continuous process of setting up and undermining thus characterize this writing. In the 'Grenzhund' cycle this is achieved by the anomalous consciousness of the dog as a lyric subject. The cycle immediately suggests a parallel with Hans-Eckardt Wenzel's 1991 poem 'Die herrenlosen Hunde des

---

reason was denied the opportunity to study German literature at university). See Naumann, 'Poetry from the bad side', p.443.
[28]Heinz Czechowski, 'Was mich betrifft', *Was mich betrifft: Gedichte* (Halle-Leipzig: mdv, 1981), p.17.

Mittags' which, although set in Managua, Nicaragua, has a lyric 'ich' which similarly identifies with roaming dogs:[29]
ihr Mittagshunde, meine Brüder, wir,
Die Vergessenen, die abgesprengten Legionen,
Wir wußten nicht mehr, wie herzlich das Wasser
In unseren Mündern schmeckt, vergaßen
Die einfache Not, vertrieben die träumenden Katzen
Und dünkten und herrisch in unserer reichen Armut.

Jetzt streunen wir heimatlos über diesen Planeten,
        Durch Mülldeponien und Mangel geht unsere Suche   (lines 18-26)

Wenzel picks up the same idea of an ex-GDR doggish consciousness, which is central to Grünbein's 'Grenzhund' cycle. The dogs, deprived in the past and now homeless, wandering the world in an undirected quest, seem to be ex-GDR poets.

The 'wir' in Grünbein's poems more generally tends not be a GDR collective however, but invariably 'we humankind'. Human consciousness as the determiner of human fate is a central idea in Grünbein's poetry.[30] The poem 'Biologischer Walzer' (Falten, p.71) traces the passage of humanity into civilization as a result of this consciousness. Thus evolution has been a waltz, a rule-governed dance of patterns which bring one back to the starting-point. The closing stanza of 'Biologischer Walzer' also comes back to a bon mot from the first:

Wenn es stimmt, daß wir schwierige Tiere sind
Sind wir schwierige Tiere weil nichts mehr stimmt.   (lines 3-4 or 19-20)

In his commentary on this poem for the Frankfurter Anthologie, Alexander von Bormann compares these lines to Bloch's statement 'Das in den Geschichten nicht stimmt, weil es mit uns und allem nicht stimmt'.[31] Bormann's comparison underplays Grünbein's divergence from Bloch: Grünbein's chiasmus has as its focus the repeated phrase 'wir sind schwierige Tiere'. Bloch does not mention animals, whereas for Grünbein, it is the renunciation of animal origins which makes human life 'difficult'. The renunciation of animal instinct is the departure from 'dieser Wald / Aus

---

[29]Hans-Eckardt Wenzel, 'Die herrenlosen Hunde des Mittags', ndl, 39 (1991), No.2, 41-42.

[30]The prose piece which appeared in Falten und Fallen as 'Aus einem alten Fahrtenbuch' in 1994 was first published without its 'Herausgeberfiktion' in 1991 under the title of the work Bewußtsein als Verhängnis by the expert in depressive psychology Alfred Seidel. Durs Grünbein, '(Bewußtsein als Verhängnis)', ndl, 39 (1991), No.10, 53-59.

[31]Alexander von Bormann, 'Schwierige Tiere', in Frankfurter Anthologie, xix, ed. by Marcel Reich-Ranicki (Frankfurt a.M. and Leipzig: Insel, 1996), pp.246-248 (p.246).

Begierden', which may be Freudian desires. Elsewhere poetic language provides 'das Alphabet der Begierden' ('Point of no return', I:10). This poem, however, focuses on the beginnings of human language as a troubling development. 'Nichts mehr stimmt' and 'niemand kennt' in the first stanza foreshadow 'nichts erklärt' in the second:

> Steter Tropfen im Mund war das Wort der Beginn
> Des Verzichts, einer langen Flucht in die Zeit.
> Nichts erklärt, wie ein trockener Gaumen Vokale,
> Wie ein Leck in der Kehle Konsonanten erbricht.   (lines 5-8)

The biblical 'in the beginning was the word' flashes an association which is promptly denied, for here it is 'der Beginn / Des Verzichts'. In Grünbein's poetry, this point of departure from the animal to the human is picked up again and again as a point at which consciousness, memory and language evolved. In his exchanges with Brigitte Oleschinski and Peter Waterhouse concerning poetology, Grünbein refers to the forgotten ape from which the human animal descended:

> In dem Augenblick, wo das Bewußtsein auftritt
> Ist der Affe vergessen, der mit den Ästen ging.
> Das Vermögen, den Baum zu denken, wird teuer bezahlt.[32]

This of course takes up the idea of the human experiencing a costly loss of innocence, which interested various German writers over the centuries (Schiller and Kleist for instance). The decisive turning-point which Grünbein looks back to is not 1989/90, as for the majority of his contemporaries, but a 'Wende' valid for all people, of all eras. Grünbein's perspective is rooted in an evolutionary explanation of human behaviour, rather than sociological explanations which locate the human in a particular society. Indeed, in an interview with Sven Michaelsen, Grünbein stated, 'Soziologisches stößt mich ab, Zoologisches tröstet mich. Das Tier im Menschen ist vielleicht die Hoffnung'.[33] Of what does this hope in the human animal consist?

Alongside the animal as an image of the human in general, it is also specifically an image of the poet. The 'Grenzhund' cycle of poems are after all entitled 'Porträt des Künstlers'. Here lies the hope in animal influence. In an aside from an article he wrote pertaining to the 'Literaturstreit', Grünbein cites Aristotle's distinction between the *zoon politikon* and the *idiotes*.[34] The social animal 'in seinem Staatskäfig' is contrasted with the self-contained idiot.

---

[32]Durs Grünbein, Brigitte Oleschinski, and Peter Waterhouse, *Die Schweizer Korrektur*, ed. by Urs Engeler (Basel: Urs Engeler Editor, 1995), p.51.
[33]Sven Michaelsen, 'Rebell mit Röntgenblick', *Stern*, 19 October 1995, pp.228-231 (p.231).
[34]Durs Grünbein, 'Im Namen der Füchse: Gibt es eine neue literarische Zensur?', *FAZ*, 26 November 1991, p.33.

Grünbein's positive reception of the *idiotes* contrasts with Braun's despair and horror at the 'nützlicher Idiot' in 'Die Verstellung'. The idiot, and Grünbein describes himself as 'bestenfalls ein ästhetischer Idiot', possesses 'tierhafter Charme'. Without this, the social-political animal becomes a 'Bestie'. His civilization, training and conditioning return him to the wild. 'Tierhafter Charme' is a key term which Grünbein scatters throughout his writing. In his speech upon receiving the 'Bremer Literaturförderpreis' of 1992 Grünbein spoke of his 'Vision vom Dichter als elektronischem Dandy, der mit tierhaftem Charme durch die Bildwelten streift'.[35] Again roaming, the poet aspires to atavistic charm. At the beginning of his collected essays, Grünbein's translation from Dante's *Inferno*, Canto xxvi, concludes, 'Aus welchem Samen ihr / Geschaffen seid, bedenkt. Daß ihr Erkenntnis folgt / Und nicht dahinlebt wie das wilde Tier' (*Galilei*, p.7). Animal charm is connected with the ability to pursue 'Erkenntnis' and is the opposite of the wild beast. Grünbein presents the modern world as a return to the wild in its chaos of media and technology, and its dehumanization. Against these things the poet's innocence and idiocy is an alternative. In the third poem of Grünbein's cycle 'Morgenandacht and Ketzerei', lovers make a pact 'naiv und vom tierhaften Charme' (15).[36] 'Wahnsinn zu zweit' (13), it is suggested, is also an alternative, 'ein Drittes'(13).

'Hoffnung' and 'ein Drittes', normally part of socialist discourse, become tags in Grünbein's zoological discourse. The word 'Reise' functions in the same way in the first poem of the 'In utero' cycle (*Falten*, pp.50-51). Here, the journey is not a moral progress through socialism, but the biological journey of human birth. The *Falten* of the collection's title become the folds of a newborn baby's skin: 'Hautfalten kräuseln sich, daß man den Säugling erkennt' (I:14). The birth is accompanied by references to the evolutionary process, so that the pregnancy becomes a micro-version of macro-evolution.

In utero, 1
Niemand berichtet vom Anfang der Reise, vom frühen Horror
Betäubt in den Wassern zu schaukeln, vom Druck
In der Kapsel, vom Augenblick, der sie sprengt.
Wochenlang blutig, und das Fleisch wächst amphibisch
5   Zuckend wie die Frösche Galvanis, in Folie eingeschweißt.
Horchen ist trügerisch und das Strampeln vergeblich

---

[35]Durs Grünbein, 'Reflex und Exegese: Rede anläßlich des Bremer-Literatur-Förderpreises 1992 der Rudolf-Alexander-Schröder-Stiftung', *Galilei*, pp.61-66 (p.66).
[36]Durs Grünbein, 'Morgenandacht und Ketzerei', *Literarischer März: Lyrik unserer Zeit*, 6 (1989), 52-57 (p.54). This is not the same as the cycle of the same name in *Schädelbasislektion*.

Wo Liebe erwidert und ein Herz schlägt, so nah.
Über Kloschüsseln hängend wie über offenem Grab
Erwacht bald die Scham. Und es gibt kein Zurück
10   Für die Hände, die Füße, Farnblättchen gleich eingerollt
Oder schlafenden Mücken, für Jahrmillionen im Bernstein.
Bis es die ersten Namen gibt, später, herrscht Dunkel,
Ein Chorus aus Lauten wie Alkohol, Hoden und Elektroden.
Hautfalten kräuseln sich, daß man den Säugling erkennt.
15   Alles ist vorstellbar, und ein Gehirn schaut herab.
Ein Blitz zaubert Landschaft in leere Augen.
Um als Lurch zu beginnen und zu enden als Mensch ...

The unfinished sentence of the last line, an exclamation at the evolution from amphibian to human, is effectively continued in the first line of the following poem in the cycle: 'Wer hätte gedacht, daß es so einfach ist, schließlich?' (II:1). This is typical of Grünbein's ambivalent expression of wonder: it is immediately debunked in a colloquial register. In the midway line of the poem, the expression 'es gibt kein Zurück' (I:9) draws together the evolution of the race and the individual human birth. The brain, here personified, makes the human: 'Ein Gehirn schaut herab. Ein Blitz zaubert Landschaften in leere Augen' (II:15-16). This is then again Grünbein's cerebral landscape, the fateful consciousness of the human being. An awareness of the primal waters is not completely lost however even in the modern world. Waters (2) and darkness (12) evoke both inside the human body and also the primal swamp. Such evolutionary origins seem to be present elsewhere in evocations of the depths of the sea. The radio's sound recalls 'vertraute Tiefseegeräusche' (*Grauzone*, p.14) and the human subject is 'Meerestief abgesenkt' (*Schädelbasislektion*, p.122). Writing involves a diving back down to these depths to find 'das belebende Sprudeln / das Luftblasen aus einer / Seele auf Tauchstation' (*Grauzone*, p.82). Peter Hamm picks out these last lines as surprisingly positive terms for a dark, chaotic submarine world.[37] It seems to me that what is 'vertraut' and 'belebend' is the bottom of the sea as the origin of evolution. The human being who is 'unten am Schlammgrund' (*Schädelbasislektion*, pp.27-30) is figuratively in a mire of twentieth-century life, but perhaps more than that is still, at some level, in the primal mud. The depths of the sea, the primal mud and the jungle are important locations in Grünbein. They represent the problematic animal origin of the civilized human, 'das schwierige Tier', an animal origin which has been forgotten in the

---

[37]Peter Hamm, 'Vorerst - oder: Der Dichter als streunender Hund: Lobrede auf Durs Grünbein', *Manuskripte*, 33 (1993), No.122, 103-106.

rush to progress. They are places where evolution occurred and places which still exist beside the technology and the media of human sophistication. The resonant phrase 'es gibt kein Zurück' which occurs in 'In utero, 1' and also in 'Point of no return' is, amongst other things, a dismissal of nostalgia and of Braun's declarations 'Sie können aus ihrer Haut' ('Der Eisenwagen') and 'Noch kann ich aus meiner Haut ('Meine Damen und Herrn'). Grünbein makes this point through parody in 'Homo sapiens correctus' (*Falten*, pp.75-76). This poem sets out as a narrative farce about a Dutchman, Joe, who cut a hole in his own skull to drain his brain fluid. The poem tells the story of his attempt to thus cure himself of human adulthood:

> Dampf aus dem Rückenmark abzulassen
> Setzte sich Joe ein Loch in den Kopf.
> Zapfte den Liquor ab, füllte Flaschen und Tassen.
> Und alle dachten sie "Nicht zu fassen".
> Aber Joe war entschlossen und heimlich,
> Die Badtür von innen verschlossen,
> Nahm er sein Werkzeug und bohrte los.   (lines 1-7)

The tripping rhymes create a kinship with nursery rhyme or fable. Joe is already considered to be '*cet enfant terrible*', and mad and alien. In Grünbein's collected essays, this poem appears after the prose notes 'Neun Variationen zur Fontanelle' (*Galilei*, pp.247-259), which substantially illuminate the subject of the poem. The fontanelle is the soft part of an infant's head, a gap which allows the head to be crushed in childbirth and which closes up by around the second year of life. It has been seen as a half-open gateway to the unconscious, a sixth sense or a third eye. Its closure entails a loss of sensitivity, which is also symbolic of the conditioning which marks the human. Joe's pursuit of the *homo sapiens correctus* – a new, man-made evolution, or a correction to the naturally evolved human – is an attempt to find 'großes Erwachen', to recapture what has become lost to the educated, adult human being.

The child occupies a place in Grünbein's thought nearer to human origins than the adult. In the poem 'In einer anderen Tonart', the lyric 'ich' is an infant, 'Nahe der Erde'.[38] Elsewhere it is the child who can play at being an 'Urmensch' (*Falten*, p.26), near to nature and near to self:

> Doch vor allem erwachsen, voraus
> Diesen schmächtigen Fesseln, der Ohnmacht
> Von Geschlecht und Statur. Flach
> Auf den Wiesen warst du, von frischer Erde
> Betäubt, in den Mulden aus Gras
> Dir selbst so nah wie die Birnen dem Stamm.   (*Falten*, p.26, lines 6-11)

---

[38]Durs Grünbein, 'In einer anderen Tonart', *FAZ*, 16 September 1995, p.31.

The child is 'betäubt', both without language and anaesthetized, spared the
stimuli to which the adult human is trained to respond. Feeble fetters (7) are
the conventions and sophistications of human interaction, to which the
instincts are sublimated through education and growing-up. In the following
poem such education is 'Netze' and 'Zwang', creating the 'du'-child according
to the saying 'Was ein Häkchen werden will, krümmt sich beizeiten':

> Doch der wahre Spuk war das Einmaleins
> Das die Träume in Netze legte,
> Tagtäglich, das Schwirren von Bumerangs
> Um die zahllosen Dinge, der Zwang
> 5   Zu Gemenge und Handlung, das Rechnen
> Im Schlaf, algebraisch gelähmt.
> Seit du, ein Häkchen, stumm überm Heft,
> Ziffern in Kästchen sperrtest
> Bist du selbst dieses vielfache Ganze, geteilt
> 10   In sezierbare Glieder, der Kopf
> Zwischen Minus und Plus, Haut und Hirn
> So unendlich gefaltet. Die Tage
> Gezählt, wird das Leben zum Intervall.   (*Falten*, p.41)

Human life is rendered 'gelähmt' (6), 'stumm' (7), 'geteilt' (9), 'gefaltet' (12)
and 'gezählt' (13). It is ordered, by language and learning, grammatically ('der
Zwang / Zu Gemenge und Handlung') and mathematically ('das Einmaleins',
'Ziffern in Kästchen sperren'). The self too, 'dieses vielfache Ganze' (9) is
divided into parts. In another poem (*Falten*, p.42), this human training creates
'die Masken des Wissens', rigid, artificial faces, which are set beside
'Fahrpläne, Skalen' (4) and correspond to being 'traumlos' (3). Only in adults'
nonsensical monologues does 'das Süße Singen / Des Kindes' (9-10) survive.
Aspects of Grünbein's self-understanding as a poet also relate to his positive
conception of childhood. Grünbein uses the image of the child in nature as a
metaphor for the *idiotes*-poet: the poet is a child with burrs stuck to his clothes,
which carry seed between one area and another.[39] The burrs are his poetic
images. A fascination for classical myth and for science in Grünbein's poetry
puts one in mind of the schoolchild, avidly absorbing these things, for surely it
is only at school that a person is normally occupied with both Latin and
Physics, Orpheus and Brownian motion all at the same time. Also, the new
jargon of compact discs and bungee jumps, which the poems incorporate, is
the language of youth more than the language of any other generation. In the

---

[39]Durs Grünbein, 'Katze und Mond', *Galilei*, pp.55-61 (p.60).

poem 'French kiss' (*Schädelbasislektion*, p.18) we learn that 'Plötzlich wird Pfeifen im Wald zur besten Methode' (3). This child's method of vanquishing fear is also a method for writing poetry. For all the sophisticated frame of reference which Grünbein has at his disposal, for all the sarcasm, there is also a strategy at odds with this. In a poem of the 'Variation auf kein Thema' cycle (*Falten*, p.42) the poet is a 'Sarkast', 'traumlos', knowledgeable and cynical, sitting at his computer monitor. This most intellectual poet nonetheless also seems to present himself as the childlike, innocent poet.

The evolution of the cerebrum, or 'Großhirn', produced human memory and intellect. Grünbein's cycle of three poems entitled 'Mensch ohne Großhirn' (*Falten*, pp.72-74) looks back to pre-cerebrum-evolution, an era of 'Vergeßlichkeit' (I:6). In the present, 'diesseits der Zoologie' (I:17), the 'ich' half wishes, half wonders, whether one could make a 'Rückzug aus der Borniertheit Sprache' (I:15). The head-versus-heart cliché is re-worked: an animal heart, 'mein Hasenherz' (I:8), is set against the brain which is source of that narrowing language. This cycle picks up the brain motif which was central in *Schädelbasislektion*. There in 'Zerebralis' (pp.134-136) the brain is what we humans essentially are: '*Singende Hirne* / [...] Das sind wir' (p.136). In the second poem of the cycle 'Mensch ohne Großhirn' (p.73), the brain evolves 'Qualen verschalend', by suppressing pain, so that instinctive reactions to it are invalidated.

> Zweites Arkanum, das war
> Indifferenz, die totale, Qualen verschalend und Male
> Wie sie die Herkunft verschreibt.
> Unsichtbar tätowiert
> 5   Ist es die Haut die in Schweigen hüllt, Blau
> Eine Spannung von Adern und nackter Gewalt.
> Welche Freude macht vor dem Schauhaus Halt,
> Vorm zerstückelten Leib?
> Jeder bessere Witz
> 10   Bohrt sich ins Stirnbein ein. Nur allein zu sein
> Ist schon Spuk genug.
> Hinter dünner Schläfenwand
> Unerkannt, war das Bewußtsein ein rohes Ei?
> Blätternd in Röntgenbildern sprüht dir der Wind
> 15   Silbrige Tröpfchen ins Haar, Gelatine und Chrom.
> Komm schon, Stimme im telephonischen Wirrwarr
> War das Blabla ein Versteck vor dem Tod
> Symbolisch oder banal?

The body is marked, by the brain's 'Male / Wie sie die Herkunft verschreibt' and by the veins forming tattoos, further writing. Indifference, joy and wit are literally 'embodied'. Mental activity, 'Geist' itself, seems demystified in Grünbein's brain poems as physiological: the mind consists of substances and surfaces. The word 'Haut' echoes through the second paragraph above in assonating with 'Blau' and 'Schauhaus', and in alliterating with 'hüllt' and 'Halt'. Against such lulling sound repetitions (another 'Verschalung' perhaps) a number of phrases stand out by virtue of their sound, location and sense: 'nackter Gewalt', 'bohrt sich' and 'ein rohes Ei'. There is a brutality here, which is heightened by references to dismembering the corpse. Grünbein suggests language might be a means of humans hiding from their own mortality, again 'Qualen verschalend'. Such language is 'das Blabla' (echoing the [a:l] assonance in line 2 of 'totale', 'Qualen', 'verschalend' and 'Male'), only dull, monotonous words, whereas wit (9) can penetrate into the head. The third poem of this cycle (p.74) concludes by confronting mortality, an utter mortality where no element of the human lasts:

> Nicht bevor er bricht
> Wird dir klar, wie zerbrechlich dein Knöchel war.
> Keine Zelle bleibt was sie ist. Alle sieben Jahre
> Ist der Körper ein andrer, die Haut unverwandt
> Wie im Spiegel der Fingernägel das eigne Fleisch.
> Entzogen der Boden, totcodiert der enorme Raum
> Und die Skelette zerfallen im Labyrinth.
> Also allein, also blank,
> Also was?   (lines 10-18)

Rimbaud's 'je est un autre', taken up post-'Wende' by Drawert in 'Ortswechsel' (as discussed in Chapter 4), here becomes 'der Körper [ist] ein andrer': the self is the body. This body, 'totcodiert', is indeed the 'Spuk' of the second poem: human life is fragile flesh, decaying bones and cells, nothing more. Likewise, the collection *Schädelbasislektion* opens 'Was du bist steht am Rand / Anatomischer Tafeln' (p.11). These cold, anatomical pictures of the human being resemble modern 'vanitas' poetry, although here no moral injunction is made.

The images of brains and other parts of the body are, in contrast to the mechanical 'Panzer'/'Eisenwagen', organic images which, unlike landscapes and cityscapes, focus on the internal, not the external. Anatomy tends to point back to our Darwinian evolution and forward to our mortality. The poem 'Biologischer Walzer' (*Falten*, p.71) presents the human as 'Mund' (4), 'Gaumen' (6), 'Kehle' (7), 'Ohr' (9), 'Nerven' (12) and 'Hirn' (15), thus ironizing the human pursuit of sophistication by foregrounding anatomy. The past is documented biologically in the cycle 'Die leeren Zeichen'. Thus the mouth gives a measure of repression in the phrase 'die beste Zuflucht – ein geschlossener Mund' (*Schädelbasislektion*, p.69), and in the lines 'Der Mund, elektrisiert von Floskeln / Saugt sich aus Überdruß am Schweigen fest' (p.85).

In the sibilant sounds here one hears the mouth buzzing and suckling. 'Sich festsaugen' suggests the mouth kept shut, but also the suckling mouth of the dependent infant. The poem 'Mantegna vielleicht' focuses on the subject's hands which reveal human mortality and barbarity:[40]

Mantegna vielleicht
Einmal im Halbschlaf ... zwischen Nehmen und Geben
Habe ich meine Hände gesehn, ihre gelbrote Haut
Wie die eines Andern, einer Leiche im Schauhaus.
Beim Essen hielten sie Messer und Gabel, das Werkzeug

5   Des Kannibalen, mit dem die Jagd sich vergessen ließ
Und das Getöse beim Schlachten.
        Leer wie der Teller
Lag eine Handfläche vor mir, der fleischige Ballen
Des letzten Affen, dem alles erreichbar geworden war

10 In einer Welt von Primaten. Mantegna vielleicht
Hätte sie unverklärt malen können in ihrer Grausamkeit,
Diese fettigen Schwielen.
        Was war die Zukunft,
Die aus den Handlinien folgte, Glück oder Unglück,

15 Gegen den Terror der Poren, in denen der Schweiß stand
Wie die Legende vom stillen Begreifen auf einer Stirn.

These hands evoke processes from ape to human, from hunting cannibal to civilized eater, and from living body to corpse. The body is grotesque – 'gelbrote Haut' (2), 'fleischige Ballen' (8), 'fettige Schwielen' (12) – perhaps reflecting the lyric subject's self-disgust. As the hands in this poem point to mortality (3), so the chin in 'Physiognomischer Rest' recalls a jawbone exhibited in a museum.[41] In 'Erdenleicht' it is the feet which evoke a body of 'Schleim' and 'Aschenrest'; the poem 'Ostrakon Dresden 3048' describes skin, flesh, breath and pulse, which constitute 'ein sterblicher Körper'.[42] The poem occurs at the moment of denouement, when the body jolts one into recognition. In poetry of anatomy, language becomes, in the words of a poem from Schädelbasislektion (p.73), a tool for inspecting this body: 'Sprache / Die sich an Knochen bricht wie Echolot' (2-3).

[40]Durs Grünbein, 'Mantegna, vielleicht', FAZ, 24 October 1995, p.35. Paintings by the fifteenth-century Italian Andrea Mantegna are known for their physionomical exactness, such as is exemplified by his works in the Staatliche Museen, Berlin-Dahlem and the Gemäldegalerie, Dresden.
[41]Durs Grünbein, 'Physiognomischer Rest', FAZ, 3 April 1995, p.33.
[42]Durs Grünbein, 'Erdenleicht', FAZ, 18 September 1995, p.39. 'Ostrakon Dresden 3048', Neue Zürcher Zeitung, 30 September 1995, p.50.

In the poems which focus on parts of the human anatomy, the poet paints a visual image, as the comparison with Mantegna suggests. A poem describes what it is to see the familiar in an unfamiliar way, like a sonar trace. Grünbein's museum poems also describe such seeing. In 'Requiem für einen Höhlenmenschen' (*Falten*, pp.111-114) a skull is an exhibit in a museum:

> Welcher Schock,
> Als im Licht der Museen für dich die Steinzeit begann
> Beim Anblick des Schädels, in der Vitrine rotierend
> Auf rotem Samt. (p.112)

The shock is an illuminating moment, which brings the past into the present, 'für dich'. In another poem, the exhibit is an entire scene from prehistory:

> Seltsam, als Kind schon zog ihn Erstarrtes an.
> In den Museen blieb er lange vorm Diorama
> Mit den Tieren im Stillstand, natürlich gruppiert
> Vor gemalte Fernen, Urwaldszenen und Himalayas.
> 5 Wie im Märchen, verzaubert, horchten die Rehe auf,
> Trat man im Neonlicht näher mit funkelnden Augen.
> Am Schädel des Höhlenmenschen gleich nebenan
> Sah er das Loch und vergaß den Keulenhieb
> Des Rivalen, den Kampf um die Feuerstelle.
> 10 Die ägyptische Mumie hielt Jahrtausenden stand
> Mit entferntem Gehirn. Erst beim Schmelzen
> Des Ewigen Eises kam dieses Mammut ans Licht.
> Die schönsten Schmetterlinge, handtellergroß,
> Fand er auf Nadeln gespießt. Einmal schien ihm
> 15 Als ob ihre Flügel noch bebten, wie in Erinnerung
> An die gefällten Bäume, den tropischen Wind.
> Vielleicht daß ein Luftzug durch Schaukästen ging. (*Galilei*, p.116)

In contrast to the technological world, the diorama is a lost paradise. It is at once 'natürlich' (3), yet 'verzaubert' (5). The magical moment described in the last lines of the poem is an epiphany – the butterfly seems alive, its movement in the breeze functions 'wie in Erinnerung' (16). The caveman's skull and the mummy preserved without a brain recur as *memento mori* in other Grünbein poems. A different time-scale exists in the museum: life is placed in the context of 'Urwaldszenen' (4) and 'das Ewige Eis' (12), and the mammoth which is the embodiment of extinction. Like the 'Märchen' to which the diorama is compared in this poem, the museum is described as a collection of archetypal dream images or geographical 'Urmotive' in Grünbein's essay 'Kindheit im Diorama' (*Galilei*, pp.117-128). In this essay, Grünbein calls the diorama 'eine *Augenweide*', '*wie aus dem Leben gegriffen*' (p.123). The museum makes visible a lost moment. In the same way, some

poems describe images found at moments in contemporary life. In one poem
from the 'Variation auf kein Thema' cycle (*Falten*, p.12), the living human
seems to be already in a glass display case:

> Wieder vorm Telephon, in der Vitrine
> Wie unterm Glassturz, kaum
> War die Tür zu, erstarrt, ein Objekt
> Für Passanten am Straßenrand,
> Starrst du auf dieses Tastenfeld   (lines 1-5)

Here the human exhibit is an object for passers-by to observe: in the fifth
poem of the love cycle 'Im Zweieck' (*Falten*, p.62), the diorama is reversed so
that eyes look in on the human lovers: 'Draußen am Fensterglas standen die
Regentropfen wie Augen' (1). Other poems describe looking at one's image in
a mirror (*Falten*, p.22), in a shiny car bonnet, reflected in sunglasses (both,
Falten, p.33), or in a photograph:

> Befangen
> Vom Unbekannten, fixiert auf
> Längst Fernes, weist dein Blick dich zurück.   (*Falten*, p.25)

This 'Blick', so reminiscent of the deer's, 'befangen' and 'fixiert' in the
diorama, disturbs human complacence. This is the purpose of 'Blick' /
'Augenblick', namely turning the human back to the nature of his being as an
evolved creature and as a mortal one. In 'Im Zweieck' the moment exposes the
individual's insignificance: 'Der Schock / Über das wenige, das ich war, gab
mir Halt', (3-4). The shock functions to give one a foothold, a point of solidity
and certainty paradoxically, for it is also at that moment that one sees precisely
how little one is.

Grünbein has stated that the English word 'glimpses' captures a
poetological idea which manifested itself in his early poems.[43] In 'Point of no
return', the poet is marked out by his magical 'Blick':

> Der Blick des Zauberers
>   (Poeten)
>   in die Welt
> so wie sie ist,
>   entzaubert,
>   nichtig,
>   abgebrannt,
> müßte ein Blick sein, der
>   durch Schlitze fällt
> aus Tier-
>   oder Dämonenmasken. (II:1-11)

'Der Blick' is an important motif in this cycle and in Grünbein's work
generally. Here 'der Blick' 'behält nichts, / sagt nichts' (II:13-14). Animal or

---

[43]Naumann, 'Poetry from the bad side', p.446.

demon masks seem to be the opposite of 'die Masken des Wissens'. They represent a certain way of seeing, as through the slits of the 'Panzer der Sprache' – the poet's way is that of the 'Zauberer' in a world that is 'entzaubert' (Grünbein takes Max Weber's term).[44] A comment inspired by Grünbein's exchanges with Oleschinski and Waterhouse sets the magic of poetry against anatomy: 'Dichten ist ein Abwehrzauber gegen die Macht des Realen, ein Angriff aufs eigene Zentrum' (*Die Schweizer Korrektur*, p.50). The 'real' here is the physical body: 'das eigene Zentrum' or 'leere Mitte' (*Schädelbasislektion*, p.39) is the so-called soul, which anatomically does not exist. What Heiner Müller taught the 'ich', it is claimed in 'Point of no return', is that the magic of writing is to see: an image can expose everything for what it is (I:13-15). Grünbein takes up Müller's definition of seeing, '*Sehen heißt, die Bilder töten*'.[45] Grünbein's phrase 'Illusionen, gesprengt' (21) alludes to 'Sehen' as the destruction of false images. The idea of images which can kill (the other way of reading Müller's definition) is made literal in 'Blick' as a primitive and brutal weapon:

> Kein Tier sucht sein Gesicht
>> zu wahren, nur
> sein Blick schlägt zu,
>> Blick der den Weg freihaut
> wie ein Machetenhieb, ein Blitz der Armatur.
> [...]
> Heute
> gibt sich der Blick obskur,
>> lähmt
>> und errettet seine Beute. (II:21-25, 27-30)

'Der Blick' is personified, itself an active subject, committing violence. The 'Machetenhieb', which becomes a 'Messerstich' in the 'Buna' version of the cycle, has resonances of the primitive barbarian. Looking becomes itself an animal, which acts lame so that it can gather its prey. When the poet is described as '(ein deutscher / Tiresias) im Totenreich des Jahrhunderts' (IV:3-4), it seems that 'der Blick' has become superseded by Tiresias's blindness. His 'sight', that of wisdom, came in a crippled body. Wise Tiresias is thus a personification of the 'Blick'.

---

[44]In 'Buna, 2' (*Schadelbasislektion*, p.145), a different version of this poem, the word 'Poet' is replaced by 'Trickster', a substitution which may suggest that the two words are equivalent.
[45]Heiner Müller, 'Bilder', *Gedichte*, p.13.

Grünbein's three 'In der Provinz' poems are visual moments of realization, which occur not in the city, but in the provinces.[46] These poems perpetuate the opposition between child-poet-dream-countryside on the one hand and adult-city-dreamlessness-technology-speed on the other. This cycle works with single images, or pictures, which expose everything for what it is – the ideal alluded to in 'Point of no return'. The frozen scene of 'In der Provinz, I' is almost a diorama itself. The 'du'-self looks at a dead dog lying on a railway line, 'erstarrt':

> In der Provinz, I
> Gefallen am Bahndamm
> Liegt ein Hundekadaver quer im Gebiß
> Kreideweiß numerierter Schwellen, erstarrt.
>
> Je länger du hinsiehst, je mehr
> 5   Zieht sein Fell in den Staub ein, den Schotter
> Zwischen den Inseln aus frischem Gras.
>
> Dann ist auch dieses Leben, ein Fleck,
> Gründlich getilgt.

The 'Gebiß' of line 2 is not, grammatically, that of the dog, but describes the white markings along the track, although the dog's jaw must be seen by the observing 'du'. By this device the scene becomes a whole of interconnectedness, not partial and piecemeal. 'Staub' (5) and 'Gras' (6) recall the biblical occurrence of these words in the context of human mortality. 'Dieses Leben, ein Fleck' is the living grass, like the dog's small existence, and by extension the small existence of the human 'du'. The reader is not immediately sure to what occurrence the last two lines refer: after 'getilgt' there is nothing. It seems likely that a train comes, suddenly annihilating the scene. The 'Schwellen' of line 3 are also then thresholds between life and death, for life exists only as islands, here islands of grass amid the gravel. The second 'In der Provinz' poem gives a buzzard's eye view, which focuses on a rabbit's foot in the bushes below. The view is also however human, as is clear in comparison of the rabbit's foot with a baby bird in one's hand. The human hunter and the bird of prey coalesce. Out of a close inspection of the 'kleiner Knöchel, winkend mit dem Fetzchen Fell' (10) the predator's attack is reconstructed. The subject's distance from this violent event is shockingly clear in the lines 'Unbequem / Muß dieser Tod gewesen sein' (14-15):

---

[46]Durs Grünbein, 'In der Provinz' I-III, in *Der heimliche Grund*, ed. by Ahrend, pp.167-169.

Was vom Gemetzel übrigblieb, hing in den Zweigen,
Die sich an nichts erinnern wie bestochne Zeugen.
Das Gras, längst wieder aufgerichtet, sorgt dafür,
Daß es auf lange Sicht nur dies gab hier, den Hasenfuß. (17-20)

The poem captures what is forgotten and covered over by nature. An object, one of the 'Dinge', is a trace or clue which allows the occurrence to unfold, upon protracted observation. Like the train track of 'In der Provinz, I' or the 'Wellenfluß / Von Landschaft' (1-2) of 'In der Provinz, II', the third poem also focuses on a small object frozen amidst a continuum, a dead frog on a road:

> In der Provinz, III
> Wie der Gekreuzigte lag dieser Frosch
> Plattgewalzt auf dem heißen Asphalt
> Der Landstraße. Offenen Mauls,
>
> Bog sich zum Himmel, von Sonne gedörrt,
> 5   Was von fern einer Schuhsohle glich -
> Ein Amphibium aus älterer Erdzeit
> Unter die Räder gekommen im Sprung.
>
> Keine Auferstehung als in den Larven
> Der Fliegen, die morgen schlüpfen werden.
>
> 10   Durch welche Öffnung entweicht der Traum?

The simile here, which continues from the opening 'Wie ein Gekreuzigte' (1) to 'Himmel' (4) and 'Auferstehung' (8) is almost unbearably absurd: a frog like Christ? Again this is a view 'von fern' (5) which finds, in close observation of the small and overlooked, something shockingly profound. Like the dog, or the rabbit, the frog has been crushed 'im Sprung' (7) and the poem begs the human parallel. For us too, there is no resurrection, no dream, according to these poems, only the primal material of flesh.

The diorama is a model for poems like the 'In der Provinz' ones. In an interview with Dorothea von Törne, Grünbein spoke of the poem as a kind of 'Déjà-Vu-Erlebnis', implying its relationship to memory.[47] Many moments of realization in Grünbein's poetry are based on frozen visions, which are preserved in the poem. In an inspiring speech upon receiving the 'Bremer Literaturförderpreis' (*Galilei*, pp.61-66), Grünbein described himself as a poet who is 'einer von vielen Jägern und Sammlern, unterwegs durch den

---

[47]Dorothea von Törne, 'Mir kann die ganze Ostnostalgie gestohlen bleiben', *Wochenpost*, 27 April 1995, pp.44-46 (p.45).

anthropologischen Alltag' (p.66). The 'Herausgeberfiktionen' of the prose piece 'Aus einem alten Fahrtenbuch' and of the poetry collection *Den teuren Toten* literally present the poet as a collector, who is showing off his finds.[48] Grünbein's poetic finds may be aural, as well as visual. Such instances include the 'Zungenschlag wie das Quietschen von Gummistiefeln' in a love poem in *Schädelbasislektion* (p.18) or the sound of a man's head being crushed in a mangle in *Den teuren Toten* (p.20): 'Das Geräusch // Beschrieb ein Zeuge als das Knirschen einer Autopresse, / Sämtliche Wände bis zum zweiten Stock durchdringend' (lines 12-14). *Grauzone morgens* opens with the sound of thousands of paper-shredding machines (p.9), which becomes a metaphor for one's lifetime disappearing at every instant. In his Kavafis essay, Grünbein suggests the poem as an obituary for the moment: 'Eine Dichtung, die aus allen Situationen das zeitliche Wirken heraushört, neigt fast von selbst dazu, episodisches Erleben in Epitaphe zu bannen, den Augenblick als Nachruf zu monumentalisieren'.[49] This is something more general than Braun's 'Nachruf', which is an obituary for the GDR and for socialist ideals. Many Grünbein poems seem to be an obituary for a lost moment (itself of course a traditional theme of poetry). In connection with falling in love, the paradigm is the same:

> der begehrliche Traum
> Wie er dem einzelnen zustößt, im Bett
> Oder offenen Auges beim Gehn:
> Etwas blitzt auf, macht sich rar, intrigiert   (*Falten*, p.18)

Again it is a visual impact which strikes, as in the museum. The phrase 'sich rar machen', for all its colloquialism (and in fact highlighted by that register), connects with the rare creatures of the diorama. These epiphanal moments of seeing are breaks in an otherwise limited, closed horizon: 'Seltsam, woran sich das Auge gewöhnt. / Der geschlossene Horizont,' Grünbein comments laconically in *Falten und Fallen* (p.28). The 'Augenblick', a sight, a phrase, or love, can wake one from the grey boredom and from overfamiliarity.[50]

---

[48]Durs Grünbein, *Den teuren Toten: 33 Epitaphe* (Frankfurt a.M.: Suhrkamp, 1994). Apparently this poetry is partly inspired by tabloid newspaper cuttings about deaths, collected by Grünbein. See Bednarz, 'Durs Grünbein', p.207.

[49]Grünbein, 'Körper erinnere dich!', p.257.

[50]The way of understanding things here is to look at them. In 'Vorerst - oder: Der Dichter als streunender Hund', dated 'Pfingsten 1993', Peter Hamm suggested that Grünbein's poems were not fully developed with respect to observation: 'noch ist er vom Durchschauen nicht zum Anschauen oder gar Wie-zum-erstenmal-Anschauen gelangt, noch beschreiben seine Gedichte vorwiegend Fluchtbewegungen' (p.105). I would argue that Grünbein certainly achieves these things in the 'In der Provinz' poems and in the collection *Falten*.

Grünbein's finds include ideas from science and ancient philosophy, but also clichés from the cinema: the hairdryer in the bath (*Toten*, p.15) or the leap from the fifth storey (*Toten*, p.16) are 'old favourites' from detective films; a hardened sailor's death from fright at the sight of a mouse (*Toten*, p.26) is a cartoon motif. Light-heartedness is probably one of the features which has made Grünbein more attractive to poetry-readers than the relentless lamentation and hyper-sensitivity of other ex-GDR poets. Grünbein's humour is casually sprinkled in asides and throwaway lines. Hence we find blow-drying a guinea-pig in 'Falten und Fallen' (*Falten*, p.97) or the light-hearted opening of the poem 'Badewannen' (*Grauzone*, p.50) in the middle of the dull, seedy city of *Grauzone morgens*. Treatment of major and solemn themes, such as the animal nature of humankind and our inability to go back, is also frequently comic: think of the proudly talking dog, the slapstick killings, and Joe cutting his skull open. In an interview with Annette Pfeiffer, Grünbein spoke of the poem as a form which is 'unendlich dehnbar... Ich habe die Überzeugung, ein Gedicht ist die Form, die sich literarisch am besten anpaßt an alle Wechselfälle des Lebens, an alle Ereignisse. Insofern findet sich natürlich idealerweise im Gedicht auch alles wieder'.[51] The stretchy or elastic poem can include everything – the political, private, existential, philosophical, scientific, humorous and satirical. 'Ein Maximum an Idee bei einem Minimum an Worten, dabei die größte Theatralität im Kommen und Gehen der Motive, das ist es was das Gedicht, sekundenlang, allen anderen Formen voraushat' (*Die Schweizer Korrektur*, p.25). For Grünbein the poem is a dramatic concentration of motifs which stand in tension to one another or perhaps reverse expectations. In his Canetti essay, Grünbein traces the origin of the Greek *sarkazein*: 'Das Sarkastische war das gründlich Abgenagte, der Schädel, aus dem Wüstensand ausgegraben [...] der unbeirrte Blick auf die zoologische Maschinerie' (*Galilei*, pp.202-203). The sarcastic mode is thus neatly linked to the skull and bones which are elsewhere images of mortality, evolutionary history and forgetting. The poetry is designed to elicit 'Erstaunen' through juxtaposition of banality and brutality, tragi-comedy, through revelations about human evolution and confrontations with human mortality. 'Erstaunen' is a crucial prerequisite for realization and remembering in Grünbein's world:

Bald
Wirst du völlig erledigt sein, rufen
Die Jahre dem Staunenden zu. (*Falten*, p.15)

It is the 'Staunender' who realizes his own mortality: the years are personified as calling out a *memento mori*. Some poems in the collection *Den teuren Toten*

---

[51]Annette Pfeiffer, 'Streunen auf beiden Seiten: Ein Gespräch mit Büchner-Preisträger Durs Grünbein', *SZ*, 13 March 1996, p.25.

shock by their apparent mockery of the dead. Such poems articulate a sarcastic *memento mori*. Deaths which would otherwise be haphazard, undignified and unlikely are here presented as paradigmatic. The perspective is almost that of a curious alien, amazed at what human beings do. Perhaps it also reflects an ex-GDR perspective, which is not yet desensitized to the obsessions of western pulp media. Poems bluntly tell of bizarre ways to die, such as from a culture shock (*Toten*, p.13), from cold foam at a Wet T-shirt Competition (p.22), or shot by one's dog (p.32). The poems also mock people's reactions to death, giving them a voice so that they make themselves ridiculous, which is in itself a shocking strategy. Like the skull in the museum case, which can shock the observer, so sarcasm too is designed to shock in *Den teuren Toten*. This is often in the very last word of a poem – for example, the dismissive comment 'Schade' in 'Ein Mann in Belgien' (*Toten*, p.32). In 'Mit einer Kettensäge' (*Toten*, p.24) the last line is 'Das Mädchen schloß sich in ihr Zimmer ein und masturbierte'. In both these examples the violent deaths themselves are announced at the outset and thus made less shocking than the reactions which are encapsulated in the single words which close the poems.

Death is a major theme in Grünbein's poetry and not as a metaphor but as real, everyday human deaths. I focus here on one of his most beautiful, but most ignored poems. The poem which commences 'Und nachher' (*Toten*, p.31) is never quoted by critics, perhaps because it goes against the bald, blunt satire which is supposed to characterize *Den teuren Toten*; critics have tended, I would claim, to reduce *Den teuren Toten* to a homogeneity which it does not really possess.[52] The opening 'Und nachher' indicates that one is breaking into an ongoing process: it is the process of burying the dead and digging up the old graves to make space for the new.

> *Und nachher werden sie eingedeckt*
> *Jedes Jahr wieder, im Sommer,*
> *Im Winter, kommt Grün darüber,*
>
> *Zweige von Efeu, ein Nest*
> 5 *Aus Tannenreisig und Lorbeer,*
> *Milchweiße Alpenveilchen im Schnee.*
>
> *Pünktlich werden sie eingedeckt,*
> *Als ob sie noch frieren, als ob*
> *Sie noch hören könnten. Das Ohr*

---

[52]The only interesting review of this collection is by the poet Ulrike Draesner, 'Reden vom Sterben und vom Grab', *SDZ*, 19/20 November 1994, p.4.

Einer Calla bleibt offen, ihr Stiel
10   *Wie ein Hörrohr im Erdreich ...*
      Mit Blumen werden sie eingedeckt,

      Mit Kerzen und Sprüchen, sogar
      Mit Gebeten, gefalteten Händen
      Entspringend wie Fliegen.

15   *Und nachher werden sie abgeräumt,*
      Jedes Jahr wieder, im Sommer,
      Im Winter, wird Platz gemacht

      Für die nächsten, wird ausgefegt.
      Eingeholt werden die Knochen,
20   *Die Schädel verbrannt. Asche*

      Ist was noch übrigbleibt, bald
      Verstreut, eine Tafel mit Namen
      Und Zahlen, ein Memento mori

      Am falschen Ort.

The sense of a cycle is developed by repetitions, such as 'werden sie eingedeckt' (1, 7 and 12) or 'Jedes Jahr wieder, im Sommer, / Im Winter' (2-3 and 17-18). Nouns are strategically piled up: in stanzas 1-2 they relate to nature; in the following stanzas they evoke the funeral. These piled-up nouns represent the layers and significances piled upon the corpse. Near-synonymous participles in stanzas 6-7 pertain to the removal of the dead – 'abgeräumt', 'Platz gemacht', 'ausgefegt', 'eingeholt' and 'verbrannt'. And finally the last mortal remains are listed: 'Knochen', 'Schädel', 'Asche' and a 'Tafel mit Namen und Zahlen'. 'Was noch übrigbleibt' is actually hardly anything at all. The poem thematizes thus the problem of remembrance. The graveyard list of names and dates is described as the wrong place for a *memento mori* (23-24), because the body is not there (let alone the soul). The close of the poem invites the question of where the right place would be – perhaps in poetry itself.

Grünbein places himself in the tradition of the poem as an epitaph, which will survive the human mortal. The poems of the collection *Den teuren Toten* manifest quite literally the idea of poetry 'jenseits des Todes'.[53] In *Schädelbasislektion*, one of the cycles is entitled 'Posthume Innenstimmen',

---

[53]Durs Grünbein, 'Zu Kieseln gehärtet: Über das lyrische Sprechen', *Neue Zürcher Zeitung*, 30 September 1995, p.50.

suggesting the poem as a ghostly echo from the grave. At the close of the cycle 'Point of no return' the voice of the 'Autopoet', the late Heiner Müller, is preserved:

> Seine diskrete Stimme, noch höre ich sie,
> wie Nachtwind der durch ein Autowrack
> fährt, ganz ohne Bitterkeit, fern
> "Kann sein, ich bin ein Fossil".   (IV:21-24)

The metaphorical vehicle ('Auto'/'Panzer') is now a car wreck, but the poet's voice survives like a ghost, or a fossil, the petrified mark of a creature which is now extinct.[54] Direct speech in the last line offers self-deprecating sarcasm, but the fossil here might also signify a positive quality. In his interview with Dorothea von Törne, Grünbein referred to 'überzeitliche Korrespondenz': 'Jedes halbwegs erzählerische Gedicht, ob bei Juvenalis oder Leopardi, Hölderlin oder T. S. Eliot, hat mein begrenztes Zeiterleben rückwärts erweitert, gebrochen und vervielfacht'.[55] His own poems tend, I would suggest, to aspire to this extension back to the forgotten. In the poem 'Falten und Fallen' (*Falten*, p.97), forgetting marks the faces and brains of modern humanity: 'Deutlich / War diese Spur von Vergessen in allen Hirnen, Falten, Gesichtern' (14-15). The poet works against the forgetting and 'die sanften / vergeßlichen Technologien' (III:5-6). In one of the 'Variation auf kein Thema' poems (*Falten*, p.35) the psalm is a search to fill the gaps, to find what has been lost:

> Das Spaltungsirresein täuscht sich gewitzt
> Vor zerbrochenen Spiegeln
> In der Pose Vergeßlichkeit: jede Lücke
> Ein verlorenes Fundstück,
> Die Mühe, es wiederzufinden, ein Psalm. (lines 9-13)

In these lines the colon serves as an axis, on one side of which is the negative development from 'Spaltungirresein' to 'Vergeßlichkeit' and, on the other, the positive response which is finally 'ein Psalm'. 'Spaltungsirresein' is postmodern fragmentation personified as a vain figure. Gaps and forgetting, symbolized by the shattered mirror, are overcome by the 'Fundstücke' and 'wiederfinden' of the psalm. In the essay 'Mein babylonisches Hirn' (*Galilei*, pp.18-33), Grünbein also presents the poet's task in connection with overcoming forgetting and fragmentation. It is a searching amongst the voices from history and fragments of the present to find elements of poetry. Poets such as Czechowski, Drawert and Hilbig in Chapter 4, and such as Braun in Chapter 5, also demonstrate an understanding of the poem as memory, but

---

[54]Compare the Müller line 'Den Engel ich höre ihn noch', from 'Glückloser Engel, 2', discussed in Chapter 3.
[55]Dorothea von Törne interview, p.46 and p.45.

they look back specifically to Germany in the second half of the twentieth century. Theirs is a return to a post-war childhood, to memories of the GDR and, in Braun's case, to memories of an unattained ideal. For Grünbein, poetry is more generally about finding lost emotion and lost 'Erkenntnis'. Establishing memory is a poetological principle for all time (a very traditional idea of course): 'Erst die Emphase der Dichtung hat aus dem Gemurmel, dem lebensbegleitenden Singsang von Emotionen und Erkenntnis etwas Erinnerbares heraufgeholt und zu Kieseln gehärtet' (p.23). The pebbles, like the fossil, represent a solid object, which is the opposite of 'die sanften vergeßlichen Technologien'. In his essay for *Die Schweizer Korrektur*, Grünbein describes the poem as a 'Gedächtnismaschine, präzis wie ein Insektenauge, eine Maschine zum Wiederfinden gelebter Zeit'.[56] Grünbein takes another image of the poet as memory from Cicero's anecdote about Simonides of Keos.[57] (Simonides of Keos is also cited as a forefather in the afterword of *Den teuren Toten*.) The poet who survives the collapsing roof, personifies the poem which survives through the ages.

From the publication of *Schädelbasislektion* onwards, many literary names have been linked to Grünbein's by critics: Auden, Bachmann, Baudelaire, Benn, Eliot, Goethe, Hofmann von Hofmannswaldau, Joyce, Kafka, Mandelstamm, Rilke, Stevens. The variety of these comparisons is perhaps their most illuminating aspect. Grünbein's poetry often throws up connections, sometimes acknowledgements, rarely quotations, at other times just faint echoes. Grünbein's title 'Hälfte des Ohres' (*Falten*, pp.121-123) thus echoes Hölderlin's 'Hälfte des Lebens'. He cannot allude to 'der Weg in ein künstliches Paradies' ('Point of no return', III:11) without echoing Baudelaire's title *Les Paradis Artificiels*.[58] Grünbein's poems contain few direct quotations, but there is a frame of allusion, which consists of such things as the phrase '*la vita nuova*' from Dante (*Falten*, p.66), or mottoes taken from Ludwig Wittgenstein (*Falten*), T.S. Eliot (*Schädelbasislektion*, p.146), Immanuel Kant (*Falten*, p.103) and Leonardo da Vinci (*Schädelbasislektion*, p.67). One cycle of two poems is a 'Meditation nach Descartes' (*Falten*, pp.78-79), another poem is written 'In Gedanken an

---

[56]Durs Grünbein, 'Mein babylonisches Hirn', *Galilei*, pp.18-33 (p.19).
[57]Grünbein, 'Zu Kieseln gehärtet'. Simonides was giving a reading when the roof of the building collapsed, killing the audience, but the poet, who was in the doorway, survived and, though the corpses were unrecognizable, was able to recall who had sat where, and thus to identify the dead for their families.
[58]Charles Baudelaire, *Les Paradis Artificiels*, ed. by Yves Florenne (Paris: Librairie Générale Française, 1972).

Marcus Aurelius'.[59] Individual poems are dedicated to poets John Ashbery, Friederike Mayröcker, Arno Widmann and Thomas Kling. By these means Grünbein sets up correspondences with contemporary writers and with writers from the past. The reader is often unsure about an allusion; it tends to hover as a slight echo. Nicolai Riedel, for example, is put in mind by Grünbein's 'nekrophiles Hallo' of Goethe's 'Ihr Mann ist tot und läßt Sie grüßen'.[60] In Grünbein's 'Xylophon aus verborgnen Knochen' he hears an echo from Wolfgang Borchert's 'Heimkehrer' play, *Draußen vor der Tür*. Similarly, Michael Braun recalls in the 'Origami-Kranich' of the poem 'Falten und Fallen', the colourful paper cranes made by Japanese peace campaigners in remembrance of the atom bomb victims of Hiroshima.[61] Immediately however Braun asks, 'Führt eine solche Lesart schon ins Reich der Spekulation?' (p.47). Grünbein's echoes are possible rather than necessary connections and, as in the examples briefly cited above, stem from diverse sources. Clearly, this poet likes to present himself as an intellectual, well-read in history, philosophy and the natural sciences, as well as literature. His articles and essays provide further indications of the *poeta doctus*. I have not addressed the question of literary allusion and influences as part of the thematic discussion of Grünbein's work, because it seems that more important than the source of an allusion within a poem is the general principle: Grünbein picks out an intellectual heritage for himself as a poet. Poetry is a matter, for Grünbein, of finding images, moments, words in the present world but also in the world of past writers and thinkers.

Grünbein is concerned with reworking ideas which have a strong cultural tradition, and presenting these neglected finds anew. This applies, for instance, to the personification of death in 'Meditation nach Descartes, II' (*Falten*, p.79), or to the four temperaments in 'Mit einer roten Zipfelmütze' (*Toten*, p.36). The conceit in the face of death that it would be better never to have been born at all – a tradition Heine carries into the nineteenth century in his poem 'Morphine' – is taken up by Grünbein in 'Einem Schimpansen im Londoner Zoo' (*Falten*, p.115): 'O weh, diese Trauer, geboren zu sein und nicht als Tier' (12). The ancient lament, played up in the exclamation 'o weh', is set against something new, in the continuation 'und nicht als Tier'. The whole statement becomes faintly absurd, and yet alarmingly convincing. In his

[59]Grünbein, 'In Gedanken an Marcus Aurelius', *FAZ*, 28 April 1995, p.14.
[60]Nicolai Riedel, 'Durs Grünbein: Falten und Fallen', *Passauer Pegasus*, 12 (1994), No.23, 146-149.
[61]Michael Braun, 'Schädelbasislektionen', in *Jahrbuch der Lyrik 1996/97: Welt, immer anderswo*, ed. by Michael Braun, Christoph Buchwald and Michael Buselmeier (Munich: Beck, 1996), pp.46-48.

Spiegel interview, Grünbein talked about turning to world literature as an attempt 'zu den Quellen zurückzuschwimmen'.[62] More important than utter originality as a goal (an impossible goal in any case) is the poet as an archaeologist, rediscovering the ideas, the words, the sights and the figures which form archetypes that cross the boundaries of historical eras. As a collection of epitaphs, *Den teuren Toten* is, for example, in the Baroque tradition of Christian Hofmann von Hofmannswaldau's poetic grave inscriptions; thirty three as in the Christian tradition of recalling the number of years of Christ's life.[63] Grünbein's concern with 'was bleibt' is thus less a question of what survives when a system and a state fall, that is the contemporary question, and more a question of what remains from all the eras of human projects.

Grünbein's poems can be read in the tradition of many figures simultaneously. His kinship with Gottfried Benn, the doctor-poet and 'Medizyniker' has been widely recognized in reviews and articles. It reflects the influence of scientific knowledge on his work. Grünbein himself indicated his fascination with the work of the young medic-writer Georg Büchner. His speech upon receiving the 'Büchner Preis' in 1995 includes two quotations from *Dantons Tod*, Danton's statements 'Wir müssen uns die Schädeldecken aufbrechen und die Gedanken einander aus Hirnfasern zerren' and 'Es wurde ein Fehler gemacht, wie wir geschaffen worden, es fehlt uns was'.[64] Both are perhaps recalled by Grünbein's poem 'Homo sapiens correctus' (*Falten*, pp.75-76) for instance. Another doctor, the American paediatrician-poet William Carlos Williams, is a largely unrecognized kinsman of Grünbein. Williams writes his own 'Dinggedichte', and poems of visual observation, such as his cycle 'Pictures from Brueghel'.[65] And his notion of the poem is congruent with Grünbein's: 'The poem is a small (or large) machine made of words [...] Its movement is intrinsic, undulent, a physical more than a literary character'.[66] As in Kafka's story 'In der Strafkolonie', fate, in Grünbein's poetry, is written on the body:[67] Grünbein's variations on this idea include

---

[62]Martin Doerry and Volker Hage, 'Tausendfacher Tod im Hirn', *Der Spiegel*, 41 (1995), 221-230 (p.224).
[63]See Christian Hofmann von Hofmannswaldau, *Gedichte* (Stuttgart: Reclam, 1964).
[64]Durs Grünbein, 'Den Körper zerbrechen: Rede zur Verleihung des Georg-Büchner-Preises 1995', *Galilei*, pp.75-86 (p.77).
[65]William Carlos Williams, 'Pictures from Brueghel' (1962), *Collected Poems*, ii, ed. by Christopher MacGowan (London: Paladin, 1991), pp.385-394.
[66]William Carlos Williams, quoted by Randall Jarrell in 'Introduction', *Selected Poems* (New York: New Directions, 1949), p.xvi.
[67]Franz Kafka, 'In der Strafkolonie', *Die Erzählungen* (Frankfurt a.M.: Suhrkamp, 1961), pp.94-123.

physical organs determining consciousness, exploration of anatomy as enlightenment, and poetry as a permanent mark or memory. Grünbein's 'Grenzhund' is akin to Kafka's 'Forschungen eines Hundes' and the civilized monkey of 'Ein Bericht für einer Akademie'. His cycle is named after Dylan Thomas's *Portrait of the Artist as a Young Dog*, another collection which concerns the writer's place of origin.[68] In the articles Grünbein has written on other writers one can also trace his own poetology.[69] On the journal of the twenty-one-year-old Gerard Manley Hopkins, Grünbein asks, 'Ist es nicht, als würde die Welt hier zum ersten Mal wirklich gesehen?'.[70] Grünbein appreciates in Hopkins the imaginative observation of natural phenomena. He presents the following as an insight of Hopkins's, paraphrased by himself, but it is also a statement which goes to the core of his own poetic endeavour: 'Die Welt ist zerfallen in unverbundene Einzelheiten, aus denen sie, Leidenschaft des Betrachters vorausgesetzt, wieder rekonstruiert werden kann'. Although one can talk of a cold, distanced voice, there is also wonder and enthusiasm for the 'finds'. Grünbein demonstrates this 'Leidenschaft des Betrachters' in his own 'Dinggedichte'. Naturally these and the zoo poems recall Rilke. Rilke's 'Duineser Elegie, VIII', which Grünbein acknowledges in a throwaway allusion in 'Aus einem alten Fahrtenbuch', particularly foreshadows ideas in Grünbein's poetry: the contrast between the 'Falten und Fallen' of human consciousness and animal consciousness – 'Mit allen Augen sieht die Kreatur / das Offene. Nur unsre Augen sind / wie umgekehrt und ganz um sie gestellt / als Fallen, rings um ihren freien Ausgang'.[71] Rilke's

---

[68]Franz Kafka, 'Forschungen eines Hundes' and 'Ein Bericht für eine Akademie', *Die Erzählungen*, pp.333-371 and pp.154-164. Dylan Thomas, *Portrait of the Artist as a Young Dog* (London: Dent, 1940). Reviewers were quick to link Grünbein's title to James Joyce, *Portrait of the Artist as a Young Man* (London: Cape, 1956), but less quick to make the closer connection with Thomas, who, interestingly, also wrote some 'anatomical' poems.

[69]Consider also Stefan Themerson, *Bayamus und das Theater der semantischen Poesie: Roman*, trans. by Durs Grünbein (Leipzig: Reclam, 1992). The novel, first published in London in 1945, complements Grünbein's own writing. From the Theatrum Anatomicum of the first chapter to the theatre of semantic poetry which is pursued in the rest of the novel, the functioning of the human body is repeatedly compared to the way language functions. Grünbein makes this point in his afterword (pp.117-123). The novel also addresses themes of evolution and mutation.

[70]Durs Grünbein, 'Ein Schwungbild, vom Besen gemalt: Gerard Manley Hopkins' "Journal" in der ersten vollständigen Übersetzung', *FAZ*, 21 November 1994, unnumbered page.

[71]Rainer Maria Rilke, 'Die achte Elegie', *Duineser Elegien*, ed. by Wolfram Groddeck, nach den Erstdrucken von 1923 (Stuttgart: Reclam, 1997), p.35.

animal is also 'Frei von Tod' (p.35) and the child is soon trained and
conditioned – 'denn schon das frühe Kind / wenden wir um und zwingens, daß
es rückwärts / Gestaltung sehe, nicht das Offne' (p.35). Also in this elegy, one
finds the supreme statement of the human as observer: 'Und wir: Zuschauer,
immer, überall, / dem allen zugewandt und nie hinaus!' (p.37). Hermann Korte
has suggested that Grünbein's apparent reworking of such poetic motifs and
poetological ideas with a strong literary tradition places him in a GDR
tradition:

> Indes sind solche Traditionalismen für einen Lyriker aus der ehemaligen DDR
> keineswegs ungewöhnlich. Von Brechts später Lyrik über die Vielzahl von
> Adaptionen historischer Gedichtgenres in der Sächsischen Dichterschule führt
> die Linie schließlich bis zu Grünbein.[72]

Whilst this is an interesting connection, one must acknowledge that Grünbein
is not a Brechtian as Braun is after unification. GDR literature and the GDR
experience are one part of Grünbein's poetry, but not all: the context in which
his lyric subject is 'ein Ariel / Ohne Auftrag und unter niemands Vaterblick'
(*Falten*, p.21) is wider. It does not primarily point to the poet's loss of role,
but to general human insubstantiality in urban darkness.

Grünbein has affinities with numerous great writers and poets. His
poem then, as a meeting of the ancient and the new, exists at a point 'jenseits
des Todes': 'Was sollte ein Gedicht in den neunziger Jahre ausdrücken?
Dasselbe wie im Jahre 96 nach Christus, nur neu. [...] Der Zusammenhang
zwischen Lyrik und Bundesrepublik ist ein temporärer. Die Lyrik wird auch
diesen Staat überleben'.[73] In this way Grünbein applies a model of human
evolution to the poem: as genetic material is passed on, so the same poetic
material is taken up in new manifestations. Wolfgang Rath's outline of the
literary 1980s, within which Grünbein's portrayal of a 'Welt der Simulation'
seems typical, corresponds to the human as 'ein bezugloses IchKäfig'.[74]
Grünbein describes this too. However he goes further, providing an
explanation of what has been lost, an explanation based on evolutionary
theory, and finding in memory, and the poem as a 'Gedächtnismaschine', an
answer. The 'Bezuglosigkeit' of the 'ich' in the postmodern world is set
against a poet who stands in a dense web of associations to poets and painters,
to philosophers and scientists, from the ancient world to the present day.
Poetic material is passed on from generation to generation. Political shifts do

---

[72]Hermann Korte, *Lyrik von 1945 bis zur Gegenwart: Interpretationen* (Munich:
Oldenbourg, 1996), p.132.
[73]Letter to me, 30 November 1998.
[74]Rath, 'Entgrenzung ins Intersubjektive', p.259.

not invalidate it. It adapts, mutates, and survives, so that the poet's role is thus to contribute to an evolution and to memory.

CHAPTER 7
CONCLUSION

In October 1989, Braun and Grünbein seemed to represent two typical positions for ex-GDR poets: the poet on the political rostrum for whom 1989/90 was ultimately going to be an endpoint and the would-be poet, senselessly imprisoned, for whom 1989/90 would represent a beginning to his real writing. In their poetry after 1989, both Braun and Grünbein take up Baudelaire's intellectual dandy, although in contrasting treatments. Modern culture, Baudelaire suggested, is a culture of separation and loss, mourning the loss of ideals, of permanent truth and moral stability. His flâneur is an asocial and apolitical figure, not serving a cause or a country, but characterized by his irony and caprice.[1] The bohemian figure, who roams the edges of society, is part of an expression of despair where he is Braun's beggar-poet, whereas for Grünbein the poet's location on the periphery, disconnected in a centreless, urban world is taken for granted; he would not expect to be anywhere else at the end of the twentieth century. From the survey chapters, it is clear that Braun's post-unification sense of loss is typical for ex-GDR poets. In Grünbein's poetry, it is the thematization of death and the underground imagery which are part of wider trends in poetry of the time. In conclusion, whilst addressing whether and how 1989/90 is a literary turning-point, I shall also acknowledge the prevalence of typical features and trends which unite ex-GDR poets as a group.

At the end of Chapter 2, I characterized GDR poets in the 1980s before the 'Wende' as negotiators of boundaries, who stood at the windows, looking out. Grünbein's 'Grenzhund' patrolling his border is a related image, as is Braun's image of the mountaineer. Both indicate the poet's role as a charter of territory and both simultaneously reveal their authors' opposed beliefs as to the possibilities available under GDR socialism: Grünbein's lyric subject feels the edges (as is the case in many poets' work of the 1980s), whereas Braun's feels the space to explore upwards within the territory. A line from Czechowski's poem 'Lyriker in der Mitte der neunziger Jahre' is particularly interesting set beside this territorial imagery: 'Ich bin isoliert. Mein Ich kennt keine Grenzen'.[2] It links the removal of the GDR borders to an unbounded ego: the only boundaries left in the mid-1990s are those of the self – a point which may be implicit in much of Grünbein's anatomical poetry, and is certainly explicit in some of the poetry of self-analysis and self-address, discussed in Chapter 4.

---

[1] Leeder calls Grünbein 'a flâneur of sorts' in *Breaking Boundaries* p.56.
[2] Heinz Czechowski, 'Lyriker in der Mitte der neunziger Jahre', *Mein westfälischer Frieden: Ein Zyklus 1996-1998* (Cologne: Nyland, 1998), pp.58-59 (p.58).

As well as this territorial representation of the change brought by unification, there are many temporal representations of 1989/90. As indicated in Chapter 3, the 'Wende' is associated with a new sensitivity to time and especially to the speed of modern life in the new Germany. The 'Zeitgedichte' of 1989/90 are poems both about time as a force and about the unification period.

In 1999 the publishers Bertelsmann offered 250,000 DM to the author who would write the great German novel about the 'Nachwendezeit'. Poetry was, in the main, overlooked. The genre of poetry is not 'about' events in the same way as a lengthy prose narrative; it takes a more oblique approach to history and bears witness to fragments of experience rather than transition as a whole. But recent history is at the centre of contemporary poetry by ex-GDR poets. What is interesting about the lyric response to 1989/90 is that some very different poets are drawn together by a shared concern: firstly they articulate their 'Wende' experiences and then examine their role as poets. In *La recherche d'une identité dans la poésie de R.D.A. de 1960 à 1989*, Anne-Marie Pailhes emphasized the gradual erosion of the poet's role in society over the three decades preceding 1989.[3] Without looking at the poetry written in 1989 and thereafter, she concluded (p.394) that the political caesura confirmed a shift from collective identity to personal identity that had already been indicated in the poetry. My discussions of the 'Wende' poetry, however, suggest that far from anticipating the political caesura, poetry responds to it, following events with some shock. Chapter 3 sought to demonstrate, amongst others things, that autumn 1989 polarized the positions of writers politically and led to a clarifying and re-stating of their role. This is particularly clear in the 'old' texts republished by Braun, which called the populace to climb the mountain of socialism alongside him. (But even Grünbein, scarcely acknowledged officially, became an out-and-out dissident figure at the last moment, when he was arrested and imprisoned for the first time and drew on this experience in his poetry.) As GDR monolithic power was breaking up, the question of a connection between 'Geist' and 'Macht', the defining question of GDR cultural life, was renewed.[4] Very quickly thereafter, this heightened sense of role was superseded by its utter collapse. Mensching, for instance, has articulated this contrast between the early 'Wende' and unification as a shift

---

[3] Anne-Marie Pailhes, *La recherche d'une identité dans la poésie de R.D.A. de 1960 à 1989* (Stuttgart: Heinz, 1998).
[4] Ursula Heukenkamp calls this 'ein Wechselverhältnis von schriftstellerischem Selbstverständnis und Dirigat durch die Staatsmacht, das konstituierend für die Literaturverhältnisse in der DDR war', in '*Eine* Geschichte oder *viele* Geschichten der deutschen Literatur seit 1945? Gründe und Gegengründe', *ZfG*, N.F. 5 (1995), 22-37 (p.27).

from opening to closure, or from flux to fixity:
> Die politische Wende 89 bedeutete eine Öffnung, eine Befreiung von Zwängen, Privilegien, Neurosen, Überfrachtung. Sie warf mich, also auch 'den Dichter', zurück in eine Normalität, die Gewinn bedeutete, neue Orientierung forderte, neue Denk- und Verhaltensweisen provozierte. Die Wiedervereinigung 1990 begriff ich viel mehr als Schlußpunkt, als Fixierung dieses offenen, ungekannten, teils anarchischen Prozesses.[5]

Contemporary poetry tends to articulate this closure as a loss of dialogue and location, indeed as a loss of identity. On the evidence of close textual analysis then, poetry confirms Kolbe's description of 1989/90 as 'ein Umbruch auch fürs Schreiben'.[6]

This 'Umbruch' does not represent an end to poetry-writing nor an end to GDR poetry: rather it has demonstrably given it a new impulse. 1989/90 is a turning-point within GDR poetry which casts what has gone before in a different context. Many post-'Wende' texts move backwards, as if to recapture meaning which has been put in doubt. This is described in Rainer Kirsch's epigrammatic poem 'Protokollnotiz' in the lines 'Und jeder neue Vers ist wie ein Rücklicht / der alten Zukünfte'.[7] Poetry does indeed seem to return to socialist idealism from a new angle. Numerous poems of the period focus on poets' own experiences of life and writing. This seems to be a reflection of being under attack, as poets were at the time of the 'Literaturstreit', and a reflection of the radical indeterminacy of life in the new Germany, by comparison with GDR life. Even in 1997 then, Kirsch's poem, like other 'new' poetry for the new Germany, invokes the 'old futures' of the GDR. Typically, Drawert's poem 'Das letzte Bild' (*Wo es war*, p.99) describes a last picture of the GDR: the singers who go from the political rostra to the markets represent the shift from the poets' role under socialism to their role in the figurative marketplace of a capitalist economy:

> Das letzte Bild
> Jetzt singen sie auf den Märkten
> des Westens. Ich sah sie noch auf hohen Tribünen,
> wir waren gerade verkleidet und spielten Pioniere im Land,
> Adoptivenkel stolzer, russischer Folkloresoldaten.
>
> 5 Wie faules Obst von den Zweigen
> stürzten später die Engel. Wer erwachsen genug war,

[5] Letter to me, 9 December 1998.
[6] Ingo R. Stoehr, ' "Das Konkrete wird alle Klischees wegwischen": Ein Gespräch mit Uwe Kolbe', *Dimension*[2], 1 (1994), 456-469 (p.458).
[7] Rainer Kirsch, , 'Protokollnotiz', *ndl*, 45 (1997), No.1, 5.

schaufelte die Gräber. Ihre Lieder änderten sich nicht.
Eine rote Nase aus Pappe aber vollendet das Bild

und erklärt, was die Texte verschweigen. Danke.

The 'Bild' of this ambiguous poem is a picture but also the poet's public image. The 'sie' of line 1 could be interpreted as the older GDR poets, who were almost elevated as angels. The 'wir' are then the younger poets; in the first stanza they are children in fancy dress, then in the second stanza the older generation seems to take on fancy dress, with red cardboard noses: from being important messengers they have become fallen, rotten and ridiculous. In addition, however, the final 'Danke' suggests the status of the 'wir' is also that of the paid entertainer or even busker, thus blurring the distinction between 'sie' and 'wir'.

The fall of the GDR is an important topic for poetry, both amidst the events and thereafter. In the 'Wendezeit (1989-95)' section of the *Kleine Literaturgeschichte der DDR*, Emmerich discusses poetry under the subtitle 'Keine Zeit für Lyrik' (p.507). He suggests that poets in the GDR had no time for poetry in 1989 because they were doing other things. The material discussed in this thesis, however, gives a different impression. In conclusion I would like to draw particular attention to the way that the fall of the GDR has also continued to be a reference point throughout the 1990s. In a sense it is difficult to conclude this project, because the corpus of poetry in question is still being augmented: the newest collections by Braun, Czechowski, Grünbein, Mensching and Papenfuß published in 1998 and 1999, arguably demonstrate a continuation of these poets' lyric response to the 'Wende'.[8] I shall briefly outline here some indications of why I see this to be so. Whilst there can be a sense of 'Neuer Staat, neues Gedicht' (a line from Rathenow's poem 'Deutschland'), there is also a prevalent concern with memory.[9] Papenfuß's 1998 collection is not named after the new Germany, but after the 'sowjetische Besatzungszone' – *SBZ Land und Leute*. It is furthermore dedicated to 'unsere Mittäter, Verräter und Väter', roles which implicitly refer to the GDR past. Czechowski's 1998 poem 'Lyriker in der Mitte der neunziger Jahre' exemplifies a thematic continuation of his reaction to 1989/90, typified by a line such as 'Ich sehe keinen Sinn mehr im Schreiben. Trotzdem schreibe ich noch immer' (p.58). In Mensching's 1999 cycle 'New York Lines', the

---

[8]Volker Braun, *Tumulus: Gedichte* (Frankfurt a.M.: Suhrkamp, 1999). Czechowski, *Mein westfälischer Frieden*. Durs Grünbein, *Nach den Satiren: Gedichte* (Frankfurt a.M.: Suhrkamp, 1999). Steffen Mensching, 'New York Lines', *ndl*, 47 (1999), No.3, 46-52. Bert Papenfuß, *SBZ Land und Leute* (Berlin: Galrev, 1998).
[9]Lutz Rathenow, 'Deutschland', in *Grenzfallgedichte*, p.112.

English titles of the poems trace the urban localities which the ex-GDR traveller observes. Their number and exclusively American origin give the impression that the German poet's world has become American. Literature as the 'Stoff zum Leben' (Braun) has become 'Stoff zum Vergessen' in Mensching's poem 'Columbia Campus' (p.47). The motif of losers, from *Berliner Elegien*, also returns in the 1999 cycle, especially where the word 'Verlierer' is repeated in the poem 'Milano's Bar' (p.50):

> Du bist ein Verlierer […]
>   Verlierer,
> sagt Frank, glauben nicht an Amerika, weil
> sie nicht an Amerika glauben, sind sie
> Verlierer, sagt Frank   (lines 1-6)

These lines point to the loss of ideals and beliefs: the lyric 'du' does not believe in 'America'. As in the many post-unification poems which use English words, especially brand names like Coca Cola or Marlboro, as symbols of American colonization, so these lines equate America with a victorious, but ultimately amoral and belief-less, social order. Mensching also takes up Braun's desert motif in the poem 'Harlem, dawn' (p.45):

> In dieser Wüste
> erwartet dich niemand
> als Rufer.   (lines 6-8)

John the Baptist was the original voice in the wilderness, sent to the people as a messenger;[10] now there is no 'good news' of socialism to come, only the moral desert of capitalism. In the late 1990s, Braun's poetry also articulates the same kind of rejection of western society as that articulated earlier by him and by poets such as Mensching and Müller. Braun's 1999 collection focuses on the fall of socialism as a turning-point of violent disillusionment: everything after 1989/90 is 'Nach dem Massaker der Illusionen'.[11] Continuity with Braun's earlier poetry may be suggested by the surtext 'Der Stoff zum Leben 4', the continuation of an old cycle, but this 'stuff of life' contrasts with the title *Tumulus*, which is an ancient burial mound or barrow. Graves and tombs are in fact the collection's central motif. One poem focuses on the 'Totenmaske' (*Tumulus*, p.13), another on a 'Totenhügel' (*Tumulus*, p.16): both may be metaphors for the poem. Braun's lyric subject is repeatedly facing a turning-point between life and death, between 'die Vorzeit' and 'die Nachwelt' or 'Das Nachleben' (*Tumulus*, pp.13-15):

> Ich fühlte jetzt die Nachwelt auf mich starren
> Und lächelte gelassen VOLLER HOFFNUNG
> Ins Finstre, ein Verrückter

---

[10]See Mark 1.2-4.
[11]Volker Braun, 'Nach dem Massaker der Illusionen', *Tumulus,* p.28.

Aus der Vorzeit, die die Hoffnung kannte
Insgeheim   (p.14)
Hope is felt to be untimely still. 'Nachwelt' refers both to concerns about posterity and to a sense of being 'after' or coming late. There are many references back to 1989/90, including a quotation from Braun's own 1988 poem 'Die Wende' in 'Der Totenhügel'. In the same poem, 1989/90 is the crucial turning-point, and also 'Eine Minute in Meiner Zeit' (17). Like the repetition of 'mein' at the end of 'Das Eigentum', the first person possessive is emphasized in this final line: the GDR term 'Unsere Zeit' has become the individual's 'Meine Zeit'. The present brings deathliness and, in the poem 'Strafkolonie' (*Tumulus*, pp.31-35), torture. Braun makes Kafka's punishment machine the instrument of history, which prints out the admission 'ICH GLAUBTE'. This is reminiscent of Wolf's and Kahlau's post-'Wende' poems about nails piercing flesh and there being no salvation.[12] The massacre of illusions is also then the massacre of the self: this sense is still predominant ten years after the 'Wende'.

The prolonged response to 1989/90 in poetry was not obvious at the outset; on the contrary, some commentators opined that a distinctive GDR literature would quickly disappear after the fall of the GDR.[13] In 1990 Jurek Becker represented the opinion that the sole difference between GDR and other German literature was the conditions under which it had been produced: in Becker's view GDR literature would lose its 'Eigenarten' after unification.[14] The question of GDR literature constituting a separate development within German literature became acute at the turning-points of 1949 and 1976, that is at the founding of the GDR and after the 'Biermann-Ausbürgerung' when so many writers from the GDR re-settled in West Germany. It is also an acute question after the turning-point of 1989/90. In 1985, Anneli Hartmann came to the conclusion that as long as the GDR existed, its literature must follow a separate development.[15] After the fall of the GDR, this conclusion must be re-assessed. As discussed in Chapter 2, literature in the GDR became increasingly diverse over its forty-year history: on the one hand, this departure from the easily-characterized GDR literature of the 1950s suggests convergence with

---

[12]Wolf's 'Prinzip Hoffnung' and Kahlau's 'Folter' are discussed in Chapter 4.
[13]Karl Deiritz and Hannes Krauss state 'so sehr die Literatur der DDR, gerade ihr bester Teil, mit diesem Land verklammert war, so unrettbar ist sie auch mit dem Zusammenbruch verklammert', in *Der deutsch-deutsche Literaturstreit*, ed. by Deiritz, p.7.
[14]Jurek Becker, 'Die Wiedervereinigung der deutschen Literatur', *German Quarterly*, 63 (1990), 359-366 (p.364).
[15]Anneli Hartmann, 'Was heißt heute überhaupt noch "DDR-Literatur"?', *SGCS*, 5 (1985), 265-280 (p.275).

other German literature. Rather than a homogeneous strand, however, a separate national literature would arguably be defined by its extensiveness and diversity. However the increasing diversity of GDR literature was interpreted, writers' self-understanding was always central to the debate: hence commentators referred to whether GDR émigrés saw themselves as 'West German', 'German', or 'GDR writers resident in West Germany'. Writers themselves seemed to perceive an increasing divergence between GDR literature and West German literature, as the two states became surer of their separate identities and a generation grew up which had only written in divided Germany. In 1986 Christoph Hein referred to the importance of different biographies in East and West:

> Ich glaube, daß beginnend mit meiner Generation, spätestens beginnend mit meiner Generation, man schon von zwei verschiedenen Literaturen sprechen muß. [...] Meine Biographie ist drüben nicht denkbar.[16]

This sense of a different biography, the GDR biography, is reflected in poems after 1989/90 which go back to childhood and in search of identity. Even Grünbein, many of whose poems do convey a sense of becoming free of the past, makes this trip back to a childhood GDR in a poem from his latest collection ('Vita brevis', *Nach den Satiren*, pp.117-118). Identities proliferate in this poem, where the lyric subject recalls being the clown, the choir-boy, doubting Thomas, St Peter, an army deserter and finally the traveller. Biography was identified early on by Colin B. Grant as a crucial text of the former GDR or 'neue Länder':

> The first signs indicate that writers from the eastern *Länder* will continue to address the history of their country as part of the texture of the socialist utopia, to which some illustrious predecessors had been attracted (from Büchner to Brecht); they will continue to engage with their own texts, both as part of the utopian texture and as part of their own biographical textuality.[17]

In poetry these points are most clearly true of Braun's work, where his contemporary texts are in dialogue with his own past texts and the themes of utopia and biography are foregrounded in this connection.

Inasmuch as GDR poetry was ever a separate development in German poetry, it remains distinct after 1989/90. Kunert stated in 1992, 'Man kann nicht vierzig Jahre in einem Teich herumschwimmen, ohne Schuppen und Schwimmhäute zu kriegen. Doch das Rückkehr an Land erweist sich danach als schwierig – metaphorisch gesprochen'.[18] Here Kunert uses animal evolution as a metaphor for social adaptation, suggesting that GDR writers

---

[16]Krzysztof Jachimczak, 'Gespräch mit Christoph Hein', *SuF*, 40 (1988), 342-359 (pp.358-359).
[17]Grant, *Literary Communication*, p.177.
[18]Kunert, *Der Sturz vom Sockel*, p.7.

became different creatures, not best adapted to western conditions. Brigitte Burmeister has also suggested that GDR writers have not been swallowed up into the literary life of the 'Bundesrepublik' in such a way that they are indistinguishable:

> Das Ende der nationalen Teilung hat den Partikularismus, die Gegensätze der Berufsauffassungen und der ideologischen Standpunkte nicht aufgehoben, sie nicht auf neue Gemeinsamkeiten [...] hingewendet.[19]

The 'Berufsauffassungen' of ex-GDR poets, as expressed in their poetry, are central to my project. They represent a distinctively GDR perspective on life in the new Germany. Peter Geist draws a related conclusion with respect to poetry:

> The nuances which distinguish the state of having-not-yet-gotten-used-to and the uneasy adaptation make it possible to tell which texts are from the East and which are from the West.[20]

The misery of the simulacrum thematized in Mensching's *Berliner Elegien* perhaps especially exemplifies this point. I would suggest that individual texts cannot always be so segregated, but that the many poems which thematize poetry writing itself or the figure of the poet do give this impression of distinctness. The treatment of the poet's role as a lyric theme illustrates Geist's 'state of having-not-yet-gotten-used-to'. Since the 1970s literary historians have treated GDR literature separately: to an extent, poetry after the GDR reflects poets' own sense of separateness, their own sense that they have undergone Kunert's evolution. The GDR poet who was typically a political poet, born into the present, conscious of being at a peak in history, gives way to the 'nachgeborener Dichter', a poet who comes after. Rather than this being a generational shift, it has occurred within GDR poets' own lifetimes and work.

Lyric subjects tend to be acutely conscious of the poet's approach to 1989/90 and the changes it brought: in the 1989 poem 'Zeitlos', Kahlau's subject, for instance, explicitly suggests the past as a retreat from an incomprehensible present. His title points less to a timeless principle and rather to a sense of being out of step with one's time and not of the present.[21]

> Gegenwart scheint unverständlich –
> drum aufs Vergangne gerichtet
> ist unser fragender Eifer   (lines 9-11)

The 'we' here seem to be 'we ex-GDR writers'. The quality 'Eifer' is strange and uncalled-for, in the present. In his telegram poem '31/12/89', Grünbein seems to diagnose a preoccupation with signs of the 'late' GDR as characteristic

---

[19]Burmeister, 'Schriftsteller in gewendeten Verhältnissen', p.650.
[20]Geist, 'Voices from No Man's Land', p.144.
[21]Heinz Kahlau, 'Zeitlos', *Kaspers Waage*, p.11.

of 'Wende' writing and symbolizes this by the old-fashioned characters of a
typewriter (as opposed to a word-processor): [22]

> Aus jeder Schreibmaschine, abgehackt, ein Nachruf...
> Bis zum Beginn der Neuzeit nichts als alte Zeichen.   (lines 7-8)

Resonances particular to the GDR are also 'alte Zeichen'. They perpetuate the
past by looking again at ways it established for talking about existence, history
and writing.

My examination of the poetry suggests that the 'Neuzeit' did not begin
with the founding of the new Germany. Indeed in 1994, Rathenow referred to
'eine starke DDR-Bezogenheit' amongst ex-GDR intellectuals: 'Die DDR lebt
als Gespenst fort'.[23] This spirit is evident in the poetry. It is present, for instance,
in the prominence given to place-names which lie in the territory of the former
GDR: Richter's *Die kleinen mecklenburgischen Meere* or Czechowski's 'Riesa,
Umgebung' are titles which illustrate this. In Czechowski's new collection many
poems refer to GDR cities, although these places have been left behind both by
Czechowski and by his lyric subject. There is a recurrent concern with not being
free from the GDR past: in the poem with the evocative title 'Mein Herz' (*Mein
westfälischer Frieden*, p.60), Dresden and Leipzig are abbreviated to initials,
almost like lovers' names or family names in a diary, suggesting great
familiarity:

> Geblieben sind
> Anfälle von Trunksucht, Bobrowskis
> Bücher in den Regalen, zwei, drei
> Gedichte von dir, Kurt,
> Der du auch in Darmstadt
> Dich nicht losmachen kannst
> Von einer Vergangenheit
> Mit den Kürzeln
> D. oder L.   (lines 22-30)

The question of what remains after the GDR is still urgent in the later 1990s, it
seems. Czechowski's reference here to the early GDR poet Johannes
Bobrowski and to fellow ex-GDR poet Kurt Drawert (who now lives in
Darmstadt) is not an anomaly: in this collection the poem 'Stille, saubere
Vorstadtstraße' (*Mein westfälischer Frieden*, pp.100-101) refers ruefully to
Grünbein's successes. In their post-'Wende' collections, Hensel and Kolbe
both write poems to Braun, and Mensching's cycle 'New York Lines' is
dedicated to him. Braun dedicates 'Die Verstellung' to Christa Wolf, his Pliny
poem to Heiner Müller, and invokes Müller and Karl Mickel in 'Schreiben im

---

[22]Durs Grünbein, '31/12/89', *Schädelbasislektion*, p.63.
[23]Both quotations are taken from an interview with Lutz Rathenow by H. Ohligschläger
and R. Vernier, 'Ein Gespenst lebt fort', *Focus*, 26 (1994), 40-41 (p.40).

Schredder'. Kunert and Drawert write poems for each other, Kunert writes 'Herbstgang der Dichter' for Reiner Kunze,[24] Papenfuß dedicates the poem 'die kompostierung des blühenden lebens' to matthias baader holst (*SBZ*, pp.39-40) and Wüstefeld writes 'Im Februar über die Salzach' to Wulf Kirsten (*Deutsche Anatomie*, pp.28-30). Mensching's ode to Czechowski, 'Öde an einen klemmenden Buchstaben und Heinz C.', and 'Point of no return', one of Grünbein's several poems to Müller, have been discussed in some detail in previous chapters. Groups were always very important in the GDR, in particular the 'sächsische Dichterschule', but also Prenzlauer Berg and other underground groups. Several commentators have suggested that writers' collective activity disappeared after 1989: Emmerich makes the lack of group identity a distinguishing feature of the 'Wende' period: 'Eine Eigenheit der Wendejahre ist, daß sich das lyrische Sprechen weiter individualisiert und von Schulen oder Gruppen nun kaum die Rede sein kann'.[25] Erik Grimm argues that the underground writers' collective praxis ended when western media and the western bookmarket took over in 1990.[26] However, there are vestiges of a group-identification which contradict these impressions. The dedications and some instances of intertextuality in poetry after 1989 reflect a sense of comradeship with other ex-GDR poets. These identifications often cross the boundaries of the older groupings based on age and instead seem to be based on a shared GDR origin. In the work of these post-GDR 'GDR poets', Brecht's influence is particularly striking, as is suggested by the frequency with which his poetry arises as an influence, in my discussions of the poems. To a lesser extent, the same applies to Hölderlin, whose importance for GDR poetry before 1989 is well attested.

As well as in place-names and group-identification, the 'Gespenst' also survives in the lyric perspective. These kinds of continuity suggest that post-'Wende' poetry is a sub-set of GDR poetry. Drawert has located his post-1989 perspective in the GDR experience:

> Ich will sagen, ich kann die Gegenwart nur aus der Vergangenheit heraus sehen, das heißt, ich schaue auf die Bundesrepublik wie aus dem Fenster einer Zelle.[27]

The writer's perspective remains trapped, Drawert suggests, imprisoned in the past. Drawert's cell contrasts with Hilbig's domestic image of the GDR as source of his literary material:

---

[24]Günter Kunert, 'Herbstgang der Dichter', in *"mit dem wort leben hängen": Reiner Kunze zum 65. Geburtstag*, ed. by Marek Zybura (Heidelburg: Winter, 1998), p.133.
[25]Emmerich, *Kleine Literaturgeschichte der DDR*, p.511.
[26]Erik Grimm, 'Der Tod der Ostmoderne oder Die BRDigung des DDR-Untergrunds: Zur Lyrik Bert Papenfuß-Goreks', *ZfG*, N.F. 1 (1991), 9-20.
[27]Herzog, 'Erinnern und erzählen', p.71.

Ich habe einen bestimmten Haushalt von Themen, oder von Ideen, den ich mit mir herumtrage und der darauf wartet, bearbeitet zu werden. Diese Komplexe von Stoffen stammen – es ist leicht einzusehen – aus der ehemaligen DDR.[28] Both as a perspective and as a source of themes and ideas the GDR is resurrected in poetry. It perhaps constitutes evidence for what Drawert terms 'Die Geburt des Mythos'.[29] The point he makes is best explained through two substantial quotations from *Haus ohne Menschen*:

In dem zähen Versuch, die Mechanismen der Macht zu verschweigen, liegt bereits ein neuer Anspruch auf Macht, und mitunter scheint es, als sei die DDR gerade erst geboren. Nur eben nicht als Utopia, sondern als eine Ruine, aus der niemand mehr auferstehen wird. Denn der Körper ist tot, den der Geist noch verteidigt. (p.85)

Die Stabilität also, die die DDR in der Weise, ihr Mythos zu sein, heute besitzt, wird die Dauer ihrer tatsächlichen Vergangenheit weit überholen. Sie ist nun das, was sie zu Zeiten ihrer fiktiven Souveränität nicht sein konnte: *real, weil sie nicht ist*. Dieses Realsein wird, so paradox es klingt, gerade dadurch geschützt, daß die Mauer gefallen ist. [...] War die Mauer einmal geschaffen, um die Lebensfähigkeit einer Idee zu garantieren, was den Körper der Idee, den Staat, kaputtmachen mußte, so ist es nun die gefallene Mauer, die Leerstelle, in die hinein die jetzt körperlos gewordene Idee projiziert werden kann. (pp.33-34)

In Drawert's view then the GDR has taken on life as a myth precisely because the concrete experience, which would contradict a myth, no longer exists. Returning to the ruins of Germany after the Second World War and to Becher's anthem, in the first quotation, is typical of the ex-GDR poet's perspective on 1989/90. In the poetry of the 1990s, remarkable resonances of Germany in 1945, such as ruined landscapes and the return to childhood homes, suggest a sense of going back to where Germany started from after Hitler. Equally, the 'Leerstelle' in the second quotation, according the GDR a certain space which has not been filled by the new Germany, is a motif in this poetry.

What is the vacuum or gap left by the end of the GDR? In 1990 the critic Bernd Leistner contended that GDR literature is more German than the rest of so-called German literature, because of the 'Goethe-Geist' and 'Klassik-Kult' in the GDR.[30] He characterized GDR literature as concerned with 'erstrebte Mündigkeit' and 'Utopie' (p.98), with the whole question of a 'Deutsche Gelehrtenrepublik' (p.100), which defined German literature around 1800. As I have indicated, these aspirations are still in evidence in 1989; in

---

[28]Hilbig, 'Zeit ohne Wirklichkeit', p.15.
[29]Kurt Drawert, 'Die Geburt des Mythos', *Haus ohne Menschen*, pp.30-47.
[30]Bernd Leistner, 'DDR-Literatur – die "deutschere" Literatur?', *ndl*, 38 (1990), No.12, 93-101 (p.95).

some ways they are not only 'still in evidence', but rather are invoked in every subsequent allusion to loss. In Czechowski's poem 'Verkommen' (*Mein westfälischer Frieden*, p.71) what remains is not a practical question about social mechanisms, but the memory of these aspirations:

Was bleibt,
Ist das Gedenken
An eine Zeit,
Die es niemals gab. (lines 16-19)

This is like Braun's line 'Was ich nicht lebte, werd ich ewig missen' in 'Das Eigentum' of course. Memory, the great German theme of post-war literature, is not now memory of atrocities that actually happened, but memory of an unrealized GDR. Hopes and illusions are central to poets' understanding of themselves as ex-GDR poets. They are bound to places which no longer exist and, ironically, to places that never existed. Hartmannn points out that émigrés write more than ever about the home country which they have been forced to leave behind.[31] The ex-GDR poets do the same, and in this respect resemble the exiled poets who had to leave the GDR before 1989. Poets in the GDR became émigrés in that they crossed the boundaries through their work. When the GDR is gone, the poetry suggests that they go back as 'Heimkehrer' to seek out what has been lost. Their distinctive, interrogative poetry is no longer turned to the truth or falsity in society (for they are now in a society which makes no claim to truth), but rather turned to the purpose of writing and searching at all.

---

[31]Hartmann, 'Was heißt heute überhaupt noch "DDR-Literatur"?', p.272.

BIBLIOGRAPHY

a. Poetry of the 'Wende' and Unification......... 287
-   Primary sources

Poetry collections, anthologies, and individual poems published in newspapers and journals, by poets from the GDR, except Volker Braun and Durs Grünbein who have separate bibliographies below. In the main restricted to poetry published 1989-1996, although a few later works are also included as I refer to them.
-   Secondary sources

Reviews, articles and books pertaining to the primary texts above, including relevant writing by the poets in other genres at the time.

b. Volker Braun's Poetry 1988-1998...305
-   Primary sources
-   Secondary sources

c. Durs Grünbein's Poetry 1988-1998......................................311
-   Primary sources
-   Secondary sources

d. The 'Wende', Unification and the 'Literaturstreit'.........................318
History books, articles and socio-political texts. 'Wende' prose literature other than works included in a., b. or c. above.

e. GDR Literary History..331
-   Primary sources

Poetry written 1949-1989, and other genres where relevant.
-   Secondary sources

As pertain to topics and perspectives addressed in Chapter 2.

f. Other Sources Used..350
Poetry in languages other than German, German literature outside GDR literature, literary theory.

Short references are given for individual poems in the following anthologies:

Chiarloni, Anna, ed., 'Die Dichter und die Wende', *GDR Monitor*, 23 (1990), 1-12
= 'Die Dichter und die Wende'

Chiarloni, Anna, and Helga Pankoke, eds., *Grenzfallgedichte: Eine deutsche Anthologie* (Berlin and Weimar: Aufbau, 1991)
= *Grenzfallgedichte*

Conrady, Karl Otto, ed., *Von einem Land und vom andern: Gedichte zur deutschen Wende 1989/1990* (Leipzig: Suhrkamp, 1993)
= *Von einem Land*

a. POETRY OF THE 'WENDE' AND UNIFICATION

Primary sources

Anderson, Sascha, *Jewish Jetset: Gedichte 1989-1991* (Berlin: Galrev, 1991)
-- *Rosa Indica Vulgaris: Gedichte und ein Essay* (Berlin: Galrev, 1994)

Arfmann, Paul, and G.E. König, eds., *Der Morgen nach der Geisterfahrt: Neue Literatur aus Thüringen* (Greiz: Weisser Stein, 1993)

Bartsch, Wilhelm, 'Gedichte', *SuF*, 44 (1992), 543-547
-- *Gen Ginnungagap: Gedichte* (Halle: mdv, 1994)

Biermann, Wolf, 'Dideldumm', in *Von einem Land*, p.82
-- 'Ballade von verdorbenen Greisen' and 'Mein Bauch ist leer', in *Alle Lieder* (Cologne: Kiepenheuer & Witsch, 1991), pp.412-413 and 429-430

"...bin ich um den Schlaf gebracht": Literarische Texte von vierzehn Autorinnen und Autoren (Lüneberg: Heinrich-Heine-Haus, 1993)

Böhme, Thomas, 'die kuckucks verschweigen den mai', in 'Die Dichter und die Wende', pp.10-11, and in *Von einem Land*, p.53
-- *ich trinke dein. plasma november: 2 dreizehnzeilige und 100 zwölfzeilige gedichte (1987-1990)* (Berlin and Weimar: Aufbau, 1991)
-- *ballett der vergeßlichkeit: Gedichte* (Leipzig: Connewitz, 1992)
-- *heimkehr der schwimmer* (Berlin: Galrev, 1996)

Braun, Michael, Christoph Buchwald and Michael Buselmeier, eds., *Jahrbuch der Lyrik 1996/97: Welt, immer anderswo* (Munich: Beck, 1996)

Braun, Volker - see separate bibliography

Buchwald, Christoph, and Joachim Sartorius, eds., *Jahrbuch der Lyrik 1995/96: Poesie der Poesie* (Munich: Beck, 1995)

Bundesministerium für Bildung, Wissenschaft, Forschung und Technologie, ed., *Von Abraham bis Zwerenz: eine Anthologie*, 3 vols ([Berlin]: Cornelsen, 1995)

Chiarloni, Anna, ed., 'Die Dichter und die Wende', *GDR Monitor*, 23 (1990), 1-12
-- and Helga Pankoke, eds., *Grenzfallgedichte: Eine deutsche Anthologie* (Berlin and Weimar: Aufbau, 1991)

Cibulka, Hanns, 'Ohne Titel' and 'Jahrgang 20', in *Die sanfte Revolution: Prosa, Lyrik, Protokolle, Erlebnisberichte, Reden*, ed. by Stefan Heym and Werner Heiduczek (Leipzig and Weimar: Kiepenheuer, 1990), pp.296-297

-- 'Jahrgang 20', *ndl*, 38 (1990), No.3, 118-123

Conrady, Karl Otto, ed., *Von einem Land und vom andern: Gedichte zur deutschen Wende 1989/1990* (Leipzig: Suhrkamp, 1993)

Czechowski, Heinz, 'Historische Reminiszenz', in 'Die Dichter und die Wende', pp.7-8, and in *Grenzfallgedichte*, pp.74-75
-- 'Die überstandene Wende', in *Von einem Land*, p.7
-- *Nachtspur: Ein Lesebuch aus der deutschen Gegenwart: Gedichte und Prosa 1987-1992* (Zurich: Ammann, 1993)
-- 'Riesa, Umgebung', *ndl*, 43 (1995), No.2, 32-38
-- 'Orpheus hat einen Fehler gemacht', *die horen*, 40 (1995), 183-187
-- *Wüste Mark Kolmen: Gedichte* (Zurich: Ammann, 1997)
-- *Mein westfälisches Frieden: Ein Zyklus 1996-1998* (Cologne: Nyland, 1998)

Dieckmann, Friedrich, 'Konditionen', *ndl*, 43 (1995), No.2, 71-73

Drawert, Kurt, 'Politisches Gedicht, Januar 1990', in 'Die Dichter und die Wende', p.6, and in *Die sanfte Revolution: Prosa, Lyrik, Protokolle, Erlebnisberichte, Reden*, ed. by Stefan Heym and Werner Heiduczek (Leipzig and Weimar: Kiepenheuer, 1990), p.172
-- 'Ortswechsel', *ndl*, 41 (1993), No.7, 21-26
-- *Fraktur: Lyrik, Prosa, Essay* (Leipzig: Reclam, 1994)
-- 'Gedichte', *Akzente*, 41 (1994), 108-110
-- 'Tauben in ortloser Landschaft', *ndl*, 43 (1995), No.6, 5-11
-- 'Betriebsnachrichten. Intern', *ndl*, 44 (1996), No.2, 103-106
-- *Zwei Gedichte: Tauben in ortloser Landschaft; Geständnis* (Meran: Offizin S. Meran, 1996)
-- *Wo es war: Gedichte* (Frankfurt a.M.: Suhrkamp, 1996)
-- 'Engel', *FAZ*, 10 February 1997, p.29

Einhorn, Hinnerk, 'Fragen eines trauernden Arbeiters', *ndl*, 38 (1990), No.3, 124-127
-- 'Friedensfeier Paraphrase', in 'Die Dichter und die Wende', p.12

Erb, Elke, *Winkelzüge, oder Nicht vermutete, aufschlußreiche Verhältnisse* (Berlin: Galrev, 1991)
-- *Unschuld, du Licht meiner Augen: Gedichte* (Göttingen: Steidl, 1994)

Faktor, Jan, *Henry's Jupitergestik in der Blutlache Nr. 3 und andere positive Texte aus Georgs Besudelungs- und Selbstbesudelungskabinett: Texte, Manifeste, Stücke und ein Bericht* (Berlin: Janus, 1991)
-- 'wir brauchen eine neue lyrik', *Litfass*, 16 (1992), 4-9

Gerlach, Harald, 'Exodus', in 'Die Dichter und die Wende', p.11, and in *Grenzfallgedichte*, p.58
-- *Einschlüsse. Aufbrüche: Blätter zu sechs Monaten deutscher Geschichte* (Rudolstadt: burgart, 1991)

-- 'Aufbrüche, deutsch', in *Von einem Land*, p.11, or under the title 'November' in *Grenzfallgedichte*, p.67

Gosse, Peter, 'Jener Herbst', *ndl*, 38 (1990), No.11, 41

Gröschner, Annett, *Herzdame Knochensammler: Gedichte, Fotografie* (Berlin: Kontext, 1993)

Grosz, Christiane, *Die asoziale Taube* (Berlin and Weimar: Aufbau, 1991)
-- 'die blonde frau auf der behörde', in *Von einem Land*, p.39

Grünbein, Durs - see separate bibliography

Grüneberger, Ralph, 'Das Geringste', *ndl*, 40 (1992), No.11, 81-86

Grüning, Uwe, 'Heimfahrt von Prag' and 'Fahrt zum Palast der Republik', in *Von einem Land*, pp.8-9 and pp.48-49

Hensel, Kerstin, *Gewitterfront: Lyrik* (Halle-Leipzig: mdv, 1991)
-- 'Poetik', *ND*, 20/21 April 1991, p.14
-- *Angestaut: Aus meinem Sudelbuch* (Halle: mdv, 1993)
-- 'Trauer Arbeit', *ND*, 2/3 October 1993, p.14
-- *Freistoß: Gedichte* (Leipzig: Connewitz, 1995)

Heym, Stefan, and Werner Heiduczek, eds., *Die sanfte Revolution: Prosa, Lyrik, Protokolle, Erlebnisberichte, Reden* (Leipzig and Weimar: Kiepenheuer, 1990)
Hilbig, Wolfgang, 'prosa meiner heimatstraße', *NR*, 101 (1990), 81-99, and completed in *Sprache im technischen Zeitalter*, (1991), No.119, 99-102
-- *Das Meer in Sachsen: Prosa und Gedichte*, ed. by Hans-Jürgen Schmitt (Frankfurt a.M.: Büchergilde Gutenberg, 1991)
-- 'Neue Gedichte', *ndl*, 39 (1991), No.9, 5-8

holst, "matthias" BAADER, 'ich weiss nicht was soll es bedeuten', *Temperamente* (1990), No.1, 33

Hultenreich, Jürgen, 'Grenzübergang Berlin, Januar 1990', in *Dissidenten? Texte und Dokumente zur DDR-"Exil"-Literatur*, ed. by Maria Sonnenberg (Berlin: Volk und Wissen, 1991), p.73

Jansen, Johannes, *prost neuland: spottklagen und wegzeug* (Berlin and Weimar: Aufbau, 1990)
-- 'zusammen gekommen', in *Grenzfallgedichte*, p.72

Kahlau, Heinz, *Kaspars Waage: Gedichte* (Berlin: Aufbau, 1992)
-- 'Tag der Einheit', in *Von einem Land*, p.95

Kirchner, Annerose, 'Im Reich der Stühle', 'Sonntag', 'Legende', 'Zwischen den Ufern', *Der Literatur Bote*, 5 (1990), No.19, 27-30
-- 'Wolfsspur', *Der Literatur Bote*, 5 (1990), No.20, 27
-- *Zwischen den Ufern* (Rudolstadt: burgart, 1991)
-- 'Unterwegs', 'Halbzeit', 'Alexander Grin', in *Der Morgen nach der Geisterfahrt: Neue Literatur aus Thüringen*, ed. by Paul Arfmann and G.E. König (Greiz: Weisser Stein, 1993), pp.51-53

Kirsch, Rainer, 'Ich-Soll 1991', *Jahrbuch der Lyrik 8*, ed. by Christoph Buchwald and Thomas Rosenlöcher (Hamburg and Zurich: Luchterhand, 1992), pp.43-45
-- 'Drei Gedichte', *ndl*, 45 (1997), No.1, 5-6

Kirsch, Sarah, *Erlkönigs Tochter: Gedichte* (Stuttgart: DVA, 1992)

Kirsten, Wulf, *Stimmenschotter: Gedichte 1987-1992* (Zurich: Ammann, 1993)

Köhler, Barbara, *Deutsches Roulette* (Frankfurt a.M.: Suhrkamp, 1991)
-- *Blue Box* (Frankfurt a.M.: Suhrkamp, 1995)

Kolbe, Uwe, *Vaterlandkanal: Ein Fahrtenbuch* (Frankfurt a.M.: Suhrkamp, 1990)
-- *Nicht wirklich platonisch: Gedichte* (Frankfurt a.M.: Suhrkamp, 1994)

Königsdorf, Helga, 'Drehn wir die Zeit um', *ndl*, 38 (1990), No.1, 74-78

Koziol, Andreas, *Bestiarum literaricum* (Berlin: Galrev, 1990)
-- *mehr über raunten und türme: gedichte* (Berlin and Weimar: Aufbau, 1991)

Kraft, Gisela, 'Senftenberg' and 'Bitte des Karlmarxkopfes an das rotliegende Chemnitz', in 'Die Dichter und die Wende', pp.4-5 and p.5

Kunert, Günter, *Fremd daheim* (Munich: Hanser, 1990)
-- 'Ja zum November', in *Nie wieder Ismus! Neue deutsche Satire!*, ed. by Christine and Manfred Wolter (Berlin: Eulenspiegel, 1992), p.58
-- 'Durch die leeren Häuser der Dichter: Vier neue Gedichte', *NR*, 104 (1993), 147-150
-- 'Fortgesetzt was geht', *ndl*, 41 (1993), No.6, 5-11
-- 'Gedichte', *Akzente*, 41 (1994), 104-107
-- *Mein Golem* (Munich and Vienna: Hanser, 1996)

Kunze, Reiner, 'die mauer: zum 3. oktober 1990', in *Von einem Land*, p.86
-- *ein tag auf dieser erde: Gedichte* (Frankfurt a.M.: Fischer, 1998)

Leising, Richard, *Gebrochen deutsch: Gedichte* (Ebenhausen: Langewiesche-Brandt, 1990)
-- *Die Rotzfahne: Gedichte und kleine Prosa* (Ebenhausen: Langewiesche-Brandt, 1998)

Mensching, Steffen, 'Unvollendete Tag', *ndl*, 38 (1990), No.3, 50-56
-- 'Simulis simulis', *ndl*, 40 (1992), No.4, 31-36
-- *Berliner Elegien* (Leipzig: Faber & Faber, 1995)
-- 'New York Lines', *ndl*, 47 (1999), No.3, 46-52

Müller, Heiner, 'Fernsehen', *Temperamente*, (1990), No.1, 31 and in *Grenzfallgedichte*, p.55
-- *Gedichte* (Berlin: Alexander, 1992)
--'Mommsens Block', *SuF*, 45 (1993), 206-211 and in *Drucksache 1*, ed. by Berliner Ensemble (Berlin: Alexander, 1993), pp.1-9
-- 'Glückloser Engel 2', in *Von einem Land*, p.77
-- *Die Gedichte, Werke*, i, ed. by Frank Hörnigk (Frankfurt a.m.: Suhrkamp, 1998)

'Neue Lyrik vom literarischen März', *Der Literat*, 31 (1989), 105-106

Oktober 1989: Texte, Temperamente (1990), No.1

Papenfuß, Bert, [also publishing as Bert Papenfuß-Gorek – see below] *tiské* (Göttingen: Steidl, 1990)
-- *mors ex nihilo* (Berlin: Galrev, 1994)
-- *SBZ Land und Leute* (Berlin: Galrev, 1998)
-- *hetze: gedichte 1994 bis 1998* (Berlin: Janus, 1998)

Papenfuß-Gorek, Bert, *LED Saudaus: notdichtung, karrendichtung* (Berlin: Janus, 1991)
-- endart and novemberklub, *nunft: FKK/IM* (Göttingen: Steidl, 1992)

Pietraß, Richard, 'die vertriebene zeit', *ndl*, 44 (1996), No.5, 21-24

Rathenow, Lutz, *Oder was schwimmt da im Auge: Gedichte* (Weilerswist: Landpresse, 1994)
-- *Verirrte Sterne oder Wenn alles wieder ganz anders kommt: Gedichte* (Gifkendorf: Merlin, 1994)

Rennert, Jürgen, 'Chopiniade', *ndl*, 40 (1992), No.1, 109-116
-- 'Lied vom fröhlichen Inzest', in *Von einem Land*, p.55

Richter, Armin, *Die kleinen mecklenburgischen Meere* (Frankfurt a.M.: Fischer, 1991)
-- 'Herbstsonate 89' and 'Rotes Kirschlaub', in *Von einem Land*, p.10 and p.12

Rosenlöcher, Thomas, *Schneebier: Gedichte* (Halle: mdv, 1991)
-- 'Ostbarbar', *ndl*, 43 (1995), No.2, 124-128
-- *Die Dresdener Kunstausübung: Gedichte* (Frankfurt a.M.: Suhrkamp, 1996)

Rost, Helgard, and Thorsten Ahrend, eds., *Der heimliche Grund: 69 Stimmen aus Sachsen* (Leipzig: Kiepenheuer, 1996)

Schacht, Ulrich, *Lanzen im Eis. Gedichte* (Stuttgart: DVA, 1990)
-- 'Das Brandenburger Tor' and 'Rosenhagen am Meer' in *Von einem Land*, p.40 and p.142

Schedlinski, Rainer, 'der rückfall der blicke ins auge', *ndl*, 39 (1991), No.1, 78-80
-- *die männer der frauen* (Berlin: Galrev, 1991)

Schmidt, Kathrin, 'Flußbild mit Engel', in *Grenzfallgedichte*, p.83
-- *Flußbild mit Engel: Gedichte* (Frankfurt a.m.: Suhrkamp, 1995)

Stötzer, Gabriele, [also publishing as Gabriele Stötzer-Kachold – see below] *Erfurter Roulette* (Munich: Kirchheim, 1995)

Stötzer-Kachold, Gabriele, *grenzen los fremd gehen* (Berlin: Janus, 1992)

Teschke, Holger, 'Freitagmorgen über den bleiernen Fluß', *Temperamente* (1990), No.1, 137
-- *Jasmunder Felder / Windschlucht / New York* (Berlin and Weimar: Aufbau, 1991)
-- 'Berliner November' and 'Elegie nach Virgil' in *Von einem Land*, p.13 and p.64

Tietze, Oliver, 'Berlin – 5. Oktober 1989', *Temperamente* (1990), No.1, 46

Tragelehn, B. K., 'Einrichtung einer Idylle', *ndl*, 41 (1993), No.10, 23
-- 'Schluß der Reise' and 'Die Niederlage', *SuF*, 6 (1993), 988-989
-- 'Drei Gedichte', *ndl*, 43 (1995), No.5, 5-6
-- *NÖSPL: Gedichte 1956-1991* (Basel and Frankfurt a.M.: Stroemfeld, 1996)

Walter, Ursula, *Mein kleines bißchen Leben: Gedichte* (Frankfurt a.M.: Fischer, 1991)

Wenzel, Hans-Eckardt, 'Die herrenlosen Hunde des Mittags', *ndl*, 39 (1991), No.2, 41-47

Werner, Walter, 'Gebirgsschlag', *ndl*, 39 (1991), No.3, 67-70
-- 'An einem siebten Oktobertag' and 'Die verlassenen Türme' in *Grenzfallgedichte*, p.56 and p.68

Willingham, Heike, *vom fegen weiß ich wird man besen* (Berlin: Janus, 1992)

Wolf, Christa, 'Prinzip Hoffnung', in 'Nagelprobe', *ndl*, 40 (1992), No.5, 34-44, p.44

Wolter, Christine and Manfred, eds., *Nie wieder Ismus! Neue deutsche Satire* (Berlin: Eulenspiegel, 1992)

Wüstefeld, Michael, 'Abbau einer Lösung von hinten', *Sondeur* (1991), No.12, 16

-- 'Gedichte', *SuF*, 44 (1992), 833-838
-- *Amsterdamer Gedichte* (Dresden: Hellerau, 1994)
-- *Deutsche Anatomie: Gedichte* (Schöppingen: tende, 1996)

Secondary sources

Ammann, René, 'Eine Tragodie der Dummheit', *Freitag*, 16 November 1990, p.3

Berendse, Gerrit-Jan, ' "Ändern sich die Umstände, zeigen sich die Konstanten!"
Deutsche Lyrik in der "Wende" zum Regionalen', *GR*, 67 (1992), 146-152
-- 'Mit der Lücke leben', *SuF*, 44 (1992), 1055-1061
-- 'The Poet in a Cage: On the Motif of Stagnation in Poems by Heiner Müller and Ezra
Pound', in *Heiner Müller: ConTEXTS and HISTORY: A Collection of Essays from the
Sydney German Studies Symposium 1994*, ed. by Gerhard Fischer (Tübingen:
Stauffenburg, 1995), pp.249-257

Berg, Anna, 'Immer auf der Kippe: Braun und Mensching lasen in der Berliner
LiteraturWerkstatt', *ND*, 29 January 1996, p.10

Biermann, Wolf, 'Aktenkundig', in *Aktenkundig*, ed. by Hans Joachim Schädlich
(Berlin: Rowohlt, 1992), pp.51-61
-- 'Nur wer sich ändert, bleibt sich treu', in *"Es geht nicht um Christa Wolf": Der
Literaturstreit im vereinten Deutschland*, ed. by Thomas Anz (Munich: Spangenberg,
1991), pp.139-156
-- 'Der gräßliche Fatalismus der Geschichte', in *Büchner-Preis-Reden 1984-1994*, ed.
by Deutsche Akademie für Sprache und Dichtung (Stuttgart: Reclam, 1994), pp.176-
189

Bohl, Inka, 'Leicht bis mittelschwer trägt der junge Dichter an der Last der Welt: Der
Darmstädter Wettbewerb um den Leonce-und-Lena-Preis', *Der Literat*, 31 (1989), 103-
104

Bormann, Alexander von, 'Grüsse von einem anderen Stern', *Neue Zürcher Zeitung*, 28
May 1993, p.31
-- 'Nirgendwo war ich zuhaus', *Der Tagesspiegel*, 28 August 1994, p.7

Braun, Michael, 'Die zusammengebrochene Generation', *Die Weltwoche*, 27 May
1993, p.56
-- 'Nichts geht mehr', *Die Woche*, 15 July 1993, p.18
-- 'In aufgerissenen Sprachräumen: Eine Begegnung mit Gedichten der neunziger
Jahre', in *Deutschsprachige Gegenwartsliteratur: Wider ihre Verächter*, ed. by
Christian Döring (Frankfurt a.M.: Suhrkamp, 1995), pp.271-286

Broos, Susanne, 'Lyrik im Spiegelkabinett', *FR*, 30 April 1992, p.31

Bungart, Florian, 'Ein halber Abschied von der Nische', *die taz*, 17 August 1993, p.16

Buselmeier, Michael, 'Sehnsucht nach Anwesenheit', *Freitag*, 13 March 1992, p.12

Chiarloni, Anna, 'Die Dichter und die Wende', *GDR Monitor*, 23 (1990), 1
-- 'Zwischen gestern und morgen: DDR-Gedichte aus der Zeit des Mauerfalls', *SGCS*, 11/12 (1993), 89-103
--'From the Ramparts of History: Two Versions of a Poetic Text by Heiner Müller', in *Heiner Müller: ConTEXTS and HISTORY: A Collection of Essays from the Sydney German Studies Symposium 1994*, ed. by Gerhard Fischer (Tübingen: Stauffenburg, 1995), pp.243-248

Conrady, Karl Otto, 'Deutsche Wendezeit', in *Von einem Land*, pp.173-248

Cosentino, Christine, ' "Die Gegensätze Übergänge": Ostdeustche Autoren Anfang der neunziger Jahre', *GR*, 69 (1994), 146-155

Cramer, Sibylle, 'Hölderlin möchte ich sein', *Die Zeit*, 4 June 1993, p.7

Czechowski, Heinz, 'Gehen die Uhren jetzt anders herum? Zur Situation von Literatur und Schriftstellern in der DDR aus heutiger Sicht', *Sondeur* (1990), No.1, 46-48
-- 'Stichwörter: Ein Nachwort', in *Von Leipzig nach Deutschland: Oktober '89 / Oktober '90: Zeittafel und Fotografien* (Leipzig: Forum, 1991), pp.187-190
-- 'Abgebrochene Biographien, vergessene Orte', *ndl*, 41 (1993), No.10, 27-34
-- 'Das Vergängliche überlisten? Ein lyrisches Ich am Ende des zweiten Jahrtausends', in *Das Vergängliche überlisten: Selbstbefragungen deutscher Autoren*, ed. by Ingrid Czechowski (Leipzig: Reclam, 1996), pp.60-75

'Das Neue Gedicht', *Der Tagesspiegel*, 16 June 1996, p.26

Deiritz, Karl, 'Ich halt's halt mit der Kunst: Ein Gespräch mit Gerhard Wolf', in *Verrat an der Kunst? Rückblicke auf die DDR-Literatur*, ed. by Karl Deiritz and Hannes Krauss (Berlin: Aufbau, 1993), pp.255-272

Delius, Friedrich Christian, 'Die Unfähigkeit zu loben', *SuF*, 46 (1994), 655-657
-- 'Gute Zeichen Fragezeichen', *Dimension*[2], 1 (1994), 444-451

'Die Umwälzung in der DDR und die Schriftsteller – eine Umfrage bei Autoren in der DDR', *Literatur für Leser* (1990), No.2, 122-129

Domdey, Horst, 'Writer's Block, or 'John of Patmos in the Haze of a Drug High': Heiner Müller's Lyrical Text Mommsens Block', trans. by Colin Hall, in *Heiner Müller: ConTEXTS and HISTORY: A Collection of Essays from the Sydney German Studies Symposium 1994*, ed. by Gerhard Fischer (Tübingen: Stauffenburg, 1995), pp.233-241

Döring, Christian, ed., *Deutschsprachige Gegenwartsliteratur: Wider ihre Verächter* (Frankfurt a.M.: Suhrkamp, 1995)

Drawert, Kurt, 'Leipzig, eine Situation in Frankfurt', *Temperamente* (1990), No.1, 167-169
-- 'Niemand braucht sie', *Monatshefte*, 4 (1990), 399-402
-- 'Veränderung des Hintergrundes', *ndl*, 38 (1990), No.11, 50-53
-- 'Die Ungeklärtheit der Revolution', *SDZ*, 6 November 1991, p.8
-- 'Es gibt keine Entschuldigung: Offener Brief an Rainer Schedlinski', *SDZ*, 11/12 January 1992, p.14
-- 'Wenn Dichter mit der Urne spielen', *Freitag*, 20 March 1992, p.13
-- 'Dieses Jahr, dachte ich, müßte das Schweigen der Text sein', *Freitag*, 15 May 1992, p.13
-- *Spiegelland: Ein deutscher Monolog* (Frankfurt a.M.: Suhrkamp, 1992)
-- *Haus ohne Menschen: Zeitmitschriften* (Leipzig: Suhrkamp, 1993)
-- 'Ohne Antwort: "Nachtspur" ', *Freitag*, 30 July 1993
-- 'Ich bin ein Feind von Utopien', *Nordkurier*, 24 September 1994, p.3
-- 'Die Abschaffung der Wirklichkeit', *FR*, 22 October 1994, p.ZB4
-- 'Osten, Westen, Finale', *SuF*, 47 (1995), 499-504
-- 'Mein arbeitloser Sisyphos', *Freitag*, 17 January 1997, p.2

Durrani, Osman, Colin Good and Kevin Hilliard, eds., *The New Germany: Literature and Society after Unification* (Sheffield: Sheffield Academic Press, 1995)

Emmerich, Wolfgang, 'Wendezeit (1989-95)', *Kleine Literaturgeschichte der DDR*, rev. edn. (Leipzig: Kiepenheuer, 1996), pp.435-525

Engler, Jürgen, 'Vom Herzversagen der Poesie', *ndl*, 43 (1995), No.5, 152-155

Ertl, Wolfgang, 'Grenzfallgedichte', *GR*, 67 (1992), 183
-- 'Refugium und Ortsbestimmung: Zu Wulf Kirstens neuer Lyrik', *Colloquia Germanica*, 30 (1997), 323-333

Fuld, Werner, 'Ausharren und fremdgehen', *FAZ*, 17 August 1991, unnumbered page

Garbe, Joachim, 'Hanns-Josef Ortheil und Kurt Drawert: Abschied von den Vätern', in *Deutschsprachige Gegenwartsliteratur*, ed. by Hans-Jörg Knobloch and Helmut Koopmann (Tübingen: Stauffenburg, 1997), pp.167-180

GDR Writers since the 'Wende', GLL, 50 (1997)

Geisel, Sieglinde, 'In der Gegenwart verwunschen', *Neue Zürcher Zeitung*, 26 July 1991, p.33

Geist, Peter, 'Voices from No Man's Land: Recent German Poetry', trans. by Friederike Eigler, in *Cultural Transformations in the New Germany: American and*

German Perspectives, ed. by Friederike Eigler and Peter C. Pfeiffer (Columbia, South Carolina: Camden House, 1993), pp.132-153
-- ' "mit würde holzkekse kauen" – neue Lyrik der jüngeren Generation nebst Seiten- und Rückblicken', *ndl*, 41 (1993), No.2, 131-153
-- 'Asphodelen im Kühlschrank: Poetische Urszene und Lyrik der neunziger Jahre', *ndl*, 47 (1999), No.3, 168-172

Goodbody, Axel, 'Review Article', *GM*, 26 (1992), 95-104

Görner, Rüdiger, 'Die Anrufung der Hälfte des Lebens', *Die Presse*, 13 April 1996, p.8

Görtz, Günter, 'Beifall und Blumen für Wolf Biermann', *ND*, 14 December 1989, p.16
-- 'Die Maske paßt', *ND*, 30 April 1993, p.17

Greiner, Vera, 'Inventur', *FR*, 2 September 1993, p.10

Grimm, Erik, 'Der Tod der Ostmoderne oder die BRDigung des DDR-Untergrunds: Zur Lyrik Bert Papenfuß-Goreks', *ZfG*, N.F. 1 (1991), 9-20

Grimm, Erk, 'Das Gedicht nach dem Gedicht: Über die Lesbarkeit der jüngsten Lyrik', in *Deutschsprachige Gegenwartsliteratur: Wider ihre Verächter*, ed. by Christian Döring (Frankfurt a.M.: Suhrkamp, 1995), pp.287-304

Gutschke, Irmtraud, 'Einer geht aufs Ganze', *ND*, 10 November 1995, p.12

Hammer, Klaus, 'Gespräch mit Harald Gerlach', *WB*, 36 (1990), 1931-1948
-- 'Gespräch mit Kerstin Hensel', *WB*, 37 (1991), 93-110

Hartung, Harald, 'Placebos, Kwerdeutsch, Vaterlandkanal: Anmerkungen zur jungen Lyrik', *Merkur*, 45 (1991), 1145-1152
-- 'Was bleibt von Connewitz', *FAZ*, 16 June 1993, p.32
-- 'Leere hinterm Trauerrand', *FAZ*, 29 July 1995, p.26

Heimberger, Bernd, 'Wenn die Flammen der Sprache lodern', *NZ*, 7 June 1994, p.14

'Heiner Müller', *The Times*, 2 January 1996, p.17

Heise, Hans-Jürgen, 'If I were a shark', *SDZ*, 15 July 1995, p.4
-- 'Die verdrängten Inhalte: Zur Lyrik unserer Zeit', *die horen*, 40 (1995), No.4, 193-196

Hensel, Kerstin, 'Ich teste meine Grenzen aus', *Deutsche Volkszeitung/die tat*, 3 November 1989, p.9
-- 'Das Eine und nicht das Andere: Zum Thema: Schreiben in der DDR', *ndl*, 43 (1995), No.4, 19-23

Herzog, Andreas, 'Erinnern und erzählen: Gespräch mit Kurt Drawert', *ndl*, 42 (1994), No.4, 63-71

Hilbig, Wolfgang, 'Grünes, grünes Grab', in *Grünes, grünes Grab: Erzählungen* (Frankfurt a.m.: Fischer, 1993), pp.99-122
-- 'Zeit ohne Wirklichkeit: Ein Gespräch mit Harro Zimmermann', *TuK*, 123 (1994), 11-18
-- *Abriß der Kritik: Frankfurter Poetikvorlesungen: Collection* (Frankfurt a.m.: Fischer, 1995)

Hilton, Ian, ' "Erlangte Einheit, verfehlte Identität": Reflections on lyric poetry of the 1990s', in *The New Germany: Literature and Society after Unification*, ed. by Osman Durrani, Colin Good and Kevin Hilliard (Sheffield: Sheffield Academic Press, 1995), pp.252-273
-- 'Heinz Czechowski: "Streit mit dem weißen Papier" ', *GM*, 40 (1997), 209-225
-- 'Heinz Czechowski: Die überstandene Wende?', *GLL*, 50 (1997), 214-226

Jäger, Manfred, 'Eine Flaschenpost wird angespült', *Deutsches Allgemeines Sonntagsblatt*, 30 July 1993, p.24

Jansen, Johannes, 'bleibt auf der straße', *Temperamente* (1990), No.1, 130

Jordan, Lothar, and Winfried Woesler, eds., *Lyriker Treffen Münster: Gedichte und Aufsätze 1987-1989-1991* (Bielefeld: Aisthesis, 1993)

Kalkreuth, Ulf, 'Doppelt spannend zu erleben: DDR-Autoren in diesem Herbst: Eine politische Poetik-Reihe an Leipzigs Karl-Marx-Universität', *Wissenschaftliche Zeitschrift der Karl-Marx-Universität*, 39 (1990), No.4, 3-4

Kane, Martin, 'Regeneration of the Language or "gequirlter Stumpfsinn" (Wolf Biermann): The Poetry of Bert Papenfuß-Gorek', *GM*, 35 (1995), 67-86

Kaufmann, Eva, 'Developments in East German Women's Writing since Autumn 1989', in *Postwar Women's Writing in German: Feminist Critical Approaches*, ed. by Chris Weedon (Providence, USA and Oxford: Berghahn, 1997), pp.211-222

Kiedaisch, Petra, ed., *Lyrik nach Auschwitz? Adorno und die Dichter* (Stuttgart: Reclam, 1995)

Kirsch, Rainer, 'Das Rad der Geschichte: Gesellschaftlicher Status und soziale Situation der Schriftsteller in den neuen Bundesländern', *ndl*, 39 (1991), No.8, 164-169

Klussmann, Paul Gerhard, 'Antworten der Literatur auf den Prozeß der deutschen Widervereinigung', in *Umgestaltung und Erneuerung im vereinten Deutschland*, ed. by Dieter Voigt and Lothar Mertens (Berlin: Duncker & Humboldt, 1993), pp.151-165

Knobloch, Hans-Jörg, and Helmut Koopmann, eds., *Deutschsprachige Gegenwarts-literatur* (Tübingen: Stauffenburg, 1997)

Kolbe, Uwe, 'Die Heimat der Dissidenten: Nachbemerkungen zum Phantom der DDR-Opposition', in *Der deutsch-deutsche Literaturstreit oder "Freunde, es spricht sich schlecht mit gebundener Zunge": Analysen und Materialien*, ed. by Karl Deiritz and Hannnes Krauss (Hamburg and Zurich: Luchterhand, 1991), pp.33-39
-- 'Frau Wolf, warum lächeln Sie nicht?', in *Jenseits der Staatskultur: Traditionen autonomer Kunst in der DDR*, ed. by Gabriele Muschter and Rüdiger Thomas (Munich: Hanser, 1992), pp.250-258
-- *Die Situation* (Göttingen: Wallstein, 1994)

Koneffke, Jan, 'Stunt-Ort-Dichtung: Kerstin Hensels "Freistoß" ', *Freitag*, 5 April 1996, p.12
-- 'Leer-Jahre', *Freitag*, 20 September 1996, p.11

Koopmann, Helmut, 'Tendenzen der deutschen Gegenwartsliteratur (1970-1995)', in *Deutschsprachige Gegenwartsliteratur*, ed. by Hans-Jörg Knobloch and Helmut Koopmann (Tübingen: Stauffenburg, 1997), pp.11-30

Kopplin, Wolfgang, 'Ein tiefer, neuer Ton', *Bayern Kurier*, 25 January 1992, p.16

Korte, Hermann, 'Ein neues Jahrzehnt des Gedichts? Deutschsprachige Lyrik der neunziger Jahre', *Der Deutschunterricht*, 51 (1999), No.4, 21-36

Kraft, Thomas, 'Geregelt', *SZ*, 13 September 1996, p.28

Kramp, Uwe, 'wort für wort um kopf und kragen', *ND*, 5/6 October 1991, p.14

Kratschmer, Edwin, *Dichter Diener Dissidenten: Sündenfall der DDR-Lyrik* (Jena: Universitätsverlag, 1995)

Krättli, Anton, ' "Ich habe mein Land verloren": Beobachtungen an deutschen Gedichten 1990', *Schweizer Monatshefte*, 70 (1990), 953-958

Kulturstreit – Streitkultur: German literature since the Wall, GM, 38 (1996)

Kundera, Ludvik, 'Die lyrische Reaktion auf die stillen Revolutionen von 1989/90 in Ost- und Südosteuropa', in *Lyriker Treffen Münster: Gedichte und Aufsätze 1987-1989-1991*, ed. by Lothar Jordan and Winfried Woesler (Bielefeld: Aisthesis, 1993), pp.515-542

Kunert, Günter, *Die letzten Indianer Europas* (Munich and Vienna: Hanser, 1991)
-- *Der Sturz vom Sockel: Feststellungen und Widersprüche* (Munich: Hanser, 1992)
-- 'Zu Kurt Drawert', *Akzente*, 41 (1994), 107-108

Küntzel, Heinrich, 'Verlieren Gedichte aus der DDR ihren Reiz?', *Deutschland Archiv*, 23 (1990), 1774-1779

Kurzke, Hermann, 'Lauter abgeschnittene Ohren', *FAZ*, 25 May 1996, p.28

Labroisse, Gerd, 'The Literature of the GDR and the Revolution of 1989/90', trans. by Ian Wallace, *GM*, 26 (1992), 37-49
-- 'Heiner Müllers "Endzeit" oder Wie die Wirklichkeit den Schriftsteller verrät', *GM*, 32 (1994), 229-247
-- 'Verwortete Zeit-Verflechtungen: Zu Heinz Czechowskis neuen Texten', *GM*, 32 (1994), 29-85

Langner, Beatrix, 'Abschied eines Clowns', *SDZ*, 27 March 1996, p.3

Lau, Jörg, 'Unsere Presse: Literarischer Osten: Die Bestellten und nicht Abgeholten', *Merkur*, 48 (1994), 364-369

Leeder, Karen, ' "Eine Abstellhalle des Poetischen": Postmodernism and Poetry in the New Germany', in *The Individual, Identity and Innovation: Signals from Contemporary Literature and the New Germany*, ed. by Arthur Williams and Stuart Parkes (Bern, Berlin, Frankfurt a.M., New York, Paris and Vienna: Lang, 1994), pp.201-220

Leistenschneider, Peter, 'Spiegelfrau und Rapunzel: Gedichte von Kerstin Hensel und Barbara Köhler', *Freitag*, 13 September 1991, p.20

Literarische Antworten auf die deutsche Einigung und den Untergang der DDR, *Colloquia Germanica*, 27 (1994)

Magenau, Jörg, and Stefan Reinecke, 'Verlust ist eine Herausforderung: Gespräch mit Bert Papenfuß', *Freitag*, 24 December 1993, p.21

Mennemeier, Franz Norbert, 'Eine poetische Minimalutopie: Barbara Köhlers Gedicht "traum hinter dem irrgarten" im Kontext', in *Gedichte und Interpretationen*, vii (Stuttgart: Reclam, 1997), pp.136-144

Mensching, Steffen, 'Notate im November 1989', *Sondeur*, (1990), No.1, 43-45
-- and Hans-Eckardt Wenzel, 'Entwürfe einer anderen Welt: Gespräch mit Frauke Meyer-Gosau', *TuK* (1990), No.108, 86-94

Michalzik, Peter, 'Wo es war, soll nichts werden', *SZ*, 17 August 1996, p.4

Michaelis, Rolf, 'Rufe vom Niemandsufer', *Die Zeit*, 15 November 1991, p.83

Müller, Heiner, ' "Nicht Einheit, sondern Differenz": Gespräch zur Revolution in der DDR', *Deutsche Volkszeitung/die tat*, 24 November 1989, pp.13-14
-- 'Plädoyer für den Widerspruch', *ND*, 14 December 1989, p.5

-- ' "Ich bin kein Held, das ist nicht mein Job" ', *SDZ*, 14/15 September 1991, p.15
-- 'Bautzen oder Babylon?', *SuF*, 43 (1991), 664-665
-- 'Was wird aus dem größeren Deutschland?', *SuF*, 43 (1991), 666

Néy, Karin, ' "Letztlich will ich nichts, als Aufklärer sein...": Ein Gespräch mit Kerstin Hensel', *Temperamente* (1989), No.3, 3-7

Ohligschläger, H., and R. Vernier, 'Ein Gespenst lebt fort', *Focus*, 26 (1994), 40-41

Ortheil, Hanns-Josef, 'Zum Profil der neuen und jüngsten deutschen Literatur', in *Spätmoderne und Postmoderne: Beiträge zur deutschsprachigen Gegenwärtsliteratur*, ed. by Paul Michael Lützeler (Frankfurt a.M.: Fischer, 1991), pp.36-51

Overrath, Angelika, 'Mein braves Schindluder', *Neue Zürcher Zeitung*, 14 November 1995, p.38

Popp, Fritz, 'Legoland ist noch nicht in Sicht', *Die Presse*, 14 August 1993, p.8

Pulver, Elsbeth, 'Der Freispruch des Sisyphos', *Neue Zürcher Zeitung*, 23 July 1996, p.39

Rath, Wolfgang, 'Entgrenzung ins Intersubjektive: Zu den literarischen achtziger Jahren', in *Tendenz Freisprache: Texte zu einer Poetik der 80er Jahre*, ed. by Ulrich Janetzki and Wolfgang Rath (Frankfurt a.M.: Suhrkamp, 1992), pp.258-276

Rathenow, Lutz, 'Nachdenken über Deutschland', in *Aufbruch in eine andere DDR*, ed. by Hubertus Knabe (Reinbek bei Hamburg: Rowohlt, 1989), pp.285-293
-- 'Die Überwindung eines Zustandes glücklicher Unzufriedenheit', *Deutsche Volkszeitung/die tat*, 12 October 1990, p.13
-- 'Eine Denkpause oder die neue Sensibilität', *Stuttgarter Nachrichten*, 4 May 1991, p.50
-- 'Hut ab vor dem Kollegen Spitzel!', *Die Welt*, 1 June 1991, p.16
-- ' "Schreiben Sie doch für uns!" Was sich die Staatssicherheit einfallen ließ, um die Literatur zu bändigen', *FAZ*, 27 Novmber 1991, p.36
-- 'Tatsächlich: er hat was getan', *FR*, 15 January 1992, p.8
-- 'Wie lassen wir Vergangenheit vergehen?', in *Vergangenheitsklärung an der Friedrich-Schiller-Universität Jena: Beiträge zur Tagung "Unrecht und Aufarbeitung" am 19. und 20.6.1992*, ed. by Hans Richard Böttcher (Leipzig: Evangelische Verlagsanstalt, 1994), pp.231-238

Reif, Adelbert, 'Mit geschlossenen Augen vor der unerträglichen Wahrheit: Gespräch mit dem Schriftsteller Günter Kunert', *Universitas*, 45 (1990), 484-495

Rietzschel, Thomas, 'Revolution im Leseland: Begreifen die DDR-Autoren das Volk nicht mehr?', *FAZ*, 10 February 1990, unnumbered page

-- 'Kalauer und geliehene Fragmente: Gedichte aus der DDR verlieren ihren Reiz', *FAZ*, 12 February 1990, p.30
-- 'Jeden Tag eine Nachricht von Kriegen', *Die Presse*, 14 June 1997, p.6

Riha, Karl, 'Es ist Zeit, daß Zeit ist', *FR*, 21 October 1993, p.12
-- 'Wende im Gedicht', in *Wende-Literatur: Bibliographie und Materialien zur Literatur der deutschen Einheit*, ed. by Jorg Fröhling, Reinhild Meinel and Karl Riha, 2nd edition (Frankfurt a.m., Berlin, Bern, New York, Paris, Vienna: Lang, 1997), pp.127-128

Romero, Christine Zehl, 'No Voices – New Voices? Literature and Literary Climate in the Former GDR since the Wende', *SGCS*, 13 (1994), 139-164

Rosenlöcher, Thomas, *Die verkauften Pflastersteine* (Frankfurt a.m.: Suhrkamp, 1990)
-- *Die Wiederentdeckung des Gehens beim Wandern: Harzreise* (Frankfurt a.m.: Suhrkamp, 1991)

Ryan, Judith, 'Deckname Lyrik: Poetry after 1945 and 1989', in *Wendezeiten, Zeitenwende: Positionsbestimmungen zur deutschsprachigen Literatur 1945-1995*, ed. by Robert Weninger and Brigitte Rossbacher (Tübingen: Stauffenburg, 1997), pp.37-54

Sartorius, Joachim, 'Vorwort', in *Atlas der modernen Poesie*, ed. by Joachim Sartorius (Reinbek bei Hamburg: Rowohlt, 1995), pp.7-16
-- 'Die Poetik der Poesie oder vom Schauder der Berührung des Apfels mit dem Gaumen', in *Jahrbuch der Lyrik 1995/96: Poesie der Poesie*, ed. by Christoph Buchwald and Joachim Sartorius (Munich: Beck, 1995), pp.97-108

Schedlinski, Rainer, 'Die Furcht der DDR-Autoren vor der offenen Gesellschaft', *FAZ*, 6 December 1989, unnumbered page
-- 'gibt es die ddr überhaupt?, *Temperamente* (1990), No.1, 4-9
-- *die arroganz der ohnmacht: aufsätze und zeitungsbeiträge 1989 und 1990* (Berlin and Weimar: Aufbau, 1991)

Scheer, Udo, ' "Ich bin dafür, ihn nicht weiter zu beachten" ', *Das Parlament*, 21 June 1996, p.20

Schlenstedt, Dieter, 'Integration-Loyalität-Anpassung: Über die Schwierigkeit bei der Aufkündigung eines komplizierten Verhältnisses', in *Literatur der DDR: Rückblicke*, ed. by Heinz Ludwig Arnold (Munich: TuK, 1991), pp.172-189

Schmidt-Mühlisch, Lothar, 'Im Gespräch: Lutz Rathenow', *Die Welt*, 14 March 1990, p.8

Scholz, Hannelore, 'Literature of the "Wende": Changes in Aesthetic Perception among German Male and Female Writers', in *Germany Reunified: A Five- and Fifty-Year Retrospective*, ed. by Peter M. Daley, Hans Walter Frischkopf, Trudis Goldsmith-Reber and Horst Richter (New York, Washington, Boston, Bern, Frankfurt a.m., Berlin, Vienna and Paris: Lang, 1997), pp.93-103

Schönwald, Heino, 'Das Ende vom Lied', *ND*, 3-6 June 1993, p.1

Schubert, Hans, 'Als wollte er etwas sagen', *ND*, 17 June 1994, p.12

Schuler, Ralf, 'Melancholie ist mit vorhanden', *NZ*, 8 August 1990, p.9

Sharp, Ingrid, 'Male privilege and female virtue: Gendered representations of the two Germanies', *New German Studies*, 18 (1994), 87-106

Sommerhage, Claus, 'Einsätze: Barbara Köhlers Gedichte', *SuF*, 44 (1992), 668-678

'Sorgen', *FAZ*, 31 March 1990, p.27

Stoehr, Ingo R., ' "Das Konkrete wird alle Klischees wegwischen": Ein Gespräch mit Uwe Kolbe', *Dimension*[2], 1 (1994), 456-469

Theobaldy, Jürgen, 'Im Niemandsland der Zeiten', *FAZ*, 10 February 1990, unnumbered page

Tok, Uta, and Thomas Hartwig, 'Gespräch mit Rainer Kirsch', *ndl*, 38 (1990), No.7, 7-12

Törne, Dorothea von, 'Adam in Hades der Bilder', *Der Tagesspiegel*, 9 July 1995, p.W5

Treichel, Hans-Ulrich, 'Spiegelscherben eines Melancholikers', *Die Welt*, 3 April 1995, p.G5

Tresch, Christine, 'Einsichten vom Rande', *Die Wochenzeitung*, 10 September 1993, p.21

Tuk, Cornelius, 'Gedichte "zur Wende" in der Klasse', *Amsterdamer Beiträge zur neueren Germanistik*, 36 (1993), 117-130

Umbricht, Clemens, 'Nachrufen unter leeren Himmel', *Schweizer Monatshefte*, 75 (1995), 43-45

Verdorfsky, Jürgen, 'Sachsen am Meer – Ahoi!', *FR*, 11 June 1991, p.13
-- 'Die Zeit hat keine Ohren', *SZ*, 18 June 1993, p.27

Wald, Hans, ed., *Tiefe Eindrücke und andere Gedichte von Erich Honecker* (Siegen: Universität, 1993)

Wallmann, Jürgen P., 'Fernbedienung für den Gottesbeweis', *Die Welt*, 15 July 1995, p.G5

Welke, Dunja, 'Kraftvolle Nüchternheit', *Berliner Zeitung*, 27 August 1993, p.27

Widmann, Arno, 'Totenrede auf den Mauerspringer: Eine bunte Trauergemeinde nahm Abschied von Heiner Müller, den ersten gesamtdeutschen Dichter', *Die Zeit*, 19 January 1996, p.8

'Wieviel Literatur im Leben, wieviel Politik in der Poesie? Eine Umfrage unter deutschsprachigen Schriftstellern der Jahrgänge 1950 bis 1966', *NR*, 103 (1992), 95-103

Williams, Arthur, Stuart Parkes and Roland Smith, eds., *German Literature at a Time of Change 1989-1990: German Unity and German Identity in Literary Perspective* (Bern, Berlin, Frankfurt a.M., New York, Paris and Vienna: Lang, 1991)
-- and Stuart Parkes, eds., *The Individual, Identity and Innovation: Signals from Contemporary Literature and the New Germany* (Bern, Berlin, Frankfurt a.M., New York, Paris and Vienna: Lang, 1994)

Wittstock, Uwe, 'Ab in die Nische? Über die neueste deutsche Literatur und was sie vom Publikum trennt', *NR*, 104 (1993), 45-53
-- ' "Ich bin ein Neger": Zum Tode von Heiner Müller', *NR*, 107 (1996), 156-159

Wolf, Christa, *Was bleibt: Erzählung* (Frankfurt a.M.: Luchterhand, 1990)
-- *Im Dialog: Aktuelle Texte* (Berlin and Weimar: Luchterhand, 1990)
-- *Auf dem Weg nach Tabou: Texte 1990-1994* (Cologne: Kiepenheuer & Witsch, 1994)

Wolf, Gerhard, 'Die eigene Spur', *NZ*, 3 June 1993, p.2

Würtz, Hannes, ' "Herübergefallen" ', *ND*, 11 October 1996, p.12

Wüstefeld, Michael, 'Notiz zur Lurik', *SuF*, 43 (1991), 712-719
-- *Grenzstreifen* (Warmbronn: Keicher, 1993)

Zenke, Jürgen, 'Vom Regen und von den Traufen: Bert Papenfuß-Gorek: die lichtscheuen scheiche versunkener reiche', in *Gedichte und Interpretationen*, vii (Stuttgart: Reclam, 1997), pp.146-157

Zimmermann, Albrecht, 'Zwischen politischer Poesie und westlicher Privatdichtung', *Badische Neueste Nachrichten*, 5 October 1992, p.12

Zimmermann, Hans Dieter, 'Eine Landschaft ohne Orte', *Der Tagesspiegel*, 17 November 1996, p.W5

Zingg, Martin, 'Gute Zeiten für Lyrik', *Drehpunkt*, 25 (1993), 66-67

Zipser, Richard, 'Literary Portrayals of Postunification Germany', *Colloquia Germanica*, 30 (1997), 305-306

Zybura, Marek, ed., *"mit dem wort leben hängen"*: *Reiner Kunze zum 65. Geburtstag* (Heidelberg: Winter, 1998)

b. VOLKER BRAUN'S POETRY 1988-1998

Primary sources

Collections of poetry
-- *Training des aufrechten Gangs: Gedichte* (Halle: mdv, 1979)
-- *Gedichte* (Frankfurt a.m.: Suhrkamp, 1979)
-- *Langsamer knirschender Morgen: Gedichte* (Halle: mdv, 1987)
-- *Die Zickzackbrücke: Ein Abrißkalender* (Halle: mdv, 1992)
-- *Lustgarten Preußen: Ausgewählte Gedichte* (Frankfurt a.m.: Suhrkamp, 1996)
-- *Tumulus: Gedichte* (Frankfurt a.m.: Suhrkamp, 1999)

In addition, *Texte in zeitlicher Folge*, 10 vols (Halle-Leipzig: mdv, 1989-1993) contains Braun's published work until 1993.

Individual poems
-- 'Der Eisenwagen', *Monatshefte*, 78 (1986), 7
-- 'Aus dem dogmatischen Schlummer geweckt', *Das Argument* (1988), No.170, 474
-- [7 poems], *Bizarre Städte*, Sonderheft, October 1989
-- 'Die Zickzackbrücke', *ndl*, 38 (1990), No.1, 5-13
-- 'Das Eigentum', *ND*, 4-5 August 1990, p.1
-- 'O Chicago! O Widerspruch!', *Thüringer Allgemeine*, 26 August 1990, p.17
-- 'Wüstenstrurm', *Berliner Zeitung*, 21 January 1991, p.26
-- 'Rot ist Marlboro', *ndl*, 39 (1991), No.12, 5-8
-- 'Das Verschwinden des Volkseigentums', *Freibeuter*, 59 (1994), 125-127
-- 'Die Verstellung', in *Ein Text für CW* (Berlin: Janus, 1994), pp.18-22, and *Theater der Zeit*, 49 (1994), No.3, 2-4
-- 'Schreiben im Schredder', *ndl*, 43 (1995), No.4, 5-7
-- *Der Weststrand. Eine Veröffentlichung zur Lesung am 9. Juli 1995 im Christian-Wagner-Haus Warmbronn* (Warmbronn: Keicher, 1995)

Collections of Essays
-- *Es genügt nicht die einfache Wahrheit: Notate* (Leipzig: Reclam, 1975)
-- *Verheerende Folgen mangelnden Anscheins innerbetrieblicher Demokratie: Schriften* (Frankfurt a.m.: Suhrkamp, 1988)
-- *Wir befinden uns soweit wohl. Wir sind erst einmal am Ende. Äußerungen* (Frankfurt a.M.: Suhrkamp, 1998)

Articles and Essays
-- 'Rimbaud. Ein Psalm der Aktualität', *SuF*, 37 (1985), 978-998
-- 'Der Mensch ohne Zugehörigkeit', *Das Argument* (1986), No.157, 327-329
-- 'Die Erfahrung von Freiheit', *ND*, 11/12 November 1989, p.13
-- 'Notizen eines Publizisten: Vom Besteigen hoher Berge oder: Kommt Zeit, kommt Räte', *ND*, 8 December 1989, p.4, and reprinted in *SDZ*, 12 December 1989, p.33
-- 'Monströse Banalität', *Die Zeit*, 22 November 1991, p.63

-- ' "...solang Gedächtnis haust / in this distracted globe" ', *Freitag*, 30 April 1993, p.9

Speeches and Lectures
-- [Braun's speech] *X. Schriftstellerkongreß der Deutschen Demokratischen Republik, Berlin 24.-26- November 1987, ndl,* 36 (1988), No.3, 44-47
-- 'Das Unersetzliche wird unser Thema bleiben', *ndl,* 38 (1990), No.6, 6-9
-- 'Leipziger Poetik-Vorlesung, gehalten am 12.12.1989 an der Karl-Marx-Universität Leipzig', *kopfbahnhof. Almanach,* 3 (1991), 256-274

Prose and Drama
-- *Die Kipper: Schauspiel* (Berlin, GDR, and Weimar: Aufbau, 1972)
-- *Böhmen am Meer, Texte in zeitlicher Folge,* x (Halle-Leipzig: mdv, 1989-1993), pp.61-111
-- *Iphigenie in Freiheit* (Frankfurt a.M.: Suhrkamp, 1992)
-- *Der Wendehals: Eine Unterhaltung* (Frankfurt a.M.: Suhrkamp, 1995)
-- *Das Nichtgelebte: Eine Erzählung* (Leipzig: Faber & Faber, 1995)

Secondary sources

Arnold, Herbert, 'The Third World in the Work of Volker Braun and Heiner Müller', *Seminar,* 28 (1992), No.2, 148-158

Berendse, Gerrit-Jan, 'Volker Braun', *Die "Sächsische Dichterschule": Lyrik in der DDR in den sechziger und siebziger Jahre* (Frankfurt a.M.: Lang, 1990), pp.217-246
-- 'Fünfundzwanzig Jahre politischer Poesie von Volker Braun: Von einem heftigen Experimentator, der immer neue Wege sucht', *Wirkendes Wort,* 41 (1991), 425-435
'Zu neuen Ufern: Lyrik der "Sächsischen Dichterschule" im Spiegel der Elbe', *SGCS,* 10 (1991), 197-212

Böttiger, Helmut, 'Gebrochen, zerstückelt, versandt', *FR,* 8 August 1992, p.ZB4

Braun, Michael, 'Die Erde wird rot', *Jahrbuch der Lyrik 1996/97: Welt, immer anderwo,* ed. by Michael Braun, Christoph Buchwald and Michael Buselmeier (Munich: Beck, 1996), pp.59-60

Cosentino, Christine, and Wolfgang Ertl, *Zur Lyrik Volker Brauns* (Königstein: Forum Academicum, 1984)
-- ' "ich bin kein artist": Volker Braun and Sascha Anderson zur Position des Dichters in der DDR', *Germanic Notes,* 17 (1986), No.1, 2-4
-- 'Volker Brauns Essay "Rimbaud. Ein Psalm der Aktualität" im Kontext seiner Lyrik', *SGCS,* 7 (1987), 171-184
-- 'Ostdeutsche Autoren mitte der neunziger Jahre: Volker Braun, Brigitte Burmeister und Reinhard Jirgl', *GR,* 71 (1996), 177-194

Costabile-Heming, Carol Anne, *Intertextual Exile: Volker Braun's Dramatic Re-Vision of GDR Society* (Hildesheim, Zurich and New York: Olms, 1997)

Domdey, Horst, 'Volker Braun und die Sehnsucht nach der Großen Kommunion: Zum Demokratiekonzept der Reformsozialisten', *Deutschland Archiv*, 23 (1990), 1771-1774

Emmerich, Wolfgang, 'solidare – solitaire. Volker Braun: Drei Gedichte', in *Verrat an der Kunst? Rückblicke auf die DDR-Literatur*, ed. by Karl Deiritz and Hannes Krauss (Berlin: Aufbau, 1993), pp.195-205
-- *Kleine Literaturgeschichte der DDR*, rev. edn. (Leipzig: Kiepenheuer, 1996)

Fiedler, Theodore, 'Trauma, Mourning, Laughter: Volker Braun's Response to the "Wende" ', *Colloquia Germanica*, 30 (1997), 335-347

Geist, Peter, Christel and Walfried Hartinger and Klaus Werner, 'Unerhörte Nachrichten: Wilhelm Bartsch, "Übungen im Joch", Uwe Kolbe, 'Bornholm II', Volker Braun, "Langsamer knirschender Morgen"', in *DDR-Literatur '87 im Gespräch*, ed. by Siegfried Rönisch (Berlin, GDR, and Weimar: Aufbau, 1988), pp.128-157

Goodbody, Axel, 'The Romantic Landscape in Recent GDR Poetry: Wulf Kirsten and Volker Braun', in *Neue Ansichten: The Reception of Romanticism in the Literature of the GDR*, ed. by Howard Gaskill, Karin McPherson and Andrew Barker (Amsterdam: Rodopi, 1990), pp.191-211

Grauert, Wilfried, *Ästhetische Modernisierung bei Volker Braun: Studien zu Texten aus den achtziger Jahren* (Wurzburg: Königshausen und Neumann, 1995)

Hartinger, Walfried, and Christel Hartinger, 'Nachwort', in *Volker Braun: Gedichte*, ed. by Walfried and Christel Hartinger (Leipzig: Reclam, 1976), pp.141-158
-- 'Gesellschaftsentwurf und ästhetische Innovation – Zu einigen Aspekten im Werk Volker Brauns', in *Volker Braun*, ed. by Rolf Jucker (Cardiff: University of Wales Press, 1995), pp.30-54

Hartung, Harald, 'Der Feind im Spiegel', *FAZ*, 4 August 1992, p.24

Hensel, Kerstin, 'Jetzt kenn ich alles das', *ND*, 28-31 March 1996, Literaturbeilage, p.2

Herzinger, Richard, 'Empörte Zickzack-Literatur gegen Johnny Walker', *NZ*, 3 July 1992, p.14

Jacquemoth, Jos, *Politik und Poesie: Untersuchungen zur Lyrik Volker Brauns* (Berlin: Schmengler, 1990)

Jäger, Manfred, 'Das Handeln als Basis und Ziel dichterischer Praxis: Zu Volker Brauns Reflexionen über Poesie und Politik', *TuK*, 55 (1977), 12-21

Jarmatz, Klaus, 'Wiederholte Lektüre des jungsten Gedichtbandes von Volker Brauns', *ND*, 28 November 1989, p.4
-- 'Ideale ohne Namen', *ND*, 7-10 May 1992, p.1

Jucker, Rolf, ed., *Volker Braun* (Cardiff: University of Wales Press, 1995)
-- 'Von der "Ziehviehlisation" (1959) zur "ZUVIELISATION" (1987): Zivilisationskritik im Werk Volker Brauns', in *Volker Braun*, ed. by Rolf Jucker (Cardiff: University of Wales Press, 1995), pp.55-67

Juhre, Armin, 'Zorngesänge', *Deutsches Allgemeines Sonntagsblatt*, 9 October 1992, p.27

Kolbe, Uwe, 'Der größte Anspruch: Über ein paar Zeilen bei Volker Braun', *NR*, 101 (1990), No.4, 46-52

Kopka, Fritz-Jochen, 'Taxieren der Erbmasse', *Wochenpost*, 7 May 1992, p.17

Leistner, Bernd, 'Braun oder Die Verteidigung der Utopie', in *Lyriker Treffen Münster: Gedichte und Aufsätze 1987-1989-1991*, ed. by Lothar Jordan and Winfried Woesler (Bielefeld: Aisthesis, 1993), pp.365-377

Marquardt, Hans-Jochen, 'Mit den Kopf durch die Wende: Zu Volker Brauns Gedicht "Das Eigentum" ', *Acta Germanica*, 22 (1994), 115-130

Meinel, Reinhild, ' "Mein Luftkoffer, mein politisches Gepäck..." ', in *Wende-Literatur: Bibliographie und Materialien zur Literatur der deutschen Einheit*, ed. by Jörg Fröhling, Reinhild Meinel and Karl Riha, 2nd ed. (Frankfurt a.M., Berlin, Bern, New York, Paris, Vienna: Lang, 1997), p.105

Meyer-Gosau, Frauke, ' "Links herum nach Indien!" Zu einigen Hinter-lassenschaften der DDR-Literatur und den jüngsten Verteilungskämpfen der Intelligenz', *Literatur in der DDR: Rückblicke*, ed. by Heinz Ludwig Arnold (Munich: TuK, 1991)

Pergande, Ingrid, ' "Doch die eigenen armen Entwürfe gelten jetzt nichts": Alltag, Politik und Literatur bei Volker Braun', *Juni*, 4 (1990), No.2-3, 136-143

Rosellini, Jay, *Volker Braun* (Munich: Beck, 1983)

Schlenstedt, Dieter, 'Vorwort', in *Im Querschnitt: Volker Braun: Gedichte, Prosa, Stücke, Aufsätze*, ed. by Holger J. Schubert (Halle-Leipzig: mdv, 1978), pp.8-20
-- 'Ein Gedicht als Provokation', *ndl*, 40 (1992), No.12, 124-132

Schuhmann, Klaus, 'Lagebericht zur ökologischen Situation – Beobachtungen zur Lyrik der achtziger Jahre', in *DDR-Literatur '85 im Gespräch*, ed. by Siegfried Rönisch (Berlin, GDR, and Weimar: Aufbau, 1986), pp.23-43

-- 'Landeskunde im Gedicht: Zeitwandel und Zeitwende in der Lyrik Volker Brauns', *ZfG*, N.F. 3 (1993), No.1, 134-145

Subiotto, Arrigo, 'Die Entwicklung eines Dichters: Zu Volker Brauns neuester Lyrik', in *Ein Moment des erfahrenen Lebens: Zur Lyrik der DDR*, ed. by John L. Flood (Amsterdam: Rodopi, 1987), pp.140-161
-- 'Volker Braun: Literary Metaphors and the Travails of Socialism', in *Socialism and the Literary Imagination: Essays on East German Writers*, ed. by Martin Kane (New York and Oxford: Berg, 1991), pp.195-212

Visser, Anthonya, ' "Ost-itis"? Zu Volker Brauns "Wende"-Texten in "Rot ist Marlboro" ', *WB*, 42 (1996), 68-88
-- ' "Die Hoffnung lag im Weg wie eine Falle": Die Auseinandersetzung mit der sozialistischen Diktatur in Gedichten Volker Brauns', in *Literatur in der Diktatur: Schreiben im Nationalsozialismus und DDR-Sozialismus*, ed. by Günther Rüther (Paderborn, Munich, Vienna and Zurich: Schönigh, 1997), pp.421-443

Wallace, Ian, 'Teacher or Partner? The Role of the Writer in the GDR', in *The Writer and Society in the GDR*, ed. by Ian Wallace (Tayport: Hutton, 1984), pp.9-20
-- *Volker Braun: Forschungsbericht*, Forschungsberichte zur DDR-Literatur, iii (Amsterdam: Rodopi, 1986)

Wichner, Ernst, and Herbert Wiesner, eds., *Zensur in der DDR: Ausstellungs-buch: Geschichte, Praxis, und "Ästhetik" der Behinderung von Literatur* (Berlin: Brinkmann & Bose, 1991)

Wirsing, Sibylle, 'Im Todesjahr', *Frankfurter Anthologie*, xv, ed. by Marcel Reich-Ranicki (Frankfurt a.M. and Leipzig: Insel, 1992), pp.264-266

Wolf, Gerhard, 'Die gebrochene Ode oder: Training des aufrechten Gangs: Zur Lyrik Volker Brauns', *Wortlaut Wortbruch Wortlust: Dialog mit Dichtung: Aufsätze und Vorträge* (Leipzig: Reclam, 1988), pp341-357

Interviews

Berger, Peter, 'Das Nichtgelebte und das Wirklichgewollte', *ND*, 23 December 1993, p.13

'Darum sieht diese neue Welt so alt aus', *Budapester Rundschau*, 20 November 1989, p.9

Funke, Christoph, ' "Jetzt wird der Schwächere plattgewalzt" ', *Der Morgen*, 21 February 1991, p.3

'Halbheiten kommen teuer zu stehen', *Unsere Zeit*, 7 November 1989, p.7

Jucker, Rolf, ' "Wir befinden uns soweit wohl. Wir sind erst einmal am Ende": Volker Braun im Gespräch', in *Volker Braun*, ed. by Rolf Jucker (Cardiff: University of Wales Press, 1995), pp.21-29

Lehmann, Andreas, [untitled interview], *Freitag*, 21 June 1991, p.19

Schütt, Peter, 'Trost bei der Nüchternheit der Aufklärer', *Deutsche Volkszeitung/die tat*, 4 July 1986, p.11

Vörös, Karoly, 'Lösungen für alle', *Der Morgen*, 28/29 October 1989, and reprinted in *Wir befinden uns soweit wohl. Wir sind erst einmal am Ende. Äußerungen* (Frankfurt a.M.: Suhrkamp, 1998), pp.14-17

c. DURS GRÜNBEIN'S POETRY 1988-1998

Primary sources

Collections of poetry
-- *Grauzone morgens: Gedichte* (Frankfurt a.m.: Suhrkamp, 1988)
-- *Schädelbasislektion: Gedichte* (Frankfurt a.m.: Suhrkamp, 1991)
-- *Den teuren Toten: 33 Epitaphe* (Frankfurt a.m.: Suhrkamp, 1994)
-- *Falten und Fallen: Gedichte* (Frankfurt a.m.: Suhrkamp, 1994)
-- *Nach den Satiren: Gedichte* (Frankfurt a.m.: Suhrkamp, 1999)

In addition, *Von der üblen Seite* (Frankfurt a.m.: Suhrkamp, 1994) contains *Grauzone morgens* and *Schädelbasislektion*.

Individual poems
-- 'Gedichte', *SuF*, 40 (1988), 818-824
-- 'Morgenandacht und Ketzerei', in *Literarischer März: Lyrik unserer Zeit*, 6 (1989), 52-57
-- 'Point of no return: Für Heiner Müller', *Jahrbuch zur Literatur in der DDR*, 7 (1990), 47-50
-- 'Schöner Sterben', *FAZ*, 12 January 1993, p.27
-- 'Alba', *Manuskripte*, 33 (1993), No.122, 30
-- 'Deutsche Landschaft: Für Burgel Zeeh', *ND*, 9 September 1994, p.12
-- 'Club of Rome: Für Arno Widmann', *FAZ*, 24 October 1994, p.35
-- 'In der Provinz', *FAZ*, 6 February 1995, p.27
-- 'Avenue of the Americas', *FAZ*, 8 February 1995, p.29
-- 'In der Provinz', *FAZ*, 25 March 1995, p.27
-- 'Vom Tauchen', *Wochenpost*, 27 April 1995, p.45
-- 'In Gedanken an Marcus Aurelius', *FAZ*, 28 April 1995, p.14
-- 'Physiognomischer Rest', *FAZ*, 3 April 1995, p.33
-- 'In einer anderen Tonart', *FAZ*, 16 September 1995, p.31.
-- 'Erdenleicht', *FAZ*, 18 September 1995, p.39.
-- 'Ostrakon Dresden 3048', *Neue Zürcher Zeitung*, 30 September 1995, p.50
-- 'Mantegna, vielleicht', *FAZ*, 24 October 1995, p.35
-- 'Fragment', in *Jahrbuch der Lyrik 1995/96: Poesie der Poesie*, ed. by Christoph Buchwald and Joachim Sartorius (Munich: Beck, 1995), pp.22-23
-- 'In der Provinz I-III', in *Der heimliche Grund: 69 Stimmen aus Sachsen*, ed. by Helgard Rost and Thorsten Ahrend (Leipzig: Kiepenheuer, 1996), pp.167-169
-- 'Zum Abschied Heiner Müller', *FAZ*, 2 January 1996, p.25
-- 'Historien 1', *SuF*, 49 (1997), 35-40

Collection of essays
Galilei vermißt Dantes Hölle und bleibt an den Maßen hängen: Aufsätze 1989-1995 (Frankfurt a.M, Suhrkamp, 1996)

Articles and Essays
-- 'Völlig daneben', 'Protestantische Rituale', and 'Nach dem Fest', in *abriß der ariadnefabrik*, ed. by Andreas Koziol and Rainer Schedlinski (Berlin: Galrev, 1990), pp.258-261, pp.297-306 and pp.306-313
-- 'Ameisenhafte Größe', *Die andere Sprache: Neue DDR-Literatur der 80er Jahre*, ed. by Heinz Ludwig Arnold (Munich: TuK, 1990), pp.110-113
-- 'Ilya Kabakov in Berlin', in *Die Endlichkeit der Freiheit: Ein Handbuch zur Ausstellung* (Berlin: Akademie der Künste, 1990)
-- 'Im Namen der Füchse: Gibt es eine neue literarische Zensur?', *FAZ*, 26 November 1991, p.33
-- 'Brillen, Drogen, zoomorphe Träume: Über David Cronenbergs Film "Naked Lunch" ', *die taz*, 2 May 1992, p.13
-- 'Unruh aus Silben: Oskar Pastiors lyrische Uhrwerke', *Die Zeit*, 4 December 1992, p.6
-- 'Bis ans Ende der Linie: Über Eugen Gottfried Winckler (1912 bis 1936)', *FAZ*, 30 October 1993, unnumbered pages
-- 'Etwas wird von dem Strom der Dinge entrissen: Der Vesuv und der Müllberg von Dresden', *FAZ*, 27 May 1994, p.33
-- 'Bevor der Mensch mit sich allein ist: Besuch im Laderaum der Arche Noah', *FAZ*, 27 July 1994, p.25
-- 'Meine Jahre mit Helmut Kohl', *Die Zeit*, 23 September 1994, p.76
-- 'Ein Schwungbild, vom Besen gemalt: Gerard Manley Hopkins' "Journal" in der ersten vollständigen Übersetzung', *FAZ*, 21 November 1994, unnumbered page
-- 'Feldpost', *Schreibheft*, (1995), No.46, 191-192
-- 'Mein Kino', *Der Tagesspiegel*, 15 January 1995, p.22
-- 'Unser Verwandte unter der Tarnkappe: Man muß die Vernichtung Europas aus der Nähe sehen: Erinnerung an Felix Hartlaub', *FAZ*, 9 March 1995, p.35
-- 'Nicht zu ermüden durch die Zeit: Hundert Jahre, drei Generationen: Stimmen zu Ernst Jüngers heutigem Geburtstag', *FAZ*, 29 March 1995, p.37
-- 'Zu Kieseln gehärtet: Über das lyrische Sprechen', *Neue Zürcher Zeitung*, 30 September 1995, p.50
-- 'Körper erinnere dich!', *Der Spiegel*, 25 October 1997, pp.254-259

Speeches and Lectures
-- 'Reflex und Exegese: Rede anläßlich des Bremer-Literatur-Förderpreises 1992 der Rudolf-Alexander-Schröder-Stiftung', *Galilei vermißt Dantes Hölle und bleibt an den Maßen hängen: Aufsätze 1989-1995* (Frankfurt a.M, Suhrkamp, 1996), pp.61-66
-- 'Büchners Fischnerven und was daraus folgt: Dankrede zur Verleihung des Georg-Büchner-Preises 1995', *Die Weltwoche*, 2 November 1995, pp.74-75 and *Rede zur Entgegennahme des Georg-Büchner-Preis* (Frankfurt a.M.: Suhrkamp, 1995)

Miscellaneous

Grünbein, Durs, (Texts) and Via Lewandowsky (Graphics), *Ghettohochzeit* (Berlin: Ursus, 1988) [Künstlerbuch im Eigenverlag]

Grünbein, Durs, '(Bewußtsein als Verhängnis)', *ndl*, 39 (1991), No.10, 53-59

Grünbein, Durs, Brigitte Oleschinski, and Peter Waterhouse, *Die Schweizer Korrektur*, ed. by Urs Engeler (Basel: Urs Engeler Editor, 1995)

Themerson, Stefan, *Bayamus und das Theater der semantischen Poesie: Roman*, trans. by Durs Grünbein (Leipzig: Reclam, 1992)

Winckler, Eugen Gottlob, *Die Erkundung der Linie*, ed. by Durs Grünbein (Leipzig: Reclam, 1993)

Secondary sources

Auffermann, Verena, 'Söhne des Kalten Krieges', *SDZ*, 23 October 1995, p.13

Basse, Michael, 'Augen auf – und durch!', *SDZ*, 30 March 1994, p.15
-- 'Durs Grünbein', *SDZ*, 10 May 1995, p.4
-- 'Körper an Hirn: Ab nach New York!', *SDZ*, 4 May 1996, p.4

Baumgart, Richard, 'Frühgereift, unzart, doch traurig', *Die Zeit*, 10 May 1996, p.51

Böker, Carmen, 'Im Schatten des Sauriers', *Berliner Zeitung*, 19 January 1996, p.29

Bormann, Alexander von, 'Schwierige Tiere', in *Frankfurter Anthologie*, xix, ed. by Marcel Reich-Ranicki (Frankfurt a.M. and Leipzig: Insel, 1996), pp.246-248
-- 'Also weiter im Vers', *Der Tagesspiegel*, 15 May 1994, p.4

Böttiger, Helmut, 'Das Ich als Chirurgenwitz', *FR*, 16 April 1994, p.ZB2
-- 'Durs Grünbein: Die sibirischen Abenteuerplätze', *Rausch im Niemandsland: Es gibt ein Leben nach der DDR* (Berlin: Fannei und Walz, 1994), pp.86-95

Braun, Michael, 'Was alles hat Platz in einem Gedicht', *Badische Zeitung*, 12 June 1989
-- 'Fröstelnd unter den Masken des Wissens', *Freitag*, 18 March 1994, p.19
-- 'Kleine, verwunderte Fußnote zu einer Polemik von Franz Josef Czernin', *Schreibheft*, (1995), No.46, 192-195
-- 'Schädelbasislektionen', in *Jahrbuch der Lyrik 1996/97: Welt, immer anderswo*, ed. by Michael Braun, Christoph Buchwald and Michael Buselmeier (Munich: Beck, 1996), pp.46-48

Camartin, Iso, 'Das Veto der Eingeweide', *Neue Zürcher Zeitung*, 6/7 May 1995, p.53

Czernin, Franz Josef, 'Falten und Fallen: Zu einem Gedichtband von Durs Grünbein', *Schreibheft*, (1995), No.45, 179-188

'Der Lyriker Durs Grünbein erhält den Büchner-Preis: Leserbriefe', *Die Zeit*, 13 October 1995, p.105

Detering, Heinrich, 'Hin wie nichts', *FAZ*, 4 October 1994, p.6

Draesner, Ulrike, 'Reden vom Sterben und vom Grab', *SDZ*, 19/20 November 1994, p.4

Drawert, Kurt, 'Die leeren Zeichen', *ndl*, 40 (1992), No.6, 132-137

Engler, Jürgen, 'Nicht heimisch', *ndl*, 42 (1994), No.4, 139-145

Falcke, Eberhard, 'Lyrischer Landmesser', *Die Zeit*, 1 April 1994, p.58

Fricke, Harald, 'Sein Vergnügen war die Logik des anderen: Der Schriftsteller Durs Grünbein kannte Heiner Müller als einen boshaften Humoristen', *die taz*, 2 January 1996, p.3

Goetsch, Monika, 'Täglicher Reflex', *Das Sonntagsblatt*, 12 May 1995, p.33

Görner, Rüdiger, 'Ausflug in die Quere', *Die Presse*, 9 April 1994, p.7

Grimm, Erk, 'Durs Grünbeins Depeschen über den Atavismus Mensch', in 'Das Gedicht nach dem Gedicht: Über die Lesbarkeit der jüngsten Lyrik', in *Deutschsprachige Gegenwartsliteratur: Wider ihre Verächter*, ed. by Christian Döring (Frankfurt a.M.: Suhrkamp, 1995), pp.300-304

Guschke, Irmtraud, 'Ritterschlag', *ND*, 10 May 1995, p.2

Hamm, Peter, 'Vorerst – oder: Der Dichter als streunender Hund: Lobrede auf Durs Grünbein', *Manuskripte*, 33 (1993), No.122, 103-106
-- 'O Tod, wie trivial bist du', *Die Zeit*, 7 October 1994, p.13

Hartung, Harald, 'Tagträume in der Grauzone', *FAZ*, 24 October 1988, p.28
-- 'Dichter sind Dornauszieher: Die Schweizer Korrektur', *FAZ*, 13 November 1995, p.38

Heise, Hans-Jürgen, 'S-Bahn-Surfing oder Wie still ist der See', *Die Welt*, 2 July 1994, p.5

Hell, Cornelius, 'Ein genauer Blick auf unsere Zeit', *Die Furche*, 22 September 1994, p.23

Jenny-Ebeling, Charitas, 'Zwischen den Spalten: Poetologische Essays', *Neue Zürcher Zeitung*, 7 November 1995, p.34

Koburg, Roland, 'Blutdurst sagt: Komm Leberdurst!', *Die Zeit*, 27 October 1995, p.69

Köhler, Andrea, 'Sezieren am Nerv der Zeit', *Neue Zürcher Zeitung*, 5 June 1994, p.14

Krieg, Karl, 'Durs Grünbein: Grauzone morgens', *Passauer Pegasus*, 8 (1990), No.15, 137-138

Kunze, Heinz-Rudolf, 'Er schreibt, wie Miles Davis spielt', *Berliner Zeitung*, 10 September 1994, p.38

Langner, Beatrix, 'Neugier auf Katastrophen', *Berliner Zeitung*, 23 October 1995, p.27

Lau, Jörg, 'Der Dichter als grausamer kleiner Junge', *die taz*, 17 March 1994, p.19
-- 'Zoologisch kühler Blick', *die taz*, 13/14 May 1995, p.15

Lindner, Burkhardt, 'Lyrische Schwundstufe', *FR*, 5 October 1994, p.B13
-- 'Kryptische Sehnsucht, von Heimweh zerfressen', *FR*, 16 March 1994, p.B2

Magenau, Jörg, 'Der Schatten des Körpers des Dichters', *Freitag*, 27 October 1995, p.9

Martin, Marko, 'Im Schatten des Sauriers', *Der Tagesspiegel*, 19 January 1996, p.21

Meyer-Gosau, Frauke, 'Assoziationsgestöber', *Freitag*, 29 March 1996, p.23

Michaelsen, Sven, 'Rebell mit Röntgenblick', *Stern*, 19 October 1995, pp.228-231

Michalzik, Peter, 'Club der lebenden Dichter: Drei Lyriker auf dem Weg zum Dialog', *SDZ*, 13/14 April 1996, p.5

Müller, Lothar, 'Das Herbarium als Quelle neuer Bilder', *Der Tagesspiegel*, 18 July 1995, p.19

Overath, Angelika, 'Genaues Vermessen vermisst: Durs Grünbeins Essays', *Neue Zürcher Zeitung*, 23 April 1996, p.35

Peukert, Tom, 'Metaphern für eine neue Wildnis: Im Dickicht des Nicht-Ich: Die Gedichte von Durs Grünbein', *Der Tagesspiegel*, 17 May 1992, p.ix
-- 'Bedrängender Sog', *Der Tagesspiegel*, 19 May 1995, p.21

Pickerodt, Gerhart, 'Durs Grünbein und der Aschermittwoch der DDR', in *Verrat an der Kunst? Rückblicke auf die DDR-Literatur*, ed. by Karl Deiritz and Hannes Krauss (Berlin: Aufbau, 1993), pp.99-103

Pfeiffer, Annette, 'Der Jugend den Vorzug', *SZ*, 23 October 1995, p.14

Plath, Jörg, 'Bilder blitzen auf', *Berliner Zeitung*, 20 October 1995, p.26

Raddatz, Fritz J., 'Nicht Entwurf der Moderne, sondern Faltenwurf der Mode', *Die Zeit*, 22 September 1995, pp.65-66

Riedel, Nicolai, 'Durs Grünbein: Falten und Fallen', *Passauer Pegasus*, 12 (1994), No.23, 146-149

Ritter, Henning, 'Wolken, vermessen', *FAZ*, 2 April 1996, p.14

Sartorius, Joachim, 'Durs Grünbein', *die taz*, 3 April 1992, p.17
-- 'Grünbein schöner Gotterfunke!', *Die Weltwoche*, 19 October 1995, p.73

Schirrmacher, Frank, 'Jugend: Büchner-Preis für Grünbein', *FAZ*, 9 May 1995, p.35

Schmidt, Thomas E., 'Aufhorchen und Weitergehen oder: Die Fallgesetze der Poesie', *FR*, 27 March 1996, Literaturbeilage p.14

Schubert, Matthies, 'Gute Lyrik in schlechter Zeit', *Deutsches Allgemeines Sonntagsblatt*, 1 July 1994, p.22

Siebt, Gustav, 'Mit besseren Nerven als jedes Tier', *FAZ*, 15 March 1994, p.L1
-- 'In den Albtraum erwachen. Über Durs Grünbeins Gedicht *Alba*', in *Gedichte und Interpretationen*, vii (Stuttgart: Reclam, 1997), pp.56-62

Sprang, Stefan, 'Fröhliche Mörder vorm Monitor', *Rheinische Merkur*, 29 April 1994, p.21

Steiner, Uwe, 'Abseits von Abseits: Randgänge der neuren deutschsprachigen Stadt-Literaur', *Manuskripte*, 38 (1998), No.139, 91-97

Steinfeld, Thomas, 'Falten und Fallen', *FAZ*, 13 May 1995, p.10

Törne, Dorothea von, 'Sterbefälle', *Wochenpost*, 8 September 1994, p.28
-- 'Pornographie des Sterbens', *Der Tagesspiegel*, 31 December 1994 / 1 January 1995, p.5
-- 'Codiert bis in die Zehenspitzen', *NZ*, 4 June 1994, p.14

Tresch, Christine, 'Maximum an Idee, Minimum an Worten', *Die Wochenzeitung*, 17 May 1996, pp.17-18

Verdorfsky, Jürgen, 'Vom Ruhm verwöhnt und davon unberührt', *SZ*, 9 May 1995, p.23

Wallmann, Hermann, 'Immer schon vor dir da', *Wochenpost*, 17 March 1994, p.8

Würtz, Hannes, 'Wißbegier eines Klosterschülers', *ND*, 15 May 1996, p.9

Transcripts of radio broadcasts

Altmann, Gerhard, [Review of *Falten und Fallen*], in 'Ex libris', presented by Volkmar Parschalk, *Österreichischer Radio*, 14 August 1994

Franke, Konrad, 'Hirn-Poesien: Durs Grünbeins Aufsatzsammlung "Galilei vermißt Dantes Hölle" ', *Radio Bremen*, 21 July 1996

Matt, Hubert, [Review of *Schädelbasislektion*], in 'Ex libris', presented by Volkmar Parschalk, *Österreichischer Radio*, 8 March 1992

Interviews

Bednarz, Klaus, 'Durs Grünbein: Den teuren Toten', in Klaus Bednarz and Gisela Marx, *Von Autoren und Büchern: Gespräche mit Schriftstellern* (Hamburg: Hofmann und Campe, 1997), pp.204-210

Doerry, Martin, and Volker Hage, 'Tausendfacher Tod im Hirn', *Der Spiegel*, 41 (1995), 221-230

Moser, Gerhard, 'Im Fach der Orchidee', *Die Presse*, 20 May 1995, p.7

Naumann, Thomas, 'Poetry from the bad side', *Sprache im technischen Zeitalter* (1992), No.124, 442-449

Pfeiffer, Annette, 'Streunen auf beiden Seiten: Ein Gespräch mit Büchner-Preisträger Durs Grünbein', *SZ*, 13 March 1996, p.25

Törne, Dorothea von, 'Mir kann die ganze Ostnostalgie gestohlen bleiben', *Wochenpost*, 27 April 1995, pp.44-46

d. THE 'WENDE', UNIFICATION AND THE 'LITERATURSTREIT'

Abbey, William, ed., *Two into one: Germany 1989-1992: A bibliography of the 'Wende'* (London: Institute of Germanic Studies, 1993)

Andress, Reinhard, ' "das Gefühl, mitten in einem riesigen Ozean auf einem kleinen Schiff zu sein": Zur DDR-Protokolliteratur während und nach der Wende-Zeit', *Colloquia Germanica*, 27 (1994), 49-62

Anz, Thomas, ed., *"Es geht nicht um Christa Wolf": Der Literaturstreit im vereinten Deutschland* (Munich: Spangenberg, 1991)

Arnold, Heinz Ludwig, ed., *Vom gegenwärtigen Zustand der deutschen Literatur* (Munich: TuK, 1992)
-- and Frauke Meyer-Gosau, eds., *Die Abwicklung der DDR* (Göttingen: Wallstein, 1992)

Ashbrook, B., and P. P. Hasler, eds., *The New Germany: Divided or United by a Common European Culture?* (Glasgow: Goethe-Institut, 1992)

Bahrmann, Hannes, and Christoph Links, *Wir sind das Volk: Die DDR im Aufbruch – Eine Chronik* (Berlin and Weimar: Aufbau, 1990 and Wuppertal: Hammer, 1990)
-- *Chronik der Wende: Die DDR zwischen 7. Oktober und 18. Dezember 1989* (Berlin: Links, 1994)

Baier, Lothar, *Volk ohne Zeit: Essays über das eilige Vaterland* (Berlin: Wagenbach, 1990)

Bannas, Günter, Klaus Broichhausen, Carl Graf Hohenthal and Kerstin Schwan, *Der Vertrag zur deutschen Einheit: Texte und Erläuterungen. Mit einer Chronik der deutschen Geschichte von 1949 bis 1989 von Eckhard Fuhr* (Frankfurt a.M. and Leipzig: Insel, 1990)

Barthélemy, François, and Lutz Winkler, eds., *Mein Deutschland findet sich in keinem Atlas: Schriftsteller aus beiden deutschen Staaten über ihr nationales Selbstverständnis* (Frankfurt a.M.: Luchterhand, 1990)

Bathrick, David, 'The End of the Cold War Intellectual', *German Politics and Society*, 27 (1992), 77-87

Baume, Brita, ' "Mein Thema war nie die DDR" (Hensel): Zur Literatur junger Autorinnen der DDR vor und nach 1989', in *"Ich will meine Trauer nicht leugnen und nicht meine Hoffnung": Veränderungen kultureller Selbstwahrnehmungen von ostdeutschen und osteuropäischen Frauen nach 1989*, ed. by Helga Grubitzsch, Eva Kaufmann and Hannelore Scholz (Bochum: Winckler, 1994), pp.57-69

Baumgart, Reinhard, 'Wir sind das Volk – nicht Halbzeit im ersten Jahrzehnt der Wieder(un)vereinigung – Ein Fastenpredigt für Rechts-links-Intellektuelle', *Die Zeit*, 12 October 1995, pp.57-58

Biechele, Werner, 'Das alles ist unsere Geschichte: Der deutsch-deutsche Literaturstreit und die Autoren', *GM*, 40 (1997), 32-45

Blaschke, Rosi, and Adolf Sturzbecher, 'DDR-Aufbruch in eine neue Zeit', *ND*, 30/31 December 1989, p.11

Blohm, Frank, and Wolfgang Herzberg, eds., *Nicht wird mehr so sein wie es war: Zur Zukunft der beiden deutschen Republiken* (Leipzig: Reclam, 1990)

Blum, Mechthild, and Thomas Nesseler, eds., *Deutschland einig Vaterland? Geschichte(n), Probleme und Perspektiven* (Bonn: Zeitlupe, 1992)

Bohn, Rainer, Knut Hickethier and Eggon Müller, eds., *Mauer-Show: Das Ende der DDR, die deutsche Einheit und die Medien* (Berlin: Sigma Bohn, 1992)

Bondy, François, 'Nach dem Zusammenbruch der DDR – deutscher Intellektuellen-streit', *Schweizer Monatshefte*, 70 (1990), 710-715

Böttcher, Hans Richard, ed., *Vergangenheitsklärung an der Friedrich-Schiller-Universität Jena: Beiträge zur Tagung "Unrecht und Aufarbeitung" am 19. und 20.6.1992* (Leipzig: Evangelische Verlagsanstalt, 1994)

Brockmann, Stephen, 'A Literary Civil War', *GR*, 68 (1993), 69-78
-- 'German Literary Debates after the Collapse', *GLL*, 47 (1994), No.2, 201-210
-- '...And then there was Sascha', *Dimension*[2], 1 (1994), 423-435

Brückner, Dieter, and Heiner Schulz, 'Unser Schiff zieht seinem Kurs fest und stolz dahin – bis zum Sieg', *ND*, 21 September 1989, p.3

Bullivant, Keith, *The Future of German Literature* (Oxford and Providence: Berg, 1994)

Burmeister, Brigitte, 'Schriftsteller in gewendeten Verhältnissen', *SuF*, 46 (1994), 646-654

Carr, Godfrey, and Georgina Paul, 'Unification and its Aftermath: The Challenge of History', in *German Cultural Studies: An Introduction* (Oxford: OUP, 1995), pp.325-347

Childs, David, *Germany on the road to unity: The determination which has forced the pace and the huge obstacles still to be overcome* (London and New York: Economist Intelligence Unit, 1990)

Corino, Karl, 'Vor und nach der Wende: Die Rezeption der DDR-Literatur in der Bundesrepublik und das Problem einer einheitlichen deutschen Literatur', *ndl*, 39 (1991), No.8, 146-164

Dahn, Daniela, *Westwärts und nicht vergessen: Vom Unbehagen in der Einheit* (Berlin: Rowohlt, 1996)

Deiritz, Karl, and Hannes Krauss, eds., *Der deutsch-deutsche Literaturstreit oder "Freunde, es spricht sich schlecht mit gebundener Zunge": Analysen und Materialien* (Hamburg and Zurich: Luchterhand, 1991)

Dennis, Mike, 'Civil Society, Opposition and the End of the GDR', *SGCS*, 11/12 (1993), 1-18

Durrani, Osman, Colin Good and Kevin Hilliard, eds., *The New Germany: Literature and Society after Unification* (Sheffield: Sheffield Academic Press, 1995)

Eigler, Friederike, and Peter C. Pfeiffer, eds., *Cultural Transformations in the New Germany: American and German Perspectives* (Columbia, South Carolina: Camden House, 1993)

Ein Text für C.W. (Berlin: Janus, 1994)

Emmerich, Wolfgang, and Lothar Probst, eds., *Intellektuellen-Status und intellektuelle Kontroversen im Kontext der Wiedervereinigung* (Bremen: Universitat, 1993)
-- 'Zwischen Hypertrophie und Melancholie: Die literarische Intelligenz der DDR im historischen Kontext', in *Intellektuellen-Status und intellektuelle Kontroversen im Kontext der Wiedervereinigung*, ed. by Wolfgang Emmerich and Lothar Probst (Bremen: Universitat, 1993), pp.5-21

Famler, Walter, 'Wiederverwendungsfähig? Ein Gespräch über DDR-Literatur und deutsche Politik', *Wespennest* (1990), No.78, 12-16

Fest, Joachim, 'Nach dem Scheitern der Utopien: Probleme der offenen Gesellschaft', *SuF*, 49 (1997), No.3, 410-421

Fischer, Alexander, and Maria Haendcke-Hoppe-Arndt, eds., *Auf der Weg zur Realisierung der Einheit Deutschlands* (Berlin: Duncker & Humblot, 1991)
-- and Manfred Wilke, eds., *Probleme des Zusammenwachsens im wiedervereinigten Deutschland* (Berlin: Duncker & Humblot, 1994)

Fischer, Erica, and Petra Lux, *Ohne uns ist kein Staat zu machen: DDR-Frauen nach der Wende* (Cologne: Kiepenheuer & Witsch, 1990)

Fischer, Ludwig, 'Zwischen Aufbruch und Zukunftsangst: Beobachtungen und Dokumente zur Situation der Künstler in der Noch-DDR', *deutsche studien*, 28 (1990), 122-142

Förster, Peter, and Günter Roski, *DDR zwischen Wende und Wahl: Meinungsforscher analysieren den Umbruch* (Berlin: Links, 1990)

Fries, Fritz Rudolf, 'Linke Nostalgie und großes Fressen', *Freibeuter*, 45 (1990), 32-35

Fröhling, Jörg, Reinhild Meinel and Karl Riha, eds., *Wende-Literatur: Bibliographie und Materialien zur Literatur der deutschen Einheit*, 2nd ed. (Frankfurt a.m., Berlin, Bern, New York, Paris, Vienna: Lang, 1997)

Gann, Lewis, 'German Unification and the Left-Wing Intelligentsia: A Report', *German Studies Review*, 15 (1992), 99-110

Giesen, Bernd, and Claus Leggewie, 'Sozialwissenschaften vis-à-vis: Die deutsche Vereinigung als sozialer Großversuch', in *Experiment Vereinigung: Ein sozialer Großversuch*, ed. by Bernd Giesen and Claus Leggewie (Berlin: Rotbuch, 1991), pp.7-18

Glaessner, Gert-Joachim, and Ian Wallace, eds., *The German Revolution of 1989: Causes and Consequences* (Oxford and Providence, USA: Berg, 1992)
-- *The Unification Process in Germany: From Dictatorship to Democracy*, trans. by Colin B. Grant (London: Pinter, 1992)

Gorbachev, Mikhail, *Perestroika: New Thinking for Our Country and the World* (London: Collins, 1987)

Grass, Günter, *Rede vom Verlust: Über den Niedergang der politischen Kultur im geeinten Deutschland* (Göttingen: Steidl, 1992)

Greiner, Ulrich, 'Der Potsdamer Abgrund: Anmerkungen zu einem öffentlichen Streit über die "Kulturnation" Deutschland', *Die Zeit*, 22 June 1990, p.59
-- 'Die deutsche Gesinnungsästhetik', *Die Zeit*, 2 November 1990, p.59

Grimm, Reinhold, 'The Travails of the Plains: On Some Consequences of German Unification', *German Studies Review*, 15 (1992), 87-98

Grosser, Dieter, Stephan Bierling and Friedrich Kurz, *Die sieben Mythen der Wiedervereinigung: Fakten und Analysen zu einem Prozeß ohne Alternative* (Munich: Ehrenwirth, 1991)

Grunenberg, Antonia, 'Das Ende der Macht ist der Anfang der Literatur', *Aus Politik und Zeitgeschichte*, 26 October 1990, pp.17-26
-- ' "Ich finde mich überhaupt nicht mehr zurecht...": Thesen zur Krise in der DDR-Gesellschaft', in *DDR: Ein Staat vergeht*, ed. by Thomas Blanke and Rainer Kirsch (Frankfurt a.M.: Fischer, 1990), pp.171-182

Habermas, Jürgen, *Die nachholende Revolution*, Kleine politische Schriften, vii (Frankfurt a.M.: Suhrkamp, 1990)

Hallberg, Robert von, ed., *Literary Intellectuals and the Dissolution of the State: Professionalism and Conformity in the GDR*, trans. by Kenneth J. Northcott (Chicago and London: University of Chicago Press, 1996)

Hannemann, Ernst, 'Geschichtsschreibung nach Aktenlage? Bemerkungen anläßlich der Debatte um die Stasikontakte von Christa Wolf und Heiner Müller', *GM*, 38 (1996), 19-34

Hartung, Klaus, *Neunzehnhundertneunundachtzig: Ortsbesichtigungen nach einer Epochenwende* (Frankfurt a.M.: Luchterhand, 1990)

Heidenreich, Gerd, 'Volk ohne Traum: Die deutsche Intellektuellen-Debatte', *ndl*, 40 (1992), No.8, 56-67

Hein, Christoph, *Die fünfte Grundrechenart. Aufsätze und Reden 1987-1990* (Frankfurt a.M.: Luchterhand, 1990)
-- 'Kein Seeweg nach Indien', in *Christoph Hein. Texte, Daten, Bilder*, ed. by Lothar Baier (Frankfurt a.M.: Luchterhand, 1990), pp.13-19
--'Der Name der Anpassung: Stasi-Spitzel, die spezielle Form des politischen Opportunismus', in *Deutschland einig Vaterland? Geschichte(n), Probleme und Perspektiven*, ed. by Mechthild Blum and Thomas Nesseler (Bonn: Zeitlupe, 1992), pp.8-13

Hellmann, Manfred W., 'Linguistics, Politics and the German Language: Changes in the Linguistic Debate on the German-German Language Problem', *SGCS*, 9 (1989), 189-208

Henrich, Rolf, *Der vormundschaftliche Staat: Vom Versagen des real existierenden Sozialismus* (Reinbek bei Hamburg: Rowohlt, 1989)

Herberg, Dieter, Doris Steffens and Elke Tellenbach, *Schlüsselwörterbuch der Wendezeit: Wörter-Buch zum öffentlichen Sprachgebrauch 1989/90* (Berlin and New York: de Gruyter, 1997)

Herminghouse, Patricia, 'Whose German literature?', *GDR Bulletin*, 16 (1990), No.2, 6-11

Heym, Stefan, *Einmischung: Gespräche, Reden, Essays* ([Munich]: Bertelsmann, 1990)

Hübner, Peter, 'Von der friedlichen Herbstrevolution 1989 bis zur deutschen Einheit – das Erbe', in *Auf der Weg zur Realisierung der Einheit Deutschlands*, ed. by Alexander Fischer and Maria Haendcke-Hoppe-Arndt (Berlin: Duncker & Humblot, 1991), pp.61-93

Hutchinson, Peter, and Alan G. Jones, eds., *Wende '89: Von der DDR zu den fünf neuen Ländern* (Bristol: Bristol Classical, 1992)

Huyssen, Andreas, 'After the Wall: The Failure of German Intellectuals', *New German Critique*, 52 (1991), 109-143

James, Harold, and Marla Stone, eds., *When the Wall came down: Reactions to German Unification* (London and New York: Routledge, 1992)
-- 'The landscape that didn't bloom', *Times Literary Supplement*, 13 June 1997, 5-6

Jones, Alun, *The New Germany: A Human Geography* (Chichester, England: Wiley, 1994)

Kasper, Elke, 'Untergangs- oder Überlebenskunst? Ein Lyrikdebatte und ihre Folgen', in *Günter Kunert: Beiträge zu seinem Werk*, ed. by Manfred Durzak and Helmut Steinecke (Munich and Vienna: Hanser, 1992), pp.102-118

Keller, Ernst, 'Fallen Idols – German Intellectuals and Writers facing the demise of the GDR', *GM*, 38 (1996), 35-50

Kershaw, Ian, *Germany's Present, Germany's Past: The 1992 Bithell Memorial Lecture* (London: Institute of Germanic Studies, 1992)

Kirschey, Peter, *Wandlitz / Waldsiedlung – die geschlossene Gesellschaft: Versuch einer Reportage, Gespräche, Dokumente* (Berlin: Dietz, 1990)

Klein, Thomas, Vera Vordenbäumen, Carsten Wiegrefe and Udo Wolf, *Keine Opposition. Nirgends? Linke in Deutschland nach dem Sturz des Realsozialismus* (Berlin: Links, 1991)

Knabe, Hubertus, ed., *Aufbruch in eine andere DDR: Reformer und Oppositionelle zur Zukunft ihres Landes* (Reinbek bei Hamburg: Rowohlt, 1989)

Knoell, Dieter R., *Kritik der deutschen Wendeköpfe: Frontberichte vom publizistischen Feldzug zur Herbeiführung des Endsiegs über die zersetzende Gesellschaftskritik* (Münster: Westfälisches Dampfboot, 1992)

Kogel, Jörg-Dieter, Wolfram Schütte and Harro Zimmermann, eds., *Neues Deutschland: Innenansichten einer wiedervereinigten Nation* (Frankfurt a.m.: Fischer, 1993)

Kohler, Georg, and Martin Meyer, eds., *Die Folgen von 1989* (Munich and Vienna: Hanser, 1994)

Korte, Karl-Rudolf, 'Schriftsteller', in *Handwörterbuch zur deutschen Einheit*, ed. by Werner Weidenfeld and Karl-Rudolf Korte (Frankfurt a.m. and New York: Campus, 1992), pp.575-581

Krenz, Egon, *Wenn Mauern fallen: Die friedliche Revolution: Vorgeschichte – Ablauf – Wirkungen* (Vienna: Neff, 1990)

Krieger, Hans, 'Monologe zum Prophetensturz: Ein internationales Literatur-Symposium in München', *ndl*, 40 (1992), No.1, 153-157

Krone, Tina, Irena Kukutz and Henry Leide, *Wenn wir unsere Akten lesen: Handbuch zum Umgang mit den Stasi-Unterlagen* (Berlin: BasisDruck, 1992)

Krüger, Hans-Peter, 'Ohne Versöhnung handeln, nur nicht leben: Zur Diskussion um DDR-Intellektuelle', *SuF*, 44 (1992), 40-50

Kügelgen, Dirk von, 'Aus und weiter: Die Situation des Schriftstellerverbandes der ehemaligen DDR', *Der Literat*, 32 (1990), 309-311

Kukral, Michael Andrew, *Prague 1989: Theater of Revolution* (New York: Columbia University Press, 1997)

Kunze, Reiner, *Am Sonnenhang: Tagebuch eines Jahres* (Frankfurt a.m.: Fischer, 1993)

Lang, Ewald von, ed., *Wendehals und Stasi-Laus: Demo-Sprüche aus der DDR* (Munich: Heyne, 1990)

Lang, Jochen von, *Erich Mielke: Eine deutsche Karriere* (Berlin: Rowohlt, 1991)

Lasky, Melvin, *Voices in a Revolution: Intellectuals (& others) in the collapse of the East German Communist Regime* ([London]: [International Association for Cultural Freedom], 1991)

Lauckner, Nancy A., 'Christa Wolf's Efforts on behalf of "Mündigwerden nach langer Sprachlosigkeit"', *SGCS*, 11/12 (1993), 125-142

Lewis, Alison, 'The Writers, Their Socialism, The People and Their Bad Table Manners: 1989 and the Crisis of East German Writers and Intellectuals', *German Studies Review*, 15 (1992), 243-266
-- 'Unity begins together: Analyzing the Traumas of German Unification', *New German Critique* (1995), No.64, 135-159

Lewis, Derek, and John R.P. McKenzie, eds., *The New Germany: Social, Political and Cultural Challenges of Unification* (Exeter: University of Exeter Press, 1995)

Lilienthal, Volker, 'Links liegen gelassen: Die Buchverlage der ehemaligen DDR', in *Mauer-Show: Das Ende der DDR, die deutsche Einheit und die Medien*, ed. by Rainer Bohn, Knut Hickethier and Eggon Müller (Berlin: Sigma Bohn, 1992), pp. 243-256

Literatur und politische Aktualität, Amsterdamer Beiträge zur neueren deutschen Literatur, 36 (1993)

Loest, Erich, *Nikolaikirche: Roman* (Leipzig: Linden, 1995)

Löw, Konrad, ed., *Ursachen und Verlauf der Deutschen Revolution 1989* (Berlin: Duncker & Humblot, 1991)

Maaz, Hans-Joachim,'Die sozialpsychologischen Schwierigkeiten der deutschen Vereinigung', in *Probleme des Zusammenwachsens im wiedervereinigten Deutschland*, ed. by Alexander Fischer and Manfred Wilke (Berlin: Duncker & Humblot, 1994), pp.9-12

Malchow, Helga, and Hubert Winkels, eds., *Die Zeit danach: Neue deutsche Literatur* (Cologne: Kiepenheuer & Witsch, 1991)

Maron, Monika, *Nach Maßgabe meiner Begreifungskraft: Artikel und Essays* (Frankfurt a.M.: Fischer, 1993)

Matthies, Frank-Wolf, 'Wiedervereinigung im Aldi-Rausch', in *Die Geschichte ist offen: DDR 1990: Hoffnung auf eine neue Republik: Schriftsteller aus der DDR über die Zukunftschancen ihres Landes*, ed. by Michael Naumann (Reinbeck bei Hamburg: Rowohlt, 1990), pp.137-141

Meier, Christian, 'Nicht Zerstörung, aber die Herausforderung der Vernunft: Erwartungen an deutsche Intellektuelle nach 1989', in *Intellektuellendämmerung? Beiträge zur neuesten Zeit des Geistes,* ed. by Martin Meyer (Munich and Vienna: Hanser, 1992), pp.77-95

Mellis, James, 'Writers in Transition: The End of East German Literature?', in *The New Germany: Social, Political and Cultural Challenges of Unification*, ed. by Derek Lewis and John R.P. McKenzie (Exeter: University of Exeter Press, 1995), pp.220-242

Meyer, Martin, ed., *Intellektuellendämmerung? Beiträge zur neuesten Zeit des Geistes* (Munich and Vienna: Hanser, 1992)

Meyer-Gosau, Frauke, ' "Linksherum, nach Indien!" Zu einigen Hinterlassenschaften der DDR-Literatur und den jüngsten Verteilungskämpfen der Intelligenz', in *Literatur in der DDR: Rückblicke*, ed. by Heinz Ludwig Arnold (Munich: TuK, 1991), pp.267-279

Michelis, Julia, ed., *Die ersten Texte des Neuen Forum* (Berlin: Neues Forum, 1990)

Miller, Barbara, ' "Wiederaneignung der eigenen Biographie": The Significance of the Opening of the "Stasi" files', *GLL*, 50 (1997), 369-377

Möbius, Regine, *Autoren in den neuen Bundesländern: Schriftsteller-Porträts* (Leipzig: Thon, 1995)

Morrison, Susan S., 'The Feminization of the German Democratic Republic in Political Cartoons 1989-1990', *Journal of Popular Culture*, 25 (1992), No.4, 35-51

Naumann, Michael, ed., *Die Geschichte ist offen: DDR 1990: Hoffnung auf eine neue Republik: Schriftsteller aus der DDR über die Zukunftschancen ihres Landes* (Reinbeck bei Hamburg: Rowohlt, 1990)

New German Critique, 52 (1991), 'Special Issue on German Unification'

The Observer, *Tearing down the Curtain: The People's Revolution in Eastern Europe* (London, Sydney, Auckland and Toronto,: Hodder & Stoughton, 1990)

Oktober 1989: Texte, Temperamente (1990), No.1 and reprinted as *Oktober 1989: Wider den Schlaf der Vernunft* (Berlin, FRG: Elefanten Press, 1989 and Berlin, DDR: Neues Leben, 1989)

Opie, Gerald, 'Views of the "Wende" ', in *The New Germany: Social, Political and Cultural Challenges of Unification*, ed. by Derek Lewis and John R.P. McKenzie (Exeter: University of Exeter Press, 1995), pp.31-51

Opp, Karl-Dieter, and Peter Voß, *Die volkseigene Revolution* (Stuttgart: Klett-Cotta, 1993)

Oschlies, Wolf, *Wir sind das Volk: Zur Rolle der Sprache bei den Revolutionen der DDR, Tschechoslowakei, Rümanien und Bulgarien* (Cologne: Böhlau, 1990)

Osmond, Jonathan, *German Reunification: A Reference Guide and Commentary* (Essex: Longman, 1992)

Pape, Walter, ed., *1870/71-1989/90: German Unifications and the Change of Literary Discourse* (Berlin and New York: de Gruyter, 1993)

Peitsch, Helmut, 'Der 9. November und die publizistische Reaktion westdeutscher Schriftsteller', in *Mauer-Show: Das Ende der DDR, die deutsche Einheit und die Medien*, ed. by Rainer Bohn, Knut Hickethier and Eggon Müller (Berlin: Sigma Bohn, 1992), pp. 201-226

Pischel, Joseph, 'Das Ende der Utopie? Zur aktuellen Diskussion um die DDR-Literatur und zum Streit um Christa Wolf', *ndl*, 38 (1990), No. 9, 138-147

Prins, Gwyn, ed., *Spring in Winter: The 1989 revolutions* (Manchester and New York: Manchester University Press, 1990)

Probst, Lothar, 'Die Revolution entläßt ihre Schriftsteller', *Deutschland Archiv*, 23 (1990), 921-925
-- 'Mythen und Legendenbildung: Intellektuelle Selbstverständnisdebatten nach der Wiedervereinigung', in *Intellektuellen-Status und intellektuelle Kontroversen im Kontext der Wiedervereinigung*, ed. by Wolfgang Emmerich and Lothar Probst (Bremen: Universitat, 1993), pp. 23-44

Rathjen, Friedhelm, 'Crisis? What crisis?', in *Deutschsprachige Gegenwarts-literatur: Wider ihre Verächter*, ed. by Christian Döring (Frankfurt a.M.: Suhrkamp, 1995), pp.9-17

Rauschenbach, Brigitte, ed., *Erinnern, Wiederholen, Durcharbeiten: Zur Psycho-Analyse deutscher Wenden* (Berlin: Aufbau, 1992)

Reed, T. J., 'Another Piece of the Past', in *1870/71-1989/90: German Unifications and the Change of Literary Discourse*, ed. by Walter Pape (Berlin and New York: de Gruyter, 1993), pp.233-250
-- 'Disconnections in the 1990 Literaturstreit: "Keine akademische Frage"?', in *Connections: Essays in Honour of Eda Sagarra*, ed. by Peter Skrine, Rosemary E. Wallbank-Turner and Jonathan West (Stuttgart: Heinz, 1993), pp.211-217

Reich, Jens, 'Reflections on becoming an East German dissident, on losing the Wall and a country', in *Spring in Winter: The 1989 revolutions*, ed. by Gwyn Prins (Manchester and New York: Manchester University Press, 1990), pp.65-97
-- *Abschied von den Lebenslügen: Die Intelligenz und die Macht* (Berlin: Rowohlt, 1992)

Reid, J.H., 'Right hand, left hand – both hands together: German writers and the challenges of unification', in *The New Germany: Divided or United by a Common European Culture?* ed. by B. Ashbrook and P. P. Hasler (Glasgow: Goethe Institut, 1992), pp.1-24

Reiher, Ruth, and Rüdiger Läzer, eds., *Wer spricht das wahre Deutsch?* *Erkundungen zur Sprache im vereinigten Deutschland* (Berlin: Aufbau, 1993)

Richter, Michael, *Die Staatssicherheit im letzten Jahr der DDR* (Weimar, Cologne and Vienna: Böhlau, 1996)

Rietzschel, Thomas, ed., *Über Deutschland: Schriftsteller geben Auskunft* (Leipzig: Reclam, 1993)

Roberts, Geoffrey K., *The Reunification of Germany* (Manchester: University of Manchester, [1992])

Rose, Richard, and Edward C. Page, *German Responses to Reunification: A Contextual Analysis* (London: Anglo-German Foundation, 1996)

Schirrmacher, Frank, 'Abschied von der Literatur der Bundesrepublik', *FAZ*, 2 October 1990, Buchmesse Beilage, p.1.
-- ed., *Im Osten erwacht die Geschichte: Essays zur Revolution in Mittel- und Osteuropa* (Stuttgart: DVA, 1990)

Schlesak, Dieter, 'Alles ist so, wie es ist: Reicher denn je an jeder Art Armut: Normalitätslüge und innere Spaltung', *Literaturmagazin*, 31 (1993), 68-85

Schmid, Thomas, 'Pinscherseligkeit', *Die Zeit*, 10 April 1992, pp.13-14

Schneider, Michael, *Die abgetriebene Revolution: Von der Staatsfirma in die DM-Kolonie* (Berlin: Elefanten Press, 1990)

Schneider, Rolf, 'Das Schweigen der Schafe: Über den ostdeutschen Kulturbetrieb', *Merkur*, 48 (1994), 537-543

Schüddekopf, Charles, ed., *"Wir sind das Volk": Flugschriften, Aufrufe und Texte einer deutschen Revolution* (Reinbek bei Hamburg: Rowohlt, 1990)

Schulz, Marianne, and Jan Wielgohs, 'DDR-Identität zwischen Demokratie und DM', in *DDR: Ein Staat vergeht*, ed. by Thomas Blanke and Rainer Erd (Frankfurt a.M.: Fischer, 1990), pp.123-136

Schumann, Frank, ed., *100 Tage, die die DDR erschütterten* (Berlin: Neues Leben, 1990)

Seeßlen, Georg, 'Die Banane: Ein mythologischer Bericht', in *Mauer-Show: Das Ende der DDR, die deutsche Einheit und die Medien*, ed. by Rainer Bohn, Knut Hickethier and Eggon Müller (Berlin: Sigma Bohn, 1992), pp.55-69

Simon, Annette, 'East goes West', in *Ein Text für C.W.* (Berlin: Janus, 1994), pp.186-192

Smith, Ken, *Berlin: Coming in from the Cold* (London: Penguin, 1991)

Sprink, Rolf, 'Zur Situation der neuen Verlage', *ndl*, 39 (1991), No.8, 188-191

Strasser, Johano, 'Intellektuellendämmerung? Anmerkungen zu einem Macht-kampf im deutschen Feuilleton', *ndl*, 40 (1992), No.10, 110-127

Swoboda, Jörg, *Die Revolution der Kerzen* (Wuppertal and Kassel: Oncken, 1990)

Szaruga, Leszak, 'Danach (Alles Vorbei). Die polnische Lyrik um die Wende', in *Lyriker Treffen Münster: Gedichte und Aufsätze 1987-1989-1991*, ed. by Lothar Jordan and Winfried Woesler (Bielefeld: Aisthesis, 1993), pp.543-548

Teubert, Wolfgang, 'Sprachwandel und das Ende der DDR', in *Wer spricht das wahre Deutsch? Erkundungen zur Sprache im vereinigten Deutschland?*, ed. by Ruth Reiher and Rüdiger Läzer (Berlin: Aufbau, 1993), pp.28-51

Thierse, Wolfgang, *Mit eigener Stimme sprechen* (Munich and Zurich: Piper, 1992)

Treichel, Hans-Ulrich, 'Ein Grabstein für die Zukunft', *Die Welt*, 8 October 1991, p.6

Von Leipzig nach Deutschland: Oktober '89 / Oktober '90: Zeittafel und Fotografien (Leipzig: Forum, 1991)

Wagner, Herbert, 'Die Novemberrevolution 1989 in Dresden: Ein Erlebnis-bericht', in *Ursachen und Verlauf der Deutschen Revolution 1989*, ed. by Konrad Löw (Berlin: Duncker & Humblot, 1991), pp.9-15

Wallace, Ian, 'Deutscher Literaturstreit aus britischer Sicht', *ndl*, 39 (1991), No.3, 150-155

Warneken, Bernd Jürgen, ' "Aufrechter Gang": Metamorphosen einer Parole des DDR-Umbruchs', in *Mauer-Show: Das Ende der DDR, die deutsche Einheit und die Medien*, ed. by Rainer Bohn, Knut Hickethier and Eggon Müller (Berlin: Sigma Bohn, 1992), pp.17-30

Wehdeking, Volker, *Die deutsche Einheit und die Schriftsteller: Literarische Verarbeitung der Wende seit 1989* (Stuttgart, Berlin and Cologne: Kohlhammer, 1995)

Weidenfeld, Werner, and Karl-Rudolf Korte, eds., *Handwörterbuch zur deutschen Einheit* (Frankfurt a.M. and New York: Campus, 1992)

Wilke, Manfred, 'Die bundesdeutschen Parteien und die demokratische Revolution in der DDR – oder: Die Bewährung des demokratischen Kern-staates', in *Ursachen und Verlauf der Deutschen Revolution 1989*, ed. by Konrad Löw (Berlin: Duncker & Humblot, 1991), pp.105-122

Wimmer, Micha, ed., *"Wir sind das Volk!" Die DDR im Aufbruch: Eine Chronik in Dokumenten und Bildern* (Munich: Heyne, 1990)

Wittek, Bernd, *Der Literaturstreit im sich vereinigenden Deustchland: Eine Analyse des Streits um Christa Wolf und die deutsch-deutsche Gegenwarts-literatur in Zeitungen und Zeitschriften* (Marburg: Tectum, 1997)

Wittstock, Uwe, 'Die Dichter und ihre Richter: Literaturstreit im Namen der Moral: Warum Schriftsteller aus der DDR als Sündenböcke herhalten müssen', *SZ*, 13/14 October 1990 and reprinted in *"Es geht nicht um Christa Wolf": Der Literaturstreit im vereinten Deutschland*, ed. by Thomas Anz (Munich: Spangenberg, 1991), pp.198-207

Woods, Roger, 'Civil Society, Critical Intellectuals, and Public Opinion in the new *Bundesländer*', *SGCS*, 11/12 (1993), 53-70

Zimmermann, Monica, ed., *Was macht eigentlich...? 100 DDR-Prominente heute* (Berlin: Links, 1994)

Zipser, Richard, ed., *Fragebogen Zensur: Zur Literatur vor und nach dem Ende der DDR* (Leipzig: Reclam, 1995)

e. G.D.R. LITERARY HISTORY

Primary sources

Anderson, Sascha, *Jeder Satellit hat einen Killersatelliten: Gedichte* (Berlin, FRG: Rotbuch, 1982)
-- and Elke Erb, eds., *Berührung ist nur eine Randerscheinung: Neue Literatur aus der DDR* (Cologne: Kiepenheuer & Witsch, 1985)

Auswahl 64: Neue Lyrik – Neue Namen (Berlin, GDR: Neues Leben, 1964)

Bartsch, Wilhelm, *Übungen im Joch* (Berlin, GDR, and Weimar: Aufbau, 1986)

Becher, Johannes R., *Über Literatur und Kunst* (Berlin, GDR: Aufbau, 1962)
-- *Gedichte 1949-1958, Gesammelte Werke*, vi (Berlin, GDR: Aufbau, 1973)

Bender, Hans, ed., *Was sind das für Zeiten? Deutschsprachige Gedichte der achtziger Jahre* (Frankfurt a.M.: Fischer, 1990)

Berenberg, Heinrich von, and Klaus Wagenbach, eds., *Deutsche Demokratische Reise: Ein literarischer Reiseführer durch die DDR* (Berlin, FRG: Wagenbach, 1989)

Biermann, Wolf, *Nachlaß 1* (Cologne: Kiepenheuer & Witsch, 1977)
-- *Preußischer Ikarus: Lieder/Balladen/Gedichte/Prosa* (Cologne: Kiepenheuer & Witsch, 1978)
-- *Affenfels und Barrikade: Gedichte/Lieder/Balladen* (Cologne: Kiepenheuer & Witsch, 1986)
-- *Klartexte im Getümmel: 13 Jahre im Westen: Von der Ausbürgerung bis zur November-Revolution*, ed. by Hannes Stein (Cologne: Kiepenheuer & Witsch, 1990)

Braun, Volker – see separate bibliography

Brecht, Bertolt, 'Mutter Courage und ihre Kinder, *Gesammelte Werke*, iv (Frankfurt a.M.: Suhrkamp, 1967), pp.1347-1443
-- 'Gedichte', *Gesammelte Werke*, viii, ix, x (Frankfurt a.M.: Suhrkamp, 1967)
-- 'Fünf Schwierigkeiten beim Schreiben der Wahrheit', *Gesammelte Werke*, xviii, pp.222-239

Brinkmann, Hans, *Poesiealbum 170* (Berlin, GDR: Neues Leben, 1981)

Czechowski, Heinz, *Wasserfahrt: Gedichte* (Halle: mdv, 1967)
-- *Scharfe und Sterne: Gedichte* (Halle: mdv, 1974)
-- *Was mich betrifft* (Halle-Leipzig: mdv, 1981)
-- *Kein näheres Zeichen* (Halle-Leipzig: mdv, 1987)
-- *Ich und die Folgen* (Reinbek bei Hamburg: Rowohlt, 1987)

-- *Mein Venedig: Gedichte und andere Prosa* (Berlin, FRG: Wagenbach, 1989)

Cibulka, Hanns, *Losgesprochen: Gedichte aus drei Jahrzehnten* (Leipzig: Reclam, 1986)

Deicke, Günther, *Ortsbestimmung: Ausgewählte Gedichte* (Berlin, GDR: Verlag der Nation, 1972)

Deisler, Guillermo, and Jörg Kowalski, eds., *wortBILD: Visuelle Poesie in der DDR* (Halle-Leipzig: mdv, 1990)

Döring, Stefan, *Heutmorgestern* (Berlin, GDR, and Weimar: Aufbau, 1989)
-- *Zehn* (Berlin: Galrev, 1990)

Drawert, Kurt, *Zweite Inventur* (Berlin, GDR, and Weimar: Aufbau, 1987)
-- *Privateigentum* (Frankfurt a.m.: Suhrkamp, 1989)

Drews, Jörg, ed., *Das bleibt: Deutsche Gedichte 1945-1995* (Leipzig: Reclam, 1995)

Eine Zukunft ohne Kriege: 13 Plakate für den Frieden (Berlin, GDR, and Weimar: Aufbau, 1986)

Endler, Adolf, and Karl Mickel, eds., *In diesem besseren Land: Gedichte der Deutschen Demokratischen Republik seit 1945* (Halle: mdv, 1966)
-- *Tarzan am Prenzlauer Berg: Sudelblätter 1981-1983* (Leipzig: Reclam, 1994)

Faktor, Jan, *Georgs Versuche an einem Gedicht und andere positive Texte aus den Dichtergraben des Grauens* (Berlin, GDR, and Weimar: Aufbau, 1989)

Geist, Peter, ed., *Ein Molotow-Cocktail auf fremder Bettkante: Lyrik der siebziger/achtziger Jahre von Dichtern der DDR* (Leipzig: Reclam, 1991)

Gerlach, Harald, *Mauerstücke: Gedichte* (Berlin, GDR: Aufbau, 1986)
-- *Wüstungen: Gedichte* (Berlin, GDR, and Weimar: Aufbau, 1989)

Greßmann, Uwe, *Der Vogel Frühling: Gedichte*, 2nd ed. (Halle: mdv, 1967)

Grünbein, Durs – see separate bibliography

Grüning, Uwe, *Spiegelungen: Gedichte* (Berlin, GDR: Union, 1981)

Häfner, Eberhard, *Excaliburten: Gedichte 1979-1991* (Berlin: Galrev, 1992)

Hensel, Kerstin, *Poesiealbum 222* (Berlin, GDR: Neues Leben, 1986)
-- *Stilleben mit Zukunft* (Halle-Leipzig: mdv, 1988)

Herwegh, Georg, *Werke in einem Band*, Ausgewählt und eingeleitet von Hans-Georg Werner (Berlin, GDR: Aufbau, 1967)

Hesse, Egmont, ed., *Sprache und Antwort: Stimmen und Texte einer anderen Literatur aus der DDR* (Frankfurt a.m.: Fischer, 1988)
-- and Christoph Tannert, eds., *Zellinnendruck* (Leipzig: Eigen+Art, 1990)

Heukenkamp, Ursula, Heinz Kahlau and Wulf Kirsten, eds., *Die eigene Stimme: Lyrik der DDR* (Berlin, GDR, and Weimar: Aufbau, 1988)

Hilbig, Wolfgang, *abwesenheit* (Frankfurt a.m.: Fischer, 1979)
-- *Stimme Stimme: Gedichte und Prosa* (Leipzig: Reclam, 1983)
-- *versprengung* (Frankfurt a.m.: Fischer, 1986)
-- *zwischen den paradiesen: Prosa, Lyrik*, ed. by Thorsten Ahrend (Leipzig: Reclam, 1992)

Jentzsch, Bernd, *Die alte Lust, sich aufzubäumen: Lesebuch* (Leipzig: Reclam, 1992)

Kirchner, Annerose, 'Klopstock in Langensalza', in *Ästhetik heute*, ed. by Erwin Pracht (Berlin, GDR: Dietz, 1978), p.90
-- *Mittagsstein* (Berlin, GDR, and Weimar: Aufbau, 1979)
-- *Im Maskensaal* (Berlin, GDR, and Weimar: Aufbau, 1989)

Kirsch, Rainer, 'Osymandias', *SuF*, 27 (1975), 633-636

Kirsch, Sarah, *Zaubersprüche* (Ebenhausen: Langewiesche-Brandt, 1974)

Kolbe, Uwe, *Hineingeboren: Gedichte 1975-1979* (Berlin, GDR, and Weimar: Aufbau, 1980)
-- *Abschiede und andere Liebesgedichte* (Berlin, GDR, and Weimar: Aufbau, 1983)
-- *Bornholm II: Gedichte* (Berlin, GDR, and Weimar: Aufbau, 1986)
-- Lothar Trolle and Bernd Wagner, eds., *Mikado oder Der Kaiser ist nackt: Selbstverlegte Literatur in der DDR* (Darmstadt: Luchterhand, 1988)
Kuczynski, Jürgen, *Ein linientreuer Dissident: Memoiren 1945-1989* (Berlin and Weimar: Aufbau, 1992)

Kunert, Günter, *Wegschilder und Mauerinschriften: Gedichte* (Berlin, GDR: Aufbau, 1950)
-- *Unschuld der Natur* (Berlin, GDR: Aufbau, 1966)
-- *Unterwegs nach Utopia* (Munich and Vienna: Hanser, 1977)
-- *Ein anderer K.: Hörspiel* (Stuttgart: Reclam, 1977)
-- *Verlangen nach Bomarzo: Reisegedichte* (Munich: Hanser, 1978)
-- *Abtötungsverfahren: Gedichte* (Munich and Vienna: Hanser, 1980)
-- *Stilleben: Gedichte* (Munich: Hanser, 1983)
-- *Berlin beizeiten* (Munich: Hanser, 1987)

-- ed., *Aus fremder Heimat: Zur Exilsituation heutiger Literatur* (Munich: Hanser, 1988)
-- *Schatten entziffern: Lyrik, Prosa, 1950-1994* (Leipzig: Reclam, 1995)

Kunze, Reiner, *Sensible Wege: Achtundvierzig Gedichte und ein Zyklus* (Reinbek bei Hamburg: Rowohlt, 1969)

Kutulas, Asteris, and Udo Tietz, eds., *Ausdrückliche Klage aus der inneren Immigration: Texte und Grafiken aus der DDR* (Luxemburg: Edition Phi, 1992)

Lorenc, Kito, *Struga: Bilder einer Landschaft* (Bautzen: Domowina, 1967)

Mangel, Rüdiger, Stefan Schnabel and Peter Staatsmann, eds., *DEUTSCH in einem anderen LAND: Die DDR (1949-1990) in Gedichten* (Berlin: Edition Hentrich, 1990)

Mensching, Steffen, *Poesiealbum 146* (Berlin, GDR: Neues Leben, 1979)
-- *Erinnerung an eine Milchglasscheibe: Gedichte* (Halle-Leipzig: mdv, 1984)
-- 'Traumhafter Ausflug mit Rosa L.' and 'Lied für meine Freunde', in *Poetenseminare 1970-1984* (Berlin, GDR: Neues Leben, 1985), pp.49-50 and p.55
-- *Tuchfühlung: Gedichte* (Halle-Leipzig: mdv, 1986)

Michael, Klaus, and Thomas Wohlfahrt, eds., *Vogel oder Käfig sein: Kunst und Literatur aus unabhängigen Zeitschriften in der DDR 1979-1989* (Berlin: Galrev, 1992)

Mickel, Karl, *Gelehrtenrepublik: Aufsätze und Studien, Essay* (Halle: mdv, 1976) and republished (Leipzig: Reclam, 1990)

Müller, Heiner, 'Die Hamletmaschine', in *Mauser* (Berlin, FRG: Rotbuch, 1978), pp.89-97
-- *Rotwelsch* (Berlin, FRG: Merve, 1982)
-- *Krieg ohne Schlacht: Leben in zwei Diktaturen* (Cologne: Kiepenheuer & Witsch, 1992)

Oehme, Dorothea, ed., *Fluchtfreuden Bierdurst: Letzte Gedichte aus der DDR* (Berlin: UVA, 1990)

Pankoke, Helga, and Wolfgang Trampe, eds., *Selbstbildnis zwei Uhr nachts: Gedichte: Eine Anthologie* (Berlin, GDR, and Weimar: Aufbau, 1989)

Papenfuß, Bert, [also publishing as Bert Papenfuß-Gorek – see below], *Gesammelte Texte*, i, ii, iii, v (Berlin: Janus, 1993-1996)

Papenfuß-Gorek, Bert, *dreizehntanz: Gedichte* (Berlin, GDR, and Weimar: Aufbau, 1989)

Pech, Kristian, *Abschweifungen über Bäume* (Rostock: Hinstorff, 1976)

Poetenseminare 1970-1984, Poesiealbum Sonderheft (Berlin, GDR: Neues Leben, 1985)

Samoilow, David, *Poesiealbum 145* (Berlin, GDR: Neues Leben, 1984)

Schedlinski, Rainer, *die rationen des ja und des nein: Gedichte* (Berlin, GDR, and Weimar: Aufbau, 1988)

Schmidt, Kathrin, *Ein Engel fliegt durch die Tapetenfabrik: Gedichte* (Berlin, GDR: Neues Leben, 1987)

Teschke, Holger, *Bäume am Hochufer* (Berlin, GDR, and Weimar: Aufbau, 1985)

Törne, Dorothea von, ed., *Vogelbühne: Gedichte im Dialog* (Berlin, GDR: Verlag der Nation, 1984)

Wolf, Christa and Gerhard, eds., *Wir, unsere Zeit: Gedichte aus zehn Jahren* (Berlin, GDR: Aufbau, 1959)

Wüstefeld, Michael, *Heimsuchung: Gedichte* (Berlin, GDR, and Weimar: Aufbau, 1987)
-- *Stadtplan: Gedichte* (Berlin and Weimar: Aufbau, 1990)
-- *Nackt hinter der Schutzmaske: Erinnerungen* (Berlin and Weimar: Aufbau, 1990)

Secondary sources

Abusch, Alexander, 'Hölderlins poetischer Traum einer neuen Menschengemeinschft', *WB*, 15 (1970), No.7, 10-26

Adel, Kurt, *Die Literatur der DDR: Ein Wintermärchen?* (Vienna: Braunmüller, 1992)

Adorno, Theodor, 'Rede über Lyrik und Gesellschaft', *Noten zur Literatur*, i (Frankfurt a.M.: Suhrkamp, 1958), pp.73-104

Aesthetics and Politics: Ernst Bloch, Georg Lukács, Bertolt Brecht, Theodor Adorno, trans. ed. Ronald Taylor (London: Verso, 1980)

Ahrend, Thomas, 'Was ging uns die DDR-Kulturpolitik an? Biographische Notizen eines "Hineingeborenen" ', *Aus Politik und Zeitgeschichte*, 11 March 1994, pp.23-29

Ahrends, Martin, 'The Great Waiting, or The Freedom of the East: An Obituary for Life in Sleeping Beauty's Castle', in *When the Wall came down: Reactions to German Unification*, ed. by Harold James and Marla Stone (London and New York: Routledge, 1992), pp.157-164

Arnold, Heinz Ludwig, ed., *Die andere Sprache: Neue DDR-Literatur der 80er Jahre* (Munich: TuK, 1990)
-- ed., *Literatur in der DDR: Rückblicke* (Munich: TuK, 1991)

Ballusak, Lothar von, ed., *Dichter im Dienst: Der sozialistische Realismus in der deutschen Literatur* (Wiesbaden: Limes, 1956)

Barck, Simone, Martina Langermann and Siegfried Lokatis, eds., *"Jedes Buch ein Abenteuer": Zensur-System und literarische Öffentlichkeit in der DDR bis Ende der sechziger Jahre* (Berlin: Akademie, 1997)
-- 'Ein Genre wird öffentlich', in *"Jedes Buch ein Abenteuer": Zensur-System und literarische Öffentlichkeit in der DDR bis Ende der sechziger Jahre*, ed. by Simone Barck, Martina Langermann and Siegfried Lokatis (Berlin: Akademie, 1997), pp.286-317

Barthomes, Herbert, *Das Wort "Volk" im Sprachgebrauch der SED* (Düsseldorf: Pädagogischer Verlag Schwann, 1964)

Bathrick, David, *The Powers of Speech: The Politics of Culture in the GDR* (Lincoln and London: University of Nebraska, 1995)

Baumann, Christiane, 'Anthologien erforschen? Versuch über Spezifik und Geschichte von Anthologien zur DDR-Literatur', *WB*, 35 (1989), 618-636

Bender, Peter, *Unsere Erbschaft: Was war die DDR – was bleibt von ihr?* (Hamburg and Zurich: Luchterhand, 1992)

Berendse, Gerrit-Jan, *Die "Sächsische Dichterschule": Lyrik in der DDR in den sechziger und siebziger Jahre* (Frankfurt a.M.: Lang, 1990)
-- 'Outcast in Berlin: Opposition durch Entziehung bei der jüngeren Generation', *ZfG*, N.F. 1 (1991), 21-27

Bloch, Ernst, *Das Prinzip Hoffnung: in fünf Teilen* (Frankfurt a.M.: Suhrkamp, 1959)

Bormann, Alexander von, 'Wege aus der Ordnung', in *Jenseits der Staats-kultur: Traditionen autonomer Kunst in der DDR*, ed. by Gabriele Muschter and Rüdiger Thomas (Munich: Hanser, 1992), pp.83-107
-- ' "Wir lachen sie kaputt": Subversion und Utopie in der DDR-Lyrik, mit besonderem Hinweis auf Thomas Rosenlöcher', *Wespennest* (1991), No.82, 33-40

Böthig, Peter, 'Aufbrüche in die Vielfalt' (1988), in *Zellinnendruck*, ed. by Egmont Hesse and Christoph Tannert (Leipzig: Eigen+Art, 1990), pp.9-10
-- 'Und, undsoweiter, undsofort ...: Bibliophile Zeitschriftenprojekte und Siebdruckbücher', *Marginalien*, (1990), No.120, 53-60
-- 'die verlassene sprache', in *Die andere Sprache: Neue DDR-Literatur der 80er Jahre*, ed. by Heinz Ludwig Arnold (Munich: TuK, 1990), pp.38-48

-- 'Grammatische Experimente: Selbstverlegte Literarisch-Originalgrafische Editionen in der DDR', in *NON KON FORM: Künstlerbücher, Text-Grafik-Mappen und autonome Zeitschriften der DDR 1979-1989 aus der Sammlung der Sächsischen Landesbibliothek, Dresden*, ed. by Renate Damsch-Wiehager, Knut Nievers and Helgard Sauer (Kiel: Kulturamt / Stadtgalerie and Esslingen: Galerie der Stadt, 1992), pp.26-31

-- 'über den prenzlauer berg und andere', in *Tendenz Freisprache: Texte zu einer Poetik der 80er Jahre*, ed. by Ulrich Janetzki and Wolfgang Rath (Frankfurt a.m.: Suhrkamp, 1992), pp.248-257

-- and Klaus Michael, *MachtSpiele: Literatur und Staatssicherheit im Fokus Prenzlauer Berg* (Leipzig: Reclam, 1993)

Brady, Philip, 'Prenzlauer Berg – Enklave? Schrebergarten? Powerhouse?', *GM*, 35 (1995), 1-17

-- ' "Wir hausen in Prenzlauer Berg" On the very last generation of GDR poets', in *1870/1871 - 1989/90 German Unifications and the Change of Literary Discourse*, ed. by Walter Pape (Berlin and New York: de Gruyter, 1993), pp.278-301

Braun, Matthias, 'Führungsoffiziere, Operative Vorgänge, Inoffizielle Mitarbeiter – der Einfluß des MfS auf die Literatur- und Kunstentwicklung in der DDR', in *Stasi, KGB und Literatur: Beiträge und Erfahrungen aus Rußland und Deutschland*, ed. by Heinrich-Böll-Stiftung (Cologne: Heinrich-Böll-Stiftung, 1993), pp. 60-96

Braun, Michael, and Hans Thill, eds., *Punktzeit: Deutschsprachige Lyrik der achtziger Jahre* (Heidelberg: Wunderhorn, 1987)
-- 'Poesie in Bewegung: Kleine Abschweifung über Sprachbesessenheit in der jüngsten Lyriker-Generation', *Manuskripte*, 30 (1990), No.108, 69-72

Braune-Steininger, Wolfgang, 'Das Fremde im Eigenen: Zur lyrischen Biographie der achtziger Jahre', in *Lyriker Treffen Münster: Gedichte und Aufsätze 1987-1989-1991*, ed. by Lothar Jordan and Winfried Woesler (Bielefeld: Aisthesis, 1993), pp.250-271

Brettschneider, Werner, *Zwischen literarischer Autonomie und Staatsdienst: Die Literatur in der DDR* ([Berlin, FRG]: Schmidt, [1972])

Brie, Michael, 'The Difficulty of Discussing the GDR', trans. by Christopher Upward, *SGCS*, 13 (1994), 1-23

Büscher, Wolfgang, Peter Wensierski and Klaus Wolschner, eds., *Friedensbewegung in der DDR* (Hattingen: Scandia, 1982)

Bundesbeauftragter für Unterlagen des Staatssicherheitsdienstes der ehemaligen Deutschen Demokratischen Republik, *Die Inoffiziellen Mitarbeiter: Richtlinien, Befehle, Direktiven* (Berlin: Der Bundesbeauftragte für Unterlagen des Staatssicherheitsdienstes der ehemaligen Deutschen Demokratischen Republik, 1992)

Cerny, Jochen, ed., *Wer war wer, DDR: ein biographisches Lexikon* (Berlin: Links, 1992)

Cosentino, Christine, 'Gedanken zur jüngsten DDR-Lyrik: Uwe Kolbe, Sascha Anderson und Lutz Rathenow', *GR*, 60 (1985), 82-90
-- *"Ein Spiegel mit mir darin": Sarah Kirschs Lyrik* (Tübingen: Francke, 1990)
-- and Wolfgang Müller, eds., *"im widerstand / in mißverstand"? Zur Literatur und Kunst des Prenzlauer Bergs* (New York, Washington DC, San Francisco, Bern, Frankfurt a.M., Berlin, Vienna, Paris: Lang, 1995)

Dahlke, Birgit, ' "Die Chancen haben sich verschanzt": Die inoffizielle DDR-Literatur-Szene der DDR', in *Mauer-Show: Das Ende der DDR, die deutsche Einheit und die Medien*, ed. by Rainer Bohn, Knut Hickethier and Eggon Müller (Berlin: Sigma Bohn, 1992), pp.227-242
-- ' "Im Brunnen vor dem Tor": Autorinnen in inoffiziellen Zeitschriften der DDR 1979-90', in *Neue Generation – Neues Erzählen: Deutsche Prosa-Literatur der achtziger Jahre*, ed. by Walter Delabar, Werner Jung and Ingrid Pergande (Opladen: Westdeutscher Verlag, 1993), pp.177-193
-- *Papierboot: Autorinnen aus der DDR – inoffiziell publiziert* (Würzberg: Konigshausen und Neumann, 1997)
-- ' "Temporäre autonome Zone": Mythos und Alltag der inoffiziell publizierenden Literaturszene im letzten Jahrzehnt der DDR', in *Literatur in der Diktatur: Schreiben im Nationalsozialismus und DDR-Sozialismus*, ed. by Günther Rüther (Paderborn, Munich, Vienna and Zurich: Schönigh, 1997), pp.463-478

Dahn, Daniela, *Kunst und Kohle: Die "Szene" am Prenzlauer Berg Berlin, DDR* (Darmstadt and Neuwied: Luchterhand, 1987)

Damsch-Wiehager, Renate, Knut Nievers and Helgard Sauer, *NON KON FORM: Künstlerbücher, Text-Grafik-Mappen und autonome Zeitschriften der DDR 1979-1989 aus der Sammlung der Sächsischen Landesbibliothek, Dresden* (Kiel: Kulturamt / Stadtgalerie and Esslingen: Galerie der Stadt, 1992)

DDR-Lyrik im Kontext, Amsterdamer Beiträge zur neueren Germanistik, 26 (1988)

DDR-Schriftsteller sprechen in der Zeit. Eine Dokumentation, GM, 27 (1991)

Deiritz, Karl, 'Zur Klärung des Sachverhalts – Literatur und Staatssicherheit', in *Verrat an der Kunst? Rückblicke auf die DDR-Literatur*, ed. by Karl Deiritz and Hannes Krauss (Berlin: Aufbau, 1993), pp.11-17
-- and Hannes Krauss, eds., *Verrat an der Kunst? Rückblicke auf die DDR-Literatur* (Berlin: Aufbau, 1993)

Deppe, Jürgen, 'Literaturinstitut Johannes R. Becher', in *Literatur in der DDR: Rückblicke*, ed. by Heinz Ludwig Arnold (Munich: TuK, 1991), pp.63-71

Drescher, Horst, *Aus dem Zirkus Leben: Notizen 1969-1990* (Berlin and Weimar: Aufbau, 1990)

Durzak, Manfred, and Helmut Steinecke, eds., *Günter Kunert: Beiträge zu seinem Werk* (Munich and Vienna: Hanser, 1992)

Ecker, Hans-Peter, 'Weltwandel oder Brillenwechsel? und dann sind da noch die kids von Prenzlauer Berg (Bemerkungen zur aktuellen DDR-Literatur)', *Passauer Pegasus*, 8 (1990), No.15, 56-62

Emmerich, Wolfgang, *Die andere deutsche Literatur: Aufsätze zur Literatur aus der DDR* (Opladen: Westdeutscher Verlag, 1994)
-- *Kleine Literaturgeschichte der DDR*, rev. edn. (Leipzig: Kiepenheuer, 1996)

Erb, Elke, 'Dichter und Denunziant', in *Stasi, KGB und Literatur: Beiträge und Erfahrungen aus Rußland und Deutschland*, ed. by Heinrich-Böll-Stiftung (Cologne: Heinrich-Böll-Stiftung, 1993), pp.185-195

Erbe, Günter, 'Zum Selbstverständnis junger DDR-Lyriker', *SGCS*, 4 (1984), 171-185
-- *Die verfemte Moderne: Die Auseinandersetzung mit dem "Modernismus" in Kulturpolitik, Literaturwissenschaft und Literatur der DDR* (Opladen: Westdeutscher Verlag, 1993)

Faktor, Jan, 'Diese 80er gingen zwei Jahre früher zu Ende: Über die inoffizielle Literatur der DDR in den achtziger Jahren', *Wespennest* (1990), No.78, 21-25
-- 'Was ist neu an der jungen Literatur der 80er Jahre?', in *Vogel oder Käfig sein: Kunst und Literatur aus unabhängigen Zeitschriften in der DDR 1979-1989*, ed. by Klaus Michael and Thomas Wohlfahrt (Berlin: Galrev, 1992), p.367
-- 'Realität von nebenan: Der besondere Stand der jungen, linken DDR-Intellektuellen im ehemaligen Ostblock', in *Über Deutschland: Schriftsteller geben Auskunft*, ed. by Thomas Rietzschel (Leipzig: Reclam, 1993), pp.72-81
-- 'Intellektuelle Opposition und alternative Kultur in der DDR', *Aus Politik und Zeitgeschichte*, 11 March 1994, pp.30-37

Fehervary, Helen, 'The Literature of the German Democratic Republic (1945-1990)', in *The Cambridge History of German Literature*, ed. by Helen Watanabe-O'Kelly (Cambridge: CUP, 1997), pp.393-439

Fischer, Gerhard, ed., *Heiner Müller: ConTEXTS and HISTORY: A Collection of Essays from the Sydney German Studies Symposium 1994* (Tübingen: Stauffenburg, 1995)

Flores, John, *Poetry in East Germany: Adjustments, Visions and Provocations 1945-1970* (New Haven and London: Yale Universtity Press, 1971)

Forschungsstelle Osteuropa, ed., *Eigenart und Eigensinn. Alternative Kulturszenen in der DDR (1980-1990)* (Bremen: Edition Temmen, 1993)

Fuchs, Jürgen, *"...und wann kommt der Hammer?" Psychologie, Opposition und Staatssicherheit* (Berlin: BasisDruck, 1990)

Fulbrook, Mary, *The two Germanies 1945-1990: Problems of Interpretation* (Basingstoke and London: Macmillan, 1992)
-- *Anatomy of a Dictatorship: Inside the GDR 1949-1989* (Oxford and New York: OUP, 1995)

Gansel, Carsten, *Parlament des Geistes: Literatur zwischen Hoffnung und Repression 1945-1961* (Berlin: BasisDruck, 1996)

Gaskill, Howard, Karin McPherson and Andrew Barker, eds., *Neue Ansichten: The Reception of Romanticism in the literature of the GDR*, GDR Monitor Special Series (Amsterdam: Rodopi, 1990)

Gauck, Joachim, *Die Stasi-Akten: Das unheimliche Erbe der DDR* (Reinbek bei Hamburg: Rowohlt, 1991)

Gaus, Günter, *Wo Deutschland liegt. Eine Ortsbestimmung* (Hamburg: Hoffmann und Campe, 1983)

Geist, Peter, 'Die Schatten werfen ihre Ereignisse voraus: Nachsichtendes zur Lyrik aus der DDR', *GM*, 33 (1994), 129-151

Gill, David, and Ulrich Schröter, *Das Ministerium für Staatssicherheit: Anatomie des Mielke-Imperiums* (Berlin: Rowohlt, 1991)

Grant, Colin B., *Literary Communication from Consensus to Rupture: Practice and Theory in Honecker's GDR* (Amsterdam and Atlanta: Rodopi, 1995)

Graves, Peter J., *Three Contemporary German Poets: Wolf Biermann, Sarah Kirsch, Reiner Kunze* (Leicester: Leicester University Press, 1985)

Greiner, Bernhard, *Literatur der DDR in neuer Sicht: Studien und Interpretationen* (Frankfurt a.M.: Lang, 1986)

Groth, Joachim-Rudiger, and Karin Groth, *Materialien zu Literatur im Widerspruch: Gedichte und Prosa aus 40 Jahre DDR: Kulturpolitischer Überblick und Interpretationen* (Cologne: Wissenschaft und Politik, 1993)

Grunenberg, Antonia, 'Entgrenzung und Selbstbeschränkung: Zur Literatur der DDR in den achtziger Jahren', in *Liebes- und andere Erklärungen: Texte von und über DDR-Autorinnen*, ed. by Christel Hildebrandt (Bonn: Kleine Schritte, 1988), pp.137-156

-- *Aufbruch der inneren Mauer: Politik und Kultur in der DDR 1971-1990* (Bremen: Edition Temmen, 1990)
-- ' "Vogel oder Käfig": Zur zweiten Kultur und zu den inoffiziellen Zeitschriften der DDR', in *Eigenart und Eigensinn. Alternative Kulturszenen in der DDR (1980-1990)*, ed. by Forschungsstelle Osteuropa (Bremen: Edition Temmen, 1993), pp.75-92

Gumpel, Liselotte, *Concrete poetry from East and West Germany: The Language of Exemplarism and Experimentalism* (New Haven: Yale University Press, 1976)

Günther, Heinz, *Wie Spione gemacht wurden* (Berlin: Aufbau, [1992])

Günther, Thomas, 'Derwisch & Co. oder: Die Klammer der Staatssicherheit', in *NON KON FORM: Künstlerbücher, Text-Grafik-Mappen und autonome Zeitschriften der DDR 1979-1989 aus der Sammlung der Sächsischen Landesbibliothek, Dresden*, ed. by Renate Damsch-Wiehager, Knut Nievers and Helgard Sauer (Kiel: Kulturamt / Stadtgalerie and Esslingen: Galerie der Stadt, 1992), pp. 32-36

Hähnel, Ingrid, ed., *Lyriker im Zwiegespräch: Traditionsbeziehungen im Gedicht* (Berlin, GDR, and Weimar: Aufbau, 1981)

Hartinger, Walfried and Christel, and Peter Geist, ' "Eine eigene Sprache finden": Gespräch mit den Lyrikern Thomas Böhme, Kurt Drawert, Kerstin Hensel, Dieter Kerschak, Bert Papenfuß-Gorek und Kathrin Schmidt', *WB*, 36 (1990), 580-616

Hartmann, Anneli, 'Neuere Tendenzen in der DDR-Lyrik', *deutsche studien*, 22 (1984), 5-29
-- 'Der Generationswechsel – ein ästhetischer Wechsel? Schreibweisen und Traditionsbezüge in der jüngsten DDR-Lyrik', *Jahrbuch zur Literatur in der DDR*, 4 (1985), 109-134
-- 'Schreiben in der Tradition der Avantgarde: Neue Lyrik in der DDR', *Amsterdamer Beiträge zur neueren Germanistik*, 26 (1988), 1-37

Haus, Heinz-Uwe, 'Brecht in Post-Wall Germany', in *Brecht Unbound*, ed. by James K. Lyon and Hans-Peter Breuer (Newark: University of Delaware Press, 1995), pp.89-97

Heinrich-Böll-Stiftung, ed., *Stasi, KGB und Literatur: Beiträge und Erfahrungen aus Rußland und Deutschland* (Cologne: Heinrich-Böll-Stiftung, 1993)

Heising, Bärbel, *"Briefe voller Zitate aus dem Vergessen": Intertextualität im Werk Wolfgang Hilbigs* (Frankfurt a.M.: Lang, 1996)

Henkel, Jens, and Sabine Russ, *D1980D1989R: Künstlerbücher und Originalgrafische Zeitschriften im Eigenverlag. Eine Bibliografie* (Gifkendorf: Merlin, 1991)

Henrich, Rolf, *Der vormundschaftliche Staat: Vom Versagen des real existierenden Sozialismus* (Reinbek bei Hamburg: Rowohlt, 1989)

Herminghouse, Patricia, 'New Contexts for GDR Literature: An American Perspective', in *Cultural Transformations in the New Germany: American and German Perspectives*, ed. by Friederike Eigler and Peter C. Pfeiffer (Columbia, South Carolina: Camden House, 1993), pp.93-101

Herzinger, Richard, and Heinz-Peter Preußer, 'Vom Äußersten zum Ersten: DDR-Literatur in der Tradition deutscher Zivilisationskritik', in *Literatur in der DDR: Rückblicke*, ed. by Heinz Ludwig Arnold (Munich: TuK, 1991), pp.195-209

Hesse, Egmont, and Christoph Tannert, eds., *Zellinnendruck* (Leipzig: Eigen+Art, 1990)

Heukenkamp, Ursula, 'Ohne den Leser geht es nicht: Gespräch mit Gerd Adloff, Gabriele Eckart, Uwe Kolbe, Bernd Wagner', *WB*, 25 (1979), No.7, 41-52

Hinderer, Walter, ' "Schaffen heißt: seinem Schicksal Gestalt geben": Apokalyptische Aspekte in Günter Kunerts Gedichtsammlungen *Unterwegs nach Utopia*, *Abtötungsverfahren*, *Stilleben* and *Fremd daheim*', in *Günter Kunert: Beiträge zu seinem Werk*, ed. by Manfred Durzak and Helmut Steinecke (Munich and Vienna: Hanser, 1992), pp.22-39

Hirdina, Karin, 'Debatten um Politik und Kunst', in *Literatur in der DDR: Rückblicke*, ed. by Heinz Ludwig Arnold (Munich: TuK, 1991), pp.85-92

Hofacker, Erich P., 'Faltering Steps: Günter Kunert's "Unterwegs nach Utopia"', *GR*, 57 (1982), 1-8
-- 'Günter Kunert and Socialism: A "Classic Experiment" in New Perspective', *GR*, 61 (1986), 65-71

Hörnigk, Frank, ' "Kein Verlaß auf die Literatur?" – "Kein Verlaß auf die Literatur!": Fünf Sätze zum Werk Heiner Müllers', in *Literatur in der Diktatur: Schreiben im Nationalsozialismus und DDR-Sozialismus*, ed. by Günther Rüther (Paderborn, Munich, Vienna and Zurich: Schönigh, 1997), pp.445-462

Jaekel, Ursula, '40 Jahre Staatssicherheit - Ziele, Tätigkeit, Auswirkungen', in *Ursachen und Verlauf der Deutschen Revolution 1989*, ed. by Konrad Löw (Berlin: Duncker & Humblot, 1991), pp.141-158

Jäger, Manfred, ' "Wem schreibe ich?" Adressen und Botschaften in Gedichten jüngerer Autoren aus der DDR seit dem Beginn der achtziger Jahre', in *Die andere Sprache: Neue DDR-Literatur der 80er Jahre*, ed. by Heinz Ludwig Arnold (Munich: TuK, 1990), pp.61-71
-- *Sozialliteraten: Funktion und Selbstverständnis der Schriftsteller in der DDR* (Düsseldorf: Bertelsmann, 1993)
-- 'Schriftstellers Unsicherheit und Staates Sicherheit: Bemerkungen über eine Mesalliance zwischen Geist und Macht', in *MachtSpiele: Literatur und Staatssicherheit*

im Fokus Prenzlauer Berg, ed. by Peter Böthig and Klaus Michael (Leipzig: Reclam, 1993), pp.37-43
-- *Kultur und Politik in der DDR 1945-1990* (Cologne: Edition Deutschland Archiv, 1995)

Janetzki, Ulrich, and Wolfgang Rath, eds., *Tendenz Freisprache: Texte zu einer Poetik der 80er Jahre* (Frankfurt a.m.: Suhrkamp, 1992)

Jarmatz, Klaus, *Wirklichkeit und Poesie* (Halle-Leipzig: mdv, 1989)

Keith-Smith, Brian, 'Little Magazines from the former German Democratic Republic: A Survey', *GM*, 26 (1992), 65-93

Kerschek, Dieter, 'Wer schreibt wie das aus uns geworden ist', *Temperamente* (1988), No.2, 154-156

Keune, Manfred E., 'Fremd und daheim: Gedanken zur Ortsbestimmung und lyrischen Kommunikation in Günter Kunerts Gedicht "Biographie"', in *Günter Kunert: Beiträge zu seinem Werk*, ed. by Manfred Durzak and Helmut Steinecke (Munich and Vienna: Hanser, 1992), pp.85-101

Klotz, Volker, 'Was war anders, besser? Rückblick auf Eigenarten der DDR-Kultur', *SuF*, 43 (1991), 322-332

Koch, Hans, ed., *Zur Theorie des sozialistischen Realismus* (Berlin, GDR: Dietz, 1974)

Krätzer, Jürgen, ' "sprachgeflacker in den schläfen der selbstsucht": Zwischen den Paradisen', *die horen*, 37 (1992), 233-236

Kunert, Günter, *Vor der Sintflut: Das Gedicht als Arche Noah: Frankfurter Vorlesungen* (Munich and Vienna: Hanser, 1985)

Labroisse, Gerd, 'Neue Positionen in der DDR-Lyrik der 80er Jahre?', in *The GDR in the 1980s*, ed. by Ian Wallace (Dundee: GDR Monitor, 1984), pp.101-119

Leeder, Karen, 'Towards a Profane Hölderlin: Representations and Revisions of Hölderlin in some GDR Poetry', in *Neue Ansichten: The Reception of Romanticism in the Literature of the GDR*, ed. by Howard Gaskill, Karin McPherson and Andrew Barker (Amsterdam: Rodopi, 1990), pp.212-231
-- ' "ich fühle mich in grenzen wohl": The Metaphors of Boundary and the Boundaries of Metaphor in Prenzlauer Berg', *GM*, 35 (1995), pp.19-44
-- 'Hineingeboren: A New Generation of Poets in the German Democratic Republic (1979-1989)' (D. Phil. thesis, Oxford, 1993)
-- *Breaking Boundaries: A New Generation of Poets in the GDR* (Oxford: Clarendon, 1996)

Lewis, Derek, *The GDR: A background to East German studies* (Scotland: Lochee, 1988)

Links, Roland, 'Literatur als Lebenswelt: Frühe Erfahrungen eines späteren Verlegers in der DDR', *Aus Politik und Zeitgeschichte*, 11 March 1994, pp.3-11

Lübbe, Peter, ed., *Dokumente zur Kunst-, Literatur- und Kulturpolitik der SED 1975-1980* (Stuttgart: Seewald, 1984)

Maaz, Hans-Joachim, *Der Gefühlsstau: Ein Psychogramm der DDR* (Berlin: Argon, 1991)

Mann, Ekkehard, *Untergrund, autonome Literatur und das Ende der DDR: Eine systemtheoretische Analyse* (Frankfurt a.M., Berlin, Bern, New York, Paris and Vienna: Lang, 1996)

Matt, Peter von, 'Günter Kunert: denkende Dichter', in *Günter Kunert: Beiträge zu seinem Werk*, ed. by Manfred Durzak and Helmut Steinecke (Munich and Vienna: Hanser, 1992) , pp.14-21

Mayer, Hans, *Der Turm von Babel: Erinnerung an eine Deutsche Demokratische Republik* (Frankfurt a.M.: Suhrkamp, 1991)

McElvoy, Anne, *The Saddled Cow: East Germany's Life and Legacy* (London: Faber and Faber, 1992)

Mechtenberg, Theo, 'Existenz und Sprache: Ulrich Schacht und sein erster Lyrikband "Traumgefahr"', *deutsche studien*, 22 (1984), 30-42
-- 'Von Odysseus bis Sisyphos: Zur Rezeption und Brechung mythischer Gestalten in der DDR-Lyrik', *Deutschland Archiv*, 18 (1985), 497-506
-- 'Thomas Rosenlöcher: Ein Dichter, dem "das Wenige viel und das Geringe groß ist"', in *Im Dialog mit der interkulturellen Germanistik*, ed. by Hans-Christoph Graf von Nayhauss and Krzysztof A. Kuczynski (Wroclaw: Universität, 1993), pp.401-411

Michael, Klaus, 'Samisdat-Literatur in der DDR und der Einfluß der Staatssicherheit', in *Stasi, KGB und Literatur: Beiträge und Erfahrungen aus Rußland und Deutschland*, ed. by Heinrich-Böll-Stiftung (Cologne: Heinrich-Böll-Stiftung, 1993), pp. 158-177

Mohr, Heinrich, 'Der 17. Juni 1953 als Thema der Literatur in der DDR', in *17. Juni 1953: Arbeiteraufstand in der DDR*, ed. by Ilse Spittmann and Karl Wilhelm Fricke (Cologne: Edition Deutschland Archiv, 1982), pp.87-111
-- 'Mein Blick auf die Literatur in der DDR', *Aus Politik und Zeitgeschichte*, 11 March 1994, pp.12-22

Muschter, Gabriele, and Rüdiger Thomas, eds., *Jenseits der Staatskultur: Traditionen autonomer Kunst in der DDR* (Munich: Hanser, 1992)

Neis, Edgar, *Politisch-soziale Zeitgedichte* (Hollfeld: Bange, 1983)

Oschlies, Wolf, *Würgende und wirkende Wörter: Deutschsprechen in der DDR* (Berlin, FRG: Gbr. Holzapfel, 1989)

Packalen, Sture, *Zum Hölderlinbild in der Bundesrepublik und der DDR*, Studia Germanistica Upsaliensia, 28 (Uppsala, Sweden: Acta Universitatis Upsaliensis, 1986)

Pergande, Ingrid, ' "Volker Braun? Da kann ich nur sagen, der Junge quält sich..." New Voices in the GDR Lyric of the 1980s', in *Socialism and the Literary Imagination: Essays on East German Writers*, ed. by Martin Kane (New York and Oxford: Berg, 1991), pp.229-246

Pietraß, Richard, 'Lyrisch Roulette: Zensur als Erfahrung', in *"Literaturentwicklungsprozesse": Die Zensur der Literatur in der DDR*, ed. by Ernest Wichner and Herbert Wiesner (Frankfurt a.M.: Suhrkamp, 1993), pp.178-198

Pischel, Joseph, *Zur theoretischen Selbstverständigung der DDR-Schriftsteller in den sechziger und siebziger Jahren* (Rostock: Wilhelm-Pieck-Universität, 1978)

Prenzlauer Berg: Bohemia in East Berlin?, *GM*, 35 (1995)

Reich, Jens, *Abschied von den Lebenslügen: Die Intelligenz und die Macht* (Berlin: Rowohlt, 1992)

Reimann, Brigitte, *Ankunft in Alltag* (Berlin, GDR: Neues Leben, 1961)

Retrospect and Review: Aspects of the Literature of the GDR 1976-1990, *GM*, 40 (1997)

Riedel, Nicolai, 'Michael Wüstefeld: Stadtplan', *Passauer Pegasus*, 8 (1990), No.16, 106-109

Riedel, Volker, 'Gedanken zum Verhältnis von Germanistik und Altertumswissenschaft, dargestellt an Hand der Antike-Rezeption in der Literatur der DDR', *Antikerezeption, Antikeverhältnis, Antikebegegnung in Vergangenheit und Gegenwart: Eine Aufsatzsammlung*, iii (Stendal: Winckelmann Gesellschaft, 1983), pp.783-810

Rundell, Richard J., 'The Brechtian Influence and DDR Poetry of Political Criticism', in *Bertolt Brecht: Political Theory and Literary Practice*, ed. by Betty Nance Weber and Hubert Heinen (Manchester: MUP, 1980), pp.147-158

Ruß, Gisela, ed., *Dokumente zur Kunst-, Literatur- und Kulturpolitik der SED 1971-1974* (Stuttgart: Seewald, 1976)

Rüther, Günther, *'Greif zur Feder, Kumpel': Schriftsteller, Literatur und Politik in der DDR 1949-1990* (Düsseldorf: Droste, 1991)
-- *Literatur in der Diktatur: Schreiben im Nationalsozialismus und DDR-Sozialismus* (Paderborn, Munich, Vienna and Zurich: Schönigh, 1997)

Sang, Jürgen, 'Heiner Müller: A Lyric Poet? The Dialectic Process of Aesthetic Self-Recognition', in *Heiner Müller: ConTEXTS and HISTORY: A Collection of Essays from the Sydney German Studies Symposium 1994*, ed. by Gerhard Fischer (Tübingen: Stauffenburg, 1995), pp.259-269

Sauer, Helgard, 'Nonkonforme Kunst – illegale Bücher in der DDR', in *NON KON FORM: Künstlerbücher, Text-Grafik-Mappen und autonome Zeitschriften der DDR 1979-1989 aus der Sammlung der Sächsischen Landesbibliothek, Dresden*, ed. by Renate Damsch-Wiehager, Knut Nievers and Helgard Sauer (Kiel: Kulturamt / Stadtgalerie and Esslingen: Galerie der Stadt, 1992), pp. 9-24

Schedlinski, Rainer, *Innenansichten DDR: Letzte Bilder*, Fotos von Jonas Maron (Reinbek bei Hamburg: Rowohlt, 1990)

Schlenker, Wolfram, *Das kulturelle Erbe in der DDR: Gesellschaftliche Entwicklung und Kulturpolitik 1945-1965* (Stuttgart: Metzler, 1977)

Schlenstedt, Dieter, 'Entwicklungslinien der neueren Literatur in der DDR', *Positionen 5: Wortmeldungen zur DDR-Literatur*, ed. by Hinnerk Einhorn and Eberhard Günther (Halle-Leipzig: mdv, 1989), pp.7-39
-- 'Der aus dem Ruder laufende Schriftstellerkongreß von 1987', *GM*, 40 (1997), 16-31

Schlenstedt, Silvia, 'Fragen der Nachgeborenen', *SGCS*, 9 (1989), 85-99
-- 'Beobachtungen an neuen Gedichtbänden in der DDR', in *Positionen 5: Wortmeldungen zur DDR-Literatur*, ed. by Hinnerk Einhorn and Eberhard Günther (Halle-Leipzig: mdv, 1989), pp.141-153

Schmidt, Claudia, *Rückzüge und Aufbrüche: Zur DDR-Literatur in der Gorbatschow-Ära* (Frankfurt a.M., Berlin, Bern, New York, Paris, Vienna: Lang, 1995)

Schmidt, Ulrich, 'Abschied von der "Literaturgesellschaft"? Anmerkungen zu einem Begriff', in *Literatur in der DDR: Rückblicke*, ed. by Heinz Ludwig Arnold (Munich: TuK, 1991), pp.45-52

Schubbe, Elimar, ed., *Dokumente zur Kunst-, Literatur- und Kulturpolitik der SED 1946-1970* (Stuttgart: Seewald, [1972])

Schwarz-Scherer, Marianne, *Subjektivität in der Naturlyrik der DDR (1950-1970)* (Frankfurt a.M.: Lang, 1992)

Segebrecht, Wulf, 'Gedichte über die Mauer. Wie Lyriker aus der DDR die Mauer berührten und von ihr berührt wurden oder: Zur Geschichte eines Syndroms', in *Lyriker Treffen Münster: Gedichte und Aufsätze 1987-1989-1991*, ed. by Lothar Jordan and Winfried Woesler (Bielefeld: Aisthesis, 1993), pp.285-305

Serke, Jürgen, *Zu Hause in Exil: Dichter, die eigenmächtig blieben in der DDR* (Munich and Zurich: Piper, 1998)

Simpson, Patricia Anne, 'Entropie, Ästhetik und Ethik im Prenzlauer Berg', in *MachtSpiele: Literatur und Staatssicherheit im Fokus Prenzlauer Berg*, ed. by Peter Böthig and Klaus Michael (Leipzig: Reclam, 1993), pp.50-59

Solms, Werner, ed., *Begrenzt glücklich: Kindheit in der DDR* (Marburg: Hitzeroth, 1992)

Sonnenberg, Maria, ed., *Dissidenten? Texte und Dokumente zur DDR-"Exil"-Literatur* (Berlin: Volk und Wissen, 1991)

Stephan, Alexander, 'Cultural Politics in the GDR under Erich Honecker', in *The GDR under Honecker 1971-1981*, ed. by Ian Wallace (Dundee: GDR Monitor, 1981), pp.31-42

Tannert, Christoph, 'Frischwärts' (1986), in *Zellinnendruck*, ed. by Egmont Hesse and Christoph Tannert (Leipzig: Eigen+Art, 1990), pp.6-7

Thomas, Rüdiger, 'Selbstbehauptung', in *Jenseits der Staatskultur: Traditionen autonomer Kunst in der DDR*, ed. by Gabriele Muschter and Rüdiger Thomas (Munich: Hanser, 1992), pp.11-42

Thomson, Philip, *The Poetry of Brecht: Seven Studies* (Chapel Hill and London: University of North Carolina Press, 1989)

Thulin, Michael, 'Die Imagination der poetischen Sprache: dichtung und arkdichtung von Bert Papenfuß-Gorek', in *Die andere Sprache: Neue DDR-Literatur der 80er Jahre*, ed. by Heinz Ludwig Arnold (Munich: TuK, 1990), pp.114-119

Trebeß, Achim, ' "wir würschten" in den Kämpfen unserer Zeit: Porträtgedichte junger Autoren' *Lyriker im Zwiegespräch: Traditionsbeziehungen im Gedicht*, ed. by Ingrid Hähnel (Berlin, GDR, and Weimar: Aufbau, 1981), pp.312-344
-- ' "im rechten augenblick das linke tun": Spracherneuerung in Texten von Bert Papenfuß-Gorek', *WB*, 36 (1990), 617-636

Ullmann, Wolfgang, 'Kontext: Über die Rolle der Kunst im Zeitalter antagonistischer Diktaturen', in *MachtSpiele: Literatur und Staatssicherheit im Fokus Prenzlauer Berg*, ed. by Peter Böthig and Klaus Michael (Leipzig: Reclam, 1993), pp.20-27

348   Lyric Responses to German Unification

-- 'Der Ort der Staatssicherheit im System der SED-Diktatur', in *Stasi, KGB und Literatur: Beiträge und Erfahrungen aus Rußland und Deutschland*, ed. by Heinrich-Böll-Stiftung (Cologne: Heinrich-Böll-Stiftung, 1993), pp.12-20

Visser, Anthonya, *"Blumen ins Eis": Lyrische und literaturkritische Innovationen in der DDR: Zum kommunikativen Spannungsfeld ab Mitte der 60er Jahre* (Amsterdam and Atlanta: Rodopi, 1994)

Volckmann, Silvia, *Zeit der Kirschen? Das Naturbild in der deutschen Gegenwartslyrik: Jürgen Becker, Sarah Kirsch, Wolf Biermann, Hans Magnus Enzensberger* (Königstein/Ts: Forum Academicum, 1982)

Wagner, Bernd, *Der Griff ins Leere: Elf Versuche* (Berlin, FRG: Transit, 1988)

Wallace, Ian, ed., *The Writer and Society in the GDR* (Tayport: Hutton, 1984)

Walter, Joachim, ed., *Protokoll eines Tribunals: Die Ausschlüsse aus dem DDR-Schriftstellerverband 1979* (Reinbek bei Hamburg: Rowohlt, 1991)

Whitaker, Peter, *Brecht's Poetry: A Critical Study* (Oxford: Clarendon, 1985)

Wichner, Ernest, and Herbert Wiesner, eds., *Zensur in der DDR: Geschichte, Praxis und "Ästhetik" der Behinderung von Literatur. Ausstellungsbuch* (Berlin: Literaturhaus, 1991)
-- eds., *'Literaturentwicklungsprozesse': Die Zensur der Literatur in der DDR* (Frankfurt a.M.: Suhrkamp, 1993)

Wiesbach, Reinhard, *Wir und der Expressionismus* (Berlin, GDR: Akademie, 1973)

Wittstock, Uwe, *Von der Stalinallee zum Prenzlauer Berg: Wege der DDR-Literatur 1949-1989* (Munich: Piper, 1989)
-- ed., *Wolfgang Hilbig: Materialien zu Leben und Werk* (Frankfurt a.M.: Fischer, 1994)

Wolf, Gerhard, ed., *Sonnenpferde und Astronauten: Gedichte junger Menschen* (Halle: mdv, 1964)
-- *Wortlaut Wortbruch Wortlust: Dialog mit Dichtung: Aufsätze und Vorträge* (Leipzig: Reclam, 1988)

Wolfgang Hilbig, TuK (1994), No.123

Woods, Roger, *Opposition in the GDR under Honecker, 1971-85: An Introduction and Documentation* (London: Macmillan, 1986)
--'Public Judgement versus Private Reflection: Critical East German Intellectuals as Interpreters of the Past', *GM*, 33 (1994), 101-114

Wurm, Carsten, *Jeden Tag ein Buch: 50 Jahre Aufbau-Verlag 1945-1995* (Berlin: Aufbau, 1995)

Wüst, Karl Heinz, *Sklavensprache: Subversive Schreibweisen in der Lyrik der DDR 1961-1976* (Frankfurt a.m., Bern, New York, Paris: Lang, 1989)

X. Schriftstellerkongreß der Deutschen Demokratischen Republik, Berlin 24.-26 November 1987, ndl, 36 (1988), No.3

Zentralrat der FDJ, ed., *Lieder der FDJ* (Berlin, GDR: Lied der Zeit, 1979)

Zipser, Richard, *DDR-Literatur im Tauwetter: Wandel-Wunsch-Wirklichkeit,* 3 vols. (New York, Bern and Frankfurt a.M.: Lang, 1985)

f. OTHER SOURCES USED

Bakhtin, Mikhail, *The Dialogic Imagination*, trans. by Caryl Emerson and Michael Holquist (Austin: University of Texas, 1981)

Baudelaire, Charles, *Les Paradis Artificiels*, ed. by Yves Florenne (Paris: Librairie Générale Française, 1972)
-- *Oeuvres complètes*, 2 vols. (Paris: Gallimard, 1975-76)

Benjamin, Walter, *Gesammelte Schriften*, ed. by Rolf Tiedemann and Hermann Schweppenhäuser (Frankfurt a.M.: Suhrkamp, 1974)

Bodkin, Maud, *Archetypal Patterns in Poetry: Psychological Studies of Imagination* (London: OUP, 1934)

Böhler, Dietrich, 'Geleitwort zum Thema', in *Erinnern, Wiederholen, Durcharbeiten: Zur Psycho-Analyse deutscher Wenden*, ed. by Brigitte Rauschenbach (Berlin: Aufbau, 1992), pp.17-24

Breuilly, John, ed., *The State of Germany: The national idea in the making, unmaking and remaking of a modern nation state* (London and New York: Longman, 1992)

Brinkmann, Rolf Dieter, *Westwärts 1&2: Gedichte* (Reinbek bei Hamburg: Rowohlt, 1975)

Brüggemann, Heinz, *Das andere Fenster: Einblicke in Häuser und Menschen: Zur Literaturgeschichte einer urbanen Wahrnehmungsform* (Frankfurt a.M.: Fischer, 1989)

Büchner, Georg, *Lenz, Sämtliche Werke*, i (Frankfurt a.M.: Deutsche Klassiker, 1992), pp.223-250
-- 'Der Hessische Landbote', *Sämtliche Werke*, ii (Frankfurt a.M.: Deutsche Klassiker, 1992), pp.53-66

Bullmore, Edward, 'The Millennium Brain', *The Independent on Sunday*, 17 January 1999, pp.14-16

Bürger, Peter, *Theorie der Avantgarde* (Frankfurt a.M.: Suhrkamp,1974)

Canetti, Elias, *Masse und Macht* (Frankfurt a.M.: Fischer, 1995)

Celan, Paul, *Der Meridian und andere Prosa* (Frankfurt a.M.: Suhrkamp, 1988)

Chadwick, Charles, *Symbolism* (London: Methuen, 1971)

Conrad, Joseph, *Heart of Darkness, Three Short Novels* (New York: Bantam, 1960), pp.1-94

Conrady, Karl Otto, ed., *Das große deutsche Gedichtbuch: Von 1500 bis zur Gegenwart* (Düsseldorf and Zurich: Artemis & Winckler, 1997)

Coote, Stephen, *T. S. Eliot's 'The Waste Land'* (Harmondsworth and New York: Penguin, 1985)

Demandt, Alexander, *Metaphern für Geschichte: Sprachbilder und Gleich-nisse im historisch-politischen Denken* (Munich: Beck, 1978)

Demandt, Barbara and Alexander, eds., *Römische Kaisergeschichte. Nach Vorlesungs-Mitschriften von Sebastien und Paul Heusel 1882/86* (Munich: Beck, 1992)

Easthope, Antony, and John O. Thompson, eds., *Contemporary Poetry Meets Modern Theory* (Hemel Hempstead: Harverster Wheatsheaf, 1991)

Eliot, T. S., *The Waste Land and other poems* (London: Faber and Faber, 1972)

Enzensberger, Hans-Magnus, *Einzelheiten* (Frankfurt a.M.: Suhrkamp, 1962)
-- 'Vorwort', *Museum der modernen Poesie*, 2nd edn. (Munich: dtv, 1966), pp.8-20

Faulkner, Peter, *Modernism* (London and New York: Routledge, 1980)

Forster, Leonard, ed., *Penguin Book of German Verse* (London: Penguin, 1959)

Foucault Reader, ed. by Paul Rabinow (Harmondsworth: Penguin, 1986)

Freud, Sigmund, 'Neue Folge der Vorlesungen zur Einführung in die Psychoanalyse', *Studienausgabe*, i (Frankfurt a.M.: Fischer, 1969)
-- 'Trauer und Melancholie', *Studienausgabe*, x (Frankfurt am Main: Fischer , 1969)

Frühsorge, Gotthardt, 'Fenster: Augenblicke der Aufklärung über Leben und Arbeit: Zur Funktionsgeschichte eines literarischen Motivs', *Euphorion*, 77 (1983), 346-358

Goethe, Johann Wolfgang von, *Werke in sechs Bänden* (Munich: Artemis und Winckler, 1992)

Gnüg, Hiltrud, ed., *An Hölderlin: Zeitgenössische Gedichte* (Stuttgart: Reclam, 1993)

Grimm, Günter, ed., *Metamorphosen des Dichters: Das Selbstverständnis deutscher Schriftsteller von der Aufklärung bis zur Gegenwart* (Frankfurt a.M.: Fischer, 1992)

Grimm, Hans, *Volk ohne Raum* (Munich: Langen, 1928)

Hackett, C.A., *Rimbaud* (London: Bowes and Bowes, 1957)

Hamburger, Michael, *Das Überleben der Lyrik* (Munich: Hanser, 1993)

Hartung, Harald, ed., *Luftfracht: Internationale Poesie 1940 bis 1990* (Frankfurt a.m.: Eichborn, 1991)
-- *Masken und Stimmen: Figuren der modernen Lyrik* (Munich and Vienna: Hanser, 1996)

Havel, Václav, *Living in Truth*, ed. by Jan Vladislav (London: Faber and Faber, 1987)

Heaney, Seamus, *The Redress of Poetry: Oxford Lectures* (London: Faber and Faber, 1995)

Heine, Heinrich, 'Deutschland, ein Wintermärchen', *Sämtliche Werke*, i (Munich: Winckler, 1969), pp.411-478

Heissenbüttel, Helmut, 'Zum Gelegenheitsgedicht', in *Lyrik-Katalog Bundesrepublik: Gedichte, Biographien, Statements*, ed. by Jan Hans, Uwe Herms and Ralf Thenior (Munich: Goldmann, 1978), pp.440-443

Hinck, Walter, *Von Heine zu Brecht: Lyrik im geschichtlichen Prozeß* (Frankfurt a.m.: Suhrkamp, 1978)
-- *Das Gedicht als Spiegel der Dichter: Zur Geschichte des deutschen poetologischen Gedichts* (Opladen: Westdeutscher Verlag, 1985)
-- *Magie und Tagtraum: Das Selbstbild des Dichters in der deutschen Lyrik* (Frankfurt a.M. and Leipzig: Insel, 1994)

Hobsbaum, Philip, *Metre, Rhythm and Verse Form* (London and New York: Routledge, 1996)

Hofmann von Hofmannswaldau, Christian, *Gedichte* (Stuttgart: Reclam, 1964)

Hofmannstal, Hugo von, 'Ein Brief' (1902), *Gesammelte Werke*, vii (Frankfurt a.m.: Fischer, 1986), pp.461-472

Hölderlin, Friedrich, *Poesiealbum 17* (Berlin, GDR: Neues Leben, 1969)
-- *Sämtliche Gedichte: Studienausgabe in zwei Bänden*, ed. by Detlev Lüders (Bad Homburg: Athenäum, 1970)
-- *Hyperion oder der Eremit in Griechenland* (Stuttgart: Reclam, 1980)

Howatson, M. C., ed., *The Oxford Companion to Classical Literature*, 2nd ed. (Oxford and New York: OUP, 1989)

Jameson, Frederic, *The Prison-House of Language: A Critical Account of Structuralism and Russian Formalism* (Princeton: Princeton University, 1972)

Joyce, James, *Portrait of the Artist as a Young Man* (London: Cape, 1956)

Juvenal and Persius, 'Satires', trans. by G.G. Ramsay (London: Heinemann, 1918)

Kafka, Franz, *Die Erzählungen* (Frankfurt a.m.: Suhrkamp, 1961)
-- *Sämtliche Erzählungen*, ed. by Paul Raabe (Frankfurt a.m. and Hamburg: Fischer, 1970)

Kaiser, Gerhard, *Geschichte der deutschen Lyrik*, 3 vols (Frankfurt a.m. and Leipzig: Insel, 1996)

Kant, Immanuel, 'Beantwortung der Frage: Was ist Aufklärung?' (1784), *Werke*, xi (Frankfurt a.m.: Insel, 1964), pp.53-61

Kermode, Frank, *Poetry, Narrative, History* (Oxford: Blackwell, 1990)

Korte, Hermann, *Geschichte der deutschen Lyrik seit 1945* (Stuttgart: Metzler, 1989)

Krauß, Angela, 'Das Poetische am Politischen', *Monatshefte*, 82 (1990), 403-407

Kundera, Milan, *The Book of Laughter and Forgetting*, trans. by Michael Henry Heim (London: Faber, 1981)

Lessing, Gotthold Ephraim, *Nathan der Weise: Ein dramatisches Gedicht* (Munich: Goldmann, 1979)

Maiwald, Peter, *Wortkino: Notizen zur Poesie* (Frankfurt a.m.: Fischer, 1993)

Marx, Karl, *Werke, Schriften, Briefe*, ed. by Hans Joachim Lieber (Stuttgart: Cotta, 1960-71)

Milosz, Czeslaw, *The Witness of Poetry* (Cambridge, Massachusetts and London, England: Harvard University Press, 1983)

Mitscherlich, Alexander and Margarete, *Die Unfähigkeit zu trauern: Grundlagen kollektiver Verhaltens* (Munich: Piper, 1977)

Muecke, D.C., *Irony and the ironic* (London and New York: Methuen, 1982)

New Encyclopaedia Britannica: Micropaedia, iv (Chicago, London, Toronto, Geneva, Tokyo, Manila, Seoul, Johannesburg: Encyclopaedia Britannica, 1974)

Owen, Wilfred, *The Collected Poems* (London: Chatto & Windus, 1968)

Petersdorff, Dirk von, *Wie es weitergeht: Gedichte* (Frankfurt a.m.: Fischer, 1992)

Plinius der Jungere, *Briefe in einem Band*, trans. by Werner Krenkel (Berlin, GDR: Aufbau, 1984)

Pound, Ezra, *The ABC of Reading* (London: Faber, 1951)
-- *Collected Shorter Poems* (London and Boston: Faber and Faber, 1984)

Prawer, Siegfried, ed., *Seventeen Modern German Poets* (Oxford: OUP, 1971)

Riese, Utz, 'Postmodern Culture: Symptom, Critique or Solution to the Crisis of Modernity? An East German Perspective', *New German Critique* (1992), No.57, 157-169

Rilke, Rainer Maria, *Der Neuen Gedichte anderer Teil* (Leipzig: Insel, 1923)
-- *Die Aufzeichnungen des Malte Laurids Brigge* (Wiesbaden: Insel, 1952)
-- *Duineser Elegien*, ed. by Wolfram Groddeck, nach den Erstdrucken von 1923 (Stuttgart: Reclam, 1997)

Rimbaud, Arthur, *Sämtliche Dichtungen des Jean Arthur Rimbaud: Nachdichtungen von Paul Zech* (Frankfurt a.M.: Fischer, 1990)
-- 'Lettre à Paul Demeny', *Oeuvres* (Paris: Classiques Garnier, 1991), pp.346-352

Russell, Charles, *Poets, Prophets and Revolutionaries: The Literary Avantgarde from Rimbaud through Postmodernism* (New York and Oxford: OUP, 1985)

Sartorius, Joachim, ed., *Atlas der neuen Poesie* (Reinbek bei Hamburg: Rowohlt, 1995)

Schneider, Peter, *Extreme Mittellage: Eine Reise durch das deutsche Nationalgefühl* (Reinbek bei Hamburg: Rowohlt, 1990)

Schwitters, Kurt, *Anna Blume und Ich: Die gesammelten "Anna Blume"-Texte*, ed. by Ernst Schwitters (Zurich: Arche, 1965)
-- *Das literarische Werk*, ed. by Friedhelm Lach (Cologne: DuMont Schauberg, 1973)

Segebrecht, Wulf, *Das Gelegenheitsgedicht: Ein Beitrag zur Geschichte und Poetik der deutschen Lyrik* (Stuttgart: Metzler, 1977)

Shelley, Percy Bysshe, *The Complete Poetical Works*, ed. by Neville Rogers (Oxford: Clarendon, 1975)

Steinbeck, John, *The Grapes of Wrath* (London: Arrow, 1998)

Thomas, Dylan, *Portrait of the Artist as a Young Dog* (London: Dent, 1940)

Thompson, Kenneth, ed., *Readings from Emile Durkheim* (Chicester, London and New York: Ellis Horwood, 1985)

Thwaite, Antony, *Poetry Today: A Critical Guide to British Poetry 1960-1995* (London and New York: Longman, 1996)

Tighe, Carl, 'Die polnischen Schriftsteller und der Übergang von der sozialistischen "Unwirklichkeit" zur kapitalistischen "Wirklichkeit" 1980-1992', *SuF*, 47 (1995), 638-668

Wellershoff, Dieter, *Die Auflösung des Kunstbegriffs* (Frankfurt a.m.: Suhrkamp, 1976)

Wertheimer, Jürgen, ed., *Von Poesie und Politik: Zur Geschichte einer dubiösen Beziehung* (Tubingen: Attempto, 1994)

Willard, N. M., 'A Poetry of Things: Williams, Rilke, Ponge', *Comparative Literature*, 17 (1965), 311-324

Williams, William Carlos, *Selected Poems* (New York: New Directions, 1949)
-- 'Pictures from Brueghel' (1962), *Collected Poems*, ii, ed. by Christopher MacGowan (London: Paladin, 1991), pp.385-394

Wittgenstein, Ludwig, *Tractatus logico-philosophicus: Tagebücher 1914-16. Philosophische Untersuchungen* (Frankfurt a.M.: Suhrkamp, [1969])

Index of Names

Adorno, Theodor, 10, 41, 188
Anderson, Sascha, 20, 23, 44, 48, 49, 55, 65, 66, 71, 234
Arendt, Erich, 33, 110
Ashbery, John, 234, 268

Bartsch, Wilhelm, 186-187
Baudelaire, Charles, 267, 273
Becher, Johannes R., 31-32, 34, 41, 118, 283
Becker, Jurek, 278
Berendse, Gerrit-Jan, 7-8, 193, 208
Biermann, Wolf, 20, 21, 23, 30, 34, 40, 41, 42-43, 87, 110, 126-127, 141, 278
Bloch, Ernst, 32, 41, 56, 139, 191, 197, 205-206, 207, 224, 246, 248
Bobrowski, Johannes, 41, 281
Böhme, Thomas, 45-46, 78, 124
Bohrer, Karl Heinz, 20, 22, 23
Bormann, Alexander von, 45, 248
Böthig, Peter, 48, 49-50
Braun, Volker, 6, 8, 21, 22, 34-35, 36, 38-39, 42, 43, 53-54, 56, 75-76, 78, 85-86, 90, 91, 95, 98, 100, 109, 113, 116, 122, 131, 132, 137, 138, 144-146, 158, 191-231, 233-236, 241, 243-245, 246, 250, 252, 262, 267, 271, 273, 276-278, 279, 281-282, 284
Brecht, Bertolt, 12, 28-29, 32, 34, 35, 42, 61, 63, 82, 84, 86, 87-89, 96, 100, 102, 103, 109, 120, 169, 191, 212, 216-218, 222, 228, 239, 271, 279
Brinkmann, Hans, 143, 165, 166
Büchner, Georg, 29, 170, 201-202, 269, 279
Burmeister, Brigitte, 3, 196, 280

Canetti, Elias, 244, 263
Cato, the Elder, 146
Chiarloni, Anna, 7, 8, 78, 95, 121
Cibulka, Hanns, 32, 35, 79, 84-85, 102
Conrad, Joseph, 147-148, 150, 158
Conrady, Karl Otto, 5, 79, 109
Cosentino, Christine, 63, 66, 71
Czechowski, Heinz, 15, 34, 36, 37, 39, 55, 76, 78, 91-92, 100, 108-109, 110, 119, 123, 126, 132, 133, 135, 136, 141-142, 146, 161-162, 176-178, 181, 187, 189, 231, 239, 247, 266, 273, 276, 284

Dante, 184, 241-242, 250, 267
Deiritz, Karl, 21, 27, 137
Dieckmann, Friedrich, 126-128
Domdey, Horst, 140, 159, 202-203
Döring, Stefan, 45, 48, 52, 118
Drawert, Kurt, 1, 12, 14-15, 54, 69, 76, 77, 78, 99, 101, 115, 119, 122, 123, 129, 131-132, 143, 156-157, 159, 161-165, 173-174, 178-182, 183, 187-188, 255, 265, 275-276, 281-283
Durkheim, Emile, 153

Eich, Günter, 180
Emmerich, Wolfgang, 3, 10-11, 18, 19, 20, 167, 168, 203, 234, 276, 282
Endler, Adolf, 30, 33, 34, 36, 44, 47, 48
Ertl, Wolfgang, 78

Faktor, Jan, 43-45, 48, 51, 52, 143, 164-165
Faust, Siegmar, 35, 41
Freud, Sigmund, 19, 146, 180, 249
Fühmann, Franz, 12, 37, 188

Gaus, Günter, 145
Geist, Peter, 5, 6, 49, 131, 143, 280
Gerlach, Harald, 66, 78, 95, 104-105, 106-107, 115, 138-139, 142, 159
Goethe, Johann Wolfgang von, 12, 29, 39, 155, 213, 228, 229, 267, 283
Gorbachev, Mikhail, 83, 85, 91-92, 208-209
Greiner, Ulrich, 20, 21, 22, 203
Grosz, Christiane, 128, 132
Grotewohl, Otto, 30
Grünbein, Durs, 6, 12, 16, 50-51, 54, 67, 76, 111-112, 114-115, 119-120, 129, 132, 205, 233-272, 273-274, 276, 279-281
Grunenberg, Antonia, 3, 54, 55, 169
Grüning, Uwe, 35, 79, 80-83, 85, 94, 102, 132
Gysi, Gregor, 147

Hager, Kurt, 195
Hallberg, Robert von, 23, 177
Havel, Václav, 90
Heaney, Seamus, 10
Hein, Christoph, 58, 90, 91, 137-138, 193, 279
Heine, Heinrich, 12, 29, 39, 82-83, 206, 212, 225, 228, 268
Hensel, Kerstin, 1, 12, 68-69, 136, 143, 144-145, 156, 162, 164, 169-170, 281

Herwegh, Georg, 145
Heym, Stefan, 21, 90, 91, 137, 192, 193, 215
Hilbig, Wolfgang, 1-2, 7, 47, 69-70, 101, 124, 130, 170, 182-189, 266, 282
Hilton, Ian, 24, 132
Hitler, Adolf, 93-94, 148, 239, 283
Hofmann von Hofmannswaldau, Christian, 267, 269
Hölderlin, Friedrich, 12, 39, 40, 110, 113, 139, 201, 217, 266, 267, 282
Holst, Matthias, 46, 79, 82, 85, 282
Honecker, Erich, 39, 41, 43, 93, 107-108, 120-121, 123, 218, 219
Hopkins, Gerard Manley, 270

Jäger, Manfred, 212
Janka, Walter, 90
Jansen, Johannes, 76, 107
Jentzsch, Bernd, 38
Joyce, James, 267

Kachold, Gabriele, 52, 69 – see also Stötzer
Kafka, Franz, 129, 150, 221, 226, 267, 269-270, 278
Kahlau, Heinz, 21, 55, 126, 132, 140, 142, 168-169, 278, 280
Kant, Hermann, 55, 196
Kant, Immanuel, 191, 267
Kirchner, Annerose, 39, 89-90, 98-100, 111-112, 125, 126, 133
Kirsch, Rainer, 34, 55, 275
Kirsch, Sarah, 34, 38, 41, 65-66
Kleist, Heinrich von, 39, 40, 146, 249
Kling, Thomas, 234, 268
Klopstock, Friedrich Gottlieb, 39-40, 139, 146, 224
Kohl, Helmut, 76, 123, 218
Köhler, Barbara, 70, 72, 76, 101, 143, 180
Kolbe, Uwe, 23, 42, 47, 50, 61-63, 71, 75, 76, 92, 143, 165, 275, 281
Korte, Hermann, 53, 271
Krauß, Angela, 136
Krenz, Egon, 92, 103, 122, 137, 147
Kuczynski, Jürgen, 230
Kunert, Günter, 11, 13, 14, 21, 34, 38, 58-60, 89, 102, 115-116, 118, 119, 164, 165, 167-168, 279, 282
Kunze, Reiner, 34, 38, 41, 58, 65, 116, 132, 282

Labroisse, Gerd, 77, 142, 160
Leeder, Karen, 110, 129

Lenin, 131, 158, 194
Lessing, Gotthold Ephraim, 222-223, 224
Lewis, Alison, 155-156
Liebknecht, Karl, 101
Luxemburg, Rosa, 153

Maaz, Hans-Joachim, 189
Maurer, Georg, 12, 34
Marx, Karl, 40, 56, 148, 151, 160, 161, 192
Matthies, Frank-Wolf, 50-52, 215
Mayakovsky, Vladimir, 30
Mayer, Hans, 135
Mensching, Steffen, 52, 54, 55, 60, 68, 76, 125, 130, 132, 144, 146-149, 150-
152, 155, 156, 158-159, 168, 274-277, 280-281
Meyer-Gosau, Frauke, 202
Mickel, Karl, 34, 36, 38, 44, 204, 210, 281
Mielke, Erich, 103
Milosz, Czeslaw, 17
Modrow, Hans, 137
Mohr, Heinrich, 137
Mommsen, Theodor, 147, 160, 200
Momper, Walter, 113, 122
Müller, Heiner, 1, 15-16, 21, 36, 55, 56, 57, 76, 85, 87-88, 90, 91, 94, 102,
106, 109, 113, 117, 120-122, 138, 147-150, 155, 157-163, 171, 187, 200, 204,
231, 236, 259, 281-282

Naumann, Michael, 188
Nagy, Imre, 87

Oleschinski, Brigitte, 249, 259

Papenfuß (or Papenfuß-Gorek), Bert, 1, 44, 46, 48, 49, 51, 52, 54, 56, 64, 153-
155, 189, 276, 282
Pietraß, Richard, 55, 59-60
Plato, 102, 184
Pliny, 199-200
Pound, Ezra, 120

Rathenow, Lutz, 60-61, 63, 71, 131, 132, 166-167, 276, 281
Rennert, Jürgen, 126-127, 132
Richter, Armin, 89, 96-97, 106, 108, 112-113, 116, 132, 186, 281

Rilke, Rainer Maria, 75, 149, 267, 270
Rimbaud, Arthur, 150, 174, 225, 229, 255
Rosenlöcher, Thomas, 76, 186
Rossetti, Christina, 121

Schabowski, Günter, 96
Schacht, Ulrich, 103-104, 119, 132
Schedlinski, Rainer, 12, 23, 48, 52, 55, 67, 234
Schiller, Friedrich, 29, 89, 249
Schirrmacher, Frank, 20, 22
Schlenstedt, Dieter, 55, 201, 206
Schmidt, Kathrin, 88-89, 132
Schorlemmer, Friedrich, 103, 118, 219
Seneca, 187
Stalin, 31, 93, 173, 209
Stephan, Peter M., 170-171
Stötzer, Gabriele, 8 – see also Kachold

Tacitus, 161, 199
Teschke, Holger, 78, 93-95, 102, 113, 119, 132
Thomas, Dylan, 270
Tietze, Oliver, 79-80, 85, 102
Tragelehn, B.K., 93, 102-103, 120, 217-218

Uhland, Ludwig, 159
Ulbricht, Walter, 31, 41, 90

Wallace, Ian, 23, 223
Wenzel, Hans-Eckardt, 8, 76, 247-248
Werner, Walter, 110, 119
Weskott, Martin, 204
Williams, William Carlos, 269
Wolf, Christa, 4, 8, 20, 21-22, 55, 57, 77, 78, 87, 90, 91, 137, 138, 139-141, 142, 144, 278, 281
Wolf, Gerhard, 36, 233
Wüstefeld, Michael, 97-98, 171-173, 175-176, 180, 282

Yeats, W. B., 146, 174

Index of Subjects

Advertising, 148, 152-153, 158-159, 217, 227
Akademie der Künste, 36
Alexanderplatz, 75, 91, 92, 94, 102, 154, 156, 192
America, 120, 121, 125, 130, 148, 158, 159, 187, 204, 210, 216, 217, 277 – see also New York
Angels, 105-106, 133, 275-276
Animal imagery, 245-250, 251, 260-261, 268, 270-271
Atlantis, 102, 215, 220-221
Aufbau, 28, 31, 42, 110, 117, 196, 233
Aufklärer – see Enlightenment
Aufrechter Gang, 98-99, 191-192, 206, 238, 244-245, 246
Auschwitz, 188, 221
Autumn, 81-82, 95-97, 162, 175, 221
Avant-garde, 33-34, 48-49, 50, 55

Beggar figures, 81, 156-158, 224-225, 273
Berlin, 6, 23, 33, 36, 43-44, 59, 75-76, 79, 85, 87, 90, 91, 94, 96, 102-103, 113, 118, 122, 125, 132, 143, 155, 156, 170, 204, 233, 236, 241
Berlin Wall, 1, 34, 75, 103, 115-117, 219, 233, 240, 283
Biography, 179-181, 186, 279
Bitterfeld Conference, 33-34
Bible, Old Testament, 32, 82, 100, 101, 107, 115-116, 125-126, 204, 206, 209, 215-216, 244
Bible, New Testament, 95, 140, 99, 143, 153, 158, 207, 217, 219, 249, 261, 277
Brain imagery, 239-240, 254-255, 266, 269

Censorship, 21, 38, 41, 56, 57-62, 91, 154, 164, 172, 177, 197, 225
China, 84, 120, 124, 197, 218 – see also Tienanmen Square
Commemoration – see Memory
Computer jargon, 151
Czechoslovakia, 1, 18-19, 75, 80-82, 102, 143 – see also Prague Spring

Death, 52, 59, 76, 82, 83, 118, 121, 125, 148, 149, 150-151, 154-155, 178, 184, 187, 200, 219, 220, 235, 242, 260, 263-266, 271, 277-278
Demonstrations, 5, 56, 75-76, 77, 79-81, 85-87, 91-95, 100-101, 105, 106, 112, 114, 115-116, 144-145, 184, 192-194, 198, 208, 215, 220, 238-239
Dissidents, 45, 47, 59-63, 80, 81, 230, 274

Dreams, 15, 31, 40, 41, 70, 94, 100, 111-113, 129, 137-139, 198, 201, 225, 227, 229, 246, 253, 254, 260, 261, 262
Dresden, 6, 23, 76, 97, 123, 132, 142, 156, 221, 233, 236, 256, 281

East Berlin – see Berlin
Elections, 75, 125
Émigré writers – see Exile
Enlightenment, 145, 159, 170, 186, 191, 205-208, 212, 216, 224, 236, 270
Evolution, 248-249, 250-252, 254-256, 258, 259, 263, 271-272
Exile, 2, 6, 21, 28, 41, 59, 72, 76, 110, 120, 139, 156, 174, 176, 178-179, 185, 237, 279, 284
Exodus, 8, 75, 80, 85, 87, 97, 98, 106, 107, 111, 133, 137, 196

Fall, 97, 109-111, 115, 117-119, 131-132, 178, 184, 198-199, 200, 260, 275-276
Files – see Stasi
Film, 94, 113-115, 129, 151, 180, 237, 263
Flood, 70, 85, 100-101
Fool, 212-215, 228
FDJ, 28, 36, 54
French Revolution, 94, 124-125, 202

Gauck-Behörde, 205
Geist und Macht, 23, 30, 43, 54, 55, 135-136, 184, 195, 210, 215, 233, 274
Gelegenheitsgedichte, 76-77, 102, 133
Generations, 27, 34-36, 41, 43-45, 50-54, 62, 71, 110, 143, 205, 233, 276
Gulf War, 210, 219, 221

Heimkehrer, 181, 187, 284
House imagery, 40, 65-66, 71, 73, 119, 130, 164, 195-196
Hungary, 1, 75, 87, 94
Hunger motif, 208-209, 226, 230

Icarus, 60, 85, 109-110
Identity, 8, 24-25, 30, 48, 88, 114, 115, 128, 135, 153, 156, 157, 174-177, 181-183, 186-187, 189, 198-199, 201-203, 206, 214-215, 219, 221, 228, 239, 274-275, 279, 280, 282
Inner immigration, 64-66

Journey, 37, 81, 101-102, 120, 138, 182-186, 222, 225-227, 250
Judgement Day, 24, 86, 184

Kahlschlag, 29, 142, 178, 187

Landscape – see Nature
Language, 4, 5, 13, 17, 33, 44, 47-50, 54, 64, 79, 89, 91, 104, 105, 124, 130, 155, 158-159, 180, 183, 195, 207, 219, 233, 235-236, 242, 245, 246, 249, 254-255, 256, 259
Leipzig, 12, 23, 32, 34, 76, 91, 104, 105, 142, 170, 192, 204, 226, 281
Leseland, 3, 4
Literaturinstitut, 12, 62
Literaturstreit, 20-24, 140, 234, 249, 275
Lyrikwelle, 34, 196

Memento mori – see Death
Memory, 15, 81, 101, 108, 121, 159, 162, 174, 175, 180, 181-182, 184, 225, 240, 242, 249, 254, 257, 261, 266-267, 271-272, 275, 284
Montage, 48, 130, 155, 159, 204, 221

Nature, 41-43, 98-101, 108, 116, 133, 178, 194, 198-200, 236-237, 252, 260-261, 265
Nazism, 18, 30, 32, 36, 64, 121, 141 – see also Auschwitz
Neues Forum, 94, 219
New York, 50, 146, 148, 281
November 1989, 1, 8, 19, 89-91, 94-96, 107, 109, 113-116, 119, 124, 126, 137, 148, 191, 192, 193, 202, 220, 231

Occasional poetry – see Gelegenheitsgedichte
Opposition in the GDR, 38, 58, 61, 62, 75, 137, 196-197
Orpheus, 118, 185, 253

Poetry as a genre, 10-17, 27, 57, 77, 267, 274
Poland, 1, 18-19, 75
Prague Spring, 1, 40, 94
Prenzlauer Berg, 23, 33, 44-50, 52, 79, 234, 235, 282
Publishing, 3, 4, 29, 47, 52-53, 56, 57-60, 63, 64, 193, 194, 196-197, 233-234, 236, 274

Quotation, 39, 88, 93-95, 114, 122, 139, 151-153, 158-159, 161, 192, 195, 200, 209, 216-218, 233, 267, 278

Romanticism, reception of, 39-40, 44
Ruins, 29, 31, 92, 105, 117-118, 130, 181, 219, 221, 283

Russian Revolution, 15, 82, 97, 208

Sächsische Dichterschule, 34-42, 43, 44, 79, 177, 234, 271, 282
Schriftstellerverband, 12, 33, 55, 58, 90, 138, 193, 196, 213
Second World War, 31, 105-106, 117, 123, 181, 187, 283
SED, 1, 29, 34, 36, 43, 53, 54, 55, 57, 71, 94, 101, 103, 122, 124, 125, 138, 142, 145, 155, 195, 196, 199, 212, 213, 230
Ship imagery, 101-102, 138
Sisyphus, 164-168
Slogans – of the 'Wende', 75, 92-95, 98, 112, 221
Slogans – of the GDR, 60, 92-94, 219
Slogans – other, 92, 217, 221
Socialist Realism, 28
Soviet Union, 28, 37, 77, 85, 120, 195, 208, 219
Speed, 130-131, 133, 144-145, 260, 274
Stasi, 20-23, 55-60, 87, 94, 102, 103, 128-129, 154, 164, 173, 205, 220, 234

Tienanmen Square, 84, 87, 102, 209
Time, 68, 85, 110, 111, 115, 129-133, 274
Tiresias, 259
Traffic, 79-80, 144, 148-149
Translations, 30, 119-121, 174, 250
Treuhand, 211, 221

Utopia, 15, 19, 37, 41-42, 44, 46, 88, 102, 117, 122, 129, 136, 138-139, 141, 142-143, 149-150, 152, 163, 188, 193, 212, 213, 219, 228, 229, 241, 244-245, 279, 283

Volk, 28, 31, 33-34, 71, 75, 87, 91-94, 96, 98, 103, 113, 114, 122, 123, 135, 170-174, 194, 195, 202, 211, 218-219, 225, 231

West Germany, 1, 22, 30, 47, 75, 78, 80, 82, 102, 103, 113, 126, 143, 147, 173, 174, 176, 217, 234, 236, 237, 241, 247, 275, 278, 279
Windows, 65-72, 274
Writers' Union – see Schriftstellerverband

Zeitgedichte, 10, 77, 83, 85, 104, 133, 189, 274